T0212039

Communications in Computer and Information Science 1448

More information about this series at http://www.springer.com/series/7899

Alla G. Kravets · Maxim Shcherbakov ·
Danila Parygin · Peter P. Groumpos (Eds.)

Creativity in Intelligent Technologies and Data Science

4th International Conference, CIT&DS 2021
Volgograd, Russia, September 20–23, 2021
Proceedings

 Springer

Editors
Alla G. Kravets 🆔
Volgograd State Technical University
Volgograd, Russia

Danila Parygin 🆔
Volgograd State Technical University
Volgograd, Russia

Maxim Shcherbakov 🆔
Volgograd State Technical University
Volgograd, Russia

Peter P. Groumpos 🆔
University of Patras
Patras, Greece

ISSN 1865-0929   ISSN 1865-0937 (electronic)
Communications in Computer and Information Science
ISBN 978-3-030-87033-1   ISBN 978-3-030-87034-8 (eBook)
https://doi.org/10.1007/978-3-030-87034-8

This Springer imprint is published by the registered company Springer Nature Switzerland AG
The registered company address is: Gewerbestrasse 11, 6330 Cham, Switzerland

Preface

Creativity is the powerful engine of humanity to move forward and overcome global challenges in changing environments. Creativity is the process of breaking out of established patterns; it is the reorganization, recombination, or reinterpretation of concepts and ideas to get something unique and previously unknown in a fast modifying world due to new unforeseen hazards. First, a shift to a new technological paradigm requires a velocity of adaptation to the new reality, merging physical and virtual components; therefore, creativity is probably one of the essential components of humankind, and is becoming more crucial in the new digital Society 5.0. Second, 2020 brought new challenges due to the COVID-19 pandemic, and finding a new normality requires the identification novel and non-trivial solutions, which could influence the whole world. So, in this case, artificial intelligence and data science can be considered as new tools for creativity in achieving the new normality.

This book contains the proceedings of the fourth Conference on Creativity in Intelligent Technologies and Data Science (CIT&DS 2021). Despite the worldwide turbulence, we continued the successful series of previous conferences that took place in 2015, 2017, and 2019. The main objective of CIT&DS 2021 was to bring together researchers and practitioners to share ideas in applying creativity to theory and practice for designing brand new intelligent systems for engineering and decision-making. Readers will find results on creating cutting-edge intelligent technologies based on state-of-the-art research.

The following topics are covered in the proceedings. Section 1 includes papers on knowledge discovery in patent and open sources, open science semantic technologies, and IoT and computer vision in knowledge-based control. Section 2 contains papers on pro-active modeling in intelligent decision-making support, design creativity in CASE/CAI/CAD/PDM, and intelligent technologies in urban design and computing. Section 3 covers data science in social networks analysis and cyber security, educational creativity and game-based learning, intelligent assistive technologies, and software design and application.

We do hope these proceedings will help stimulate your creativity and bring new insights to you.

July 2021

Alla Kravets
Maxim Shcherbakov
Danila Parygin
Peter Groumpos

Organization

Program Chairs

Alla Kravets	Volgograd State Technical University, Russia
Maxim Shcherbakov	Volgograd State Technical University, Russia
Danila Parygin	Volgograd State Technical University, Russia
Peter Groumpos	University of Patras, Greece

Program Committee

Adriaan Brebels	KU Leuven, Belgium
Alena Zakharova	Institute of Control Sciences of Russian Academy of Sciences, Russia
Alexander Bolshakov	Saint-Petersburg State Institute of Technology (Technical University), Russia
Alexander Bozhday	Penza State University, Russia
Alexander Priven	Corning, South Korea
Alexandr Bershadskii	Penza State University, Russia
Alexey Finogeev	Penza State University, Russia
Alexey Kizim	Volgograd State Technical University, Russia
Alin Moldoveanu	University Politehnica of Bucharest, Romania
Anatoly Karpenko	Bauman Moscow State Technical University, Russia
Andrey Andreev	Volgograd State Technical University, Russia
Andrius Zhilenas	INVENTSHIP, Lithuania
Anna Matokhina	Volgograd State Technical University, Russia
Anton Anikin	Volgograd State Technical University, Russia
Anton Ivaschenko	Samara National Research University, Russia
Anton Tyukov	Volgograd State Technical University, Russia
Bal Krishna	Bal Kathmandu University, Nepal
Carla Oliveira	Lisbon University, Portugal
Christos Malliarakis	University of Macedonia, Greece
Dang Phuong	University of Science and Technology - The University of Danang (UST-UD), Vietnam
Danish Ather	Sharda University, Uzbekistan
David Moffat	Glasgow Caledonian University, UK
Dmitriy Korobkin	Volgograd State Technical University, Russia
Eduardo Sarmento	Lusofona University, Portugal
Edwin Gray	Glasgow Caledonian University, UK
Elena Rusyaeva	Institute of Control Sciences of Russian Academy of Sciences, Russia
Evgeniya Cheremisina	Dubna State University, Russia

Vadim Stefanuk	Institute for Information Transmission Problems RAS, Russia
Vibhash Yadav	Rajkiya Engineering College, India
Victor Kureychik	Southern Federal University, Russia
Victor Toporkov	National Research University "MPEI", Russia
Vladimir Gorodetsky	St. Petersburg Institute for Informatics and Automation of the RAS, Russia
Vladimir Tsyganov	Institute of Control Sciences Russian Academy of Sciences, Russia
Wolfram Hardt	Chemnitz Technical University, Germany
Yasemin Allsop	University College London, UK

Contents

**Artificial Intelligence and Deep Learning Technologies for Creative
Tasks. IoT and Computer Vision in Knowledge-Based Control**

**Cyber-Physical Systems and Big Data-Driven World. Pro-Active
Modeling in Intelligent Decision Making Support**

**Cyber-Physical Systems and Big Data-Driven World. Design
Creativity in CASE/CAI/CAD/PDM**

**Cyber-Physical Systems and Big Data-Driven World. Intelligent
Technologies in Urban Design and Computing**

Intelligent Technologies in Social Engineering. Educational Creativity and Game-Based Learning

Intelligent Technologies in Social Engineering. Intelligent Assistive Technologies: Software Design and Application

Keynotes

The Meta COVID-19 Pandemic Period: A Data Science Driven Wise Future Planet?

Peter P. Groumpos[✉]

Department of Electrical and Computer Engineering, University of Patras, 26500 Patras, Greece
groumpos@ece.upatras.gr

Abstract. The COVID-19 pandemic is a sign of how vulnerable and fragile our world is. The virus has upended societies, put the world's population is in grave danger, and exposed deep inequalities. Data have been generated since Ancient times. A historical review of the data information explosion landscape is very interesting. A new scientific area has emerged due to the big number of data been generated every day: The Big Data-Driven World (BDDW) dominates all planet's activities. The arrival of COVID-19 has complicated the BDDW. Creating new knowledge has always been a challenging issue. The role of BDDW in creating new knowledge is important and briefly explained. The need to differentiate between knowledge and wisdom is dictated by the BDDW. New "Wise Knowledge" (WK) and the "Wise Data Science" (WDS) scientific field is formulated and defined for the first time. A new generic decision-making algorithm is proposed for generating the WK and the WDS. The way to build in the future a "Wise Planet driven by Data Science" based on the "Wise Data Science" and "Wise Knowledge" is provided for the first time. Finally, how to avoid the new phenomenon "My Current Knowledge, my Tomorrow's Delusion?!" is stressed.

Keywords: COVID-19 · Pandemic · Big data-driven world · Complexity · Knowledge · Data science · Wisdom · Cognition · Data mining · Learning · Philosophy of science · Social media

1 Introduction

COVID-19 has cast a nearly insufferable strain upon every facet of our society, undoubtedly influencing the way we will live, interact, grow families, govern societies, perform religious services, manage health care systems and conduct business for decades to come. And, in a time when agility and resilience are necessary norms, societies that had already embraced data analytics found themselves positioned to combat the disease and its consequences with a big amount of data.

This was the first global crisis that relied on tech to get us through it. After all, as the world locked down, our lives went almost entirely online [11, 12]. Scientists explain how it was the boom in big data that enabled this world of remote working, online shopping, distance learning, home entertainment, and home delivery. Without the algorithms behind them, the logistics of these services would be impossible [6–9]. Fifteen years ago, ten years ago, we would have been living in a much less comfortable locked-down world.

© Springer Nature Switzerland AG 2021
A. G. Kravets et al. (Eds.): CIT&DS 2021, CCIS 1448, pp. 3–15, 2021.
https://doi.org/10.1007/978-3-030-87034-8_1

The tools of Artificial Intelligence (AI), (mainly machine and deep learning) and data analytics allowed us to continue our lives even the way we did [24–28]. We have seen governments take charge to protect citizens, citizens take responsibility for protecting one another, and companies do their best to help the people. But one pivotal actor driving change behind the scenes of this story has been that of intelligent technology - and the data science that underpins it. The race for the adoption of data analytics has been under way for years, but strengthened digital disruptors such as technological advancements and improved data accessibility, when paired with the COVID-19 pandemic, have, in just a few short months, catapulted an increasingly Big Data-Driven World (BDDW) forward a few years to data-science reliance and optimization. Data science was the architect behind many of the COVID-19 public health mandates [19–23]. Advice to stay at home, wear masks, and adhere to social distancing was the result of analyzing an enormous set of data of the pandemic's behavior worldwide. Many scientists argue: had there been larger and more accurate data sets from initially infected countries and better international cooperation, we could have created better and more sufficient scientific models using data science to predict and curtail the COVID-19 spread.

In this Keynote paper, the whole spectrum of scientific approaches and technological methods in tackling the COVID-19 pandemic are reviewed and presented analytically. Their effects and impacts and all faces and business conduct during the pandemic period are analyzed. We have many lessons to draw from the events of COVID-19 but perhaps one of the most critical is the importance of being able to use "Big Data" to prepare for potential scenarios and guide our decision-making process. The new BDDW is challenging us. There is a real and urgent need for those with the skills to crunch data quickly, and to implement the data strategy needed for this analysis and processing. As the world prepares for 'the new normal' post-pandemic, and all the economic, social, and political question marks that loom above it, many are looking to the BDDW tools or simply the "Data Science" to continue helping us and guide our future trajectories. Advanced "Data Science", beyond the BDDW and AI methods, and the technology it powers, is rapidly becoming an essential component of nearly every activity in both our public and private sectors. Let us be honest: the meta-COVID (or post….as some people call it) will be much different than the pre-pandemic period.

A huge area for further work in data science post-COVID will of course be in healthcare with the introduction of contact tracing apps, remote consultations, and remote monitoring devices. Development of medical solutions and understanding the patterns of a pandemic involve large, complex data sets which are perfect for the new tools of "Data Science" that will be developed. Similar work must be done for all activities of our life (education, entertainment, family life, governing, managing business, and companies to mention a few). On a public level, local and regional governments under new economic strain are looking to make a rapid transition to smart city infrastructure with intelligent solutions for traffic control, crime prediction, and data sensors that could lead to more effective policing and administrative efficiencies. However, a key concern with developing and rapidly deploying these new models are the vulnerabilities that come with them and risks to security and privacy as a result. Ensuring that these systems are ethical and transparent will be more important than ever. If we use the new "Data

Science" developed tools in a wise way, then we can hope to have in the near future a peaceful and wise planet.

This keynote paper is as follows: Sect. 2 provides a historical review in creating the Big Data-Driven World (BDDW). Section 3 discusses the COID-19 pandemic and its impact on the BDDW. Section 4 addresses the important challenge of creating new knowledge from the BDDW. Section 5 covers the heart of this paper which is the creation of the meta COVID-19 new sustainable model driven by a "Wise Data Science" scientific field. Finally, Sect. 6 provides meaningful conclusions and some future research directions.

2 A Historical Review of the Data Information Explosion Landscape

Perhaps the most dramatic outcome of the "digital revolution" (which is one of the driving forces of INDUSTRY 4.0) is the amount of data been collected and analyzed worldwide. The International Data Corporation (IDC) and the World Economic Forum (WEF) calculated that in 2010 the world created more than two (2) zettabytes (ZB) and in 2020 around 45 ZB. That sounds impressive until you consider that the World Economic Forum (WEF) estimates that the global data sphere will grow to 210 ZB or even more by 2025 [1], (in just less than 4 years from now). Nearly 70% of the world's data will need real-time processing. COVID-19 affecting all facets of our lives will be a big contributor to this data explosion. Thus, the Big Data-Driven World (BDDW) has been generated and is all around us. However, there is some very interesting and challenging question: do Data Equal Information? I personally say NO! Do you trust all given data? Furthermore, what do you do with unreliable and/or fake data? How new knowledge is generated from the BDDW?

The story of how data became Big, starts many years before the current buzz around Big Data. Already seventy years ago we encounter the first attempts to quantify the growth rate in the volume of data or what has popularly been known as the "information explosion" (a term first used in 1941, according to the Oxford English Dictionary). Data have been collected and stored since ancient times. Most of them are on books and encyclopedias. Libraries and archives were known to many ancient civilizations in Egypt, Mesopotamia, Syria, Asia Minor, and Greece. The Library of Alexandria, a universal library, the most famous library of Classical antiquity, was considered to be the largest one in those times [2]. It formed part of the research institute at Alexandria in Egypt that is known as the Alexandrian Museum. Unfortunately, it was destroyed as a result of wars early on the first century AC. A lot of historic and valuable information was lost.

It is very informative and useful to briefly review some major milestones in the history of sizing data during the 29th century. The interesting scientist by looking carefully at these milestones and how the "firsts" in the evolution of the idea of "big data" and observations pertaining to data or information explosion, will be able to better analyze, study and comprehend the unfolding BDDW, in front of him/her. In 1944, Fremont Rider, [3], estimated that American university libraries were doubling in size every sixteen years. Given this growth rate, Rider speculated, that the Yale Library in 2040

(100 years later) will have "approximately 200,000,000 volumes, which will occupy over 7,000 miles of shelves and requiring a cataloging staff of over six (6) thousand persons."

Derek Price in 1961, publishes Science Since Babylon, [4], in which he charts the growth of scientific knowledge by looking at the growth in the number of scientific journals and papers. He concludes that the number of new journals has grown exponentially rather than linearly, doubling every fifteen years and increasing by a factor of ten during every half-century. Price, calls this the "law of exponential increase," explaining that "each [scientific] advance generates a new series of advances at a reasonably constant birth rate so that the number of births is strictly proportional to the size of the population of discoveries at any given time". A few years later, in 1967, Marron and Maine, [5], publish "Automatic data compression" in the Communications of the ACM, stating that "a fully automatic and rapid three-part compressor which can be used with 'any' body of information to greatly reduce slow external storage requirements and to increase the rate of information transmission through a computer."

The term Big Data sees the scientific and academic world, for the first time in 1999 by John R. Mashey, Chief Scientist at SGI [6]. He presented at a USENIX meeting a paper titled "Big Data… and the Next Wave of Infrastress"[6]. A few years later in 2001 Laney [7] made the first attempt to define big data, describing Big Data as having volume, velocity, and variety as primary characteristics. In September 2008 a special issue of Nature on Big Data "examines what big data sets mean for contemporary science", [8]. This special issue features and opinion pieces on one of the most daunting challenges facing modern science: how to cope with the flood of data now being generated. Eighteen months later, in February 2010 Kenneth Cukier publishes in The Economist a Special Report titled, "Data, data everywhere" [9]. Writes, Cukier: "…the world contains an unimaginably vast amount of digital information which is getting ever vaster more rapidly… The effect is being felt everywhere, from business to science, from governments to the arts. Scientists and computer engineers have coined a new term for the phenomenon: 'big data'.

In May 2012, Boyd and Crawford publish "Critical Questions for Big Data" in Information, Communications, and Society [10]. They define big data as "a cultural, technological, and scholarly phenomenon that rests on the interplay of (1) Technology: maximizing computation power and algorithmic accuracy to gather, analyze, link, and compare large data sets. (2) Analysis: drawing on large data sets to identify patterns in order to make economic, social, technical, and legal claims. (3) Mythology: the widespread belief that large data sets offer a higher form of intelligence and knowledge that can generate insights that were previously impossible, with the aura of truth, objectivity, and accuracy."

Since 2012 many academicians, scientists and scholars have published numerous studies which describe big data as large data sets whose size is beyond the ability of traditional data processing tools to manage (it is easy to find these sources). The arrival of COVID-19 makes the whole BDDW situation much more complex and complicated. Data generated by the COVID-19 pandemic are spread at an exponential rate across all aspects of our life and all scientific fields. Now, the primary focus lies on the complexity of data and a change in data and information management. In the context of local government, big data is referred to, for example, registers such as health care and education, electronic board protocols, geographic information, and sensor data. External sources are in use within local government as well, such as data from national statistics centers, unemployment rates, and population structure. The combination of internal and external data creates a new foundation of information and knowledge. This new foundation must be analyzed and studied with new technologies of AI, BDDW, and Cognitive Sciences.

3   The Impact of COVID-19 on the BDDW

In late December 2019, COVID-19 officially, SARS-CoV-2, an outbreak of mysterious pneumonia characterized by fever, dry cough, and fatigue, and occasional gastrointestinal symptoms happened in a seafood wholesale wet market, in Wuhan, Hubei, China [11, 12]. Experts say SARS-CoV-2 originated in bats. That's also how the coronaviruses behind the Middle East respiratory syndrome (MERS) and severe acute respiratory syndrome (SARS) got started some years ago. Some believe that COVID-19 was around as early as September of 2019 in China but was never reported and are certain suspicions that it was the product of a Lab in Wuhan, without this to be proven. The initial outbreak was reported in the market in December 2019 and involved about 66% of the staff there. The market was shut down on January 1, 2020, after the announcement of an epidemiologic alert by the local health authority on December 31, 2019. However, in the following month (January) thousands of people in China, including many provinces (such as Hubei, Zhejiang, Guangdong, Henan, Hunan, etc.) and cities (Beijing and Shanghai) were attacked by the rampant spreading of the disease. Furthermore, the disease traveled to many other countries on the planet. On March 11 of 2020, the World Health Organization (WHO), after many hesitations, declared the outbreak a pandemic [12]. As of September of 2020, more than 135 countries were reporting millions of cases and deaths. The recent news from the USA, United Kingdom, Brazil, South Africa, China, Vietnam, and other countries are scaring the whole of humankind, especially with the different mutations of the coronavirus pandemic. More recently, the Indian mutation, DELTA, has left everyone who believed that the COVID-19 pandemic was under control, speechless. The placing of entire cities and/or countries in "lockdown: directly affects urban economies and whole societies. However, many believe that the "lockdown" has not been and cannot be the solution to COVID-19.

History has proven that world pandemics have been either totally eliminated or controlled to a satisfactory level by massive vaccination of the people as were the cases for TB, Malaria, AIDS, uterine cancer of women, polio, flu, and other ones. To bring this COVID-19 pandemic to an end, a large share of the world needs to be immune to the virus. The safest way to achieve this is with a vaccine. Vaccines are a technology that humanity has often relied on in the past to bring down the death toll of infectious diseases.

Prior to COVID-19, a vaccine for an infectious disease had never been produced in less than several years – and no vaccine existed for preventing a coronavirus infection in humans. However, vaccines have been produced against several animal diseases caused by coronaviruses, including (as early as 2003) infectious bronchitis virus in birds, canine coronavirus, and feline coronavirus [13, 14]. Previous projects to develop vaccines for viruses in the family Coronaviridae that affect humans have been aimed at severe acute respiratory syndrome (SARS) and the Middle East respiratory syndrome (MERS). Vaccines against SARS and MERS have been tested in non-human animals [15]. According to studies published in 2005 and 2006, the identification and development of novel vaccines and medicines to treat SARS was a priority for governments and public health agencies around the world at that time [16, 17]. As of 2020, there was no cure or protective vaccine proven to be safe and effective against SARS in humans. This was the case for COVID-19.

Since February 2020, vaccine and medical developments have been expedited via unprecedented collaboration between governments, research laboratories, and the multinational pharmaceutical industry [18]. Within less than 12 months after the beginning of the COVID-19 pandemic, several research teams rose to the challenge and developed vaccines that protect from SARS-CoV-2, the virus that causes COVID-19. Since last November (2020) a number of vaccines have been approved by the appropriate medical authorities and vaccination of people had started middle of December 2020, in the USA and England. Today there are a number of approved and used COVID:19 Vaccines: Phizer, Sputnik V, Astra-Zeneca, Moderna, Johnson&Johnson, Sinovac/China, COVAX, and some others. It is of interest to note that the Russian Sputnik-V vaccine is the world's first registered vaccine based on a well-studied human adenoviral vector-based platform. Sputnik V is already registered in more than 65 countries. The ongoing Sputnik V post-registration clinical trial in Russia involved more than 31,000 volunteers. Phase 3 clinical trials of Sputnik V have been conducting in the UAE, India, Venezuela, and Belarus. Sputnik V is one of the three vaccines in the world with an efficacy of over 90%. The Vaccine's efficacy is confirmed at 91.6% based on the analysis of data on 19,866 volunteers, who received both the first and second doses of the Sputnik V vaccine or placebo at the final control point of 78 confirmed COVID-19 cases. According to the analysis of data from 3.8 million vaccinated persons in Russia, Sputnik V demonstrated 97.6% efficacy.

Now the challenge is to make these vaccines available to people around the world. It will be key that people in all countries — not just in rich countries — receive the required protection. With what are we really confronting NOW? No one denies that the COVID-19 epidemic has caused a large number of human losses and havoc in the economic, social, societal, health, defense, communication, energy, and environmental systems around the world. Controlling such an epidemic requires understanding its characteristics and behavior, which can be identified only by collecting and analyzing the related big data. Earlier, it was pointed out that the generated data which will be part of the BDDW, was estimated before the COVID-19 pandemic to reach 210 ZB by 2025. This estimation is going to be surpassed. First of all, we must accept that our life will never return to pro-COVID-19 "regularity". Our life will be different and no one knows what will look like. The generated BDDW will be so complicated and data generated from different aspects of all activities and processes of our everyday life will have an impact on many aspects of our life, that were not taking place in the pro-COVID-19.

Fortunately, a host of organizations and research centers were already well-versed in the power of Big Data analytics when the COVID-19 pandemic presented itself [19–21].

However, we are very far to be able to use BDDW methods and tools to battle the many problems of COVID-19. Research has been recently reported to show that the BDDW and AI experts need to get closer to the physicians and clinical doctors to be able to create the needed tools for tackling COVID-19 [22, 23]. "Data Science" will play a vital role in building new knowledge required in making decisions and precautionary measures. However, due to the vast amount of data available on COVID-19 from various sources, there is a need to review the roles of big data analysis in controlling the spread of COVID-19, presenting the main challenges and directions of COVID-19 data, as well as providing a framework on the related existing applications and studies to facilitate future research on COVID-19 analysis and implications. This can be accomplished only by generating new knowledge.

4 Creating New Knowledge from the BDDW: A Serious Challenge

Creating New Knowledge in these difficult times is difficult and a serious challenge. BDDW methods and tools, advanced methods of AI and cognitive sciences, will be used to create the required new knowledge leading to a "Wise Data Science" (WDS) scientific field. This is also our final objective: to formulate such a WDS scientific field. You've probably have heard the old quote, "Knowledge is Power," That's truer than you can ever imagine. Few people understand how important knowledge can be. We need to understand ourselves, our strengths, and our weaknesses. We need to learn the art of life. Knowledge accounts for the success of people. The more knowledgeable you are the more advantage you have over the other people. Sometimes we have problems with knowledge because we have difficulties obtaining it. Being in school, gaining knowledge is mandatory, and people can respond negatively to being forced to learn, but the knowledge you gain in that class can actually help you succeed further down the line. It sounds strange, but it's possible that you can forget how to learn. Learning is the most important process that all living creatures are performing. Knowledge is the basis for all-natural and human-made systems. All teaching and all intellectual learning come about from already existing knowledge. However new knowledge is created every day and the BDDW methodologies become more important in this process.

The BDDW is the universe (in probability and logic set theories) of knowledge. With the COVID-19 period not yet reaching the top of data generation, the new landscape is uncertain and ambiguous. The known methodologies of data mining and AI tools generate important and useful new knowledge. However, they are not as effective as needed to address all problems of the world on this difficult time facing our societies. The new landscape is large and complex. The interaction and direct relations between the subsystems comprising a scientific field are beyond any simple understanding and comprehension. Let us take the case of health care systems. Systems that affect it besides the already difficult medical challenges, many other systems and factors affect it such as environment, nutrition, pharmaceutical, engineering, research, economics, business, government policies, work, international crisis, education, phycology, ecology, religion, tourism, entertainment, and every other aspect of our every-day life. Everything is affecting all other activities of our life. Or take the case of business: every day to day business practices have changed drastically with unknown long-term effects on the business cycles. What would be the effect of this change on the world and the individual societies.

Let us see some peculiarities of COVID-19, that make the new BDDW very complex. Unfortunately, some mutations can be more harmful, an amino acid difference (from aspartic acid to glycine) can make the virus more easily penetrate our cells. This differs from patient to patient. The ability to enter the cells of a person is different from the pathological reaction it can cause, another more infectious and another deadlier. And this depends on the value of our own good genetic construction. By knowing the biology of the virus, we can learn both its "Achilles heel" and the chess strategies that it plays with us in order to "win". For example, if in some areas of the genome there are no mutations, it means that they are very important for its life cycle and these unaltered parts are the best targets for the development of drugs and vaccines. Just a few weeks ago, researchers found that due to mutations, it takes longer from infection to the onset of the first symptoms, so a 14-day quarantine may not be enough! All these must be taken into consideration before immunization and/or medical treatment is performed on a patient. However, we do not have yet this knowledge.

The reason this keynote paper is written is to emphasize the value of continuous research, how much more we have to learn. Knowledge is our only and best weapon, knowledge resulting from research and analyzing the new BDDW landscape has been transformed by COVID-19. A microorganism one-millimeter-thick of a human hair will not defeat us. We don't have an alternative other than winning against the COVID-10 challenge. Let us continue our research efforts with our experts. We need the experts that dare to change the instructions from month to month, from day today. This is a sign of high scientific responsibility. The right scientist when he/she opens his/her mouth and speaks incorporates the knowledge he/she has until the previous night; the next day is another day. We all discover secrets second by second!

Therefore, what can we do? We can only turn to science, but wisely and with caution!

The era of Big Data-Driven World (BDDW) is underway and active. Computer scientists, engineers, physicists, physicians, chemists, pharmacists, economists, politicians, health managers, researchers, educators, mathematicians, statisticians, political scientists, bio-informaticists, sociologists, and other scholars are clamoring for access to the massive quantities of data = information produced by and about people, things, and their interactions. Diverse groups argue about the potential benefits and costs of analyzing genetic sequences, social media interactions, health records, phone logs, government records, and other digital traces left by "people". Significant questions emerge. Will large-scale search data help us create better tools, services, and public goods? Or will it guide the world in a new wave of privacy incursions and invasive marketing? Will Big Data analysis help us understand online communities and political movements? Or will it be used to track protesters and suppress speech? Will it transform how we study human communication and culture, or narrow the palette of research options and alter what 'research' means? Given the rise of Big Data as a socio-technical phenomenon, we argue that it is necessary to critically interrogate its assumptions and biases. Definitely, all these will generate new knowledge! NOW, the serious question: can the new knowledge be trusted? How reliable will it be? Or we might experience a new phenomenon been said by me for the first time:

"My Current Knowledge, my Tomorrow's Delusion?!".

All the above create a new environment on how new knowledge will be created during and/or on the meta COVID-19 landscape. Creating new knowledge is not enough. For new knowledge to be useful and effective it needs also to be wise as will be seen in the next section.

5   The Meta COVID-19: A New Sustainable Model is Driven by "Wise Data Science"

Humankind has never had a more urgent task than creating effective medicine and broad immunity for COVID-19. One of the questions been asked the most these days, is when the world will be able to go back to the way things were before December 2019, before the COVID-19 pandemic. Most answers are always the same: when we have an almost safe and perfect drug to treat COVID-19, or when almost every person on the planet has been vaccinated against COVID-19 and all its mutations and is 100% immune to future pandemics. Realistically, if we're going to return to normal, we need to develop both and as quickly as possible. That sounds daunting because it is. Although vaccines and drugs have been developed in the last 12 months or so. However, they are by far to meet the desired objectives. Only miracles can achieve them, but it is not realistic to happen. And this is because it will require a global cooperative effort like the world has never seen and will not see in the near future. There is one more reason: many people believe (I also do so) that the world will NEVER return to the pro-COVID-19 "way of life". Most if not all of the meta COVID-19 activities of our societies will be different than those of the pro pandemic period.

In the previous section, the issue of creating new knowledge was discussed in many details. However, it was also said that just knowledge is not enough. However, we need to repeat that without knowledge, one cannot be successful in life. To grow in one's career, gaining as much knowledge as possible is important. Knowledge is also very important to shape our personality and perfect our behavior and dealings with people. Knowledge is the only way to introduce us to the world. Without knowledge, we can't achieve anything in our life. It is the only way to make us a better person compared to others. So, without "such power" a person can't judge and decide between what is good and what is bad and make decisions voluntarily. It is the power for a person to learn from his/her past mistakes and avoid repeating them. But again, all these are not enough. For example, in the case of not repeating mistakes a wise person might avoid such a mistake altogether by listening to the wisdom of others and/or by wisely choosing to seek information and "Wise Knowledge" on how to properly avoid making a mistake on the first place. It becomes obvious that we seek to define how "Wise Knowledge" can be generated from existing big data sets.

Thus, we need to create a new world order. A new economic and social model will be needed. It must be centered around the human. Furthermore, a "Wise Data Science" (WDS) theoretical base is needed. The proposed model will be called: the new Wise Decision-Making Support System (WMDSS) model. One such model will need to use Big Data analytics, classical Fuzzy Cognitive Maps, and the new advanced Fuzzy Cognitive Maps [29–35].

Such a Decision-Making Support System (DMSS) is proposed in Fig. 1. Looking at Fig. 1, it is proposed to use it for developing the "Wise Data Science" mathematical-scientific theory. However, this needs a lot of explanation and serious mathematical formulation, which is behind the scope of a plenary paper. Still, the first steps and useful directions can be pointed out.

Definition 1. A "Wise Knowledge" (WK) is defined as the outcome of a Decision-Making process, according to Fig. 1 and for all selected: scientific fields, business, and economic activities and every day of all aspects of the life of the whole planet. The outcome of this process would constitute the universal set of a "Wise Data Science" of a scientific field.

Definition 2. The created "Wise Knowledge" (WK) according to figure one must have enough data for each case and follow the three parallel paths of Fig. 1. Given the initial set for each case follow 1) quantitative analysis and the appropriate decision tree algorithm 2) Perform for the same data a DSS and 3) obtain qualitative data for the same initial data and using FCM's theories proceed to make a final decision for an acceptable outcome. In the last step, the inductive knowledge generated by the first knowledge will be taken into consideration.

Lemma 1: The generated "Wise Knowledge" (WK) been the outcome of Fig. 1 will be acceptable to the universal set of "Wise Data Science" scientific field only if the minimum number of experts is not less than three (3). Preferably five (5) or more.

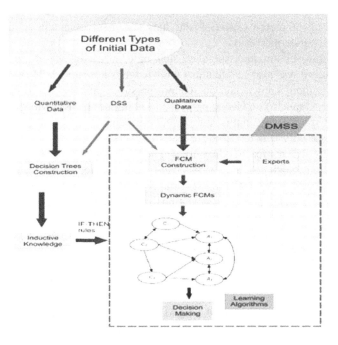

Fig. 1. Generic approach of a Decision-Making system constructed by Decision Trees and Fuzzy Cognitive Maps.

In order to proceed and exploring further the WDS scientific field, we need to remember Plato's wise phrase: «πᾶσά τε ἐπιστήμη χωριζομένη δικαιοσύνης καὶ τῆς ἄλλης ἀρετῆς πανουργία, οὐ σοφία φαίνεται» in plain English: «Every science, when separated from justice and the rest of virtue, becomes cunning and not wisdom».

Lemma 2. The "Wise Data Science" scientific field will be a valid one if and only if provides for all problems of the planet solutions that will be just, fair and useful to humankind. To continue to be valid it must be updated once every year for all its sets.

Finally, the last definition seems appropriate with the title of this Keynote paper.

Definition 3. The planet will be defined as a "Wise Planet driven by Data Science" if and only if the majority of the World's state holders help to create the "Wise Data Science" according to the above Definitions and Lemmas.

6 Conclusions and Future Research

This keynote paper is addressing the aspects affecting the Big Data-Driven World (BDDW) as a result of the recently emerged catastrophic for the world the COVID-19 pandemic. It presents the issues of the pandemic and the new COVID-19 landscape. A historical overview of the generated Big Data-Driven World (BDDW) and the data explosion due to pandemics is presented for the first time. Creating new knowledge is always a challenging task. The arrival of COVID-19 makes the whole BDDW situation much more complex and complicated. Data generated by the COVID-19 pandemic are spread at an exponential rate across all aspects of our lives and all scientific fields. Now, the primary focus lies on the complexity of data and a change in data and information management practices. The known methodologies of data mining and AI tools generate important and useful new knowledge. However, they are not as effective as needed to address all problems of the world in this difficult pandemic time facing our societies. The new landscape for the planet is large and complex. However, the planet needs urgently new viable and realistic solutions in battling the pressing problems of our societies. Generating every hour millions of data is useless unless they are processed to obtain information that will be further processed to create new knowledge. However, this is not enough either. This keynote paper brings up the urgent need for developing new sustainable models for the steady growth of the world. A new "Wise Data Science" is proposed for the first time. A new Generic approach of a Decision-Making system constructed by Decision Trees and Fuzzy Cognitive Maps is proposed as the tool for creating "Wise Knowledge" (WK). First definitions and Lemmas for developing the new "Wise Data Science" are proposed which eventually will lead to a "Wise Planet driven by Data Science". Is this feasible? YES. Indeed, we can have a "Wise Planet driven by Data Science". It is not just a wish or a dream, but instead a realistic proposition to the future generations of our planet. We ought it to our children.

Future research directions are wide open. All theories, practices, and tools of AI, BDDW, cognitive learning, Intelligent Control, and human mind modeling must be revised and updated taking into consideration the new scientific area of "Wise Data Science". Putting in the center of studies the human being, new studies must be undertaken and new models must be developed. For example, the Machine Learning and Deep Learning methods must be updated keeping in mind that new "Wise Knowledge" must be created using the generic approach of a Decision-Making system constructed by Decision Trees and Fuzzy Cognitive Maps. New concepts and algorithms for Wise learning must be defined and mathematically formulated. Using the new generic Decision-Making system create new "Wise Knowledge" for all scientific fields. Compare these new models with classical AI methods for specific applications e.g. Health, Energy, Environment, and others. The new proposed "Wise Data Science" scientific field needs a lot of basic research for its development. Finally, studies are needed for developing the "Wise Planet driven by Data Science".

References

1. World Economic Forum. The Global Competitiveness Reports, 2012–2013 and 2020–2021 Insight Reports, Klaus Schwab, World Economic Forum
2. El-Abbadi, M. "Library of Alexandria". Encyclopedia Britannica, Invalid Date. https://www.britannica.com/topic/Library-of-Alexandria. Accessed 2 June 2021
3. Rider, F.: Guy Stanton Ford, the scholar and the future of the research library: a problem and its solution. (New York: Hadham Press. 1944. pp. xiv, 236.). Am. Hist. Rev. **50**(2), 303–304 (1945)
4. Price, D.: Science Since Babylon Unknown Binding – 1 January 1961
5. Marron, B., Maine, P.: Automatic data compression. Commun. ACM (1967). https://doi.org/10.1145/363790.363813
6. Mashey, J.R.: "Big Data and the Next Wave of InfraStress, Problems, Solutions, Opportunities", 1999 {USENIX} Annual Technical Conference ({USENIX} {ATC} 99), Monterey, CA, June 1999
7. Laney, D.: Application delivery strategies (2001). https://blogs.gartner.com/doug-laney/files/2012/01/ad949-3D-Data-Management-Controlling-Data-Volume-Velocity-and-Variety.pdf
8. NATURE. A Special Issue of Nature on Big Data, Science on the PetaBite Era, 4 September 2008, vol. 455 no. 7209 (2008)
9. Curier, K.: The Economist: Data, data everywhere A special report on managing information, February 2010
10. Boyd, D., Crawford, K.: Critical questions for big data provocations for a cultural, technological, and scholarly phenomenon. Inf. Commun. Soc. **15**(5), 662–679 (2012)
11. Huang, C., Wang, Y., Li, X., Ren, L., Zhao, J., Hu, Y., et al.: Clinical features of patients infected with 2019 novel coronavirus in Wuhan, China. The Lancet **395**(10223), 497–506 (2020). https://doi.org/10.1016/S0140-6736(20)30183-5
12. World Health Organization (WHO). Novel Coronavirus (2019-nCoV): Data. https://www.who.int/emergencies/diseases/novel-coronavirus-2019. Accessed 7 Feb 2020
13. Cavanagh, D.: Severe acute respiratory syndrome vaccine development: experiences of vaccination against avian infectious bronchitis coronavirus. Avian Pathol. **32**(6), 567–82 (2003)
14. Gao, W., et al.: Effects of a SARS-associated coronavirus vaccine in monkeys. Lancet **362**(9399), 1895–96 (2003)
15. Kim, E., Okada, K., Kenniston, T., Raj, V.S., AlHajri, M.M., Farag, E.A., et al.: Immunogenicity of an adenoviral-based Middle East Respiratory Syndrome coronavirus vaccine in BALB/c mice. Vaccine **32**(45), 5975–5982 (2014)
16. Greenough, T.C., et al.: Development and characterization of a severe acute respiratory syndrome-associated coronavirus-neutralizing human monoclonal antibody that provides effective immunoprophylaxis in mice. J. Infect. Dis. **191**(4), 507–514 (2005)

17. Roberts, A., et al.: Therapy with a severe acute respiratory syndrome-associated coronavirus-neutralizing human monoclonal antibody reduces disease severity and viral burden in golden Syrian hamsters. J. Infect. Dis. **193**(5), 685–692 (2006)
18. Le, T.T., Cramer, J.P., Chen, R., Mayhew, S.: Evolution of the COVID-19 vaccine development landscape. Nat. Rev. Drug Discov. **19**(10), 667–668 (2020)
19. Bean, R.: CIO Network, "Big Data in the Time of Coronavirus (COVID-19)" FORBES, 30 March 2020
20. Zwitter, A., Gstrein, O.J.: Big data, privacy and COVID-19 – learning from humanitarian expertise in data protection. J. Int. Humanit. Act. **5**(1), 1–7 (2020)
21. Shah, H., Jiles, L.: "A Data-Driven Approach to the Pandemic" Strategic Finance Magazine, 1 September 2020
22. Alsunaidi, S.J., et al.: Applications of Big Data Analytics to Control COVID-19 Pandemic. Sensors, MDPI **21**, 2282 (2021)
23. Jones, M., Fishman, S., Reschechko, Y.: The World Bank's Development Impact Evaluation (DIME), Published on Data Blog, 26 April 2021
24. McCorduck, P.: Machines Who Think, 2nd edn. CRC Press Taylor & Francis Group, Routledge (2004)
25. Russell, S.J., Norvig, P.: Artificial Intelligence: A Modern Approach, 3rd edn. Prentice Hall, Upper Saddle River (2009)
26. Luger, G., Stubblefield, W.: Artificial Intelligence: Structures and Strategies for Complex Problem Solving, 5th edn. The Benjamin/Cummings Inc., San Francisco (2004)
27. Shalev-Shwartz, S., Ben-David, S.: Understanding Machine Learning: From Theory to Algorithms, 1st edn. Cambridge University Press, Cambridge (2014)
28. Poole, D., Mackworth, A.: Artificial Intelligence: Foundations of Computational Agents, 2nd edn. Cambridge University Press, Cambridge (2017)
29. Kosko, B.: Fuzzy cognitive maps. Int. J. Man Mach. Stud. **24**(1), 65–75 (1986)
30. Groumpos P.P., Fuzzy cognitive maps: basic theories and their application to complex systems, Glykas, M. (ed.) Fuzzy Cognitive Maps: Advances in Theory, Methodologies, Tools and Applications, vol. 247, pp. 1–22. Springer, Berlin, Heidelberg (2010). https://doi.org/10.1007/978-3-642-03220-2_1
31. Mpelogianni, V., Groumpos, P.P.: Re-approaching fuzzy cognitive maps to increase the knowledge of a system. Intern. J. AI Soc. **33**(2), 175–188 (2018)
32. Vergini, E.S., Groumpos, P.P.: A new conception on the fuzzy cognitive maps method. IFAC-Papers OnLine **49**(29), 300–304 (2016)
33. Anninou, A.P., Groumpos, P.P., Poulios, P., Gkliatis, I.: A new approach of dynamic fuzzy cognitive knowledge networks in modelling diagnosing process of meniscus injury. IFAC-Papers OnLine **50**, 5861–5866 (2017)
34. Groumpos, P.P.: Intelligence and fuzzy cognitive maps: scientific issues, challenges and opportunities. Stud. Inf. Control **27**(3), 247–264 (2018)
35. Keen, P.G., Morton, S., Michael, S.: Decision Support Systems: An Organizational Perspective. Addison-Wesley Pub. Co., Reading (1978)

Adapting, Learning, and Control the Supply of a Vital Commodity Such as COVID-19 Vaccine

Vladimir V. Tsyganov[✉]

V.A. Trapeznikov Institute of Control Sciences of the Russian Academy of Sciences, 65, Profsoyuznaya Str., Moscow 117997, Russia
bbc@ipu.ru

Abstract. The article examines the problem of managing a democratic socio-economic system in the face of a shortage of a vital commodity (such as the COVID-19 vaccine). The citizens' approval of the actions of the authorities to increase the production and supply of this product contributes to political stability. The possibilities of increasing the supply of a vital commodity depend on random factors. In the face of such uncertainty, in the age of artificial intelligence, the management of a socio-economic system can be based on machine learning and adaptation. In this case, it is necessary to take into account the activity of the elements of the system associated with the presence of their own goals, which do not necessarily coincide with the goal of the system as a whole. These elements can influence adaptation and machine learning procedures to achieve their goals. The research is carried out on a three-level model of a democratic socio-economic system. At its top level is a member of society - a citizen who evaluates the politician who is at the middle level of the system. In turn, the politician can influence the increase in the supply of a vital commodity, including both its purchase on the market and production at a local plant belonging to the lower level of the system. Political stability is guaranteed if the citizen regularly approves the actions of the politician to increase the supply of vital goods. But the plant's management knows its own production potential better than the politician. Thus, this leadership can manipulate the volume of its own production in order to gain more support from the politician. A politician may also manipulate the opportunities available to him in order to achieve personal goals. To avoid manipulation of the supply of a vital product under conditions of uncertainty, a socio-economic management mechanism is proposed, including an economic and political mechanism. The economic mechanism includes a procedure for adaptive forecasting of the production of a vital commodity, as well as a procedure for supporting this production. The political mechanism includes a procedure for machine self-learning of a citizen, as well as a procedure for assessing the activity of a politician. Sufficient conditions for the synthesis of the optimal mechanism of socio-economic management are found, in which random opportunities to increase the supply of a vital commodity are fully used, including both purchases on the market and production at a local plant. An example of such a socio-economic mechanism is considered on the example of the supply of the COVID-19 vaccine to England.

A. G. Kravets et al. (Eds.): CIT&DS 2021, CCIS 1448, pp. 16–26, 2021.
https://doi.org/10.1007/978-3-030-87034-8_2

Keywords: Socio-economic system · Political stability · Control · Adaptation · Machine learning · COVID-19 vaccine

1 Introduction

1.1 Socio-Economic System and Political Stability

In the face of a crisis caused by a shortage of a vital commodity (such as the COVID-19 vaccine), the authorities must take the job of monitoring and supporting its production and supply in the right quantities. Therefore, authorities need to control the supply of this commodity in the face of change and associated uncertainty. First of all, this concerns the development and production at factories that are located in the territory they control. The authorities also have other opportunities to increase the supply of the commodity, for example, through procurement from the external market or through production under license in the economic system they control.

Unfortunately, however, market fundamentalism leads to a crisis of the values of politicians and their attempts to pursue personal rather than public goals [1]. Therefore, it is necessary to organize public control in order to motivate the authorities to use all available opportunities to overcome the social crisis. Lack of proper social control leads to the emergence of toxic leaders and corrupt politicians [2], oligarchy [3], leaders without ethics [4], hedonistic politicians [5], and wire-pullers creating phobias [6].

In a democracy, society controls politicians through elections, politicians' ratings, protests, etc. Political stability is fostered by public acceptance of politicians' actions to secure supplies of a vital commodity such as the COVID-19 vaccine. Taking into account the above, we will consider the hierarchical organizational structure of the socio-economic system "Society - Power - Economy", schematically shown in Fig. 1a).

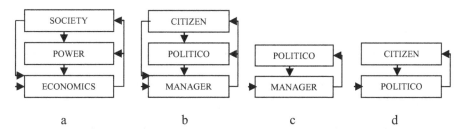

Fig. 1. Hierarchical organizational structures: a. Society – Power – Economy; b. Citizen – Politico – Manager; c. Politico – Manager; d. Citizen – Politico.

1.2 Artificial Intelligence, Adaptation, and Machine Learning

To manage production under conditions of uncertainty, in accordance with the concept of Industry 4.0, artificial intelligence (AI) is used [7]. AI involves adaptation and learning.

For example, for sustainable development, adaptive control mechanisms are proposed [8]. Learning mechanisms are used in the digital control of industrial systems [9].

In the long term, AI will become not only the prerogative of production managers but also members of society. The Economic World Forum White paper (2019) concludes that "The increasing use of AI … will have revolutionary effects on human society … thereby preserve a human-centric society." [10]. AI makes it possible to implement the prediction paradigm "as a technological dream of public safety, national security" [11]. Related to AI is the concept of a digital society adopted by the European Commission to access citizens to better social care, health monitoring, etc. [12]. Members of the digital society are modeled as digital voters [13].

However, there are difficulties on the way to the effective use of AI in society. First of all, there is a need for algorithmic accountability and transparency in the use of artificial intelligence for making public decisions [14]. It is necessary to initiate a conversation on public accountability frameworks, including issues of governance, and the cultivation of a culture of algorithmic accountability arising from concerns of opaqueness, transparency, and responsibility [11]. In seeking an insight into issues of accountability, de Laat asks 'How to install a culture of accountability?' [15].

Spiegelhalter says that perhaps a more basic issue is whether we should believe what we hear about AI and what the algorithm tells us [16]. For those interested in the design of trustworthiness of AI algorithms, he proposes seven criteria for the evaluation of claims of trustworthiness: (1) is it any good when tried in new parts of the real world? (2) Would something simpler, and more transparent and robust, be just as good? (3) Could I explain how it works (in general) to anyone who is interested? (4) Could I explain to an individual how it reached its conclusion in their particular case? (5) Does it know when it is on shaky ground, and can it acknowledge uncertainty? (6) Do people use it appropriately, with the right level of skepticism? (7) Does it actually help in practice? In seeking the trustworthiness of the AI system, Spiegelhalter asks to be mindful in that "It is important not to be mesmerized by the mystique surrounding AI."

1.3 Human Factor

In addition to the above, the use of AI is hampered by the gap between machine learning (ML) and control theory [17]. It is also necessary to take into account the activity of the elements of the socio-economic systems associated with the presence of their own goals. In industry, they can manipulate production to influence AI in their favor [9]. In this regard, there is a need to control the activities of production management.

For their part, as mentioned above, the authorities may not fully use the opportunities of outsourcing - purchases of vital commodities in foreign markets, acquisition of production licenses, etc. Indeed, in the face of changes, a politician knows his capabilities better than a citizen. Using this insight, the politician can manipulate. In [18], such a politician is called Politico. His unwanted activity can lead to the failure to use existing opportunities in which the citizen is interested. In this regard, there is a need to control and evaluate the actions of the authorities in a crisis on the part of society.

Thus, in order to ensure political stability in a social crisis caused by a shortage of vital commodities, it is necessary to take into account the human factor. For this, the theory of organizational control is traditionally used [19]. One of the directions in this theory is associated with learning and adaptation. On their basis, adaptive mechanisms for improving international stability developed [20]. A behavioral model for control mechanism design including individual evolutionary learning was developed [21].

The idea of integration of different learning & control systems is based on systems engineering [22]. Particular attention is directed toward adaptations of the widely used self-learning algorithms to increase the efficiency of control with the aid of AI methodology [9].

1.4 The Investigated Model and Its Decomposition

In line with the concept of a digital society [12], we will assume that both citizens and politicians are using appropriate AI procedures. For simplicity, let's assume that citizens learn and make decisions independently using the same optimal procedure. Likewise, policymakers use the same best adaptation procedures. Then, without limiting the generality, it is enough to consider a socio-economic system consisting of one citizen, a politician, and a manager (Fig. 1b). At the top level of this organizational structure is a member of the community (Citizen). At the middle level, there is a representative of the government responsible for supplying the Citizen with the commodity (Politician). To do this, the Politician conducts both purchases of this commodity and supports its products in a factory belonging to the lower level of this structure.

Both the purchases and the production of the commodity are affected by random environmental factors. Therefore, the Citizen does not know the maximum supply possibilities. In addition, Politico does not know the maximum possibilities of its production at the plant (in short - the potential). In the face of such uncertainty, the Citizen and the Politician must use AI procedures to make optimal decisions.

To solve this problem, we will use the method of decomposition of the hierarchical structure, which is widely used in systems engineering [22]. Figure 1c) shows the structure "Politician – Manager" obtained as a result of such decomposition. Also, Fig. 1d) shows the structure "Citizen-Politico" obtained as a result of this decomposition. After describing and analyzing these structures, the composition is produced. This approach provides a combination of adaptive and learning procedures in the development of intelligent mechanisms for regulating the evolution of organizations.

2   Adaptive Mechanism of Production Control

Consider the structure of the "Politician – Manager" (Fig. 1c). At the upper level of it, there is the Politico, on the lower level - the Manager of the factory producing the commodity. Denote v_t the volume of the factory production (in short, output) in period t, t $= 1, 2,..., v_t \in B_t = [v, V_t]$. There V_t is the maximal output (in short, potential) which is a stationary stochastic value $V_t \in B = [\sigma, l]$, s $\geq$ v.

If Politico knows V_t exactly, then he can use some kind of adaptive algorithm to predict factory performance from time-series observations. For example, for forecasting time series Brown's adaptive model [23] is used.

However, in reality, Politico knows less about the possibilities of production in the factory than the factory management. In such cases, one speaks of asymmetric awareness

[24]. Therefore we need to consider the activity of the management associated with the presence of its own target, which does not necessarily coincide with the target of Politico. To achieve this target, the management can manipulate output.

To consider this problem, assume the potential V_t becomes known to the factory management at the beginning of period t. After that, the factory management chooses the output v_t, $v_t \leq V_t$. Then Politico becomes known v_t. For the estimates of the output, Politico uses the adaptive Brown's model [23]. Then the estimate (n_t) of factory production output in period t is calculated by the recurrent equation:

$$n_t = N(n_{t-1}, v_t) = (1 - e)n_{t-1} + ev_t, \ 0 < e < 1, \ t = 1, \ 2..., \ n_0 = n^0. \tag{1}$$

We will call $N(n_{t-1}, v_t)$ - the forecasting procedure, and e - elasticity. If the output is below the potential ($v_t < V_t$ t = 1, 2,....,), then the estimate n_t will differ from the optimal estimate obtained when $v_t = V_t$, $t = 1, 2, ...$

Consider the practical aspects of increasing the factory management's interest in using its own potential. In the practice of production planning & control in large-scale hierarchical organizations, usually support grows on the increase in output of production with respect to forecasted plan [9]. Thus, the higher the plan the more difficult it is to get support. Also in such organizations, often plan increased by a certain percentage of the achieved production output. This is called planning "from the level has been achieved" [9]. Then plan in the future will be the higher, the higher the output today. Therefore, the factory management may not be interested in increasing output. Thus, there is a problem of lack of interest in the disclosure of production potential. So it is necessary to arrange control to motivate the factory management to unleash its own potential.

Consider such control with the following order of operations. At the beginning of period t, the factory management becomes aware of the potential V_t, and chooses the metric v_t, $v_t \leq V_t$. Then comparing v_t with the estimate n_{t-1}, Politico determines the factory support:

$$s_t = S(n_{t-1}, v_t) = \alpha(v_t - n_{t-1}) + const, \ \alpha > 0, t = 1, \ 2..., \tag{2}$$

where $S(\cdot)$ is the support procedure.

The set of the procedures of forecasting (1) and support (2) of production in the factory will be called the economic mechanism and denoted by $E = (N, S)$.

Below we suppose that the factory management seeks to increase the sum of support in current and T future periods with the discount factor λ:

$$D_t = \sum_{\tau=t}^{t+T} \lambda^{\tau-t} s_\tau, \ 0 < \lambda < 1, \tag{3}$$

Then the factory management chooses a metric v_t^* that maximizing (3): $v_t^* = \arg \max_{v_t \leq V_t} D_t$.

3 Citizen Learning and Control of Politico

In addition to manufacturing in local factories, the authorities have other opportunities to increase the supply of the vital commodity, for example, by purchasing them from the external market. At the same time, the authorities are more informed about the available opportunities (potential) than citizens and other stakeholders. In this case, we can also talk about asymmetric awareness [24].

In addition, we need to consider the impact of expectations that are fundamental to people's lives. The fact is that a politician's rating rises if his effectiveness exceeds the expectations of citizens. But the higher these expectations, the more difficult it is for a policy to maintain and improve its rating. In addition, the nature of man is such that his desires grow over time: «It is human nature to evolve—people are never content with what they have, but always strive for the next thing». High humanitarian technologies are based on the use of such dynamics of expectations [25].

Thus, the expectations of citizens in each subsequent period can grow in relation to the result achieved by Politico today. Consequently, the future expectations of citizens will be higher, the higher the efficiency of Politico achieved today [18]. But then Politico may not be interested in raising efficiency beyond Citizens' expectations. Otherwise, Citizens' expectations will accelerate and it will be more difficult for Politico to maintain and improve its rating. Thus, the problem arises of Politico's disinterest in using all the possibilities in the interests of Citizens. This problem is typical of social systems. As a result, "estimations of policy effectiveness fail to account for dynamics that are fundamental in human life and central to many public policy challenges" [26].

With this in mind, we need to develop digital public policy control using AI and ML. In [27], a model of supervised learning and voter decision-making on voting for or against a politician in a digital society is considered. With insufficient voter awareness, an unscrupulous politician may not use the available opportunities to achieve his goals. To avoid this, the voter learns using the recommendations of a mentor (who also does not know about all the possibilities of a politician). The voter uses obtained knowledge to evaluate and vote under conditions of uncertainty caused by both random influences of the external environment and undesirable activities of a politician. The evaluation and voting procedure constitutes the mechanism for making a decision by the voter. With this mechanism, a set of politician's choices is determined, at which the maximum of his objective function is achieved. Sufficient conditions have been found for the synthesis of an optimal mechanism in which a politician fully uses his capabilities in the interests of the voter.

Taking this approach, consider a model of Citizen unsupervised learning and assessment of Politico actions to increase the supply of the vital commodity. Suppose the total supply q_t is the sum of the factory's output v_t^* and the purchase $a_t q_t = v_t^* + a_t$. $a_t \in A_t = [a, A_t]$, where A_t is the maximum purchase of the commodity in a market. There A_t is a stationary stochastic value, $A_t \in A = [\eta, \iota]$, $\eta \geq a$. From $v_t \in B_t = [v, V_t]$ and $V_t \in B = [\sigma, /]$, $s \geq v$, it follows that $v_t \in \hat{B} = [v, /]$, $q_t \in \Pi = [a + v, \iota + /]$.

The Citizen can monitor both the estimate n_t and the metric v_t^* but does not know A_t. In this situation, the Citizen should rating Politico in such a way as to increase total supply q_t. Namely, the Citizen gives Politico 1st rating if Politico's work is satisfactory (or 0th rating if not).

To determine the rating of Politico in period t, it is necessary for Citizen to assign total supply q_t to one of the two sets Π_1 and Π_2 which make up the set Π, $\Pi_1 \cup \Pi_2 = \Pi$.

An incorrect rating leads to losses of Citizen. The problem is to determine the separation of the set Π which minimizes overage losses.

Assume the Citizen knows both the maximum supply $Q_t = A_t + V_t$ and the density of its stochastic distribution. Then for each unknown set Π_1 and Π_2, the Citizen can introduce loss functions $L_1(c, Q_t) = Q_t - cm$ and $L_2(c, Q_t) = f(c - Q_t)$, $0 < m < 1$, $f > 0$. There c is an unknown parameter minimizing the overage losses. For obtaining its estimate, the optimal algorithm of learning can be used [9]. Suppose the Citizen only knows the supply q_t determined by Politico. Then the estimate z_t of an unknown parameter c can be calculated by the recurrent formula:

$$z_{t+1} = Z(z_t, q_t) = \begin{cases} z_t + \omega_t m \ if \ q_t < p_t \\ z_t - \omega_t f \ if \ q_t \geq p_t \end{cases}, \ p_t = z_t(f + m)/(f + 1), z_1 = c*, \quad (4)$$

where $0 < \omega_{t+1} < \omega_t$, $\sum\limits_{\tau=1}^{\infty} \omega_\tau < \infty$. Using (4), the Citizen determines Politico rating:

$$r_t = R(z_t, q_t) = \begin{cases} 1 & if \quad q_t \geq p_t \\ 0 & if \quad q_t < p_t \end{cases}. \quad (5)$$

In fact, p_t is the minimum quantity of a vital commodity that Politico must supply in order to receive a higher rating of 1. This means that the Citizen approves of the policy to increase the supply of the commodity, assuming the supply p_t is normal for period t. Therefore for brevity, we will call p_t the supply rate, $Z(z_t, q_t)$ - rationing procedure, and $R(z_t, q_t)$ - the rating procedure.

If the supply q_t is not lower than the rate p_t ($q_t \geq p_t$) then Politico gets a rating 1 ($r_t = 1$) otherwise - rating zero ($r_t = 0$). In the case of zero-rating, the Citizen accuses Politico, voted and protested against him, etc. So the support of Politico from Citizen rises with this rating.

The set of rationing procedure $Z(z_t, q_t)$ and rating procedure $R(z_t, q_t)$ will be called political mechanism and denoted $P = (Z, R)$.

Assume that maximal supply A_t becomes known to Politico before selecting a_t^*. Then Politico chooses such a_t^* from the set A_t which maximizing target function depending on both on the current rating and μ future ratings:

$$W_t = W[r_t, r_{t+1}, ..., r_{t+\mu}], W_t \uparrow r_i, \ i = \overline{1, \mu}, \quad (6)$$

where $W[\cdot]$ is a non-decreasing function. Below we assume Politico supportive of the Citizen: if $v_t^* + A_t \in Arg \max\limits_{a_t \in A_t} W_t$ then $a_t^* = A_t$.

4   Socio-Economic Control Mechanism

The set of economic mechanism $E = (N, S)$ and Political mechanism $P = (Z, R)$ will be called socio-economic control mechanism and denoted $C = \{N, S, Z, R\}$. Consider the problem of synthesis of optimal mechanism $C = \{N, S, Z, R\}$, which fully exploits the capabilities of supply of vital commodity: $q_t^* = V_t + A_t, t = 1, 2...$

Theorem. Socio-economic control mechanism $C = \{N, S, Z, R\}$ ensures the highest possible supply: $q_t^* = V_t + A_t$, $t = 1, 2...$

Proof. Substitute s_t from (2) into expression (3) for Dt. Then we substitute the expressions for $n\tau$ from (1) into the obtained expression for Dt, $\tau = \overline{t+1, t+T}$. Using (1) as a recurrent equation, it is easy to obtain the expression for Dt as a function of vt: $D_t = \{1 - \lambda + e\lambda[\lambda(1-e)]^T\}v_t + const$. Hence $\partial D_t/\partial v_t = 1 - \lambda + e\lambda[\lambda(1-e)]^T$. Considering that $0 < e < 1$ by (1) and $0 < \lambda < 1$ by (3), we get: $\partial D_t/\partial v_t > 0$. Thus by (3) the maximum of D_t is reached at $v_t = V_t : v_t^* = \arg\max\limits_{v_t \leq V_t} D_t = V_t$. Therefore $q_t = V_t + a_t$. Taking this into account, we get that, according to (5), the rating $r_t = R(v_t, q_t)$ is a non-decreasing function of a_t. From (4), v_τ does not increase with growth a_t when $\tau = \overline{t+1, t+\mu}$. Consequently by (5), the future rating $r_\tau = R(v_\tau, q_\tau)$ does not decrease with growth a_t when $\tau = \overline{t+1, t+\mu}$. So target function (6) do not decrease with growth a_t. Due to assumption that Politico supportive of the Citizen, we have $a_t^* = A_t$. Taking into account that $q_t = V_t + a_t$, we have $q_t^* = V_t + A_t$, QED.

5 Example: Socio-Economic Control of COVID-19 Vaccine Supply in England

A multidisciplinary approach to AI and COVID-19 is discussed in [28]. AI vs COVID-19 is associated with limitations, constraints, and pitfalls [29]. Consider how we can use the approach developed above to use AI to develop the production and procurement of a vital COVID-19 vaccine when demand for it exceeds supply.

Suppose there is a factory in an area where the population has empowered a politician with some potential to produce a COVID-19 vaccine. This potential is influenced by random factors. Therefore, the exact potential of vaccine production is not known to either the politician or the citizens. Then, to solve the problem of unlocking the potential of vaccine production at this factory, an economic mechanism $E = (N, S)$ can be used that satisfies the condition of the theorem. Guided by the Theorem, to increase COVID19 vaccine production, Politico should be used the procedures of forecasting (1) and support (2) of this product in the factory. Moreover, as shown in the proof of the Theorem, the sum of support (3) increases with an increase in the volume of vaccine production. This will interest factory management in unlocking the potential of vaccine production.

5.1 Political Mechanism

Suppose now that the authorities have solved the problem of unlocking the potential of vaccine production in factories located in the territory under the jurisdiction of the politician. However, in addition to production at local factories, the politician has other opportunities to increase the supply of products that are vital for the population, for example, by purchasing them on the foreign market. In this regard, the problem of building a political mechanism arises, which would interest the politician in using all his available opportunities for the benefit of society. For this, a political mechanism $P = (Z, R)$ satisfying the Theorem condition can be used. Let us illustrate its functioning with the example of vaccination against COVID-19 in England from January 10 to March

31, 2021 [30]. During this period, the demand for vaccination from the population exceeded the supply of vaccine doses. Therefore, all receipts of the vaccine were spent. For this reason, the number of delivered vaccine doses will be considered equal to the number of people vaccinated during this period.

Formally, Citizen observes daily vaccination data q_t which is equal to the number of people vaccinated in day t, where t is the day and month of 2021 (black line on Fig. 2a). Then Citizen uses the political mechanism $P = (Z, R)$ to control vaccine supply with the procedures of rationing (4) and rating (5). The results of this mechanism's functioning are illustrated in Fig. 2. The Citizen calculates rate p_t using (4) (blue line on Fig. 2a). The daily rating of Politico r_t (pink line on Fig. 2b) is determined by comparing the daily vaccination data q_t and rate p_t according to (5).

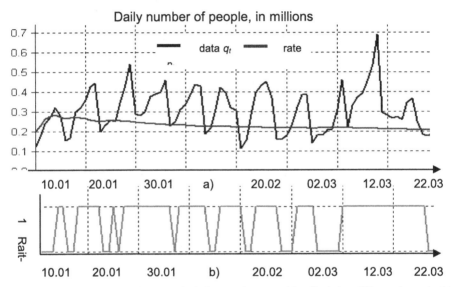

Fig. 2. a) Daily vaccination data q_t (black line) and rate p_t (blue line), in millions of people; b) daily rating r_t (pink line). (Color figure online)

5.2   Political Stability and Dual Channel Politico Stimulation

As can be seen from Fig. 2.b, periods of time have arisen (in late January and early February, as well as in the second half of March) in which the daily ratings are 1. In fact, these are the times when citizens are satisfied with the pace of vaccination. Regular citizen approval of government action to secure a vital vaccine contributes to political stability.

Let's see how the mechanism $P = (Z, R)$ encourages Politico to increase the pace of vaccination. Firstly, the Politico rating r_t is determined according to (5) If $q_t \geq p_t$ then $r_t = 1$, and Politico obtains rating 1. Otherwise, Politico obtains zero ratings ($s_t = 0$). So Politico's rating is growing q_t.

Secondly, according to (4) the higher the number of people vaccinated q_t, the lower rate p_τ for the future period τ, $\tau = \overline{t+1, t+T}$. But, according to (5), this rate p_τ plays the role of the threshold value of the number q_t of people vaccinated in the future period τ at which Politico will receive rating 1 in the period τ, $\tau = \overline{t+1, t+T}$. Consequently, it becomes easier for Politico to get rating 1 in period τ even with a smaller value of the random potential of vaccination p_τ, $\tau = \overline{t+1, t+T}$.

In other words, Citizen stimulates Politico to accelerate vaccination, with an increase of the number of vaccinated people (q_t) through 2 channels - today and in the future. Firstly, Politico receives the best rating today. Secondly, the threshold values for obtaining Citizen best ratings in the future are decreased. This means 2-channel stimulation of Politico in supplying vaccination.

As a result of combining the above economic and political mechanisms, we get an optimal socio-economic control mechanism $C = \{N, S, Z, R\}$. This mechanism satisfies the Theorem and encourages Politico to increase the number of vaccinated people. However, the politician is interested in taking full advantage of all the opportunities of the supply of the vaccine. In fact, this mechanism forms the progressive consciousness of Politico in the interests of citizens and aims to reconcile the interests of society and Politico. This example illustrates the simplicity and transparency of the socio-economic mechanism $C = \{N, S, Z, R\}$.

6 Conclusions

Political stability is determined by the loyalty of citizens. With a vital commodity shortage (such as a coronavirus vaccine), citizens need to meet their vital needs quickly. It is important for the loyalty of citizens. For example, in connection with the COVID-19 pandemic, it is necessary to establish and adjust the system, structure, and mechanisms for the supply of the vaccine. To process big data, it is advisable to use such elements of artificial intelligence as adaptive procedures and machine learning. This requires transparency and accountability of the use of artificial intelligence in decision-making. To avoid abuse of power and monopoly position in the market, modern management methods should be used in the event of conflicts of interest.

This article illustrates a simple and transparent approach to ensuring political stability when a vital commodity (such as the vaccine) is in short supply, based on the theory of organizational management, on the one hand, and layered artificial intelligence, on the other. Further research in this direction can be associated with the system engineering of a more complex model of socio-economic systems.

References

1. Soros, G.: The Crisis of Global Capitalism. Little, Brown & Company, USA (1998)
2. Lipman-Blumen, J.: The Allure of Toxic Leaders. Oxford University Press, USA (2004)
3. Schultz, V.: Oligarchy, ontology, cycles, and change in a globalizing world. Sotsiologicheskie Issledovaniya **2**, 3–15 (2009)
4. Boddy, C., Ladyshewsky, R., Galvin, P.: Leaders without ethics in global business: corporate psychopaths. J. Public Aff. **10**, 121–138 (2010)

5. Tsyganov, V.: Limits of global growth, stagnation, creativity and international stability. AI Soc. **29**(1), 259–266 (2013). https://doi.org/10.1007/s00146-013-0483-x
6. Tsyganov, V.: Socio-political stability, voter's emotional expectations, and information management. AI Soc. (2020). https://doi.org/10.1007/s00146-020-01017-8
7. Blanchet, M., Rinn, T., Thaden, G., Thieulloy, G.: Industrie 4.0 - the new industrial revolution. How Europe will succeed. Roland Berger Strategy, München (2014)
8. Borodin, D., Gurlev, I., Klukvin, A.: Adaptive mechanisms for sustainable development. Syst. Sci. **30**, 89–95 (2004)
9. Tsyganov, V.: Learning mechanisms in digital control of large-scale industrial systems. In: Proceedings of the Global Smart Industry Conference, pp. 1–6. IEEE, Chelyabinsk (2018)
10. AI governance: a holistic approach to implement ethics into AI. White Paper. World Economic Forum Homepage. https://www.weforum.org. Accessed 12 Apr 2021
11. Gill, K.S.: Prediction paradigm: the human price for instrumentalism. AI Soc **35**, 3 (2020)
12. Creating a digital society. EU Homepage. https://ec.europa.eu/digital-single-market/en/creating-digital-society. Accessed 19 Oct 2020
13. Tsyganov, V.: Intelligent information technologies in social safety. Commun. Comput. Inf. Sci. **1084**, 270–284 (2019)
14. De Fine Licht, K., de Fine Licht, J.: Artificial intelligence, transparency, and public decision-making. AI Soc. **35**(4), 917–926 (2020). https://doi.org/10.1007/s00146-020-00960-w
15. De Laat, P.B.: Algorithmic decision-making based on machine learning from big data: can transparency restore accountability? Philos. Technol. **31**, 525–541 (2018)
16. Spiegelhalter, D.: Should we trust algorithms? Harv. Data Sci. Rev. **2**(1), 1–12 (2020)
17. Recht, B.: Reflections on the learning-to-control renaissance. In: Proceedings of the 21st IFAC World Congress, p. 4707. Elsevier, Berlin (2020)
18. Tsyganov, V.: Emotional expectations and social stability. IFAC-PapersOnLine **51**(30), 112–117 (2018)
19. Burkov, V., Gubko, M., Kondratiev, V., Korgin, N., Novikov, D.: Mechanism Synthesis and Management. NOVA Publishers, New York (2013)
20. Bagamaev, R., Gurlev, I.: Adaptive mechanism for mastering capital and improving international stability. IFAC-PapersOnLine **16**, 42–45 (2005)
21. Arifovic, J., Ledyard, J.: A behavioral model for mechanism design: individual evolutionary learning. J. Econ. Behav. Organ. **78**, 375–395 (2011)
22. Kossiakoff, A., Sweet, W., Seymour, S., Biemer, S.: Systems Engineering: Principles and Practice. John Wiley, New York (2011)
23. Dibrivniy, O., Onyshchenko, V., Grebenyuk, V.: Forecasting based on the trend model and adaptive Brown's model. In: 14th International Conference on Advanced Trends in Radio-electronics, Telecommunications and Computer Engineering, pp. 944–947. Lviv University, Ukraine (2018)
24. Auster, S.: Asymmetric awareness and moral hazard. Games Econ. Behav. **82**, 503–521 (2013)
25. Schultz, V.: Humanitarian high technologies in political system of society. Sotsiologicheskie Issledovaniya **8**, 85–93 (2012)
26. Diallo, S.Y., Shults, F.L., Wildman, W.J.: Minding morality: ethical artificial societies for public policy modeling. AI Soc. **36**(1), 49–57 (2020). https://doi.org/10.1007/s00146-020-01028-5
27. Tsyganov, V.: Models of voters and the politicians in a digital society under uncertainty. IFAC PaperOnline **52**(25), 275–280 (2019)
28. Ahuja, S., Reddy, V., Marques, O.: Artificial intelligence and COVID-19: a multidisciplinary approach. Integr. Med. Res. **9**, 100434 (2020)
29. Naudé, W.: Artificial intelligence vs COVID-19: limitations, constraints and pitfalls. AI Soc. **35**(3), 761–765 (2020). https://doi.org/10.1007/s00146-020-00978-0
30. Coronavirus (COVID-19) in the UK. GOV.UK Homepage. https://coronavirus.data.gov.uk/details/vaccinations. Accessed 12 Apr 2021

Artificial Intelligence and Deep Learning Technologies for Creative Tasks. Knowledge Discovery in Patent and Open Sources

Development of a Method for Intellectual Support of Inventive Activity Based on Deep Machine Learning

Alla G. Kravets[1,2]([⊠]), Natalia Salnikova[3], Irina P. Medintseva[3], and Vladimir Shinkaruk[4]

[1] Volgograd State Technical University, 28 Lenin Av., Volgograd 400005, Russia
agk@gde.ru
[2] Dubna State University, 19 Universitetskaya St., Dubna, Moscow Region 141982, Russia
[3] Volgograd Institute of Management – Branch of the Russian Presidential Academy of National Economy and Public Administration, 8 Gagarin St., Volgograd 400131, Russia
[4] Volgograd State University, 100 Universitetskiy Av., Volgograd 400062, Russia

Abstract. This paper describes a software and information method for intellectual support of an inventive activity, which is characterized by the implementation of mechanisms for identifying interdisciplinary classes of inventions based on deep machine learning. The problem of classification of patent texts and predictions of trends in technological development is solved using a neural network with long short-term memory. To obtain better results, the selection of the optimal parameters of this network is provided. The process of forming a training sample of a neural network is described and trained for the classification of patent documents. The analysis of the parameters influencing the results of the work of the recurrent neural network, intended for thematic classification of the patent array, and the selection of their optimal values are carried out. An optimal configuration of a recurrent neural network has been obtained, which has improved the results of the developed software.

Keywords: Neural network · Recurrent neural network · Machine learning · Deep learning · Training samples · Patent structure · Patent search of images · Patent image processing · Data set generation

1 Introduction

The number of patentsSearch increases every year. With the increase in the number of patents, the time for consideration of an application for registration of a patent also increases. The inventor needs to establish the uniqueness of the patented technology. To do this, he must make a comparison with similar patents and make sure that there are no analogs of the invention. In the course of such work, the inventor can check several thousand patents.

Due to the increasing flow of patent applications, the processing time for inventors is also increasing. In some cases, it reaches several years. One of the main operations of

© Springer Nature Switzerland AG 2021
A. G. Kravets et al. (Eds.): CIT&DS 2021, CCIS 1448, pp. 29–44, 2021.
https://doi.org/10.1007/978-3-030-87034-8_3

the analysis of the prior art for a patent application is the search for patents for analogs that could refute the novelty of the application and make it impossible to issue a patent on it [1, 2]. In many cases, the inventor spends tens of hours conducting a search, while looking through thousands of existing patents and other documents. Throughout the entire period of the patent examination, the applicant does not know whether he will be granted a patent or not. At the same time, the average percentage of refusals for the grant of patents is more than 60%, which is a problem in conditions of many years of waiting. The past decades have seen rapid market changes and widespread technology diffusion. As a result, the product life cycle is shortened. In such a rapidly changing environment, monitoring of technology changes or trend analysis becomes a strategic necessity [3, 4]. In this case, patent documents are one of the best sources of technological and commercial knowledge for organizing such monitoring, since more than 80% of all technological information can be found in patents. Currently, decision support systems are actively developing in the analysis of the state of the art for patents and patent applications, and new methods are being developed to automate the classification of applications and search for patent analogs [5, 6]. However, the currently existing methods of automating the search for analog patents do not have sufficient accuracy to reduce the search time compared to manual search using keywords. Thus, the development of a software-informational method of intellectual support is an urgent task.

The aim of this work is to develop a toolkit for a software-information method for intellectual support of the inventive activity.

To achieve this goal, it is necessary to solve a number of tasks:

- investigate the process of inventive activity;
- study the structure of patent documents;
- analyze existing patent search systems;
- analyze the architectures of neural networks and deep learning libraries;
- form a training sample;
- train the neural network to classify patent documents;
- evaluate the work of the developed system.

2   Research of Inventive Activity and Analysis of Patent Search Methods

2.1   Features of Patent Search

Patent searches are currently carried out using special information retrieval systems. Conducting a search using electronic databases on the Internet is considered to be quite complete and objective, but, nevertheless, it must be supplemented with a "manual" search by carefully "filtering" the information received.

A patent search is a procedure for selecting information on patents corresponding to a specific request, which can be carried out on one or several grounds. In particular, a patent search makes it possible to establish the novelty of an invention.

The search is carried out on an array of patent documents or data. This kind of information retrieval is rather narrow, since it is carried out only on the basis of patent documentation, which contains specific data on a technical solution, is sufficiently uniform, has the necessary completeness, contains a critical assessment of the level of technology and, most importantly, is reliable, since it is verified as a result of an examination of the patentability of an invention [7, 8].

The search results will contain information that formally, to a greater or lesser extent, coincides with the query. The most effective algorithm for working with search results involves viewing additional information on the items found, including descriptions, images, etc., as well as identifying firms and authors that are most often found in the obtained material, and studying patents in similar areas [9, 10].

The usefulness and effectiveness of a patent search depend on many factors: the competence of the search specialist; from a competent choice of request and search criteria; from database capabilities; from the thoroughness of the "sampling" of the information received and others. As a result of a patent search, ideally, there should be a clear idea of the possibility or impossibility of registering a new invention, as well as the possibility or impossibility of using or not using an already registered one [11, 12].

2.2 Patent Search Procedures

When conducting a patent search, a very lengthy query is often used, the wording of which requires referring to the entire text of the patent application. It can take a long time to translate such requests into different languages. Therefore, a method is proposed for preliminary processing of the text of a search request to determine the prior art, since it is focused on identifying all relevant documents that can discredit the novelty of the submitted application. When using this method, the full text of the patent application is perceived as a search query, and the documents cited in it are perceived as relevant documents subject to automated identification [13, 14].

Pre-processing of the text of the application includes standard procedures used in most information retrieval systems: normalization of vocabulary, truncation of word forms, and removal of common words. It is assumed that in this way, a faster setup of a machine translation system can be provided.

Currently distributed patent and license search software systems provide users with search capabilities based on standard (attributive) query formation or on the so-called "substring" search. In rare cases, a partial analytical analysis of documents is carried out.

2.3 Analysis of Patent Search Methods

The system analysis of patent search methods is performed in the form of a structural-functional model, a fragment of which is shown in Fig. 1.

As can be seen from the figure, the investigated area of image patent search methods can be divided into three subcategories:

- the use of neural network architectures;
- search for patents using images;
- search for patents without images.

Most patents also include a pictorial section, consisting of figures, drawings, and diagrams, used as an additional means of displaying the features of the invention [15]. Therefore, today in the field of intellectual property protection there is a great interest in research and experiments related to information retrieval in this area.

The textual descriptions contained in the patent document are used to obtain the textual features of the images. They are considered as an unordered collection of words (bag-of-words), used to construct a vector function by counting word formations most often found in text descriptions. For this, common words are removed, and the remaining keywords, after adding weight coefficients to them, are indexed. Only those words that have overcome the weight barrier are involved in the construction of the vector function [16, 17].

The study of images can be very important when trying to get to the essence of patents and establish their relevance. When searching for a patent, sometimes you have to look through thousands of patents using only the images they contain. This process could be accelerated using automated systems for searching for patent images, including using neural networks [17–19].

Fig. 1. Mind-map of the investigated methods of patent search.

3　Analysis of Patent Search Systems and Study of the Specifics of Processing Patent Arrays

3.1　Automated Patent Search Systems

All large patent offices have their patent databases and automated systems that process them. Patent offices can be national (FIPS - Russian Patent Office, USPTO - US Patent

Office, PAJ - Japan Patent Office), and international (WIPO - World Intellectual Property Organization, ESPACENET - European Patent Office). There are also search engines that are not related to patent offices (FPO, FindPatent.ru, Google Patents). A brief description of the search engines is presented below.

Espacenet is the system of the European Patent Office [20]. The database currently contains over 80 million patent applications and patents. The system makes it possible to search for patents in the following databases: European Patent Organization (EPO), World Intellectual Property Organization (WIPO), Japan, Austria, Belgium, Cyprus, Denmark, Finland, France, Germany, Greece, Ireland, Italy, Liechtenstein, Luxembourg, Monaco, Netherlands, Portugal, Spain, Sweden, Switzerland, England. Search by keywords and by metadata of the application is possible.

The patent scope is a search engine from the World Intellectual Property Organization. Contains 36 million patients [21]. You can search for patent documents: Japan, Canada, USA, European Patent Organization (EPO), France, India, China, Latin American countries, and PCT applications. Also available are databases for international trademarks, industrial designs, and databases of patent-associated literature (JOPAL). When searching, it is necessary to indicate on which part of the patent to search for keywords. You can search by the first page, by the entire text of the patent, by number, by name, by date, by class.

USPTO is the system of the US national patent office. The patent database contains about 8 million patients search [22]. You can access the full-text database of patents since 1976, the abstract database of patents since 1976, and the database of trademarks. You can search by bibliographic data and the text of the document, as well as view facsimile copies of pages, found documents in graphic format. The Office actively cooperates with the European Patent Office and the Japan Patent Office. The search is organized by two terms that can be connected by operators: AND, or. You can set the time frame for granting a patent: from 1976 to the present.

Google Patents - Searches the patent databases of the USPTO, EPO, JPO, SIPO, WIPO, DPMA, and CIPO offices. [23] The main advantage of this system is the built-in ability to recognize text in images. The search interface Google Patent Search is the simplest of all the systems presented.

FIIP (Federal Institute of Industrial Property) is the system of the Russian Patent Office - the Federal Service for Intellectual Property, Patents and Trademarks [24]. More than 2 million patents are numbered. Search by keywords, by metadata of the application is possible.

Free Patents Online is a free search engine with access to full-text patents of the European Patent Office and the World Intellectual Property Organization [25]. When compiling a query, you can select a database of agencies for which the search will be carried out, the time period (for the entire time, the last 20 years), the launch of the Stemming algorithm, the mode of sorting the results (by the date of the patent, by relevance).

SIPO is the system of the State Intellectual Property Office of the PRC [26]. Provides open access to documents in Chinese and English. There is a possibility of machine translation from Chinese into English. The search is performed by metadata and keywords. Terms can be connected by logical operators.

After analyzing the above patent search systems, a comparative analysis of the functionality of these systems was made. The results are shown in Table 1.

All of these systems have the same disadvantage. The inventor must himself form the query from the keywords. Keywords are words that, according to the inventor, reflect the essence of the novelty of the patent. If you automate this process, then the inventor's work will become more efficient, since he will not waste time compiling a request.

Table 1. Comparative characteristics of search engines.

System	Keywords search	Metadata search	Keyword highlighting	Machine translation	Text recognition in images	Fulltext search
ESPACENET	+	+	+	−	−	−
PATENT SCOPE	+	+	+	−	−	−
USPTO	+	+	−	−	−	−
Google Patent Search	+	−	+	+	+	−
FIIP	+	+	−	−	−	−
Free Patents Online	+	+	+	−	−	−
SIPO	+	+	−	+	−	−

3.2 Methods for Processing Large Text Arrays and Information Retrieval

Information retrieval (data search) is the process of finding, selecting, and issuing information (including documents, their parts, and/or data) from arrays and records of any kind, defined by predetermined attributes.

It is proposed to use parsing to process the text of a patent application since this process of collecting information solves problems associated with large amounts of information that even a group of people cannot solve [27]. For example, if you need to collect the necessary content, the parser program itself will collect the necessary data from many documents and provide them to the user in the desired form. Parsing programs greatly speed up and simplify the process of collecting information, which makes life much easier for optimizers, copywriters, and rewriters.

3.3 Parsing Phases

Any parser consists of three parts, which are responsible for three separate parsing processes:

- Getting content in its original form. Getting content most often means downloading the code of the web page from which you want to extract data or content. One of the most advanced solutions for getting the code of the required page is the PHP cURL library.
- Extraction and transformation of data. In this phase, the required data is extracted from the page code obtained at the first stage. Regular expressions are most commonly used for extraction. Also at this stage, the extracted data is converted to the desired format, if required.
- Generation of the result. The final stage of parsing. It displays or writes the data received at the second stage in the required format. Most often, the recording is done directly to the database.

The algorithm for parsing the patent file is shown in Fig. 2, the action diagram of the search algorithm is shown in Fig. 3.

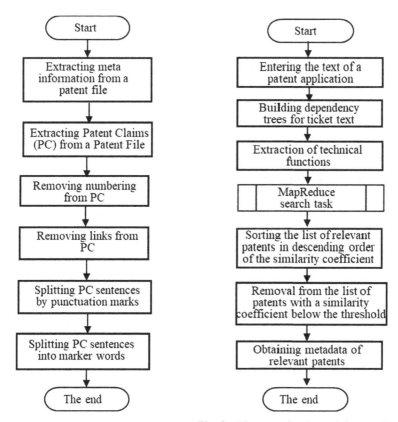

Fig. 2. Algorithm for parsing a patent file.   **Fig. 3.** Diagram of actions of the search algorithm.

To load data from an XML document into a java object, you can use different data binding methods, one of which is JAXB. Such options are suitable if the format of the original XML document is known in advance. If you need to parse XML of an arbitrary format, you can use SAX or DOM parsers. These parsers are similar in functionality, the approaches differ - the DOM parser first loads the entire source document into a java object, which can then be worked with; The SAX parser uses the event-driven model of document parsing, parsing occurs "on the fly" and there is no need to load all XML into memory at once.

SAX parser works when an opening tag is encountered in the source document, the startElement method is called with the appropriate parameters. When reading the content of the tag, characters are called. When closing the tag - endElement. Thus, the document is parsed without first loading it into memory. To use the DOM parser, a class is created that works with an object of the Document type and determines the format of the output data. There are no events here, there is an already loaded object of the Document type, which is a representation of the initial data.

4   Experiments and Results

4.1   Selected Patent Offices for Research

The Patent Office is an organization that provides legal services for the patenting of inventions, industrial designs, and utility models.

There are many patent offices around the world that review and register new inventions:

- The U.S. Patent and Trademark Office (USPTO),
- European Patent Office (EPO),
- Canadian Intellectual Property Office (CIPO),
- Google Patents,
- State Intellectual Property Office (SIPO),
- Japan Patent Office (JPO) etc.

The scheme for filing applications and describing patents is the same for all offices. For USPTO, the text of the patent is supplied in the XML file, graphic illustrations - in the tiff files. For EPO, CIPO, Google Patents, patents, along with text and illustrations, are supplied in PDF files.

This paper discusses patents from the United States Patent and Trademark Office (USPTO), which provides open access to a database of patents. Arrays of patents are in XML format, which in turn are stored in zip archives.

For the study, 62 zip files were downloaded, which have a total weight of 7.20 GB (7 736 950 293 bytes).

4.2   Vector Text Representation

Computers cannot understand the text. You need to convert the text to numeric vectors before any text analysis such as clustering or text classification. The classic well-known model is the bag of words (BOW). With this model, there is one dimension for each unique word in the dictionary. We represent the document as a vector with 0 and 1. Use 1 if a word from the dictionary exists in the document.

Recently, new models with the embedding of words in machine learning have gained popularity, since they allow you to preserve semantic information. With word nesting, we can get a smaller dimension than with the BOW model. There are several such models, for example, Glove, word2vec, Seq2Seq, which are used in the analysis of machine learning texts [28].

Word2vec is a tool (set of algorithms) for calculating vector representations of words, it implements two main architectures - ContinuousBagofWords (CBOW) and Skip-gram. The input is a text corpus, and the output is a set of word vectors.

Finding connections between contexts of words according to the assumption that words in similar contexts tend to mean similar things, i.e. be semantically close. More formally, the problem is as follows: maximizing the cosine proximity between vectors of words (dot product of vectors) that appear next to each other and minimizing the cosine proximity between vectors of words that do not appear next to each other. Next to each other in this case means in close contexts.

For example, the words "analysis" and "research" often appear in similar contexts, such as "Scientists have done an analysis of algorithms" or "Scientists have done research on algorithms." Word2vec analyzes these contexts and concludes that the words "analysis" and "research" are similar in meaning. Since word2vec draws similar conclusions based on a large amount of text, the conclusions turn out to be quite adequate [29].

The Seq2Seq model [30] consists of two multilayer LSTMs - an encoder and a decoder. The encoder maps the input sequence to a fixed-length vector. The decoder decodes the target vector using the output of the encoder. When trained, an autoencoder is a model in which the target values are set the same as the input values. The basic architecture is shown in Fig. 4.

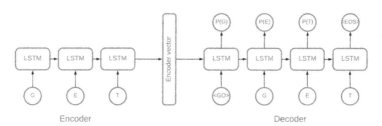

Fig. 4. The architecture of the Seq2Seq model.

Each rectangle in the picture above represents a cell in the RNN, usually a GRU cell, a managed recurrent block, or an LSTM cell, long short-term memory.

4.3 How the Parser Works

Several stages have been implemented:

- The corpus is read, and the occurrence of each word in the corpus is calculated (i.e., the number of times a word has occurred in the corpus - and so on for each word).

- The array of words is sorted by frequency (words are stored in a hash table), and rare words (gapaxes) are removed.
- A Huffman tree is being built. The HuffmanBinaryTree is often used to encode a dictionary - this greatly reduces the computational and time complexity of the algorithm.
- the so-called sub-sentences were read from the corpus, and sub-sampling of the most frequent words are carried out. A sub-sentence is some basic corpus element, usually just a sentence, but it could be a paragraph, for example, or even an entire article. Subsampling is the process of removing the most frequent words from the analysis, which speeds up the learning process of the algorithm and contributes to a significant increase in the quality of the resulting model.
- According to the sub-sentences, we slide the window (the window size is set to the algorithm as a parameter). In this case, the window means the maximum distance between the current and predicted word in the sentence.
- A feedforward neural network is used with the activation function for Hierarchical-Softmax and/or NegativeSampling.

4.4 Algorithm Description

Preparation of a training sample for a neural network, based on patents in the selected categories. To do this, we first process the archive of patents of the required categories, and then process the documents and present the document as a vector of numbers.

Execution algorithm:

- Get a directory with patents in a zip archive.
- Unpack zip archives.
- Carry out the processing of internal XML files for subsequent processing by an XML parser.
- Create JSON files with information about each patent of the selected categories. This includes the patent number, short description, full description, claims, IPC classification of the patent.
- Saving the obtained results.

4.5 Patent Classes and Subclasses for Training Set

The international patent classification includes 8 sections [31]:

- Section A: SATISFACTION OF HUMAN LIFE NEEDS;
- Section B: VARIOUS TECHNOLOGICAL PROCESSES; TRANSPORTATION;
- Section C: CHEMISTRY; METALLURGY;
- Section D: TEXTILE; PAPER;
- Section E: CONSTRUCTION; MINING;
- Section F: ENGINEERING; LIGHTING; HEATING; ENGINES AND PUMPS; WEAPONS AND AMMUNITION; IMPLODING WORKS;
- Section G: PHYSICS;
- Section H: ELECTRICITY.

Each section has its own hierarchy.

For the formation of the new class, the four most appropriate sections were selected:

- Section B: VARIOUS TECHNOLOGICAL PROCESSES; TRANSPORTATION
- Section F: ENGINEERING; LIGHTING; HEATING; ENGINES AND PUMPS; WEAPONS AND AMMUNITION; IMPLODING WORKS
- Section G: PHYSICS
- Section H: ELECTRICITY

Table 2 shows the selected classes of each section for the parser to work.

Table 2. Selected classes and sub-classes.

Sections	Classes	Subclasses
B	B06B, B60Q	–
F	F03B, F15B, F15C	–
G	G06C, G06F, G01S, G08C, G08G, G06N, G06K, G06Q, G08B, G06T, G99Z	G05B 13/00, G05B 15/00, G05B 19/00, G05B 17/00, G05B 23/00, G05B 24/00
H	H04W	H04L 1/00, H04L 7/00, H04L 29/00, H02J 13/00, H02J 3/00, H04B 7/00, H04L 9/00

4.6 Parsing Results

At the output, after the software is running, we get a textual description of each patent in a separate JSON file (Fig. 5).

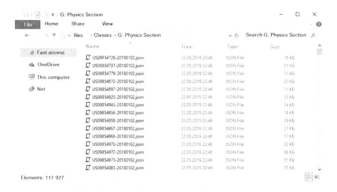

Fig. 5. Results of the parsing software.

At this stage, we already have ready-made representations of patent texts obtained from JSON files. The t-SNE algorithm was used to graphically represent the obtained results of the seq2seq model.

t-SNE is a machine learning visualization algorithm developed by Laurens van der Maaten and Jeffrey Hinton [32]. It is a non-linear dimensionality reduction technique well suited for embedding high-dimensional data for visualization in a low-dimensional space (two- or three-dimensional). In particular, the method models each high-dimensional object with a two or three-dimensional point in such a way that similar objects are modeled by closely spaced points, and dissimilar points are modeled with a high probability by points that are far from each other. The t-SNE algorithm has two main steps. First, t-SNE creates a probability distribution over pairs of high-dimensional objects in such a way that similar objects will be selected with a high probability, while the probability of selecting dissimilar points will be low.

4.7   Graphical Presentation of Intermediate Results

The t-SNE then determines a similar probability distribution over points in a low-dimensional space and minimizes the distance between the two distributions based on the position of the points. The t-SNE algorithm is able to detect clusters that are well separated from each other, which are the classes selected as a result of selection:

- Section B: VARIOUS TECHNOLOGICAL PROCESSES; TRANSPORTATION (Technology);
- Section F: ENGINEERING; LIGHTING; HEATING; ENGINES AND PUMPS; WEAPONS AND AMMUNITION; EXPLOSIVE WORKS (Machines);
- Section G: Physics;
- Section H: Electricity.

The view of a randomly distributed sample is shown in Fig. 6. The display of each text from the training sample using the t-SNE algorithm is shown in Fig. 7. Where each text of the patent is colored in one of four colors, depending on the class: 0 - Section H (Electricity), 1 - Section F (Machines), 2 - Section G (Physics), 3 - Section B (Technology). A large amount of data does not allow you to see the full picture, since each point (patent text) has its own color and overlap occurs.

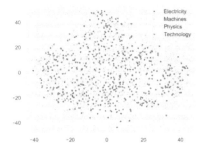

Fig. 6. Graphical representation of class vectors without t-SNE.

In Fig. 7, the main cluster of points (patent texts) of different classes is highlighted with a black rectangle, therefore, the allocated area is a new class - cyber-physical systems. We train the neural network on the selected area.

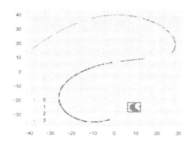

Fig. 7. t-SNE Patent Classification Chart.

4.8 Selecting a New Class and Training the Neural Network

The sample was split 80% by 20%. 80% - training sample, 20% - test sample. The results of the trained neural network on the test sample are shown in Fig. 8.

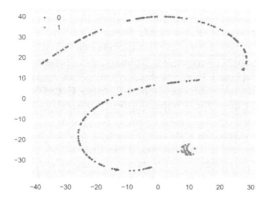

Fig. 8. Graphical presentation of the results on the test sample.

5 Conclusion

As a result of the experiments, the following results were obtained: selected a neural network model; the parameters influencing the operation of the neural network are highlighted; revealed the parameters of the neural network that improve the result of the work the optimal configuration of the recurrent network has been compiled.

The task of eliminating problems of an interdisciplinary nature that appear as a result of working with patent documents has been successfully solved.

Thus, the constructed configuration of a recurrent neural network can be used in the framework of classification problems for patent texts.

After the completion of the work, the optimal configuration of the recurrent neural network was obtained, which improved the results of the developed software.

Acknowledgments. The reported study was funded by RFBR according to research project # 19-07-01200.

References

1. Korobkin, D., Fomenkov, S., Kravets, A., Kolesnikov, S.: Methods of statistical and semantic patent analysis. In: Kravets, A., Shcherbakov, M., Kultsova, M., Groumpos, P. (eds.) CIT&DS 2017. CCIS, vol. 754, pp. 48–61. Springer, Cham (2017). https://doi.org/10.1007/978-3-319-65551-2_4

2. Fomenkov, S., Korobkin, D., Kolesnikov, S.: Method of ontology-based extraction of physical effect description from Russian text. In: Kravets, A., Shcherbakov, M., Kultsova, M., Iijima, T. (eds.) JCKBSE 2014. CCIS, vol. 466, pp. 321–330. Springer, Cham (2014). https://doi.org/10.1007/978-3-319-11854-3_27

3. Fomenkov, S.A., Korobkin, D.M., Kolesnikov, S.G., Dvoryankin, A.M., Kamaev, V.A.: Procedure of integration of the systems of representation and application of the structured physical knowledge. Res. J. Appl. Sci. **9**(10), 700–703 (2014)

4. Kamaev, V.A., Salnikova, N.A., Akhmedov, S.A., Likhter, A.M.: The formalized representation of the structures of complex technical devices using context-free plex grammars. In: Kravets, A., Shcherbakov, M., Kultsova, M., Shabalina, O. (eds.) CIT&DS 2015. CCIS, vol. 535, pp. 268–277. Springer, Cham (2015). https://doi.org/10.1007/978-3-319-23766-4_22

5. Kravets, A., Shumeiko, N., Lempert, B., Salnikova, N., Shcherbakova, N.: "Smart queue" approach for new technical solutions discovery in patent applications. In: Kravets, A., Shcherbakov, M., Kultsova, M., Groumpos, P. (eds.) CIT&DS 2017. CCIS, vol. 754, pp. 37–47. Springer, Cham (2017). https://doi.org/10.1007/978-3-319-65551-2_3

6. Korobkin, D.M., Fomenkov, S.A., Kolesnikov, S.G., Voronin, Y.F.: System of physical effect extraction from natural language text in the internet. World Appl. Sci. J. **24**(24), 55–61 (2013)

7. Korobkin, D.M., Fomenkov, S.A., Kravets, A.G.: Methods for extracting the descriptions of sci-tech effects and morphological features of technical systems from patents. In: 9th International Conference on Information, Intelligence, Systems and Applications (IISA 2018), pp. 1–6 (2019)

8. Kravets, A.G., Kolesnikov, S., Salnikova, N., Lempert, M., Poplavskaya, O.: The study of neural networks effective architectures for patents images processing. In: Kravets, A.G., Groumpos, P.P., Shcherbakov, M., Kultsova, M. (eds.) CIT&DS 2019. CCIS, vol. 1084, pp. 27–41. Springer, Cham (2019). https://doi.org/10.1007/978-3-030-29750-3_3

9. Kravets, A.G., Skorobogatchenko, D.A., Salnikova, N.A., Orudjev, N.Y., Poplavskaya, O.V.: The traffic safety management system in urban conditions based on the C4.5 algorithm. In: Moscow Workshop on Electronic and Networking Technologies (MWENT 2018), art. No. 8337254, pp. 1–7 (2018)

10. Kravets, A.G., Vasiliev, S.S., Shabanov, D.V.: Research of the LDA algorithm results for patents texts processing. In: 9th International Conference on Information, Intelligence, Systems and Applications (IISA 2018), pp. 1–6 (2019)

11. Kizim, A.V., Matokhina, A.V., Vayngolts, I.I., Shcherbakov, M.V.: Intelligent platform of monitoring, diagnosis and modernization of technical systems at various stages of life cycle. In: Proceedings of the 5th International Conference on System Modeling and Advancement in Research Trends (SMART 2016), vol. 5, pp. 145–150 (2016)

12. Korobkin, D.M., Fomenkov, S.A., Kolesnikov, S.G.: A function-based patent analysis for support of technical solutions synthesis. In: 2016 2nd International Conference on Industrial Engineering, Applications and Manufacturing (ICIEAM 2016), p. 7911581 (2016)

13. Korobkin, D.M., Fomenkov, S.A., Kravets, A.G.: Extraction of physical effects practical applications from patent database. In: 2017 8th International Conference on Information, Intelligence, Systems and Applications (IISA 2017), pp. 1–5 (2018)

14. Lecun, Y., Bottou, L., Bengio, Y., and Haffner, P.: Gradient-based learning applied to document recognition. In: Proceedings of the IEEE, vol. 86 (1998)

15. Kravets, A.G., Burmistrov, A.S., Zadorozhny, P.A.: Experimental determination of the optimal parameters of the recurrent neural network for the tasks of patent classification. In: Modeling, Optimization and Information Technology. **7**(2) (2019). https://moit.vivt.ru/wp-content/uploads/2019/05/KravetsSoavtors_2_19_1.pdf. https://doi.org/10.26102/2310-6018/2019.25.2.027.

16. Tiwari, A., Bansal, V.: PATSEEK: content based image retrieval system for patent database. In: The Fourth International Conference on Electronic Business, at Tsinghua University, Beijing, China (2004)

17. Koch, G., Zemel, R., Salakhutdinov, R.: Siamese neural networks for one-shot patent image recognition. In: CA: Department of Computer Science (2015)

18. Lecun, Y., Bottou, L., Bengio, Y., Haffner, P.: Gradient-based learning applied to document recognition. In: Proceedings of the IEEE, vol. 86 (1998)

19. Simard, P.Y., Steinkraus, D., Platt, J.C.: Best practices for convolutional neural networks applied to visual document analysis. In: Proceedings of the IEEE Conference Publications, pp. 958–963 (2003)

20. System of the European Patent Office. Access mode: https://worldwide.espacenet.com/. Accessed 20 May 2021

21. Search Engine from the World Intellectual Property Organization. Access mode: https://patentscope.wipo.int. Accessed 20 May 2021

22. Search Engine of the US Patent and Trademark Office. Access mode: https://www.uspto.gov/patents-application-process/search-patents. Accessed 20 May 2021

23. Patent Search System Google Patent Search. Access mode: https://patents.google.com/. Accessed 20 May 2021

24. System of the Russian Patent Office of the Federal Service for Intellectual Property, Patents and Trademarks. Access mode: http://www1.fips.ru. Accessed 20 May 2021

25. FPO: Search, Tools and Resources. Access mode: https://www.freepatentsonline.com/. Accessed 20 May 2021

26. SIPO: Protection of Intellectual Property Rights in the PRC. Access mode: http://www.russchinatrade.ru/assets/files/ru-useful-info/Intelektual_sobstvennost.pdf. Accessed 20 May 2021

27. Alla, K., Nikita, L., Maxim, L.: Patent images retrieval and convolutional neural network training dataset quality improvement. ITSMSSM **72**, 287–293 (2017)

28. Vector Representation of Text. Word Embeddings with word2vec. Text Analytics Techniques. Access mode: http://ai.intelligentonlinetools.com/ml/text-vectors-word-embeddings-word2vec/. Accessed 20 May 2021

29. Word2vec: Useful Theory – NLPx. Access mode: http://nlpx.net/archives/179. Accessed 20 May 2021

30. Sequence to Sequence Learning with Neural Networks. Access mode: https://arxiv.org/abs/1409.3215. Accessed 20 May 2021

31. Library of Patents for Inventions. Access mode: http://www.freepatent.ru/. Accessed 20 May 2021

32. Stochastic Embedding of Neighbors with t-Distribution. Access mode: https://ru.wikipedia.org/wiki/. Accessed 20 May 2021

The Software for Identifying Technological Complementarity Between Enterprises Based on Patent Databases

Alexey Bezruchenko, Dmitriy Korobkin[(✉)] [iD], Sergey Fomenkov[iD],
Sergey Kolesnikov, and Sergey Vasiliev

Volgograd State Technical University, 28 Lenina Ave, Volgograd 400005, Russia

Abstract. In this paper, it is proposed to identify the technological complementarity of enterprises. The process of identifying potential partners is based on the comparison of cluster information, clustered with hLDA algorithm. To analyze an array of patents, it must first be loaded, parsed, and filtered by a specific class of patents. Then technical terms are extracted from data and clustered using the hLDA algorithm, and after clustering, an enterprises complementarity matrix is constructed. We developed software for clustering USPTO patent documents based on the hLDA method and identifying the technological complementarity of enterprises based on the comparison of cluster information.

Keywords: Technological complementarity · hLDA

1 Introduction

Nowadays, information is an important factor in the success of a company, and many companies invest a lot of money in research. At the same time, several companies often research in the same area, and they can benefit from a partnership, acquisition, or merging. It is known that the best results are obtained with a high complementarity of technologies in these companies. However, there are currently no open-source solutions for an automated finding of complementary businesses.

Although there are some architectures for similar systems [9], we use our own. The designed system can be divided into several modules:

- Module for loading XML files from the USPTO database and parsing them.
- Clustering module.
- Analysis module.
- Visualization module.

2 State-of-Art

There were no open access programs with similar functions (search for potential patent partners). There is a study [1], the authors of which developed such a program, but it is

© Springer Nature Switzerland AG 2021
A. G. Kravets et al. (Eds.): CIT&DS 2021, CCIS 1448, pp. 45–54, 2021.
https://doi.org/10.1007/978-3-030-87034-8_4

not publicly available. For this reason, programs were analyzed to search for patents for subsequent manual analysis.

We made a final comparison of the existing solutions to the patent search problem according to the following criteria:

- Current data.
- Downloading a patent.
- Named search.
- Numbering search.
- Subject search.
- View full patent information.
- Availability of patents from different countries of the world.

The results of the comparative analysis of the above solutions are presented in Table 1.

Table 1. Results of comparison of existing solutions.

Criterion\solution	uspto.gov	Google Patents	Yandex.Patents
Current data	+	+	+
Downloading a patent	+	+	+
Named Search	−	+	+
Numbering search	−	+	+
Subject search	−	+	+
View full patent information	+	+	+
Availability of world patents	+	+	−

3   Designing the Software for Identifying Technological Complementarity

Based on the analysis of existing solutions, as well as the list of tasks, it was decided to implement a system that allows you to calculate and analyze the technological complementarity between enterprises. It is proposed to create a GUI software, as well as a command-line interface.

An array of patents is submitted to the input, and the system starts processing it. After processing, a line is entered into the system — the name of the company whose potential partners need to be identified.

At the output, the user receives a list of potential partners formed based on the complementarity matrix.

3.1 Architecture of Software

The program can perform the following functions:

- Parsing of patent documents in XML format to form a patent database.
- Clustering a patent array.
- Formation of the matrix "Enterprises-Clusters (Topics)".
- Visualization of technological complementarity of enterprises.

The architecture of the program can be illustrated by a data flow diagram (Fig. 1).

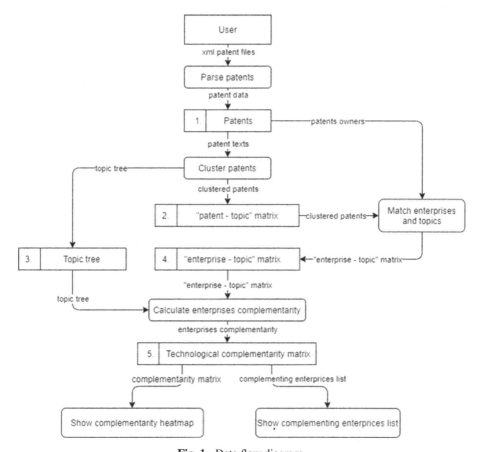

Fig. 1. Data flow diagram.

The program consists of the following modules:

- Parsing module that takes input XML files and extracts data for further processing.
- Clustering module that takes patent texts and clusters them.
- Analysis module that takes parsed and clustered data and makes companies complementarity matrix.
- Visualization module that allows controlling processing and view results.

3.2 Parsing Module

The patent parser input is a patent file (or files). Patent files must be in the USPTO format [3].

The parser outputs to the parser_output folder:

- In the "data" subfolder, the text of the fields "abstract", "claims", "description", all three fields in one file, the text of each patent in a separate file. The name of each file is a unique patent number.
- In the "info" subfolder, file or several files with information on patents. In the file, each line contains info about 1 patent: id, classification type, number, or class according to this classification. If a class consists of several elements (class, subclass, section, etc.), they are separated from each other by a tab character (Fig. 2).
- In the "companies" subfolder, a file or several files with information on companies publishing patents. File (s) format: each patent is written on a separate line, with the patent ID separated by a tab, followed by the company names separated by a tab (Fig. 3).

```
29327626    classification-locarno    1505
29335412    classification-locarno    0707
29333252    classification-locarno    0707
29331743    classification-locarno    0909
11400453    classification-ipcr  A    61   M
12077553    classification-ipcr  A    01   H
12077554    classification-ipcr  A    01   H
12012112    classification-ipcr  A    01   H
12313048    classification-ipcr  A    01   H
```

Fig. 2. Example of patent information file.

```
29324776    Acme United Corporation
29307999    Samsung Electronics Co., Ltd.
29324459    Kabushiki Kaisha Sato   Kabushiki Kaisha Sato Chishiki Zaisan Kenkyusho
29305551    Ricoh Company, Ltd.
29305555    Ricoh Company, Ltd.
29308001    Samsung Electronics Co., Ltd.
29312220    Seiko Epson Corporation
29328541    Seiko I Infotech Inc.
```

Fig. 3. Example of a file with companies information.

3.3 Clustering Module

The patent clustering module takes as input a set of hyper-parameters of the algorithm. At the output, it outputs three files to the cluster_output folder:

- A file with the classification of patents. File format: each patent on a separate line with the patent ID and the corresponding topic number separated by a tab (Fig. 4).
- A file with a description of the topics. File format: each topic on a separate line, which contains the topic number and keywords of this topic (Fig. 5).
- A file with a description of the topic tree. File format: a pair of topic numbers separated by a tab character, each pair on a separate line. The first number of the pair is the number of the parent topic of the topic with the second number (Fig. 6).

```
10007730    170
10010245    11
10013543    171
10020162    172
10024432    171
10035987    56
10036566    15
10058122    130
10085528    173
10088683    8
10106298    174
10121976    166
10133653    166
10143498    145
```

```
0    one, system, invent, wherein, method,
1    includ, wherein, provid, data, accord,
56   trade, pair, imag, request, parcel,
170  forecast, member, data, organ, submit,
171  devic, content, mobil, languag, wax,
172  display, screen, help, area, button,
178  data, imag, modifi, gener, present,
179  batteri, mold, yarn, region, elast,
186  file, spool, print, data, font,
194  color, sampl, gamut, valu, identifi,
196  frame, inform, featur, unit, imag,
197  order, scan, scanner, comput, process,
198  email, address, commun, first, partner,
199  transfer, fund, system, paye, may,
3    invent, one, may, provid, includ,
```

```
0    1
1    56
1    170
1    171
1    172
1    178
1    179
1    186
1    194
1    196
1    197
1    198
1    199
0    3
3    15
```

Fig. 4. Example of patent classification.

Fig. 5. Example of topic descriptions.

Fig. 6. Example of a topic tree description.

We use an optimized version of the "hlda" python library for clustering. The most notable modification is a replacement of one of the inner loops with a formula (Fig. 7). This improved speed of clustering by almost 30%.

It is possible because the inner loop can be interpreted as a difference of logarithms of products of arithmetic progressions (which can be calculated with gamma-function):

$$\sum_{w=0}^{wc} \sum_{i=0}^{c} \ln\left(\frac{\eta + wc_w + i}{\eta_{sum} + tw_n + tw_0 + i}\right) = \sum_{w=0}^{wc} \left(\begin{array}{l} \ln(\Gamma(\eta + wc_w + c)) - \\ \ln(\Gamma(\eta + wc_w)) - \\ \ln(\Gamma(\eta_{sum} + tw_n + tw_0 + c)) + \\ \ln(\Gamma(\eta_{sum} + tw_n + tw_0)) \end{array} \right) \quad (1)$$

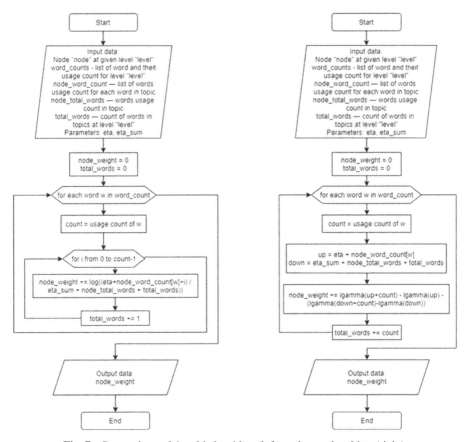

Fig. 7. Comparison of the old algorithm (left) and new algorithm (right).

3.4 Analysis Module

The input data of the analysis module is:

- Info and companies from the parser.
- The output of the clustering module.

The output is a complementarity matrix. Complementarity is calculated using the formula from [1]:

$$Compl(A \leftarrow B) = \sum \frac{TN(B) - TN(A\&B)}{TN - TN(A)} \times \frac{PN(Ci)}{PN}$$

where Compl $(A \leftarrow B)$ is the complementarity of B for A, Ci is the i-th main technological topic (i.e., a higher-level topic in the hierarchy), TN is the number of subtopics in Ci, TN (A), TN (B), TN (A&B) is the number of subtopics in Ci for which enterprise A, B, A&B have patents, PN (Ci) is the number of patents in Ci, PN is the number of patents.

According to the formula, the following algorithm was written (Fig. 8).

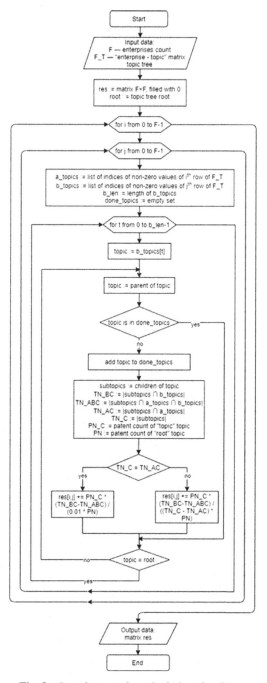

Fig. 8. Complementarity calculation algorithm.

3.5 Visualization Module

The visualization module can start other modules and visualize the results of the analysis module. It can show complementarity matrix heatmap (Fig. 9) or some of the most complementary companies (Fig. 10).

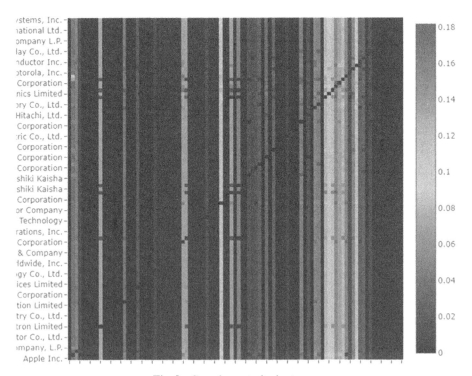

Fig. 9. Complementarity heatmap.

Fig. 10. Most complementary companies.

4 Conclusion

In this paper, it is proposed to identify the technological complementarity of enterprises. There are many different approaches for analyzing patent data [8, 10, 11]. Here the process of identifying potential partners is based on the comparison of cluster information, clustered with hLDA algorithm. To analyze an array of patents, it must first be loaded, parsed, and filtered by a specific class of patents. Then technical terms are extracted from data (there are many approaches for this [7, 12], in this software we use tokenizing, stemming, and stop words filtering). This data is then clustered using the hLDA algorithm, and after clustering, an enterprise complementarity matrix is constructed.

We developed software for clustering USPTO patent documents based on the hLDA method and identifying the technological complementarity of enterprises based on the comparison of cluster information.

Acknowledgments. The reported study was funded by RFBR and the Administration of the Volgograd region according to the research projects 19-47-340007, 19-41-340016, and was funded by RSF according to the research projects 22-21-00855, 22-1-00808.

References

1. Wang, X., Qiao, Y., Hou, Y., Zhang, S., Han, X.: Measuring technology complementarity between enterprises with an hLDA topic model. IEEE Trans. Eng. Manage. (2019). https://ieeexplore.ieee.org/document/8937531. Accessed 14 Apr 2021
2. Standard St.36 Version 1.2 Recommendation for the Processing of Patent Information Using XML (Extensible Markup Language); 23.11.2007. WIPO, 2007. 14 p. (International Standard)
3. Patent Grant Full Text Data/XML Version 4.5 ICE (2021). https://bulkdata.uspto.gov/data/patent/grant/redbook/2015/us-patent-grant-v45-2014-04-03.dtd. Accessed 17 Apr 2021
4. Mallet 2 API (2021). http://mallet.cs.umass.edu/api/. Accessed 17 Apr 2021

5. GitHub. joewandy/hlda: Gibbs Sampler for the Hierarchical Latent Dirichlet Allocation Topic Model (2021). https://github.com/joewandy/hlda. Accessed Apr 17 2021

6. GitHub. tankistqazwsx/hlda: Gibbs sampler for the Hierarchical Latent Dirichlet Allocation Topic Model (2021). https://github.com/tankistqazwsx/hlda Accessed 22 Apr 2021

7. Korobkin, D., Shabanov, D., Fomenkov, S., Golovanchikov, A.: Construction of a matrix "physical effects – technical functions" on the base of patent corpus analysis. In: Kravets, A.G., Groumpos, P.P., Shcherbakov, M., Kultsova, M. (eds.) CIT&DS 2019. CCIS, vol. 1084, pp. 52–68. Springer, Cham (2019). https://doi.org/10.1007/978-3-030-29750-3_5

8. Fomenkova, M., Korobkin, D., Kravets, A.G., Fomenkov, S.: Extraction of knowledge and processing of the patent array. Commun. Comput. Inf. Sci. **1084**, 3–14 (2019)

9. Vayngolts, I., Korobkin, D., Fomenkov, S., Kolesnikov, S.: The software and information complex which uses structured physical knowledge for technical systems design. Commun. Comput. Inf. Sci. **1084**, 42–51 (2019)

10. Fomenkova, M., Korobkin, D., Fomenkov, S.: Extraction of physical effects based on the semantic analysis of the patent texts. Commun. Comput. Inf. Sci. **754**, 73–87 (2017)

11. Korobkin, D., Fomenkov, S., Kravets, A., Kolesnikov, S.: Methods of statistical and semantic patent analysis. Commun. Comput. Inf. Sci. **754**, 48–61 (2017)

12. Vayngolts, I., Korobkin, D., Fomenkov, S., Golovanchikov, A.: Synthesis of the physical operation principles of technical system. Commun. Comput. Inf. Sci. **754**, 575–588 (2017)

13. Seshadri, K., Shalinie, S., Kollengode, C.: Design and evaluation of a parallel algorithm for inferring topic hierarchies. Inf. Process. Manage. **51**, 662–676 (2015). https://doi.org/10.1016/j.ipm.2015.06.006

14. Patents I USPTO (2021). https://www.uspto.gov/patents. Accessed 14 Apr 2021

15. Google Patents (2021). https://patents.google.com. Accessed 14 Apr 2021

16. Yandex.Patents (2021). https://yandex.ru/patents. Accessed 14 Apr 2021

17. blei-lab/hlda: This implements hierarchical latent Dirichlet allocation, a topic model that finds a hierarchy of topics. The structure of the hierarchy is determined by the data. https://github.com/blei-lab/hlda

18. Beautiful Soup 4.9.0 documentation. https://www.crummy.com/software/BeautifulSoup/

19. bs4/doc.ru/bs4ru.html. Accessed 14 Apr 2021

20. Natural Language Toolkit. NLTK 3.6.2 documentation (2021). https://www.nltk.org. Accessed 14 Apr 2021

21. The Web framework for Perfectionists with Deadlines I Django (2021). https://www.djangoproject.com. Accessed 14 Apr 2021

Analyzing and Forecasting Emerging Technology Trends by Mining Web News

Nguyen Thanh Viet[1,2(✉)] and Vladislav Gneushev[1]

[1] Volgograd State Technical University, Volgograd, Russia
[2] Pham Van Dong University, Quang Ngai, Vietnam

Abstract. Monitoring the development of existing technologies and discovering new and promising technologies help enterprises or firms obtain competitiveness in an environment of rapidly changing science. In other words, it is significant for a firm to promote a technology development strategy based on forecasting emerging technologies to gain competitive advantages while utilizing finite resources. In addition to the prospective changes, the speed and directions of technologies are considered to forecast future technology. Analyzing technically relevant historical information can be applied to identify how changes in technological developments are influenced by current and past changes in related technologies. An important aspect for identifying technological trends is the data. Among large amounts of data generated every day, Web news is an important data resource for studying social public awareness of emerging technologies. For this reason, this paper presents results of analyzing and forecasting emerging technology trends in Web news by utilizing burst detection algorithm, which is still impactful and significant in recent researches. After applying burst detection algorithm and clustering burst terms manually, we are able to detect and infer some main technological development trends for the near future, which are evaluated later by domain experts. That means the proposed method is effective and prospective for analyzing and forecasting technology trends.

Keywords: Data mining · Emerging technology · Technology analysis · Technology trend · Burst detection algorithm · Linear regression · Clustering

1 Introduction

The technological progress has been occurring at rapid speed since the past decades; the accelerating modularity and complexity of productions (e.g. Transportation and Information Communication Technology goods); and the interdisciplinary combination of scientific branches contributing to latest technology evolutions demands methods to detect new emerging technological fields, and to examine their progressions. The ability to identify new technological prototypes, the emergences of novel technologies, and to predict the diffusion of next technological productions has been the main focus of policy makers and researchers for many decades.

The evolutions of emerging technologies not only have shifted existing productions but also have generated new ones that retain important influences on the socioeconomic

© Springer Nature Switzerland AG 2021
A. G. Kravets et al. (Eds.): CIT&DS 2021, CCIS 1448, pp. 55–69, 2021.
https://doi.org/10.1007/978-3-030-87034-8_5

construction. Detecting upcoming shifting tendencies of those technological emergences as soon as possible is vital for strategic planning in research and development (R&D) of governments and enterprises to gain dominance in the competitive commerce domains. Many decision makers and employers are conscious of the importance of understanding about the emergence patterns, and exploring the upcoming development tendencies of relating technological emergences for corporation's competitiveness and sustained evolution.

Hence, in this condition, with the evolution of big data epoch, technology forecast significantly has been gained from data analysis techniques for many years, which are expected to utilize the fast enlargement of accessible data and latest progresses in computer science. Specifically, data analytics techniques process, examine, discover and extract meaningful patterns, insights and relations from massive amount of data over diverse sources [1, 2], not only have enhanced the accuracy and efficiency of current approaches but also proposed novel methods to technology forecast [3].

Subsequently, scholars have performed a numerous studies on the evolutional tendencies of technological emergence. Comprehending the technology history is the foundation for detecting technology variations. Investigating appropriate historical data and information can help determine how shifts in technological evolutions are affected by current and past innovations in relevant technologies. A significant facet for discovering technological tendencies is data. For the reason that patents and scientific publications are essential carriers of engineering knowledge, researchers have performed analysis of these data sources to examine the evolutional tendencies of technological emergence. Specifically, early technological trends are usually disseminated firstly in scientific publications and researches. Therefore, these data have been significant knowledge sources for premature signals and tendencies [4, 5].

Likewise, patents provide a source of up-to-date and reliable information for revealing technological information and development [6]. Through the analysis of the technological information available in patents, we may better reveal and understand the path of technological evolution and be able to identify the development trends of technology with the help of domain experts. Thus, researchers have begun to use patent data for analyzing and studying technology trends [7, 8].

However, most studies have focused on publications and patents – data that are not only sensitive to time, but also provide limited perspectives on the multifaceted phenomenon of emerging technologies. Moreover, because of the uncertainty and vagueness of emerging technologies, there are limitations to the study of development trends by analyzing only scientific papers or patents. Therefore a few studies have focused on the use of news articles and big data sources (e.g. Google Trends). These are clearly emerging streams in scientometric and data-mining researches, however so far little attention has been paid to these novel data sources in the context of emerging technologies. Hence, researchers should pay more attention to social awareness data, such as web news, business reviews, social public's expectations, views, and attitudes toward the development of emerging technologies; this information can reflect the emergence and development trends of emerging technologies and even change the future trends of such technologies [9, 10].

In this regard, the paper presents analysis results of detecting and forecasting emerging technology trends by mining Web news. The remainder of this paper is structured as follows. Section 2 describes the primary approach of the analysis. Section 3 details the processes of the research framework and presents results of analysis on use case data. Concluding remarks, with implications and future research, appear in Sect. 4.

2   Burst Detection Method of Analysis

The Burst detection algorithm devised by Kleinberg [11] focuses on streams of documents and aims to identify features that occur with high frequency over limited periods of time – i.e. 'bursts' of activity. In the case of sets of messages, bursts can be understood as short periods characterized by relatively higher volumes of them. Once in a bursting 'mode', the frequency of messages can further increase, reaching a next level or intensity, and trigger a hierarchy of levels or states that can progress recursively. Kleinberg's finite state algorithm seeks to replicate the behavior of these streams of documents, so that each state corresponds to a different level or rate of activity. This results in a set of state transitions that identify points in time where the frequency of activity changes following a hierarchy of levels. Up till now this algorithm and the study [11] have been cited in numerous researches (559 citations from 2004 to 2020) whose citation trend is presented in Fig. 1. The upward citation trend means that the algorithm is still impactful and significant in recent researches.

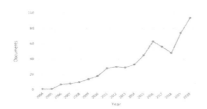

Fig. 1. Trend of citations to Kleinberg's study

2.1   Review of Studies Adopting Burst Detection Algorithm

Chen [12] also relied on this algorithm to identify emergent research-front concepts. In this context, a detected burst can be understood as a period of higher relative frequency of usage of a term as compared to other periods, normalized with respect to the overall volume of scientific production in the years considered. In the context of patents, a burst can be understood as a period of higher relative frequency of patent applications in a certain technology class compared to previous years.

Guo et al. [13] presented a mixed model that combines different indicators to describe and predict key structural and dynamic features of emerging research areas. Three indicators are combined: sudden increases in the frequency of specific words, which were identified by burst detection algorithm; the number and speed by which new authors are attracted to an emerging research area, and changes in the interdisciplinarity of cited references. Results show that the indicators are indicative of emerging areas and they exhibit interesting temporal correlations: new authors enter the area first, then the interdisciplinarity of paper references increases, and then word bursts occur.

Additionally, authors [14] applied the mixed approach of Social Network Analysis techniques and Triple Helix indicators on scholarly papers obtained from the Web of Science database. Further, burst detection algorithm is applied on keywords appearing in the titles of the South Asian ICT (Information Communication Technology) scholarly papers to understand the emerging trends in the ICT research domain. Thus the study helps better understanding of current trends, strengths, and weaknesses of ICT in South Asia, which provides better insights to bridge the digital divide and achieve socioeconomic development through ICT.

In the work [15] authors detected the emergence of science and technology fields to characterize science and technology trajectories. They proposed a new data mining approach based on burst detection algorithm, called 'DETECTS', for the identification of those research and innovative activities whose intensity increases sharply compared to previous levels and to other developments. This approach also allows monitoring the extent to which field and topic-specific activities further accelerate, stabilize or abate, and the time it takes for such dynamics to unfold. The results further suggest, somewhat unexpectedly, that in some focal technology fields considered, the acceleration in the development of science seems to closely follow the acceleration in the development of technologies, and not vice versa.

Sohrabi et al. [16] analyzed the content of validated journal articles related to Knowledge Management (KM) in more than 18,000 papers of the Web of Science (WoS) database and then provided the most recent specific trends in KM field using text mining and burst detection to help researchers invest in the most challenging and fruitful areas of KM research domain. This study could be valuable for researchers and KM specialists as well as managers since they may study the history of a subject by getting the structure of its scientific productions, thus to plan purposefully and determine the research priorities in KM.

In paper [17] authors present Trendy Keyword Extraction System (TKES), which is designed for extracting trendy keywords from text streams. The system also supports storing, analyzing, and visualizing documents coming from text streams. Specifically, the system first collects automatically daily articles, and then it ranks the importance of keywords by calculating keyword's frequency of existence in order to find trendy keywords by using the Burst detection algorithm.

2.2 Burst Detection Algorithm

In each period, the algorithm built to model the behavior of a term can assume two states, i.e. q_0(baseline state) and q_1 (burst state) corresponding, respectively, to a low relative frequency p_0, and to a high relative frequency p_1.

The frequency p_0 corresponds to the overall proportion R/D of the number of documents having the term R under analysis over the number of documents in the collection D. Conversely, p_1 is the value of p_0 scaled by a parameter s, so that $p_1 = p_0 \, s$. Denoting by r_t the number of documents having the term under analysis in period t and by d_t the total number of documents in the period, the cost for adopting the state q_i is given by:

$$\sigma(i, r_t, d_t) = -ln\left[\binom{d_t}{r_t}p_i^{r_t}(1 - p_i)^{d_t - r_t}\right] \tag{1}$$

where i corresponds to the state (in a two-state system, $i = 0$ corresponds to the baseline state and $i = 1$ corresponds to the burst state), and

$$\binom{d_t}{r_t} = \frac{d_t!}{r_t!(d_t - r_t)!} \tag{2}$$

The selection of the sequence of states – each corresponding to the time periods considered – which defines the sequential algorithm and minimizes the cost, is further restrained by applying a transition cost τ whenever the system moves from the lower frequency state (q_0) to the higher frequency one (q_1). This allows reducing the number of state transitions that are ultimately selected for each sequential algorithm. The transition cost from state i to state j is defined as:

$$\tau(i, j) = (j - i)\gamma \ln(D) \tag{3}$$

where the parameter γ accounts for the cost of having an additional transition.

With the cost function we can find the optimal state sequence q. The optimal state sequence is the sequence of states that minimizes the total cost or, in other words, the sequence that best explains the observed proportions. We find q with the Viterbi algorithm. The basic idea is following: first, we calculate the cost of being in each state at $t = 1$ and we choose the state with the minimum cost; then we calculate the cost of transitioning from our current state in $t = 1$ to each possible state at $t = 2$, and again we choose the state with the minimum cost. Likewise we repeat these steps for all time points to get a state sequence that minimizes the cost function. The state sequence presents when the system was in a heightened (burst) state.

Once the sequential algorithm has been run for each term, the mined bursts are sorted and ranked using the weight of the bursts. Such weights are defined as the gain in cost obtained by adopting the higher frequency state q_1 over the initial state of q_0 for the burst period, i.e. the continuous period of time when the algorithm assumes the state q_1:

$$weight = \sum_{t=t_1}^{t_2}[\sigma(0, r_t, d_t) - \sigma(1, r_t, d_t)] \tag{4}$$

3   Analyzing and Forecasting Technology Trends by Mining Web News

Web news is an important data resource for studying social public awareness of emerging technologies [18]. Web news, which refers to recent changes, renovating realities, and reports reviews spread by the Internet, has the characteristics of real-time updating.

Web news covers the history and status of an event and social public's attitudes toward it. In other words, Web news contain topics of social public concern, corresponding expectations, and this social awareness information is valuable for studying the future development trends of technologies (events) [19].

In this paper we adopt dataset "Keyword frequencies in popular tech media (01.2016–01.2020)" of Kristóf Gyódi et al. [20] for technology trend analysis and forecast. Authors of the dataset collected all articles from 8 famous technological and news websites: Ars technica, Euractiv, Fastcompany, The Register, Techcrunch, The Guardian, Venturebeat, The Verge. Table 1 describes details of these websites (information was collected in May 4th, 2021).

Table 1. Detail information about websites collected for the dataset

№	Media name	Website address	Topic categories	Start	Alexa rank
1	Ars technica	https://arstechnica.com	News and opinions in technology, science, politics, and society	1998	3,904
2	Euractiv	http://www.euractiv.com	Investigation of European policies in tech policy, environment and energy, transport, food safety, and agriculture	1999	47,262
3	Fastcompany	http://www.fastcompany.com	Leadership and innovation in business, environmental and social issues, entertainment and marketing	1995	4,624
4	The Register	https://www.theregister.com	Information technology news and opinions, computer business and trade news	1994	25,628
5	Techcrunch	http://techcrunch.com	High tech, startup companies, technology news and analysis	2005	1,051
6	The Guardian	https://www.theguardian.com	Daily news (world, environment, science, technology, business), opinion, sport, culture, lifestyle	1999	183
7	Venturebeat	https://venturebeat.com	Technology news and analysis, social media, big data, mobile, business, deals, cloud, enterprise, entrepreneur, security, marketing, and small bisiness	2006	4,104
8	The Verge	https://www.theverge.com	Technology news, feature stories, guidebooks, product reviews, and podcasts	2011	943

Eight aforementioned media sources were used for collecting data with the same number of articles per source. The dataset contains number of appearances of every string terms (words, keywords, expressions, henceforth will be referred as terms), which are all unigrams and bigrams in the texts, divided by the number of published articles (for every month and all media sources). In other words, this measure reveals how many times a term has been mentioned on average per article. Columns of the dataset consist of freq_months (e.g. freq_2020-01, which is the average frequency of the term in January, 2020). The original dataset contains 109928 rows and 49 columns.

Procedures of applying Burst detection algorithm on this dataset for technology analysis and forecast includes following steps: data cleaning; explanatory data analysis; fitting linear regression model for data and sorting data by slope (regression coefficient); applying Burst detection for the refined dataset; and forecasting technology trend. The entire proposed method is illustrated in Fig. 2 below.

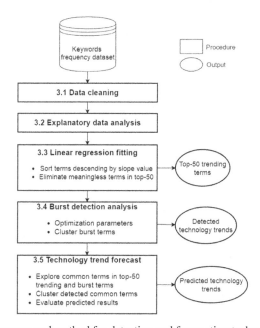

Fig. 2. The proposed method for detecting and forecasting technology trends

3.1 Data Cleaning

It is decided to perform data cleaning in the first stage in order to remove outliers and noisy data. Hence we eliminated 6572 string terms whose lengths are more than 25 (e.g. "http://www.cpubenchmark.net/cpu.php", "an-absolute-beast-in-every-way", "your-best-photographs-of-the-week-with-us", "iphone-xr-dual-camera-a13-smartphon", etc.) or less than 3 (e.g. "ice", "opt", "5", "act", "urg", "lie", "15", "-", etc.), because these terms are meaningless, only characters, only numbers, or hyperlinks. Then 3615 stop words, such as "i", "me", "my", "myself", "we", "our", "ours", "ourselves", "in", "out", etc., and strings containing only numbers or punctuations (e.g.

"2020", "2017", "2050", "1-800-273-8255", "250,000", etc.) were also removed. Additionally, terms with so many zero frequency columns (≥40 over 49 independent columns) were also eliminated. Finally, a dataset was retrieved with 62372 rows from the result of data cleaning, as shown in Fig. 3.

keyword	2020-01	2019-12	2019-11	2019-10	2019-09	2019-08	2019-07	2019-06	2019-05
https	0.811841	1.381482	1.185203	1.204652	1.255377	1.316972	0.999107	1.024407	1.124163
facebook	0.415763	0.654422	0.844343	0.874471	0.511986	0.544226	0.805396	0.773171	0.721004
huawei	0.501025	0.304817	0.120662	0.134158	0.216222	0.158398	0.317285	0.265185	0.617306
said	1.928487	1.901630	1.916028	1.858476	1.686843	1.647025	1.890645	1.830844	1.913166
amazon	0.420389	0.386964	0.392924	0.340698	0.504365	0.478240	0.442490	0.314209	0.321004
...	...	...	...	...	...	...	...	...	...
work	1.160508	1.202837	1.139493	1.188132	1.194413	1.065297	1.093664	1.162073	1.136014
uber	0.078942	0.098680	0.222369	0.108874	0.158265	0.185065	0.086597	0.172365	0.429160
want	0.599707	0.665391	0.716445	0.733284	0.789770	0.588810	0.644144	0.673474	0.713944
peopl	0.899982	1.035337	1.111957	1.208005	1.128501	1.073018	1.045138	1.036683	1.079602
http	0.014510	0.010330	0.025444	0.031092	0.030115	0.028479	0.021743	0.021595	0.023867

Fig. 3. Values of first 10 columns in the dataset

3.2   Explanatory Data Analysis

Herein exploratory data analysis summarizes some of main data characteristics by using histogram statistical graphics (Fig. 4) and scatter plot (Fig. 5).

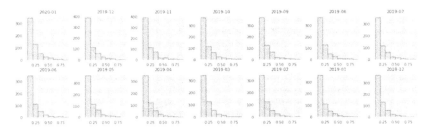

Fig. 4. Histogram of first 14 columns in the dataset

In Fig. 4, the histogram bins are sequence (0.1, 0.2, 0.3, …, 0.9), one can observe that most of average frequency values are less than 0.1. Besides, Fig. 5 presents that values between columns have positive correlation.

3.3   Fitting Linear Regression Model

In general, the linear regression model allows for a linear relationship between the forecast variable y_t and a single predictor variable x_t:

$$y_t = b + Ax_t + \varepsilon_t \tag{5}$$

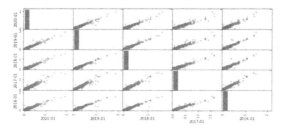

Fig. 5. Scatter matrix between 5 columns of the dataset

where ε_t is a deviation from the underlying straight line model; the coefficients b and A denote the intercept and the slope of the line respectively. The intercept b represents the predicted value of y_t when $x_t = 0$. The slope A represents the average predicted change in y_t (string term frequency) resulting from a one unit increase in x_t (month). More specifically, the regression coefficient (slope A) will be calculated by Ordinary least square (OLS) regressions. The dependent variable of the estimation is the frequency index, while the number of months since the beginning of the analyzed period (January 2016) is the independent variable. Hereby the regression coefficient shows by how much on average the analyzed term's frequency changed with every observed month (marginal change of the frequency), revealing which term had the biggest monthly growth.

After fitting linear regression model for every time series of each term frequency and sorting data descending by slope, we demonstrate in Fig. 6 time series values and fitting lines of 6 selective highest slope terms.

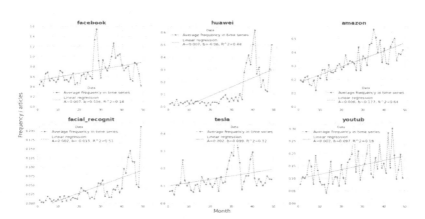

Fig. 6. Time series values and fitting lines of 6 selective highest slope terms

In particular, terms that appeared at the same rate throughout the time period should have slopes around zero, terms that became less prevalent should have negative slopes, conversely, terms that became more prevalent should have positive slopes. The higher slope of fitting line is, the more trending term is. Consequently, after eliminating some meaningless string terms, we can find top-50 most frequent terms (by summing up all frequencies) and top-50 trending (steep upward) terms, which are illustrated in Fig. 7.

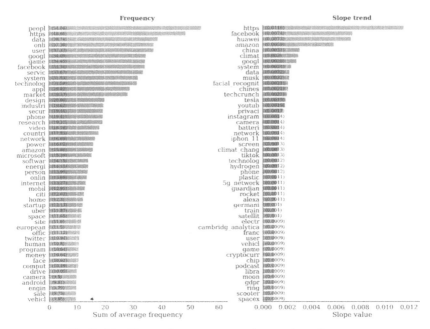

Fig. 7. Top-50 most frequent terms and upward trending terms

3.4 Burst Detection Analysis

Burst detection finds periods of time in which a target is uncharacteristically popular, or, in other words, when it is "bursting". In this case, the target is one of the unique terms in the dataset and we are looking for periods in which the term appears in a greater proportion of articles than usual. The two-state model assumes that a target can be in one of two states: a baseline state, in which the target occurs at some baseline or default rate, and a bursty state, in which the target occurs at an elevated rate. For every time point (month), the algorithm is adopted to compare the frequency of the target term to the frequency of all the other terms in the same time point, and try to guess whether the target is in a baseline state or a bursty state. The algorithm returns its best guess of which state the target was in at each time point during the time period (49 months, from January 2016 to January 2020).

There are 2 parameters that can be optimized in burst detection. The first is the "distance" s between the baseline state and burst state. In our analysis, s is also fixed at 2, which is the same value that Kleinberg used in his experiment [11]. The parameter s = 2 means that a word has to occur with a frequency that is more than double its baseline frequency to be considered bursting.

The second parameter is the difficulty γ associated with moving up into a bursty state. Herein we used $\gamma = 0.02$, which makes it relatively easy to enter a bursting state. The reason γ is quite small because the distribution values mostly less than 0.1, which was revealed in Sect. 3.2 – explanatory data analysis, hence the rate between target term and all other terms becomes smaller. Moreover, the optimal value $\gamma = 0.02$ is chosen after considering with burst term results, which presented more meaningful terms.

The program code for burst detection algorithm implementation was written on Python language with the utilization of popular libraries, such as: numpy, matplotlib, pandas, nltk, re, scikit-learn. Finally we applied the abovementioned burst detection model to all 62372 unique string terms in the dataset to determine which terms were associated with bursts of activity and when those bursts occurred. Figure 8 below is a timeline of all the bursts.

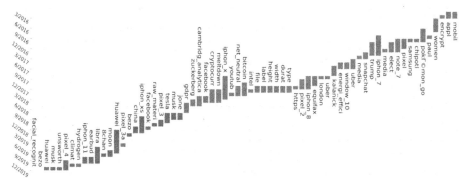

Fig. 8. Timeline of bursty terms

The vast majority of terms were not associated with any bursts, but a handful of terms did exhibit bursting activity. Each bar represents one burst, with previous bursts in violet and current bursts (those that are still in a burst state after June 2018) in blue. By observing burst terms, we are able to cluster these terms into some main technology trend categories (terms are listed ascending by start time of burst):

1. Smartphones: mobil (mobile), samsung, note_7, iphon_7 (iPhone 7), iphon_8 (iPhone 8), pixel_2, iphon_x (iPhone X), pixel_3, iphon_xs (iPhone XS), pixel_3a, huawei, earbud, iphone_11 (iPhone 11), pixel_4;
2. Application, software, system: pokГ©mon_go (Pokémon GO), snapchat, window_10, facial_recognit (Facial recognition);
3. Hardware: intel, meltdown;
4. Finance, digital currencies: encrypt, equifax, bitcoin, cryptocurr (cryptocurrency), libra;
5. Politics, policies: elect, trump, cambridg_analytica (Cambridge Analytica), gdpr (General Data Protection Regulation), china;
6. Transportation industry: uber, energi_effici (energy efficiency), kalanick (Travis Kalanick), musk (Elon Musk), tesla;
7. Internet, media: net_neutral (net neutrality), youtub (youtube), 8chan;
8. Tech giants: appl (Apple), facebook, zuckerberg (Mark Zuckerberg), bezo (Jeff Bezos).

3.5 Technology Trends Forecast

Herein, in order to predict technological development trends, we will explore appearances of burst terms (Fig. 8) in top-50 most trending terms (Fig. 7), which are (sorted from oldest to newest burst): "cryptocurr", "youtub", "cambridg_analytica", "gdpr", "tesla", "facebook", "china", "huawei", "libra", "moon", "iphon_11", "climat", "hydrogen", "musk", "huawei", "facial_recognit". From these keywords, one could infer some technological development trends for the near future (2020–2022) by manual clustering as below, and these trends can be evaluated by experts in respective links:

1. Cryptocurrency trends: (keywords: "cryptocurr", "libra"). Blockchain technology is highly secure with default protective mechanisms and anti-fraudulent. As we know, crypto is always a trendy one in the blockchain world. Also, the profits that are made through digital currencies are endless. At this present time, there are millions of crypto traders globally, and compared to other traders, bitcoin traders are more across the world. So the usage of altcoins and bitcoins are growing day by day rapidly. Today, in 2021, the number of cryptocurrencies in the market has more than 6000. Companies, startups, and entrepreneurs are all trying to get into this cryptocurrency trend and are willing to create their own crypto coin that can take the market by storm like bitcoin [21, 22].

2. Data privacy (keywords: "cambridg_analytica", "gdpr"). The Facebook – Cambridge Analytica data breach is one of the most notorious data privacy scandals in recent years. Interestingly, the scandal unraveled around the same time that the EU General Data Protection Regulation (GDPR) was about to come into effect. Under the GDPR, sensitive personal data is subject to stricter regulations around collection and usage, given that such information could be used in ways that could potentially endanger, blackmail, or discriminate against the individual in question. In an era where privacy is now at the forefront of consumer's concerns online, companies must evolve their practices and processes, and implement significant changes to their platform design and communications around user privacy [23, 24]. Besides, recently TikTok has faced strong criticism for its extensive, uninformed data collection and other GDPR violations. Consumer protectionists have particularly criticized the lack of adequate protection for children and young people against hidden advertising and harmful content [25, 26]. For this reason, nowadays Data Privacy problems are becoming more and more important.

3. Electric vehicle and battery technology (keywords: "tesla", "musk"). Elon Musk has become a household name synonymous with the future. Whether he's working on electric vehicles (Tesla) or sending rockets into space (SpaceX), his larger-than-life reputation attracts its fair share of attention and scrutiny. The Tesla Model 3 – Tesla's first true mass market electric vehicle – became the best-selling electric vehicle globally in March 2020. Moreover, expecting electric vehicles to become mass market makes sense. Great Britain and France voted to ban diesel and gasoline auto sales starting in the year 2040. China has said that 20% of cars sold in the country should run on some alternative source of fuel by 2025. Hence, though electric vehicles like Teslas still rely on the grid for energy, they could help reduce gasoline burden [27]. Thus, the future of the battery is coming, and Tesla wants to be at the forefront of this race to fully electrify global transportation [28].

4. Facial recognition ("facial_recognit"). We know for sure is that this feature is becoming increasingly popular in our devices – not just in home security cameras, but also our phones and as efficiency tools helping to automate airport check-ins. In light of

the Covid-19 outbreak, the tech is superseding tickets as a touchless way to enter stadiums and enjoy sporting events in New York and Los Angeles. Facial recognition is also a powerful instrument for law enforcement agencies to track down criminals, and for governments to surveil their citizens. It is a stronghold of the Skynet mass monitoring system deployed in China, with more than 600 million cameras having been installed across the country [29]. As law enforcement becomes more invested in facial recognition technology, it's already raising serious questions about surveillance technology, privacy and civil rights across the board, and bringing calls for governmental regulation [30].

5. Clean energy (keywords: "climat", "hydrogen"): Climate change includes both global warming driven by human-induced emissions of greenhouse gases and the resulting large-scale shifts in weather patterns. The largest driver of warming is the emission of greenhouse gases, of which more than 90% are carbon dioxide (CO_2) and methane. Fossil fuel burning (coal, oil, and natural gas) for energy consumption is the main source of these emissions, with additional contributions from agriculture, deforestation, and manufacturing. Hence, green hydrogen, an alternative fuel generated with clean energy, is experiencing a global resurgence and has been identified as the clean energy source that could help bring the world to net-zero emissions in the coming decades [31, 32]. Billions of dollars of investment capital and taxpayer support has flowed into the industry, and company share prices have soared [33].

4   Conclusions

Technological developments have an essential impact on strategic decision making. The early awareness of possible upcoming or emerging technological trends could lead to strengthening the competitiveness and market positioning of enterprises. Hence, if innovation-driven companies ignore emerging technological developments, they may not tap the full potentials of their own products or technologies. Furthermore, Web news is an important data resource for studying social public awareness of emerging technologies. Web news, which refers to recent changes, renovating realities and reports reviews spread by the Internet, has the characteristics of real-time updating and is valuable for studying the future development trends of technologies.

In this paper we proposed a method that helps analyze and forecast technological development trends by adopting burst detection algorithm and linear regression. The algorithm devised by Kleinberg focuses on streams of documents and aims to identify features of burst activity that occur with high frequency over limited periods of time. In the case of sets of messages, bursts can be understood as short periods characterized by relatively higher volumes of them. Up till now, citation trend analysis shows that the algorithm still has been impactful and significant in recent researches. After applying burst detection algorithm and clustering burst terms manually, we obtained some main technology trends that occurred in recent years from January 2019 to January 2020. Furthermore, by examining appearances of burst terms in top-50 most trending terms detected by linear regression fitting, and then implementing manual clustering, we inferred some technological development trends for the near future, which can be evaluated later by domain experts. That means the proposed method is effective and promising for analyzing and forecasting technology trends. In future plan, we will develop burst terms clustering method, apply burst detection algorithm for publication and patent data to explore relationship patterns between science and technology, and help comprehend more about technology life cycle.

Acknowledgments. The reported study was funded by RFBR, projects No. 19-07-01200 and 20-37-90092.

References

1. Iqbal, W., Qadir, J., Tyson, G., Mian, A.N., Hassan, S., Crowcroft, J.: A bibliometric analysis of publications in computer networking research. Scientometrics **119**(2), 1121–1155 (2019). https://doi.org/10.1007/s11192-019-03086
2. Chen, H., Chiang, R.H.L., Storey, V.C.: Business intelligence and analytics: from big data to big impact. MIS Q. Manag. Inf. Syst. (2012). https://doi.org/10.2307/41703503
3. Lee, C., Kwon, O., Kim, M., Kwon, D.: Early identification of emerging technologies: a machine learning approach using multiple patent indicators. Technol. Forecast. Soc. Change (2018). https://doi.org/10.1016/j.techfore.2017.10.002
4. Nazemi, K., et al.: Visual trend analysis with digital libraries. ACM Int. Conf. Proc. Ser. (2015). https://doi.org/10.1145/2809563.2809569
5. Viet, N.T., Kravets, A.G., Analyzing recent research trends of computer science from academic open-access digital library. In: Proceedings of the 2019 8th International Conference on System Modeling and Advancement in Research Trends, SMART 2019 (2020). https://doi.org/10.1109/SMART46866.2019.9117215.
6. Noh, H., Jo, Y., Lee, S.: Keyword selection and processing strategy for applying text mining to patent analysis. Exp. Syst. Appl. (2015). https://doi.org/10.1016/j.eswa.2015.01.050
7. Kravets, A.G., Vasiliev, S.S., Shabanov, D.V.: Research of the LDA algorithm results for patents texts processing. In: 2018 9th International Conference on Information, Intelligence, Systems and Applications, IISA 2018 (2019). https://doi.org/10.1109/IISA.2018.8633649.
8. Kravets, A., Gneushev, V., Biryukov, S., Skorikov, D., Marinkin, D. Research of the LDA algorithm processing results on high-level classes of patents. In: CEUR Workshop Proceedings (2020).
9. Rotolo, D., Hicks, D., Martin, B.R.: What is an emerging technology? Res. Policy (2015). https://doi.org/10.1016/j.respol.2015.06.006
10. Xie, Q.-Q., Li, X., Huang, L.-C.: Identifying the development trends of emerging technologies: a social awareness analysis method using web news data mining. In: PICMET 2018 - Portland International Conference on Management of Engineering and Technology: Managing Technological Entrepreneurship: The Engine for Economic Growth, Proceedings (2018). https://doi.org/10.23919/PICMET.2018.8481813.
11. Kleinberg, J.: Bursty and hierarchical structure in streams. Data Min. Knowl. Disc. (2003). https://doi.org/10.1023/A:1024940629314
12. Chen, C.: CiteSpace II: detecting and visualizing emerging trends and transient patterns in scientific literature. J. Am. Soc. Inf. Sci. Technol. (2006). https://doi.org/10.1002/asi.20317
13. Guo, H., Weingart, S., Börner, K.: Mixed-indicators model for identifying emerging research areas. Scientometrics (2011). https://doi.org/10.1007/s11192-011-0433-7
14. Swar, B., Khan, G.F.: Mapping ICT knowledge infrastructure in South Asia. Scientometrics **99**(1), 117–137 (2013). https://doi.org/10.1007/s11192-013-1099-0

15. Dernis, H., Squicciarini, M., de Pinho, R.: Detecting the emergence of technologies and the evolution and co-development trajectories in science (DETECTS): a 'burst' analysis-based approach. J. Technol. Transf. **41**(5), 930–960 (2015). https://doi.org/10.1007/s10961-015-9449-0

16. Sohrabi, B., Vanani, I.R., Jalali, S.M.J., Abedin, E.: Evaluation of research trends in knowledge management: a hybrid analysis through burst detection and text clustering. J. Inf. Knowl. Manage. (2019). https://doi.org/10.1142/S0219649219500436

17. Vo, T., Do, P.: TKES: a novel system for extracting trendy keywords from online news sites. J. Oper. Res. Soc. China (2021). https://doi.org/10.1007/s40305-020-00327-4

18. Breitzman, A., Thomas, P.: The Emerging Clusters Model: A tool for identifying emerging technologies across multiple patent systems. Res. Policy (2015). https://doi.org/10.1016/j.respol.2014.06.006

19. Yoon, J.: Detecting weak signals for long-term business opportunities using text mining of Web news. Expert Syst. Appl. (2012). https://doi.org/10.1016/j.eswa.2012.04.059

20. Gyódi, K., Nawaro, Ł., Paliński, M.: Keyword frequencies in popular tech media (01.2016–02.2020) (Version 1.0). Zenodo (2020). https://doi.org/10.5281/zenodo.3715353

21. Top 8 Blockchain and Cryptocurrency Trends that You Must Look Out in 2021 (2021). https://dev.to/mathew_b/top-8-blockchain-and-cryptocurrency-trends-that-you-must-look-out-in-2021-3bog. Accessed 7 May 2021

22. The 10 Most Important Cryptocurrencies Other Than Bitcoin (2021). https://www.investopedia.com/tech/most-important-cryptocurrencies-other-than-bitcoin. Accessed 7 May 2021

23. Could the GDPR have helped prevent the Cambridge Analytica data breach? (2021). https://getterms.io/blog/could-the-gdpr-have-helped-prevent-the-cambridge-analytica-data-breach. Accessed 8 May 2021

24. Data Privacy Scandal, Anyone? (2021). https://terranovasecurity.com/data-privacy-scandal-facebook. Accessed 8 May 2021

25. TikTok's lack of adherence to data privacy regulations: what online advertisers need to know (2021). https://usercentrics.com/knowledge-hub/tiktoks-lack-of-adherence-to-data-privacy-regulations-what-online-advertisers-need-to-know. Accessed 8 May 2021

26. TikTok could be facing some serious GDPR charges (2021). https://www.techradar.com/news/tiktok-could-be-facing-some-serious-gdpr-charges. Accessed 8 May 2021

27. From Energy to Transport to Healthcare, Here are 8 Industries Being Disrupted by Elon Musk and His Companies (2020). https://www.cbinsights.com/research/report/elon-musk-companies-disruption. Accessed 9 May 2021

28. What Does Elon Musk's New Tesla Battery Technology Mean for the Future? (2020). https://www.motorbiscuit.com/what-does-elon-musks-new-tesla-battery-technology-mean-for-the-future. Accessed 9 May 2021

29. Facial recognition technologies see significant advancements (2020). https://www.securityinfowatch.com/access-identity/biometrics/facial-recognition-solutions/article/21152899/serious-advancements-in-facial-recognition-technologies. Accessed 10 May 2021

30. The best facial recognition security cameras of 2021 (2021). https://www.cnet.com/home/security/best-facial-recognition-security-cameras. Accessed 10 May 2021

31. In-depth Q&A: does the world need hydrogen to solve climate change? (2020). https://www.carbonbrief.org/in-depth-qa-does-the-world-need-hydrogen-to-solve-climate-change. Accessed 10 May 2021

32. Why green hydrogen is the renewable energy source to watch in 2021 (2021). https://abcnews.go.com/Technology/green-hydrogen-renewable-energy-source-watch-2021/story?id=74128340. Accessed 10 May 2021

33. What is green hydrogen, how is it made and will it be the fuel of the future? (2021). https://www.abc.net.au/news/science/2021-01-23/green-hydrogen-renewable-energy-climate-emissions-explainer/13081872. Accessed 10 May 2021

Relevant Image Search Method When Processing a Patent Array

Alla G. Kravets[1,2(✉)], Natalia Salnikova[3], Ilya Mikhnev[3], and Natalia Solovieva[4]

[1] Volgograd State Technical University, 28 Lenin Avenue, Volgograd 400005, Russia
agk@gde.ru

[2] Dubna State University, 19 Universitetskaya Street, Dubna, Moscow Region 141982, Russia

[3] Volgograd Institute of Management – Branch of the Russian Presidential Academy of National Economy and Public Administration, 8 Gagarin Street, Volgograd 400131, Russia
mkmco@list.ru

[4] Volgograd State University, 100 Universitetskiy Avenue, Volgograd 400062, Russia

Abstract. In this paper, the specificity of patent images was studied, a method was developed that uses a neural network for image preprocessing (classification) and their subsequent comparison, the architectures of neural networks for working with images and deep learning libraries were analyzed, and a comparative analysis of existing methods for searching and classifying patent images was carried out. A number of practical tasks have been completed for the search and collection of patent images, the selection of the main classes of patent images, the formation of a training sample; the training of the neural network for the recognition of the selected classes of patent images was carried out, the analysis of the trained model was carried out; a software module was created based on the developed method.

Keywords: Neural network · Neural network architecture · Machine learning · Deep learning · Training samples · Patent images search · Patent image processing

1 Introduction

A patent search is a procedure for selecting information on patents corresponding to a specific request, which can be carried out on one or several grounds. In particular, a patent search makes it possible to establish the novelty of an invention.

This is a time-consuming process that is often entrusted to intellectual property professionals, but it is necessary - both for those who wish to obtain a patent and for those who wish to use an already patented invention.

In addition, patent search allows one to determine the general state of research in an area of interest. Analysis of search results allows making forecasts, identifying trends in the future development of the invention and its analogs, and the industry as a whole [1, 2].

The number of patents increases every year. More than 3 million patent applications were filed in 2019. This is a record number that is 8.3% higher than in 2018. If you

© Springer Nature Switzerland AG 2021
A. G. Kravets et al. (Eds.): CIT&DS 2021, CCIS 1448, pp. 70–84, 2021.
https://doi.org/10.1007/978-3-030-87034-8_6

analyze the global trend in filing applications, you can see that the number of applications is steadily increasing from year to year.

With the increase in the number of patents, the time for consideration of an application for registration of a patent also increases. The expert of the patent office needs to establish the uniqueness of the patented technology. To do this, he must make a comparison with similar patents and make sure that there are no analogs of the invention. In the course of such work, an expert can check more than a thousand patents, using only the images they contain [3, 4]. So the study of images can be very important when trying to establish the relevance of patents.

Further confirmation of the importance of searching for patent images is the fact that images, by their very nature, are independent of the applicant's language and are not affected by changes in scientific terminology over time that affects search quality. In addition, the use of patent images in search would facilitate the identification of relevant documents published in different languages without resorting to insufficiently high-quality machine translation [5, 6].

Insufficient accuracy and productivity of traditional methods of searching for relevant images do not allow automated analysis of drawings contained in patent documents. To solve it, it is necessary to develop a new method of automated patent search.

The work aims to improve the accuracy and productivity of the process of analyzing drawings when processing a large patent array.

To achieve this goal, it is required to solve several theoretical problems:

- study the specifics of patent images;
- study and analyze the architectures of neural networks for working with images and deep learning libraries;
- analyze the existing methods of searching and classifying patent images.

And also it is necessary to solve a number of practical tasks:

- conduct a search and collection of patent images, highlight the main classes of patent images, form training samples;
- provide training of the neural network for recognizing the selected classes of patent images, analyzing the trained model;
- develop a method for finding relevant patent images;
- create a software module based on the developed method.

2   Methods for Searching Patent Images from Existing Analogues

Most of the patents contain drawings. They are necessary to fully disclose the essence of the invention. The absence of figures may indicate an incomplete description of the invention and entail the return of the patent application and other problems [7, 8]. In patent documents, there is an association between figures and texts. Figures, as in most technical documents, are numbered sequentially and are called "FIG. X" in the text. However, the figure designation numbers are part of the figure, so its designation is not always easy to extract automatically due to the different fonts used.

The difficulty of viewing many inventions is compounded by the set of black and white drawings that are used in patents. Also currently distributed software systems of patent and license search to provide users with search capabilities based only on standard (attributive) query formation or on the so-called "substring" search [9, 10]. Most of the image search methods are based on image comparisons. Patent offices with the current development of information retrieval tools should accept electronic 3D models and other electronic supplementary material in order to provide completeness of information about the invention and to make the search process more efficient.

Classifying patent images is challenging. Since patent images, even if we consider images of the same type, class, etc., are unique, different from each other. Patent images can only be classified with great precision on the main classes of patent images. This classification can be done using a neural network or based on the text in the headings of the figures. But such a classification would not provide any information to the patent office. It can be used for primary image processing, and only then apply search. Consider a number of existing methods for searching and classifying patent images.

PATSEEK is a patent image retrieval system for US patent databases. It consists of two subsystems: one for extracting features of images, the other for searching images based on the loaded one [11]. Extraction of image features is done using the Edge Orientation Auto Correlogram (EOAC) method. It classifies parts of an image based on their orientations and correlations between adjacent parts around the center of the image. Graphics content is used to compute a vector of image features. PATSEEK uses EOAC because it is computationally good and doesn't depend on translation. The feature vector size is small, 144 real numbers. The PATSEEK search engine interacts with the user through a simple interface, showing the loaded search image and a series of visually similar images.

ImageSeeker is an accessible image search tool created by LTU Technologies. Their technology has been used by the French Patent Office (INPI) to build an image-based search engine and has also been applied to the European project eMARKS, which seeks to develop services for accessing trademark and image databases [12]. The developers of the system claim that it is better than the existing image classification system. Since LTU technology is proprietary, it is difficult to assess how image search is performed and its scalability. But you can see the available ImageSeeker architecture, it consists of several modules. When a new image is loaded into the system, the image commenting module processes the image and assigns labels to different segments of the image. The annotated image is stored in a database with all keywords (labels) and records a rank for each keyword so that it can be used in image searches that have a specific keyword or object. Image Search Module, like other search engines, ImageSeeker has a database containing category images. Each image saved in the database has its own keywords (labels) attached to it. The user uploads an image, and then the system starts searching for images in the database using the object's keywords. And displays images according to their rating of existing counterparts.

PIRs are search algorithms that have not been tested extensively in large-scale databases and have not been applied in search engines, where images must be extracted from patent documents before searching can be applied [13]. One such algorithm is to investigate a method for efficiently selecting patents from a database based on the visual content of technical drawings. The algorithm extracts lines from the drawing for two different searches. One is based on the relative measure of the similarity of the graph, the other - on the structural histogram comparison. Experiments have shown that these methods work well for some images and not for others. The algorithm is only used for technical drawings.

PatMedia is a hybrid search engine created in the multimedia knowledge laboratory at the Institute of Informatics and Telematics. This search engine supports four searches: visual, text, hybrid, and patent image browsing. The system classifies each patent image by class [14]. This classification is based on the text in the figure headings, but the heading does not always contain the name of the picture class. Visual search is based on the extracted AdaptiveHierarchicalDensityHistograms (AHDH) feature vectors. Advanced visual search is based on visual information. The precision provided by the classifiers is used to generate a vector that is based on the final SVM classifier structure for the final search.

Automated system for support of patent and licensing activities (AS SPLA) - data exchange between the user and the system occurs through the web interface. The search subsystem includes three blocks, each of which consists of functional modules: standard attributive search, semantic search, pattern recognition, and image analysis [15]. The last block is provided by the following modules:

- The module for image processing and recognition is designed for filtering, smoothing, color clustering, outline and skeleton highlighting, transformation into vector form, image compression, highlighting informative features, and recognizing objects of a given class.
- The graphical search module searches for graphical information contained in the texts of titles of protection and other publications by recognizing visual images.
- The module for analyzing and interpreting images analyzes the image converted to a vector form and writes a brief description in the database in the form of a verbal description.
- The module for searching images by verbal portrait is designed to search for titles of protection and publications that contain graphic information corresponding to the interpreted verbal portrait.

The results of the analysis of the search systems discussed above are shown in Table 1, which displays a comparative analysis of the functionality of these systems. The criteria available for external testing are text search support, image search method, interface complexity, and the number of different types of searches. During the analysis of analogs, five systems were considered: PATSEEK, ImageSeeker, PIR, PatMedia, AS PPLD. Of all the systems, only one PIR is a search algorithm that has not been extensively tested in large-scale databases and has not been applied in search engines, where images must be extracted from patent documents before searching can be applied. Also, the algorithm is used only for technical drawings.

The AS PPLD system has a rather complex interface, but it has two different methods of searching for images in the patent database.

Table 1. Comparison of analogs of search and classification methods for patent images.

	PATSEEK	Image Seeker	PIR	PatMedia	AS SPLA
Text search	Absent	Present	Absent	Present	Present
Image search method	Edge orientation autocorrelogram (EOAC)	By keywords	Based on the visual content of technical drawings	On extracted feature vectors Adaptive Hierarchical Density Histograms (AHDH)	1) By graphic information using visual recognition 2) By verbal portrait
Number of search types	1	1	2	4	5

PATSEEK and PIR are highly specialized programs, as they only work with images of patents. All of the above systems have a common property, before searching, they pre-analyze the loaded images and images stored in the database. Pre-processing is performed, converted to vector form, objects are extracted from the image, and the class or category of the patent image is classified. Then there is a search in the patent database.

3   Analysis of Existing Deep Learning Libraries

To implement algorithms for working with neural networks in the developed system, it was decided to use one of the existing libraries. In our review of deep learning libraries for the Python programming language, we looked at four libraries: Theano, Caffe, TensorFlow, and Keras [16–19]. A comparative analysis of the capabilities of these libraries is shown in Table 2.

For comparison, the following criteria were identified: name, creator, operating system, programming language, providing the ability to create fully connected neural networks (FC NN), convolutional neural networks (CNN), autoencoders (autoencoders, AE), and recurrent neural networks. networks (Recirrentneuralnetwork, RNN), support for openMP technology, and the possibility of cloud computing [20, 21].

Table 2. Library functionality for Keras, Caffe, Theano, and TensorFlow.

Title	Keras	Caffe	Theano	TensorFlow
Creator	Francois Chollet	University of Berkeley	Montreal University	Google
OS	Linux, Windows, macOS	Linux, Windows, macOS, Android	Cross platform	Linux, Windows, macOS

(continued)

Table 2. (*continued*)

Title	Keras	Caffe	Theano	TensorFlow
Language	Python	C++, Python, Matlab	Python	C++, Python
FCNN	+	+	+	+
CNN	+	+	+	+
AE	+	−	+	+
RNN	+	+	+	+
Support OpenMP	−	−	+	−
Cloud computing	+	+	+	+

3.1 Structural and Functional Model of the Patent Image Search Method

For the patent image search method, functional requirements must be presented. The context diagram for the patent search task is shown in Fig. 1.

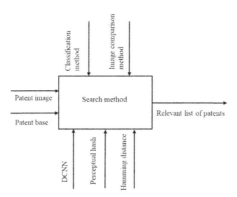

Fig. 1. Structural and functional model of the patent image search method (IDEF0 methodology).

The following is used as the initial information on the basis of which the ranked list is formed:

- Patent base on which the search takes place.
- Patent image to be checked.

Control data are:

- Image classification method.
- Image comparison method.

The mechanisms are:

- Deep Convolutional Neural Network (DCNN) architecture, for image classification.
- Perceptual hash, for its subsequent comparison.
- Hamming distance, for comparing perceptual hashes.

The result of the system should be a relevant list of patents.

The functions of the system that must be implemented within the framework of the main function are shown in Fig. 2.

The queue for performing functions for solving the problem under consideration is as follows:

- Image classification.
- Obtaining images with a given class.
- Comparison of images.

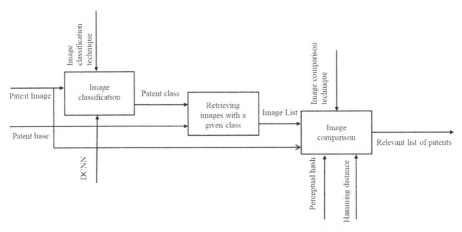

Fig. 2. Decomposition diagram of the structural-functional model of the patent image search method (IDEFO methodology).

3.2 Algorithm of the Method of Searching for Relevant Patent Images

To implement the method of searching for relevant images, an algorithm for comparing patent drawings was developed. The idea is to assign a class to patent images that are in the search base and submitted to the application using the architecture of the deep convolutional neural network (DCNN). Next, we get all images with the same classes. For each image, its own perceptual hash is calculated. The computation of perceptual hashes is very fast. Hamming distance is used to compare images. We count the number of different bits, if the distance is zero, then these are most likely the same images. If the distance is in the region of 10, then the images are different from each other, but in general, they are still quite close to each other. If the distance is more than 20, then these are probably completely different images. Perceptual hash is calculated to find identical images with minor modifications.

The execution of the method for searching for relevant images is divided into three stages: classification of the patent image, calculation of perceptual hashes, and comparison of images (Fig. 3).

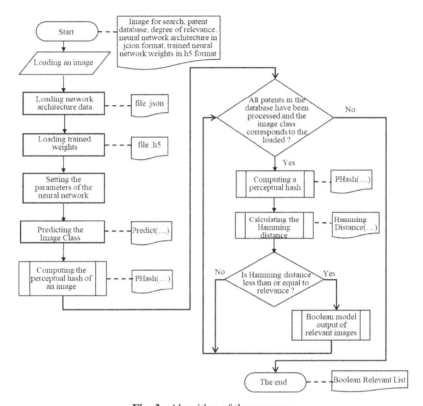

Fig. 3. Algorithm of the program.

The image enters the program through a graphical user interface. The expert needs to check the uniqueness of the information.

The most used search model is the Boolean model, which provides the ability to construct logical expressions from a set of arguments. The corresponding images are found using the logical operations described by the query on the set of images. The expert receives only those images whose sets of arguments exactly match the corresponding combinations of query arguments.

Based on the Boolean model, images and queries are represented as multiple arguments. All images being searched are indexed relative to the arguments. This results in a "dictionary" - this is the index base of all arguments: $A = \{a_1, a_2, ..., a_n\}$.

Searches bind arguments using the basic boolean operators OR, AND, NOT. These operations are combined with each other and performed on sets of images containing one or another argument specified by the query.

The query might look like this: $a_3 OR a_6 AND NOT a_{10}$, which means you need to find images that include the third or sixth arguments of the dictionary, but not the tenth. If the formula is executed for any image, then this document is considered to meet the request.

The main disadvantage of the Boolean model is extreme rigidity.

4   Image Comparison

4.1   Perceptual Hash (pHash)

A perceptual hash (Fig. 4) is a "fingerprint" of a multimedia file derived from various features from its content. Unlike hash functions, which are fast and simple but may not find a duplicate image after gamma correction or color histogram changes, perceptual hashes use a more robust algorithm that uses discrete cosine transform (DCT) to eliminate high frequencies. Perceptual hashes are evolving and are at the center of computer science research, as they must be robust enough to find the same files when rotated, distorted, contrast-adjusted, and various compression/formatting, while flexible to distinguish between them.

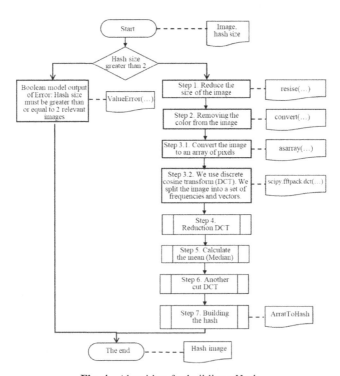

Fig. 4. Algorithm for building pHash.

Perceptual hashes are used for copyright protection, searching for similarities between media files, or in digital forensics. For example, YouTube maintains a database of hashes from major movie producers to maintain copyright. If a user uploads a video to YouTube, and the hash is almost identical, then we can talk about a possible copyright infringement. Audio hashes can be used to automatically find duplicate mp3 files, while ID3 tags (information contained in mp3) are processed to detect plagiarism.

The input to this method is images (to build a hash) and the size of the hash (the standard value is 8). The output is the hash of the image.

At the very beginning, you need to reduce the size of the image. pHash is used on small image sizes. The standard image is set to 32 by 32. This is to simplify the discrete cosine transform (DCT), not to remove high frequencies. The next step is to convert the image from RGB to pure black and white, for easier calculations. In step 3, convert the image to a pixel array and use DCT. We split the image into a set of frequencies and vectors.

Reduce DCT (Fig. 5). The original array was 32 by 32 in size. From it, we select only the upper left values, which are in the 8 by 8 block. They contain the lowest frequencies from the picture.

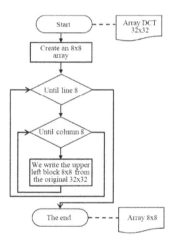

Fig. 5. Step 4. Reducing DCT.

We calculate the average value (Median) for random variables (Fig. 6). The median is the number from the sample, where half of the elements are less than it, and the other half is greater.

We make another abbreviation DCT (Fig. 7). We assign True or False to each of the 64 DCT values, whichever is greater or less than the mean (Median). Using this option will allow you to withstand gamma correction or histogram changes without any problems.

In the end, we build a hash. Converting 64 bits (True, False), obtained in step 6, into a 64-bit value, the order does not matter here. In order to see how the hash looks visually, you need to assign each pixel the values −255 and +255, depending on whether True or False, and convert the 32 × 32 DCT back to a 32 × 32 image.

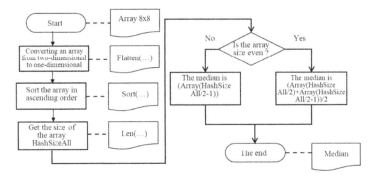

Fig. 6. Step 5. Calculate the Median.

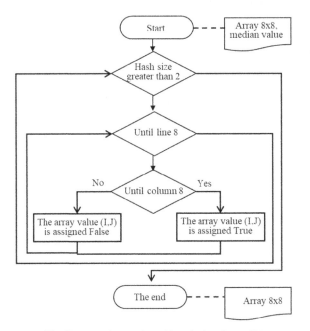

Fig. 7. Step 6. Another abbreviation for DCT.

4.2 Comparing Hashes Using Hamming Distance

Hamming distance is the number of positions in which the corresponding characters of two words of the same length are different. In this application, it is the number of positions at which the corresponding bits of the two arrays are different.

The computed perceptual hash (Fig. 6) will be assigned to all images, after which the hashes will be compared using the Hamming distance.

Hamming distance determines the number of distinct positions between two binary sequences. This method of comparing hash values is used in the DCT BasedHash method.

The hash is 8 bytes in size, so the Hamming distance lies in the segment [0, 64]. The lower the value, the more similar the images are.

Hamming distance is used to compare images (Fig. 8).

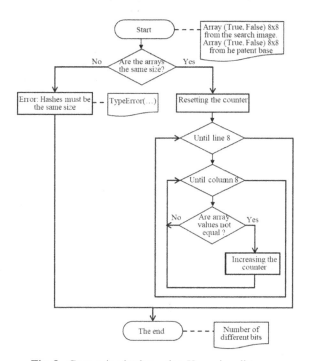

Fig. 8. Comparing hashes using Hamming distance.

5   Designing a Software Module Based on the Developed Method

The Python programming language was chosen to implement the program module. Python is a high-level programming language that is widely used in web development, scripting, scientific computing, artificial intelligence programs, and other fields.

Python code is processed by an interpreter program directly at runtime. There are three main versions of Python: 1.x, 2.x, and 3.x.

Language changes that are compatible with earlier versions are introduced, but only between major versions. Code written in Python 3.x will always be compatible with future versions. Python versions 2.x and 3.x is currently used.

To implement a qualitative search method for relevant images, it is necessary to develop a comparison algorithm for each class of patent images. This is a big task. Within the framework of this study, it was decided to implement a software module, the task of which is to assign a class to patent images located in the search database and submitting an application using the architecture of a deep convolutional neural network

(DCNN). And also assigning the computed perceptual hash to all images for subsequent comparison.

The Keras library was used to develop the program. It uses the Theano library to perform efficient computations. Keras makes it quick and easy to describe a neural network. Keras builds a neural network and calls highly efficient methods from the Theano library for computation. Keras uses Python as its programming language.

The Theano library is used for the computational backend. The library is designed by YoshuyaBengio. It allows you to work with multidimensional matrices (tensors) and allows you to perform efficient calculations with them. Python is used as the programming language.

The Grab library was used to parse the FreePatent site. Grab is a python framework for building web scrapers. This library allows you to build web scrapers of varying complexity from simple scripts to complex asynchronous website crawlers that process millions of web pages. Grab provides an API for making network requests and handling the resulting content, such as interacting with the DOM tree of an HTML document.

The PyQt5 library was used to create the graphical user interface. PyQt5 is one of the most popular sets of Python libraries for building a graphical interface based on the Qt5 platform from Digia. It is available for Python 2.x and 3.x. The Qt library is one of the most powerful GUI (Graphical User Interface) libraries. PyQt5 is implemented as a collection of python modules. PyQt contains over 620 classes and 6000 functions and methods that cover GUIs, XML processing, network communication, SQL databases, web browser, and other technologies available in QT. It is a multi-platform library that runs on all major operating systems, including Unix, Windows, and Mac OS.

6 Conclusion

The specificity of patent images has been studied, the main classes of patent images have been determined, which will be determined by a neural network for comparing the classes corresponding to each other.

The existing automated systems based on the search for images of patents are analyzed, their advantages and disadvantages are highlighted. The common thing in all systems is that before searching, they pre-analyze the loaded images and images stored in the database. Then there is a search in the patent database.

Different methods of image classification are considered, classification will be performed only on the basis of visual information.

The existing architectures of neural networks for working with images and machine learning libraries are analyzed, the architecture of a deep convolutional neural network and the open library Keras, Theano are selected.

Patent images were obtained using web scraping. Collected statistics of downloaded and remaining images after processing based on the International Patent Classification (IPC) classification. This leaves 45168 images, 86.25% of the images from the Freepatent website are not suitable for the training sample. Based on the remaining images, training, validation, and testing samples were formed for the selected classes of patent images.

A method for searching for relevant patent images is developed, which compares the corresponding classes of patent images determined on the basis of a deep convolutional neural network using a perceptual hash and Hamming distance.

The developed method and module for the formation of a set of data for training in the form of an automated system is implemented in software.

The accuracy of the neural network was assessed depending on the size of the images, the number of epochs, and the size of the training sample. Control over the training of the neural network was ensured with the help of validation and test samples so that the neural network was not retrained and worked correctly on images that it did not see.

Acknowledgments. The reported study was funded by RFBR according to research project # 19-07-01200.

References

1. Kravets, A., Shumeiko, N., Lempert, B., Salnikova, N., Shcherbakova, N.: "Smart queue" approach for new technical solutions discovery in patent applications. In: Kravets, A., Shcherbakov, M., Kultsova, M., Groumpos, P. (eds.) CIT&DS 2017. CCIS, vol. 754, pp. 37–47. Springer, Cham (2017). https://doi.org/10.1007/978-3-319-65551-2_3
2. Kamaev, V.A., Salnikova, N.A., Akhmedov, S.A., Likhter, A.M.: The formalized representation of the structures of complex technical devices using context-free plex grammars. In: Kravets, A., Shcherbakov, M., Kultsova, M., Shabalina, O. (eds.) CIT&DS 2015. CCIS, vol. 535, pp. 268–277. Springer, Cham (2015). https://doi.org/10.1007/978-3-319-23766-4_22
3. Kravets, A.G., Kolesnikov, S., Salnikova, N., Lempert, M., Poplavskaya, O.: The study of neural networks effective architectures for patents images processing. In: Kravets, A.G., Groumpos, P.P., Shcherbakov, M., Kultsova, M. (eds.) CIT&DS 2019. CCIS, vol. 1084, pp. 27–41. Springer, Cham (2019). https://doi.org/10.1007/978-3-030-29750-3_3
4. Korobkin, D.M., Fomenkov, S.A., Kravets, A.G.: Methods for extracting the descriptions of sci-tech effects and morphological features of technical systems from patents. In: 9th International Conference on Information, Intelligence, Systems and Applications (IISA 2018), pp. 1–6 (2019)
5. Kravets, A.G., Lebedev, N., Legenchenko, M.: Patent images retrieval and convolutional neural network training dataset quality improvement. In: ITSMSSM, vol. 72, pp. 287–293 (2017)
6. Kizim, A.V., Matokhina, A.V., Vayngolts, I.I., Shcherbakov, M.V.: Intelligent platform of monitoring, diagnosis and modernization of technical systems at various stages of life cycle. In: Proceedings of the 5th International Conference on System Modeling and Advancement in Research Trends (SMART 2016), vol. 5, pp. 145–150 (2016)
7. Kravets, A.G., Vasiliev, S.S., Shabanov, D.V.: Research of the LDA algorithm results for patents texts processing. In: 9th International Conference on Information, Intelligence, Systems and Applications (IISA 2018), pp. 1–6 (2019)
8. Lecun, Y., Bottou, L., Bengio, Y., Haffner, P.: Gradient-based learning applied to document recognition. Proc. IEEE **86**, 2278–2324 (1998)
9. Simard, P.Y., Steinkraus, D., Platt, J.C.: Best practices for convolutional neural networks applied to visual document analysis. In: Proceedings of the IEEE Conference Publications, pp. 958–963 (2003)
10. Koch, G., Zemel, R., Salakhutdinov, R.: Siamese Neural Networks for One-shot Patent image Recognition. In: CA: Department of Computer Science (2015)
11. Tiwari, A., Bansal, V: PATSEEK: content based image retrieval system for patent database. In: The Fourth International Conference on Electronic Business, At Tsinghua University, Beijing, China (2004)

12. Hemayed, E., Tawfik, A., Megahed, R., Hemayed, E.: ImageSeeker: a content-based image retrieval system. In: SPIE Proceedings, vol. 7255 (2009)
13. Huet, B., Kern, N.J., Guarascio, G., Merialdo, B.: Relational skeletons for retrieval in patent drawings. In: International Conference, Image Processing (2001)
14. Vrochidis, S., Papadopoulos, S., Moumtzidou, A., Sidiropoulos, P., Pianta, E., Kompatsiaris, I.: Towards content-based patent image retrieval: a framework perspective. World Patent Inf. **32**(2), 94–106 (2010)
15. Vrochidis, S., Moumtzidou, A., Kompatsiaris, I.: Concept-based patent image retrieval. World Patent Inf. **34**(4), 292–303 (2012)
16. Theano 2018. Universite de Montreal. http://deeplearning.net/software/theano/. Accessed 20 May 2021
17. Caffe 2017. Berkeley Center. http://caffe.berkeleyvision.org/ Accessed 20 May 2021
18. Tensorflow 2018. Google. https://www.tensorflow.org/ Accessed 20 May 2021
19. Keras Documentation. Keras: Available models (2018). https://keras.io/applications/ Accessed 20 May 2021
20. Korobkin, D., Fomenkov, S., Kravets, A., Kolesnikov, S.: Methods of statistical and semantic patent analysis. In: Kravets, A., Shcherbakov, M., Kultsova, M., Groumpos, P. (eds.) CIT&DS 2017. CCIS, vol. 754, pp. 48–61. Springer, Cham (2017). https://doi.org/10.1007/978-3-319-65551-2_4
21. Adams, S.: Electronic non-text material in patent applications-some questions for patent offices, applicants and searchers. World Patent Inf. **27**, 99–103 (2005)

Artificial Intelligence and Deep Learning Technologies for Creative Tasks. Open Science Semantic Technologies

Chomsky Was (Almost) Right: Ontology-Based Parsing of Texts of a Narrow Domain

Boris Geltser[1] , Tatiana Gorbach[1] , Valeria Gribova[2] , Olesya Karpik[3] ,
Eduard Klyshinsky[4]([⊠]) , Dmitrii Okun[2] , Margarita Petryaeva[2] ,
and Carina Shakhgeldyan[1,5]

[1] Far East Federal University, Vladivostok, Russia
boris.geltser@vvsu.ru
[2] Institute of Automation and Control Processes, FEB, RAS, Moscow, Russia
gribova@iacp.dvo.ru
[3] Keldysh Institute of Applied Mathematics, RAS, Moscow, Russia
[4] National Research University Higher School of Economics, Moscow, Russia
eklyshinsky@hse.ru
[5] Vladivostok State University of Economics and Service, Vladivostok, Russia

Abstract. The common approach to the analysis of natural texts implies that semantic analysis should following the stage of parsing. However, medical texts are known as very complicated and written in a very specific language. Traditional parsers are demonstrating relatively small productivity here. In this article, we are demonstrating an opposite approach: ontology-based entailing of words in combination with simple shallow parsing rules. It allows us to increase UAS metrics from 0.82 for SpaCy to 0.834 for our approach.

Keywords: Parsing · Ontology · Patients' complaints

1 Introduction

There are many theories that explain human speech as a reflection of processes in our mind. N. Chomsky wrote: *"Universal grammar, then, constitutes an explanatory theory of a much deeper sort than particular grammar, although the particular grammar of a language can also be regarded as an explanatory theory."* [1, p. 24] Freely interpreting the ideas of Chomsky, we can say that semantics should be first, and the syntax just shapes the ideas we want to express.

Speaking about grammar, we imply dependency structures that restoring syntactic (and shallow semantic) connections between head and tail words, as we did at school time. If we will parse the phrase "The quick brown fox jumps over the lazy dog", we will find out the following facts: that is the fox which is quick and brown, that is the dog which is lazy, and that is the fox which carries out the action over the dog as an object of such action. Parsing of this sentence, we create a list of connections between words (fox is quick, a fox is brown, fox jumps, …) and tag them by semantic relations (quick is a property of fox, a fox is the subject of jumping, …) using both our knowledge about the

A. G. Kravets et al. (Eds.): CIT&DS 2021, CCIS 1448, pp. 87–96, 2021.
https://doi.org/10.1007/978-3-030-87034-8_7

world (foxes have some specific colors, foxes and dogs are animals and animals have some temper, …) and rules of grammar (subject precedes predicate, the object follows predicate, …).

The common approach to natural text processing conducts in the following way. In the first stages, one should tag a text, then parse it, and, finally, conduct semantic processing. Neural networks are trying to make these steps altogether or at least entail them as tough as they can. However, neural networks try to infer such information as verbal government, words co-occurrences, multi-word terms, etc., which are statistical in their nature and can be just collected in dictionaries, but dictionaries of huge size.

The aim of this article is to demonstrate that if one has an ontology of a narrow domain, then he or she can construct the dependency structure of a sentence using just simple rules of shallow parsing. For our experiments, we used an ontology of patients' complaints applied to medical records written in the Russian language. We achieved a higher quality in comparison to modern parsers.

2   Review

There are several options for natural text parsing; the choice of an option depends on the purposes of a constructed system. In the case of such systems as machine translation, one needs a powerful subsystem providing complete parsing and semantic labeling [2]. However, in some cases, one could use a shallow parsing system that aims to extract a list of connected clauses from a text. Such an approach names chunking [3] or shallow parsing depending on the output of the algorithm in hand. There is no need for reconstruction of dependencies structure for such tasks as terms or named entities recognition [4] and fact extraction [5] because a system just needs to define the borders of a clause. Chunking increases the speed of a system by reducing the number of rules and extracted patterns and by using less complicated methods such as Hidden Markov Models [5], Conditional Random Fields [6], context-free grammars [4], and finite automatons [7].

There are two different approaches to creating such systems: empirical and machine learning ones. The empirical approach is a more robust and controlled one; however, it implies a lot of manual jobs which consists of writing many concrete rules for a variety of language phenomena. Machine learning methods presuppose that one has a corpus, and this corpus is big enough and allows training a model with high precision. Modern neural networks can successfully solve all the stated tasks [8–10], but for some tasks, their speed or precision is too low; another option is the lack of tagged corpora mentioned above. Empirical approaches could increase the quality of results but in a narrow domain or task only.

Ontologies are one of the solutions for the task of semantic processing of texts. We will mention here some of the alternatives used for the processing of medical texts, the domain which was selected for our experiments. The biggest medical ontology here is Unified Medical Language System (UMLS) [11] which consists of Metathesaurus (hierarchy of terms collected from many vocabularies), Semantic Network (relationships among these terms and their categories), and SPECIALIST Lexicon and Lexical Tools (a large syntactic lexicon of biomedical and general English combined with natural language processing tools). Metathesaurus vocabulary (Medical Subject Headings - MeSH) was translated into 15 languages including Russian [12]. MeSH was used in such projects as MetaMap - a program for information extraction from medical texts [13]. MetaMap algorithm consists of two stages: 1) processing of a medical text and fact extraction and 2) notions refinement. The first stage starts with tokenization and finishes with syntactic analysis. It includes an acronym/abbreviation identification, multi-word terms extraction, and their identification in dictionaries. The result of the medical text processing is a tagged text with links to Metathesaurus. Exactus system [14] used a UMLS dictionary translated into Russian. The main purpose of this project is a logical inference for the diagnosis of chronic diseases. Using machine learning algorithms allows the authors to increase the precision of fact extraction up to 82\% for the severity of disease and 99\% for a flow of disease.

Note that both of the mentioned systems are using parsing of medical texts before entailing extracted terms to articles in their thesauri. Medical texts should be considered as texts written in a very specific language. Some parts of such texts do not have any verbs at all, but consist of long sequences of homogeneous parts: lists of complaints, diseases, pharmacy, etc. That is why the real performance of parsers falls down to 80–85\%. The ambiguity of terms decreases performance as well. A combined solution [15], which tries to correct the structure of the dependency tree according to the information from an ontology, also demonstrated small performance.

Despite its notorious quality, parsing of medical texts keeps its practical and theoretical importance. Creating a precise dependency structure of a medical text allows drawing a correct picture of disease and its flow. Such results could be used, for example, for quantitative research of historical data, inference of a diagnosis, and in other tasks.

Note that most of the modern medical text processing systems are not so sensitive to the quality of parsing. For example, the paper [16] introduces a method for processing medical records. However, this method is devoted to the extraction of such facts as medication, diseases, indications, and some other and relations among them. The output of the method is the list of such facts and their tags. Thus, the need for deep parsing in such a system is very doubtful. The same is true for the system described in [17] which extracts named entities.

In our project, we investigate an approach that is opposite to the one mentioned above. Our goal was to create algorithms that will infer the structure of a medical text mainly using information from an ontology with help of just a few simple shallow syntactical rules. We hope that this approach allows gather all the advantages and increase the productivity of the system.

3 Database of Terms and Observations

The main part of our system is the Database of Terms and Observations [18]. It is formed on the basis of ontology with the same name. This ontology contains definitions of all concept classes and consists of two main types of medical terms descriptions – symptoms and factors. Symptoms characterize the current functional state of a patient, and factors are used to describe the risks of various diseases. Symptoms and factors can be combined into logically related groups to make them easier to navigate. A symptom can be simple or composite. The first ones are described by name and a set of qualitative, numeric, or interval values. A composite symptom has a name and a set of characteristics. Each characteristic is also described by its name and a set of possible values (qualitative, numerical, or interval). Thus, the Database of Terms and Observations have the form of a tree, where values are leaves that are subordinated to a name of a characteristic, a name of a characteristic subordinated to a name of the feature, and a name of the feature is subordinated to the Complaints node, e.g. *Notalgia → Localization → Dorsal Spine*. Each medical term could have several synonyms.

The "Symptom" section of this database contains several groups of symptoms: "Complaints", "Objective examination", "Laboratory and instrumental examination". In this article, we use only the "Complaint" group of symptoms which describes the subjective feelings of the patient, characterizes his or her current functional status and the state of individual systems: digestive, respiratory, circulatory, nervous system, etc. This group contains a subgroup "General complaints", which includes those that occur in many diseases (dizziness, weakness, nausea, sweating, etc.). Subgroup "Pain" is a part of the subgroup "General complaints"; it includes such symptoms as headache, back pain, neck pain, sore throat, etc. The most of composite symptoms in the "Complaints" group have such characteristics as "localization", "severity", "cause", "time of occurrence", "intensity", "frequency", etc. Characteristics of the "Pain" group also include additional characteristics: "irradiation", "increasing", "increasing", etc.

A fragment of the Database of Terms is presented in Fig. 1. Group of symptoms Pains includes a symptom Back Pain that has synonyms Spinal Pain and Lumbodynia. The symptom Back Pain has such characteristics as Localization (possible values are Lumbar Region and Lumbar Spine) and Amplification (possible values are a Deep Breath and In a Strong Position).

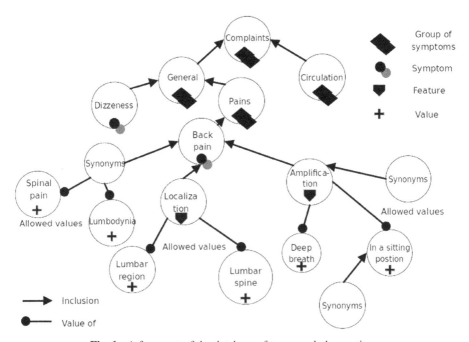

Fig. 1. A fragment of the database of terms and observations.

The section of the Database in the neurology domain was created according to 3000 anonymized medical records from the Department of Neurosurgery of Far Eastern Federal University. The information resources described above are stored in a heterogeneous repository developed by the authors [18]. The Database was created by a team consisting of both doctors in the neurosurgical domain and ontology creation specialists.

4   The Algorithm of Parsing of Patients' Complaints

As it was mentioned above, patients' complaints are written in a very specific language. We used the following presuppositions for parsing such texts.

- A feature should be introduced before its characteristics; a characteristic should be introduced before its values: *Complains to a notalgia localized in the dorsal spine.*
- In a text of a complaint, a value can be syntactically subordinated to a feature or characteristic; a characteristic can be subordinated to a feature: *Complains to a notalgia* ($\rightarrow$) *localized in* ($\rightarrow$) *dorsal spine* VS *Complains to a notalgia in* ($\rightarrow$) *dorsal spine.*
- A sequence of medical terms with the same first or last words (a packed form of terms usage) can be joined using a conjunction or without it: *dorsal and lumbar spine*, or *dorsal, lumbar spine*, or *dorsal aorta and artery.*
- In a Russian text, relations between nouns should be governed by defined prepositions and grammatical cases, an adjective should be governed by a noun: *a notalgia localized in* the *dorsal spine.*

The two last presuppositions were implemented in a form of syntactical rules. Every rule can be presented as a tuple

$$R = \langle t_h,\ p_h,\ v_h,\ t_t,\ p_t,\ v_t,\ prep,\ case \rangle,$$

where t_h is a token of a head term, p_h - a path in the Database of Terms and Observations that defines a feature or a characteristic to which belongs the head term, v_h - type of head term (value, characteristics, and feature), *prep* and *case* – a preposition (if any) and a grammatical case by which governs a tail token, t_t, p_t, and v_t – the same variables defined for a tail word.

Totally, we have written 44 such rules; 41 of them describing verbal government for the used terms. For example, a rule

```
<"", ".+/Pains", "", "", ".+/Pains/.+/Localization/.+",
"", "in", "Case=Loc" >
```

means that any term which belongs to pains can be connected with any term which belongs to the localization of pains (both of them are placed on any level of the Database) using the preposition "*in*", the tail word should be in the prepositional case.

The overall algorithm of parsing a patient's complaint is following.

1. Tag the text of a patient's complaint.

2. Find terms in the tagged text. Every multi-word term should be joined in one token and subscribed by grammatical parameters of its headword. The sequence of terms in packed form should be restored to a sequence of full terms.
3. Connect words according to the set of rules.

    a. Create an empty list of candidate's heads.
    b. Iterating over words in the tagged text.
    c. Starting from the tail of the list of candidate's heads, find the first head with the "active" tag which can be applied to the current word. If such a rule was found, remove all the rules after it; create a new connection between head and tail word; a preposition, if any in the rule, connected to the tail word.
    d. Put into the end of the list of candidate heads all the rules which can be successfully applied to the current word. If a rule needs a preposition, mark this rule by the "suspend" tag, otherwise mark it by the "active" tag.
    e. In case of the current word is a preposition, mark all the candidate heads which are waiting for this preposition by the "active" tag; mark all the candidate heads which need no preposition by the "suspend" tag until the next noun.

4. Iterate over all adjectives in the tagged text. Every adjective should be connected to a neighboring noun that coordinates it or to a noun in the right position if there is no coordination to any neighboring noun.
5. Create a dependency tree using the list of connections between words.

By removing rules in item 3c, we try to keep the projectivity of the resulting tree. Connecting adjectives to nouns, we follow the statistics of such connections in medical records. We try to "reuse" prepositions since we found out that doctors tend to write just one preposition followed by several terms. The same is true for a sequence of terms restored from packed form. Note that we ignore all the punctuation marks because of a variety of mistakes found in real texts. The same is true for terms; that is why we use fuzzy algorithms for the comparison of words.

Let us consider an example of parsing taken from one of the patient's complaints.

Complaints on the significant levels of pain in the lumbar and dorsal spine, increased pain on exertion, ambulation disorder.

At the first stage, we tag the text and process terms, including multi-word ones. Let us denote the extracted terms by square braces, non-term tokens by curly braces. Note that English "significant levels of" corresponds to one Russian adjective. The result should be as following.

```
[Complaints] {on} {the} [significant levels of] [pain]
{in} [lumbar spine] {and} [dorsal spine], [increased
pain] {on} [exertion], [ambulation disorder].
```

After analyzing the first two words (*Complaints on*), we have one active rule in the list of candidate heads which corresponds to the connection between a feature "Complaints" to its characteristics. Then we pass over the text "the significant levels of". The word "pain" can be connected to "complaints on"; it also adds a set of rules to the list of candidate rules: "pain + in + localization in prepositional case" and "feature + characteristic".

The former rule will be activated after the preposition "in". This rule will be applied on terms "lumbar spine" and "dorsal spine" and will create proper connections. The term "increased pain" creates a connection between "pain" and "increased pain" and removes the rule "pain in". It also adds the rule "increased pain + on + value in prepositional case" which will be activated by "on" and applied to the next word "exertion". Finally, the term "ambulation disorder" is connected to "complaints on" and removes proper rules from the list.

The result of our algorithm is the following list of connections:

```
[complaints → pain → on,
 pain → lumbar spine → in,
 pain → dorsal spine → in,
 pain → increased pain,
 increased pain → exertion → on,
 complaints → ambulation disorder]
```

In the next stage, we connect to the term "pain" the term corresponding to "significant levels of". After that, we construct the resulting dependency tree.

As was mentioned above, our aim was the comparison of such a simple ontology-based approach to the traditional parsing of a natural language sentence. However, we make some steps in our algorithm which make impossible the direct comparison of results. That is why we created a procedure that aligns the resulting trees.

First of all, we created a "gold standard" containing manually parsed trees consisting of terms instead of sole words. We compared just these connections which were found in this "gold standard", instead of comparison of resulting trees. For trees provided by traditional parsing algorithms, we reduced terms into one node and restore terms written in packed form. Since we always add a preposition to a term, including the situation when we process terms in packed form, we excluded prepositions from the resulting list of connections. These steps allow us to compare our results to results provided by other parsing algorithms.

5 Results of Experiments and Discussion

As it was mentioned above, we had manually tagged a "gold standard" consisting of 80 texts of patient's complaints and 1036 connections. All these patient's complaints were extracted from medical records written by different doctors and describing a flow of neurological diseases for different patients. All texts were collected at the same hospital. Since our task was to connect correctly terms that are already tagged by our ontology, we evaluated our results using unlabeled attachment score (UAS, percentage of correctly connected pairs of words) instead of labeled attachment score (LAS, percentage of correctly connected and labeled pairs of words). We used for our comparison UDPipe version 2.5 (released in December 2019) [19] and SpaCy 3.0. (released in March 2021) [20]. Both of them built using LSTM neural networks. For training, UDPipe used Universal Dependencies corpora [21], while SpaCy trained on a bunch of different corpora and provides a lot of models for different purposes. In our experiments, we used the "ru_core_news_sm" SpaCy model which provides more precise results.

The results of our experiments were following. UDPipe correctly parsed 11 out of 80 sentences and creates 780 correct connections out of 1036; SpaCy correctly parsed 23 sentences and created 850 correct connections; our algorithm correctly parsed 26 sentences and created 864 correct connections. Thus, the resulting UAS of the systems is 0.753 for UDPipe, 0.82 for SpaCy, and 0.834 for our approach.

Note that authors of SpaCy claim for 0.96 UAS on regular texts, while for patients' complaints their system demonstrated results as low as 0.83. The reason for such break-down was already discussed above: that is lack of verbs, the formal listing of claims and symptoms with sudden transitions among different groups of terms, introducing just one preposition for a sequence, some grammatical mistakes. However, such text has very strict inner logic: any subordinated term should be introduced after its main term only, convolution of several terms with a common prefix or postfix, etc. Note that some of the drawbacks of such texts can be simply described in very short rules; that is why their analysis can be easily implemented, but only in case if you know what you should wait as an input. Thus, some of the drawbacks can be considered as hints, but in the case of parsing common texts, such peculiarities could lead to over-specification and redundant complexity. That is why we can say that parsers compete on the uneven played field - a common parser VS a specialized one in the case of very special texts.

Note again that modern parsers, which are based on neural networks, can be easily trained on existing syntactically tagged corpora. Creating such corpora takes long years; but once created and published, they can be re-used for a long. Creating an ontology takes much more time. Putting the same effort, one is able to create an ontology for just a small domain. Creating a complete ontology takes decades. That is why the ontology-based approach is much more expensive than a traditional one. However, if one already has an ontology that reflects relations in a domain, then it can be used for parsing as well.

If we will consider such syntactic structure as a gerundial group, we will found that it reflects such relations as "owner-property" (hand of a human), "object of a process" (publishing of orders), and so on. That is why the opposite process can help us describe syntactical relations between terms using semantic relations from an ontology; but currently, for a narrow domain only.

Thus, we can state that idea of using semantics as syntactic instrumentation could lead to success. However, this way is very expensive and still unproved on a wide domain or common knowledge texts.

6   Conclusion

In this paper, we use an old idea that semantics could play the first role in text parsing. Modern parsers are demonstrating pretty high accuracy, but their productivity falls down from 0.96 to 0.85 UAS in the case of medical texts, more precisely - in the case of patient's complaints. We introduce an ontology-based method of text parsing which uses connections in an ontology in order to restore connections in a text. However, the used ontology has a structure that differs from a traditional one, consisting of synonyms, associations, etc. The used ontology contains the same logical relations among terms one can see in a text: locations, reasons, etc. In order to take into account syntactical relations, we introduce a small set of simple rules. Most of these rules are describing verbal governance combined with semantic tags.

Our system demonstrates the same productivity as modern parsers, but its aim was to demonstrate a new approach to parsing special text. Now we can state that such an approach can be successfully applied to short text parsing, in case, if one already has a big and complete ontology of a domain. However, our approach needs a new automatic method for the extraction of verbal governance.

References

1. Chomsky, N.: Language and Mind, 3rd edn. Cambridge University Press, Cambridge (2006)
2. Apresjan, Ju., et al.: ETAP-3 linguistic processor: a full-fledged NLP implementation of the MTT. In: Proceedings of the First International Conference on Meaning-Text Theory, Paris, École Normale Supérieure, pp. 279–288 (2003)
3. Abney, S.: Parsing by chunks. In: Berwick, R., Abney, S., Tenny, C., (eds.) Principle-Based Parsing. Kluwer Academic Publishers (1991)
4. Bolshakova, E.I., Baeva, N.V., Bordachenkova, E.A., Vasilyeva, N.E., Morozov, S.S.: Lexicosyntactic patterns for automatic text processing. In: Proceedings of International Conference on Computational Linguistics and Intellectual Technologies "Dialog-2007", pp. 70–75 (2007). (in Russian)
5. Molina, A., Pla, F.: Shallow parsing using specialized HMMs. J. Mach. Learn. Res. **2**, 595–613 (2002)
6. Sha, F., Pereira, F.: Shallow parsing with conditional random fields. In: Proceedings of HLT-NAACL, Edmonton, pp. 134–141 (2003)
7. Nozhov, I.M.: Implementation of an automatic syntactical segmentation of a Russian sentence. Ph.D. thesis, RSUH, Moscow (2003)
8. Anastasyev, D.G.: Exploring pretrained models for joint morpho-syntactic parsing of Russian. In: Proceedings of International Conference on Computational Linguistics and Intellectual Technologies "Dialog-2020", pp. 1–12 (2020)
9. Korzun, V.A.: R-BERT for relationship extraction on Russian business documents. In: Proceedings of International Conference on Computational Linguistics and Intellectual Technologies "Dialog-2020", pp. 467–463 (2020)
10. Lyashevskaya, O.N., Shavrina, T.O., Trofimov, I.V., Vlasova, N.A.: GRAMEVAL 2020 shared task: Russian full morphology and universal dependencies parsing. In: Proceedings of International Conference on Computational Linguistics and Intellectual Technologies "Dialog-2020", pp. 553–569 (2020)
11. Current Bibliographies in Medicine. https://www.nlm.nih.gov/archive/20040831/pubs/cbm/umlscbm.html. Accessed 20 Apr 2021
12. MSHRUS (MeSH Russian) – Statistics. https://www.nlm.nih.gov/research/umls/sourcereleasedocs/current/MSHRUS/stats.html. Accessed 20 Apr 2021
13. Aronson, A.R., Lang, F.M.: An overview of MetaMap: historical perspective and recent advances. J. Am. Med. Inform. Assoc. **17**(3), 229–236 (2010)
14. Shelmanov, A.O., Smirnov, I.V., Vishneva, E.A.: Information extraction from clinical texts in Russian. In: Proceedings of International Conference on Computational Linguistics and Intellectual Technologies "Dialog-2015", pp. 560–572 (2015)
15. Klyshinsky, E., et al.: Formalization of medical records using an ontology: patient complaints. In: van der Aalst, W.M.P., et al. (eds.) AIST 2019. CCIS, vol. 1086, pp. 143–153. Springer, Cham (2020). https://doi.org/10.1007/978-3-030-39575-9_14

16. Jagannatha, A., Yu., H.: Bidirectional RNN for medical event detection in electronic health records. In: Proceedings of Association for Computational Linguistics. North American Chapter, pp. 473–482 (2016)
17. Miftahutdinov, Z., Alimova, I., Tutubalina, E.: On biomedical named entity recognition: experiments in interlingual transfer for clinical and social media texts. In: Jose, J., et al. (eds.) Advances in Information Retrieval, vol. 12036, pp. 281–288. Springer, Cham (2020). https://doi.org/10.1007/978-3-030-45442-5_35
18. Gribova, V.V., Moskalenko, Ph.M., Shahgeldyan, C.I., Gmar', D.V., Geltser, B.I.: A concept for a heterogeneous biomedical information warehouse. Inf. Technol. **2**(25), 97–106 (2019). (in Russian)
19. Straka, M., Straková, J., Haji, J.: UDPipe at SIGMORPHON 2019: contextualized embeddings, regularization with morphological categories, corpora merging. In: Proceedings of the 16th SIGMORPHON Workshop on Computational Research in Phonetics, Phonology, and Morphology, pp. 95–103 (2019)
20. Whats New in v3.0 (2021). https://spacy.io/usage/v3. Accessed Apr 2020
21. Nivre, J., et al.: Universal dependencies v1: a multilingualtreebank collection. In: Proceedings of the 10th International Conference on Language Resources and Evaluation (LREC 2016), pp. 1659–1666 (2016)

Creative Knowledge Representation for Knowledge Management: The Dialectical Approach

Elena Rusyaeva[1]([⊠]) [iD] and Alla G. Kravets[2,3] [iD]

[1] Institute of Control Sciences, Moscow, Russian Federation
rusyaeva@ipu.ru
[2] Dubna State University, Dubna, Moscow Region, Russia
agk@gde.ru
[3] Volgograd State Technical University, Volgograd, Russian Federation

Abstract. The dialectical approach to the knowledge representation in general form consists in the possibility of synthesizing new knowledge based on the explication of meaningful contradictions in the antinomic poles of dichotomies. The scientific novelty of the research lies in the fact that the dialectical approach is combined with new information technologies. This is how the "bridge" of reasoning is thrown from the concept of "knowledge management" to machine learning based on large, expertly labeled data. This is the basis of the synthesis carried out in the expert-metric approach, which is a special case of the dialectical approach. Now, with the development of the Internet, big data, there is a technological opportunity to use the creative potential of dialectics more fully. The basis of the synthesis depth is the representation of the management decision-making process by a set of decision trees. In this case, the metric approach is the use of a small number of decision trees, often presented explicitly, and the expert approach is the use of a very large number of trees that exist only in the head of an expert in an implicit, non-reflected form.

Keywords: Dialectical approach · Knowledge representation · Machine learning · Expert-metric approach · Substantive-formal principle · Decision trees

1 Introduction

In connection with the creation of artificial intelligence technologies, there is now a surge of interest in the study of the creative, intellectual activities of people. This forces us to turn to classical theories of knowledge, to re-examine the issues of knowledge generation, aspects of the mental activity of people.

As is known from the classics [1, 2], the logical forms of resolving contradictions lie on the basis of the mental, cognitive activity of people. Thus, cognitive, intellectual activity is based on the search for various ways of meaningful and/or formal arguments in favor of a particular point of view. This is how the architecture of the cognitive act is arranged, and it is designed for the perception of the other (it is basically dialogical [3], even if it is an internal dialogue). That is, in fact, the content of any scientific research

© Springer Nature Switzerland AG 2021
A. G. Kravets et al. (Eds.): CIT&DS 2021, CCIS 1448, pp. 97–109, 2021.
https://doi.org/10.1007/978-3-030-87034-8_8

is based on the use of dialectics as a logical form of proof. Speaking in the language of philosophy, dialectics is a way of reflective theoretical thinking, which has as its subject the contradictions of its conceivable content [4].

The main thing that follows from the above definition, which we will focus on in this study, is that understanding is possible only in the search for an initial semantic unity for contradictory opposites [4]. Simply put, the dialectical approach in the logic of resolving contradictions is based on the fact that the division of concepts (content) should proceed from a single basis.

In a formalized approach in the language of graphic representation, this position can be demonstrated in the form of a graph, which has one single base, and two edges emanating from this base form a dichotomy, that is, a dialectical pair of opposites. Also, in the form of a graph, it is possible to demonstrate the logic of proof in science, namely, the resolution of contradictions in the spirit of Hegel: thesis, antithesis, synthesis [2].

Moving on to the topic of our research, in the knowledge management, in the case of decision making by a decision-maker, in a control system, the correctness of the formation of a decision tree lies precisely in the fact that the edges of the graph are clearly distinguished from a single base. The problem of modeling a real managerial situation is, in our opinion, among other things, that the branches (edges) of the graph in the content plan run into different semantic foundations. This pattern of cognitive biases is, unfortunately, inherent in the expert approach. People are mistaken for various reasons, one of which lies in the fact that the verbal language, the words of the language are becoming more and more polysemous, therefore one word, the term can have several variants of meaning. It is not always clear to which of them the antinomical pair is built, what kind of fork in the contradictions should be considered. This requires a rigorous semantic analysis, which in reality does not always happen. Therefore, sometimes complex and beautiful mathematical models are built on constructions that are rather dubious from a substantive point of view.

Nowadays many terms are becoming meta-terms, and sometimes "umbrella brands" [5], "covering" several meanings. Additional explanations are constantly required, in what sense this concept is used, broadly or narrowly, in what meaning, for what purpose, etc. Below we will give examples of the division of terms according to a single and not quite satisfying the requirement of unity, the basis for research in the field of management. Let us also consider the logic of constructing separately taken expert and formal-metric approaches, show the relevance of the dialectical approach, which makes it possible to take into account the merits of each and resolve their contradictions by using the new possibilities of computer data representation. That is, by including the modern capabilities of machine learning on huge data from the Internet, we will show the relevance of the logic of resolving contradictions in the dialectical approach. At the time of Hegel, there was no such possibility, which is why his method is idealistic in nature. Now, when existence (reality) has acquired a discourse (real dialogue) in the form of the Internet [6], It is possible with the help of dialectics to activate the intellectual, creative activity of people to resolve contradictions.

The basis of the depth of synthesis, the point of dialectical removal of these two approaches is the presentation of the process of making managerial decisions by a set of decision trees. In this case, the metric approach is the use of a small number of decision trees, often presented explicitly, and the expert approach is the use of a very large number of trees that exist only in the head of an expert in an implicit, unreflected form. The approach under consideration is that for the management of organizations in the knowledge economy, it is necessary to obtain by machine learning formula for evaluating the control object, "folding" the values of a large number of different metrics characterizing the control object into an integral value, using for this a training sample, which is made up of values these metrics and expertly labeled.

2 A Dialectical Approach to Knowledge Management

Modern scientific knowledge is basically technological. Now even purely substantial, humanitarian knowledge must be strictly substantiated and, if possible, formalized - this is one of the main requirements, a trend of the time. In the most general form, approaches to the explication of some basic cognitive techniques of cognition for the possibility of formalizing cognitive tools were presented by us in [7].

Now the classical dialectical approach, one might say, is experiencing a renaissance as one of the effective ways of solving creative problems. The fact is that once the basic tool of the dialectic approach, the method of dialectical removal of essential contradictions through the productive synthesis of new knowledge, formulated by Hegel, could not be actively used for various reasons. One of the significant obstacles was the lack of an extensive and adequate database for the possibility of choices for decision-making. also, the expert analysis of information parameters took a lot of time.

With the advent of information and digital technologies, the issues of scalability and efficiency when choosing solutions have ceased to be a stumbling block. But creative problems cannot be solved directly with algorithms; end-to-end artificial intelligence technologies serve to support decision making.

All the more relevant, in our opinion, is the conceptual-formal principle (as rule [8]), when the advantages of the formal and content way are used for solving creative problems. So problems of scalability (input of a large number of parameters) and efficiency (speed of computer search) are overcome. The dialectic approach finds a new embodiment and application to find a new non-trivial solution for representing knowledge in knowledge management in the information economy in the form of the expert-metric approach. It can be applied when compiling a rating of parameters for adequate analysis (process algorithmization) of a phenomenon in the knowledge economy. The representation of knowledge in the form of algorithms is gradually becoming more and more popular, and it is the dialectic approach that allows the creation of adequate algorithms [9].

In other words, the dialectic nature of our approach to solving creative problems lies in the fact that many factors are taken into account to form the rating of the most significant estimation parameters, machine learning is carried out on large expertly marked samples, as a result of which a long formula is determined, for example, similar to the Yandex formula for the search ranking of sites [10]. We will consider methods of constructing algorithms capable of learning as machine learning. There are two types of training: 1) learning from precedents or inductive learning based on the identification of general patterns from particular empirical data; 2) deductive learning involves the formalization of expert knowledge and their transfer to a computer in the form of a knowledge base [11]. Deductive learning is commonly referred to as expert systems, so the terms machine learning and use case learning can be considered synonymous.

In the dialectical approach, it is proposed to use the entire arsenal of factors, to use all indicators. In this case, one should not be afraid of an overabundance of information; on the contrary, one should use all known approaches when analyzing the available textual information content to assess the most meaningful parameters for a particular phenomenon. In addition, it is important, as was emphasized at the beginning, that decision trees should be built on the basis of graphs, the branches of which originate from a single basis. As a result, the more material for analysis is provided, the more accurately the indicators for evaluation will be determined. Thus, in the future, it will be possible to automatically screen-out, "reject" material that is not valuable in the assessment system and is not meaningful.

So, the removal of antinomies in the dialectical approach to knowledge management occurs due to the use in one machine learning of both all formal indicators and the goal obtained by expert ranking.

3   Knowledge Representation in Knowledge Management

As you know, in knowledge management, as one of the most relevant modern advanced platforms of management theory and practice, it can be considered that knowledge management is reduced either to restructuring, reconfiguring knowledge itself as such, or to knowledge-based management of business entities. Further, speaking about knowledge management, we will keep in mind exactly this second understanding of knowledge management. It is knowledge-based management that can be called management in the knowledge economy or management in the information economy.

Management in the knowledge economy will be called such a process of managing organizations in which a significant, decisive role is played by taking into account semi-structured, implicit knowledge about the object of management.

Indeed, when taking into account explicit knowledge in the process of managing business entities, expert assessments are not needed; one can entirely confine oneself to a formal, metric approach. If the mechanism for using some data in management together with the context is presented explicitly, then it should be followed, no expert is needed here. But as soon as a part of this mechanism turns out to be implicit, inexplicable, the need immediately arises to supplement the formal metric approach with an expert one.

For what type of control objects is the accounting of implicit knowledge in decision-making and management fundamental? We hypothesize that such management objects are high-tech and/or science-intensive industries. Thus, it is for such industries that the antinomy of the expert and metric approaches is essential.

It is well known that there are two main, in some sense diametrically opposite, "polar" approaches to accounting for implicit knowledge in the process of managing business entities, namely, expert and metric. In the broadest, partly in a philosophical sense, knowledge is considered "a certain image of the reality of the subject in the form of concepts and representations." Moreover, such a broad understanding of knowledge practically identifies it with the concept of information [12]. The very same philosophical analysis of knowledge is associated, first of all, with understanding it not as "information about external and independent reality", but, on the contrary, as "an element of the human world, speaking about his ability to bring ideal order and meaning into reality, thereby creating the prerequisites its practical transformation" [4].

R. Ackoff developed the DIKW-pyramid, at the base of which is data, on the next "floor" is information - it adds context to the data. Knowledge is located one floor higher in the pyramid, it adds the answer to the question "how", that is, it essentially determines the mechanism for using information. On the top floor is wisdom, it adds the answer to the question "when", that is, it determines the conditions for using knowledge. It is believed that as one moves from the lower floor of the pyramid to the upper one, the degree of utility increases [13].

Thus, according to R. Ackoff, knowledge is data together with a context and a mechanism for its application. What, then, is implicit knowledge, if knowledge is generally understood in this way? Implicit knowledge is such data, together with a context, the mechanism of application of which exists and effectively works "in the head" of an expert, but this mechanism is not presented explicitly either verbally, mathematically, or in any other way.

Traditionally, knowledge is divided into substantive and formal knowledge. Indeed, since the opposition to formal and substantive knowledge has existed for a very long time, its antinomic nature seems self-evident. Many people think that formal knowledge cannot be substantive, and truly substantive knowledge cannot be fully formalized. Substantive and formal are perceived as mutually exclusive: often, from the fact that something is formal, it is immediately concluded that it is not substantive. Therefore, in particular, it does not contribute to effective management.

But if you think about it, is it always like this? In fact, it turns out that the formal and substantive are not the result of a division on one basis. Thus, if we divide knowledge by the degree of formalization, then the formal is opposed to the undiscovered, inexplicable, hidden, implicit knowledge. And if we divide by the closeness to the essence of the phenomenon, by the extent to which something reflects the essence of the phenomenon, and by the extent to which a certain concept embraces the entire diversity of the real multitude of objects, then the substantive knowledge is opposed to the scholastic one [4]. The latter, by definition, is artificial, detached from the realities of life, and irrelevant to the complex phenomenon it tries to embrace.

Formal and substantive are not the poles of a single antinomy, so why are they so often contradicted? Apparently, they do not have to be mutually exclusive at all times, but they are often. Indeed, formal knowledge is often scholastic (and therefore inconsequential), and substantive is often implicit, hidden, unexplored, and therefore informalized.

It turns out that although this is not strictly necessary, the concepts of "formal" and "substantive" are often mutually exclusive. But, on the other hand, what are the conditions for the existence of substantive-formal knowledge? What will help to carry out dialectical sublation and to combine in one phenomenon seeming to be antinomic poles?

4   Antinomy of Substantive and Formal Knowledge

Let's show that for this we need to look deeper into the category of substantive. As strange as it may seem, the modern information age allows us to do it. The experience of the last decades has shown that a significant part of the substantive representations of decision-making processes can be described by the forest of decision trees. Description of a meaningful decision-making process by a set of decision trees is, in the framework of the dialectical approach, the moment of sublation, which will allow describing the transition from scholastic to substantive in unified terms. Thus, the zone of mediation is indicated, which will allow constructing already sufficiently substantial, but at the same time formalized solutions.

It should be noted that this is possible for the first time in history, and only because "the existence has acquired a discourse in the form of the Internet" [6]. The Internet has made it possible to digitize (and thus make measurable) not only a huge amount of knowledge but also people's behavior and how people interact with content. This has enabled a huge learning sample to be formed, and the problem of a "narrow neck of knowledge" could be at least partially solved. Now, the decades-old methods of machine learning have been able to work to their full potential, and it has become possible to expose a set of decision trees close to real life. The specific numerical characteristics of the trees in this set turned out to be quite interesting and indicative (Table 1). Firstly, it turned out that these trees are not so deep (4–8 depth levels) [14]. But, secondly, the number of factors used in trees is very large (thousands) [15]. Thirdly, the number of decision trees in the set is simply huge - hundreds of thousands [10, 16]. These are the numerical characteristics of the formalized representation of "almost substantial".

Table 1. The bases of the division of the formalized and substantial knowledge

Antinomy	Informal	Formal
Scholastic	Explication set (up to ten) of decision trees	Explication set of decision trees
Substantial	Explication forest (thousands, tens of thousands) of decision trees	Explication forest of decision trees

Thus, in Table 1, the direction of development of representations from proto-science to modern scientific knowledge, and from modern scientific knowledge to substantial and explication future scientific knowledge.

Thus, the point of sublation for formal and substantive decision-making will be the set of decision trees. The logic here is as follows: if the set contains some (up to ten) trees it is perceived by us as a formal approach to decision-making. But if we use thousands, tens of thousands of decision-making trees (as, apparently, a human neural network), then we perceive it as substantive decision-making. Here the law of transition of quantity in quality operates: increase in the number of trees of decision-making leads to change of its quality, and, thereby, translation from formal to substantive.

Such a dialectical sublation makes it possible to formulate the conditions for the existence of substantive-formal knowledge, firstly, and, accordingly, the expert-metric approach, and secondly. Explication of a large number of decision trees (e.g., by methods of machine learning) creates prerequisites for making expert-like substantive, but at the same time strict, poorly manipulated, verified, carefully "measured" decisions, the logic of which can be justified and presented in an explicit form.

5 Expert and Metric (Formal) Approaches

Let us describe in more detail these two approaches to knowledge management. Thus, the first one, which has long been known and widely used, is the so-called expert or expert assessment method. It consists of the fact that some authorities in a certain field of activity evaluate certain parameters. The second one, which appeared later but has been actively used recently, is metric (sometimes it is called computational, statistical, etc.). Both of these approaches have their advantages and disadvantages, which are as follows.

In the first, expert approach [17], the high quality of assessments is apparently due to the fact that the expert's neural network takes in and processes a very large number of factors, which is a property of the human cognitive mechanism. But the same human nature leads to systematic cognitive distortions: for example, expert assessments are too easily manipulated. Experts, like many people, can be "greedy and untruthful" by their very nature [18], and since no one forces them to explicate the logic of reasoning, there is a great temptation to distort the expert opinion for their own good.

In the second - the metric, formalized approach - the logic of using evaluation factors is explicit, but fewer factors are used than the neural network of the expert advisor implicitly uses.

Due to the small number of factors, there is a problem with the quality and adequacy of evaluation. The existing lists of formal indicators cannot fully reflect neither the non-triviality nor the entire complexity of the real economic activity. This is a disadvantage of the metric approach.

On the other hand, explicitness as a factor of evaluation, as well as the clarity of the evaluation formula itself, in general, allows reducing the manipulation, "the gap of expert arbitrariness" compared to the expert approach. This is the advantage of the metric approach.

However, despite the fact that the metric approach slightly reduces the probability of manipulation of the expert approach, it still remains essentially manipulated. Indeed, the desire for higher metric indicators often runs counter to the truly creative, non-standard approach to the work performed, which requires time and serious intellectual effort. "Rules of the game", given by metrics of work for people are such that now it is more profitable for them to duplicate the standard receptions of activity, than each time to create something new, to achieve original, nontrivial results. This is exactly what leads to the manipulation of formal parameters, which has been repeatedly criticized [19].

Nevertheless, each of the approaches – expert and metric – has pluses and minuses, there is a question: how to use the advantages of these approaches and at the same time to avoid the specified shortcomings?

The answer, in our opinion, is in development mediation's approach in which the expert quality does not contradict the formalized quantity, and, on the contrary, supplements advantages, dialectically arises from it (under the law of transition of quantity to quality).

Let's assume that it is possible to connect pluses of metric approach where formal processing on the small volume of data, and advantages of expert approach where there are a lot of data takes place, but they are absent formal processing. Now technical capabilities [17] quite allow using such a dialectical approach.

6 Basic Provisions of Expert and Metric Approach

When assessing the integrated indicator of the control object, it is proposed to use machine learning on large expertly marked samples containing the values of a large number of factors for a large number of already expertly evaluated control objects, as a result of which a long formula is determined.

That is, the sublation of antinomies in the expert metric approach is achieved through the use in single machine learning as all the formal indicators, and the target obtained by the expert ranking.

Such an approach allows replicating the knowledge and experience of experts in integrated assessment of complex phenomena by identifying (explication) the contribution of values of various aspects of this phenomenon to its integral assessment, as well as identifying the mutual influence of these aspects. The formula obtained, which "reduces" the values of parameters (factors) characterizing individual aspects of this phenomenon into an integral value, will allow us to evaluate the control objects that are not included in the training sample and, accordingly, are not evaluated by experts directly as qualitatively as the best experts do (Table 2).

Table 2. Methodological principles of data evaluation in knowledge management

Methodological principles of assessment data	Completeness of data accounting	Non-manipulation, objectivity of data assessment
Formal	−	+
Substantial	+	−
Substantial-Formal	+	+

When assessing big data according to a formal methodological principle, the completeness of data accounting is most often missing, as it requires a very large evaluation formula, and it is difficult to agree on such a large formula in organizational terms. On the other hand, the use of the formula achieves some non-manipulation and objectivity of the assessment due to the explicability of the assessment formula.

When assessing data in accordance with the substantial methodological principle, the opposite is often the case: there is the completeness of data accounting, but there is no non-manipulation and objectivity of data assessment due to the non-formalization of the assessment procedure. And only following the substantial-formal principle makes it possible to combine both the completeness of data accounting and some objectivity and non-manipulation of data evaluation. So, it seems to be at a high level of abstraction, let's see what the picture will be if we descend from the level of methodological principles to the level of methodological approaches (Table 3).

Table 3. Methodological approaches to data evaluation in knowledge management (with the prospect of development)

Methodological approaches to data assessment	Completeness of data aspects	Non-manipulation, objectivity of data assessment
Expert	+++	+
Metric before the Big Data era ("old metric")	+	++
Expert metric in the Big Data era	++	+++
Expert metric approach in 5–7 years	++++	++++

Some conclusions regarding the relationship between different methodological approaches to assessment are the same as the relatively higher-abstract principles of assessment, so let us focus only on the differences. We see that despite the fact that the expert-metric approach as it is possible now has some advantages and can replace the "old metric" approach [20], it still cannot completely replace the expert approach. It happens because although the completeness of data aspects accounting has increased in the modern expert-metric approach in comparison with the metric one, the level of the expert approach is most likely not yet reached. That is, the expert will take into account more aspects necessary for a qualitative assessment. Therefore, at the moment, modern expert-metric and "pure" expert approaches form a non-dominant set, it makes sense to combine these two approaches in order to develop practically used assessment methods.

However, we can assume that in a decade (and perhaps, in 5–7 years) the completeness of accounting for the aspects of the evaluated object in the expert-metric approach will not be inferior to the "pure" expert approach [21], and then the methods of assessment already used in practice can be designed on the basis of the exclusively expert-metric approach.

7 Algorithm of Expert-Metric Estimation

Consider a generalized algorithm that allows us to determine and make a rating of parameters that are relevant for evaluating a particular phenomenon of the knowledge economy using an expert-metric method (see Fig. 1). The operation of this algorithm is carried out in several cycles, which makes it possible to determine the final parameters, their rating with the greatest accuracy. In the future, it will probably be possible to determine ratings for assessing any phenomena of the knowledge economy, based on the dialectical approach, with even greater adequacy.

Let us describe the sequence of operation of the algorithm for expert-metric estimation of the parameters of a phenomenon in the knowledge economy, for example, tutoring. At the first stage, block 1 receives the initial set of parameters for evaluating tutoring, for example, education, work experience, feedback from former students, etc., up to the area of residence (important for individual face-to-face studies). Note that we collect these factors (parameters) from all currently available sources. These are official documents (for example, university graduation diplomas and other documents), the content of Internet sites where tutoring services are offered, data from social networks, instant messengers, etc., etc. A sufficient condition for inclusion in this list is that some of the experts suggested that this factor could be useful for the assessment.

Further, in the next step (in block 2), we collect the reference expert estimates for the training sample - this will be the marking of the training sample. This is also where the cycle returns if you need to add estimates of new experts. This cycle will not end until we have a stable top 10 indicators that are relevant for assessing the phenomenon. This will be an indication of the need to exit the first cycle.

Then (block 3) we sift through the available estimates with axioms. This process boils down to weeding out or rejecting those grades that do not correspond to any consensus judgment regarding the parameters of tutoring.

In block 4, machine learning of a formula containing a vector of already available parameters is carried out. Here, at this stage, the cycle returns if we update the set of parameter values collected, including with the help of the information system (IS).

At the next step (block 5), we need to conduct a meaningful analysis of the residual. Here we analyze the largest deviations that exist between expert estimates and the result that a machine-trained formula gives.

Then we get to block 6, in which we ask the question: "Is it necessary or possible to improve the estimation by introducing new parameters?" If the answer is "Yes", then we move on to the next stage, block 7, when it is necessary to develop new factors. After that, in block 8, we need to collect the values of new factors, possibly with the involvement of IS, and after that, we enter a new cycle of machine learning (block 4) and go through all the stages that follow in the course of this cycle again.

If the answer to the question of block 6 is "No", then we proceed to the stage of determining a new pool of reference expert estimates of parameters using a machine-trained formula - block 9. Upon completion of this stage, we again find ourselves in another fork with a question (block 10): "Has the pool of reference expert parameters changed since the previous iteration?" If the answer is "Yes", then we carry out the next iteration, returning to block 2, where we re-collect expert estimates of the newly identified parameters. Now we can include the estimates of already new experts, we ask you to give estimates for the training sample, repeating the whole cycle. Let us remind you that only the stable top 10 parameters serve as an indicator of the need to exit the cycle. If the answer to the question in block 10 is "No", then we received the final formula (block 11) for determining the rating of the evaluation parameters of a certain phenomenon.

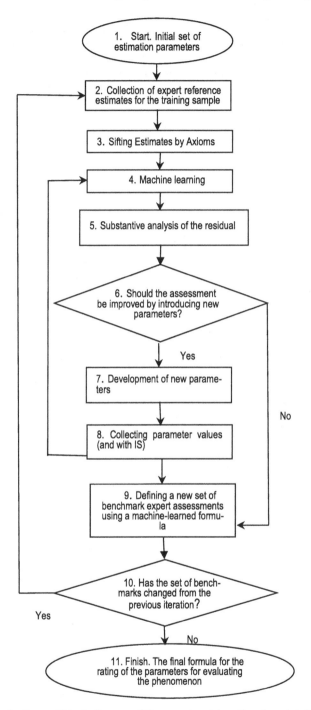

Fig. 1. General block diagram of the expert-metric estimation algorithm

In general, the expert-metric representation of knowledge will most likely require the creation of a whole cascade of algorithms in order to introduce, take into account and agree on the values of all newly identified parameters and factors. This work must be carried out in order to make the final formula for determining the rating of the parameters for evaluating any phenomenon of the knowledge economy the most adequate.

8   Conclusion

So, we have shown that the dialectical approach is, as the top general floor, the basis of the creative aspect for knowledge management in the knowledge economy. The dialectical approach is based on the subjective-formal principle, which is completely and corresponds to the modern ethics of knowledge representation. here, formalized data (metric indicators) and content (experts, subjective) are taken into account. The problem of scaling and efficiency allows solving the expert-metric approach, which is a special case of the dialectical approach - the ascent from the abstract to the concrete representation of knowledge. Algorithms based on the expert-metric approach not only include substantive and formal criteria but also by means of machine learning make it possible to create a final formula for determining the rating of the parameters for evaluating any phenomenon of the knowledge economy in the most adequate way. Now, in modern conditions, the explication of a large number of decision trees (using machine learning) creates the prerequisites for making meaningful, but at the same time, strict, poorly manipulated, verified, carefully "weighed" decisions, the logic of which can be justified and stated in an explicit form. That is, in our opinion, modern information technologies make it possible to solve the problems of knowledge management more and more adequately, provided that the rules of the dialectical approach are observed.

Acknowledgment. This research was supported by the Russian Fund of Basic Research (grant No. 19-07-01200).

References

1. Kant, I.: Critique of Pure Reason, 784 p. AST (2019). (in Russian)
2. Hegel, G.G.: Science of logic, 912 p. AST (2018). (in Russian)
3. Bakhtin, M.M.: The problem of the text. Collected works in 7 volumes, vol. 5 (1997). (in Russian)
4. New philosophical encyclopedia. Scholasticism (2010). https://iphlib.ru/greenstone3/library/collection/newphilenc/document/HASHd77bb8e881b4426890ced7. Accessed 25 Jan 2021
5. Novikov, D.A.: Cybernetics 2.0. Advances in Systems Science and Application, vol. 16, no. 1, pp. 1–18 (2016)
6. Pelipenko, A.A.: Comprehension of culture. Part 1. Culture and sense, 607 p. ROSSPEN (2012). (in Russian)
7. Rusyaeva, E.Yu.: Cognitive techniques of knowledge formation. In: Kravets, A., Shcherbakov, M., Kultsova, M., Iijima, T. (eds.) JCKBSE 2014. CCIS, vol. 466, pp. 40–48. Springer, Cham (2014). https://doi.org/10.1007/978-3-319-11854-3_4
8. Novikov, D.A.: Control Methodology, 101 p. Nova Science Publishers, New York (2013)

9. Rusyaeva, E.Yu., Poltavsky, A.V., Ahobagze, G.N.: Basics of algorithms intelligent system. In: Proceedings of the 2019 International Multi-Conference on Industrial Engineering and Modern Technologies (FarEastCon). Vladivostok, Russia. IEEE (2019). https://ieeexplore. ieee.org/document/8934296. https://doi.org/10.1109/FarEastCon.2019.8934296

10. Academy of Yandex. Machine learning searching: infrastructure and algorithms (answers to questions). https://youtu.be/g-bPnhKU0P8?t=1606. Accessed 20 June 2019

11. Kizim, A.V., Kravets, A.G.: On systemological approach to intelligent decision-making support in industrial cyber-physical systems. In: Kravets, A.G., Bolshakov, A.A., Shcherbakov, M.V. (eds.) Cyber-Physical Systems: Industry 4.0 Challenges. SSDC, vol. 260, pp. 167–183. Springer, Cham (2020). https://doi.org/10.1007/978-3-030-32648-7_14

12. Dictionaries and Encyclopedias at the Academy. Knowledge. https://dic.academic.ru. Accessed 25 Jan 2021

13. Akoff, R.L.: Management in the 21st century. Transformation of corporation, 418 p. TGU, Tomsk (2006)

14. Parameter tuning. https://catboost.ai/docs/concepts/parameter-tuning.html. Accessed 23 June 2019

15. Safronov, A.: How to find the best answers. https://youtu.be/oBVdFTRidg8?t=11m14s. Accessed 20 June 2019

16. Dorogush, A.V.: Machine learning searching: infrastructure and algorithms. https://youtu.be/ g-bPnhKU0P8?t=736. Accessed 20 June 2019

17. Saltykov, S.A., Rusyaeva, E.Yu.: Mediation in Science of Science: Expert-Scientometric Approach. Control Sci. **6**, 63–67 (2017). (in Russian)

18. Burkov, V.N.: Bases of the mathematical theory of active systems, 255 p. Science (1977). (in Russian)

19. Saltykov, S.A., Rusyaeva, E.Yu.: Approaches to determination of priority in science and innovations, 151 p. ICS (2018). (in Russian)

20. Korobkin, D., Fomenkov, S., Kravets, A., Kolesnikov, S.: Methods of statistical and semantic patent analysis. In: Kravets, A., Shcherbakov, M., Kultsova, M., Groumpos, P. (eds.) Communications in Computer and Information Science, vol. 754, pp. 48–61. Springer, Cham (2017). https://doi.org/10.1007/978-3-319-65551-2_4

21. Korobkin, D.M., Fomenkov, S.A., Kravets, A.G.: Extraction of physical effects practical applications from patent database. In: 2017 8th International Conference on Information, Intelligence, Systems and Applications, IISA 2017, pp. 1–5 (2018)

Improvement of Intent Classification Using Diacritic Restoration for Text Message in Chatbot

Trang Nguyen[(✉)] and Maxim Shcherbakov

Volgograd State Technical University, 28 Lenin Avenue, 400005 Volgograd, Russia

Abstract. Today, chatbots or conversational agents are increasingly being used in various fields. In recent years, governments, organizations, and businesses have invested in dialogue systems to improve the engagement of their users. A smart chatbot is a chatbot that can understand the user's intents. To achieve this goal, the developer always needs to improve the ability to classify the user's intents. However, the user's raw text usually contains spelling errors, abbreviations, or slang that the chatbot cannot understand. Therefore, processing the input text is also an urgent task of natural language understanding (NLU). In the Vietnamese dialogue system, there are always cases when users enter questions without signs. These questions greatly affect the understanding of the user's intents. In this paper, an improvement in the intent classification for a Vietnamese chatbot is presented. We propose the Encoder-Decoder Bidirectional Long Short-Term Memory (BiLSTM) model for the diacritic restoration. On our evaluation dataset, this approach has an accuracy of 99.12% by using the pre-trained language model for word embedding. Then, the proposed model is applied as a custom component in the NLU pipeline. Using the proposed approach for constructing a model of intent classification is considered, comparison with basic models has shown the best results for the proposed model.

Keywords: Diacritic restoration · Intent classification · Rasa NLU · Pipeline · NLP · Chatbot · Vietnamese · Encoder-Decoder BiLSTM · Transformer

1 Introduction

In recent years, advances in artificial intelligence have led to advances in natural language processing (NLP). Neural network-based models performed better on language tasks compared to traditional machine learning models such as support vector machine (SVM) or logistic regressions. NLP tasks are very important and necessary for chatbots. The use of deep learning models for the chatbot improves the results of tasks such as sentiment analysis [1–3], intent classification [4, 5], and entity extraction [6].

Understanding the text entered by the user is determined by the chatbot's intelligence. In many languages, diacritics are used in writing which is omitted by convention or for convenience. However, the lack of accents in the text causes problems with reading and understanding from easy to serious, as well as problems that are difficult to solve for

© Springer Nature Switzerland AG 2021
A. G. Kravets et al. (Eds.): CIT&DS 2021, CCIS 1448, pp. 110–123, 2021.
https://doi.org/10.1007/978-3-030-87034-8_9

natural language processing systems. Detecting and correcting spelling errors will especially help the chatbot better understand the user's intent in Vietnamese. Because of the complexity of the language, many Vietnamese prefer to use non-diacritical Vietnamese to make typing easier and faster on any computer or phone. Therefore, Vietnamese diacritic restoration is a very challenging task that is one of the first tasks to be solved in Vietnamese natural language processing.

There are many options to restore the appropriate diacritics for an unsigned sentence in Vietnamese and still make it meaningful. For example, a sentence "Toi doi chiec xe do" is "Tôi đợi chiếc xe đó"/I'm waiting for that car. However, each syllable has several variants to transform to the form with full diacritic marks. We can restore as follows: Toi - tôi, tội, tồi, tối, tơi, tợi, tời, tới, tòi; doi - đòi, đói, đọi, đợi, đời, đội, đổi, đối, đồi, đỗi; chiec - chiếc; xe - xé, xẻ, xè, xê, xế, xệ; do - đo, đỏ, đó, đò, đọ, đơ, đờ, đớ, đở, đợ, đô, đồ, đố, độ, đổ. Then from the unsigned sentence, we can restore some variants as follows: "Tôi đợi chiếc xe đó" (I'm waiting for that car), "Tôi đòi chiếc xe đó" (I claim that car), "Tôi đổi chiếc xe đó" (I changed that car), "Tôi đợi chiếc xe đỏ" (I'm waiting for the red car) and there are still some variants of the recover but the restore sentence would be meaningless. Therefore, we always need a powerful approach to restoring diacritical marks in Vietnamese.

There are two main approaches are studied on diacritic restoration: character-based [7, 8] and word-based [9, 10]. Both approaches require several factors to build useful models: first, they require large arrays of grammatical correction tags, and second, they also require significant processing time for tokenization, tagging, etc. In Vietnamese diacritic restoration researches, many methods are applied [11–15]. In work [11], a method using the Encoder-Decoder LSTM model is proposed, which gives an excellent result in comparison with other methods. However, in the model's structure author used the LSTM layer which has not achieved the highest efficiency in improving the performance of the model. In [13], a method of using the n-gram language model is proposed, which also gives relatively accurate results for diacritic restoration. But it will take a long time to restore the diacritic and using this model in constructing a chatbot will slow down the response process. In [14] the authors proposed a method of combination convolutional neural network and bidirectional gated recurrent unit (GRU) and this approach achieved the word accuracy of 94.77%. On the use of a machine translation-based approach for Vietnamese in [15], they achieved an accuracy of 96.15% and an accuracy of 97.32% by a phrase-based approach. The authors also pointed that the neural-based method is twice faster than the phrase-based method. In [29] the authors used a novel combination of a character-level recurrent neural-network-based model and a language model to recovery diacritics. This approach achieved the highest accuracy of 97.73% on Vietnamese.

To classify user's intent, there are some different approaches: rule-based, machine learning, and hybrid approach [16]. The traditional solution is to classify intents based on rules. This approach is to create specific rules, but one of the major problems here is defining too many rules. The machine learning approach is to train a classifier and using the trained classifier to predict the intent. This approach requires a training set of intents, based on which a classifier is built. The hybrid method combines all the previous principles (rule-based and machine learning-based) and comprises the application of the classifier. In work [17], methods for classifying intents were proposed: Bag-of-Words (BOW) in combination with Naïve Bayes, Continuous Bag-of-Words coupled with Support Vector Machines (SVM), Long Short-Term Memory (LSTM), and then the effectiveness of methods was compared on an open-sourced academic dataset. The author showed that using the SVM models outperforms the LSTM models. Deep learning approaches are significantly useful for text classification, summarization, machine translation, and intent classification [18–20]. In [20], the author evaluated the data set for intent classification and showed that the method BERT-based is the best method in the classification framework.

In this paper, we propose a deep learning approach for automatically restoring diacritics in Vietnamese. We use the Rasa platform for building a conversational agent (chatbot) based on machine learning. So we suggested the proposed diacritic restoration model as a component of the Rasa NLU pipeline [21] to classify user intents.

2 Methodology

For natural language understanding of the chatbot, we propose a model that involves two steps: restoring diacritics and classifying intents. At the first stage, we used FastText for word embedding on the BiLSTM for diacritic restoration. At the second stage, the created model was used as a component of the NLU pipeline for building the chatbot NLU model. In this paper, to create a chatbot we experimented on the Rasa platform which is easy to design a chatbot and quite popular recently.

2.1 Vietnamese Spelling

Vietnamese script based on the Latin alphabet consists of 29 letters, including 11 vowels and 18 consonants. In Vietnamese, 22 letters from Latin are used (the letters "f, j, w, z" are removed), and the rest of the letters with a sign are created (ă, â, đ, ê, ô, ơ, ư).

Compared to other languages, Vietnamese is much more complex. Statistics on the difficulty of the Vietnamese language are presented below:

– more than 95% of Vietnamese words contain accents, while French only 15%, and Romanian is 35% [11];
– more than 80% of Vietnamese syllables are found in repeated and unclear words (for example: "ban" maybe "bạn"/friend or possibly "bán"/sell, etc.).

All the characters contain diacritics when unmarked according to the rule in Table 1.

Table 1. The rule of the changing from diacritical characters to non-diacritical characters.

Diacritical characters	Non-diacritical characters
a, à, ả, ã, á, ạ, ă, ằ, ẳ, ẵ, ắ, ặ, â, ầ, ẩ, ẫ, ấ, ậ	a
e, è, ẻ, ẽ, é, ẹ, ê, ề, ể, ễ, ế, ệ	e
i, ì, ỉ, ĩ, í, ị	i
o, ò, ỏ, õ, ó, ọ, ơ, ờ, ở, ỡ, ớ, ợ, ô, ồ, ổ, ỗ, ố, ộ	o
u, ù, ủ, ú, ụ, ư, ừ, ử, ữ, ứ, ự	u
y, ỳ, ỷ, ỹ, ý, ỵ	y
d, đ	d

2.2 Models

Word Embedding. NLP techniques such as Word2Vec, GloVe, FastText transform words into fixed dimensional vectors. When referring to deep learning, word embedding is an important technology in NLP. The word embedding methods learn a real-valued vector representation for a predefined fixed-sized vocabulary from a corpus of text. In this work, word embedding was calculated with GloVe, FastText, and a combination of both models.

Encoder-Decoder Model. In this work, we used the Encoder-Decoder (or Seq2seq) model to solve the problem of diacritic restoration. Initially, this model was developed to create a machine translation system. Applying the model to our task is justified since this task is to convert the original sentence without signs into a sentence with signs. Thus, special architecture of the recurrent neural network (RNN) was developed—a network of BiLSTM. The main advantage of LSTM over a conventional feedforward neural network is that it can store information about previous output data. Figure 1 shows a diagram of a simple LSTM cell. A cell is a memory with five main elements: input gate i, output gate o, forget gate f, hidden state h, and updated cell-state c. Given a sequence of vectors $(x_1, x_x, ..., x_n)$, σ- is a logistic sigmoid function, h_t the latent state of the LSTM at time t is calculated as follows:

$$h_t = o_t * \tanh(c_t) \tag{1}$$

$$o_t = \tanh(Wx_o x_t + Wh_o h_{t-1} + Wc_o c_t + b_o) \tag{2}$$

$$c_t = f_t * c_{t-1} + i_t * \tanh(Wx_c x_t + Wh_c h_{t-1} + b_c) \tag{3}$$

$$f_t = \sigma(Wx_f x_t + Wh_f h_{t-1} + Wc_f c_{t-1} + b_f) \tag{4}$$

$$i_t = \sigma(Wx_i x_t + Wh_i h_{t-1} + Wc_i c_{t-1} + b_i) \tag{5}$$

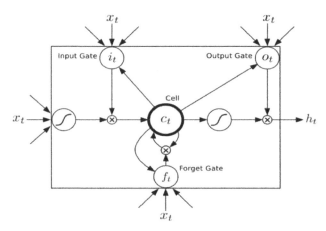

Fig. 1. LSTM cell (source [24]).

A BiLSTM is a modified version of LSTM which consists of two LSTMs: one talking the input in a forward direction, and the other in a backward direction (see Fig. 2). So BiLSTM-based model offers better performance than regular LSTM-based models. The word embedding of each word $(x_1, x_2, ..., x_n)$ of the sentence is taken as input for BiLSTM at each time step t. The forward pass will produce the hidden states $(\overrightarrow{h}_1, \overrightarrow{h}_2, ..., \overrightarrow{h}_n)$ of the output forward LSTM and the backward pass will encode the hidden states $(\overleftarrow{h}_1, \overleftarrow{h}_2, ..., \overleftarrow{h}_n)$ of the backward LSTM. The resulting hidden state is combined at each time step $h_t = [\overrightarrow{h}_t, \overleftarrow{h}_t] \in R^m$. Then a complete hidden state sequence is formed:

$$(h_1, h_2, ..., h_n) \in R^{n \cdot m} \tag{6}$$

The m-dimensional hidden state vector is mapped with the k-dimensional one, and k is the number of labels. So, the extracted sentence features are denoted as a matrix $Y = (y_1, y_2, ..., y_n) \in R^{n \cdot k}$.

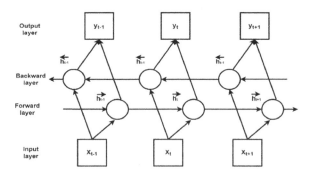

Fig. 2. Illustration of a BiLSTM model.

An overview of our Encoder-Decoder BiLSTM architecture is presented in Fig. 3.

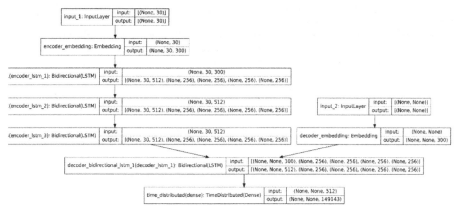

Fig. 3. The architecture of the Encoder-Decoder BiLSTM model.

Transformer. Introduced by Vaswani et al. Transformers [22] have now become the most modern architecture in NLP. It is built on top of the Seq2seq architecture, consisting of an encoder and a decoder. Before the appearance of transformers, the Seq2seq model based on RNN (such as LSTM, GRU) with attention mechanisms to handle the input sequence and the output without a fixed length and avoids the gradient vanishing. However, the transformer model with only attention mechanisms (see Fig. 4) and the additional training parallelization allow training on a larger dataset, which gives better results with less time.

Key, Value, and Query. The major component in the transformer is the unit of the multi-head self-attention mechanism. The transformer views the encoded representation of the input as a set of key-value pairs, (K, V), both of dimension n (input sequence length). In the decoder, the previous output is compressed into a query (Q of dimension m) and the next output is produced by mapping this query and the set of keys and values.

The transformer adopts the scaled dot-product attention: the output is a weighted sum of the values, where the weight assigned to each value is determined by the dot-product of the query with all the keys:

$$Attention(Q, K, V) = soft\max(\frac{QK^T}{\sqrt{d^k}})V \tag{7}$$

where d^k is the key dimensionality

Multi-Head Attention lets the model jointly attend to information from different representation subspaces at different positions.

$$MultiHead(Q, K, V) = [head_1; ...; head_h]W^o \tag{8}$$

Where

$$head_i = Attention(QW_i^Q, KW_i^K, VW_i^V)$$

where W_i^Q, W_i^K, W_i^V and W^O are parameter matrices to be learned.

Position Embedding. Since RNN was removed from the Transformer's architecture, to use the order of the sequence, it is necessary to include some information about the tokens' position in the sequence. The authors added "positional encodings" to the input embedding at the bottoms of the encoder and decoder stacks. Positional encoding can be learned or fixed.

The transformer is used in many tasks of NLP. In this paper, we will experiment with Transformer for diacritic restoration and intent classification.

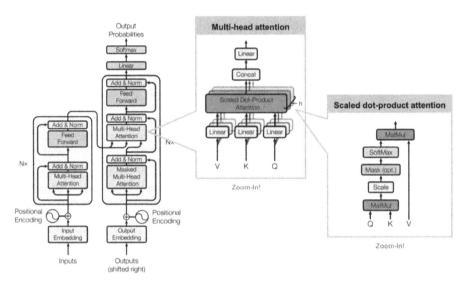

Fig. 4. The architecture of the Transformer (source [23]).

2.3 Intent Classification

The Effect of Missing Diacritics in Intent Detection. Normally Vietnamese people can read the simple text without diacritical marks with no ambiguity, but for the machine, it is a hard task. As we mentioned, the unsigned sentences will make the chatbot misinterpret the user's intentions in Vietnamese. For example, an utterance about the symptoms of covid-19 is entered without diacritics "Nhung trieu chung bieu hien cua mac covid-19 la gi?" (What are the symptoms of covid-19?). The chatbot's intent detection is shown in Fig. 5 with three cases. Obviously, the lack of diacritics reduces the confidence of intent detection to only 0.33, while the restored sentence with 2 errors (underlined in red) still gives confidence of 1.

We consider another example if the utterance (A) is similar to the target utterance (T), and the utterance (B) is (A) without diacritics.

(T): những triệu chứng biểu hiện của mắc covid-19 là gì?
(A): những triệu chứng biểu hiện của covid-19
(B): nhung trieu chung bieu hien cua covid-19

Figure 6 shows us that, utterance (T) gave confidence of 1, utterance (A) gave confidence of 1, and utterance (B) gave confidence only 0.25 of another intent (seriousillness). Moreover, since we have chosen the threshold of action confidence is 0.5, for utterance (A) the chatbot answered, and for utterance (B) the chatbot was silent and did not give any answer. Thus, restoring diacritics is important for detecting user's intent in Vietnamese chatbots.

Fig. 5. Examples of chatbot's intent detection in different cases of an utterance: 1) with full diacritics; 2) without diacritics; 3) restored diacritics.

Fig. 6. Example of three utterances (T), (A), (B).

Intent Classification in Rasa NLU Pipeline. The Rasa platform consists of two modules NLU and CORE. Rasa NLU defines the intent and entities from the user's source text. Rasa CORE is a dialog Manager that manages the flow of conversations and actions. So in this paper, we will focus on Rasa NLU.

Rasa NLU analyzes a user's text consisting of intents and a set of entities. The NLU itself is further modulated as a pipeline that defines how the user's utterance is processed. In particular, a user's utterance can be passed through components such as a tokenizer, a named entity recognition (NER), and then an intent classifier before being distributed to possible actions.

In this paper, we have created two custom components: a diacritic restorer and a tokenizer for the Vietnamese language. The diacritic restorer is created using the proposed model created at the previous stage. To create a Vietnamese tokenizer, we use the Vietnamese Underthesea tool [23]. Then all the custom components are added to the pipeline to build the NLU model.

For intent classification entity extraction, we used DIETClassifier (Dual Intent Entity Transformer Classifier) which is provided by Rasa. DIET is a multi-task architecture based on Transformer. DIETClassifier is also used as a component in Rasa NLU.

Figure 7 shows a schematic of a proposed pipeline for the five components. The context (training data) is passed to the diacritic restorer, which performs its training, and then persists the trained model for itself. Then the data is passed through the diacritic restorer as input to the tokenizer. The tokenizer also trains and persists, and so on for the next components. After all, components are trained and persisted, the last context dictionary is used to save the model metadata.

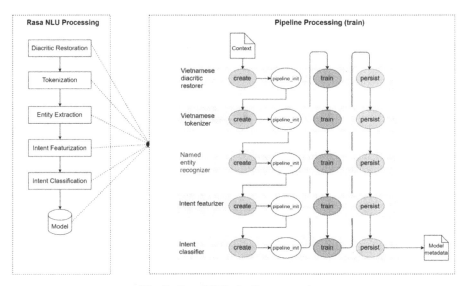

Fig. 7. Rasa NLU pipeline processing.

3   Experiment and Results

To train the proposed Encoder-Decoder BiLSTM model, we used the Vietnamese dataset from Wikipedia [25] and selected a file named "viwiki-latest-pages-articles.xml.bz2" containing the content of the articles. Then the downloaded file is extracted using WikiExtractor.

After unpacking, JSON files contain the content of articles are obtained. We then extracted the contents of the articles and saved them in a file train_data.txt. This file contains more than 3 million contents in Vietnamese. We used 500000 first content for our work. Each content consists of many sentences, so they are separated into sentences. Because the articles from Wikipedia contain many foreign words, it will falsify the restoration of Vietnamese diacritics. Since the length of the longest single word in Vietnamese is 7 [26], we only keep the sentences where the length of each token is not greater than 7.

The collected data with full signed text as the target dataset and then we removed all marks to get the source data set of unsigned text. The dataset was divided into train and test set with the ratio of 0.8 and 0.2, respectively. Figure 3 shows a brief structure of our model. Here in the proposed model, we use three BiLSTM layers in the encoder and one BiLSTM layer in the decoder. In addition, we used meta-embeddings [27] as the initial weights for the embedding layer which combined pre-trained embeddings from multiple sources (here, pre-trained model FastText for Vietnamese and Glove 6B). Adam optimizer is used with a learning rate of 0.001, the length of the sequence is 30. We also used dropout [28] of 0.3 for better generalization and stop the training of our model as soon as the accuracy on the validation set, which should at least improve 0.001 to prevent over-fitting.

We experimented with five models to compare the performance of our proposed model (BiLSTM with meta-embeddings, BiLSTM with GloVe, BiLSTM with FastText, LSTM with FastText, and Transformer model). The models were trained on a TPU v3-8 with 8 cores and a batch size of 2048. Table 2 shows the test result based on the models for recovering diacritics. From the result, it is obvious that our model has the best-performing score compared to the rest of the models. As we mentioned the approach based on the Transformer model restores diacritics faster than an approach based on neural networks. However, in fact, in a conversation, the interlocutor does not immediately answer the question and the other one can still wait for a few minutes to receive an answer. So, then we will use the proposed model (BiLSTM + meta-embeddings) in the intent classification of chatbot.

Table 2. Experimental result on the validation set.

Model	Validation accuracy (max)	Drop out	Epoch
BiLSTM + GloVe	0.929	0.3	20
BiLSTM + FastText	0.9842	0.3	16
LSTM + FastText	0.8236	0.3	20
BiLSTM + meta-embeddings	0.9912	0.3	10
Transformer	0.9651	–	8

At the next stage, the created model is used as a component in the Rasa NLU pipeline. We also created custom components for Vietnamese tokenization using the Underthesea tool [30]. Two custom components are added into the NLU pipeline as shown in Fig. 8.

```
language: "vi"
pipeline:
- name: "rasa_component.vspellchecker.CorrectSpelling"
  diacritic_model_path: "weight/max_acc.chkpt"
- name: "VietnameseTokenizer"
- name: "LexicalSyntacticFeaturizer"
- name: "CRFEntityExtractor"
- name: "CountVectorsFeaturizer"
- name: "CountVectorsFeaturizer"
  analyzer: "char_wb"
  min_ngram: 1
  max_ngram: 4
- name: DIETClassifier
  epochs: 100
```

Fig. 8. Example of the components in the Rasa NLU pipeline.

Our chatbot was created to search for information about COVID-19, as well as the number of cases of infection in countries around the world. At the stage of intent classification, the pipeline method was used [31]. The custom Rasa NLU pipeline configuration was presented in Fig. 8.

In this study, three models for intent classification were created: a baseline model without using the custom component, a model using the proposed model for recovering diacritics, and a model using the Vietnamese Toolkit Pyvi [32] for recovering diacritics. Figure 9 shows examples of testing intent classification on three models.

Source text and intent	Baseline model	Baseline + Pyvi model	Proposed model
- text: "nhung bieu hien cua benh thuong gap nhat la gi" - intent: "symptoms"	- text: "nhung bieu hien cua benh thuong gap nhat la gi" - intent: "symptoms" - confidence: 0.6311	- text: "những biểu hiện của bệnh thượng gặp nhất là gi" - intent: "symptoms" - confidence: 0.9684	- text: "những biểu hiện của bệnh thường gặp nhất là gi " - intent: "symptoms" - confidence: **0.9718**
- text: "toi muon hoi ve kiem tra covid" - intent: "test"	- text: "toi muon hoi ve kiem tra covid" - intent: "test" - confidence: 0.8220	- text: "Tôi muốn hội về kiểm tra Covid" - intent: "test" - confidence: 0.5415	- text: "tôi muốn hỏi về kiểm tra covid" - intent: "test" - confidence: **0.8249**
- text: "cho biet viruscorona lay nhiem nhu the nao" - intent: "spread"	- text: "cho biet viruscorona lay nhiem nhu the nao" - intent: "spread" - confidence: **0.7982**	- text: "cho biệt viruscorona lấy nhiệm như thế nao" - intent: "goodbye" - confidence: 0.2502	- text: "cho biết viruscorona lấy nhiễm như thế nào" - intent: "spread" - confidence: 0.3542
- text: "toi can lam gi de bao ve ban than truoc covid-19" - intent: "prevention"	- text: "toi can lam gi de bao ve ban than truoc covid-19" - intent: "prevention" - confidence: 0.9894	- text: "Tôi cần làm gì để bảo vệ bản thân trước Covid-19" - intent: "prevention" - confidence: 0.4617	- text: "Tôi cần làm gì để bảo vệ bản thân trước Covid-19" - intent: "prevention" - confidence: **0.9914**
- text: "cho toi thong ke so nguoi nhiem benh o Viet Nam hom nay" - intent: "cases"	- text: "cho toi thong ke so nguoi nhiem benh o Viet Nam hom nay" - intent: "cases" - confidence: 0.9940	- text: "Cho tới thông kê số người nhiệm bệnh ở Việt Nằm hôm Nay" - intent: "cases" - confidence: 0.9275	- text: "cho tôi thống kê số người nhiệm bệnh ở Việt Nam hôm này" - intent: "cases" - confidence: **0.9987**

Fig. 9. Testing intent detection from user's utterance on three models.

To experiment on the intent classification, we created a file of intents and utterances that comprises 11 intents and 165 examples of utterances. To evaluate the models' performance, we used the Rasa NLU quality assessment module with cross-validation. Table 3 shows the results of intent classification by three metrics (accuracy, precision, and F1-score).

Table 3. Average quality ratings for three models.

Model	Accuracy	Precision	F1-score
Baseline	0.918	0.932	0.911
Baseline + Pyvi	0.880	0.901	0.883
Proposed model	0.925	0.936	0.926

The proposed model received the highest accuracy value (0.925), precision (0.936), and F1-score (0.926) in comparison with the other models. The lowest results were shown by the baseline + Pyvi model which was constructed using The Vietnamese Pyvi Toolkit. And so that means that the Pyvi tool not good enough at recovering diacritics. Thus, when using Pyvi, the source text was changed, which led to a misunderstanding of intents.

4 Conclusion

In this paper, we investigated the Encoder-Decoder BiLSTM neural network for recovering diacritic. The diacritic recovery model is integrated into the task-oriented chatbot, which improved the intent classification performance of the NLU model. The results of the experiment showed the effectiveness of the proposed model and approach.

An Encoder-Decoder BiLSTM model is developed for recovering diacritics. Besides, the proposed model used meta-embeddings with the pre-trained model FastText and Glove 6B to initial the weights for the embedding layer that helps to improve the diacritical restoration performance. Then we used the proposed diacritic restoration model as a component of the NLU pipeline. This proposed approach achieved the best result in intent classification. Using the proposed approach is promising, as it will allow chatbots to understand text messages without diacritics and improve their ability to understand users' intents.

In future work, we will apply a modified transformer model to improve the performance as well as reduce restore time in the Vietnamese diacritic restoration task.

References

1. Nivethan, S.S.: Sentiment analysis and deep learning based chatbot for user feedback. In: Balaji, S., Rocha, Á., Chung, Y.N. (eds.) Intelligent Communication Technologies and Virtual Mobile Networks, pp. 231–237. Springer, Cham (2019). https://doi.org/10.1007/978-3-030-28364-3_22
2. Wu, X., et al.: Sentiment Analysis with Eight Dimensions for Emotional Chatbots (2017). https://www.anlp.jp/proceedings/annual_meeting/2017/pdf_dir/C5-2.pdf

3. Kulikova, Y.V., Obuhov, D.A., Orlova, Y.U.: Development of a chatbot based on a neural network. Mod. Sci. **2**(11), 253–255 (2019). (in Russian)
4. Wang, Y.C., Chang, W., Wang, Y.: Dialogue intent classification with character-CNN-BGRU networks. Multimedia Tools Appl. **79**, 4553–4572 (2020). https://doi.org/10.1007/s11042-019-7678-1
5. Meng, L., Huang, M.: Dialogue intent classification with long short-term memory networks. In: Huang, X., Jiang, J., Zhao, D., Feng, Y., Hong, Y. (eds.) Natural Language Processing and Chinese Computing, pp. 42–50. Springer, Cham (2018). https://doi.org/10.1007/978-3-319-73618-1_4
6. Qian, C.: BERT for Join Intent Classification and Slot Filling (2019). https://arxiv.org/abs/1902.10909
7. De Pauw, G., Wagacha, P.W., de Schryver, G.-M.: Automatic diacritic restoration for resource-scarce languages. In: Matoušek, V., Mautner, P. (eds.) TSD 2007. LNCS (LNAI), vol. 4629, pp. 170–179. Springer, Heidelberg (2007). https://doi.org/10.1007/978-3-540-74628-7_24
8. Simard, M., Deslauriers, A.: Real-time automatic insertion of accents in French text. Nat. Lang. Eng. **7**(2), 143–165 (2001). https://doi.org/10.1017/s1351324901002650
9. Mihalcea, R.F.: Diacritics restoration: learning from letters versus learning from words. In: Gelbukh, A. (ed.) CICLing 2002. LNCS, vol. 2276, pp. 339–348. Springer, Heidelberg (2002). https://doi.org/10.1007/3-540-45715-1_35
10. Nelken, R., Shieber, S.M.: Arabic diacritization using weighted finite-state transducers. In: Proceedings of the ACL Workshop on Computational Approaches to Semitic Languages. Association for Computational Linguistics, Ann Arbor, Michigan (2005)
11. Hung, B.T.: Vietnamese diacritics restoration using deep learning approach. In: 2018 10th International Conference on Knowledge and Systems Engineering (KSE), Ho Chi Minh City, pp. 347–351. IEEE (2018). https://ieeexplore.ieee.org/document/8573427
12. Pham, L., Tran, V., Nguyen, V.: Vietnamese text accent restoration with statistical machine translation. In: Proceedings of the 27th Pacific Asia Conference on Language, Information, and Computation ({PACLIC} 27), pp. 423–429. Department of English, National Chengchi University, Taipei, Taiwan, November 2013
13. Tung, B.T.: Language Modeling - Language model and punctuation problem in Vietnamese. https://viblo.asia/p/language-modeling-mo-hinh-ngon-ngu-va-bai-toan-them-dau-cau-trong-tieng-viet-1VgZveV2KAw#_neural-network-language-model-5. (in Vietnamese)
14. Nga, C.H., et al.: Deep learning based Vietnamese diacritics restoration. In: 2019 IEEE International Symposium on Multimedia (ISM), San Diego, CA, USA, pp. 331–3313. IEEE, December 2019
15. Pham, T.H., Pham, X.K., Le-Hong, P.: On the use of machine translation-based approaches for Vietnamese diacritic restoration. In: 2017 International Conference on Asian Language Processing (IALP), Singapore, pp. 272–275. IEEE (2017)
16. Date, S.S.: A comprehensive review on intents, intention mining and intention classification. Int. J. Sci. Res. **9**, 16–20 (2020)
17. Schuurmans, J., Frasincar, F., Cambria, E.: Intent classification for dialogue utterances. IEEE Intell. Syst. **35**(1), 82–88 (2020). https://doi.org/10.1109/mis.2019.2954966
18. Graves, A.: Supervised Sequence Labelling. Studies in Computational Intelligence Supervised Sequence Labelling with Recurrent Neural Networks (2012). https://arxiv.org/pdf/1909.02027
19. Cho, K., et al.: Learning phrase representations using RNN encoder-decoder for statistical machine translation. In: Proceedings of the 2014 Conference on Empirical Methods in Natural Language Processing, Doha, Qatar, pp. 1724–1734. Association for Computational Linguistics, October 2014
20. Larson, S., et al.: An Evaluation Dataset for Intent Classification and Out-of-Scope Prediction. arXiv abs/1909.02027 (2019)

21. Bocklisch, T., et al.: Rasa: Open Source Language Understanding and Dialogue Management. arXiv abs/1712.05181 (2017). https://arxiv.org/abs/1712.05181
22. Vaswani, A., et al.: Attention is all you need (2017). http://arxiv.org/abs/1706.03762
23. Weng, L.: Attention? Attention! (2021). https://lilianweng.github.io/lil-log/2018/06/24/attention-attention.html. Accessed May 2021
24. Joty, S., Mohiuddin, T.: Modeling speech acts in asynchronous conversations: a neural-CRF approach. Comput. Linguist. **44**, 859–894 (2018). https://www.aclweb.org/anthology/J18-4012
25. Wikimedia. https://dumps.wikimedia.org/viwiki/latest
26. Wikipedia contributors: Longest words (2021). https://en.wikipedia.org/w/index.php?title=Longest_words&oldid=1030765356. Accessed May 29
27. He, J., et al.: Learning efficient task-specific meta-embeddings with word prisms. In: Proceedings of the 28th International Conference on Computational Linguistics. International Committee on Computational Linguistics, Stroudsburg, PA, USA (2020)
28. Srivastava, N., Hinton, G., Krizhevsky, A., Sutskever, I., Salakhutdinov, R.: Dropout: a simple way to prevent neural networks from overfitting. J. Mach. Learn. Res. **15**(56), 1929–1958 (2014)
29. Náplava, J., et al.: Diacritics restoration using neural networks. In: Proceedings of the Eleventh International Conference on Language Resources and Evaluation (LREC 2018). European Language Resources Association (ELRA), Miyazaki, Japan (2018)
30. Vietnamese, N.U., Toolkit. https://pypi.org/project/underthesea/
31. Nguyen, T., Shcherbakov, M.: Enhancing Rasa NLU model for Vietnamese chatbot. Int. J. Open Inf. Technol. **9**(1), 31–36 (2021)
32. Toolkit. https://pypi.org/project/pyvi/

Numerical and Symbolic Integration in the MAPLE Package: Software for Antiplane Problems of the Non-linear Elasticity Theory

Yulia Y. Andreeva$^{(\boxtimes)}$, Natalia V. Asanova, and Irina A. Tarasova

Volgograd State Technical University, Lenin Avenue 28, 400005 Volgograd, Russian Federation

Abstract. Currently, there are many different mathematical packages. This work uses the MAPLE package as the most accessible and common. The math package specializes in the symbolic calculation, but the capabilities of the package allow you to use the numerical component. The capabilities of the MAPLE package allow you to develop on its basis. A problematic specialized calculation system, which is a combination of numerical and symbolic methods. The creation of modules is focused on their application in the nonlinear theory of elasticity. The creation of a specialized calculation system allows you to use powerful means of symbolic integration, methods of minimizing functionality, and visualization capabilities of the results inherent in MAPLE. The symbolic component allows you to write a numerical integration program for functions with parameters whose values are not specified. Therefore, it becomes possible to calculate integrals in functionals with iterative minimization methods only once. This approach avoids the calculation of integrals at each step of the iteration process. One-time integration allows you to cope with the simplest formulas of numerical integration.

Keywords: Numerical and symbolic integration · Antiplane shear deformation · Variational principle · The neo-Hookean potential

1 Introduction

The most common character calculation package is MAPLE. The package examined in this work is not only useful for theoretical study but can also be used in other spheres due to the fact that it has a numerical component [1]. The nonlinear theory of elasticity is not represented in standard mathematical packages, but many mathematical calculations are necessary to solve such problems. Therefore, one of the tasks is to develop a problematic specialized calculation system, which is a combination of numerical and symbolic methods. MAPLE [2, 3] is selected as the main basis on which the system is based. The created modules are aimed at application in the nonlinear theory of elasticity [4, 5]. The fact that the specialized system will be based on MAPLE determines the direction of its configuration as a library of author programs that are uploaded to MAPLE by the user, and the interface will have a form of the MAPLE worksheet. The uploaded libraries can be classified as algorithmic subsystems, and the programs in these libraries can be classified as numerical and symbolic blocks of the universal SACs (systems for analytical

© Springer Nature Switzerland AG 2021
A. G. Kravets et al. (Eds.): CIT&DS 2021, CCIS 1448, pp. 124–132, 2021.
https://doi.org/10.1007/978-3-030-87034-8_10

computation) which will be represented by MAPLE. All programs are written in the MAPLE programming language. In this work, the numerical and symbolic computation system will be referred to as the numerical and symbolic system (NSCS) [3]. This system is not an alternative to the renowned numerical packages as ANSYS, ABAQUS, etc. The NSCS simply broadens the MAPLE package capacity and facilitates its implementation in the mechanics.

When creating new software products that will solve problems of nonlinear theories, many problems can arise. This is due to the fact that creating new, narrowly specialized packages requires a lot of intellectual, material, and time costs. Using simple models that solve specific problems within a particular package is the most acceptable [6]. Creating modules that solve complex technical problems in the MAPLE environment allows you to talk about creating an automated work center for a mechanic.

The linear theory of elasticity is quite extensive. Therefore, two-dimensional tasks are distinguished from a plurality of three-dimensional tasks. The two-dimensional problems that we consider are problems with axisymmetric, flat, and antiplane deformation. Antiplot deformation is the simplest. Therefore, it is worth starting with the model of anti-flat deformation. In the nonlinear theory of elasticity, the problem of such separation is more complex. Thus, for the incompressible materials, antiplane shear deformation can occur only in objects with such shear energy potentials which fit the conditions mentioned in [7]. For instance, antiplane shear deformation can always occur in materials with the generalized neo-Hookean potential. There are a great number of studies that focus on non-linear antiplane shear deformation [8–12].

One practical application of final antiplane deformation is the design model of the rubber-metal shock absorber of longitudinal shear [13]. Rubber shock absorbers usually consist of metal (plane, tubular, or shaped) braces with rubber between them. Braces are held together maintaining the antiplane shear deformation of the rubber at a reasonable distance from the end faces. So, long shock absorbers are reviewed. It should be mentioned that under antiplane shear deformation, the size is maintained irrespective of the compressibility of the material. The Jacobian conversion equals one for any cross-section warping function which sets this deformation. This is a geometrical feature of the deformation. A model of the non-compressible material was chosen as it is the most developed one. It should be also mentioned that the application of the shaped braces implies the cross-section diversity of configurations that can be sophisticated enough.

2   NSCS Functional Properties

The developed NSCS is designed to numerically solve any static problems with final antiplot deformation with mixed boundary conditions and arbitrary Neo-Ukrainian potential for areas with complex configuration. In particular, the NSCS helps automate the computation of the rubber shock absorber under final deformations with a direct cursor of any neo-Hookean potential and with a sophisticated configuration of the cross-section of a shock absorber.

The NSCS performs a mixed variational principle. For this principle, all finitesimal conditions are natural, thus it facilitates the algorithm of the approximation of the desirable functions.

The NSCS helps choose the approximation method for the desirable functions through orthogonal polynomials of different types with regard to the symmetry of the problem in all set areas. Such a non-local approximation provided the accuracy is sufficient, helps reduce significantly the time of calculation compared with FEM adaptive approximations and other similar methods. A posteriori assessment of solution accuracy is conducted through the assessment of the residuals of the equations in different functional norms. The residual of the finitesimal conditions is assessed with the uniform norm, the residual of the differential equations is assessed with the energy norm.

The system of the non-linear algebraic equations (obtained through the decomposition of the stationarity conditions of the variational principle functional) is solved by the method of least squares which excludes the occurrence of the complex roots which do not have any physical sense but which sometimes occur due to the fact that the system of equations is approximate.

The inclusion of the geometrical information is made by R-functions [14–16]. This approach facilitates the process of setting the configurations of the domain of the desirable functions, finitesimal conditions, and it also automates the calculation of the multiple integrals for the complex domains.

The program algorithm implementation is made in the MAPLE programming language.

The interface and visualization tools are from the MAPLE package. The NSCS package is built using a modular architecture, which allows you to connect additional modules during operation. At the moment, several modules have been developed that allow you to solve static problems during the final antiplot deformation. One of the modules is a symbol-numerical integration module used in the calculation of integral functionality.

3 Numerical and Symbolic Integration

A symbolic package helps write a program for the numerical integration for functions with parameters which values are not set. Thus, there is an opportunity to calculate integrals in the functional only once. In other words, if the unknown functions are approximated through the set functions $u = u(x,y,c_1,c_2,...c_n)$, where c_k are not set, then, after the numerical integration, the functional transforms into a numerical function of variables $F(c_1,c_2,...c_n)$. The necessary condition of this function is the system:

$$\frac{\partial F}{\partial c_k} = 0. \tag{1}$$

This approach helps avoid calculating integrals at every step of the iterative process, which would be inevitable in the numerical integration since the coefficient values are necessary to be set while they change at every step. The fact that the integration takes place only once helps avoid using the simplest formulas of the numerical integration since there are no technical obstacles for the substantial increase in the number of the nodes of the quadrature function. Integration that occurs at the domain border is not related to the integration which occurs inside the domain, and the number of nodes in the quadrature formulas for the border and the domain does not correlate either.

Calculating the line integrals is limited to the definite integral which is calculated in the module $OprInt(f(t),t_1,t_2,n)$, where $f(t)$ is an integrand, t_1,t_2 are the lower and upper limits of integration, and n is the number of nodes of the quadrature function. For the quadrature function, the average value of the functions of the left, right, and middle rectangulars is used (all the calculations have a symbolic form):

$$I_n = \frac{h}{3}\sum_{i=1}^{n}\left\{f[t_1 + i - 1 \; h] + f\left[t_1 + ih\right] + f\left[t_1 + \left(i - \frac{1}{2}\right)h\right]\right\}, \quad h = \frac{t_2 - t_1}{n} \quad (2)$$

In Fig. 1, there are examples of the usage of the module $OprInt(f(t),t_1,t_2,n)$. The monotonous accuracy increase is shown alongside the growing number of nodes according to the known assessment $|I - I_n| < O(1/n^2)$ for the functions with the limited derivative of at least the second order [7, 16]. Then, there is the result of the integration with the NSCS module of the expression with the non-definite coefficients. This expression cannot be integrated symbolically or with the numerical integration tools of MAPLE.

Double integrals in the rectangular area are calculated with the module $Intplan(f(x, y), m_1, m_2, m_3, m_4, n)$, where $f(x,y)$ is the integrand, m_1, m_2 are the limits of the change of x, m_3, m_4 are the of the change of y, n is the number of the nodes of the quadrature function with one variable, thus the general number of the nodes is n^2. The quadrature function is used as:

$$I_n = \left[\frac{1}{2}S_0 + S_n + \sum_{k=1}^{n-1}S_k\right]h_y, \; S_k = \left[\frac{1}{2}S_{k0} + S_{kn} + \sum_{i=1}^{n-1}f_{ik}\right]h_x,$$

$$f_{ik} = f\left[m_1 + ih_x, m_3 + kh_y\right], \quad h_x = \frac{m_2 - m_1}{n}, \; h_y = \frac{m_4 - m_3}{n} \quad (3)$$

that is, the trapezoidal rule is used successively.

In Fig. 2, there are examples of using the module $Intplan(f(x, y), m_1, m_2, m_3, m_4, n)$. In the rectangular integration, there is a monotonous increase of accuracy with the increase in the number of nodes for functions with the limited partial derivative of at least the second order.

Then, in Fig. 3(a, b, c), there is the result of integration along the curve area.

As it has already been mentioned, the rectangular integration is carried out with the module, but the integrand is multiplied by the figure's indicator. There arises the problem of filling the rectangular with the figure's points. The more the figure's area differs from the rectangular's area, the lesser the accuracy of integration with an indicator is. The solution to this problem is based on the additivity of the integral. The figure is covered with the elementary rectangulars in such a way that the difference between the areas of the elementary figures and elementary rectangulars is small. The integration is evaluated along with every rectangular, and the results are summed up.

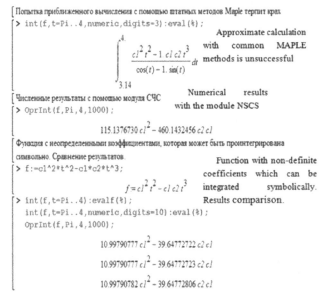

```
[> restart;
[> with(plots):with(linalg):
[> read "c:\FB.m";
[> with(FB);
  [Coord, EqvSol, FUN, FunCurv, FunPart, GlobVect, GrCon, Intplan, Norma, OprInt,
   Structure, con, diz, otr]
[ Определенный интеграл                 Definite
[> f:=t^3*cos(t);
```

$$f := t^3 \cos(t)$$

```
[ Точное значение интеграла              Accurate     value     of
[> int(f,t=Pi..4):evalf(%);
```

$$-34.11631868$$

```
[ Численные результаты  с помощью модуля СЧС для числа узлов n=10, 100, 1000
[> OprInt(f,Pi,4,10);            Numerical  results  with  the
   OprInt(f,Pi,4,100);
   OprInt(f,Pi,4,1000);          module NSCS for n=10, 100,
```

$$-34.10199036$$ 1000 number of nodes
$$-34.11617540$$
$$-34.11631743$$

```
[ Функция с неопределенными коэффициентами       Function  with  non-
[> f:=(c1^2*t^2-c1*c2*t^3)/(cos(t)-sin(t));   definite coefficients
```

$$f := \frac{c1^2 t^2 - c1\,c2\,t^3}{\cos(t) - \sin(t)}$$

```
[ Попытка символьного вычисления терпит крах      Symbolic
[> int(f,t=Pi..4);                       calculation     is
                                         unsuccessful
```

$$\int_{\pi}^{4} \frac{c1^2 t^2 - c1\,c2\,t^3}{\cos(t) - \sin(t)} dt$$

Fig. 1. There are examples of the usage of the module OprInt(f(t), t_1, t_2, n).

```
[ Попытка приближенного вычисления с помощью штатных методов Maple терпит крах
[> int(f,t=Pi..4,numeric,digits=3):eval(%);
                                         Approximate calculation
```

$$\int_{3.14}^{4.} \frac{c1^2 t^2 - 1.\,c1\,c2\,t^3}{\cos(t) - 1.\sin(t)} dt$$ with common MAPLE
methods is unsuccessful

```
[ Численные результаты с помощью модуля СЧС      Numerical     results
[> OprInt(f,Pi,4,1000);                   with the module NSCS
```

$$115.1376730\, c1^2 - 460.1432456\, c2\,c1$$

```
[ Функция с неопределенными коэффициентами, которая может быть проинтегрирована
символьно. Сравнение результатов.
                                         Function with non-definite
[> f:=c1^2*t^2-c1*c2*t^3;                 coefficients  which  can  be
```

$$f := c1^2 t^2 - c1\,c2\,t^3$$ integrated   symbolically.

```
[> int(f,t=Pi..4):evalf(%);               Results comparison.
   int(f,t=Pi..4,numeric,digits=10):eval(%);
   OprInt(f,Pi,4,1000);
```

$$10.99790777\, c1^2 - 39.64772722\, c2\,c1$$
$$10.99790777\, c1^2 - 39.64772723\, c2\,c1$$
$$10.99790782\, c1^2 - 39.64772806\, c2\,c1$$

Fig. 2. Examples of using the module Inplan(f(x, y), m_1, m_2, m_3, m_4, n).

[Двойной интеграл   **Double integral**
> f:=x*y*(cos(x)+sin(y));

$$f := x\,y\,(\cos(x) + \sin(y))$$

[Точное значение   **Accurate value**
> int(int(f,x=0..1),y=0..1):evalf(%);

0.3414709848

[Вычисление по прямоугольнику.   **Rectangular integration**
[Численные результаты с помощью модуля СЧС для числа узлов n^2=10*10, 100*100, 200*200.
> Ind:=1;

$Ind := 1$

> Intplan(f,0,1,0,1,10);   **Numerical results with the module NSCS for**
  Intplan(f,0,1,0,1,100);
  Intplan(f,0,1,0,1,200); n^2=10*10, 100*100, 200*200 number of nodes

0.3415046288

0.3414713215

0.3414710685

[Криволинейная область   **Curvilinear area**
> f:=1;
  omega:=con(x^2+y^2-1,4-x^2-y^2);
  Ind:=piecewise(omega<0,0,1);

$$f := 1$$

$$\omega := 3 - \sqrt{2x^4 + 4x^2y^2 - 10x^2 + 2y^4 - 10y^2 + 17}$$

$$Ind := \begin{cases} 0 & -\sqrt{2x^4 + 4x^2y^2 - 10x^2 + 2y^4 - 10y^2 + 17} < -3 \\ 1 & \text{otherwise} \end{cases}$$

a)

> Gr:=implicitplot(omega=0,x=-2..2,y=-2..2,numpoints=6000):
  print(Gr);

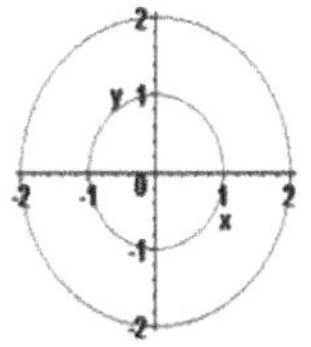

[Предварительный численный эксперимент   **Preliminary numerical experiment**
[Точное значение площади
> Pi*(2^2-1);s:=evalf(%);   **Accurate area value**

3π

$s := 9.424777962$

[Численные результаты с помощью модуля СЧС для числа узлов n^2=10*10, 200*200, 300*300, 400*400.
> Intplan(f,-3,3,-3,3,100);   **Numerical results with the module NSCS**
  Intplan(f,-3,3,-3,3,200);
  Intplan(f,-3,3,-3,3,300);   **for n²=10*10, 100*100, 200*200, 300*300,**
  Intplan(f,-3,3,-3,3,400);   **400*400 number of nodes**

9.460800000

9.414000000

9.436800000

9.428400000

b)

Fig. 3. (a, b, c) The result of integration along the curve area.

Разбивая область на подобласти вариацией пределов интегрирования, можно улучшить результат:

```
> 4*Intplan(f,0,2,0,2,100);
  4*Intplan(f,0,2,0,2,200);
  4*Intplan(f,0,2,0,2,300);
  4*Intplan(f,0,2,0,2,400);
```

Result can be improved by dividing area into subareas with the variation of integration limits

$$9.436000000$$
$$9.423000000$$
$$9.423739164$$
$$9.425350000$$

Функция с неопределенными коэффициентами

```
> f:=(c1*x^2+c2*y^3)/exp(x*y);
```

Function with non-definite coefficients

$$f := \frac{c1\,x^2 + c2\,y^3}{e^{(x\,y)}}$$

Using MAPLE procedure is unsuccessful

Попытка использования встроенной в Maple процедуры терпит крах.

```
> with(Student[MultivariateCalculus]):
> ApproximateInt(Ind*f,x=-2..2,y=-2..2,partition = [400,400]);
```

Numerical results with the module NSCS

Численный результат с помощью модуля СЧС

```
> Intplan(f,-2,2,-2,2,400);
```

$$19.16845294\,c1 - 0.1494598\;10^{-8}\,c2$$

Уточним разбивая область на подобласти

```
> i1:=Intplan(f,0,2,0,2,400);i2:=Intplan(f,0,2,-2,0,400);
  i3:=Intplan(f,-2,0,0,2,400);i4:=Intplan(f,-2,0,-2,0,400);
```

$$i1 := 1.372185694\,c1 + 1.957287441\,c2$$
$$i2 := 8.217148011\,c1 - 11.42619915\,c2$$
$$i3 := 8.217147919\,c1 + 11.42619886\,c2$$
$$i4 := 1.372185744\,c1 - 1.957287336\,c2$$

Making results more accurate by dividing area into subareas

```
> i:=i1+i2+i3+i4;
```

$$i := 19.17866737\,c1 - 0.19\;10^{-6}\,c2$$

c)

Fig. 3. (*continued*)

In Fig. 4a, there is an example of dividing the given rectangular into four parts. Then, in Fig. 4b, there is an example of the integration with the module NSCS of the expression with the non-definite coefficients. This expression cannot be calculated symbolically or with the numerical integration tools of MAPLE.

[Уточним разбивая область на подобласти

```
> i11:=ApproximateInt(Ind*f1,x=0..2,y=0..2,partition =
  [400,400]);
  i12:=ApproximateInt(Ind*f1,x=0..2,y=-2..0,partition =
  [400,400]);
  i13:=ApproximateInt(Ind*f1,x=-2..0,y=0..2,partition =
  [400,400]);
  i14:=ApproximateInt(Ind*f1,x=-2..0,y=-2..0,partition =
  [400,400]);
```

$$i11 := 1.372643509$$
$$i12 := 8.215402383$$
$$i13 := 8.215402379$$
$$i14 := 1.372643298$$

Making results more accurate by dividing area into subareas

```
> I1:=i11+i12+i13+i14;
```

$$I1 := 19.17609157$$

```
> i21:=ApproximateInt(Ind*f2,x=0..2,y=0..2,partition =
  [400,400]);
  i22:=ApproximateInt(Ind*f2,x=0..2,y=-2..0,partition =
  [400,400]);
  i23:=ApproximateInt(Ind*f2,x=-2..0,y=0..2,partition =
  [400,400]);
  i24:=ApproximateInt(Ind*f2,x=-2..0,y=-2..0,partition =
  [400,400]);
```

$$i21 := 1.958432393$$
$$i22 := -11.42402755$$
$$i23 := 11.42402842$$
$$i24 := -1.958432409$$

```
> I2:=i21+i22+i23+i24;
```

$$I2 := 0.854 \ 10^{-6}$$

a)

[Сравнение с встроенной в Maple процедурой. Разобьем функцию на две и исключим неопределенные коэффициенты

```
> f1:=x^2/exp(x*y);f2:=y^3/exp(x*y);
```

Comparison of MAPLE procedure. Now we divide the function into two and exclude non-definite coefficients

$$f1 := \frac{x^2}{e^{(xy)}}$$

$$f2 := \frac{y^3}{e^{(xy)}}$$

```
> ApproximateInt(Ind*f1,x=-2..2,y=-2..2,partition =
  [400,400]);
  ApproximateInt(Ind*f2,x=-2..2,y=-2..2,partition = [400,400]);
```

$$19.17858566$$

$$-0.48965498 \ 10^{-8}$$

b)

Fig. 4. a) An example of the dividing of the given rectangular into four parts; b) An example of the integration with the module NSCS of the expression with the non-definite coefficients.

4 Conclusion

Our chosen approach, combining direct integration, allows us to solve complex problems in one cycle of integration. As a result of these calculations, we get an expression for the functional, depending on the coefficients of the many-terms approximation. Depending on the types of approximating coefficients, the problem can be solved significantly faster with the necessary accuracy. Unlike the methods used before, our approach is faster and applies to all types of problems considered by the nonlinear theory of elasticity. Fitting of approximation coefficients can be carried out using various methods, which allows solving problems with different accuracy.

References

1. Systems of analytical calculations (computer algebra systems) in the distorted solid body mechanics, p. 168 (1990)
2. Paimushin, V.N., Kholmogorov, S.A., Badriev, I.B.: Consistent equations of nonlinear multilayer shells theory in the quadratic approximation. Lobachevskii J. Math. **40**(3), 349–363 (2019). https://doi.org/10.1134/S1995080219030156
3. Andreeva, Y.Y., Zhukov, B.A.: Combined system of numerical and symbolic methods on the basis of MAPLE in the non-linear antiplane shear deformation problems, pp. 237–244 (2016)
4. Zubov, L.M.: Stationary principle of the additional work in the non-linear elasticity theory, pp. 241–245 (1970)
5. Zubov, L.M.: Variational principles of the non-linear elasticity theory, pp. 406–410 (1971)
6. Bondar, V.D.: Modeling of the non-linear antiplane shear deformation of the cylindrical body, pp. 99–109 (2005)
7. Gent, A.N., Thomas, A.G.J.: Polymer Sci. **28**, 625 (1958)
8. Zhukov, B.A.: Non-linear interrelation of the finite longitudinal shear and the finite torsion of the sleeve from the rubber-like material. Bulletin of the Russian Academy of Sciences. Mechanics of the Solid Body, pp. 127–135 (2015)
9. De Pascalis, R., Destrade, M., Saccomandi, G.: The stress field in a pulled cork and some subtle points in the semiinverse method of nonlinear elasticity. Proc. R. Soc. A P. **463**, 2945–2959 (2007)
10. Zhukov, B.A.: Non-linear effect of interrelation between in-plane and antiplane deformations in the incompressible material, pp. 142–145 (1998)
11. Horgan, C.O.: Anti-plane shear deformations in linear and nonlinear solid mechanics. SIAM Rev. **37**(1), 53–81 (1995)
12. Horgan, C., Saccomandi, G.: Superposition of generalized plane strain on anti-plane shear deformations in isotropic incompressible hyperelastic materials. J. Elast. **73**(1–3), 221–235 (2003)
13. Chernykh, K.F.: Nonlinear singular elasticity. Part 2. Applications, p. 195 (2000). SPb: ISBN 5-7997-0181-X
14. Rvachev, V.L., Sheiko, T.I.: Introduction to the R-functions theory. Mach. Eng. 46–58 (2001)
15. Steigmann, D.J.: Finite elasticity theory. Finite Elasticity Theory, p. 184 (2017)
16. Efimov, G.B., Zueva, E.Yu., Shchenkov, I.B.: Computer algebra at the Institute of Applied Mathematics. M.V. Keldysha Mat. Modeling **13**(6), 11–18 (2001)

Artificial Intelligence and Deep Learning Technologies for Creative Tasks. IoT and Computer Vision in Knowledge-Based Control

Optimization of Internet of Things System

Igor Lvovich[1] , Yakov Lvovich[2] , Andrey Preobrazhenskiy[1](✉) ,
and Oleg Choporov[2]

[1] Voronezh Institute of High Technologies, 73a, Lenina st., Voronezh 394043, Russia
[2] Voronezh State Technical University, 14, Moscow Dist., Voronezh 394026, Russia

Abstract. The paper discusses the features of solving problems related to the modeling of complex systems of Internet of things. They can be used in different organizations. The multi-alternative optimization model that allows selection of components in the IoT system is developed. The approach that allows finding future solutions in Internet of Things systems is shown. The formation of an integrated approach when building IoT systems, taking into account promising options is carried out. The formation of an integrated approach when building IoT systems, taking into account promising options is shown. The results of the paper can be useful in choosing an effective implementation of the complex components of Internet of Things on the basis of a computational experiment. The construction of an integrated Internet of Things system is considered in the form of building a new option from among the promising ones. In this case, the implementation efficiency is achieved through the use of genetic algorithms.

Keywords: Internet of Things · Control · Optimization · Model

1 Introduction

For many companies, IoT systems are of strategic value. There is a high interest in the development and verification of methods and approaches to automate the creation of such systems. It is known that the systematic application of such methods can significantly improve the quality, reduce the cost and delivery time of IoT systems. At the same time, the increase in complexity and the increase in the level of requirements for modern information and telecommunication systems [1], the use of more complex architectural solutions leads to an increase in the volume of program code, the appearance of corresponding errors. In this regard, the design of complex systems of the IoT is impossible without modeling. The purpose of this paper is to create software that will increase the level of automation and intellectual support in the processes of making optimal design decisions in the Internet of Things systems. Such software will allow, for the early stages of design, to ensure an increase in efficiency in the choice of options for IoT systems that will most closely meet the specified requirements.

© Springer Nature Switzerland AG 2021
A. G. Kravets et al. (Eds.): CIT&DS 2021, CCIS 1448, pp. 135–148, 2021.
https://doi.org/10.1007/978-3-030-87034-8_11

2 Multi-alternative Optimization Model that Allows Selection of Components of the IoT System

The design of Internet of Things systems in modern conditions is based on the use of various standard solutions. IoT systems use software solutions. In addition, technical models are being developed. You can rely on the analogy of processes in different systems. Then we can say that standard solutions are transferred. This approach provides opportunities for new systems to be formed. It should be noted that IoT systems have some peculiarities [2]. Not in all cases for them we can rely on transfer by standard solutions. The problem is that it is difficult to meet the required performance levels. Why is this so? This is because:

1. Researchers are faced with questions regarding transfer processes, if it is important to strive for multivariate consideration.
2. It is possible to have economic limitations in the system. In this regard, the work will take place when the entire system of the Internet of Things does not change at once. The transformations will concern local components and subsystems. It follows that when this entire IoT system is considered in terms of its effectiveness, then researchers are faced with the corresponding uncertainties.
3. Users work in different ways. Designers do not always learn and function in parallel ways. Then there are difficulties in the transfer processes in IoT systems.

There are multiple optimization procedures. They allow to overcome the indicated disadvantages in the design processes. In this case, the transfer processes are taken into account. As a result, the characteristics regarding the choice of standard solutions will be simplified.

This leads to the fact that parallel development will be supported. In addition, comparative assessments related to the transfer will be implemented for alternative projects.

Problems are solved under the conditions that there are limited resources. They can also be distributed over time intervals. In the complex, it will be possible to form systems of the Internet of Things that will be integrated.

We will consider the process of transferring and using standard solutions as an active one. What will this lead to? Then there will be no development of single projects. In systems of the Internet of Things, the concept of supporting different options is being developed in an integrated parallel way.

Due to the effects of parallelism, researchers will be able to apply relevant teaching information in a simultaneous manner at different stages.

Sets that will be related to technical components:

$$\delta_{rj} = \left(\overline{1, R_j; \upsilon_j}\right), j = \overline{1, J}, \tag{1}$$

Where υ_j illustrates how the set $\overline{1, R_j}$; is numbered. Software components will be associated with the following set:

$$\delta_{vt} = (\overline{1, V_t; \upsilon_e}),\quad t = \overline{1, T}, \tag{2}$$

where υ_t illustrates how the set $\overline{1, V_t}$; is numbered.

We will use the set S. It is formed using the relation over the nonempty sets R and V:

$$\delta_s = (S, \upsilon_s), \quad \delta_s = \delta_R \times \delta_v, \tag{3}$$

where υ_s illustrates how the set S is numbered

$$\delta_R = \times \{\delta_{rj} : j = \overline{1, J}\}, \delta_v = \times \{\delta_{vt} : t = \overline{1, T}\}; \tag{4}$$

The set S_l will form. It includes components that affect the operation of both hardware and software components in the Internet of Things $W_g = (g = 1, G)$:

$$\delta_w = \left(\overline{W_1, W_G}; \upsilon_g\right),$$

In it υ_g illustrates how the set S_l is numbered. The analysis is performed with respect to each of the subsystems. The system of the Internet of Things is considered from the point of view of the implementation of active transfer processes in it. Then the implementation of the corresponding structure of the Internet of Things will be carried out. From the point of view of a formal description, we will observe that in the set δ_S the elements will be transformed to the elements included in the set δ_w.

Therefore, then modeling, we create a family of morphisms from δ_S to

$$\delta_w - Mor(\delta_S, \delta_n).$$

The task is to optimally synthesize IoT systems. Requirements $F_i (i = \overline{1, I})$ are set for them. The transformations Mor (δ_s, δ_w) will be relative to the order υ^*, allowing to achieve the fulfillment according to the specified requirements. If any numbering of the sets Mor (δ_s, δ_w) is denoted υ, then the transformation $\upsilon = \upsilon^* h$ corresponds to the optimal choice, where h is a general recursive function, i.e. reduction υ to the main computable numbering. Inside the sets Mor (δ_s, δ_w), we can consider them in the form of corresponding transformations. An optimal selection process is required. In order υ^* to achieve it, we must make a transformation. For it, it is considered as a general recursive function. Then to the main computable numbering will come.

Thus, the generalized optimal synthesis problem is reduced to the problem of finding the principal computable numbering of the sets Mor (δ_s, δ_w) (problem P for a pair (δ_s, δ_w)).

If a finite numbered set $\delta_w \left(\overline{W_1, W_G}; \upsilon_g^*\right)$, and the principal admissible υ_g^* with respect to some partial order on the list S_l, is a numbering, for any numbered set δ_s such that Mor (δ_s, δ_w) is finite, then the problem P for the pair (δ_s, δ_w) is solvable. If problem P is solvable for (δ_s, δ_w), the numbered set $Mor(\delta_s, \delta_w); \upsilon^*)$ will be denoted by (δ_s, δ_w).

Requires Mor (δ_s, δ_w) transform to be implemented. We proceed from the assumption that the equivalence condition will be satisfied:

$$Mor(\delta_s, \delta_w) \sim Mor(\delta_R, \delta_v, \delta_w) \sim Mor(\delta_R, Mor(\delta_v, \delta_w)). \tag{5}$$

We will rely on the notation

$$Mor(\delta_v, \delta_w) = \delta_{vw}; L_{j-1} = \times \{\delta_{rj} : j = \overline{1, J-1}\} \text{ if } \delta_R = \delta_{j-1} \times \delta_{rj}, \tag{6}$$

after that we will represent (1) in the following form

$$Mor\left(\delta_R, Mor\left(\delta_v, \delta_w\right)\right) \sim Mor(\delta_R, \delta_{vw})$$
$$\sim Mor\left(\delta_{j-1} \times \delta_{rj}, \delta_{vw}\right) \sim Mor\left(\delta_{j-1}, \delta_{vw}\right) \tag{7}$$

We again denote

$$Mor\left(\delta_{rj}, \delta_{vw}\right) = \delta_{rj,vw}, \delta_{j-2} = \times\left\{\delta_{rj} : j = \overline{1, J-2}\right\} \tag{8}$$

similarly to (2), we obtain

$$Mor(\delta_{J-1}, Mor(\delta_{rJ}, \delta_{vw})) \sim Mor\left(\delta_{J-2}, Mor\left(\delta_{r(J-2)}, \delta_{rJ,vw}\right)\right). \tag{9}$$

Continuing procedure (2) until $j = I$, we have

$$Mor\left(\delta_2, Mor\left(\delta_{r3}, \delta_{rJ,...,r3,vw}\right)\right) \sim Mor\left(\delta_{r1}, Mor\left(\delta_{r2}, \delta_{rJ,...r2,vw}\right)\right). \tag{10}$$

If we analyze the $j - \mathcal{M}$ step, then we will represent stage (2) as follows

$$Mor\left(\delta_j, Mor\left(\delta_{r(j+1)}, \delta_{rJ,...,r(j+1,vw)}\right)\right) \sim Mor\left(\delta_{j-1}, Mor\left(\delta_{rj}, \delta_{rJ,...,rj,vw}\right)\right). \tag{11}$$

The set $Mor(\delta_v, \delta_w)$ can be handled with (4). As a result, we (1) represent by the t–th stage

$$Mor\left(\delta_t, Mor\left(\delta_{v(t+1)}, \delta_{vt,...,v(t+1),w}\right)\right) \sim Mor\left(\delta_{vt}, Mor\left(\delta_{vt}, \delta_{vT,...,vt,w}\right)\right), \tag{12}$$

n the specified expression $\delta_t = \times\left\{\delta_\tau : \tau = \overline{1, t}\right\}$; if it is required to deduce $\delta_{vT,...,v(t+1),}, \delta_{VT,...,vt,w}$, then it will be the same as in (3).

Then the main computable numbering, if (δ_s, δ_w) is analyzed, will be obtained in the appropriate steps:

1. The problem P is solved with respect to v_j^* which will be morphisms $Mor\left(\delta_{rj}, \delta_{rJ,...,rj,vw}\right)$, $\left(j = \overline{1, J}\right)$, while we proceed from the fact that it is necessary to fulfill (4) and (5), which is associated with morphisms v_t^*.
2. Performing the transformation $Mor(\delta_s, \delta_w)$.
3. The problem P is solved for v_g^* over sets $\delta_w = \left(\overline{W_1, W_G}; v_g\right)$, after which we apply (4), (5) if $v_j = v_j^*, v_t = v_t^* u v_g = v_g^*$.

We need an implementation of active transfer. We based on alternative variables:

$$x_m = \begin{cases} 1, \textit{if for according time interval} \\ \textit{we transfer } m - \textit{th subsystem;} \\ 0, \textit{otherwise}, m = \overline{1, M}; \end{cases} \tag{13}$$

$$x_{nm} = \begin{cases} 1, \textit{if for ana} \log \textit{ of } m - \textit{th subsystem} \\ \textit{we use } n_m - \textit{th type solution;} \\ 0, \textit{ otherwise}, n_m = \overline{1, N_m}, \end{cases} \tag{14}$$

Then, given that the corresponding requirements are satisfied, we can arrive at a combinatorial choice. Considered N_m in the above expressions as the number of solutions.

A large number of subsystems need to be processed for the appropriate time. This is determined by the condition

$$\sum_{m=1}^{M} a_m x_m \rightarrow \max, \tag{15}$$

specified weight a_m - shows which of the m-th subsystems will be mastered earlier. □

Requirements are established regarding financial resources C. They are used at a certain time

$$\sum_{m=1}^{M} \sum_{n_m=1}^{Nm} C_{nm} X_m X_{nm} \leq C, \tag{16}$$

The weighting factor C_{nm} – is related to the participation nm - th component of the IoT system.

This participation is associated with costs, implementation, etc.

Summarizing the above steps, we can build an optimization model. In it, on the ba-sis of a multi-alternative approach, the selection of components

$$\sum_{m=1}^{M} a_m x_m \rightarrow \max, \sum_{m=1}^{M} \sum_{n_m=1}^{Nm} C_{nm} X_m X_{mn} \leq C,$$

$$X_m = \begin{cases} 1, \\ m = \overline{1, M} \end{cases}, X_{nm} = \begin{cases} 1, \\ n_m = \overline{1, N_m}, \\ 0, \end{cases} \sum_{n_m=1}^{Nm} Z_{mn} = 1. \tag{17}$$

3   The Approach that Allows Finding Future Solutions in Internet of Things Systems

We will solve the specified optimization problem from the condition that those x_{mn} that are deterministic $\tilde{x}_{mn}$, will become random and their distribution will be appropriate

$$P(x_{mn} = 1) = \rho_{xmn}, \sum_{n=1}^{Nm} \rho_{xmn} = 1, (m = \overline{1, M}), \tag{18}$$

is important to consider the condition

$$P(\tilde{x}_{mn} = 1) = P(A_{mn}), (m = \overline{1, M}). \tag{19}$$

We believe that there is information on the number of the corresponding disjunctive experience A_{mn}. It is seen as a consequence of experience A_m.

In this case, the values of boolean variables x_{mn} are compared to it [9].

We associate the process of simulating such a consequence with an algorithm (Θ_1), operating with the following ordered arrays:

$$(n = 1, 2, 3, ..., N) \, and \, (P_{xm1}, P_{xm1} + P_{xm2} + P_{xm3}, ..., 1). \tag{20}$$

After analyzing the results obtained, we get a uniform random search. It is constructed proceeding from the fact that we consider probabilities $A - P(A_{mn}) = \frac{1}{N_m} (m = \overline{1, M},$ $n = \overline{1, N_m})$, in an a priori way.

The search will be directed. For this we use multi-alternative optimization models. We will need the probabilities indicated in the previous paragraph in the course of the simulation experiment if $(k = 1)$.

If the experiment continues $(k\rangle1)$, then the probabilities are based on predictive estimates $B^k(x_{mn})$.

That is, the probabilities will be different, and they are associated with the scheme Θ_2:

$$P_{xmn}^{k+1} = P_{xmn}^k + B^k(x_{mn}), \sum_{n=1}^{N_m} P_{xmn}^k = 1, \sum_{n=1}^{N_m} P_{xmn}^{k+1} = 1. \tag{21}$$

In practice, it is of interest to calculate predictive estimates. They are related to the algorithm (Θ_3).

The optimization model will be dichotomous, it has no unlimited restrictions:

$$\Psi(x) \to \max, \tag{22}$$

In it $(M, N = 1)$, we also take into account $x = (x_1, x_2, ..., x_m)$, $x_m = \begin{cases} 1, \\ 0, (m = \overline{1, M}) \end{cases}$ which is a vector of Boolean variables.

We can represent the specified model (22) under the condition of randomization

$$m\{\Psi(\tilde{x})\} \to \max, \tag{23}$$

It is required to take into account that $\tilde{x}$ - will be characterized by the distribution

$$\rho(\tilde{x}_m = 1) = \rho_{xm}; P(\tilde{x}_m = 0) = q_{xm}. \tag{24}$$

In this formula, we use the notation

$$x_m = \begin{cases} 1, \, if \, \rho_{xm} \geq 0, 5, \\ \\ 0, \, if \, \rho_{xm} \langle 0, 5. \end{cases} \tag{25}$$

The process of calculating prognostic estimates is underway. It requires that it be based on the preference of local enhancements. There is a condition for them:

$$m_{\tilde{x}^{k+1}}\{\Psi(\tilde{x})\} - m_{\tilde{x}^k}\{\Psi(\tilde{x})\}\rangle0. \tag{26}$$

In it, we take into account the pseudo-gradient. What is its role? Then the algorithm (Θ_2), will converge with the attraction $B^k(x_m)$ being the estimates. As a result of the modification, the algorithm Θ_{31} will be as follows:

$$B^k_{calc}(x_m) = \left\{ P^k_{\gamma m} + P^{k+1}_{\lambda m} \left[q^k_{\gamma m} \ae \right. \right.$$

$$\left(\Delta^k_{2m} \Psi \left(\tilde{x}^k \right) \right) \times \Delta^k_{1m} \Psi \left(\tilde{x}^k \right)) - P^k_{\gamma m} \ae$$

$$\left(-\Delta^k_{2m} \Psi \left(\tilde{x}^k \right) \Delta^k_{1m} \Psi \left(\tilde{x}^k \right) \right)] \} \times \left[q^k_{xm} \ae \right. \tag{27}$$

$$\left(\Delta^k_{1m} \Psi \left(\tilde{x}^k \right) \right) - P_{xm} \ae \left(-\Delta^k_{1m} \Psi \left(\tilde{x}^k \right) \right)].$$

In the specified expression $\tilde{\gamma}_m$, $\tilde{\lambda}_m$, they will be random boolean values

$$P_{\gamma m} = P(\tilde{\gamma}_m = 1); \quad q_{\gamma m} = P(\tilde{\gamma}_m = 0);$$

$$P_{\lambda m} = P\left(\tilde{\lambda}_m = 1 \right); \quad q_{\lambda m} = P(\lambda_m = 0);$$

$$P^k_{\gamma m} = P^k_{\gamma m} + P^{k+1}_{\lambda m} \left[q^k_{\gamma m} \ae \left(\Delta^k_{2m} \Psi \left(\tilde{x}^k \right) \times \Delta^k_{1m} \Psi \left(\tilde{x}^k \right) \right) - P^k_{\gamma m} \ae \right. \tag{28}$$

$$\left(-\Delta^k_{2m} \Psi \left(\tilde{x}^k \right) \Delta^k_{1m} \Psi \left(\tilde{x}^k \right) \right);$$

$\Delta^k_{1m} \Psi \left(\tilde{x}^k \right)$, $\Delta^k_{2m} \Psi \left(\tilde{x}^k \right)$ - are considered as realizations of random variables

$$\Delta^k_m \Psi = \Psi \left(\tilde{x}^k / \tilde{x}^k_m = 1 \right) - \Psi \left(\tilde{x}^k / x^k_m = 0 \right); \tag{29}$$

$\tilde{x}^k = \{ \tilde{x}^k_\upsilon \}$, $(\upsilon = \overline{1, M}, \upsilon \neq m)$ - vector containing random boolean variables;

$$(a) = \begin{cases} 1, \text{ if } a \rangle 0, \\ \\ 0, \text{ if } a \rangle 0. \end{cases} \tag{30}$$

We use the Lagrange function in (17). Then if it is possible to calculate the variation for the variable x_m. It is necessary to take the following steps: 1) for evaluating the x_m variation (29); 2) for x_m, N_m, if $x_m = 1$ by variation (12), when we must apply $\sum_{n=1} x_{mn} = 1$ in the problem.

Based on a random approach, we make a calculation $x_m = 1$, then

$$\nabla_m F = \sum_{\substack{v=1 \\ v \neq m}}^{M} a_v x_v + \lambda \sum_{\substack{v=1 \\ v \neq m}}^{M} c_n x_v x_n - (a_m + c_{nm} x_{nm}) - \sum_{\substack{v=1 \\ v \neq m}}^{M} a_v x_v - \lambda \sum_{\substack{v=1 \\ v \neq m}}^{M} \sum_{n=1}^{N} c_{nv} x_v x_{nv}. \tag{31}$$

The distribution by variables x_{nm} will be as follows

$$p_{1m}, p_{2m}, \ldots, p_{Nm} \tag{32}$$

We proceed from the fact that $\sum_{n=1}^{N_m} p_{nm} = 1$.

4 The Formation of an Integrated Approach When Building IoT Systems, Taking into Account Promising Options

We have to build for each m-th IoT system (14). The process of ranking these systems is underway. This requires the formation of comprehensive expert assessments. Their creation is influenced by various characteristics.

Then the process of building ranks takes place β_{nm}, $m = \overline{1, M}$ $n = \overline{1, N_m}$,.. for them, the corresponding probabilities p_{nm} can be compared:

$$p_{nm} = \frac{\beta_{nm}}{\sum\limits_{n=1}^{N_m} \beta_{nm}}. \tag{33}$$

The variational simulation stops after a certain number of steps. What are the results? Perspective variants will be generated for the distributions p_{km}^* and p_{nm}^*. Then we need to aggregate the resulting variants Θ_7. Then genetic algorithms allow you to get an integrated environment.

New options among the promising ones allow you to ensure aggregation. Then we come to a situation in which there will be at least two options that will be promising

$$x_l = \{Z_{lm}\}, Z_{lm} = \begin{cases} 1 \\ m = \overline{1, M}, \quad l \in \overline{1, L}, \\ 0 \end{cases}$$

$$x_t = \{Z_{tm}\}, Z_{tm} = \begin{cases} 1 \\ m = \overline{1, M}, \quad t \in \overline{1, L}, \quad t \neq 1. \\ 0 \end{cases} \tag{34}$$

In the course of modeling, we consider the specified set x_l, $l = \overline{1, L}$ as a population $= (x_1, ..., x_l, ..., x_L)$. When the process of building it takes place, we consider the parent pair. It is described using individuals x_l, x_t. There are opportunities for their reproduction. It is important to correctly form the aggregation algorithm.

What can he depend on? A pair of parents x_l, $x_t \in \Pi$ can be formed in different ways. This will be determined by how the crossing process will take place, as well as the breeding process.

It is required to implement the specified processes correctly. Then the calculation of integral estimates of the variants F_l, $l = \overline{1, L}$ is required. In the course of calculations, we consider them in the form of degrees of fitness $\mu(x_l)$ for such individuals x_l, in which there is a genotype $E(x_l)$.

Let us give an analysis of the crossing process. On its basis, the corresponding individuals will be selected for parental pairs. We distinguish local populations $\Pi_g \neq \emptyset$, $g = \overline{1, G}(g \leq L)$. At the same time, in the process of crossing, panmixia of genotypes is taken into account. What is the peculiarity of this approach? For individuals $(x_1, ..., x_l, ..., x_L)$, the values of Hemming distances between a pair of genotypes will be 0. It is required to select a parental pair. In order to satisfy this condition, we look at two individuals $x_l \in \Pi_{g1} x_t \in \Pi_{g2}(\Pi_{g1} \neq \Pi_{g2})$ in which a random selection is made according to local populations. In this case, it is necessary to rely on probability distributions [11].

$$P_g = L_g/L, g = \overline{1, G}, \tag{35}$$

The L_g are considered in terms of the size of the local population.

Opportunities exist to apply other systems during crossbreeding. Their choice is influenced by the Hemming distances between genotypes $\mathring{A}(x_l)$ and $\mathring{A}(x_t)$ that are associated with the corresponding individuals $x_l, x_t \in \Pi$. When the condition is met:

$$d[E(x_l), E(x_t)] = \|E(x_l) + E(x_t)\| \le d_0, \tag{36}$$

in which $d_0 > 0$, as well as the $(Ex_l) = (l_0(1), ..., l_0(m), ..., l_0(M)), l_0(m)$ – allelic m-th locus, which corresponds to the l-th individual, $l_0(m) = z_{ml}$, then we consider the individuals in the form of close relatives. Additional conditions may apply. In general, this process is considered as inbreeding. But the opposite condition may be fulfilled

$$d[E(x_l), E(x_t)]\rangle d_0. \tag{37}$$

Then we talk about outbreeding. This will be another option associated with the selection of the parental pair.

The next stage is aimed at forming an assortative crossing system. To build it, information is required to quantify the degree of fitness. Let assortative cross be considered positive. Then individuals with close and high values of the degrees of fitness make it possible to ensure the creation of parental pairs. The probability distribution leads to support for the selection of individuals.

$$P_t = \mu(x_t)/\sum_{t=1}^{L} \mu(x_t), t = \overline{1, L}. \tag{38}$$

Another option is when assortative cross will be negative. Then we make a random choice of the individual. Proceed from distribution (38). The probability distribution allows you to choose another individual

$$P_t = [1/\mu(x_t)]\sum_{t=1}^{L} (1/\mu(x_l)), t = \overline{1, G}. \tag{39}$$

In an assortative cross corresponding to a positive case, there may be a special case. Then they resort to selective crossing. In the course of its implementation, an exception is made from the population P of such individuals that are characterized by a degree of fitness $\mu(x_l)$ not exceeding the average degree of fitness, which describes the population $\mu_{med} \mu_l \langle \mu_{med}$. The next step is based on the fact that in the probability distribution (16) we rely on a random choice.

The recombination of genes is at the heart of the breeding patterns of individuals. Then there are opportunities to build new aggregated options. As a result of recombination, new combinations of parental genes appear. Why is this happening? An allele in any gene of the parental homologous chromosome will be inherited to the offspring. In doing so, we apply Mendel's first law. The homologous chromosomes of the parents are compared based on the gene content. Provided that the alleles for the m-th $\left(m = \overline{1, M}\right)$ locus, as well as the maternal chromosome $\left[l_0^{OT}(m) = l_0^M(m) = l_0(m)\right]$, are the same, the process of conservation within the m-th gene in the offspring will take place. Otherwise $\left[l_0^{OT}(m) \neq l_0^M(m)\right]$, there will be a process of movement at a probability of 1/2, or the allele or allele $l_0^{OT}(m)$, inside the m-th locus of the gamete in the offspring. What will this lead to? A set of new aggregated options is being formed.

They are obtained as a result of the fact that the parental genes diverge randomly across the gametes of the offspring. There may be crossing over.

Then there is a mutual exchange of sections of homologous chromosomes. If it is simple, then the homologous chromosomes of the zygote, before they diverge into the daughter gametes of the offspring, will be broken at a point α that is random. The gap will be in 2 sections M_1^M and M_1^{OT}.

They correspond to genes 1 through α, and $M_2^M M_2^{OT}$. They also include genes from $(\alpha + 1)$ to M. After that, the necessary sections of linked genes are supported. Another option would be when restoring to its original form.

Let the degree of fitness for the new version be $\mu(X_{L+!})\rangle\mu^{\max}(X_l)$. In this case, it will be the inclusion of the specified option inside the set of promising options. In this case, the process of exclusion from the set of options will be carried out, in which $\mu^{\min}(x_l)$. The next step is related to the selection of individuals in terms of their correspondence to parental pairs. When will this process end? All possible parenting pairs should be considered.

Promising options should be shortened to speed up the task. Then we proceed from the fact that we form a reproductive group using breeding schemes. In such a case, it is required to analyze two basic schemes.

If we apply the first of them, then ordering is done for all individuals on the basis of the principle of decreasing values according to their degrees of fitness. We set the number in the reproductive group L^0. Inside the reproductive group R we will introduce individuals L^0, among those that will be ordered.

If we use the second of them, then we consider the average degree of fitness for all individuals

$$\mu^{med} = (1/L) \sum_{l=1}^{L} \mu(x_l) \tag{40}$$

We will include within the production group such individuals that are characterized by a degree of fitness with values no less than the average fitness

$$R = \left\{X_l \middle| \mu(X_l) \geq \mu^{med}(X_l), l = \overline{1, G}\right\}. \tag{41}$$

We consider the options corresponding to the reproductive group from the point of view of expert assessment [12]. As a result, opportunities arise for making the final choice according to the rational option.

In advance, in order to carry out the aggregation, we make a choice of the appropriate options. According to them, it is important to comply with the conditions for limiting financial resources. In this case, the degree of fitness is calculated according to the 1st option (1st individual):

$$
\mu_1(X = 1) = \alpha_1 \frac{\sum_{m=1}^{M} \beta_{nm1} - \sum_{m=1}^{M} \beta_{nm1}^{\min}}{\sum_{m=1}^{M} \beta_{nm1}^{\max} - \sum_{m=1}^{M} \beta_{nm1}^{\min}} + \alpha_2 \frac{\left(C - \sum_{m=1}^{M} c_{nm1}\right) - \left(C - \sum_{m=1}^{M} c_{nm1}^{\max}\right)}{\left(C - \sum_{m=1}^{M} c_{nm1}^{\min}\right) - \left(C - \sum_{m=1}^{M} c_{nm1}^{\max}\right)},
$$

$$(42)$$

In this expression, β_{nm1}, c_{nm1} - the rank of preference is considered in the form, as well as the costs for the nth component of the m-1 system of the Internet of Things, which will correlate with the 1st option, which is required in order to conduct aggregation:

$\beta_{nm1}^{\max}$, $\beta_{nm1}^{\min}$ - will be the maximum and the minimum value of the ranks by component in the m-1 IoT system. At the same time, the variants $I = \overline{1, L}$ that were involved in the course of aggregation are analyzed;

$c_{nm1}^{\max}$, $c_{nm1}^{\min}$ - are considered in the form of the maximum and minimum values of costs in order to carry out the process of moving the components of the m-th IoT system among the variants $I = \overline{1, L}$ that were involved in the course of aggregation (1). The choice of weight coefficients α_1 and α_2 we carry out, based on the fact that for the indicator of allocated financial resources for the movement of the subsystem, the options that were considered from the point of view for aggregation, we consider in the form of selected ones.

The rank values are taken into account only in the algorithm for generating random values z_{nm} associated with probabilities p_{nm}. In this regard, it is desirable in the course of calculations to proceed from the fact that $0.6 \le \alpha_1 \le 0.7$, then there will be $0.3 \le \alpha_2 \le 0.4$.

Since the ranks β_{nm} take into account complex estimates for a number of components characteristics, the basic procedures for choosing a rational choice from those obtained after aggregation are carried out for a subset of indicators using linguistic estimates (Θ_8). The structure of an integrated environment that provides a combination of procedures for multi-alternative optimization, aggregation, optimal selection and training is shown in Fig. 1.

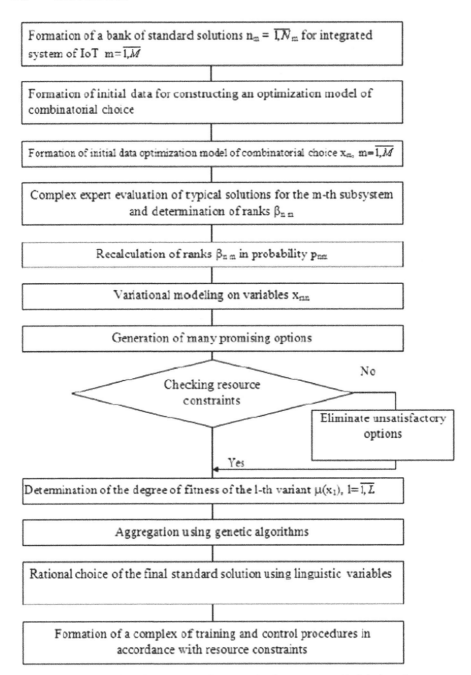

Fig. 1. The structure of the integrated environment for the computer-aided design of components of the Internet of Things systems.

5   Conclusion

The early stages of computer-aided design of complex systems of the Internet of Things represent the problem of structural synthesis on many different components, mostly based on typical solutions implemented in similar systems. It is advisable to organize the process of transfer and distribution of standard solutions in the automated selection mode as processes of active transfer. Adequate to this process is a multialternative optimization model, which in a formalized form describes the decomposition problem in accordance with a given criterion and restrictions on the classes of numbered sets and relations on them.

To build a structural synthesis algorithm, an approach based on replacing alternative variables with random Boolean variables with the organization of a three-level procedure is acceptable: the formation of a set of promising options, aggregation of the obtained options and the final choice with the involvement of expert information.

Since aggregation is considered as the construction of a new variant from among the promising ones, the implementation efficiency is achieved by using genetic algorithms used for combining, firstly, the method of selecting a pair of parents (crossing scheme), and secondly, the breeding scheme. At the same time, it is advisable to choose a rational option from those obtained after aggregation using linguistic variables for a set of indicators.

References

1. Lvovich, I.Y., Preobrazhenskiy, A.P., Choporov, O.N.: Investigation of reliability character-istics of software-defined networks. In: International Conference on Industrial Engineering, Applications and Manufacturing (ICIEAM), Sochi, Russia, pp. 1–5 (2019)
2. Abdelwahab, S., Hamdaoui, B., Guizani, M., Znati, T.: Network function virtualization in 5G. IEEE Commun. Mag. **54**(4), 84–91 (2016)
3. Lvovich, I.Ya., Lvovich, Ya.E., Preobrazhenskiy, A.P., Preobrazhenskiy, Yu.P., Choporov, O.N.: Modelling of information systems with increased efficiency with application of optimization-expert evaluation. In: Journal of Physics: Conference Series Krasnoyarsk Science and Technology City Hall of the Russian Union of Scientific and Engineering Associations; Polytechnical Institute of Siberian Federal University. Bristol, United Kingdom, p. 33079 (2019)
4. Evsyutin, O.O., Kokurina, A.S., Mescheriakov, R.V.: A review of methods of embedding information in digital objects for security in the internet of things. Comput. Opt. **43**(1), 137–154 (2019)
5. Odu, G.O., Charles-Owaba, O.E.: Review of multi-criteria optimization methods. Theory Appl. **3**, 01–14 (2013)
6. Shah, A., Ghahramani, Z.: Parallel predictive entropy search for batch global optimization of expensive objective functions. In: Advances in Neural Information Processing Systems, pp. 3330–3338 (2015)
7. Rios, L.M., Sahinidis, N.V.: Derivative-free optimization: a review of algorithms and comparison of software implementations. J. Global Optim. **54**, 1247–1293 (2013)
8. Orlova, D.E.: Stability of solutions in ensuring the functioning of organizational and technical systems. Modeling Optim. Inf. Technol. **6**(1), 325–336 (2018)
9. Lutakamale, A.S., Kaijage, S.: Wildfire monitoring and detection system using wireless sensor network: a case study of Tanzania. Wirel. Sens. Netw. **9**, 274–289 (2017)

10. Talluri, S., Kim, M.K., Schoenherr, T.: The relationship between operating efficiency and service quality: are they compatible? Int. J. Prod. Res. **51**, 2548–2567 (2013)
11. Stankovic, J.A.: Research directions for the internet of things. IEEE Internet Things J. **1**, 3–9 (2014)
12. Yao, Y., Chen, J.: Global optimization of a central air-conditioning system using (2021)

Optimization of the Intelligent Controller Rule Base Based on Fuzzy Clustering for Controlling an Object Operating in Changing Conditions

Alexandra Ignatyeva⬥, Viktor Kureychik, Vladimir Ignatyev(✉)⬥,
Viktor Soloviev⬥, Denis Beloglazov⬥, and Andrey Kovalev⬥

Southern Federal University, 105/42, Bolshaya Sadovaya Street, Rostov-on-Don 344006, Russia
vvignatev@sfedu.ru

Abstract. The paper proposes a method for optimizing the rule base of an intelligent controller based on fuzzy clustering for controlling an object operating in changing conditions. For modeling, a hybrid model of a technical object control with the action of a disturbing influence at the start is used. The model is implemented based on a PID-classical and intelligent PD-FUZZY-controller (IPD-FUZZY-controller) with the generated structure of a Sugeno-type fuzzy inference system and a developed model of an adaptive neuro-fuzzy inference system. In the developed hybrid model, the rule base for the IPD-FUZZY-controller has formed automatically based on data obtained from the PID-classical controller with subsequent training and fuzzy clustering, which allows reducing the number of membership functions and the number of fuzzy inference rules during the synthesis of the IPD-FUZZY-controller and ensuring effective and robust control of the object functioning in unforeseen external situations. A hybrid model proved the effectiveness of the proposed method before and after fuzzy clustering.

Keywords: Control · Intelligent controller · Adaptive neuro-fuzzy inference system · Rule base · Optimization · Fuzzy clustering

1 Introduction

Control systems using intelligent technologies are rapidly being introduced into automated production processes. In modern conditions, production is a complex system, the basis of which is the integration of various subsystems that require automation and trouble-free collaboration. The development of automated control systems in production is inherently associated with their intellectualization. This trend is due to the wide capabilities of the developed intelligent controllers in the development of task signals, ensuring stability to disturbances and improving the quality of transients.

More progressive controllers used in automated control systems are hybrid, synthesized based on traditional (classical) PI-PID controllers and fuzzy, neural network, and neuro-fuzzy controllers. Hybrid controllers are effective in ensuring reliability and accuracy in controlling a facility in unforeseen situations and in ensuring the desired control with maximum quality.

© Springer Nature Switzerland AG 2021
A. G. Kravets et al. (Eds.): CIT&DS 2021, CCIS 1448, pp. 149–162, 2021.
https://doi.org/10.1007/978-3-030-87034-8_12

The main tasks in the development of hybrid controllers are the task of fine-tuning all its parameters to ensure efficient control, including in emergencies, and the task of optimizing the controller parameters to reduce the load on computing resources and obtain the desired control with fewer labor costs.

The main reason for using intelligent controllers is the need to handle a large number of input and output effects. The rule base of such controllers can be up to several thousand. A detailed analysis of the need to use all the rules in the synthesis of a control model that allows one to get the desired control is a complex and urgent task, which requires new approaches and methods.

One of these methods is proposed in this work, which consists of optimizing the rule base of an intelligent controller based on fuzzy clustering to control an object operating in changing conditions.

2 Literature Review

Theoretical investigations of works in the considered subject area showed that great attention is paid to the problem of synthesis and parameters optimization of intelligent controllers.

Helem Sabina Sanchez et al. [1] developed tuning rules for robust fractional-order PID (FOPID) controllers based on multi-objective optimization using first-order-plus-dead-time (FOPDT) models. The problem of controlling the simultaneous minimization of the integrated absolute error has been solved, both for a given value and a response to a loading disturbance.

N. Xiong and L. Litz [2] presented a method for optimizing the number of control rules of a fuzzy controller. The main idea of the method is to identify and then combine conflicting rules, but not improve the efficiency of the fuzzy controller, which is its main disadvantage.

In paper [3], a method for controlling the position of wind turbine blades based on the fuzzy controller of the Takagi-Sugeno model is proposed.

In work [4], a method for automated synthesis of a fuzzy controller from a set of numerical data is proposed.

In article [5], a linear fuzzy PID controller is adjusted using the developed method for determining the optimal parameters. This method has disadvantages in training or adaptation of the controller when the parameters of the control object are changed.

In work [6], a hybrid system is developed in which the optimality of the PID controller parameters obtained using a genetic algorithm is achieved using a neural network, and then a fuzzy model rule base is constructed using a neural network.

Jeremy Kerr-Wilson and Witold Pedrycz [7] proposed a new methodology for extracting hierarchical architecture based on Takagi-Sugeno fuzzy rules from data. The architecture makes it possible to reduce the number of involved fuzzy rules and to simplify them.

Yanpeng Hu et al. [8] proposed a fuzzy controller design based on an improved genetic optimization algorithm to control an unmanned helicopter, the dynamic of which is modeled by the identification method in the frequency domain. It should be noted that the improved genetic algorithm developed by the authors is used to optimize the initial expert empirical fuzzy rules, which initially depend on the knowledge of subject matter experts, which is not an advantage over control systems in which fuzzy inference rules are generated automatically.

Nelles O. [9] proposed a method for optimizing the parameters of a fuzzy controller, which makes it possible to reduce the number of applied fuzzy rules. The main idea of the method is to reduce the term sets of the linguistic variable of a fuzzy controller to a simpler form, followed by checking the efficiency of the performed transformations.

The work [10] describes a method for synthesis the fuzzy controller rule base with its subsequent analysis and optimization using a genetic algorithm. The difference between the method is the use of two methods of encoding the parameters of the fuzzy controller and, accordingly, in the structure of the resulting chromosomes.

In work [11], a method for generating a base of fuzzy controller control rules based on cluster analysis and a genetic algorithm is proposed. A feature of the method is the ability to control the process of setting the parameters of the fuzzy controller to prevent the phenomenon of overfitting.

Z. Fan et al. [12] proposed a multi-level fuzzy model based on the clustering of fuzzy rules for forecasting problems. This approach can be useful for application in systems for monitoring operation and forecasting the technical condition of the equipment.

In work [13], fuzzy clustering is used to diagnose and predict wind turbine failures.

In work [14], the forest optimization algorithm (FOA) was used to improve the accuracy of the standard FCM algorithm.

Lei Li et al. [15] presented a new forecasting methodology called SSOFC-Apriori-WRP, which predicts wind energy and speed one day ahead. The problem of probabilistic forecasting of wind energy is solved using a combined intelligent structure and fuzzy clustering algorithm.

Mayank Baranwal and Srinivasa Salapaka [16] consider the problem of decomposition of large power grids into small and loosely coupled ones to simplify the process of managing power transmission systems. The rule-based expert control system uses fuzzy clustering to design local control actions during overload, underload, and separation.

The analysis of the works showed that one of the main directions in the development of methods for optimizing the parameters of intelligent controllers is the use of a hybrid approach, which consists of combining traditional control methods with methods based on artificial intelligence.

It should be noted that fuzzy clustering is practically not used as a tool for optimizing the parameters of intelligent controllers, which determines the scientific novelty of this work, which consists in the use of fuzzy clustering to reduce the number of fuzzy products and the number of membership functions (MF) when developing a fuzzy inference system.

To confirm the effectiveness of the method proposed in this work, a hybrid model of a technical object's control with the action of a disturbing influence at the start is used [18]. The model is synthesized using the PID-classical and IPD-FUZZY-controller with the Sugeno fuzzy inference system (SFIS) structure and the developed adaptive neuro-fuzzy inference system (ANFIS) model. In the hybrid model, the rule base for the IPD-FUZZY-controller is formed automatically based on the data obtained from the PID-classic controller, followed by training and fuzzy clustering.

The modeling task is to obtain a transient process when the object is controlled by an IPD-FUZZY-controller after fuzzy clustering (that is, with a reduced rule base and the number of MF) no worse than before fuzzy clustering.

3   Methodology Description

This work is a continuation of the research carried out by the authors on the development of methods for optimizing the procedure for the synthesis of intelligent controllers [17–20]. In particular, in [18], the authors solved the problem of obtaining better control of an object using an IPD-FUZZY-controller, which works in tandem with the PID-classical controller in the hybrid model. This hybrid model will be considered in this paper. The proposed method includes the following steps.

Step 1. Development of a hybrid control model based on a PID-classical and IPD-FUZZY-controller. The model is implemented based on a fuzzy inference system of the SFIS and an ANFIS. In the hybrid model, the rule base for the IPD-FUZZY-controller is formed automatically with the data obtained from the PID-classic controller.

Step 2. Development of ANFIS, which is a hybrid network using PID- and IPD-FUZZY controllers. When implementing a network, the indicators of the error of the output signal, its differential and control action, obtained from the PID-controller, are necessary to check the efficiency of the hybrid network. This allows determining the fact of its retraining. The indicators of the output signal's error, its control action, and differential, are necessary to form the training sample required to build a hybrid network.

Step 3. Generation of the SFIS structure.

Step 4. Fuzzy clustering of the error output signals' values, their differential, and control action, obtained from the classical and fuzzy controllers.

Step 5. Development of ANFIS, which is a hybrid network with the use of PID- and IPD-FUZZY controllers, in the implementation of which the clustered indicators of the output signal error, their differential, and control action, obtained from the PID-controller, are necessary to test the efficiency of the hybrid networks. This allows determining the fact of its retraining. The clustered indicators of the output signal error, its differential, and the control action, obtained from the fuzzy controller, are necessary to form the training sample required to build a hybrid network.

Step 6. Generation of a new SFIS structure.

Step 7. Modeling the operation of the resulting fuzzy inference systems before and after fuzzy clustering.

In the process of modeling, studies of the hybrid model are performed in the case of a disturbing effect (10% of the input effect) at the start.

The proposed method includes the following steps. The hybrid control model developed at the first step based on the PID-classical and IPD-FUZZY-controller is shown in Fig. 1.

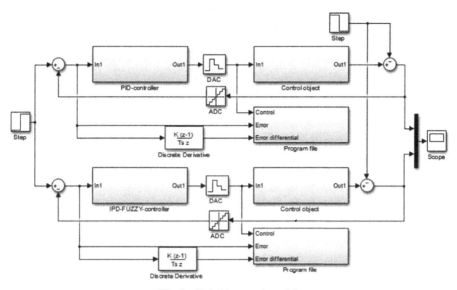

Fig. 1. Hybrid control model.

At the second step, to develop ANFIS in the form of a hybrid network, it is necessary to obtain the error output signals values, its differential, and control action as a result of the operation of the classical controller and the error output signals values, its differential, and control action as a result of the operation of the fuzzy controller. For this purpose, special software is used (Program file in Fig. 1).

Obtained after running the model, 67 values are partially presented in Table 1.

Table 1. The controller signals values.

PID-classical controller				IPD-FUZZY-controller		
Error		Error diffeential	Control	Error	Error differential	Control
1	1	0,6666	13,3761	1	0,6666	4,5572
2	1	0	3,17940	1	0	5,3905
3	1	0	3,27200	1	0	5,3905
...	...	...	...	...	...	...
66	– 0,0036	– 2,1e-05	0,8021	0,0059	– 1,0e-05	0,7953
67	– 0,0036	0	0,8021	0,0059	0	0,7953

In accordance with step 3, a SFIS is developed, as shown in Fig. 2.

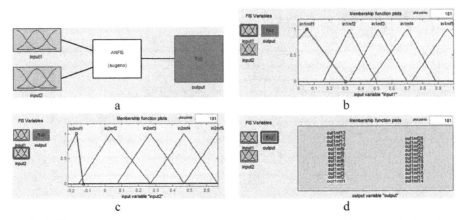

Fig. 2. SFIS: a. Generated structure; b. MF of the input deviation variable; c. MF of the input variable of the deviation differential; d. Required values of the output variable.

The hybrid network was trained using the backpropagation method. The training results are presented in Fig. 3.

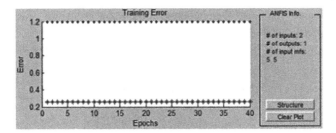

Fig. 3. Training results.

It can be seen from the graph that, using the backpropagation method, training ends after two cycles, which is confirmed by MATLAB.

The data obtained showed that the number of fuzzy rules is 25. Obtained structure of the IPD-FUZZY-regulator is shown in Fig. 4.

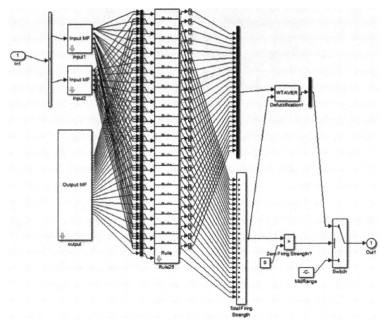

Fig. 4. Fuzzy controller structure.

The number of MF for each input linguistic variable (LV) is 5 (Fig. 5). The resulting SFIS structure is shown in Fig. 6.

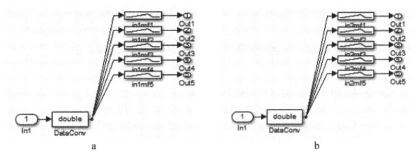

a

b

Fig. 5. LV structure: a. LV – Error; b. LV – Error differential.

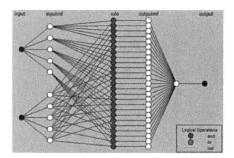

Fig. 6. Structure of the generated SFIS.

In accordance with step 4, to reduce the values for each controller for each indicator (error, error differential, and control action) fuzzy clustering of the data from Table 1 was applied. The results obtained after applying fuzzy clustering are presented graphically in Fig. 7.

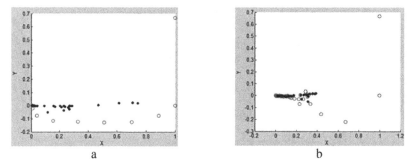

Fig. 7. Results of clustering: a. Training data; b. Validation data.

The obtained values for each controller for each indicator are presented in Table 2. The number of values decreased more than twice and amounted to 30.

At the fifth step, ANFIS is developed, but already clustered error output signals values, its differential, and control action obtained from the classical controller and the same parameters obtained from the fuzzy controller.

Table 2. Controller signals values after fuzzy clustering.

PID-classical controller			IPD-FUZZY-controller		
Error		Error differential	Control	Error	Error differential	Control
1	8,9e-01	3,5e-02	3,5e + 00	7,0e-02	4,4e-05	1,0e + 00
2	8,6e-01	3,8e-02	3,5e + 00	2,2e-02	− 5,1e-05	8,5e-01

(continued)

Table 2. (*continued*)

PID-classical controller			IPD-FUZZY-controller		
Error		Error differential	Control	Error	Error differential	Control

Error		Error differential	Control	Error	Error differential	Control
3	5,6e-02	– 4,3e-03	8,8e-01	8,9e-02	– 3,0e-04	1,1e + 00
...	...	...	...	...	...	...
29	9,7e-01	3,8e-02	3,8e + 00	2,4e-01	– 1,4e-02	2,3e + 00
30	9,6e-02	– 5,8e-03	9,5e-01	1,5e-01	– 9,2e-05	1,4e + 00

The SFIS developed in the sixth step after fuzzy clustering is shown in Fig. 8.

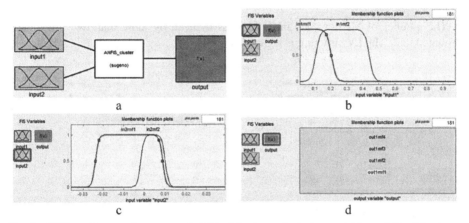

Fig. 8. SFIS: a. Generated structure; b. MF of the input deviation variable; c. MF of the input variable of the deviation differential; d. Required values of the output variable.

The hybrid network was trained using the error backpropagation method. The training results are presented in Fig. 9.

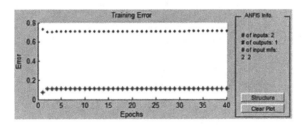

Fig. 9. Training results.

The graph shows that when using the backpropagation method, the learning process ends after two cycles, which is confirmed by MATLAB.

The data obtained showed that the number of fuzzy rules decreased more than six times and amounted to 4. Obtained structure of the IPD-FUZZY-regulator is shown in Fig. 10.

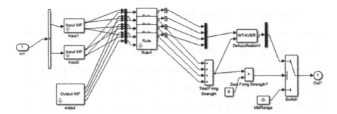

Fig. 10. IPD-FUZZY-regulator structure.

The number of MF for each input LV was reduced by more than two times and amounted to 2. The LV structure is shown in Fig. 11.

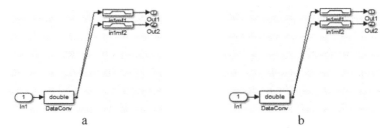

a   b

Fig. 11. LV structure: a. LV – Error; b. LV – Error differential.

The resulting SFIS is shown in Fig. 12.

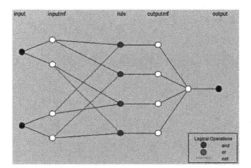

Fig. 12. Structure of the generated SFIS.

4   Results

The generated fuzzy inference systems (before and after fuzzy clustering) are integrated into the hybrid control model presented in Fig. 1. The obtained simulation results are presented in Fig. 13.

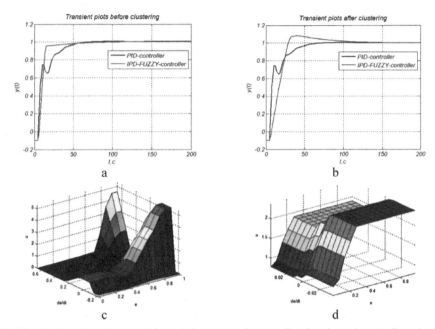

Fig. 13. Graphs of transients and fuzzy inference surfaces: a. Graphs of transients before clustering; b. Graphs of transients after clustering; c. The surface of fuzzy inference before clustering; d. The surface of fuzzy inference after clustering.

The analysis of the presented surfaces showed that the definition domains of the input variables in Fig. 13(c) and Fig. 13(d) differ, but not significantly. Definition domains of error signals, error differential and control action before fuzzy clustering [0; 1], [0,6; –0,2], [0; 5,5]. Definition domains of error signals, error differential and control action after fuzzy clustering [0; 1], [0,04; –0,035], [0,8; 2,4].

It should also be noted that the fuzzy input surface obtained after performing the fuzzy clustering procedure is more unambiguous over the entire definition domain, smooth, and does not contain discontinuities.

This suggests that the quality of the transient process when controlling the object using the IPD-FUZZY-controller obtained after starting the hybrid model presented in Fig. 1, not worse when applying fuzzy clustering. With practically the same duration of the steady-state mode, in the case of control using the IPD-FUZZY-controller, there is a slight overshoot (Fig. 13(b)).

It should be noted that the parameters of training the hybrid network before and after fuzzy clustering did not change. When generating a new (based on clustered indicators)

SFIS structure, MF were used not of a triangular shape, but the MF psigMF (product of two sigmoid MF), which showed the best modeling results.

5   Discussion

The method proposed in this work for optimizing the rule base of an intelligent controller has shown its effectiveness when implemented in a hybrid control model.

The main positive effect of the method is to optimize the parameters of the intelligent controller based on fuzzy clustering, which reduces labor costs in its development without losing the quality of regulation.

In comparison with the works [6, 8], in which a genetic algorithm is used to optimize the controller parameters, the tuning of which for a specific problem is rather complicated, the proposed method is more efficient and requires minimal calculations.

In contrast to work [11], which proposes to use expert knowledge and further cluster it in the development of FIS, in this work the values of each LV are clustered after the synthesis of the first FIS (step 3).

Next, based on the clustered values, a new FIS is synthesized (step 6). Given that the synthesis of the first FIS is performed when developing ANFIS, in which the training set for building a hybrid network is formed by an IPD-FUZZY-controller with an automatically generated rule base [18, 19], the possibility of error in the synthesis of a new FIS is significantly reduced.

The application of the developed method allowed:

1. Reduce more than two times the number of values required for the development of ANFIS for each controller for each indicator (error, error differential, and control action).
2. Reduce more than two times the number of MF for each input LV when developing an IPD-FUZZY-controller in a hybrid control model.
3. Reduce more than six times the number of fuzzy rules when developing an IPD-FUZZY-controller.

The achieved simulation results showed that the quality of object control with the proposed optimization method remains sufficiently high while reducing the developer's labor costs by several times.

6   Conclusion

With the increasing complexity of automated control systems, it is necessary to solve problems associated with their optimization during development. Currently, this is due to the high cost of equipment on which such systems are implemented and software for equipment control.

Programming a real automated control system is a complex task, depending on the number of input and output parameters.

More complex is the task of developing the scientific foundations used in automated systems for object control. Information about the behavior of a particular technical object is available to experts who can be involved in the development of intelligent controllers.

Considering the field of intelligent control based on fuzzy logic, it is difficult to determine the number of terms in the LV term-sets, which directly affects the size of the controller's rule base. A rule base consisting of hundreds or thousands of rules will be difficult for an expert to create, it will necessarily be either incomplete or redundant, and contain errors.

This will lead to additional labor costs and the use of excessive computing resources.

The approach proposed in this work, consisting of the use of a hybrid model, in which the rule base for the IPD-FUZZY-controller is formed automatically based on data obtained from the PID-classical controller with subsequent training and fuzzy clustering, allows:

- Optimize the rule base of the IPD-FUZZY-controller by reducing the number of MF required to describe linguistic variables and the number of rules when developing it.
- Increase the performance of the hybrid model by reducing the required number of computational operations in terms of issuing control actions.
- Reduce labor costs when developing an IPD-FUZZY-controller without losing the quality of regulation.

Acknowledgments. The presented research was carried out at the frames of the project "Creating a high-tech production of hardware and software systems for processing agricultural raw materials based on microwave radiation" (Agreement № 075-11-2019-083 dated 20.12.2019 with the Ministry of Education and Science of the Russian Federation, Agreement № 18 dated 20.09.2019 of Southern Federal University, work № HD/19-25-RT in Southern Federal University).

References

1. Sanchez, H.S., Padula, F., Visioli, A., Vilanova, R.: Tuning rules for robust FOPID controllers based on multi-objective optimization with FOPDT models. ISA Trans. **66**, 344–361 (2017). https://doi.org/10.1016/j.isatra.2016.09.021
2. Xiong, N., Litz, L.: Reduction of fuzzy control rules by means of premise learning – method and case study. Fuzzy Sets Syst. **132**, 217–231 (2002)
3. Civelek, Z.: Optimization of fuzzy logic (Takagi-Sugeno) blade pitch angle controller in wind turbines by genetic algorithm. Eng. Sci. Technol. Int. J. **23**(1), 1–9 (2020). https://doi.org/10.1016/j.jestch.2019.04.010
4. Dutu, L., Mauris, G., Bolon, P.: A fast and accurate rule-base generation method for Mamdani fuzzy systems. IEEE Trans. Fuzzy Syst. **26**(2), 715–733 (2018). https://doi.org/10.1109/TFUZZ.2017.2688349
5. Kudinov, Y., Kolesnikov, V., Pashchenko, F., Pashchenko, A., Papic, L.: Optimization of fuzzy PID controller's parameters. In: XIIth International Symposium «Intelligent Systems», INTELS 2016, 5–7 October 2016, Moscow, Russia. Procedia Comput. Sci. **103**, 618–622 (2017)
6. Savran, A., Kahraman, G.: A fuzzy model based adaptive PID controller design for nonlinear and uncertain processes. ISA Trans. **53**, 280–288 (2014)

7. Kerr-Wilson, J., Pedrycz, W.: Generating a hierarchical fuzzy rule-based model. Fuzzy Sets Syst. **381**, 124–139 (2020). https://doi.org/10.1016/j.fss.2019.07.013

8. Hu, Y., Yang, Y., Li, S., Zhou, Y.: Fuzzy controller design of micro-unmanned helicopter relying on improved genetic optimization algorithm. Aerosp. Sci. Technol. **98** (2020). https://doi.org/10.1016/j.ast.2020.105685

9. Nelles, O.: GA-based generation of fuzzy rules. In: Pedrycz, W. (ed.) Fuzzy Evolutionary Computation, pp. 269–295. Springer, Boston (1997). https://doi.org/10.1007/978-1-4615-6135-4_12

10. Gegov, A., Sanders, D., Vatchova, B.: Aggregation of inconsistent rules for fuzzy rule base simplification. Int. J. Knowl.-Based Intell. Eng. Syst. **21**(3), 135–145 (2017)

11. Al-Shamma, M., Abbod, M.: Automatic generation of fuzzy classification rules using granulation-based adaptive clustering. In: IEEE Systems Conference (SysCon 2015) (2015). https://doi.org/10.1109/syscon.2015.7116825

12. Fan, Z., Chiong, R., Hu, Z., Lin, Y.: A multi-layer fuzzy model based on fuzzy-rule clustering for prediction tasks. Neurocomputing **410**, 114–124 (2020). https://doi.org/10.1016/j.neucom.2020.04.031

13. de la Hermosa Gonzalez-Carrato, R.R.: Wind farm monitoring using Mahalanobis distance and fuzzy clustering. Renew. Energy **123**, 526–540 (2018)

14. Chaghari, A., Feizi-Derakhshi, M., Balafar, M.: Fuzzy clustering based on Forest optimization algorithm. J. King Saud University – Comput. Inf. Sci. **30**, 25–32 (2018)

15. Li, L., Yin, X., Jia, X., Sobhani, B.: Day ahead powerful probabilistic wind power forecast using combined intelligent structure and fuzzy clustering algorithm. Energy **192**, 116498 (2020)

16. Baranwal, M., Salapaka, S.: Clustering and supervisory voltage control in power systems. Int. J. Electr. Power Energy Syst. **109**, 641–651 (2019). https://doi.org/10.1016/j.ijepes.2019.02.025

17. Vladimir Vladimirovich, I., Tudevdagva, U., Kovalev, A.V., Borisovich, S.O., Maksimov, A.V., Sergeevna, I.A.: Model of adaptive system of neuro-fuzzy inference based on PID- and PID-fuzzy-controllers. In: Silhavy, R. (ed.) CSOC 2020. AISC, vol. 1225, pp. 519–533. Springer, Cham (2020). https://doi.org/10.1007/978-3-030-51971-1_43

18. Ignatyev, V., Kureichik, V., Spiridonov, O.: Modelirovaniye gibridnogo upravleniya na osnove algoritma samoorganizatsii robastnykh baz znaniy. [Modeling hybrid control based on a robust knowledge base self-organization algorithm]. In: Proceedings of the International Scientific and Technical Congress «Intelligent Systems and Information Technologies – 2020» («IS & IT-2020», «IS & IT'20»). Scientific edition in 2 volumes, vol. 1, pp. 328–336. Stupina S. A. Publishing House, Taganrog (2020). ISBN 978-5-6043689-8-5. ISBN 978-5-6043689-9-2

19. Ignatyev, V., Kovalev, A., Spiridonov, O., Kureychik, V., Soloviev, V., Ignatyeva, A.: A method of optimizing the rule base in the Sugeno fuzzy inference system using fuzzy cluster analysis. Int. Rev. Electr. Eng. (I.R.E.E.) **15**(4), 316–327 (2020)

20. Ignatyev, V., Soloviev, V., Beloglazov, D., Kureychik, V., Andrey, K., Ignatyeva, A.: The fuzzy rule base automatic optimization method of intelligent controllers for technical objects using fuzzy clustering. In: Kravets, A.G., Groumpos, P.P., Shcherbakov, M., Kultsova, M. (eds.) CIT&DS 2019. CCIS, vol. 1084, pp. 135–152. Springer, Cham (2019). https://doi.org/10.1007/978-3-030-29750-3_11

New Communicative Strategies for the Affective Robot: F-2 Going Tactile and Complimenting

Liliya Volkova[1,2(✉)] 📵, Andrey Ignatev[2] 📵, Nikita Kotov[2] 📵,
and Artemy Kotov[1,3,4] 📵

[1] Russian State University for the Humanities,
Miusskaya pl., 6, Moscow 125993, Russia
liliya@bmstu.ru, kotov_aa@nrcki.ru
[2] Bauman Moscow State Technical University, 2-ya Baumanskaya ul. 5-1,
Moscow 105005, Russia
[3] National Research Center «Kurchatov Institute», Pl. Akademika Kurchatova,
1, Moscow 123182, Russia
[4] Moscow State Linguistic University,
ul. Ostozhenka, 38, Moscow 119034, Russia

Abstract. This paper is dedicated to modeling affective reactions in a communicative robot via achieving communicative goals. The effective robot F-2's software processes multimodal input and facts extracted from input texts. Sentences in Russian are translated with a syntactic-semantic parser into semantic structures that represent sentences meanings and comprise valencies and semantic markers. Basing on the input, the robot changes its emotional state over time, generating effective remarks along with gestures and gazes. The emotional state is modeled via microstates, each represented as a communicative goal, which is further matched to multimodal reactions scenarios from a database. New communicative strategies are introduced. Basing on human features extraction from video, a robot implements strategies of complimenting and making friends; in both cases, it points at the addressee's look, including clothes and glasses. With tactile sensors, the robot is taught to react to touching; thus the gap in perception is filled which had previously caused the loss of interest by people inclined to tactile communication. Precision is estimated for both methods which are on the basis of new communicative strategies.

Keywords: Dialogue system · Affective robot · Communicative robot · Artificial intelligence · Tactile sensors · Computer vision · Complimenting

1 AI: Affective Companionship

I do think, in time, people will have, sort of, relationships with certain kinds of robots − not every robot, but certain kinds of robots − where they might feel that it is a sort of friendship, but it's going to be of a robot-human kind.
Cynthia Breazeal.

© Springer Nature Switzerland AG 2021
A. G. Kravets et al. (Eds.): CIT&DS 2021, CCIS 1448, pp. 163–176, 2021.
https://doi.org/10.1007/978-3-030-87034-8_13

"Empathetic computing" is addressed to the growing need for home healthcare solutions, including those for elderly people or those with disabilities [5, 9, 34]. Affective assistants are assumed to be helpful for not only entertainment purposes but for monitoring human health, for collecting and transmitting data from a patient's home. The task is set as companionship: conducting a conversation, recognizing human feelings and states, understanding user intents, and responding to one's needs dynamically [5, 41]. Moreover, due to the coronavirus pandemic, a new task arises: to support people who are obliged to stay home and who crave conversations and affection. This sets the focus to empathetic computing and to developing effective communicative agents and robots with specific social functions.

Dialogue systems are classified into task-oriented and non-task-oriented [2]. As to voice-recognizing assistants and the majority of toys, these task-oriented solutions lack affection and are limited to a set of domain-based scripts in the same way as pioneer systems of both classes were. The most effective reactions turn out to be simple *if-then* rules, e.g. Yandex Alice's voice assistant would say the phrase "Anyone can offend a robot" in case it gets offensive words as input. Modeling more natural reactions is a key to the audience's hearts. Emotions are regarded here as mediators of conversational content, allowing interlocutors to form the common ground and sometimes to understand and align each other's moods [13, 17, 19]. Hence, an effective agent would be capable of initiating the common ground effects and of captivating human beings.

The effect is a general term related to emotions, but applicable to robots. Several approaches exist to emotional state modeling, the most prominent is Ekman's basic emotions set and the representation of emotions as points in a continuous two-dimensional space, with valence and arousal as axes [28]. Attitudes can be modeled as amalgamations of emotions [18], or as a weighted combination of pleasure, arousal, and dominance, resulting in an emotion [3]. Switching states can be modeled via Petri nets [2, 27] . Another approach introduces microstates which take control one by one concurrently and stand for intentions [1], each having its activation degree at each time. In this research, the latter approach is adopted.

Basing on text semantics processing and simulating surface emotional phenomena [4], several breakthroughs have been made: IBug [14], SEMAINE [29, 31], Greta [11], and Max [3, 22]. Max changes their emotional state over time; he is taught to get offended, then to calm down, and to return to communication as time passes by. It can get offended with a special bad word 'pancake', in this case, it walks out of the screen, but calms down and returns as its *anger* emotion activation value fades.

One particularly important aspect of affective agents and robots design is their prototyping. There are different ways of visualizing an AI (or not – headliner voice assistants don't have dynamic faces). First, there were several toys: Aibo, iCat, Tamagotchi. Their appearance uncovered the problem of the limitedness of reactions scenarios: a human user gets bored and loses interest pretty fast. The most captivating of the toys was Tamagotchi: what attracted people to it was the phenomenon of behavioral cues which a human would interpret as emotions. The so-called Tamagotchi effect discovery was a milestone: the fact is, human beings tend to get attracted to toys and robots and to humanize them in case they show expressive emotional phenomena. Complicated 3D figures for computer agents have their weakness called the "uncanny valley" [24]: when an android looks more scary than natural. A niche's been found – a non-anthropomorphic affective assistant reacting rather in a human way [36]. Our project started with a computer agent, sort of a cartoon character; then it was given a body with hands and a display standing for the face. The agent became a robot called F-2 (see Fig. 1). Somehow it touches the same strings as Tamagotchi did: it shows affective reactions – it can look *sad, happy, bored,* etc. We call the intention to express something *a communicative goal.*

F-2 is an affective robot, which uses a natural language processor for understanding input sentences, changes its emotional state, and produces multimodal reactions – text and gestures (speech synthesis is powered by Yandex SpeechKit [40]). The nonverbal communicative behavior is important, as it can express up to 60% of the information [7] and gives a personal touch, allowing to show the attitude towards the addressee or the subject.

2   Understanding the Text and Reacting

> *"What do you think, Sally?".*
> *Sally's two doors opened and then shut with a cushioned slam.*
> *"What's that?" said Gellhorn.*
> *"That's the way Sally laughs."*
> *(Isaac Asimov, "Sally").*

In order to produce multimodal reactions, a robot should process natural language sentences, ending up with facts extracted, and then use some procedures and/or scenarios to show its response which is dependent not only on its rules of commenting but on its emotional state as well. This section shows the design of this mechanism.

An interlocutor gives a cue – a phrase. Our parser processes it on three layers of natural language processing: (i) morphology, (ii) syntax, and (iii) semantics. First, each token is morphologically analyzed and is associated with one or several hypotheses (in the case of homonymy) of its morphological parameters. Second, all of the tokens in the phrase serve as input for filling a stack with words. If a word is found to be morphologically ambiguous, the number of stacks increases in order to include all of the possible hypotheses. Syntactic rules are used to get a dependency tree, reduced to but one node. To form a dependency tree, the stack head is reduced (when possible) with any of the existing 450 syntactic rules: each rule can reduce a list of tokens in its right-hand side to the left-hand side head (e.g. to form a predicate group out of a predicate and its object). The parser presently operates with a morphological dictionary of 98,000 lemmas. The result is a syntactic dependency tree, where subtrees are annotated with semantic valencies, as indicated by the rules. Dependency trees are the source for facts mining. Facts are extracted assets of semantic markers, assigned to words in each valency, as specified by semantic roles (e.g., agent-predicate-patients (subject-verb-object)).

The agent's reactions are dependent on its "emotional state". To simulate the latter, we adopted the approach of specifying a set of concurrent control states, each of the states having its activation degree (changing over time). These states correspond to emotion-driven reactions, which were selected due to functional analysis of non-verbal communicative behavior from the REC multimodal corpus of human behavior in emotional situations [21]. Functional annotation of human actions is conducted, and elements of multimodal expression of communicative functions are detected on layers of text, gestures, and facial expressions (one function can be implemented via hands and/or head movements and via text, e.g. *agreement*). F-2 expresses its current emotional state with elements of communicative behavior [20] translated to the robot. Multimodal reactions are generated in BML markup [33] and include text, gestures, and gazes. BML frames are sent to the robot control subsystem and then rendered on the robot.

The abovementioned microstates are often referred to as communicative goals. Following the rules approach [3, 23, 30], we developed dominant scripts for implementing emotions and rational scripts for considering a particular situation as a problem to solve (a total of 82 scripts). A script matches each communicative goal to a fact of a given type (e.g. the 'amaze' scenario is activated for a fact where an agent gets to a big and unusual world, given as a node with the 'locative' valency). Input facts or events from other perception channels can activate more than one script, each produces a goal with a different activation level, which is variable and fades over time. The topmost goal is selected to implement the output reaction in speech and behavior (each goal is attached to a list of possible reactions; a reaction is selected randomly from such a list from the database). F-2 can pass through several emotional *microstates*, thus the goal of this approach is achieved: to make reactions most natural via producing these in real-time depending on events. Tuning the sensitivity of activations and fulfilling the database of emotional reactions is the key to reaching the most adequate model, this is a research process.

There is but one particular predefined scenario, which has a small activation that doesn't fade so that in case there is no event-activated scenario, this one would be selected for performing. In order to make the robot look sort of alive all of the time, the following strategy was introduced: F-2 doesn't freeze when nothing happens, it simulates breathing instead, along with watching its hands or the ceiling. A video of the simulation of the standby state can be found in [8].

Two classes of scenarios will be described further, both based on multimodal input.

3 F-2 Going Tactile

> *"Hi, Sally, how'd you like a drive?"*
> *Sally's motor revved up. She backed away.*
> *"Don't push her, Mr. Gellhorn," I said. "She's liable to be a little skittish."*
> *(Isaac Asimov, "Sally").*

The team conducts experiments with invited respondents giving feedback on F-2's dialogue conducting. Respondents estimate their experience in terms of "human-like", "realistic", "nice", we aggregate feedback on different stages of F-2's evolution. One particular case imposed a task to solve. In this experiment, youngsters were to make a puzzle with helpful comments and verbal and gestures directions by F-2. A special computer vision module tracks pieces of a tangram puzzle by QR-codes on them; and

F-2's strategies are to be helpful and to give hints ("Put that green piece on the left") or to point out mistakes, as well as to comment out what was done correctly (e.g., F-2 nods and says "That's right"). People in this situation act in different ways. Few cases surprised us: youngsters tried to communicate with F-2 in a tactile way as if F-2 could feel their touch. We mostly consider F-2 as an AI, as a smart and talkative creature, which is somehow distantiated from people. Perhaps this is brought up as a tradition from times when dialogue systems were young, and all of the communication was via a terminal, as with Weizenbaum's ELIZA [38] or Winograd's SHRDLU [39]. But times change, and as multiple smart toys started a trend of tactile toys (rather toys than intellectual AIs), youngsters seem to need a touch of personal touch.

The task arises to fill this gap in perception which had caused the loss of interest by people inclined to tactile communication. With tactile sensors, the robot is taught to react to touching via several communicative goals.

Four-fold tactile sensors classification is as follows.

(1) Capacitive tactile measurement.
(2) Resistive tactile sensors.
(3) Piezoelectric tactile sensors (passive and active).
(4) Optical tactile sensors.

Basing on the conducted analysis of existing tactile sensors and their characteristics [15, 25, 32, 42] and the robot model, the following conclusions are drawn on sensors' applicability for solving the task at hand. For placement on the robot's arms, flexible sensors are chosen that can bend with the arm. The shape of such sensors can be rectangular, linear, or arbitrary. Round sensors may also be suitable for placement on the palms. The ability to detect the touch location will be useful for reducing the number of sensors on one hand. In this regard, we selected small round sensors Ø 1.2 cm from the Interlink FSR 400 series [15] for placement in palms, and rectangular sensors of the same series for placement on F-2's hands, 4 by 4 cm. The robot head is covered with resistive sensors in the same way as the hands: 4 – on top, 3 – on each cheek. The F-2 robot model with tactile sensors is given in Fig. 1.

Since the selected FSR 400 Series sensors do not have an interface for connecting to a computer nor to a controller, these should be connected using a third-party programmable controller. The Arduino UNO board was chosen. The following materials are required to connect the sensor: an Arduino breadboard, jumper wires, a resistor, a USB A to B cable. Figure 2 shows a wiring diagram for connecting a sensor to an Arduino board. An Arduino controller allows reading values from its analog ports, mapping voltage values from the range 0 to 5V to integers from 0 to 1023. These values are sent via the USB port to the PC for further processing.

Fig. 1. The F-2 robot with tactile sensors.

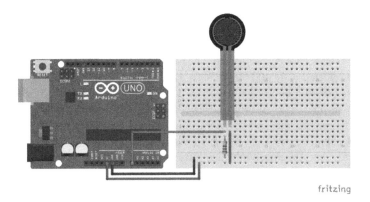

Fig. 2. The wiring diagram for connecting a sensor.

Five touch types are selected: tap, smoothing over, scratch, handshake, hit. Table 1 shows assigned communicative goals and sample reactions to each touch-type within a given zone. Given touch-types differ by duration and force of tapping; the latter is measured, the other factor is detected in program code.

Table 1. Communicative goals and sample reactions for different touch types.

Touch-type and zone	Communicative goal	Sample reaction
Tap on top of the head	Focusing on the touched zone	Turns his head up, asks "what?"
Tap on a cheek	Focusing on the touched zone	Turns the head left or right (to the tapped cheek)
Tap on a hand	Focusing on the touched zone	Looks on the tapped hand
Tap on the belly	Show discomfort	Says "ouch"
Smoothing over the head	Express pleasure	Nods, says "awesome"
Smoothing over a cheek	Express pleasure	Nods, says "it's cool"
Smoothing over the belly	Express pleasure	Raises its head, says "I like that"
Scratching over the head	Express pleasure	Raises its head and hands, says "do it again"
Scratching over a cheek	Express pleasure	Rises its hand, says "wow, cool"
Scratching over the belly	Express pleasure	Looks down, says "it tickles"
Handshake left or right hand	Express pleasure	Turns its head up or down, closes its eyes
Hit on top of the head	Express sadness and pain	Puts their hands up to cover the head, says "don't do that!"
Hit on one cheek	Express sadness and pain	Puts their hands up to cover the face, says "it hurts!"

A training set was fulfilled with a recording tool. The overall data amount is 2570 recordings. 4 classifiers were trained, the results are given in Table 2. The decision tree classifier showed the topmost quality, and its detailed precision is given in Table 3. Empty cells are for inapplicable combinations of touch type and zone. Achieved precision is acceptable. No robot was harmed during approbation.

Table 2. The precision of touch detection for four classifiers, by touch types.

Classifier	Smoothing over	Scratching	Tap	Hit	Average
Logistic regression	48.5%	97.6%	69.6%	100.0%	78.9%
Decision tree	75.7%	93.9%	81.8%	72.7%	82.0%
Bayesian	48.9%	86.8%	54.8%	0%	47.7%
Support vector machines	66.7%	100.0%	81.8%	75.0%	80.9%

Table 3. The precision of touch detection for the decision tree classifier, by touch type and zone.

Zone	Smoothing over	Scratching	Tap	Hit	Average
Head	75.7%	93.9%	81.8%	72.7%	–
Left cheek	85.0%	83.3%	81.5%	75.0%	–
Right cheek	90.6%	98.0%	76.5%	80.0%	–
Left hand	–	–	100.0%	–	96.9%
Right hand	–	–	100.0%	–	100.0%
Belly	89.5%	100.0%	100.0%	–	–

Table 4. Feedback from respondents on F-2's reactions to different touch-types and zones.

Touch-type and zone	Positive attitude	Neutral attitude	Negative attitude	Overall tests
Tap on top of the head	13/65%	3/15%	4/20%	20
Tap on left cheek	6/60%	2/20%	2/20%	10
Tap on right cheek	5/56%	2/22%	2/22%	9
Tap on left hand	5/41.5%	2/17%	5/41.5%	12
Tap on right hand	5/41.5%	2/17%	5/41.5%	12
Tap on the belly	7/47%	4/26.5%	4/26.5%	15
Smoothing over the head	18/100%	–/0%	–/0%	18
Smoothing over left cheek	14/93%	1/7%	–/0%	15
Smoothing over right cheek	13/93%	1/7%	–/0%	14
Smoothing over the belly	16/76%	4/19%	1/5%	21
Scratching over the head	5/83%	1/17%	–/0%	6
Scratching over left cheek	4/80%	1/20%	–/0%	5
Scratching over right cheek	4/80%	1/20%	–/0%	5
Scratching over the belly	5/62.5%	1/12.5%	2/25%	8
Tickling the belly (*)	3/43%	4/57%	–/0%	7
Handshake, left hand	10/59%	2/12%	5/29%	17
Handshake, right hand	11/61%	2/11%	5/28%	18
Shake/hold both hands (*)	–/0%	4/80%	1/20%	5
Hit on top of the head	14/70%	2/10%	4/20%	20
Hit on left cheek	10/84%	1/8%	1/8%	12
Hit on right cheek	12/100%	–/0%	–/0%	12
Overall	177/71%	32/13%	40/16%	249
Overall, with 2 new suggested types	180/69%	40/15%	41/16%	261

As the feedback from the respondents is the most important factor for developing the robot, 24 respondents were invited to the next stage – for *reactions evaluation*. Aggregated feedback was systematized and interpreted. Results are given in Table 4.

Two rows in Table 4 are marked with stars – these are new categories highlighted by respondents beyond basic touch types. These could be included in previous rows (tickling – to scratching the belly, and the second type – to common handshake group), but respondents expect slightly different reactions for these categories. The absence of predefined reactions to newly suggested touch-types resulted in the loss of 2% of positive opinions in the last row as compared to the previous row.

Table 5. Feedback from respondents on F-2's reactions to different touch-types, aggregated.

Touch-type, aggregated by zones	Positive attitude	Neutral attitude	Negative attitude	Overall tests
Overall, tap	41/53%	15/19%	22/28%	78
Overall, scratching	18/75%	4/17%	2/8%	24
Overall, smoothing over	61/90%	6/9%	1/1%	68
Overall, handshake	21/60%	4/11%	10/29%	35
Overall, hit	36/82%	3/7%	5/11%	44

Table 5 contains aggregated feedback by touch types. Touch categories are given without extension with two additional touch-types suggested by respondents.

Overall expressed attitude is positive. Respondents express a positive opinion of the new functionality of the robot. The following opinions are considered as most important:

(1) respondents assess positively the fact that reactions differ for different touch-types and for different touch zones;
(2) reactions are regarded as nice, cute, and interesting;
(3) most reactions met respondents' expectations.

Several disadvantages of current reactions implementation were pointed out:

(1) a number of reactions were regarded as illogical, e.g. the expected reaction to a handshake would be saying hello (not nodding or not only nodding);
(2) the tendency of repeating reactions was accentuated;
(3) respondents highlighted that not all possible touch-types have been implemented, and asked for more touch-types;
(4) a few respondents pointed out a time gap between touch and reaction;
(5) the attitude faded in a number of cases due to particular insufficient frequency for handshake/tap on a hand;
(6) most respondents were afraid to harm the robot, so the intended hit was underestimated and insufficiently tested (and unpopular: respondents do not tend to hit the robot, and if asked, they perform hits far from strong).

Respondents wrote down a number of further development directions:

(1) to adjust the reactions in order to make them closer to the expected;
(2) to increase the touch types spectrum;
(3) to increase the quality of hit and tap types classification;

(4) to adjust the gap between reactions, as only the first touch is processed in case a pair of touches is given;
(5) to introduce multi-zone touches;
(6) to introduce tickling as a new touch type;
(7) to hide the sensors in the next version, so that people wouldn't be afraid of hurting the robot.

The most arguable zone is the hand's zone: respondents expected one more touch type "to hold the hand", this can be further introduced. As respondents often do not make a difference between tap and hit, the actual difference should be decreased.

There are two paradoxes in feedback. First, one opinion is that the robot is a right-hander (perhaps that is a sensors issue). Second, two respondents said, that too many positive reactions bored them and made them lose interest because people often act differently.

In general, the aggregated feedback illustrates the whole development cycle, when reactions should be adjusted or accepted, and the introduction of new reactions leads the project to further development. The new strategy of reacting to tactile input events enhanced robot behavior evaluation and is successful in general. Thus, this approach would be adapted in beta-version, after enriching the touch types spectrum.

4 F-2 Going Complimenting

More communicative strategies are designed with computer vision methods in basis. Three communicative goals were introduced as rational scripts: *complimenting*, *greeting,* and *acquaintance*. All of the three are based on appealing to a person's look, the second one comprising complimenting itself. The latter goal would allow selecting one particular person from a crowd via narrow pointing, e.g. "Hello, how you're doing? Yes, you, the one wearing a bow-tie." This strategy is prospective in case of a crowded exhibition, e.g. in the "Sirius" scientific camp for youngsters. According to [16], complimenting gives a positive impression to humans and results in positive dynamics in human satisfaction with the dialogue with communicative robots.

A person's face is detected in an image with Haar cascade detection (as implemented in OpenCV, based on Viola-Jones algorithm [35]); its accuracy is quite high: 99.38% on the Labeled Faces in the Wild (LFW) dataset. A body location zone is selected below the face zone (3 face zone widths by not more than 12 face zone heights, as the algorithm, sometimes recognizes the face as a part of the head height) in order to further classify the pattern for clothes. The limitation is in the assumption that a person is depicted full-face. Several people can be in one image. 7 features were selected for clothes and face:

(1) plaid clothes;
(2) striped clothes;
(3) cat print on clothes;
(4) tie;
(5) bow-tie;
(6) glasses;
(7) beard.

Instead of training the neural network from scratch, the transfer learning technique was applied in order to reduce significantly the amount of data required for high-quality training [10]. The Faster-RCNN-Inception-V2 neural network [12, 26] was pretrained on the COCO (Common Objects in Context) dataset [6], containing 330k images divided into 80 categories. The neural network was trained with TensorFlow until the loss function [37] at each training iteration was stably below 0.05; 80 images per category were aggregated for learning. In order to exclude false-positive cases (e.g., glasses lying on a table), an additional step was added with matching features and body coordinates. The resulting classification quality is shown in Table 6. 50 additional images per category were aggregated as the testing set.

Table 6. Accuracy of feature detection

Feature	Number of recognized images	Accuracy
Plaid clothes	38	75%
Striped clothes	47	89%
Cat print	42	84%
Tie	42	82%
Bow-tie	41	77%
Glasses	54	96%
Beard	67	88%
Other	43	96%

During parameterization, a threshold value of the classifier confidence was selected as 0.95. The overall accuracy reduced from maximum values by 5% to 86.1%, but the number of false positives reduced as well. This is more important because during approbation respondents' feedback showed that people react more sharply to incorrect reactions than to the absence of reaction. The more confident the classifier is, the more positive the feedback on human-robot interaction.

For basic communicative goals, their weights fade over time. New goals weights should fade relatively slower, as these are background communicative goals. In the new person appearance scenario, new goals *acquaintance* and *complimenting* should be initialized with a small constant, while the *greeting* goal weight should be weighted with a maximum value so that the robot would immediately greet that person after it finishes its cue towards another interlocutor. That recommendation is formed because human beings consider paying attention to the very important. Still the current phrase shouldn't be interrupted, that's in the basic mechanism of F-2. *Greeting* and *complimenting* goals shouldn't outweigh other communicative goals during the dialogue in case the ongoing dialogue is not finished.

5 Conclusion

The F-2 robot-companion project was discussed in this article, its structure and natural text analysis principles were given. Basing on the conducted analysis of existing AIs, affective toys, and assistants, we made a decision to design F-2 resembling a cartoon character instead of a humanoid figure in order to avoid the 'uncanny valley' problem. F-2's reactions are intended to be perceived by humans as nice, realistic, and human-like. Our effective companion comprehends sentences (by means of facts extraction) and produces various affective reactions which correspond to communicative goals, or strategies. Its reactions are multimodal and consist of text and gestures executed with hands, heads, and eyes. We conduct a thorough analysis on the basis of the REC corpus in order to select behavior elements which are then translated into gestures and rendered on the robot.

The robot can be used as a healthcare solution, for it can hold a conversation. In the future with detecting a long silence or some particular human behavior, it could decide to ask a human if he or she feels well. In case if not (or no answer at all) such a robot could transmit a signal to a medical institution.

F-2 is intended to be rather a mate, and it's taught to form and express an affective attitude to the sense of the input text and to the events perceived.

In this article, a new perception channel was introduced to F-2 which filled an unexpected lacuna in perception. With tactile sensors, new communicative strategies are introduced and their implementation is investigated. The existing computer vision-based perception is enhanced with human look feature extraction, and appealing to such features allowed introducing three more communicative strategies. Precision values are estimated for classifiers which are on the basis of events detection via both perception channels.

The main directions of further research are discussed in Sect. 3, basing on the thorough analysis of the most important data required to evaluate the implemented strategies' success: the feedback aggregated from invited respondents. Most of the introduced dialogue strategies and reactions are interpreted as nice and human-like. As we performed the whole development cycle, we mined new data from the feedback, and new important accents and recommendations for further development are formulated, including consideration of negative or unexpected human reactions to what the robot responds to particular tactile communication elements. Last but not least, recommendations are given for subdividing several tactile communication elements classes.

Acknowledgments. This research is supported by the grant of the Russian Science Foundation (project № 19–18-00547).

The F-2 team wishes to express gratitude to all of our respondents, including students of the Power Engineering department of BMSTU. All of the feedback is precious for us as it shows new directions of further development for F-2.

We also wish to thank our colleague Edward Klyshinsky for pointing out Azimov's "Sally" short story for epigraphs, an inspiration to beam this article with.

References

1. Allen, S.R.: Concern processing in autonomous agents, Ph.D. thesis. The University of Birmingham, Birmingham (2001)
2. Almansor, E.H., Hussain, F.K.: Survey on intelligent chatbots: state-of-the-art and future research directions. In: Barolli, L., Hussain, F.K., Ikeda, M. (eds.) CISIS 2019. AISC, vol. 993, pp. 534–543. Springer, Cham (2020). https://doi.org/10.1007/978-3-030-22354-0_47
3. Becker, C., Kopp, S., Wachsmuth, I.: Simulating the emotion dynamics of a multimodal conversational agent. In: André, E., Dybkjær, L., Minker, W., Heisterkamp, P. (eds.) ADS 2004. LNCS (LNAI), vol. 3068, pp. 154–165. Springer, Heidelberg (2004). https://doi.org/10.1007/978-3-540-24842-2_15
4. Breazeal, C.: Designing Sociable Robots. MIT Press, Cambridge (2002)
5. Cai, Y.: Empathic computing. In: Cai, Y., Abascal, J. (eds.) Ambient Intelligence in Everyday Life. LNCS (LNAI), vol. 3864, pp. 67–85. Springer, Heidelberg (2006). https://doi.org/10.1007/11825890_3
6. COCO dataset (2021). https://cocodataset.org/. Accessed 20 Mar 2021
7. Engleberg, I.N., Wynn, D.R.: Working in Groups: Communication Principles and Strategies. My Communication Kit Series, p. 133. Allyn & Bacon, Boston (2006)
8. F-2 standby, NRCKI cognitive team (2019). http://youtube.com/watch?v=TrKh5xohBZg. Accessed 15 April 2019
9. Fung, P., et al.: Towards empathetic human-robot interactions. In: Gelbukh, A. (ed.) CICLing 2016. LNCS, vol. 9624, pp. 173–193. Springer, Cham (2018). https://doi.org/10.1007/978-3-319-75487-1_14
10. Girshick, R.: Fast R-CNN. In: IEEE International Conference on Computer Vision (ICCV), 2015, pp. 1440–1448. IEEE, Pictasaway (2015)
11. Greta, Embodied Conversational Agent (2017). http://perso.telecomparistech.fr/~pelachau/Greta/. Accessed 10 April 2017
12. Halawa, L.J., Wibowo, A., Ernawan, F.: Face recognition using faster R-CNN with inception-V2 architecture for CCTV camera. In: 2019 3rd International Conference on Informatics and Computational Sciences (ICICoS), pp. 1–6. IEEE, Pictasaway (2019)
13. Han, J.G., Campbell, N., Jokinen, K., Wilcock, G.: Investigating the use of non-verbal cues in human-robot interaction with a Nao robot. In: Proceedings of the 3rd IEEE International Conference on Cognitive Infocommunications (CogInfoCom 2012), Kosice, Slovakia, pp. 679–683. IEEE, Pictasaway (2012)
14. I·bug (2017). http://ibug.doc.ic.ac.uk/. Accessed 10 April 2017
15. InterLink Electronics. FSR 400 series (2020). https://www.interlinkelectronics.com/fsr-400-series. Accessed 18 July 2020
16. Iwashita, M., Katagami, D.: Psychological effects of compliment expressions by communication robots on humans. In: 2020 International Joint Conference on Neural Networks (IJCNN), pp. 1–8. IEEE, Piscataway (2020). https://doi.org/10.1109/IJCNN48605.2020.9206898
17. Jokinen, K., Wilcock, G.: Modelling user experience in human-robot interactions. In: MA3HMI 2014 Workshop, LNAI, vol. 8757, pp. 45–56. Springer, Heidelberg (2014)
18. Kirby, R., Forlizzi, J., Simmons, R.: Affective social robots. Robot. Auton. Syst. **58**, 322–332. Elsevier, Amsterdam (2010)
19. Kopp, S.: Social resonance and embodied coordination in face-to-face conversation with artificial interlocutors. Speech Commun. **52**, 587–597. Elsevier, Amsterdam (2010)
20. Kotov, A.A.: Patterns of emotional communicative reactions: problems of creating a corpus and translating to emotional agents (in Russian). In: Computational Linguistics and Intellectual Technologies, vol. 8, pp. 211–218. RSUH, Moscow (2009)

21. Kotov, A.A., Zinnia, A.A.: Functional analysis of non-verbal communicative behavior (in Russian). In: Computational Linguistics and Intellectual Technologies, vol. 14, no. 2, pp. 308–320. RSUH, Moscow (2015)
22. Max (2017). http://cycling74.com/products/max/. Accessed 10 April 2017
23. Minsky, M.: A framework for representing knowledge. In: Patrick Henry Winston (ed.) The Psychology of Computer Vision. McGraw-Hill, New York (1975)
24. Mori, M.: The uncanny valley (K. F. MacDorman & N. Kageki, Trans.). IEEE Robot. Autom. Mag. **19**(2), 98–100 (1970/2012)
25. Neonode AirBar (2020). https://air.bar/. Accessed 18 July 2020
26. Ren, S., He, K., Girshick, R., Sun, J.: Faster R-CNN: towards real-time object detection with region proposal networks. In: IEEE Transactions on Pattern Analysis and Machine Intelligence, vol. 39. IEEE, Pictasaway (2015)
27. Rudakov, I.V., Paschenkova, A.V.: A hierarchical method for verification of software algorithms via hierarchical Petri nets. Engineering Journal: Science and Innovations, vol. 2, no. 14 (in Russian). BMSTU Press, Moscow (2013). https://doi.org/10.18698/2308-6033-2013-2-538
28. Russell, J.: Core affect and the psychological construction of emotion. Psychol. Rev. **110**(1), 145–172. American Psychological Association, Washington (2003)
29. Semaine Project (2017). http://www.semaine-project.eu/. Accessed 10 April 2017
30. Sloman, A., Chrisley, R.: Virtual machines and consciousness. J. Conscious. Stud. **10**(4–5), 133–172. Imprint Academic, Exeter (2003)
31. Shröder, M.: The SEMAINE API: towards a standards-based framework for building emotion-oriented systems. Adv. Hum.-Comput. Interact. **2010**, 319406. Hindawi, London (2010)
32. TonTek TTP223-BA6_SPEC_V2.1 (2020). https://static.chipdip.ru/lib/949/DOC005949559.pdf. Accessed 27 Dec 2020
33. Vilhjálmsson, H., et al.: The behavior markup language: recent developments and challenges. In: Pelachaud, C., Martin, J.-C., André, E., Chollet, G., Karpouzis, K., Pelé, D. (eds.) IVA 2007. LNCS (LNAI), vol. 4722, pp. 99–111. Springer, Heidelberg (2007). https://doi.org/10.1007/978-3-540-74997-4_10
34. Vinyals, O., Le, Q.: A neural conversational model. In: Proceedings of ICML Deep Learning Workshop, July 2015. https://arxiv.org/abs/1506.05869. Accessed 15 April 2019
35. Viola, P., Jones, M.: Robust real-time face detection. Int. J. Comput. Vis. **57**, 137–154 (2004). https://doi.org/10.1023/B:VISI.0000013087.49260.fb
36. Volkova, L., Kotov, A., Klyshinsky, E., Arinkin, N.: A robot commenting texts in an emotional way. In: Kravets, A., Shcherbakov, M., Kultsova, M., Groumpos, P. (eds.) CIT&DS 2017. CCIS, vol. 754, pp. 256–266. Springer, Cham (2017). https://doi.org/10.1007/978-3-319-65551-2_19
37. Weiss, K., Khoshgoftaar, T.M., Wang, D.: A survey of transfer learning. J. Big Data, vol. 3. Springer, Heidelberg (2016)
38. Weizenbaum, J.: ELIZA. Commun. ACM **9**, 36–45 (1966)
39. Winograd, T.: Understanding Natural Language. Academic Press, New York (1972)
40. Yandex SpeechKit API (in Russian). http://api.yandex.ru/speechkit/. Accessed 10 April 2017
41. Zhou, L., Gao, J., Li, D., Shum, H.-Y.: The Design and Implementation of XiaoIce, an Empathetic Social Chatbot (2018–12–21). https://arxiv.org/abs/1812.08989. Accessed 15 April 2019
42. Zou, L., Ge, C., Wang, Z., Cretu, E., Li, X.: Novel tactile sensor technology and smart tactile sensing systems: a review. Sensors **17**(11), 2653. MDPI, Basel (2017)

The System of Intelligent Identification of Harmful Objects in the Field of Agriculture

Mohammed A. Al-Gunaid$^{(\boxtimes)}$, Maxim V. Shcherbakov, Vsevolod V. Tishchenko, and Vladislav N. Trubitsin

Volgograd State Technical University, Lenina Ave. 28, 400005 Volgograd, Russia

Abstract. One of the possible directions of digitalization of agriculture is the automatic identification of harmful objects. These include diseases and pests of plants, as well as weeds. In this paper, we compare VGG19, MobileNetV2, and InceptionResnetV2 networks to solve this problem. Determination is carried out both by classifying defects on plants and by detecting the pests themselves. For training, a set consisting of 26,000 images was collected, which are divided into 15 categories of plants and 26 defects. The data is obtained from a variety of open sources. As a result of the experiments, 97% classification accuracy was achieved. In addition to developing a universal identification algorithm, an agronomist's work automation system was created.

Keywords: Agriculture · Disease · Pests · Weed · Search

1 Introduction

Agriculture is one of the main sectors of the economy, especially important in our country. At the same time, the effectiveness in this direction depends on many different factors. Reasonable use of resources, timely decision-making can significantly increase the productivity of processes [1, 2].

A special stage in the development of agriculture is the" chemical technological revolution" of the 70s–90s of the XX century, it is based on the use of high doses of mineral fertilizers, intensive chemical treatment of plants from diseases, pests and weeds. This method allows you to effectively and quickly suppress emerging threats, but its irrational use leads to environmental pollution, the formation of resistance. In this regard, the use of chemical methods is carried out only taking into account the general analysis of crops, the prognosis of the development of harmful organisms [3].

The key figure in agriculture is an agronomist, a specialist in control of planting and harvesting, soil fertilization, and pest and disease control. The size of the territory in which the search for harmful objects is carried out is large, which requires a large amount of time to survey it. The developed program provides the ability to automatically identify plant diseases, weeds and pests from a photo. The system is intended both for analyzing the collected archive of images and for automatically filling in input fields in other applications using the API.

© Springer Nature Switzerland AG 2021
A. G. Kravets et al. (Eds.): CIT&DS 2021, CCIS 1448, pp. 177–189, 2021.
https://doi.org/10.1007/978-3-030-87034-8_14

2   Problem Statement

The aim of the work is to develop a system capable of identifying insects, weeds and diseases with maximum accuracy from a photo. To achieve this goal, it was necessary to solve the following tasks: analyze the threats to agriculture; consider existing solutions for the recognition of harmful objects in agriculture; generate data sets for identification; select and implement object recognition algorithms; implement and test a web application with an accessible and understandable interface and API.

Measures to check the presence of threats should be carried out regularly, for their early detection, as well as assessing the degree of infection and predicting further development. The program contains a library of recognizable plants and pests. The description of the plant provides a list of the various defects that can be found. Defects that appear on the leaves and stems of plants can be of a different nature. First, it can be the results of the activity of insects or their larvae. Secondly, the reason may be a lack or excess of nutrients in the soil. Thirdly, the presence of problems can be associated with external conditions, light, moisture, wind. Fourthly, the influence of various infectious diseases is possible.

The system for identifying harmful objects provides the following functions: viewing, adding, deleting elements of the library of identifiable plants, corresponding defects and animals; adding, changing, deleting object recognition models by the administrator; uploading photos to identify harmful objects, with the ability to track the process and stop it; search for harmful objects in uploaded photos, with the ability to track the search process and stop it; storing operations of searching for harmful objects in the form of protocols (each protocol is characterized by the name of the place, its coordinates, time of creation).

Plant and animal library pages must contain a search filter by title. Protocols, uploaded photos, found threats are displayed in table format with the ability to use filters. Filling out forms is carried out in a pop-up window. The service must implement both a web interface and an API.

3   Review of Analogs

3.1   Overview of Identification Approaches

One of the ways to implement the identification of harmful objects is detection using various architectures. One of such works is "A Robust Deep-Learning Based Detector for Real-Time Tomato Plant Diseases and Pests Recognition" [4]. In this work, the VGG and ResNet networks were used. The advantage of this approach is the localization of the problem in the image, however, there are diseases, the symptoms of which are not pinpoint and appear throughout the plant.

Also worth mentioning is the work "Using Deep Learning for Image-Based Plant Disease Detection" [5]. It uses the AlexNet and GoogLeNet architectures and was trained on a set of 54306 images of various leaves obtained in the laboratory, which reduces the accuracy in the field. The work does not include a search for the rest of the plant, but shows the applicability of the classification for solving the problem of identifying plant diseases.

The article "The choice of deep learning methods for solving the problem of recognizing plant diseases for cases of a small training sample" describes the application of the ResNet50 and MobileNetV2 convolutional networks, one-shot learning and Siamese neural networks are used to improve accuracy [6]. As a result, an average accuracy of 97% is achieved. The paper considers images taken in real conditions and contains both leaves and other parts of the plant.

3.2 Overview of Existing Software Solutions

Today, there are already many services for identifying harmful agricultural objects, it is worth listing the main ones. Firstly, the Plantix Vision application was developed by specialists from Germany and is used in the countries of Central Europe and the regions of South Asia. The program contains a list of various crops and is designed to recognize plant diseases [7]. Plantix provides an API, recognition occurs simultaneously by three networks: Disease Net (search for plant diseases), Crop Net (search for arbitrary objects), Object Net (modifies the image for search). The service is able to recognize more than 350 threats from 66 plant inputs with high accuracy. Among the disadvantages are the lack of the Russian language, the high cost of use (the cost of API packages starts at 15,000 euros per year), as well as the lack of obvious detection of pests by their appearance.

Secondly, the Yara app, this company is a manufacturer of fertilizers, in accordance with this, it searches for the lack of nutrients in plants and gives advice on what nutrition should be used [8]. Its application is designed to work autonomously in the field, in low communication conditions. The pluses also include support for the Russian language. The application is free, however, it is an advertising product. Among the shortcomings, one can single out the lack of search for infectious diseases, pests, and weeds. Also, Yara CheckIT does not provide an API, but is implemented only as a mobile application.

Thirdly, the PDDP project developed in Russia, its essence is to create mechanisms that allow agricultural workers to receive diagnostic data for the disease and recommendations for treatment. The application is capable of processing both an image and a textual description of the problem [9]. The project is able to distinguish 25 classes of images, among them 5 plant cultures. The total amount of images on which the classification models were trained is 934. The application searches only for diseases and does not recognize pests or weeds. Among the disadvantages, a relatively small amount of training data can be distinguished; in accordance with this, rather low accuracy of the result is possible. Also, PDDP does not provide an API.

4   Designing an Application

4.1   Data Collection

Allocate a wide variety of pests and diseases. The main share of pests is insects. There are two divisions: incompletely transformed insects and fully transformed insects. The departments are divided into groups. In accordance with the causes of disease, plants are subdivided into non-infectious (caused by unfavorable weather, soil conditions, or damage) and infectious (fungal, bacterial, actinomycotic, mycoplasma, viral, viroid) [10].

Diseases can be local and diffuse, affecting most of the plant. The process of classifying plant diseases in this project is divided into stages. In the first, the plant culture is determined, the images containing other objects are rejected, in the second, the recognition of the disease is performed. This approach allows at each stage to emphasize the search only for some of the features, which increases the final recognition accuracy. To train classification models, 26,000 images were used, which are divided into 15 categories and 26 plant defects. The data is sourced from Yandex image, pdd.jinr, various kaggle kits, as well as TFFlowers. A list of plant crops is shown in Fig. 1.

Fig. 1. Identifiable plant cultures.

Pests can inhabit both soil and vegetation. Symptoms can be various damage to the leaves, bark, stems, roots of the plant. To determine according to these characteristics, classification is also used. However, if a pest is detected, then there is the possibility of identifying it by its appearance. Detection is used for this task. The dataset is ArTaxOr, which contains 15000 images, divided into 7 orders of insects [11].

4.2 Description of the Existing Process for Identifying Harmful Objects

Pest and disease control in the fields are carried out through the use of chemicals. For their reasonable use, a comprehensive analysis of the field state is required. Monitoring is carried out using field observations and forecasting systems. An accurate definition of the threat allows you to choose the right tactics for plant protection.

An agronomist who is hired by an agricultural company is responsible for organizing threat verification activities. These activities must be carried out regularly for early detection, assessment of the degree of infection and forecasting the development of threats. This procedure is a key element of plant protection programs. When walking around the area, the agronomist fills out a status report for each field. The survey result includes a list of found threats, their volume and prevalence across the territory. It is also possible to collect damaged samples for further analysis. To determine the number and types of pests, various traps are used, which are placed in advance on the territory. The agronomist generates a report and plans for further actions. He sends the generated documents to the company.

4.3 Description of the Automated Process for Identifying Harmful Objects

Most of the time an agronomist spends in nature, the success of his work is highly dependent on weather conditions. The area of the territory that he needs to bypass is large enough. Acceleration of the agronomist's work is possible by automating the identification of threats. The developed service allows you to recognize diseases, weeds and pests by photo. The collection of images is performed at the time of traversing the fields. The creation of images can be done using a quadcopter or a phone camera. Also, the camera can be installed on devices that process crops. The collected photos are uploaded to the app for analysis. Loading is carried out separately for each field in the protocol format.

4.4 Description of the Identification Algorithm

As part of this work, it is required to create a module for recognizing plant diseases, weeds and pests. The process is broken down into two separate tasks. In the first, the determination of the plant culture and the presence of a defect is performed, the operation is carried out using classification. In the second, the identification of the animals themselves is performed, for this, detection is used. The general recognition algorithm is shown in Fig. 2.

For the classification, the structures VGG19, MobileNetV2, InceptionResNetV2 were defined. The VGG19 convolutional neural network has 19 main layers, including 16 convolutional and 3 fully connected. It also contains 1 SoftMax layer and 5 MaxPoll layers. A feature of this structure is the use of convolutions of only 3×3 size. This allows you to reduce the number of learning variables compared to using larger convolutions. Today it is quite popular, however, due to its great depth, it has a lot of weight and a slow learning rate. A detailed description of the structure is presented in Very Deep Convolutional Networks for Large-Scale Image Recognition [12].

MobileNetV2 is a convolutional neural network that has significantly fewer parameters with approximately the same accuracy. It uses deep 3×3 (channel filtering) and 1×1 point convolutions (downsize). A detailed description of the structure is provided in MobileNetV2: Inverted Residuals and Linear Bottlenecks [13].

InceptionResNetV2 is one of the most accurate convolutional neural networks that combines Inception and Residual architectures. Instead of choosing one block configuration, a list is used, and then the one that gives the best result is selected. This leads to an increase in the number of operations; to reduce them, 1×1 layers are used in front of each block. Residual scaling with factors from 0.1 to 0.3 is also applied. A detailed description of the structure is provided in Inception-v4, Inception-ResNet and the Impact of Residual Connections on Learning [14].

Algorithm 1: gettingDefectAndPests

Input: Images - list of images.
Output: Plants - a list of found plants with an indication of the defect;
          Animals - list of found animals.

1 FormattedImages = ImageProcessing (Images);
2 CropModels = LoadCropDefinitionModels();
3 FindPlants = DefineCropCulture(FormattedImages);
4 **for** *each Item in FindPlants* **do**
5   FormattedImageList = GetCultureImages(Item);
6   DefectModel = DownloadDefectModel(Piece);
7   **for** *each ItemImg in FormattedImageList* **do**
8   index = FormattedImageList.index;
9   Item[index] = ImageDefect(ItemImg, DefectModel);
10   **end**
11 **end**
12 AnimalModel = LoadDetectionModel();
13 FindAnimals = AnimalDetection(FormattedImages);
14 **return** FindPlants, FindAnimals;

Fig. 2. Algorithm of the method.

As a loss function, categorical cross-entropy is used, which is calculated by the formula [15]:

$$Loss(p, q) = -\sum_x p(x)\log q(x) \tag{1}$$

where p is the distribution of true responses; q – probability distribution of model forecasts.

Metrics are used to evaluate classification models: accuracy, Matthews correlation coefficient. The accuracy is calculated by the formula [15]:

$$Accuracy = \frac{TP + TN}{TP + TN + FP + FN} \tag{2}$$

where TP is the number of true positive responses; TN – number of true negative responses; FP – number of false-positive responses; FN – number of false-negative responses.

The Matthews correlation coefficient takes into account the values from all cells of the contingency matrix, most accurately shows the quality of the classification, is calculated by the formula [16]:

$$Matthew = \frac{TP * TN - FP * FN}{\sqrt{(TP + FP) * (TP + FN) * (TN + FP) * (TN + FN)}} \tag{3}$$

where TP is the number of true positive responses; TN – number of true negative responses; FP – number of false-positive responses; FN – number of false-negative responses.

Models from the Keras Applications set are used to classify images. They are pre-trained on the ImageNet dataset, which improves the final training accuracy. The comparison graph of the models is shown in Fig. 3 [17].

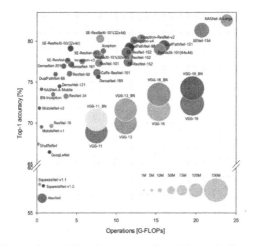

Fig. 3. Comparison of Top-1 accuracy of models on the ImageNet set.

For detection, the MobileNet architectures are also used, Ince-ptionResNet from the TensorFlow 2 Detection Model Zoo dataset. They are pre-trained on the COCO 2017 dataset. In accordance with this set, a comparison of the models in terms of speed in milliseconds and recognition accuracy using the mAP (mean Average Precision) metric is provided [18]. Model parameters are shown in Table

The table shows that the EfficientDet D7 model achieves greater accuracy, it allows processing 1536 × 1536 images, which is much more than the others. In terms of the detection speed, we can also assume the weight of the final model, this indicator is the highest for the EfficientDet D7. The MobileNet model has the least weight, when compared to InceptionResNet it has lower accuracy, but 5 times lower speed (Table 1).

Table 1. Parameters of detection models.

Model name	Speed (ms)	Accuracy (mAP)
SSD MobileNet V2 320 × 320	19	20.2
SSD MobileNet V2 FPNLite 640 × 640	39	28.2
Faster R-CNN Inception ResNet V2 640 × 640	206	37.7
Faster R-CNN Inception ResNet V2 1024 × 1024	236	38.7
EfficientDet D1 640 × 640	54	38.4
EfficientDet D4 1024 × 1024	133	48.5
EfficientDet D7 1536 × 1536	325	51.2

4.5   Service Architecture for Identifying Harmful Objects

There is the main application that aims to optimize agricultural performance. The application includes a set of microservices, each of which implements its own task. Within the framework of this microservice, an agronomist has the ability to automatically identify harmful agricultural objects that he uploads in photographs. An external service is used for registration and authentication. The general system architecture diagram is shown in Fig. 4.

The server processes user requests to add, change, delete information stored in the database, as well as requests to perform image analysis.

The files are stored on the server. All files are divided into four directories: models (models for threat recognition), images (images uploaded by the user), find (images on which objects are detected), media (images of plants and animals from the library).

The database should contain tables of plants, defects, animals, user protocols, protocol images, recognition models. Three types of models have been identified: plant classification (PlantModel), plant defect classification (Plant), animal detection (AnimalModel). However, only one PlantModel and AnimalModel are required for recognition.

The Redis component is used as a Celery broker, which serves to perform long-term background tasks and organize their execution queues [19]. The background task is to identify harmful objects in uploaded images.

5   Selecting Development Tools

The server-side source code is implemented in Python. The choice is due to the presence of a large number of libraries for creating neural networks. Django was chosen as the web framework for the server-side implementation. It is by far the most popular for large projects.

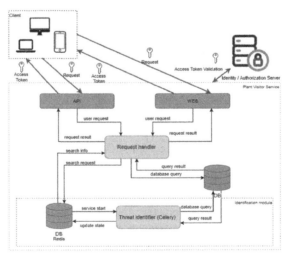

Fig. 4. System architecture.

The SQLite DBMS is used as a database, it is standard for Django and meets all the needs of this project [20]. The front-end source code must be written in the JavaScript, HTML, and CSS programming language. JQuery is used for the dynamic work of pages. Element styles and responsiveness are implemented using the Bootstrap framework.

Object identification is implemented using the TensorFlow 2 framework, as well as the Keras built into it. This choice is due to their popularity, great functionality, ease of implementation of Keras and low-level TensorFlow [21]. Architectures from the Tensorflow Keras Applications set were used for classification. Model configurations from the TensorFlow 2 Detection Model Zoo set were used for detection.

6 Experiment

6.1 Definition of Plant Culture

To train classification models, 26,000 images were used, which are divided into 15 categories of plants. When creating models, ImageNet weights are loaded into them. The t-SNE visualization for VGG19 prior to training is shown in Fig. 5.

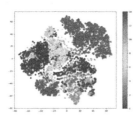

Fig. 5. Visualization of t-SNE for VGG19 before training.

As you can see from the picture, the classes are quite mixed. The trained VGG19 model has a weight of 77 MB and an accuracy of up to 85%. In comparison, MobileNetV2 has a much lighter weight (10 MB) with higher accuracy (up to 90%). The accuracy of InceptionResNetV2 is slightly higher than that of the others (up to 91%), but its size of 210 MB is significant.

Next, the models are fine-tuned, this allows you to increase the number of correct results, but this increases their weight. After additional training of the VGG19 model, the classes become relatively separated, the accuracy reaches up to 95%, and the weight is 230 MB. The t-SNE visualization is shown in Fig. 6.

After additional training of MobileNetV2, the accuracy was 96%, and its weight reached 22 MB. The separation of classes is not significantly stronger compared to VGG19. InceptionResNetV2 showed a greater accuracy of 97%, but also a greater weight of 620 MB. At the same time, this configuration shows a better separation of classes.

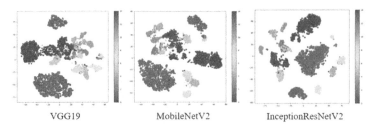

| VGG19 | MobileNetV2 | InceptionResNetV2 |

Fig. 6. Visualization of t-SNE after fine-tuning to identify the crop culture.

6.2 Determination of Corn Defects

One of the identified crops is corn. 5236 images of this plant were collected, which contain 6 types of defects. Various damages are shown in Fig. 7.

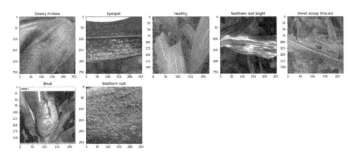

Fig. 7. Corn defects.

In the assembled set, there is a significant difference in the number of images of each class; weights are used to compensate. The visualization of the class distribution using VGG19 prior to training is shown in Fig. 8.

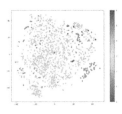

Fig. 8. Visualization of t-SNE for VGG19 before training for corn defect detection.

On the current dataset, the models also show high accuracy, while the accuracy ratio remains approximately the same as when classifying plants. The best result is shown by InceptionResNetV2 with an accuracy of 96.9%. To improve the accuracy, fine-tuning was used, the training results are shown in Fig. 9.

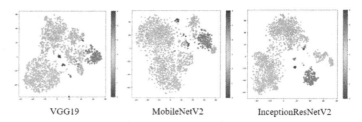

VGG19   MobileNetV2   InceptionResNetV2

Fig. 9. Visualization of t-SNE after training to detect corn defects.

6.3 Animal Identification

Detection was performed using the SSD MobileNet V2 FPNLite 640 × 640 model. The data set is ArTaxOr, which contains 15000 images, divided into 7 orders of insects [11]. The initial learning loss function is shown in Fig. 10a.

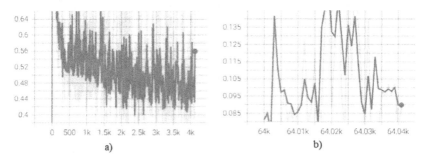

Fig. 10. Loss function of the initial (a) and the final (b) training stage of the model.

Figure 10a shows that with an increase in the number of steps, the rate of loss reduction slows down. The final training loss function is shown in Fig. 10b.

At the final stage of training, the value of the loss function reached 0.09.

7 Discussion

This paper discusses methods for identifying harmful objects. Identification operations are highlighted, including plant identification, disease identification, insect detection. A comparison of plant classification models is shown in Table 2.

Table 2. Comparison of plant crop classification models.

Model	Loss	Accuracy Matthews	Correlation
VGG19	0.2331	0.9525	0.9491
MobileNetV2	0.2107	0.9593	0.9488
InceptionResNetV2	0.1513	0.9701	0.9672

The highest determination accuracy is 97%, the best data is shown by the InceptionResNetV2 model. At the same time, the VGG19 and MobileNet-V2 models showed approximately the same results. Similar indicators are also seen in the classification of maize diseases, the results are shown in Table 3.

Table 3. Comparison of maize defect classification models.

Model	Loss	Accuracy Matthews	Correlation
VGG19	0.2639	0.9221	0.9061
MobileNetV2	0.2365	0.9190	0.9066
InceptionResNetV2	0.0972	0.9691	0.9647

At the same time, it is worth considering the practical application of the models, the total weight of InceptionResNetV2 was more than 600 MB, while the MobileNetV2 model weighs only 20 MB, which is significantly less.

The detection of orders of insects is performed with sufficiently high accuracy; however, more detailed distribution of classes is required.

8   Conclusion

As a result of the work carried out, a system for identifying harmful agricultural objects was designed and implemented. These include plant diseases, weeds and pests.

The developed system is intended for use by agronomists or other persons interested in the search for harmful objects. This system allows to reduce labor intensity and reduce the time of territory survey, improve the quality of work. The program includes methods for identifying and detecting objects in the image.

The main direction of further development and improvement of the developed system is to increase the number of recognizable objects, increase the accuracy of identification models. To collect new images and improve the quality of interaction with users, it is possible to create an interface that will allow you to submit applications for adding new crops and animals to the existing library.

References

1. Al-Gunaid, M.A., Shcherbakov, M.V., Trubitsin, V.N., Shumkin, A.M., Dereguzov, K.Y.: Analysis a short-term time series of crop sales based on machine learning Methods. In: Kravets, A.G., Groumpos, P.P., Shcherbakov, M., Kultsova, M. (eds.) CIT&DS 2019. CCIS, vol. 1083, pp. 189–200. Springer, Cham (2019). https://doi.org/10.1007/978-3-030-29743-5_15
2. Al-Gunaid, M.A., Shcherbakov, M.V., Trubitsin, V.N., Shumkin, A.M.: Time series analysis sales of sowing crops based on machine learning methods. Volgograd State Technical University (2018)

3. Sanin, S.S.: Problems of phytosanitary in Russia at the present stage. Izvestiya TSKhA **6**, 45 (2016)
4. A Robust Deep-Learning-Based Detector for Real-Time Tomato Plant Diseases and Pests Recognition. https://www.mdpi.com/1424-8220/17/9/2022/pdf
5. Using Deep Learning for Image-Based Plant Diseas Detection. https://www.frontiersin.org/articles/https://doi.org/10.3389/fpls.2016.01419/full
6. Smetanin, A.A., Goncharov, P.V., Ososkov, G.A.: The choice of deep learning methods for solving the problem of recognizing plant diseases in a small training sample. Syst. Anal. Sci. Educ. Netw. Sci. Publ. **1**, 30–38 (2020)
7. Plantix Vision Disease Recognition Offers. https://plantix.net/en/business
8. Yara CheckIT is an application for identifying possible nutrient deficiencies in crops. https://www.yara.ru/crop-nutrition/tools-and-services/yara-checkit
9. Determination of plant diseases. http://pdd.jinr.ru
10. Kogotko, L.G., Mirenkov, Y.A., Saskevich, P.A., Strelkova, E.V.: Plant protection: a tutorial, p. 340. Minsk (2016)
11. Arthropod Taxonomy Orders Object Detection Dataset, Kaggle. https://www.kaggle.com/mistag/arthropod-taxonomy-orders-object-detectiondataset
12. Very deep convolutional networks for large scale image recognition. https://arxiv.org/pdf/1409.1556
13. MobileNetV2:Inverted Residuals and Linear Bottlenecks. https://arxiv.org/pdf/1801.04381
14. Inception-v4, Inception-ResNet and the Impact of Residual Connections on Learning. https://arxiv.org/pdf/1602.07261
15. How to use binary and categorical crossentropy with TensorFlow. https://www.machinecurve.com/index.php/2019/10/22/how-to-use-binarycategorical-crossentropy-with-keras
16. The best metric for assessing the accuracy of classification models. http://datareview.info/article/luchshaya-metrika-dlya-ocenki-tochnostiklassifikacionnyx-modelej
17. Bianco, S., Cadene, R., Celona, L., Napoletano, P.: Benchmark Analysis of Representative Deep Neural Network Architectures (2018)
18. TensorFlow 2 Detection Model Zoo. https://github.com/tensorflow/models/blob/master/research/objectdetection
19. Redis Documentation. https://redis.io/documentation
20. Django documentation. https://docs.djangoproject.com/en/3.2
21. TensorFlow Core. https://www.tensorflow.org/overview

Cyber-Physical Systems and Big Data-Driven World. Pro-Active Modeling in Intelligent Decision Making Support

Formalization of the Choice for Optimal Technological Solutions

Yuri Kazakov$^{(\boxtimes)}$ and Anastasia Tishchenko

Department of Computer Technologies and Systems, Bryansk State Technical University,
7 Bulvar 50-letiya Oktyabrya, Bryansk 241035, Russian Federation

Abstract. One of the ways of increasing the efficiency of the industrial sector of the economy is the use of modern information technologies, providing integration of processes aimed at supporting the entire life cycle of products and their components. The analysis of modern research and development in the field of technological preparation of production (TPP) allows making a note of the fact that the greatest effect can be obtained with a comprehensive solution of the assigned tasks. At the same time, one of the main problems is to improve the quality of products. Being an integrated concept, quality includes various properties and characteristics of products. In general, you can think of the quality of a product as a set of properties, determining the conformity or suitability for the use of the product as intended. Tenderable grades of a product or process can vary widely, ranging from an assessment of its main purpose and reasonableness to additional by-effects, such as ergonometric, environmental, etc. When designing the technology of manufacturing processes, there is a problem of choosing the best way or design solution in terms of certain criteria. The solution to this problem is connected with the evaluation and enumeration of information bulk, which increases the complexity of technological design and reduces its efficiency. At the same time, the phenomena (criteria) that determine the final result, considered when solving this type of problem, vary in their composition and are not directly measurable. The development of automated systems can significantly reduce the complexity of design solutions, increase their efficiency and quality.

Keywords: Automated systems · Databases · Optimization · Expert assessments · Mathematical methods · Manufacturing techniques

1 Introduction

One of the ways for the improvement of the industrial sector effectiveness is the use of modern information technologies, ensuring the integration of processes aimed at supporting the whole service life of products and their components. Thus, when designing technological processes, the problem of choosing the rationale or the most suitable design solution in terms of certain criteria occurs. The solution to this problem means evaluating and sorting through a large amount of information, which increases the complexity of technological design and reduces its efficiency [1, 2]. The development of automated systems can significantly reduce the complexity of design solutions, increase their

© Springer Nature Switzerland AG 2021
A. G. Kravets et al. (Eds.): CIT&DS 2021, CCIS 1448, pp. 193–206, 2021.
https://doi.org/10.1007/978-3-030-87034-8_15

efficiency and quality. The task of optimizing the technological process involves three main elements: mathematical model of the process, target function, and the optimization algorithm. Mathematical models and target functions describe all the links between the technical, technological, and organizational limitations concerning required solutions, essential for the design. These restrictions are also used in traditional methods of solving problems, where they have the form of various regulatory guidelines and requirements, presented either in the form of tables, graphs, or in the form of functional relationships [3]. Currently, the creation of new products is increasingly becoming possible due to the development and implementation of advanced technological processes (TP) using new processing methods (PM): electrochemical, electrophysical, thermal, vacuum spraying, laser and ion treatments, etc. These methods allow solving the problems of engineering support for the quality of products, and a number of others:

- Economic: cost reduction;
- Environmental: the use of low-waste and resource-saving technology.

2   Model Evaluation and Selection PM

Exploring various PM, it can be noted that they have certain areas of application. The limiting criteria of the field can be machinability, productivity, energy demands, the initial quality of the workpiece, and others. By varying the criteria, you can go beyond the scope of the method and disrupt processing [4]. By reference to this, it can be concluded that choosing a PM, it is necessary to determine the boundaries of its rational use first of all, as a result of which should be the whole new processing [5]. Thus, in a number of studies, as criteria for evaluating methods of electrophysicochemical and combined processing (EPhCP), it was proposed to use:

- Comparative manufacturability of EPhCP methods;
- Approximate comparison of the benefits of EPhCP compared to cutting, depending on the complexity of the shape and the hardness of the material;
- Comparison of EPhCP methods by the complexity of the tool and by the nature of the tool used;
- Comparison by equipment complexity;
- Comparison of EPhCP methods, if possible, for their automation and mechanization;
- Comparison by labor costs;
- Comparison by material consumption;
- Comparison by energy consumption indicators;
- Comparison of EPhCP methods and blade processing methods in regard to best applicability
- Comparison of structural change features in the surface layer after different EPhCP methods; etc.

Thus, the evaluation and selection of PM is presented as a complex multi-criteria task [6]. As noted above, each method is characterized by a certain set of parameters. Evaluating PM as far as ensuring the required quality of the product, the main characteristics of PM will primarily be represented by physical and chemical properties of the object and its surface layer characteristics after processing, that is, the output parameters of the workpiece. All these properties, in turn, bear the impress of heredity and their achievement, depending on the initial condition of the object. Therefore, the second group of PM characteristics will be presented by physical and chemical properties and surface layer characteristics of the object before processing, that is, the input parameters of the workpiece. As it was noted, the choice of PM can be based on the analysis of expert assessments concerning their rational use [7]. The phenomena (criteria) that determine the final result, which are considered when solving this type of problem, are of various composition and cannot have a direct measurement [3, 8, 9]. Therefore, one of the stages of making a solution is the ranking and normalization of the results of expert assessments. Ranking is the assignment of positive whole numbers, when determining the relative significance to the phenomena (objects), prescribing their procedure. If there are several groups of factors, a number of methods are used to evaluate each object: simple ranking, summing weighted average ratings, ranking on the given scale, etc. Simple ranking involves placing factors in a sequence of corresponding significance groups and factors within groups. So, when evaluating PM according to a number of criteria, PM of the group with the highest rank comes first, etc. This method, being the simplest, does not allow evaluating "critical" PM with the lowest rank in the group, and also ignores the significance of individual groups. The methods of ranking according to the value, using scales, make the adjusting of factor score possible. The adjustment factor is obtained by dividing the group estimate by the sum of the factor scores within the group. The disadvantage of this method is the significant influence of a number of factors in the group. To eliminate it, a combined ranking method was used, where the factor score was determined by the sum of the group score and the given factor score was defined within the group.

$$\overline{V}_{ij} = V_j * \frac{V_j}{\sum\limits_{i=1}^{n} V_{ij}} V_{ij}, \tag{1}$$

where V_{ij} - the i-th factor score of the j-th group;
n - a number of factors within a group;
V_j - the group score.

The average estimate of an object for a group of experts was determined by dividing the normalized estimates of the object by a number of experts:

$$\overline{V} = \frac{\sum\limits_{i=1}^{k} V_i}{k}, \tag{2}$$

where $\underline{k}$ - a number of experts.

With a large number of objects (PM) and factors (criteria), ranking by methods of direct evaluation and sequential comparisons is quite time-consuming. Therefore, the method of paired comparisons was proposed to evaluate PM. The basis of the method is the formation of a matrix of paired comparisons, in which the number of rows and columns is equal to the number of compared factors, and their intersection is the estimate (ratio) of the compared factors [8, 9].

The solution of the problem of PM evaluation according to the criteria of their rational use is a rational choice of alternatives for given matrices of relations-pair comparison. As the main criteria for evaluating PM, the following factors are given:

- Comparative manufacturability of processing methods;
- Comparison of PM by the complexity of the processing form;
- Comparison of PM by tool complexity;
- Comparison of PM by the hardness of the processed material;
- Comparison of PM by complexity of the equipment;
- Comparison of PM, if possible, by their automation and mechanization;
- Comparison of PM by material consumption;
- Comparison of PM by labor costs;
- Comparison of PM by energy demands;
- Comparison of PM by the impact on the surface quality (roughness parameters, structural changes);
- Comparison of PM considering environmental factors, etc.

3   Methods for Selecting Optimal Solutions

At the first stage, a pair-wise comparison of the relative criterion weights is carried out based on the main goal of the task. The number of criteria is determined by experts in the range from 5 to 15. For each criterion, the relative weights of the pair-wise comparison of the evaluated PM are also determined. The results of pair-wise comparisons are presented in matrix form and appear as follows (Table 1):

Table 1. Pair-wise comparison matrix.

	A_1	A_2	...	A_j	...	A_n
A_1	a_{11}	a_{12}	...	a_{1j}	...	a_{1n}
A_2	a_{21}	a_{22}	...	a_{2j}	...	a_{2n}
...	...	...	...	...	...	...
A_i	a_{i1}	a_{i2}	...	a_{ij}	...	a_{in}
...	...	...	...	...	...	...
A_n	a_{n1}	a_{n2}	...	a_{nj}	...	a_{nn}

where a_{ij} – the i-th/j-th factor weight ratio.

Accordingly, the results of the pair-wise comparison of PM for each criterion are presented. In this case, the solution is reduced to finding the fare weight of the criteria together with PM, which will be determined by the eigenvector of the matrix:

$$Ax = \lambda x, \ (A - \lambda E)x = 0 \tag{3}$$

where x - eigenvector of the matrix;

E – unity matrix;
λ - matrix eigenvalue.
In expanded form, the equality will be represented by:

$$\begin{aligned}
a_{11}x_1 + a_{12}x_2 + \ldots + a_{1i}x_i + a_{1n}x_n &= \lambda x_1 \\
a_{21}x_1 + a_{22}x_2 + \ldots + a_{2i}x_i + a_{2n}x_n &= \lambda x_2 \\
a_{j1}x_1 + a_{j2}x_2 + \ldots + a_{ji}x_i + a_{jn}x_n &= \lambda x_j \\
a_{n1}x_1 + a_{n2}x_2 + \ldots + a_{ni}x_i + a_{nn}x_n &= \lambda x_n
\end{aligned} \tag{4}$$

So that a system shall have a non-zero solution, it is necessary and sufficient for the determinant of the system to be equal to zero:

$$\begin{vmatrix}
a_{11} - \lambda\ a_{12} \ldots a_{1i}\ a_{1n} \\
a_{21}\ a_{22} - \lambda \ldots a_{2i}\ a_{2n} \\
a_{j1}\ a_{j2} \ldots a_{ji} - \lambda\ a_{jn} \\
a_{n1}\ a_{n2} \ldots a_{ni}\ a_{nn} - \lambda
\end{vmatrix} = 0 \tag{5}$$

Each value λ of the characteristic equation corresponds to an eigenvector, the values of which are determined by the equation:

$$\Delta(A - \lambda E) = 0 \tag{6}$$

To determine the eigenvector of the matrix, the method of iterative calculus was used, and the determinant of the matrix was found by the Gaus method.

At the next stage, the weights of the criteria and processing methods for each criterium, obtained as a result of determining the eigenvectors of the pair-wise comparison matrices, are ordered and ranked. The average score for a group of experts is obtained as the weighted average of their scores (Table 2).

Table 2. Weighted average sum of expert ratings

	Πp_1	Πp_2	Πp_3	...	Πp_i	Πp_n
W	w_1	w_2	w_3	...	w_i	w_n
	Πp_1	Πp_2	Πp_3	...	Πp_i	Πp_n
MO_1	v_{11}	v_{12}	v_{13}	...	v_{1i}	v_{1n}
MO_2	v_{21}	v_{22}	v_{23}	...	v_{2i}	v_{2n}
MO_j	v_{j1}	v_{j2}	v_{j3}	...	v_{ji}	v_{jn}
MO_k	v_{k1}	v_{k2}	v_{k3}	...	v_{ki}	v_{kn},

where $\Pi p_1 \ldots \Pi p_n$ - criteria;
w_i - criterion weight;
v_{ji} - PM weight.

The criteria entered can be considered as target functions. The choice of processing method is a choice of alternatives, taking into account the "n" of target functions. To do this, the weighted sum of the specified criteria (target functions) is determined and a PM, having the maximum value of the resulting sum, is chosen. To determine PM weights, the matrix of relative PM weights is multiplied by the matrix-column of criteria weights. The preferred method is that one, having the maximum weight of the criteria.

The expert group assessment can be considered sufficiently reliable in case of good consistency of the responses [3]. The degree of consistency of responses can be determined taking into account the coefficient of variation, which is the ratio of the number of distinguishable pairs of events to the maximum possible number. It is defined by the following relation:

$$\omega_j = \frac{n}{n-1} \frac{(\sum\limits_{i=1}^{n} \gamma_{ji})^2 - \sum\limits_{i=1}^{n} \gamma_{ji}^2}{(\sum\limits_{i=1}^{n} \gamma_{ji})^2}, \tag{7}$$

where ω_j - the coefficient of variation of the j-th factor;
γ_{ij} – a number of factor's rate.
In this case, the expert responses are presented in the form of a table of the set of variate values of ranked assessment.

The consistency of the experts' responses on several criteria that influence the choice of PM is determined by the concordance coefficient W. The value of the coefficient varies from 0 to 1, a value close to "0" means that the relationship between expert estimation is small, a value close to "1" speaks in the favor of the agreement of estimation results.

$$W = \frac{S}{S\max}; \tag{8}$$

$$S = \sum_{i=1}^{n} \left\{ \sum_{j=1}^{m} x_{ij} - \frac{1}{2}m(n+1) \right\}^2; \tag{9}$$

$$S\max = \frac{1}{2}nm^2(n^2 - 1), \tag{10}$$

where S – sum of squared difference of rank variance.
x_{ij}- rank of the i-th criterion defined by the j-th expert;
S_{max} - sum of squared difference of rank variance in case of the best agreement;
m – a number of experts;
n - a number of criteria.
With a large number of criteria used, the distribution of χ^2 at n − 1 degrees of freedom was used to assess the significance of the concordance coefficient.

$$\chi^2 = Wm(n - 1), \tag{11}$$

The concordance coefficient is significant when the received value χ^2 is more than table one (with a given number of degrees of freedom and a confidence level).

In the formalized representation, a PM is characterized by a large number of indicators: indicators of the initial workpiece, indicators of the workpiece after processing, process indicators. In addition, these characteristics are quite heterogeneous in their structure and meaning. Therefore, the evaluation and selection of the most optimal PM becomes a time-consuming, multi-criteria task. The various characteristics of PM are almost impossible to bring under a single scale. Comparing the options according to many criteria, you have to use different scales. Moreover, according to one scale, some options may be considered the best, according to another scale other options may be the best. Also, comparison criteria used are not always equal, some are more important, others are less important.

This confirms that the solution of such problems belongs to the problems of multi-criteria optimization. The peculiarity of such tasks lies in the impossibility of achieving the optimum for all criteria simultaneously. It's reasonable to find a compromise option.

4 Principles of Building Compromise Optimization Schemes

Based on the analysis of the enumerated principles of outlining compromise optimization schemes and the characteristics of PM, a multi-level optimization structure with a criteria convolution function is proposed. Each PM quality characteristic is represented by an interval of possible values and is designed as a functional relationship or array.

The first level of optimization involves the selection of PM by quality characteristics, i.e. the assessment of PM suitability will be entering of each of the required quality values in the range of values provided by this PM. The solution to this problem is complicated by the difference in the criteria units of measurement. To eliminate this, a criteria normalized vector with dimensionless components is defined. As for estimation of PM it is reliability of providing the required parameter that is expressed by the probability of its provision and the comparison of the obtained probability with the specified one. The probability of security is dimensionless, which makes it possible to combine the criteria and transform them. Thus, the first level of optimization is the search for PMs that can ensure execution of the specified quality parameters with a given probability of their provision.

$$A_i \in \left\langle a_i^{\min}, a_i^{\max} \right\rangle;$$
$$P_i \geq P_i^3,$$

(12)

where A_i – specified quality parameter;
$a_i^{\min}$, $a_i^{\max}$ - parameter interval A_i in PM;
P_i^3 - a given probability of the provision of the parameter A_i.

Evaluating physical meaning of quality indicators, three possible options for PM estimation can be offered. The first option and the most preferable is to achieve the average value of the interval of quality parameters. Depending on the necessary requirements for the state of the surface layer this is the residual hardness or yield stress.

The criterion for this condition is the probability of a random variable P, which differs from "a" more than P^{TP} from "a"

$$P\left\{ |P - a| > \left| P^{TP} - a \right| \right\},$$

(13)

where a is the mathematical expectation of P variable;
P^{TP} is the required value of P variable.

If the parameter has a normal distribution, then geometrically it can be represented as a shaded area (Fig. 1)

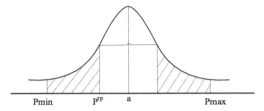

Fig. 1. Geometrical representation of probability to ensure a given quality

The higher the probability, the more reliable it is to obtain P^{TP} parameter.

$$P\{|P - a| > c\} = 1 - 2\Phi_{\prime\prime}\left(\frac{C}{\sigma}\right), \tag{14}$$

where $\Phi_{\prime\prime}$ is Laplace's function.

As examples of the second and third options, the parameters can be used, which increase or decrease is the most acceptable for PM (Figs. 2 and 3). Thus, roughness reduction Ra, achieved at a certain PM in comparison with other PM, other things being equal, makes this method the most preferable. The criterion in this case is one-sided probability value.

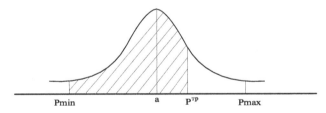

Fig. 2. Geometrical representation of probability to ensure a given quality

$$P\left\{P < P^{TP}\right\} = \frac{1}{2} + \Phi_{\prime\prime}\left\{\frac{P^{TP} - a}{\sigma}\right\},$$

$$P\left\{P < P^{TP}\right\}. \tag{15}$$

Under the condition that one PM is preferred over other PM, when they are compared by a criterion which increase is more favorable, the criterion is also a one-sided probability value. An example of such a parameter can be the degree of hardening, the relative reference length of the profile.

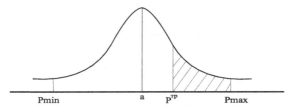

Fig. 3. Geometrical representation of probability to ensure a given quality

$$P\left\{P < P^{TP}\right\} = \frac{1}{2} - \Phi_{\prime\prime}\left\{\frac{P^{TP} - a}{\sigma}\right\},$$

$$P\left\{P < P^{TP}\right\}$$

$$(16)$$

Taking into account the different influence of the surface quality parameters and its physical and mechanical properties on the operational properties of products, the priorities of the criteria and, accordingly, the weight coefficients are determined from the condition for ensuring the specified operational properties. The designer himself directly determines the importance of a particular parameter. After determining the degree of reliability to provide the specified parameters, it is compared with the specified value of the probability to provide the parameters.

$$P^3 \leq P^P, \tag{17}$$

where P^3 is the specified value of the probability to provide Ai parameter;
P^P is the expected value of the probability to provide Ai parameter.

The resulting criteria have one dimensionless value. At the second stage of solving the first problem, the priority vector is constructed, weight coefficients are determined, and the criteria are rolled in. To obtain a generalized criterion, a convolution of criteria is used, obtained by summing individual criteria with their weight coefficients $C_1...C_m$.

$$\sum_{i=1}^{m} C_i = 1,$$

$$K_j = C_1 P_1 +, \ldots, + C_m P_m$$

$$(18)$$

Using this method of criteria convolution, it is possible to choose the optimal PM, which received the largest K_j, but has very small individual components of P_i. Thus, the selected PM can be critical according to any criterion. Therefore, it is advisable to use the minimization function as a generalized criterion.

$$K = \frac{1}{C_1 P_1} +, \ldots, + \frac{1}{C_m P_m},$$

$$\frac{optM}{M \in \Omega M} = \min(K),$$

$$(19)$$

PM, which has a low probability for any parameter, gives a sharp increase in K_j and, accordingly, reduces the possibility of choosing it as an optimal one.

The second level of optimization means the choice of mathematical expectations that provide minimum energy consumption and maximum performance.

$$\begin{cases} \dfrac{optM}{M \in \Omega_M} = \min(Q); \\[2mm] \dfrac{optM}{M \in \Omega_M} = \max(n). \end{cases} \tag{20}$$

where Ω_M is the set of possible mathematical expectations, chosen at the first level.

Since the provided parameters are random variables, described by certain distribution laws and the processing modes for providing these parameters have some boundary zones, respectively, the performance and energy consumption will also change in a certain range of values:

$$\begin{aligned} \left[\Pi^i_{\min}; \Pi^i_{\max}\right], \\ \left[Q^i_{\min}; Q^i_{\max}\right]. \end{aligned} \tag{21}$$

Analysing the task at hand we can propose three approaches to optimization.

1. Evaluation of PM by minimum energy consumption and, accordingly, maximum productivity

$$\begin{cases} \dfrac{optM}{M \in \Omega_M} = \min(Q); \\[2mm] \dfrac{optM}{M \in \Omega_M} = \max(\Pi). \end{cases} \tag{22}$$

2. Evaluation of PM by the average value of productivity and energy consumption

$$\Pi^i_{cp} = \frac{\Pi^i_{\min} + \Pi^i_{\max}}{2} \quad Q^i_{cp} = \frac{Q^i_{\min} + Q^i_{\max}}{2} \tag{23}$$

$$\frac{optM}{M \in \Omega_M} = \max(\Pi_{cp}) \quad \frac{optM}{M \in \Omega_M} = \min(Q_{cp}) \tag{24}$$

3. The third approach is to compare by a complex criterion that takes into account interval width. This is especially important when comparing mathematical expectations with different interval widths

$$K^i = \Pi^i_{-p} - \frac{1}{3}\frac{\Pi^i_{\max} - \Pi^i_{\min}}{2}, \tag{25}$$

The meaning of this criterion is that the parameter of the normal distribution σ is used to deviate to the left from the average value. At the same time, under the condition of a normal distribution, performance is guaranteed to be achieved with a probability of at least 0.841. Evaluation of PM, in this case, is formed based on the average value of the interval and its width. This is clearly seen from the following example. $K_1 < K_2$, therefore mathematical expectation MO_2 is more preferable than MO_1.

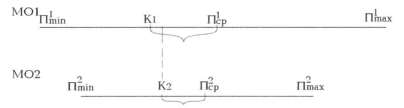

Fig. 4. The scheme of evaluation of mathematical expectations according to the complex criterion

All the proposed approaches to choosing the optimal PM in terms of performance and energy consumption can be reduced to a single criterion (Fig. 4).

$$\Pi = \Pi_{min} + K\frac{\Pi_{max} - \Pi_{min}}{6},$$

$$Q = Q_{min} + K\frac{Q_{max} - Q_{min}}{6}. \tag{26}$$

Values $K = 0, 3, 2$ bring the formula to 1, 2 and 3 variants respectively.

To optimize PM in terms of performance and energy consumption, the selected criteria are normalized, i.e. they are reduced to a dimensionless form, weight coefficients are determined and their convolution is performed. Weight factor in this case determines the priority of the impact of energy consumption or productivity.

The generalized dimensionless criterion is represented by the dependence:

$$F_i = \lambda\frac{\Pi_{i^n}}{\sum\limits_{i=1}^{n}\Pi_i} + \frac{(1-\lambda)\sum\limits_{i=1}^{n}Q_i}{nQ_i}, \tag{27}$$

where λ is weight factor;

$\frac{\Pi_{i^n}}{\sum\limits_{i=1}^{n}\Pi_i}$ is dimensionless criterion of productivity;

$\frac{(1-\lambda)\sum\limits_{i=1}^{n}Q_i}{nQ_i}$ is dimensionless criterion of energy consumption.

If $\lambda = 0$ the evaluation is done according to energy consumption, if $\lambda = 1$ the evaluation is done according to productivity. Thus, the most optimal will be PM which has the biggest F value.

One of the problems in solving the task of optimizing the choice of PM is to identify the law of distribution of quality characteristics represented by mathematical models [10]. A number of dependencies of roughness characteristics on the processing modes obtained by simulation and experimentally for a number of PM have been analyzed [4, 5]. Based on the main limit theorem, it can be assumed that the studied characteristics will have a normal distribution. Monte Carlo method was used as a mechanism for evaluating the distribution law. Thus, Pearson criterion analysis of simulation models obtained by Professor V.P. Fedorov for electromechanical processing, fine turning, diamond smoothing, round grinding showed that roughness characteristics mainly have a normal or logarithmically normal distribution.

Electromechanical Processing
The material is 45 steel after grinding and fine turning. The initial value Ra (pr) = 1.98
μm

$$
\begin{aligned}
Ra &= 0.006 \frac{Ra_{(\Pi P)}^{1.03} V^{0.37} S^{0.35} r^{0.36}}{I^{0.03} Q^{0.04} (tg\varphi_a)^{1.03}}, \\
Rp &= 0.026 \frac{Ra_{(np)}^{0.98} V^{0.257} S^{0.42}}{I^{0.04} Q^{0.336} (tg\varphi_a)^{0.88} r^{0.28}}.
\end{aligned}
\tag{28}
$$

The dependence was evaluated at the following initial values: $Ra = 1.5$–6.87 μm,
$V = 30$–80 m/min, $Q = 0.3$–0.8 kN, $S = 0.07$–0.15 mm/rev, $r = 0.5$–1.5 mm, $I = 10$–500 A, $tg\varphi a = 0.006$–0.012.

Fine Turning
The material is steel 45 HRC 48–50. The intervals of initial values of processing modes:
$S_1 = 0.05$–0.2 mm/rev, $r = 0.1$–0.8 mm, $\varphi_0 = 30$–60, $\varphi_1 = 15$–30, $\gamma + 15 = 5$–25, $V_1 = 45$–180 mm/rev, $J = 2.6$–16.7 kN/mm, $t = 0.1$–0.3 mm.

$$
\begin{aligned}
Ra &= 2.9 \frac{S_1 \varphi_1^{0.563} V_1^{0.136}}{r^{0.45} \varphi_o^{0.102} (\gamma + 15)^{0.109} J^{0.13} t^{0.25}}, \\
Rp &= 4.9 \frac{S_1^{0.87} \varphi_1^{0.52} V_1^{0.142}}{r^{0.42} \varphi_o^{0.13} (\gamma + 15)^{0.105} J^{0.123} t^{0.25}}, \\
Sm &= 1590 \frac{S_1^{0.74} \varphi_1^{0.076} V_1^{0.067}}{r^{0.13} \varphi_o^{0.5} (\gamma + 15)^{0.06} J^{0.124} t^{0.188}}, \\
tm &= 0.51 \frac{S_1^{0.021} \varphi_0^{0.1} r^{0.067}}{\varphi_1^{0.072} (\gamma + 15)^{0.02} V1^{0.142} J^{0.012}}.
\end{aligned}
\tag{29}
$$

Diamond Smoothing
The material is steel 45 HRC 48–50 after turning with composite 10, diamond SPCD,
machine oil 20. The intervals of initial values of processing modes: $S_1 = 0.05$–0.2 mm/rev,
$r = 0.1$–0.8 mm, $\varphi_0 = 30$–60, $\varphi_1 = 15$–30, $\gamma + 15 = 5$–25, $V_1 = 45$–180 m/min, $J = 2.6$–16.7 kN/mm, $t = 0.1$–0.3 mm, $Q = 50$–200 H, $S_2 = 0.05$–0.15 mm/rev, $V_2 = 45$–180 m/min, $r = 3.5$ mm

$$
\begin{aligned}
Ra &= 37 \frac{S_1^{0.9} \varphi_1^{0.51} V_1^{0.433} J^{0.164} S_2^{0.347}}{r^{0.413} \varphi_0^{0.338} (\gamma + 15)^{0.109} t^{0.467} Q^{0.745} V_2^{0.251}}, \\
Rp &= 5.21 \frac{S_1^{0.731} \varphi_1^{0.404} (\gamma + 15)^{0.008} V_1^{0.452} J^{0.143} S_2^{0.3}}{r^{0.337} \varphi_0^{0.06} t^{0.357} Q^{0.535} V_2^{0.123}}, \\
Sm &= 6207 \frac{S_1^{0.634} \varphi_1^{0.186} V_1^{0.268} S_2^{0.192}}{r^{0.172} \varphi_0^{0.623} (\gamma + 15)^{0.113} t^{0.3} Q^{0.365} V_2^{0.209}}, \\
tm &= 0.822 \frac{S_1^{0.047} \varphi_1^{0.085} J^{0.012}}{r^{0.039} \varphi_0^{0.051} (\gamma + 15)^{0.05} V_1^{0.01} t^{0.033} Q^{0.038} S_2^{0.024} V_2^{0.041}}.
\end{aligned}
\tag{30}
$$

On the basis of the analysis of developing technological process, its structural-logical and mathematical models PM, ways of formalization are considered, the criteria for evaluating mathematical expectations are proposed and an algorithm for selecting resource-saving PM is developed, based on multi-criteria optimization by quality characteristics, taking into account the probability of providing the specified criteria, as well as productivity and energy consumption.

Evaluating physical meaning of quality indicators, three possible options for PM estimation can be offered. Within the first option, the most preferred is to achieve the average value of the quality parameter interval.

As examples of the second and third options, the used parameters can increase or decrease and that is the most suitable for PM.

Taking into account that quality surface parameters and physical and mechanical properties of the surface have different effects on service characteristics of the products, the priorities of the criteria and, accordingly, the weighting factors are defined in terms of conditions for ensuring specified service characteristics. After determining the degree of reliability for ensuring the specified parameters, it is compared with the specified value of the probability of ensuring the parameters.

An intelligent computer environment is a software tool that supports programming technology with the maximum involvement of the knowledge and skills of experts and users. Thus, for designing solutions of the technological process structure synthesis, an automated system was created, including the expert data processing module and the automated data bank of processing methods (ADB PM).

References

1. Goransky, G.K.: Technological design in complex automated systems of production preparation. In: Goransky, G.K., Bendereva, E.I.-M. (eds.) Mashinostroenie, p. 456 (1981)
2. Kapustin, N.M.: Automation of design and technological design. In: Kapustin, N.M., Vasiliev, G.N.-M. (eds.) Higher School, p. 191 (1986)
3. Rumshinsky, L.Z.: Mathematical processing of experimental results. In: Rumshinsky, L.Z.-M. (ed.) Nauka, p. 192 (1971)
4. Suslov, A.G.: Technological support of parameters of the state of the surface layer of parts. In: Suslov, A.G.-M. (ed.) Mashinostroenie, p. 209 (1987)
5. Poduraev, V.N.: Technology of Physical and Chemical Processing Methods. In: Poduraev, V. N.-M. Mechanical Engineering, p. 264 (1985)
6. Averchenkov, V.I.: Automation of design of technological processes. In: Averchenkov, V.I., Kazakov Yu.M. (eds.), p. 228. Publishing house Bryansk State Technical University, Bryansk (2012). ISBN: 5-89838-130-9
7. Dvoryankin, A.M.: Methods of synthesis of technical solutions. In: Dvoryankin, A.M., Polovinkin, A.I., Sobolev, A.N.-M. Nauka, p. 104 (1977)
8. Saati, T.: Decision-making method of hierarchy analysis. In: Saati, T. (ed.) Translated from English by R.G. Vachnadze, p. 278. Radio and Communications, Moscow (1993)
9. David, G.: The Method of Paired Comparisons. In: David, G.M. (ed.) Statistics, p. 144 (1978)
10. Fedorov, V.P.: Mathematical modeling in mechanical engineering. In: Fedorov, V.P. (ed.), p. 111. Publishing house of BSTU, Bryansk (2013). ISBN 978-5-89838-656-6
11. Mitrofanov, S.P.: The use of computers in the technological preparation of serial production. In: Mitrofanov, S.P.-M. (ed.) Mechanical Engineering, p. 287 (1981)

12. Kazakov, Yu.M.: Formalization of technological decision-making when ensuring the product life cycle. In: Kazakov, Yu.M. (ed.) Izvestiya Orel State Technical University. Fundamental and Applied Problems of Engineering and Technology, vol. 3–7(271), pp. 58–65 (2008)
13. Averchenkov, V.I., Averchenkov, A.V., Bespalov, V.A., Shkaberin, V.A., Kazakov, Yu.M., et al.: Innovative Centers of High Technologies in Mechanical Engineering (3rd edn. Stereotypical), p. 180. Publishing house: "FLINT" (Moscow), Moscow (2016). ISBN 978-5-9765-1257-3
14. Kazakov, Yu.M., Tishchenko, A.A., Kuzmenko, A.A., Leonov, Yu.A., et al.: Methodology and Technology of Information Systems Design. FLINT Publishing House, Moscow, p. 136 (2018). ISBN: 978-5-9765-4013-2
15. Cherepakhin, A.A.: Processes and operations of shaping. In: Cherepakhin A.A., Klepikov, V.V. (eds.), p. 256. Kurs Publishing House (2016). ISBN 978-5-906818-28-7
16. Tsvetkov, V.D.: System of automation of design of technological processes. In: Tsvetkov, V.D.-M. (ed.) Mashinostroenie, p. 240 (1972)
17. Tsvetkov, V.D.: System-structural modeling and automation of design of technological processes. In: Tsvetkov, V.D. (ed.), p. 264. Science and Technology, Minsk (1979)
18. The technologist's handbook/under the general editorship of Suslov, A.G.M. Innovative Mechanical Engineering, p. 800 (2019). ISBN 978-5-907104-23-5
19. Stupachenko, A.A.: CAD of technological operations. In: Stupachenko, A.A.-L. (ed.) Mashinostroenie, p. 234 (1987)
20. Shpur, G., Krause, F.-L.: Computer-aided design in mechanical engineering. In: Shpur, G., Krause, F.-L.-M. (eds.) Mashinostroenie, p. 648 (1988)

Evaluating State Effectiveness in Control Model of a Generalized Computational Experiment

Alena Zakharova[1,2] , Dmitriy Korostelyov[1,3(✉)] ,
and Aleksandr Podvesovskii[1,3]

[1] Keldysh Institute of Applied Mathematics Russian Academy of Sciences, Moscow, Russia
[2] Institute of Control Sciences, Russian Academy of Sciences, Moscow, Russia
[3] Bryansk State Technical University, Bryansk, Russia
apodv@tu-bryansk.ru

Abstract. The paper investigates the problem of adaptive planning and control of a generalized computational experiment in mathematical modeling of real physical processes. A generalized computational experiment implies a multiple solution of the numerical simulation problem for different sets of values of defining model parameters. A general structure of a control model for a generalized computational experiment is proposed, the concept of the state of experiment is introduced, and a mechanism for evaluating its effectiveness is considered. A description of the concepts of reliability, representativeness, and efficiency for a generalized computational experiment is introduced. A detailed description of the algorithm for calculating the effectiveness of a generalized computational experiment based on the analysis of series of approximating curves built on subsets of modeling parameters is given. An example is given of determining the effectiveness of the state of a generalized computational experiment when assessing the accuracy of numerical models of the OpenFOAM software platform for a three-dimensional problem of inviscid flow around a cone.

Keywords: Generalized computational experiment · Experiment control · Multidimensional data · Approximation · Problem of flow around a cone · OpenFOAM

1 Introduction

In the study of mathematical models of real physical processes, in most cases, series of computational experiments are conducted within the framework of which the state of the model and its behavior in various ranges of variation of input variables and model parameters are studied [1]. With the development of computer technology and parallel computing technologies, it has become possible to construct a so-called generalized computational experiment (GCE) [2]. Its main idea is to repeatedly solve a direct or inverse problem of numerical simulation for various input data, where a set of values of simulation parameters act as the input data. As noted in [2], such an approach allows for obtaining a solution not for one but for a certain class of problems of mathematical modeling given in a multidimensional space of defining parameters. As a result,

© Springer Nature Switzerland AG 2021
A. G. Kravets et al. (Eds.): CIT&DS 2021, CCIS 1448, pp. 207–222, 2021.
https://doi.org/10.1007/978-3-030-87034-8_16

it becomes possible to simultaneously investigate the influence of several parameters on the model characteristics of interest, including investigating their joint influence in various combinations of variation ranges.

Note that both numerical values (for example some physical characteristics of the process under study) and qualitative indicators such as numerical methods, characteristics of software and hardware, etc. [3, 4] can act as defining parameters. This also makes it possible to apply a GCE for verification and assessment of accuracy of numerical methods for solving certain classes of problems in various ranges of input parameters.

Currently, there are examples of successful construction and implementation of a GCE in solving problems of computational fluid dynamics [2, 3], gas dynamics [4, 5], power plant design automation [6].

Obviously, both conducting a GCE and processing and interpreting its results are very resource-intensive tasks. Moreover, it seems impossible to conduct an experiment with all permissible combinations of models and simulation parameters. Therefore, it is necessary to resort to planning a GCE choosing a specific scenario for its implementation considering the available computing resources and time.

At the same time, following a predetermined plan for conducting a series of computational experiments may be inefficient, since significant shortcomings in the models on some areas of input data may be revealed at the early stages and, as a consequence, it may be impractical to perform the remaining computational experiments on these areas without appropriate adjustments to the models. On the other hand, in the course of processing the experimental results, some patterns may be discovered for validation and refinement of which additional computational experiments with new sets of parameters may be required. Thus, it is advisable to build a GCE on the basis of not a static, predetermined but a dynamic, adaptively changing plan. The principle of constructing such a plan can be as follows: based on the results of a series of experiments for a certain set of values of the defining parameters and processing of its results, in conjunction with the results of the previous series of experiments, the current state of the GCE is recorded. Based on the analysis and evaluation of the effectiveness of this state from the point of view of achieving the general goal of the GCE, a decision is made on the form and parameter values for which a new series of experiments should be carried out.

With this in mind, we arrive at the problem of adaptive planning and control of a generalized computational experiment. The paper proposes a control model structure, introduces a formalized representation of a GCE state, and considers a mechanism for evaluating its effectiveness. An example is given of determining the effectiveness of a GCE state when assessing the accuracy of numerical models of the OpenFOAM software platform [7] for a three-dimensional problem of inviscid flow around a cone.

2   Formalized Representation and Main Characteristics of the State of a Generalized Computational Experiment

As a rule, the purpose of a GCE is to determine or clarify characteristics and properties of models over which it is carried out. In particular, it can be a search for functional dependencies or patterns for predicting the investigated characteristics determined by the results of modeling. In addition, the goal of a GCE may be to compare the accuracy of models and also to define the areas where a particular model is more accurate than others.

Based on the formal description of a GCE for problems of computational gas dynamics given in [2], let us consider the problem statement of planning and control of a GCE and perform its formalization in a general form.

In the general case, the mathematical model of the system under study can be specified by the following set:

$$< X, Y, A, F > \tag{1}$$

where $X = (x_1, x_2, ..., x_L)$ is a vector of input variables, L is the number of input parameters, $Y = (y_1, y_2, ..., y_M)$ is a vector of output variables, M is the number of output parameters, $A = \{a_1, a_2, ..., a_N\}$ is a set of simulation parameters also called defining parameters [2], N is the number of the defining parameters, F is a mapping of the space of input variables into the space of output variables implemented using the model. The type of this mapping is determined by the structure of the model taking into account its defining parameters from set A.

As previously noted, it is supposed that both numerical values and qualitative indicators (used numerical methods, parameters of software and hardware, etc.) can act as defining parameters.

Each parameter a_k is characterized by tolerance range V_k ($k = 1, ..., N$). In the simplest case, this can be a variation range for a numeric parameter and a set of possible values for a non-numeric parameter. Also, considering the nature of the problem, the values of the parameters can be subject to joint constraints of the form

$$g_s(a_1, a_2, \ldots, a_N), s = 1, \ldots, S, \tag{2}$$

which can be specified in the form of equations, inequalities, or logical conditions. Thus, the set of ranges of parameter values together with the set of constraints of the form (2) defines the N-dimensional *space of defining parameters* **V**, which in the general case is a subset of the Cartesian product of value ranges of each parameter:

$$\mathbf{V} \subseteq V_1 \times V_2 \times \ldots V_N. \tag{3}$$

Since, as noted earlier, a GCE implies solution of a modeling problem by varying the defining parameters on some discrete set of points in the parameter space, then on the range V_k of values of each parameter a_k, a set of values $W_k = \{a_{k1}, a_{k2}, ..., a_{k,pk}\}$ is chosen, for each of which simulation will be conducted. Here a_{kj} is specific selected values of parameter $a_k, j = 1, ..., p_k$, p_k is the number of such values (it can be different for each parameter). In the simplest case, for a numerical parameter, W_k can be a set of equidistant points within the range of its values.

Space partition of defining parameters is a set of all possible tuples of the selected values of each parameter belonging to the space of parameters V, i.e. satisfying constraints (2):

$$\mathbf{W} = (W_1 \times W_2 \times \ldots W_N) \cap \mathbf{V}. \tag{4}$$

Any point belonging to this partition specifies a certain set of values of the defining parameters involved in the GCE:

$$w_i = (a_{1,i1}, a_{2,i2}, \ldots, a_{N,iN}), a_{k,ik} \in W_k. \tag{5}$$

Taking into account the introduced designations, a *single computational experiment* is characterized by a discrete vector field that defines distribution $\mathbf{Y}^*$ of the values of the vector of output variables Y for a given set $\mathbf{X}$ of values of the vector of input variables X with a certain fixed set w^* of values of the defining parameters belonging to the partition $\mathbf{W}$:

$$\mathbf{E^S} = <\mathbf{X}, \mathbf{Y}^* >, \tag{6}$$

where

$$\mathbf{Y}^* = \{Y = F(X, w^*), X \in \mathbf{X}\}. \tag{7}$$

In turn, a *generalized computational experiment* is characterized by an N-dimensional array the elements of which specify discrete vector fields corresponding to single computational experiments for all elements of the partition $\mathbf{W}$:

$$\mathbf{E^{Gen}} = <\mathbf{X}, \mathbf{Y}, \mathbf{W} >, \tag{8}$$

where

$$\mathbf{Y} = \{Y = F(X, w), X \in \mathbf{X}, w \in \mathbf{W}\}. \tag{9}$$

The resulting array of multidimensional data contains primary results of the GCE and cannot be considered as a solution to the modeling problem per se. Therefore, further processing is carried out in order to obtain useful for the researcher information about the object of modeling and the hidden patterns and relationships inherent in its defining parameters. Along with traditional methods of processing experimental data, intelligent data analysis approach is widely used including methods of visualization and visual-cognitive analytics [3, 8–10], methods of decision analysis under many criteria [11–13], expert methods [14–16], etc. In this case, integration and shared use of different approaches and methods are possible.

Thus, from the primary multidimensional array of experimental data specified by the set (8), a transition is made to some generalized indicators that represent the results of processing primary data. It is these indicators that are further used for interpretation, search for patterns, formation and testing of hypotheses.

Examples of generalized indicators include principal components in dimensionality reduction problems [17], norms of error vectors L1 and L2 in problems of estimating the accuracy of various numerical methods with varying the defining parameters of modeling [4, 5], etc.

Given these considerations, it is possible to introduce a concept of the *state of a generalized computational experiment*, which plays a key role in the problem of planning and managing it. The GCE state is determined by a set of already performed computational experiments and is set by a multidimensional array of experimental data obtained with the current partitioning of the defining parameter space, a set of generalized indicators obtained as a result of processing this array, as well as a pattern set identified on the basis of analysis and interpretation of these indicators. Formally, the GCE state can be represented as:

$$< \mathbf{X}, \mathbf{Y}, \mathbf{W}, \mathbf{P(W)}, \mathbf{R} >, \tag{10}$$

where $\mathbf{P(W)}$ is a value space of the generalized indicator set $P = \{P_1, P_2, ..., P_S\}$ for partitioning the space of defining parameters $\mathbf{W}$, $\mathbf{R}$ is a set of revealed patterns.

For problem statement of planning and control of a GCE, let us introduce the following characteristics of its state: reliability, representativeness and effectiveness.

By the *reliability* of the GCE state, we mean absence of such data and revealed patterns in it which are assessed as unreliable. Examples of such data can be the values of generalized indicators belonging to space $\mathbf{P(W)}$ for which deviations from reference or expected values exceed a certain predetermined threshold value (this situation can arise, for example, when assessing accuracy of various numerical methods). In general, these can be any data and patterns that the expert (researcher) has recognized as unreliable on the basis of his experience and understanding of model behavior.

By the *representativeness* of the GCE state, we mean presence of such a set of experimental data and revealed patterns that sufficiently allow us to judge whether or not the set goal has been achieved within a given set of defining parameters.

Note that a GCE state can be reliable, but not representative (as a rule, with a small amount of experimental data and insufficient partition coverage of the defining parameter space). Likewise, representative state may be unreliable for the reasons stated above.

The *effectiveness* of the GCE state is defined as its reliable and representative state for which the set goal has been achieved. Accordingly, achievement of effective state can be considered as the *control goal of a generalized computational experiment*.

3 General Structure of the Control Model for a Generalized Computational Experiment

In general terms, the proposed approach to GCE control can be described as follows. As noted in the previous section, the control goal is to achieve effective state. The analysis of the GCE state and the assessment of its effectiveness is carried out based on the results of a series of experiments carried out for a given set $\mathbf{X}$ of vector values of input variables and the selected partition $\mathbf{W}$ of the space of defining parameters. If the obtained state is assessed as not effective, then before carrying out a new series of experiments, partition $\mathbf{W}$ is corrected as well as set $\mathbf{X}$ if necessary (by the decision of the researcher). This is the control action. In addition, for each series of experiments, the researcher can choose methods of analysis and interpretation of generalized indicators, adjust the parameters of these methods, set or change the threshold values of deviations from the reference or expected values, as well as any other parameters that are of interest in the context of a specific computational problem. Thus, all of the above can act as additional controlled parameters.

In fact, this approach implements a set of control actions to reduce the deviation of the current GCE state from the effective state due to the adaptive adjustment of the experimental plan in a dynamic mode. With this in mind, the GCE control model can be represented as a loop with feedback that implements the principle of deviation control. The diagram of this loop is shown in Fig. 1.

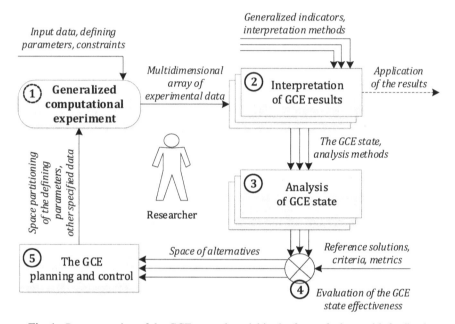

Fig. 1. Representation of the GCE control model in the form of a loop with feedback

Let us consider the general principle of this loop functioning. As a result of a series of experiments (block 1), an array of multidimensional data is formed containing the primary results of the experiment (8), which are further processed and interpreted (group of blocks 2). As noted earlier, this implies the joint use of traditional methods of processing experimental data and intelligent analysis methods, including methods of visual-cognitive analytics, decision-making methods, expert methods, etc. Based on the interpretation results, a new GCE state is recorded (10).

The resulting state is analyzed (group of blocks 3). In the process of this analysis state reliability, representativeness and other indicators are assessed, which, according to the researcher, determine the effectiveness of the experiment. A wide class of approaches and methods can also be applied here, including visualization and visual analysis of multidimensional data, approximation of dependencies between generalized indicators and defining model parameters, analysis of decisions under many criteria, expert assessment, etc., while integration and joint use of different approaches are also possible.

The stage of the GCE state analysis provides two main results. The first result is evaluation of the state effectiveness. At the same time, different methods of analysis can lead to different forms of such evaluation (in particular, it can be expressed in different scales – from binary "yes/no" to ordinal and even numerical ones, with effectiveness degree assessment). The second result is recommendations for the formation of possible control actions associated, as noted earlier, with the change and correction of the space of the defining model parameters and other conditions of the experiment. The final aggregated assessment of the GCE state effectiveness as well as the analysis and selection of control actions is performed in block 4, designated in the diagram as a comparison block. Here information can be used about previously conducted similar experiments known from the theory of reference solutions as well as various criteria and metrics.

As a result, a space of alternatives is formed describing possible solutions and recommendations for the formation of a new refined GCE plan. Based on this information, the researcher corrects space partitioning of the defining parameters, if necessary, clarifies and adjusts other conditions and proceeds to a new series of computational experiments. This is the implementation of the feedback during control.

It is easy to see that evaluation of the effectiveness of a GCE state plays a key role in the formation and adjustment of the plan. Let us proceed to considering possible methods for such evaluation.

4   Algorithm for Evaluating the Effectiveness of a Generalized Computational Experiment State

Let there be C models on which a GCE is conducted (parameter F in Eq. (1)). A single computational experiment k ($1 \leq k \leq K$, where K is the number of experiments performed) is characterized by a set of values of the simulation parameters $A_k = \{a_{k,1}; a_{k,2}; \ldots a_{k,N}\}$. The total number of computational experiments K may be unknown in advance and, in the course of computational experiments, adaptively change depending on the current results obtained. In the course of the computational experiment k on the set of all investigated models $F = \{f_1; f_2; \ldots f_C\}$ we obtain sets of results: $T_k = \{t_{k,1}; t_{k,2}; \ldots t_{k,C}\}$, where $t_{k,i} = \{y_{k,1}; y_{k,2}; \ldots y_{k,Pki}\}$, $1 \leq i \leq C$, and Q_{ki} is the number of measured results of experiment k for model f_i. In the general case, Q_{ki} may differ for different initial parameters of computational experiments. For this reason, it is a usual practice, on the basis of generalizing the set of primary results of a computational experiment, to proceed to the analysis of the set of generalized indicators $P_k = \{y'_{k,1}; y'_{k,2} \ldots y'_{k,S}\}$, where S is the number of generalized indicators, $y'_{k,t} = P_i(t_{k,i})$, $1 \leq t \leq S$, p_t is a function calculating the i-th generalized indicator based on the primary results of the computational experiment.

In the course of a series of computational experiments, the search for functional dependencies or patterns can be carried out by constructing approximating functions. In this case, various approaches are possible both to the choice of the set of approximating functions and to the approximation process itself.

So, for example, the initial set of approximating functions (let us denote it $R'_0 = \{r'_1; r'_2; \ldots r'_{D0}\}$, where r'_i is the i-th approximating function, $1 \leq i \leq D_0$, D_0 is the initial number of approximating functions) can be set before the start of a generalized computational experiment based on the hypotheses and the researcher's knowledge about the studied models, and in the course of a series of computational experiments, the set is reduced by discarding such approximating functions for which the reliability value is below the given threshold e_k. On the other hand, in the course of a series of experiments, it may become clear for the researcher that the initial set of approximating functions does not describe the revealed regularities accurately enough, or, in the course of the next computational experiment, the obtained values of the approximation reliability proved to be below the threshold, then he can add new approximating functions to this set.

The search for an approximating functional dependency on the set of input parameters A_k is not always possible or has a simple solution. Therefore, it is sometimes advisable to search for an approximating functional dependency in the context of each individual parameter from set A_k, i.e. for some changing value a_j and the rest of a_i ($i \neq j$) fixed. In this case, after each computational experiment, we obtain families of approximating functional dependencies: $R''_{c,k,p,i} = \left\{ r''_{c,k,p,i,1}; r''_{c,k,p,i,2}; \ldots; r''_{c,k,p,i,d_{c,k-1,p,i}} \right\}$, where i is the number of the defining simulation parameter, $1 \leq i \leq N$, k is the experiment number, p is the number of a generalized indicator of the result of the computational experiment, $d_{c,k-1,p,i}$ is the number of approximating functions for model f obtained after conducting k-1 computational experiment.

In the general case, approximating functions can be constructed for a different number of parameters (above, extreme cases were considered for all and for one parameter). Accordingly, we obtain the following family of approximating functional dependencies: $R_{c,k,p,j} = \left\{ r_{c,k,p,j,1}; r_{c,k,p,j,2}; \ldots; r_{c,k,p,j,d_{c,k,p,j}} \right\}$, where j defines a subset of simulation parameters A'_j ($A'_j \subseteq A_k$) used to construct an approximating function $r_{c,k,p,j}$, N'_j is the number of elements in set A'_j.

Let us consider the *algorithm for evaluating the effectiveness of the GCE state.*

1. The initial parameters for the algorithm operation include N defining simulation parameters (set A); C models; experiment number k; A'_j – subsets of parameters for modeling set A; P – a set of generalized indicators of computational experiments; R – a family of sets of approximating functions – $R_{c,k,p,j}$; e – the maximum permissible threshold values of deviations of the values of the approximating functions from those obtained in the course of computational experiments.

2. Initialize the number of the subset A'_j: $j = 1$.

3. Initialize the model number: $c = 1$; the number of the generalized indicator of the computational experiment results $p = 1$; the number of the approximating function for a given combination of model f, generalized indicator p and a subset of simulation parameters j: $i = 1$. Also initialize the set of new approximating functions for the given combination of model c, the generalized indicator p and the subset of simulation parameters j equal to a similar set obtained from the results of the previous computational experiment: $R_{c,k,p,j} = R_{c,k-1,p,j}$.

4. For function $r_{c,k,p,j,i}$, determine approximation accuracy $e_{c,k,p,j,i}$. Approximation reliability R^2 or other similar characteristics [18–20] can be used as a value that determines the approximation accuracy.

5. If the calculated approximation accuracy is less than the threshold value, i.e. $e_{c,k,p,j,I} > e_{c,k,p}$, exclude the approximating function $r_{c,k,p,j,i}$ from the set $R_{c,k,p,j}$.

6. Proceed to the next approximating function: $i = i + 1$.

7. If approximating functions for the given combination of c, p and j have not yet been exhausted ($i \leq d_{c,k-1,p,i}$), then go to step 4. Otherwise, go to the next step.

8. If the set of approximating functions $R_{c,k,p,j}$ has become empty (i.e., $R_{c,k,p,j} = \emptyset$), then inform the researcher about the need to supplement the set of approximating

functions $R_{c,0,p,j}$ or to increase $e_{c,k,p}$ (in this case, it is required to perform calculations again according to the above algorithm but with new input data: in the case of a change in the set of approximating functions $R_{c,0,p,j}$, repeat the algorithm for the results of all k computational experiments performed, and in the case of an increase of $e_{c,k,p}$, repeat the algorithm only for the k-th computational experiment); go to step 16. Otherwise, go to the next step.

9. Intelligent and visual-cognitive analysis of the obtained approximation results and curve families for the model is performed, as a result of which the researcher may find unreliable computational experiments or computational experiments with dubious results. As a result, some of the previously performed computational experiments can be repeated (in this case, go to step 16). Proceed to the next generalized indicator: $p = p + 1$.

10. If not all indicators have been considered ($p \leq S$), then go to step 4. Otherwise, go to the next model: $c = c + 1$.

11. If not all models have been considered ($c \leq C$), then go to step 4. Otherwise, go to the next step.

12. Proceed to consider the following subset of simulation parameters: $j = j + 1$.

13. If not all subsets of simulation parameters have been considered ($j \leq N'_j$), then go to step 3. Otherwise, go to the next step.

14. If the number of remaining approximating functions in all sets $R_{c,k,p,j} = 1$ (i.e., functional dependencies of simulation results on the initial parameters are uniquely established with the required accuracy), then we assume that the representativeness and the goal of the GCE have been achieved for the given reliability value. Consequently, the conclusion is made that the GCE state is effective. Go to step 16.

15. Otherwise, we believe that the effectiveness has not been achieved and additional computational experiments with new initial parameters are required.

16. The algorithm is completed.

5 An Example of Evaluating the Effectiveness of a Generalized Computational Experiment State and Discussion of the Results

Let us consider application of the proposed algorithm for analyzing the state and evaluating the effectiveness of a GCE conducted within the framework of choosing an optimal solver of the OpenFOAM platform for the three-dimensional problem of inviscid flow around a cone [5] (in OpenFOAM terminology, solvers are software modules in which various numerical models of mechanics of continua are implemented [7]). We will use three solvers as models: rhoCentralFoam, pisoCentralFoam, sonicFoam. In the course of computational experiments, primary results Y were determined, characterizing the pressure field at each point in space at each moment of time. On their basis, the corresponding generalized indicators P were calculated. The set of generalized indicators P consists of the calculated norms of deviation L1 and L2 of the numerical calculation from the known analytical solution for this problem.

The input parameters of the simulation (A) were: Mach number (a_1): 3, 5, 7; cone half-angle (in degrees) (a_2): 10, 15, 20; angle of attack (in degrees) (a_3): 0, 5, 10. A total of 24 computational experiments were carried out (no computational experiments were carried out for the combination of the half-angle = $10°$ and the angle of attack = $10°$).

Let us define subsets A'_j as follows: $A'_1 = \{a_1\}$; $A'_2 = \{a_2\}$; $A'_3 = \{a_3\}$. As the initial set $R_{c,0,p,j}$ of approximating functions for all combinations of subsets j, models c, and generalized indicators p, let us use the following set: linear ($y = ax + b$); exponential ($y = ae^{bx}$); logarithmic ($y = a\ln(x) + b$); quadratic ($y = ax^2 + bx + c$).

Let us set the threshold value of approximation accuracy e equal to 0.85. As a value that determines approximation accuracy, let us use approximation reliability R^2 [20].

Having calculated the approximation accuracy for the experiments performed and the given set of approximating functions, we have obtained the results partially presented in Tables 1–6.

Table 1. Reliability of approximation for rhoCentralFoam solver on subset $A'3$

Fixed parameter values		L1				L2			
		Linear	Exp	Log	Quad	Linear	Exp	Log	Quad
$a_1 = 3$	$a_2 = 10$	1	1	-	-	1	1	-	-
$a_1 = 3$	$a_2 = 15$	0.85490	0.85711	-	1	0.93488	0.94866	-	1
$a_1 = 3$	$a_2 = 20$	**0.18749**	**0.19313**	-	1	0.98542	0.99080	-	1
$a_1 = 5$	$a_2 = 10$	1	1	-	-	1	1	-	-
$a_1 = 5$	$a_2 = 5$	0.97911	0.98334	-	1	0.97777	0.98669	-	1
$a_1 = 5$	$a_2 = 20$	**0.05399**	**0.05416**	-	1	0.92132	0.92918	-	1
$a_1 = 7$	$a_2 = 10$	1	1	-	-	1	1	-	-
$a_1 = 7$	$a_2 = 15$	0.96513	0.96828	-	1	0.99184	0.99597	-	1
$a_1 = 7$	$a_2 = 20$	0.91134	0.91743	-	1	0.91572	0.92704	-	1

Table 2. Reliability of approximation for pisoCentralFoam solver on subset $A'2$

Fixed parameter values		L1				L2			
		Linear	Exp	Log	Quad	Linear	Exp	Log	Quad
$a_1 = 3$	$a_3 = 0$	0.90115	0.86753	0.95150	1	0.94831	0.90982	0.98279	1
$a_1 = 3$	$a_3 = 5$	0.98710	0.95472	0.99974	1	0.98831	0.96162	0.99989	1
$a_1 = 3$	$a_3 = 10$	1	1	1	-	1	1	1	-
$a_1 = 5$	$a_3 = 0$	**0.83080**	**0.82152**	0.89736	1	0.98737	0.97279	0.99978	1
$a_1 = 5$	$a_3 = 5$	0.96264	0.93841	0.99067	1	0.99097	0.97770	0.99999	1
$a_1 = 5$	$a_3 = 10$	1	1	1	-	1	1	1	-
$a_1 = 7$	$a_3 = 0$	**0.61822**	**0.62884**	**0.71038**	1	0.95852	0.94428	0.98853	1
$a_1 = 7$	$a_3 = 5$	0.95853	0.94427	0.98854	1	0.98474	0.97481	0.99932	1
$a_1 = 7$	$a_3 = 10$	1	1	1	-	1	1	1	-

Table 3. Reliability of approximation for pisoCentralFoam solver on subset A'_3

Fixed parameter values		L1				L2			
		Linear	Exp	Log	Q uad	Linear	Exp	Log	Quad
$a_1 = 3$	$a_2 = 10$	1	1	-	-	1	1	-	-
$a_1 = 3$	$a_2 = 15$	0.91702	0.92076	-	1	0.87596	0.88479	-	1
$a_1 = 3$	$a_2 = 20$	**0.10339**	**0.10975**	-	1	0.99794	0.99539	-	1
$a_1 = 5$	$a_2 = 10$	1	1	-	-	1	1	-	-
$a_1 = 5$	$a_2 = 5$	0.98832	0.98936	-	1	0.97153	0.98076	-	1
$a_1 = 5$	$a_2 = 20$	**0.44460**	**0.45927**	-	1	0.99324	0.98909	-	1
$a_1 = 7$	$a_2 = 10$	1	1	-	-	1	1	-	-
$a_1 = 7$	$a_2 = 15$	**0.59665**	**0.59444**	-	1	0.98688	0.99187	-	1
$a_1 = 7$	$a_2 = 20$	0.96393	0.95681	-	1	0.97079	0.98021	-	1

Table 4. Reliability of approximation for sonicFoam solver on subset A'_1

Fixed parameter values		L1				L2			
		Linear	Exp	Log	Quad	Linear	Exp	Log	Quad
$a_2 = 10$	$a_3 = 0$	0.99913	0.93393	0.99215	1	0.99820	0.94069	0.99427	1
$a_2 = 10$	$a_3 = 5$	0.90450	**0.83358**	0.96210	1	0.99787	0.94642	0.99482	1
$a_2 = 15$	$a_3 = 0$	0.99751	0.94378	0.99533	1	0.99712	0.95478	0.99583	1
$a_2 = 15$	$a_3 = 5$	0.99498	0.94249	0.99776	1	0.99313	0.95059	0.99876	1
$a_2 = 15$	$a_3 = 10$	0.99833	0.95377	0.99402	1	0.99364	0.95639	0.99853	1
$a_2 = 20$	$a_3 = 0$	0.99526	0.94410	0.99757	1	0.99460	0.95462	0.99800	1
$a_2 = 20$	$a_3 = 5$	0.99716	0.95508	0.99579	1	0.99730	0.96682	0.99562	1
$a_2 = 20$	$a_3 = 10$	0.99144	0.94389	0.99934	1	0.97469	0.93180	0.99828	1

Table 5. Reliability of approximation for sonicFoam solver on subset A'_2

Fixed parameter values		L1				L2			
		Linear	Exp	Log	Quad	Linear	Exp	Log	Quad
$a_1 = 3$	$a_3 = 0$	0.99234	0.95646	0.99990	1	0.99047	0.95243	1	1
$a_1 = 3$	$a_3 = 5$	0.99099	0.95830	0.99999	1	0.98868	0.95756	0.99992	1
$a_1 = 3$	$a_3 = 10$	1	1	1	-	1	1	1	-

(*continued*)

Table 5. (*continued*)

Fixed parameter values		L1				L2			
		Linear	Exp	Log	Quad	Linear	Exp	Log	Quad
$a_1 = 5$	$a_3 = 0$	0.99141	0.97308	0.99998	1	0.99281	0.97513	0.99983	1
$a_1 = 5$	$a_3 = 5$	**0.84913**	0.85610	**0.77291**	1	0.97229	0.95457	0.99518	1
$a_1 = 5$	$a_3 = 10$	1	1	1	-	1	1	1	-
$a_1 = 7$	$a_3 = 0$	0.98721	0.97176	0.99976	1	0.98889	0.97402	0.99994	1
$a_1 = 7$	$a_3 = 5$	0.98958	0.97764	0.99998	1	0.99600	0.98942	0.99881	1
$a_1 = 7$	$a_3 = 10$	1	1	1	-	1	1	1	-

Table 6. Reliability of approximation for sonicFoam solver on subset A'_3

Fixed parameter values		L1				L2			
		Linear	Exp	Log	Quad	Linear	Exp	Log	Quad
$a_1 = 3$	$a_2 = 10$	1	1	-	-	1	1	-	-
$a_1 = 3$	$a_2 = 15$	0.97719	0.96358	-	1	0.99746	0.99972	-	1
$a_1 = 3$	$a_2 = 20$	0.90949	0.89731	-	1	0.99820	0.99195	-	1
$a_1 = 5$	$a_2 = 10$	1	1	-	-	1	1	-	-
$a_1 = 5$	$a_2 = 5$	0.97084	0.96283	-	1	0.99996	0.99861	-	1
$a_1 = 5$	$a_2 = 20$	0.98047	0.97636	-	1	0.95714	0.96847	-	1
$a_1 = 7$	$a_2 = 10$	1	1	-	-	1	1	-	-
$a_1 = 7$	$a_2 = 15$	0.99736	0.99922	-	1	0.99584	0.99902	-	1
$a_1 = 7$	$a_2 = 20$	**0.66821**	**0.67059**	-	1	0.99973	0.99866	-	1

In the above tables (Tables 1–6), if the approximating curve of the corresponding type could not be built, then the corresponding cell contains a dash. Moreover, there are object reasons for the impossibility of their construction. So, for the logarithmic function, it was not possible to construct one due to the presence of points with coordinates along the $x = 0$ axis, and the quadratic function degenerated into a linear one for the cases when there were only 2 approximated points. The small number of points for constructing a quadratic approximating function indicates the insufficiency of the experiments performed for achieving representativeness of the GCE state.

Also, in the table, cells are highlighted for which approximation reliability value is below the specified threshold of 0.85, which means that a number of approximating curves can be excluded from further analysis, and it is also possible that errors were made during the experiments. Let us analyze the results obtained in more detail.

For the resulting parameter L1 in the case of rhoCentralFoam and pisoCentralFoam solvers in relation to subset A'_1 (for fixed values of the cone half-angle and angle of attack), all functions of the set $R_{c,0,p,j,i}$ showed high approximation reliability and can be used at the next GCE stages.

In the case of sonicFoam solver, for the same resulting parameters and subset A'_1, all approximating functions except the exponential one also showed high reliability (Table 4). However, for the exponential function only for $a_2 = 10$ and $a_3 = 5$, the approximation reliability was below the threshold value of 0.85. It is also noteworthy that for the linear and logarithmic approximating functions at the same values of a_2 and a_3, the approximation reliability is noticeably lower than for other values. This fact may indicate an error in one or several computational experiments for sonicFoam solver at half angle $= 10$ and angle of attack $= 5$. It is advisable to recheck these computational experiments and repeat them if necessary.

For the resulting parameter L1 in the case of rhoCentralFoam solver applied to subset A'_2 (for fixed values of the Mach number and angle of attack), all functions of set $R_{c,0,p,j}$ showed high approximation reliability and can be used at the next GCE stages.

For the resulting parameter L1 in the case of pisoCentralFoam solver in relation to subset A'_2, only the quadratic function showed high approximation reliability (Table 2) and can be used at the next GCE stages. However, low approximation reliability was obtained only for pairs ($a_1 = 5$; $a_3 = 0$) and ($a_1 = 7$; $a_3 = 0$), which may also indicate possible errors in the corresponding experiments. Such situations require additional intelligent analysis with the involvement of an expert (researcher).

As is see from Table 5 the exponential and quadratic functions showed high approximation reliability for the resulting parameter L1, sonicFoam solver, and subset A'_2. For the linear and logarithmic ones, reliability was below the threshold only for the values $a_1 = 5$ and $a_3 = 5$. Taking into account the fact that the probable error of the computational experiment in the analysis of subset A'_1 was found for the same value of parameter $a_3 = 5$, it is advisable to recheck the computational experiment for sonicFoam solver for $a_1 = 5$, $a_2 = 10$ and $a_3 = 5$.

With respect to the subset A'_3 and the resulting parameter L1, all solvers showed high approximation reliability only for the quadratic function (Tables 1, 3, 6); the logarithmic function proved to be impossible to construct at all. Therefore, it is allowed to use only a quadratic function for further computational experiments in this case.

For the resulting parameter L2 on subsets A'_1, A'_2, all functions of set $R_{c,0,p,j}$ showed high approximation reliability for all solvers, so they can be used in further computational experiments.

On the subset A'_3 for the resulting parameter L2, approximation by the logarithmic function is impossible for all solvers, and the rest of the functions showed approximation reliability above the threshold and can be used in subsequent computational experiments for this set of parameters on all solvers.

Considering the facts that there is still uncertainty in the choice of approximating functions for some combinations of solver, resulting parameter and subset, as well as the lack of data for approximation by some types of functions, it is not possible to talk about the representativeness of the GCE state. In addition, the presence of suspicious computational experiments (in particular, for sonicFoam solver with $a_1 = 5$, $a_2 = 10$ and

$a_3 = 5$) cannot characterize the current GCE state as reliable. Thus, in order to achieve effective GCE state, new series of experiments are required.

6 Conclusion

The GCE effectiveness can be achieved not only by expanding and complicating a series of experiments and increasing the amount of processed data, but also by implementing a more flexible search and establishing the order of variation of defining parameters. The paper proposes an approach to the GCE control based on adaptive adjustment of a plan for its implementation on the results of evaluating the effectiveness of its state, using intelligent and visual-cognitive methods for multidimensional data analysis.

A model of the GCE control is presented, for which an algorithm for evaluating the state effectiveness is proposed. Application of this algorithm is considered for the analysis and assessment of the GCE state effectiveness carried out within the framework of choosing the optimal solver of the OpenFOAM software platform for the three-dimensional problem of inviscid flow around a cone. The above example illustrates the situation when the GCE state effectiveness has not been achieved both due to its unreliability and insufficient representativeness.

Note that, in contrast to the classical methodology of experiment planning, used in the single experiment control, the proposed approach to the GCE control has a pronounced human-machine character and involves the researcher's active participation at all stages. At the same time, the use of intelligent (including visual-cognitive) methods of processing and analyzing data for evaluating the GCE state makes it possible to activate the researcher's cognitive and expert potential, which increases the GCE planning efficiency by reducing the volume of unsuccessful series of experiments and, conversely, conducting more detailed experimental studies on those ranges of input data that are more informative for achieve the goal of a GCE.

From this perspective, directions for further research include development of visual models for representing data which characterize the GCE state and visual analytics methods for assessing its characteristics in order to clarify and adjust the plan for its implementation.

Acknowledgements. The research has been supported by Russian Science Foundation (project No. 18-11-00215).

References

1. Kleijnen, J.P.C.: Design and analysis of computational experiments: overview. In: Bartz-Beielstein, T., Chiarandini, M., Paquete, L., Preuss, M. (eds.) Experimental Methods for the Analysis of Optimization Algorithms, pp. 51–72. Springer, Heidelberg (2010). https://doi.org/10.1007/978-3-642-02538-9_3
2. Bondarev, A.E.: On the construction of the generalized numerical experiment in fluid dynamics. Math. Montisnigri, XLII **42**, 52–64 (2018)

3. Bondarev, A.E., Galaktionov, V.A.: Generalized computational experiment and visual analysis of multidimensional data. Sci. Visual. **11**(4), 102–114 (2019). https://doi.org/10.26583/sv.11.4.09

4. Alekseev, A., Bondarev, A., Galaktionov, V., Kuvshinnikov, A., Shapiro, L.: On applying of generalized computational experiment to numerical methods verification. In: CEUR Workshop Proceedings of 30th International Conference on Computer Graphics and Machine Vision GraphiCon 2020, vol. 2744 (2020). https://doi.org/10.51130/graphicon-2020-2-3-19

5. Bondarev, A.E., Kuvshinnikov, A.E.: Analysis of the accuracy of OpenFOAM solvers for the problem of supersonic flow around a cone. In: Shi, Y., et al. (eds.) ICCS 2018. LNCS, vol. 10862, pp. 221–230. Springer, Cham (2018). https://doi.org/10.1007/978-3-319-93713-7_18

6. Andreev, S.V., et al.: A computational technology for constructing the optimal shape of a power plant blade assembly taking into account structural constraints. Program. Comput. Softw. **43**(6), 345–352 (2017). https://doi.org/10.1134/S0361768817060020

7. OpenFOAM. Free CFD Software. The OpenFOAM Foundation. https://openfoam.org. Accessed 11 May 2021

8. Zakharova, A.A., Korostelyov, D.A.: Visualizing methods of multi-criteria alternatives for pairwise comparison procedure. In: CEUR Workshop Proceedings of the 8th International Scientific Conference on Computing in Physics and Technology (CPT2020), vol. 2763, pp. 195–200 (2020). https://doi.org/10.30987/conferencearticle_5fce2770f136d9.31132653

9. Trubakova, A.A., Trubakov, A.O.: Visual analysis of dynamic changes in structured data on the basis of colour markers. Sci. Visual. **12**(4), 85–97 (2020). https://doi.org/10.26583/sv.12.4.08

10. Podvesovskii, A.G., Isaev, R.A.: Constructing optimal visualization metaphor of fuzzy cognitive maps on the basis of formalized cognitive clarity criteria. Sci. Visual. **11**(4), 115–129 (2019). https://doi.org/10.26583/sv.11.4.10

11. Zakharova, A.A., Korostelyov, D.A.: Application of visual analytics methods to reduce the dimensionality of decision-making problems. Sci. Visual. **12**(4), 23–32 (2020). https://doi.org/10.26583/sv.12.4.03

12. Figuera, J., Greco, S., Ehrgott, M. (Eds): Multiple Criteria Decision Analysis: State of the Art Surveys. Springer, New York (2005). https://doi.org/10.1007/b100605

13. Alinezhad, A., Khalili, J.: New Methods and Applications in Multiple Attribute Decision Making (MADM). Springer, Cham (2019). https://doi.org/10.1007/978-3-030-15009-9

14. Podvesovskii, A., Mikhaleva, O., Averchenkov, V., Reutov, A., Potapov, L.: A model of control of expert estimates consistency in distributed group expertise. In: Kravets, A., Shcherbakov, M., Kultsova, M., Groumpos, P. (eds.) CIT&DS 2017. CCIS, vol. 754, pp. 361–374. Springer, Cham (2017). https://doi.org/10.1007/978-3-319-65551-2_26

15. Popov, G.A., Kvyatkovskaya, I.Y., Zholobova, O.I., Kvyatkovskaya, A.E., Chertina, E.V.: Making a choice of resulting estimates of characteristics with multiple options of their evaluation. In: Kravets, A.G., Groumpos, P.P., Shcherbakov, M., Kultsova, M. (eds.) CIT&DS 2019. CCIS, vol. 1083, pp. 89–104. Springer, Cham (2019). https://doi.org/10.1007/978-3-030-29743-5_7

16. Kravets, A.G.: On approach for the development of patents analysis formal metrics. In: Kravets, A.G., Groumpos, P.P., Shcherbakov, M., Kultsova, M. (eds.) CIT&DS 2019. CCIS, vol. 1083, pp. 34–45. Springer, Cham (2019). https://doi.org/10.1007/978-3-030-29743-5_3

17. Gorban, A.N., Kegl, B., Wunsch, D., Zinovyev, A.Y. (eds.): Principal Manifolds for Data Visualisation and Dimension Reduction, Springer-Verlag, Berlin, Heidelberg (2007). https://doi.org/10.1007/978-3-540-73750-6

18. Ping, Y., Xitao, F.: Estimating R^2 shrinkage in multiple regression: a comparison of different analytical methods. J. Exp. Educ. **69**(2), 203–224 (2001). https://doi.org/10.1080/00220970109600656

19. Cheng, C.-L., Shalabh, G.G.: Coefficient of determination for multiple measurement error models. J. Multivariate Anal. **126**, 137–152 (2014). https://doi.org/10.1016/j.jmva.2014. 01.006

20. Baltagi, B.H.: Econometrics. 5th edn. Springer-Verlag Berlin Heidelberg (2011). https://doi. org/10.1007/978-3-642-20059-5

Comparative Study of the Innovative Activity Dynamics in the Russian Federation Using the Singular Spectrum Analysis

Alexey B. Simonov$^{(\boxtimes)}$ ⬡, Aleksey F. Rogachev ⬡, and Irina E. Simonova

Volgograd State Technical University, Volgograd, Russian Federation

Abstract. Analysis and modeling of innovation activity dynamics at the federal level and the regional level is a complex task of the system analysis. It requires the analysis of many indicators related to different stages of innovation activity. The dynamics of this indicators possess number of various, specific features. Singular spectrum analysis method was used in order to carry out analysis, which made it possible to reveal the essential properties of time series without using a priori assumptions. This method made it possible to identify the main components of the dynamics of innovation processes in the Russian Federation. Moreover, the trend and cyclical components anticipated by economic theory are revealed. Short-term cycles (3–4 years) were identified in the studied time series (TS) at the country and regional level. Medium-term cycles (8–12 years) were also identified for the majority of TS, with the exception of the dynamics of the number of researchers in the Volgograd region. This may be due to obsolescence and insufficient updating of fixed assets used in research activities. An economic interpretation of the obtained results is suggested. These results can be used in decision making support.

Keywords: Innovations · Singular spectrum analysis · Innovative activity · Time series · Economic development

1 Introduction

Analysis of information about the dynamics of innovation processes in the Russian economy is of great importance for planning and organizing our country's sustainable development, and ensuring its security [1]. The issues of intensifying innovative development have become of specific concern in the past two years, when the coronavirus pandemic has necessitated accelerating the introduction of a whole range of modern technologies. These innovations in telecommuting, artificial intelligence, and the Internet of Things together with new modern medical techniques and new vaccines have dramatically changed our world within hours. As the diffusion proceeds, these changes affect more and more areas of activity, which were not associated from the outset with the coronavirus, and come into use in various areas of industrial and agricultural production [2, 3]. However, large-scale innovation requires changes in decision-making support systems.

© Springer Nature Switzerland AG 2021
A. G. Kravets et al. (Eds.): CIT&DS 2021, CCIS 1448, pp. 223–237, 2021.
https://doi.org/10.1007/978-3-030-87034-8_17

The development of such a toolkit in the area of innovation faces many challenges. In particular, innovation activity is in itself quite systemic, and its indicators should be considered comprehensively in order to reflect the various aspects of innovation activity. The lack of a systemic approach in solving this problem can lead to underestimation of important factors that can significantly slow down effective innovative development, even at sufficiently high values of other factors. For example, the Russian Federation [4] is characterized by high indicators both in innovative potential and in research activity – as of 2020, Russia ranked 19th internationally for the pupil-teacher ratio, secondary, 17th for tertiary education, and 17th for the number of patents obtained. However, the indicators characterizing the conditions for conducting innovative activities in our country are quite low. The Russian Federation ranks 106th on the global stage for investment, 91st for percentage of firms offering formal training, and 95th for state of cluster development. This situation results in the following positions of Russia on the global rankings list: - 60th for creative outputs; - 46th for the generalized Global Innovation Index (GII) [4].

In addition to the systemic nature of innovation activity indicators, the study of its dynamics complicates its strategic nature. The real results of innovation activity reveal only over the long term and are largely distorted by the influence of random factors, cyclical component and other political and economic processes. It is very difficult to describe parametrically the impact of these factors; moreover, this description will be rather unstable over time since trends over a longer timeframe show significant instability. Therefore, this paper proposes to use a nonparametric method of singular spectrum analysis (SSA) used for analyzing time series (TS). The SSA method makes it possible to identify individual reconstructed series related to the trend of the phenomenon under study, as well as some cyclical components. This will allow both types of series to be economically interpreted and the relationship between the corresponding reconstructed series to be analyzed. The revealed patterns can be considered as the basis for a deeper study.

This research is aimed at studying the possibilities discovered by utilizing the SSA method in decision-making support systems in innovation management. The research objectives are to consider the process of applying the SSA method, to develop software tools for analyze by this method and to present the results obtained, to analyze the dynamics of individual indicators for innovation activity both in the Russian Federation and in the Volgograd region, to compare the results obtained, and to develop recommendations based on the analysis. At the same time, the research is not focused on identifying the correlation between the processes under study (which is theoretically substantiated and shown in many studies), but rather on qualitatively comparing various stages of innovation activity with each another, as well as the stages both at the level of the whole Russia and in an individual region.

2   Methods and Materials

The SSA method appeared at the end of the 20th century and is currently being actively developed by, among others, Soviet and Russian scientists (under the name of 'Caterpillar'-SSA [5, 6]). This method refers to nonparametric methods for analyzing time series; it allows selecting many components of TS without a priori assumptions about their presence and characteristics. This significantly increases the capabilities and quality of the analysis (for example, it makes it easier to distinguish fluctuations with varying frequency). It combines elements of conventional time series analysis, multivariate statistics, multivariate geometry, dynamical systems and signal processing [7].

The method makes it possible to predict the future values of the studied phenomena, provided that the signal will not be sufficiently distorted by noise or the nature of the selected components does not change. SSA also can interpolate the missing data. The method is effective for the spectral analysis of stationary TS, e.g., in climatology. Various modifications allow expanding the method boundaries; e.g., M-SSA (Multi-Channel SSA) is a tool for studying the relationships between the components of different time series; Monte-Carlo SSA is a tool for assessing the stability of the singular value decomposition results, and so forth.

The SSA method is increasingly being used in various scientific disciplines, including image processing, medicine, climatology, oceanology, and geophysics. The application of this method in economics is rather limited [8]. Basically, it is used to analyze data on the indicators of the system of national accounts, and on GDP in particular. Such possibility to use the method is due to the fact that in many countries there are big data arrays of GDP values over quarterly periods; and this can significantly improve the quality of the analysis being conducted.

The SSA algorithm consists of four main stages [5]. At the first stage, for the analysis of the time series, an integer parameter L is selected; i.e., the window size. This parameter is selected by an expert method, and it usually takes on a value from 4 to half the length of the N/2 series [6]. Other sources indicate either N/4 [9] or the median value [10] as the optimal L value. With a rather long series length and a rather long L, the results will not depend on the window length. For a short L [8–10], the method may not be effective enough to separate fluctuations with a period less than L, and the efficiency of the algorithm may be significantly reduced.

Then, on the basis of the series, a trajectory matrix is constructed, the columns of which are the sliding segments of length L. The next stage is the singular decomposition of the trajectory matrix into a sum of elementary matrices. Each elementary matrix is specified by a set of eigenvalues and eigenvectors. Applying diagonal averaging, we obtain the series $\tilde{F}(s) = (\tilde{f_0}(s), \tilde{f_1}(s), ..., \tilde{f_{L*}}(s))$. These series can be considered as additive components of the time series under study. They can describe a trend, cyclical components, noises, in particular, and this is in the absence of a priori assumptions about the presence and parameters of the trend and periodic components, about the stationarity of the series, and so on.

Let us consider these stages of the method in more detail.

At the first stage, the original time series of length N is transformed into a sequence of multidimensional vectors (trajectory matrix X). The matrix X has the dimension L × K, where L is the window length (traditionally selected in the range from 4 to N/2), and the K value is calculated as follows:

$$K = N - L + 1 \tag{1}$$

where K is the number of columns of the trajectory matrix; L is the number of rows of the trajectory matrix.

Then, segments of length L are selected from the initial time series. These segments are constructed sequentially. The trajectory matrix X is made up of the constructed segments. Its columns are called embedding vectors.

$$X = \begin{pmatrix} f_1 & \cdots & f_{N-L+1} \\ \vdots & \ddots & \vdots \\ f_L & \cdots & f_N \end{pmatrix} \tag{2}$$

X is Hankel matrix, as a symmetric marix with equal elements on all diagonals.

The second stage is singular value decomposition (SVD).

The result of this stage is the decomposition of the trajectory matrix X into elementary parts, i.e. representation of the matrix X as a sum of elementary matrices. Let us use λ_1, λ_2, ..., λ_L, for denoting the eigenvalues of the matrix $S = X*X^T$ taken in non-decreasing order, and d is number of $\lambda i > 0$. Then the singular value decomposition for X is

$$X = U * \Sigma * V^T \tag{3}$$

where U and V are d × d complex unitary matrixes and Σ is d × d diagonal matrix with non-negative real numbers on the diagonal. U_1, U_2, ..., U_L, are the orthonormal system of the eigenvectors of the matrix S corresponding to the ordered eigenvalues [5].

Brief SVD is as follows:

Step 2.1. Calculating the matrix S

$$S = X * X^T \tag{4}$$

where X is the trajectory matrix; X^T is the transposed trajectory matrix.

Step 2.2. Finding the eigenvalues λ_i and eigenvectors U_i (i = 1...d) of the matrix S.

Step 2.3. Finding elementary vectors V_i.

$$V_i = X^T = * \frac{U_i}{\sqrt{i}} \tag{5}$$

The singular value decomposition of the trajectory matrix X is as follows [5]:

$$X = \Sigma Xi, \tag{6}$$

Xi is the elementary matrix with rank 1. These elementary matrices are calculated by the formula:

$$X_i = \sqrt{\lambda_i} * U_i * V^T \tag{7}$$

The third stage is diagonal averaging. At this stage of the algorithm, each matrix of the grouped decomposition is translated into a series of length N. We suppose L * = min (L, K), K * = max (L, K). Let also y*ij = Yij, if L < K, and y*ij = Yji, if L > K. Diagonal averaging transforms each resulting matrix Y(s), s = 1, 2, ..., m, into a series according to the formula [5]:

$$\tilde{f}_k \begin{cases} \frac{1}{k+1} \sum_{n=1}^{k+1} y^*_{n,k-n+2}, & 0 \le k < L^* - 1, \\ \frac{1}{L^*} \sum_{n=1}^{L^*} y^*_{n,k-n+2}, & L^* - 1 \le k < K^*, \\ \frac{1}{N-k} \sum_{n=k-K^*+2}^{N-K^*+1} y^*_{n,k-n+2}, & K^* \le k < N. \end{cases} \tag{8}$$

This formula corresponds to averaging the elements along the diagonals.

So, applying the diagonal averaging to the resulting matrices Y(s), we obtain the series $\tilde{F}(s) = (\tilde{f}_0(s), \tilde{f}_1(s), ..., \tilde{f}_{L*}(s))$. The resulting series can be considered as additive components of the time series under study.

For such calculations, it is necessary to carry them out on a computer. In particular, it can be carried using the MathCAD or other math tools. However, these calculations require both some specific mathematical knowledge and particular runtime instrumentation.

Some studies use R-libraries, e.g., RSSA [11]. These libraries, among other things, can be connected by application packages using modules in this language.

To carry out research, we created a program in Python using the pyts [12] and Matplotlib [13] libraries. Our program implements the data input interface, graphical representation of the original time series and reconstructed series, and also performs the SSA singular value decomposition and shows a number of this method results. The created program allows speeding up and facilitating the analysis, making it accessible to a specialist without deep knowledge in linear algebra.

3   Results

In this study, we analyzed data on innovation activity in Russia and in the Volgograd region by using the SSA method. It should be noted that the innovation process is a multi-stage and systemic process. Therefore, a set of indicators that characterize different aspects of the innovation process should be used for its studying.

Unlike most studies (e.g., [8, 14]), we were limited to a fairly small amount of information about innovation processes in the Russian Federation, provided by the Federal State Statistics Service and related mainly to the period from 1995 till 2019 with a frequency of one year. Due to the fact that the methodology for collecting indicators of innovation activity has changed significantly during the period we study, we decided to analyze data for close, but not coinciding periods of time (e.g., 1995–2019 for the number of researchers and 2000–2019 for the proportion of innovative organizations). In this case, we proceeded from the assumption that the basic components of a time series over the period under study did not change significantly; therefore, the data can be considered sufficiently comparable. In addition, changes in the methodology for collecting information raised questions about the need of data quality (DQ) analysis. However, it was not in the focus of our research. Therefore, among a large number of DQ analysis methods described, for instance, in [2], we chose only the classical statistical methods to use.

The number of personnel employed in research and development in the Russian Federation and the Volgograd region was taken as the first indicator under study (see Fig. 1). This indicator gave a good representation of the initial stages of the innovation process associated with research and development (R&D).

The data (Fig. 1, 2, 3) were taken from the website of the Federal State Statistics Service [15]. Figure 1 shows a significant reduction in the number of researchers over the past quarter of a century (Russia experienced a 36% decrease, and the Volgograd region saw a 44% decrease). This indicates a gradual decline in innovation potential,

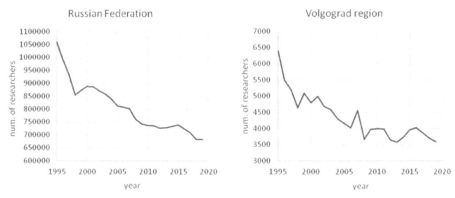

Fig. 1. Dynamics of the number of personnel engaged in R&D in the Russian Federation and the Volgograd region in 1995–2019

which is the RF's traditional area of strength. Moreover, it is often assumed that it should be accompanied by an improvement in the quality of capacities and a more active implementation of research results.

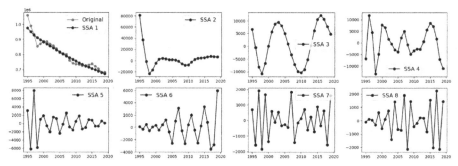

Fig. 2. The results obtained from the singular decomposition of the dynamics of the number of personnel engaged in scientific research in the Russian Federation in 1995–2019, with eight components reflected.

Let us consider in more detail the results of the singular value decomposition of the data on the dynamics of the number of researchers in the Russian Federation with window size L = 10 (see Fig. 2). The first reconstructed series named SSA1 describes a trend associated with a gradual decrease in the number of researchers in the Russian Federation over the period under study. The reconstructed series named SSA2 and SSA3 reflect medium-term periodic fluctuations, which are especially clearly visible for SSA3. The reconstructed series SSA4 can be interpreted as an autocorrelation process with a positive autocorrelation coefficient. The reconstructed series SSA5 and SSA6 reflect short-term fluctuations with a 3–4 years period.

At the same time, two features of the SSA method are well manifested on the graphs: - first, it gives rather poor description of the values at the beginning and end of the series rather poorly; - secondly, the SSA method poorly reflects short-term fluctuations, in the period of which there are a small number of data points (e.g., an increase in the data discretization step up to a quarter would make fluctuations with a period of 3–4 years much more visible).

It should be noted that both the significance of the reconstructed series and the range of variation on them rapidly decrease with an increase in the number of the reconstructed series. The range of variation in SSA1 was about 300,000 persons. For SSA3 it is 8% of this number, i.e., 20,000 persons. For SSA5 and SSA6, which can be interpreted as random fluctuations or processes with negative autocorrelation, the range of variation is about 4000 persons, which allows us to discard them (and subsequent reconstructed series) as insignificant for understanding the general picture.

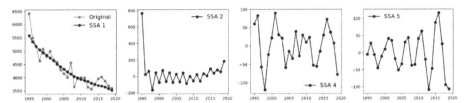

Fig. 3. Several results obtained from the singular value decomposition of the dynamics of the number of personnel engaged in scientific research in the Volgograd region in 1995–2019.

When analyzing the dynamics of the number of personnel engaged in scientific research in the Volgograd region (see Fig. 3), the method first restores TS SSA1, which characterizes the trend of TS been studied. This trend is similar to the trend of this indicator in the Russian Federation. The peculiar feature of the reconstructed series SSA2, which reflects both trend elements (a sharp drop in 1996–1998) and short-term fluctuations, deals with a very strange period of these fluctuations, which is two years. Such fluctuations, on the whole, are not predicted by economics and require additional study.

In the next two charts, we see short-term fluctuations with a period of about 4 years, similar to the same fluctuations in the Russian Federation (SSA5 in Fig. 2 and Fig. 3), and positive autocorrelation reflected in the SSA4 chart. The reconstructed series SSA3 not shown herein contains random fluctuations. It is specific that the Volgograd region, unlike the Russian Federation, demonstrates no medium-term fluctuations over a period of about 10 years. Fluctuations also was not detected when the window length was increased to the maximum possible. Fluctuations with a period of about 10 years (Juglar cycles) in the economy are traditionally considered to be related to investments in fixed assets [16], its use and renewal. The absence of Juglar cycles may indicate a significant obsolescence and lack of renewal of the instrumentation of research organizations in the Volgograd region (in contrast to the Russian Federation as a whole).

Thus, the SSA method has shown its effectiveness in analyzing the number of personnel engaged in scientific research. This method is able to identify the trend, cyclical fluctuations and autocorrelation without serious a priori assumptions and to reveal theoretically unpredicted harmonics (e.g., with a period of two years for the Volgograd region). Absent harmonics indicate problem areas in the development of the economic process being studied.

Let us study the dynamics of innovation activity indicators related to other aspects of the innovation process by using the SSA method, and compare the results obtained in the course of applying the SSA methods to these indicators.

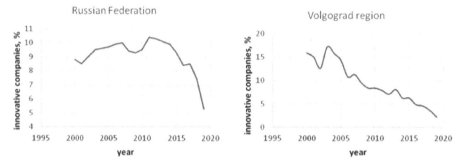

Fig. 4. Percentage of innovation organizations

Let us analyze the dynamics of the percentage of innovatively active organizations in the Russian Federation and in the Volgograd region (Fig. 4). The data were taken from the sources of the Federal State Statistics Service [15] from 2000 till 2019. For an earlier period, there were no values for this indicator. In addition, in 2017, the methodology for classifying organizations as innovative was changed to comply with the requirements in the 4th edition of the Oslo Manual [17], the international reference guide containing recommendations for collecting and analyzing data on innovation. As a result of changes in 2017, we brought the data for 2018 and for 2019 to a comparable form, which could affect the reliability of the analysis results for these years. Nevertheless, the general trend in the dynamics of innovatively active organizations in the Russian Federation is quite obvious - growth in the early 2000s, which turned into a decline in innovative activity after 2012 - and the last two points obtained by calculating do not violate this trend.

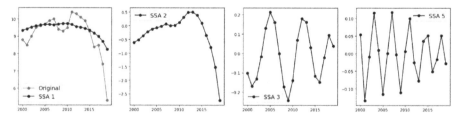

Fig. 5. Several results obtained by the singular value decomposition of the percentage of innovative organizations (%) dynamics in the Russian Federation in 2000–2019

Figure 5 shows the results obtained by analyzing the dynamics of the innovatively active organizations percentage in the Russian Federation by using the SSA method. In this case, the trend has a rather complex structure; due to this, two reconstructed series –SSA1 and SSA2 - were required to reconstruct this trend. The SSA1 method reflects dynamics close to quadratic, i.e., growth until 2012 and decline in subsequent years.

The SSA2 method models the accelerated decline of innovation activity over the past seven years at a rate well above the rate predicted by the quadratic model. The SSA3 model clearly shows medium-term fluctuations, but their period is shorter than we could see in the analysis of the number of researchers, and is about 8 years. The SSA5 model can be interpreted as short-term fluctuations over a period of 3–4 years. Thus, the main selected harmonics, for the most part, coincide with those identified by the SSA method for the number of researchers in the Russian Federation. However, the trend identified by the SSA method in this case has a more complex structure and consists of the two parts described above.

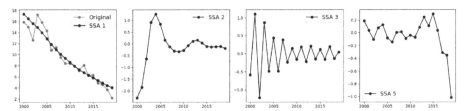

Fig. 6. Several results obtained by the singular value decomposition of the percentage of innovative organizations (%) dynamics in the Volgograd region in 2000–2019

Figure 6 shows the results obtained by analyzing the percentage of innovatively active organizations dynamics in the Volgograd region by using the SSA method. SSA1 reflects a linear trend towards a decrease in the share of innovatively active organizations in the Volgograd region. SSA2 can be interpreted as a correction to the trend identified by SSA1, but it can also be interpreted as slightly pronounced medium-term fluctuations with a period of about 10 years. SSA4 is similar to the highlighted SSA2 series in Fig. 3 and can be considered as difficult-to-interpret fluctuations with a period of 2 years (or as an even more difficult-to-interpret manifestation of autocorrelation). If the last 3 points (built on the data brought to a comparable form) are excluded, SSA5 can be interpreted as short-term fluctuations with a period of 3–4 years.

For the most part, the results of the singular value decomposition of the data related to the Russian Federation and to the Volgograd region are much closer to each other for this indicator. A trend and both medium-term and short-term fluctuations are revealed (while both are less pronounced in the Volgograd region than in Russia as a whole). The above specificity of the Volgograd region is also revealed; i.e., fluctuations with a period of 2 years.

Let us also analyze the costs for technological innovation (Fig. 7). This indicator refers to the characteristics of the innovation implementation process, which is traditionally considered the area of weakness in Russian companies. The increase in the efficiency of innovation implementation has been repeatedly proclaimed as one of the goals of innovative development in Russia, and it directly depends on the innovation implementation expenditures. The technological innovation expenditures are a cost indicator, so we converted all values to 2020 prices using the GDP deflator index. As we can see from Fig. 7, the technological innovation expenditures in the Russian Federation had a clear upward trend until 2014. The technological innovation expenditures have been

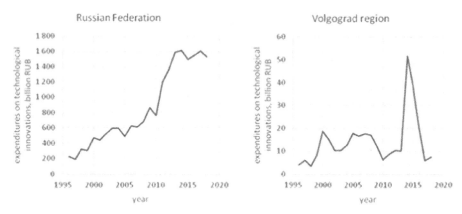

Fig. 7. Expenditures on technological innovation in prices of 2000 year, billion RUB

slowing down in subsequent years and turned into a horizontal trend. In the Volgograd region, during the entire study period, the costs for technological innovations grew but at an insignificant rate. It is necessary to highlight the sharp outburst of the extremely high costs for technological innovation in 2014–2015, which, apparently, should be analyzed by fundamental methods. This is one of the reasons that made the task of performing SSA more difficult.

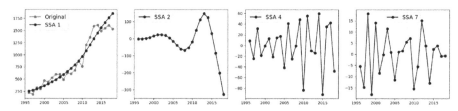

Fig. 8. Several results obtained by the singular value decomposition of the technological innovation expenditures (billion RUB) in the Russian Federation.

Let us consider the results obtained by analyzing the dynamics of technological innovation expenditures in the Russian Federation (Fig. 8) by using the SSA method. The reconstructed series SSA1 reflects a trend towards accelerated growth in technological innovation costs, which has been slowing in recent years. This trend is not very consistent with the identified trends in other indicators of innovation activity in the Russian Federation (see Fig. 2, Fig. 5); however, it should be noted that the previous indicators characterized internal innovation activity, and the cost for technological innovation can arise both when implementing domestic developments and when importing technologies.

Thus, the trend highlighted by the reconstructed series SSA1 should be considered as a result of the active introduction of advanced foreign technologies in Russia over the past 20 years.

The reconstructed series SSA2 (Fig. 8) can be considered as a manifestation of medium-term fluctuations over a period of 10–11 years, distorted by slowdown in the growth of technological innovation expenditures in recent years (the series SSA3 can be considered as belonging to the same periodical). The reconstructed series SSA7 reflects insignificant short-term fluctuations over a period of 3–4 years since 2000, or possibly just random fluctuations. Finally, the reconstructed series SSA4, as well as the series SSA5, shows the presence of a strong negative autocorrelation in the TS we are studding.

Thus, all the components, which we observed hereinbefore for other series of dynamics in the Russian Federation, were identified for the series being studied by the SSA method. This may once again testify to the close connection of the processes under study.

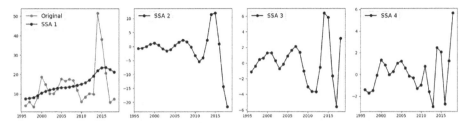

Fig. 9. Several results obtained by the singular value decomposition of the technological innovation expenditures (billion RUB) in the Volgograd region.

When analyzing of the technological innovation expenditures in the Volgograd region (Fig. 9), the SSA method identifies a linear trend (SSA1), the growth of which is much slower than in Russia as a whole, and which has also been slowing down in recent years. Medium-term fluctuations (SSA2, SSA3) with a period of 8–10 years are clearly pronounced, and they are less than for Russia as a whole. This requires an additional interpretation. The reconstructed series SSA4, which reflects a positive autocorrelation, is quite specific (recall that during this indicator analyze for Russian Federation, the autocorrelation was negative). At the same time, the SSA method did not clearly identify short-term fluctuations, which had been identified in all previous series of dynamics.

The results obtained during analyze describe the dynamics of innovation activity in the lust decades quite fully. The problems of the innovation potential and innovation activity reduction in the Russian Federation were identified. An increase in the diffusion of innovations, supposedly from the other countries, was also revealed. The results obtained by SSA method may indicate other problems, e.g., with the state of fixed asset in research organizations in the Volgograd region.

The created models can be used in decisions making at the country and regional levels management. In particular, their results can be used when making decisions on supporting innovative activities, providing grants for upgrading equipment, and making other socio-economic decisions.

The strength of the proposed method usage in management is that it does not require a priori assumptions about the composition and parameters of the time series components. This allows the methodology to be applied by managers who do not have deep knowledge in the field of time series analysis and also increases the objectivity of the results obtained. Moreover, the obtained models can be studied by other methods and can be used as a basis for building more complex predictive and regulatory models, which can also significantly increase the quality of management decisions.

4 Discussion

The use of SSA made it possible to identify the main components of the time series we were studding. It should be noted that the analysis of these components by traditional methods would require the use of a whole set of tools (regression analysis, Fourier transform, methods for detecting autocorrelation analysis, etc.). The usage of those methods would be complicated also by the fact that components similar in economic meaning (e.g., medium-term cycles) differ in period and in the type of trajectory for different indicators. For instance, the period of medium-term cycles for the number of researchers in the Russian Federation is 10–12 years, and the period for the percentage of innovative organizations is 8–10 years. We should also mention an alternative approach, that consists in the building the general dynamics of complex economic systems model similar to [18]. The use of such models can significantly increase the quality of the analysis, but it is limited by the possibility of their verification and actualization.

The simulation results are easy to interpret and can be used in decision making in innovation management. For example, at the stages of cyclic recession, it is necessary to reduce the planned values of the corresponding innovation indicators. In addition, it is necessary to increase investments in innovative research projects since the stage of recession is usually associated with the switching of the types of innovative activities. On the other hand, at the stages of recovery, it is necessary not to overestimate the role

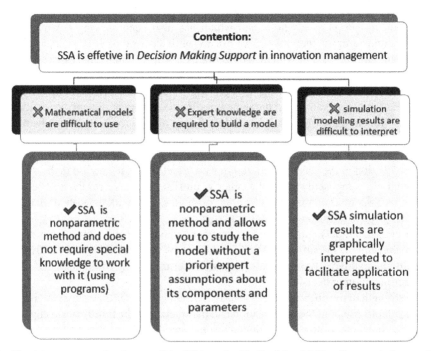

Fig. 10. Argument map for the use of the SSA method in Decision Making Support in innovation management.

of high obtained values and it is necessary in every possible way to promote the growth of innovative projects that have shown the greatest efficiency.

Particular attention should be paid to the components that were not identified during the analysis. For example, the absence of medium-term cycles in the dynamics of the number of researchers in the Volgograd region most likely indicates problems with the state of fixed assets used in research and development. Thus, this provokes an assumption about the need to make decisions related to the replacement of fixed assets in this area and about the optimization of their maintenance and repair [20].

It should be noticed that it is possible to achieve same results by other methods. However, the SSA method has shown itself to be a versatile and easy-to-use method in solving problems of decision-making support in managing innovative development. The main arguments in favor of its use are reflected in Fig. 10. However, its results should be supplemented and refined by using other methods. For example, the selected cyclic components can be verified by using the Fourier transform, and the accuracy of the obtained result can be increased by using neural network [20].

5 Conclusion

1. The SSA method is successfully being used in various scientific disciplines, including economy, image processing, medicine, climatology, oceanology, and geophysics. This method allows to effectively analyze the trend, cyclic components, and study random deviations in TS. Unlike classical statistical methods, this analysis can be carried out without a priori assumptions about the structure and parameters of these components. Moreover, the SSA method is quite versatile and can partially replace a whole range of statistical tools, including regression analysis, Fourier transform, etc.

2. The analysis of innovation activities indicators in the Russian Federation by the SSA method revealed a downward trend for the number of researchers and a quadratic trend for the innovative organizations percentage. An upward trend for the technological innovation expenditures was also revealed. Short-term cycles (3–4 years) and medium-term cycles (8–12 years) were identified in the most of studied TS.

3. During the analysis of the innovation activity indicators in the the Russian Federation region on the example of the Volgograd region, the SSA method also revealed a downward trend for the number of researchers. A long-term downward trend of the innovative organizations percentage was observed. The upward trend for the technological innovations expenditures is much less expressed than for the Russian Federation as a whole. In the studied TS, short-term cycles (3–4 years) were identified. Medium-term cycles (8–12 years) in the number of researchers wasn't identified. This may be due to obsolescence and insufficient updating of fixed assets used in research activities.

4. The results obtained can improve the quality of decision making due to the capability of prediction the value of innovation indicators and differentiate decision-making at different stages of economic cycles.

References

1. The economic security strategy of the Russian Federation for the period until 2030, approved by decree of the President of the Russian Federation No. 208 of May 13, 2017. [Electronic resource] - Access mode: http://base.garant.ru/71672608. Accessed on 21 April 2021
2. Sokolov, A., Shcherbakov, M.V., Tyukov, A., Janovsky, T.: A new approach to reduce time consumption of data quality assessment in the field of energy consumption. In: Kravets, A.G., Groumpos, P.P., Shcherbakov, M., Kultsova, M. (eds.) CIT&DS 2019. CCIS, vol. 1083, pp. 49–62. Springer, Cham (2019). https://doi.org/10.1007/978-3-030-29743-5_4
3. Simonov, A., Tarasova, I., Vinogradova, N., Stepanov, A., Fomenko, O.: Correlation study between the indicators of innovation activity and agricultural production in the Russian regions. In: International Scientific and Practical Conference on From Inertia to Develop: Research and Innovation Support to Agriculture, IDSISA 2020, Yekaterinburg; Russian Federation (2020). https://doi.org/10.1051/e3sconf/202017605017
4. Global Innovation Index 2020. Who Will Finance Innovation? 13th Edition/Soumitra, D., Bruno, L., Sacha, W.-V. (Eds.) [Electronic resource]: Official Site. - Access mode: https://www.wipo.int/edocs/pubdocs/en/wipo_pub_gii_2020.pdf. Accessed on 21 April 2021
5. Vokhmyanin, S.V.: Exploring the algorithm of the Carterpillar-SSA method for reconstructing a time series (Ispytaniye algoritma metoda "Gusenitsa-SSA" dlya vosstanovleniya vremennogo ryada), Vestnik SibGAU, 2:28 (2010)
6. Golyandina, N., Nekrutkin, V., Zhigljavsky, A.: Analysis of Time Series Structure: SSA and Related Techniques. Chapman & Hall/CRC, London (2001)
7. Zhigljavsky, A.: Singular spectrum analysis for time series. In: Lovric, M. (eds.) International Encyclopedia of Statistical Science, Springer, Berlin, Heidelberg (2011). https://doi.org/10.1007/978-3-642-04898-2_521
8. de Carvalho, M., Rua, A.: Real-time nowcasting the US output gap: singular spectrum analysis at work. Int. J. Forecast. 33, 185–198 (2017). https://www.researchgate.net/publication/292950827_Real-time_nowcasting_the_US_output_gap_Singular_spectrum_analysis_at_work. Accessed 21 April 2021
9. Isner, J.B., Tsonis, A.A.: Singular Spectrum Analysis: A New Tool in Time Series Analysis. Plenum, New York (1996)
10. Hassani, H., Mahmoudvand, R., Zokaei, M., Ghodsi, M.: On the separability between signal and noise insingular spectrum analysis. Fluctuation Noise Lett. 11, 2 (2012)
11. Golyandina, N., Korobeynikov, A., Zhigljavsky, A.: Singular Spectrum Analysis with R. Springer Verlag. https://ssa-with-r-book.github.io/. Accessed on 21 April 2021
12. Johann, F.: Pyts: a Python package for time series transformation and classification (2018). https://doi.org/10.5281/zenodo.1244152
13. Hunter, J.D.: Matplotlib: a 2D graphics environment. Comput. Sci. Eng. 9(3), 90–95 (2007). https://doi.org/10.1109/MCSE.2007.55
14. Stock, J.H., Watson, M.W.: Business cycle fluctuations in U.S. macroeconomic time series. In: Taylor, J.B., Woodford, M. (eds.) Handbook of Macroeconomics, pp. 3–64. Elsevier, Amsterdam (1998)
15. Federal State Statistics Service. [Electronic resource]: Official Site. - Access mode: https://gks.ru. Accessed on 21 April 2021
16. Daniele, B.: Clément Juglar and the transition from crises theory to business cycle theories. https://www.unil.ch/files/live/sites/cwp/files/users/neyguesi/public/D._Besomi_. Accessed 21 April 2021
17. OECD/Eurostat. Oslo Manual 2018: Guidelines for Collecting, Reporting and Using Data on Innovation, 4th Edition, The Measurement of Scientific, Technological and Innovation Activities, OECD Publishing, Paris/Eurostat, Luxemburg (2018). 10.17879789264304604-en

18. Rogachev, A.F., Lukashin, M.S.: Modeling and optimization of proactive management of the production pollutions in the conditions of information asymmetry. In: Kravets, A.G., Groumpos, P.P., Shcherbakov, M., Kultsova, M. (eds.) CIT&DS 2019. CCIS, vol. 1083, pp. 78–88. Springer, Cham (2019). https://doi.org/10.1007/978-3-030-29743-5_6
19. Kizim, A.V., Kravets, A.G.: On systemological approach to intelligent decision-making support in industrial cyber-physical systems, Cyber-physical systems: Industry 4.0 Challenges. In: Kravets, A.G., Bolshakov, A.A., Shcherbakov, M.V. (eds.) Ser. Studies in Systems, Decision and Control (SSDC), vol. 260, Springer Nature Switzerland AG, Cham (Switzerland), pp. 167–183. https://link.springer.com/book/https://doi.org/10.1007/978-3-030-32648-7
20. Al-Gunaid, M.A., Shcherbakov, M.V., Trubitsin, V.N., Shumkin, A.M., Dereguzov, K.Y.: Analysis a short-term time series of crop sales based on machine learning methods. In: Kravets, A.G., Groumpos, P.P., Shcherbakov, M., Kultsova, M. (eds.) CIT&DS 2019. CCIS, vol. 1083, pp. 189–200. Springer, Cham (2019). https://doi.org/10.1007/978-3-030-29743-5_15

Analysis of the Competitiveness Risks of Food Production Enterprises Using Mathematical Modelling Methods

Irina Veshneva[1] ⓘ, Alexander Bolshakov[2](✉) ⓘ, and Anna Fedorova[3]

[1] Saratov National Research University named after N.G. Chernyshevsky, 83, Astrakhanskaya Street, Saratov 410012, Russia
veshnevaiv@gmail.ru
[2] Peter the Great St. Petersburg Polytechnic University, 29, Polytechnicheskaya, St. Petersburg 195251, Russia
[3] Ca' Foscari University of Venice, Dorsoduro 3246, 30123 Venice, Italy
anna.fedorova@unive.it

Abstract. The increasing complexity of modern production processes necessitates the use of artificial intelligence technologies that use formalized knowledge to develop effective management tools. It is proposed to use the well-known Balance Score Card System to describe production processes based on the concepts of risks. The key performance indicators of the Balanced Scorecard are organized in a tree graph. The root of the tree graph is an event that causes a security violation. The rest of the graph vertices are unfavourable events. The branches of the tree describe the causal mechanisms between these events. A mathematical model is proposed to describe action and reaction in the form of a matrix. Its cells are functions that describe interactions at the nodes of the tree. If the result of the interaction contributes to the occurrence of an event that should be considered as unfavourable, then the sign of the event is positive. If the interaction led to the elimination of the adverse event, then the event result is zero. It is assumed that interactions can backfire and facilitate processes to prevent adverse events. The probability of realization of each combination depends on the result of interactions at the vertices of the graph, which are described by status functions. Status functions can be viewed as an extended analogy to probabilities. To develop a mathematical model of the dynamics of production processes, improve the quality and safety of food products, a system of linear differential equations of Kolmogorov-Chapman is used. The described results are obtained by solving linear differential equations. They allow you to develop scenarios and predict the dynamics of production processes when solving automation problems to improve the quality and safety of the food industry.

Keywords: Functions · Operations research · BSC · Chapmen-Kolmogorov equations · Competitiveness risks · Food safety · Creativity

© Springer Nature Switzerland AG 2021
A. G. Kravets et al. (Eds.): CIT&DS 2021, CCIS 1448, pp. 238–249, 2021.
https://doi.org/10.1007/978-3-030-87034-8_18

1   Introduction

The need to analyse competitiveness risks is becoming especially relevant both for individual enterprises and for entire regions and countries. Safety in the food industry has long been an imperishable issue of public concerns. This is due to series of scandals regarding the quality of products that are being sold and consumed, such as BSE or GMOs. While major attention of the research has been focused on development and application of food standard bodies [1], some scholars have also referred to mathematical modelling as integrated solution for spotting and preventing heterogeneous risks affiliated with the specificity of the industry.

The risks of competitiveness decreasing are one of the key components to company's overall wellbeing. However, heterogeneity and complexity of risks invites implementation of Artificial Intelligence Systems (AIS) that rely on formal knowledge for designing managerial preventive techniques. While being completely in line with HACCP prescriptions of control of critical situations in food industry [2], this approach also corresponds corporate social responsibility and sustainability principles.

Studies in the field of graph theory have proven to be widely useful in explaining complex systems such at various levels, be it the entire system, subsystem or its certain units. Not only it provides fresh angles to observe diverse phenomenon's, but also encourages to investigate interaction mechanisms. In recent studies of network science, scholars have addressed various issues, such as control principles of networks [3], contagion mechanisms [4], managing risks affiliated with plant equipment maintenance [5].

In the current paper, authors bind together Markov processes [6] and Status Functions [7] in series graph organized in accordance with Balanced Scorecard principles [8]. This model allows to track causal mechanisms and dynamics of company risks in the baking industry to increase efficiency and safety of production.

The objective of the present study is to develop a mathematical model able to chase unfavourable events occurrence and causality for the sake of quality and safety improvement in food industry. By these means a comprehensive and up-to-date picture for an enterprise in baking industry can be provided, for example. In the second part of the paper, simulations of the model are presented and results are discussed.

2   Statement of the Problem

Development of risks prevention techniques is one of the key approaches to reach safety of production in baking industry. Mathematical modelling, as a method, allows to elaborate managerial recommendations for decision makers by means of complex control of heterogeneous factors.

In order to conduct a risk analysis, they must be structured. Production processes are sorted out according to BSC structure. Let us detect key problems that may arise during the processing. It is supposed that the functioning of the enterprise is composed of complex interaction of considered processes.

It is also assumed that failure to realize one of the processes does not result in inability of mathematical model operating.

That means that within an enterprise, there exist processes due to which the system can reallocate resources and block risks in certain subsystems.

If conditions of causes and aftereffects are formulated as productions, they can be formulated as minimax operations. It is needed to design BSC-based series graph, the root of which is an event that corresponds to organizational failure and inability of enterprise's subsequent operating. Based on this graph, authors detect sets of events forming branches that lead to the root vertex and compose the system of Chapman-Kolmogorov linear differential equations. Further, authors perform analysis of the model, run modification system of Chapman-Kolmogorov simulation compare the results of computer simulation and discuss the results.

3   Causal Series Graph Based on Balanced Scorecard

Prior to suggesting mathematical model of baking company, we introduce causal series graph DS, where vertexes are risks of failure of enterprise functioning (Fig. 1). The structure of the graph is set by BSC and embraces external environment (1), financial activities (24), business processing (31), and staff (47) [8]. Hence, interconnected system of reasonable risk processes of the company is grounded in Key Performance Indicators (KPI).

BSC is the way to express that the company should be sustainable in a bunch of dimensions, each of which is evaluated with various scales. Due to that reason, comparison of heterogeneous characteristics in their absolute values appears impossible.

BCS-based series graph DS allows to tackle aforementioned issue. Each vertex of the graph represents the event that occurs due to emergence of another set of events. Thus 0-level vertex means the closedown of the baking company and its reasons are 1-level vertexes. The latter are consequential to 2-level vertexes, that, in their turn, arise from 3-level vertexes, etc. Causal mechanism operates like a logical combination of reasons. In the proposed model, «AND» ($\wedge$) and «OR» ($\vee$) operations are used. Certain probability is attributed to each event.

Figure 1 sketches possible risks in series tree-graph DS. External risks (1) originate from events beyond company's influence and control [9]. We subdivide this branch to following clusters in accordance with PEST analysis (Political, Economic, Social and Technological) and discuss each of them from risk management perspective [10].

Economic and political risks (2) include economic crisis (3), intensified competition (4) triggered by emergence of rival with competitive advantage, such as economy of scale, branding, etc. (5), emergence of a bunch of rivals in the key location (6), [11] and changes in legal regulations of baking industry operating (7).

Social network risks (8) suggest two possible scenarios of unfavourable events, involving interactions with key supplier companies and target customers, namely.

Interfirm network risks (9) tackle aspects of long-term b2b partnerships among firms in the baking industry. In this vein, unfavourable changes in reutilized logistics procedures and costs (10), existence of long-term key suppliers (11) or the quality of goods they provide (12) have disruptive impact on company well-being [12, 13].

An explanation of the risks for the corresponding indicators of the Balanced Score Card is presented in Table 1.

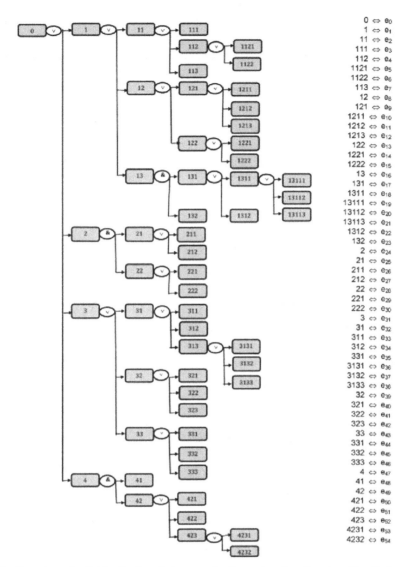

0	$\Leftrightarrow$ e_0
1	$\Leftrightarrow$ e_1
11	$\Leftrightarrow$ e_2
111	$\Leftrightarrow$ e_3
112	$\Leftrightarrow$ e_4
1121	$\Leftrightarrow$ e_5
1122	$\Leftrightarrow$ e_6
113	$\Leftrightarrow$ e_7
12	$\Leftrightarrow$ e_8
121	$\Leftrightarrow$ e_9
1211	$\Leftrightarrow$ e_{10}
1212	$\Leftrightarrow$ e_{11}
1213	$\Leftrightarrow$ e_{12}
122	$\Leftrightarrow$ e_{13}
1221	$\Leftrightarrow$ e_{14}
1222	$\Leftrightarrow$ e_{15}
13	$\Leftrightarrow$ e_{16}
131	$\Leftrightarrow$ e_{17}
1311	$\Leftrightarrow$ e_{18}
13111	$\Leftrightarrow$ e_{19}
13112	$\Leftrightarrow$ e_{20}
13113	$\Leftrightarrow$ e_{21}
1312	$\Leftrightarrow$ e_{22}
132	$\Leftrightarrow$ e_{23}
2	$\Leftrightarrow$ e_{24}
21	$\Leftrightarrow$ e_{25}
211	$\Leftrightarrow$ e_{26}
212	$\Leftrightarrow$ e_{27}
22	$\Leftrightarrow$ e_{28}
221	$\Leftrightarrow$ e_{29}
222	$\Leftrightarrow$ e_{30}
3	$\Leftrightarrow$ e_{31}
31	$\Leftrightarrow$ e_{32}
311	$\Leftrightarrow$ e_{33}
312	$\Leftrightarrow$ e_{34}
331	$\Leftrightarrow$ e_{35}
3131	$\Leftrightarrow$ e_{36}
3132	$\Leftrightarrow$ e_{37}
3133	$\Leftrightarrow$ e_{38}
32	$\Leftrightarrow$ e_{39}
321	$\Leftrightarrow$ e_{40}
322	$\Leftrightarrow$ e_{41}
323	$\Leftrightarrow$ e_{42}
33	$\Leftrightarrow$ e_{43}
331	$\Leftrightarrow$ e_{44}
332	$\Leftrightarrow$ e_{45}
333	$\Leftrightarrow$ e_{46}
4	$\Leftrightarrow$ e_{47}
41	$\Leftrightarrow$ e_{48}
42	$\Leftrightarrow$ e_{49}
421	$\Leftrightarrow$ e_{50}
422	$\Leftrightarrow$ e_{51}
423	$\Leftrightarrow$ e_{52}
4231	$\Leftrightarrow$ e_{53}
4232	$\Leftrightarrow$ e_{54}

Fig. 1. Causal graph of risks D_S for a bakery production enterprise. Based on Key Performance of Balanced Score Card

Customer network risks (13) vary from customer loyalty decrease (14) to customers' complete pastry abstinence (15) that can be fostered by such social trends as veganism and healthy lifestyle popularization and massive media coverage of those [14, 15].

Technological risks (16) refer to technological discontinuity in baking industry (17) and adaption of such technologies by competitors (23) [16], It can be due to break-through innovation regarding new products (18) or machinery (22) that have potential to completely reshape production process. The latter arises in ease of adaption of new

Table 1. The fragment of the table of indicators, decryption and logical operations of the nodes of the risk tree

No	Designation	Decoding	Logical operation
0	$0 \Leftrightarrow e_0$	impaired functioning	OR
1	$1 \Leftrightarrow e_1$	external risks	OR
2	$11 \Leftrightarrow e_2$	economic risks	OR
3	$111 \Leftrightarrow e_3$	economic crisis	
4	$112 \Leftrightarrow e_4$	increased competition	OR
5	$1121 \Leftrightarrow e_5$	advantage competitor	
6	$1122 \Leftrightarrow e_6$	group of small competitors	
7	$113 \Leftrightarrow e_7$	changes in legislation	
8	$12 \Leftrightarrow e_8$	social network risks	OR
9	$121 \Leftrightarrow e_9$	risks in the market network	OR
10	$1211 \Leftrightarrow e_{10}$	logistics disruption	
11	$1212 \Leftrightarrow e_{11}$	breach of relationships with longtermly suppliers	
12	$1213 \Leftrightarrow e_{12}$	raw material quality	
13	$122 \Leftrightarrow e_{13}$	risks in the network of buyers	OR
14	$1221 \Leftrightarrow e_{14}$	lower customer loyalty	
15	$1222 \Leftrightarrow e_{15}$	customer refusal to bake	
16	$13 \Leftrightarrow e_{16}$	technological	AND
17	$131 \Leftrightarrow e_{17}$	technological changes	OR
18	$1311 \Leftrightarrow e_{18}$	invention of new equipment	OR
19	$13111 \Leftrightarrow e_{19}$	use of new materials	
20	$13112 \Leftrightarrow e_{20}$	import of innovative equipment	
21	$13113 \Leftrightarrow e_{21}$	research intensification	
22	$1312 \Leftrightarrow e_{22}$	invention of new raw materials	
23	$132 \Leftrightarrow e_{23}$	competitors use new technologies	
24	$2 \Leftrightarrow e_{024}$	financial	AND
25	$21 \Leftrightarrow e_{25}$	significant financial losses	OR
26	$211 \Leftrightarrow e_{26}$	credit risk // bankruptcy of debtors	
27	$212 \Leftrightarrow e_{27}$	operational risk // fraud, litigation	

materials in the industry (19), import of innovative complete machinery (20), intensified research and development (21).

Financial risks (25) include credit risk (26) that is affiliated with debtor's inability to pay off debts; and operational risk (27) stands for lawsuits, frauds and other. Aforementioned categories of risks cause cash flow shocks (28), Funding risk (29) is uncertainty to get sufficient funding from investors at given financial period, while liquidity risk (30) is firm's inability to sell an asset quickly under conditions of urgent need of additional cash flow.

Organizational failures may also be caused by unskilful business processing within the firm (31) [17, 18].

Preventable risks (32) belong to a group of internal risks that are potentially controllable and can be forestalled [9]. To this category, we ascribe failures associated with low quality input purchase (33), technological breakdown (34), production process failures (35): improper sales request proceeding (36), inner logistics failure (37), improper pre-sale preparation (38).

Management failings (39) are instigated by imperfect intra-organization policy and may be related to planning (40), quality control (41), research and development (42).

Situational violations (43) are caused by improper use of the site, tools or equipment [19]. These are circulation of documents disruption (44), sanitary norms noncompliance (45), IT systems failure (46).

Personnel risks are first affiliated with the loss of staff members whose skills and expertise are crucial for the organization (48), Such circumstance normally has a set of prerequisites that it is being triggered by.

Employees' non-acceptance of managerial policy (49) can be caused by the change in business processes (50), unreadiness for other sort of deviation from organizational routine (52) or qualifications mismatch (52) that is twofold. Unqualified management versus qualified staff (53) or qualified management versus unqualified staff (54).

Each of the risks occurs with some probability. The operands of the operation are the values at the vertex-causes for the corresponding corollary. An adjacency matrix is used to represent a causal graph. Logical operations are also represented as a matrix. From the top of the graph, the graph is traversed in depth and sets of event vertices are calculated that lead to the implementation of the event of the root vertex. These sets are the minimum sections.

4 Mathematical Modelling

At the top of the graph is an event that can be implemented as a result of a combination of events. Let us imagine the relationship between the vertices of events as a cause and effect. Thus, the top of the graph is a consequence of some combination of reasons. These reasons are the vertices of level 1 graph. Reasons for Level 1 may be due to reasons of Level 2, If the cause is a consequence of the previous level, it is also implemented as a logical combination of these causes (And or Or), The implementation of the investigation occurs as a result of some logical combination of causes. Each vertex- consequence corresponds to a logical min-max operation. In the model under consideration, this can be an operation either AND (And) or OR (Or).

Minimum section of tree graph DS (Fig. 1) corresponds to critical combinations of risks, i.e., combinations of end vertexes occurrence of which results in root vertex regardless realization of other end vertexes. In infological model, they appear as end vertexes of thee-shaper series graph.

For example, vertexes 3132, 323, 332 form minimum section of series graph and will result in events 321, 31, 32, 42, 3, Series graph Gk is introduced for analysis of process of root vertex emergence. The 2k vertexes are in line with all possible combinations of events e1;...; ek. Thus, sanitary norms noncompliance e45, lack of research and development e42, inner logistics failure e37, arise production process failures e35 that, in turn, evoke preventable risks e32, management failings e39 and situational violations e49 simultaneously. All together, it brings into state unskillful business processing within the firm 31, threatening with systematic organizational failure e0.

It is possible to rely on Chapman-Kolmogorov system of linear differential Eqs. (1) for monitoring of dangerous combinations of events. This mathematical model is suitable for detecting probabilities of minimum sections occurrence and consists of 2k equations for functions of probability of events assigned to vertexes: P0(t),..., P2k-1(t). Advantages of the model are computation efficiency, relative easiness of empirical data detection and modifications with account to observed processes. The drawback, on the other side, is inability to consider infusion processes.

Let λj be intensity of event πj occurrence, μj be intensity of counteraction to this event and Pi be probabilities of these events' occurrence.

Let we consider the Chapman-Kolmogorov equations for the probabilities of the occurrence of risk events presented at the vertices of the graph. We obtain the following equations:

$$\frac{dP_0(t)}{dt} = -\sum_{j=1}^{k} \lambda_j P_0(t) + \sum_{j=1}^{k} \mu_j P_j(t)$$

$$\ldots\ldots$$

$$\frac{dP_i(t)}{dt} = -P_i(t)\pi_i^- + \sum_{j=0}^{2^k-1} \pi_{ij}^+ P_j(t) \tag{1}$$

$$\ldots\ldots$$

$$\frac{dP_{2^k-1}(t)}{dt} = \sum_{j=1}^{k} \lambda_j P_{2^k-k+j-2}(t)$$

where in (1) functions P0(t),..., P2k-1(t) are probabilities of events related to vertexes of series graph Gk, λj are values of vector intensity of event ej occurrence, and μj intensities of counteractions to those events; πi is the sum of all edges directed from i to other vertexes, i, j ∈ {0,..., 2k-1}, values of πij may be either λl if edge goes from j to i, and μ, if otherwise, or 0 is there is no edge directed from i to j.

Let us create a modification of these equations. First, we replace the characteristics of events λ_j, π_j, μ_j. Let them be combined in complex-valued Status Functions (SF) ψ_j, SF refer to the state of the object in the same way as membership functions (MF) in the theory of Fuzzy Sets.

Just like MF, SF depend on basic variables, e.g., r. However, unlike MF, the set of SF includes orthonormalized functions forming a bunch of orthogonal basic functions, SF turn out to be similar to the wave functions of quantum mechanics. They form a certain transition from the uncertainty of MF and algorithms of the theory of fuzzy sets to the methods of quantum mechanics, which can be applied to the analysis of problems of socioeconomic systems.

The SF is complex-valued. The real part is directly an estimate. There are 3 possible ratings: low, medium, high. An alternating function is introduced for each of the possible estimates. Functions are orthonormal and form the complete basis of the described system. The technology of assigning a function to estimating the state of a vertex is similar to the fuzzification procedure in the theory of fuzzy sets. The imaginary part of the status functions is built on the basis of the correspondence of the obtained assessment to the target indicator and has 3 possible values $-1, 0, +1$, This corresponds to: Below the target value, matches the target value, above the target value. These estimates are a parameter that converts the real part into a vector.

The status function satisfies the Laplace equation. They are an analogue of wave functions in quantum mechanics. Therefore, based on the SF, one can construct nonlinear differential equations, A feature of the SF is that they are rigidly localized in space. They are obtained as a result of the Gram-Schmidt orthogonalization procedure. The properties of the SF include normalization, which requires the existence in the backward range of space.

Ordered pair of arguments is the characteristic of probability of event occurrence in the vertex of the graph and its adjacent edge direction, meaning action and counteraction. Let vertexes characteristics be binary. Probability of event occurrence can be high or low, and the direction can be up to the root vertex or down. Therefore, there exist four possible values of events: low, down, low, up, high, down, high up.

Nonlinearity of Chapman-Kolmogorov equations should be considered.

Let SF be reflection that sets the rule of correspondence of ordered pair of arguments and the value associated with it [7], SF defines the status that indicates the complex of object's characteristics values, that prescribe its position in the system. These functions are fulfilled by the object according to institutional agreements of the system.

First, implementation of SF changes calculation interpretation, meaning probability is not limited to one. Herewith it is required to introduce limitations analogous to those of [20], Interfusion of investigated risks is introduced as member proportional to the product of SF of interacting processes. Let us consider Chapman-Kolmogorov equations with nonlinear members setting growth limitations and shuffling probabilities of realization of events represented in the vertexes of series graph. The first addendum remains in equation, the second sets limit to growth, the third carries out the nonlinear shuffling. Hence the following Eqs. (2) are:

$$\frac{dP_0(t)}{dt} = \int_{-1}^{1} \left(\sum_{j=1}^{k} P_0(t)(\psi_j(r) - P_0(t) - \psi_j^*(r)P_j(t)) \right) dr$$

$$\cdots\cdots$$

$$\frac{dP_i(t)}{dt} = \int_{-1}^{1} \left(\sum_{j=0}^{2^k-1} P_i(t)\left(\psi_i^* - \psi_j P_j(t) - \psi_j P_i(t) \right) \right) dr \tag{2}$$

$$\cdots\cdots$$

$$\frac{dP_{2^k-1}(t)}{dt} = \int_{-1}^{1} \left(\sum_{j=1}^{k} P_{2^k-k+j-2}(t)(\psi_j - \psi_{2^k-k+j-2} P_{2^k-k+j-2}(t)) \right) dr$$

where in (2) functions $P_0(t)$, $P_{2^k-1}(t)$ are probability density of events related to vertexes of series graph G_k, ψ_{ij} are SF. They are complex-valued, they have magnitude and direction. Therefore, they allow you to combine previously used λ_j, π_j, μ_j. The values of complex part of ψ_j may be either $exp +1 \cdot 2\pi r$ if edge goes from j to i, and $exp -1 \cdot 2\pi r$, if otherwise, or $exp -0 \cdot 2\pi r = 1$ is there is no edge directed from i to j.

Complex valued SF are written in (2). The $2^3 = 1$ equations are corresponding minimum section example suggested above. Solutions for Eqs. (1) and (2) are analogous on the short time span.

The module was validated for the implementation of a mathematical model based on the Kolmogorov-Chapman equations to assess the risks of regional competitiveness. To do this, for the analysis of regional competitiveness, including for the bakery industry, an application was developed on the Python 3.8.3 platform based on an extended set of libraries: Itertools, Matplotlib, PyPlot, Math, NumPy, SciPy, Tkinter. The functionality of the module includes specifying a section in the graph of cause-and-effect relationships, determining the size of the section, entering data. These include the levels of risks and control actions for individual indicators, the likelihood of risks for individual indicators, the level of competitiveness risk using the application interface, as well as a text file. In addition, it provides for setting a critical level for individual indicators, choosing a time interval for plotting graphs. The resulting system of differential equations is solved numerically using the Runge-Kutta method with automatic step adjustment. The developed application allows you to generate graphs of probabilities for assessing critical events and their combinations at a given time interval. In addition, it is possible to obtain numerical data corresponding to the values of probabilities for separate sets of critical events for a fixed point in time.

On the Fig. 2 is a graph of root vertex e0 realization for solution of Eqs. (2), where two initial conditions are as follows: for 1, P0 = 0.5; P1 = 0.5; P2 = 0.5; P3 = 0.5; P4 = 0.5; P5 = 0.5; P6 = 0.5; P7 = 0.5; for 2, P0 = 1; P2 = 0.5; P3 = 0.5; P4 = 0.5; P5 = 0.5; P6 = 0.5; P7 = 0.5.

On the short time span, graphs behave nearly identical. On a longer time span, however, the company with initial low probability of risks appears by far more stable and favourable. On the long run, the solution sets in same value of stable equilibrium. It is reasonable to assume that under such circumstances the infological model of series graph may fail. The simulation was run in Wolfram Mathematica software for given equations and can be considered quite an accurate approximation of reality.

It should be noted the interest and certain successes in the use of digital models based on the Kolmogorov-Chapman equations for solving various class of problems,

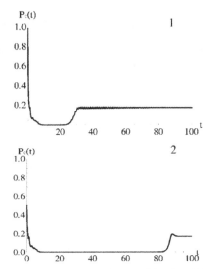

Fig. 2. The results of numerical simulation of the modification of the Chapman- Kolmogorov equations with the introduced nonlinearity for different initial conditions $1 - P_0 = 0.5$, $2 - P_0 = 1$. The probabilities of the remaining events are equal to 0.5

including for the study of regional competitiveness [21]. In addition, approaches related to the direction Society 5.0 are of interest, i.e. socio-economic and cultural strategies for the development of society, which is based on the use of digital technologies in all spheres of life [22–25].

5   Conclusions

The original mathematical approach to spotting and preventing risks in the baking industry is suggested. The model relies on Status Functions, modified Chapman-Kolmogorov equations and series graph.

The simulation exercise has shown high probability of timely reaction of the model to elementary unfavourable events at minimum sections of the graph. The output of this study can be used for development of monitoring systems and for counteraction to threats to company's sustainable functioning by means of using modern mathematical models and information technology.

A preliminary validation of the software module for the implementation of a mathematical model based on the Kolmogorov-Chapman equations, which is used to carry out the procedure for assessing the risks of regional competitiveness, including for the bakery industry, has been carried out. The software application is developed on the Python 3.8.3 platform based on an extended set of libraries.

It is convenient to use the suggested model of KPI dynamics for solving problems of industrial enterprise's resources optimization. Two following approaches can be implemented for forming target reference point, namely, standard deviations of weighted BSC values and Chebyshev Distance. Depending on selected target reference point and its continuity, convexity and other characteristics, it is required to select or develop a corresponding optimization method. Herewith the suggested mathematical model can be used for target reference points computation for detecting critical combinations of events.

Acknowledgments. This research was partially supported by the Russian Fund of Basic Research (grant No. 20-010-00465).

References

1. Trienekens, J., Zuurbier, P.: Quality and safety standards in the food industry, developments and challenges. Int. J. Prod. Econ. **113**, 107–127 (2008)
2. Pierson, M.D.: HACCP: Principles and Applications. Springer, New York (2012). https://doi.org/10.1007/978-1-4684-8818-0
3. Barabasi, A.L., Liu, Y.Y.: Control principles of complex networks. Rev. Mod. Phys. **88**, 1–61 (2016)
4. Pastor-Satorras, R., Castellano, C., Van Mieghem, P., Vespignani, A.: Epidemic processes in complex networks. Rev. Mod. Phys. **87**, 925 (2015)
5. Abbassi, P., Iyer, R., Pedro, J.-L., Rodriguez, F.: Securities trading by banks and credit supply: micro-evidence from the crisis. J. Financ. Econ. **121**(3), 569–594 (2016)
6. Bolshakov, A., Veshneva, I., Lushin, D.: Mathematical model of integration of cyber-physical systems for solving problems of increasing the competitiveness of the regions of the Russian federation. In: Kravets, A.G., Bolshakov, A.A., Shcherbakov, M. (eds.) Society 5.0: Cyberspace for Advanced Human-Centered Society. SSDC, vol. 333, pp. 129–139. Springer, Cham (2021). https://doi.org/10.1007/978-3-030-63563-3_11
7. Veshneva, I.V., Chistyakova, T.B., Bolshakov, A.A.: The status functions method for processing and interpretation of the measurement data of interactions in the educational environment. In: SPIIRAS Proceedings, vol. 6, no, 49, pp. 144–166 (2016). 10.15622. ISSN 20789181
8. Olve, N.G., Roy, J., Wetter, M.: Performance Drivers: A Practical Guide to Using the Balanced Scorecard. Wiley (1999)
9. Kaplan, R.S., Mikes, A.: Managing Risks: A New Framework. Harvard Business Review, UK (2012)
10. Ho, J.K.: Formulation of a systemic PEST analysis for strategic analysis. Eur. Acad. Res. **2**(5), 6478–6492 (2014)
11. Porter, M.E.: Competitive Advantage: Creating and Sustaining Superior Performance. The Free Press P (2008)
12. Das, T.K., Teng, B.-S.: Risk types and interfirm alliance structures. J. Manag. Stud. **33**(6), 827–843 (1996)
13. Uzzi, B.: Social structure and competition in interfirm networks: the paradox of embeddedness. Adm. Sci. Q. **42**(1), 35–67 (1997)
14. Goodman, D., Dupuis, E.M.: Knowing food and growing food: beyond the production-consumption debate in the sociology of agriculture. Sociologiaruralis **42**(1), 5–22 (2002)
15. Cherry, E.: Veganism as a cultural movement: a relational approach. Soc. Mov. Stud. **5**(2), 155–170 (2006)
16. Anderson, P., Tushman, M.L.: Technological discontinuities and dominant designs: a cyclical model of technological change. Adm. Sci. Q. **35**(4), 604–633 (1990)
17. Mellahi, K., Wilkinson, A.: Organizational failure: a critique of recent research and a proposed integrative framework. J. Recomendation Service **5**(1), 21–41 (2004)

18. Sheppard, J.P., Chowdhurv, S.D.: Riding the wrong wave: organizational failure as a failed turnaround. Long Range Plan. **38**(3), 239–260 (2005)
19. Reason, J.T., Parker, D., Lawton, R.: Organizational controls and safety: the varieties of rule-related behaviour. J. Occup. Organ. Psychol. **71**, 289–304 (1998)
20. Rogers, E.M.: Diffusion of Innovations, 4th edn. The Free Press, New York (1995)
21. Veshneva, I., Chernyshova, G., Bolshakov, A.: Regional competitiveness research based on digital models using Kolmogorov-Chapman equations. In: Kravets, A.G., Bolshakov, A.A., Shcherbakov, M. (eds.) Society 5.0: Cyberspace for Advanced Human-Centered Society. SSDC, vol. 333, pp. 141–154. Springer, Cham (2021). https://doi.org/10.1007/978-3-030-63563-3_12
22. Fomin, N.A., Meshcheryakov, R.V., Iskhakov, A.Y., Gromov, Y.Y.: Smart city: cyber-physical systems modeling features. In: Kravets, A.G., Bolshakov, A.A., Shcherbakov, M. (eds.) Society 5.0: Cyberspace for Advanced Human-Centered Society. SSDC, vol. 333, pp. 75–90. Springer, Cham (2021). https://doi.org/10.1007/978-3-030-63563-3_7
23. Galkin, A., Sysoev, A.: Controlling traffic flows in intelligent transportation system. In: Kravets, A.G., Bolshakov, A.A., Shcherbakov, M. (eds.) Society 5.0: Cyberspace for Advanced Human-Centered Society, vol. 333, pp. 91–101. Springer, Cham (2021). https://doi.org/10.1007/978-3-030-63563-3_8
24. Anokhin, A., Burov, S., Parygin, D., Rent, V., Sadovnikova, N., Finogeev, A.: Development of scenarios for modeling the behavior of people in an urban environment. In: Kravets, A.G., Bolshakov, A.A., Shcherbakov, M. (eds.) Society 5.0: Cyberspace for Advanced Human-Centered Society. SSDC, vol. 333, pp. 103–114. Springer, Cham (2021). https://doi.org/10.1007/978-3-030-63563-3_9
25. Baykina, N., Golovanov, P., Livshits, M., Tuponosova, E.: Forecast of the impact of human resources on the effectiveness of the petrochemical cyber-physical cluster of the samara region. In: Kravets, A.G., Bolshakov, A.A., Shcherbakov, M. (eds.) Society 5.0: Cyberspace for Advanced Human-Centered Society, vol. 333, pp. 116–127. Springer, Cham (2021). https://doi.org/10.1007/978-3-030-63563-3_10

System Approach in Organization of International Students' Mobility

Alexey Godenko, Grigory Boyko$^{(\boxtimes)}$, and Rashid Gadgiev

Volgograd State Technical University, Volgograd, Russian Federation
{forstud,boyko}@vstu.ru

Abstract. According to the analysis of the existing internationalization strategies, it is demonstrated that its main source is an international students' mobility, which is based on ability, willingness, and common interest in cooperation of three following subjects: countries charged with the import of education; countries connected with its export; higher educational institution of the country, exporting education, which provides its educational services for the citizens of the country, charged with the import of education. The success of this process depends on a certain set of factor indicators in politics, economics, sociology, and technology peculiar to each of the three participants. The authors propose common to all the participant's list of criteria, which evaluate indicators of the stated factors according to the unique scale: political (administrative) stability; degree of participants' cooperation; legislation in the educational sphere, mutual amiability of the subjects; level of administrative barriers, peculiarities of the demographic situation; economic performance, demand for majors of training; logistic accessibility; the number of graduate students; language attraction of training programs; level of career-oriented activities; correspondence between the level of applicants' acquirements and requirements of the country, which exports education; competition on the market of educational services; accessibility of distance educational technologies; development level and dynamics of innovations. The integral estimation of efficiency forecast for the work of exporting higher educational institutions, with the population of a particular country, charged with the import of education is carried out by the analysis of the formed multi-level hierarchical structure. The convolution of hierarchical elements on each level of the hierarchical structure is done using a generalized f-mean, proposed by Kolmogorov-Nagumo. There are given examples of implications of the proposed methodology for quantitative and comparative assessment of the potential of countries which export education, that allows international services of the university to determine the number of the most attractive countries in terms of organization of international students' mobility and therefore the concentration of administrative and financial resources in the chosen direction, in order to make a decision on promotion reasonability of the university brand on the foreign market of educational services. The model can be easily changed and modified by adding relevant parameters for a given university and time that significantly affect international students' mobility, or excluding ones, which have a low impact on it.

Keywords: Internationalization · Student mobility · Theory of qualities · Systems analysis · PEST analysis

© Springer Nature Switzerland AG 2021
A. G. Kravets et al. (Eds.): CIT&DS 2021, CCIS 1448, pp. 250–263, 2021.
https://doi.org/10.1007/978-3-030-87034-8_19

1 Introduction

Globalization of the world economy is a specific feature of the modern world.

The efficiency of any economic sector considerably depends on a variety of factors based on advanced scientific knowledge and best practices. Knowledge development cannot proceed when isolated by the frameworks of separate territories. Only large-scale integration of individual teams can lead to solutions to serious problems. These solutions are supported by up-to-date knowledge the holders of which are highly qualified professionals trained by education institutions. Globalization is typical of the education sector as well as of the other economic sectors. One of the manifestations of education globalization is internationalization, which implies the strengthening of interrelations between countries in various spheres including the following:

involvement of foreign scientists and experts - development of academic mobility, implementation of joint educational programs with foreign partners - development of student mobility,
implementation of joint scientific research with leading foreign scientific centers.

Internationalization of education is usually understood as a process in which the tasks, objectives, functions, and the procedure of rendering educational services to various target groups acquire an international aspect and dimension characterized by political, economic, social, and technological factors.

In the paper [1], four strategies for internationalization are formulated:

1. The strategy for a coordinated approach is based on the creation of favorable conditions for cooperation between research and education centers in various countries.
2. The strategy for skilled manpower involvement, including the purposeful involvement of the most talented scientists, faculty, and students. The strategy is aimed at developing the personnel potential of the organization and increasing the competitiveness of the university in the scientific and educational sphere.
3. The strategy for revenue generation.
4. The strategy for opportunities enhancement implies the import of education (considerable outbound academic and student mobility).

In various countries, the strategy for internationalization is focused on achieving the priority objectives for a particular country. Canada is interested in attracting foreign graduates to develop its own economy. Germany focuses on the support of the most talented foreign young people. Italy makes efforts to enhance the international esteem for the national education system. The United Kingdom views internationalization as an opportunity to promote British education as well as an economic aspect of training foreign students. The given examples demonstrate that all the four strategies, as well as their combinations [2], are used in the course of education internationalization.

All the internationalization strategies imply student mobility. Over the past 40 years, the number of international students in the world has increased from 800 thousand to 4500 thousand. The most intensive growth was observed at the turn of the XXI century. In recent years, the growth rates have slowed down significantly. This can be explained due to a number of objective reasons. Thus, traditional student-importing countries (China, Vietnam, South Korea, and others) make considerable efforts to improve the quality of their own national education systems. As a result, a network of world-class national universities has emerged in these countries, which have become attractive to their own students.

The statistical data on the number of foreign students, for example for the Russian Federation, show an increase in their number by 14%in 2016–2017and by 12%in 2017–2018. The main growth was due to students from Asian countries. In the 2017–2018 academic year, 256.9 thousand people studied at 703 Russian universities (an increase in the number of students by 27.5 thousand people–4.8 thousand people from Turkmenistan, 3.4 thousand people from India, 2.5 thousand people from each of China, Uzbekistan, and Tajikistan) [3]. Thus, the CIS countries are the main source of student mobility enhancement in the Russian Federation.

2 Materials and Methods

As shown above, one of the main sources of internationalization is student mobility the scope of which depends on the strategies for education export used by the countries and universities. The success of an internationalization strategy largely depends on the correct choice of partner countries for the population of which the education-exporting country and the organization of the study process by the university are attractive [4–9]. In order to solve this sort of problem, a sufficiently large number of approaches have been developed, such as the method of paired comparisons by L. Thurstone, the Analytic Hierarchy Process by Thomas L. Saaty, the method of construction of generalized Harrington's desirability function, the method of construction of Taguchi loss functions, etc. [10–13].

The present paper suggests a technique for the quantitative assessment of the degree of foreign education attractiveness for the population of an importing country, which is based on the theory of quality successfully used to assess complex objects in the problems of Mechanics, Chemical Technology, and Economics [14–16].

The total quality of the attractiveness of getting an education in an exporting country can be represented as a multilevel hierarchical system, which is formed from particular qualities determined by experts at hierarchy levels through folding them in accordance with the functional average of Kolmogorov-Nagumo [17, 18].

The suggested method of analysis is similar to the methods of Harrington and Taguchi, but in contrast to them, the quality of the system at a certain level is obtained from the qualities at a lower level of the system as the functional average of Kolmogorov-Nagumo:

$$M(x_1, x_2, \ldots, x_n) = f^{-1}\left(\frac{1}{n}\sum_{k=1}^{n} f(x_k)\right) \tag{1}$$

The functions of particular qualities and the functions of averaging are chosen by experts depending on the objectives of the analysis.

According to the suggested approach, a "failure" of the quality in one of the parameters leads to poor quality of the entire system, even if all the other parameters exhibit excellent quality. And vice versa, the excellent quality in one of the parameters cannot ensure the good quality of the entire system (it is necessary to improve the quality in other parameters as well).

The criterion of the assessment of exporting university attractiveness for foreign students (Q) is based on the PEST-analysis of the three main participants in the education internationalization process, namely: an education-importing country (a country that needs training of its professionals abroad) - quality Q_1; an education-exporting country (a country that trains professionals for foreign countries) - quality Q_2; an education-exporting university (a university that trains foreign students) - quality Q_3.

Inbound student mobility depends on the level of development and the extent of the willingness of these three subjects to interact. The degree of attractiveness of the exporting country and exporting university (Q) is described in the form of a complex multi-level hierarchical structure (Fig. 1).

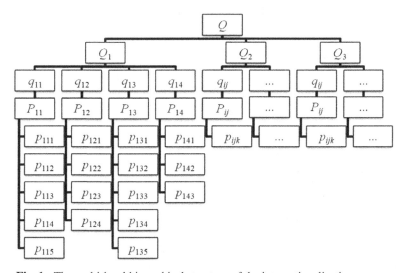

Fig. 1. The multi-level hierarchical structure of the internationalization process

The integral assessment of Q is expressed as the exponential average of Q_1, Q_2, Q_3

$$Q = -\ln\left(\frac{\alpha_1 \cdot e^{-Q_1} + \alpha_2 \cdot e^{-Q_2} + \alpha_3 \cdot e^{-Q_3}}{\alpha_1 + \alpha_2 + \alpha_3}\right) \qquad (2)$$

where
$i = 1$ – importing country;
$i = 2$ – exporting country;
$i = 3$ – exporting university;
α_1, α_2, α_3 – are the weighting factors of the integral indices of quality Q_1, Q_2, Q_3, which can take the values less than or equal to unity (depending on the degree of the expected importance of this or that group of integral indices).

The quality Q_i ($i = 1, 2, 3$) is the function of particular qualities q_{ij} ($i = 1, 2, 3, j = 1...4$) typical of the selected objects:

$$Q_i = -\ln\left(\frac{\beta_1 \cdot e^{-q_{i1}} + \beta_2 \cdot e^{-q_{i2}} + \beta_3 \cdot e^{-q_{i3}} + \beta_4 \cdot e^{-q_{i4}}}{\beta_1 + \beta_2 + \beta_3 + \beta_4}\right) \tag{3}$$

where

q_{i1} – particular quality "political factors" of the i-th object;

q_{i2} – particular quality "economic factors" of the i-th object;

q_{i3} – particular quality "social factors" of the i-th object;

q_{i4} – particular quality "technological factors" of the i-th object.

$\beta_1, \beta_2, \beta_3, \beta_4$ – are the weighting factors of the indices of the particular quality q_{ij}, which can take the values less than or equal to unity depending on the degree of the expected importance of this or that group of integral indices.

The q_{ij} included in the formula (3) are the functions of the integral properties P_{ij} of the corresponding subjects, which are taken as a linear dependence

$$q_{ij} = (A \cdot P_{ij} + B) \tag{4}$$

where the coefficients A and B are set by experts.

The particular quality q_{ij} is presented in the form of a linear dependence obtained from the condition that the particular quality q_{ij}^* corresponds to the maximum value of the property P_{ij}^* and, respectively, the particular quality q_{ij}^0 corresponds to the minimum value P_{ij}^0 (Fig. 2).

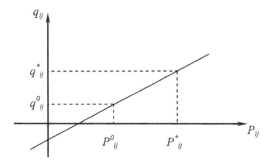

Fig. 2. Linear dependence of the particular quality q_{ij} on the property P_{ij}

In its turn, P_{ij} is determined as the arithmetic mean of the expert assessments of the particular properties p_{ijk} corresponding to the indices of politics ($k = 1...5$), economics ($k = 1...4$), sociology ($k = 1...5$), and technology ($k = 1...3$) of the corresponding subject:

$$P_{ij} = \frac{1}{k} \cdot \sum_{k=1}^{k} p_{ijk} \tag{5}$$

The properties (p_{ijk}) were assessed by experts on the basis of the three-point scale: 2 – the best value of the property, 1 – the good value of the property, 0 – the underwhelming value of the property.

Table 1 presents the elementary properties (p_{ijk}) used in the PEST-analysis [19].

Table 1. PEST-analysis of the subjects

Politics (P_{i1})	Economics (P_{i2})
1) political (administrative) sustainability of the subject (p_{i11}) 2) extent of interaction of the subjects (p_{i12}) 3) legislation in the sphere of education (p_{i13}) 4) mutual attractiveness of the subjects (p_{i14}) 5) level of administrative barriers (p_{i15})	1) subject-specific features of the demographic situation (p_{i21}) 2) economic situation of the subject (p_{i22}) 3) level of demand for the fields of study in the subject (p_{i23}) 4) logistical accessibility of the subject (p_{i24})
Sociology (P_{i3})	Technology (P_{i4})
1) number of graduates of the subject (p_{i31}) 2) language attractiveness of the subject (p_{i32}) 3) level of professional orientation activities carried out by the subject (p_{i33}) 4) equality of the competence levels of applicants for admission in the subjects (p_{i34}) 5) competition of the subjects in the educational services market (p_{i35})	1) level of use of distance education technologies (DET) by the subject (p_{i41}) 2) level of technology development in the subject (p_{i42}) 3) innovation dynamics in the subject (p_{i43})

The specific details of the expert assessment of the properties p_{ijk} of each of the subjects are described below [20].

Education-Importing Country:

Politics

p_{111} – *political (administrative) sustainability of the subject;*

2 – the political power has been unchanged for 10 years;

1 – has been unchanged for 5 years;

0 – a change in the political course.

p_{112} – *the extent of interaction of the subjects;*

2 – the goods turn over dynamics (taking into account their balance) between the importing country and the exporting country has been positive over the past 3 years;

1 – has been constant over the past 3 years;

0 – the goods turnover decreases.

p_{113} – *legislation in the sphere of education;*

2 – agreements on the mutual recognition of education documents have been signed between the importing country and the exporting country;

1 – partial recognition of education documents;

0 – the absence of recognition of education documents.

p_{114} – *mutual attractiveness of the subjects;*

2 – the confessions of the importing country are widely represented in the exporting country;

1 – are represented to a limited extent;

0 – are not represented.

p_{115} – *level of administrative barriers;*
2 – visa-free entry for the citizens of the exporting country;
1 – simplified procedure for obtaining a visa;
0 – visa is required.

Economics

p_{121} – *specific features of the demographic situation (over the past 5 years);*
2 – growth of the population of the country;
1 – the population of the country is constant;
0 – decrease in the population of the country.

p_{122} – *economic situation (over the past 5 years);*
2 – steady growth of GDP;
1 – GDP remains constant;
0 – decrease in GDP.

p_{123} – *level of demand for the fields of study in the subject;*
2 – more than 75% of the fields of study taught in the exporting country are demanded by the economy of the importing country;
1 – 40–75% of the fields of study are in demand;
0 – less than 40%.

p_{124} – *logistical accessibility of the subject;*
2 – direct flight/train/bus to the exporting country is available;
1 – one connecting flight/train/bus is necessary;
0 – two or more connecting flights/trains/buses are necessary.

Sociology

p_{131} – *number of graduates in the subject;*
2 – the share of graduates of the importing country with higher education degrees from the exporting country comprises more than 5% of the total population of the importing country with foreign higher education degrees received in the XXI century;
1 – the share of graduates of the importing country is 1–5%;
0 – less than 1%.

p_{132} – *language attractiveness of the subject;*
2 – the common official language in the education-importing country and education-exporting country;
1 – large groups of population in the importing country have a command of the language of the education-exporting country;
0 – other.

p_{133} – *level of professional orientation activities carried out by the subject;*
2 – wide support of exhibitions, Olympiads, and competitive events aimed at attracting the people of the importing country to study in the exporting country (the share of the exporting country scholarships in the importing country comprises more than 10% of the total number of state scholarships for the people of the importing country);
1 – the share of scholarships is 3–10%;
0 – less than 3%.

p_{134} – *equality of the competence levels of applicants for admission in the subjects;*
2 – the ratio of the position of the importing country in the world ranking of the level of secondary education to the position of the exporting country is more than 0.8;

1 – within the range of 0.5–0.8;

0 – less than 0.5.

p_{135} – *competition of the subjects in the educational services market;*

2 – the share of school eaves of the importing country sent to the exporting country comprises more than 2% of the total population of the country sent to study abroad in the year preceding to the year of the assessment;

1 – 0.5–2%;

0 – less than 0.5%.

Technology

p_{141} – *level of use of distance education technologies (DET) by the subject;*

2 – from 70 to 100% of the country is covered by the zone of stable internet connection;

1 – 40–69% coverage zone;

0 – less than 40%.

p_{142} – *level of technology development in the subject;*

2 – the country belongs to the type of «the least developed country»;

1 – a country with a developing economy;

0 – a country with a developed economy.

p_{143} – *innovation dynamics in the subject;*

2 – the country spends0–0.5% of its GDP on research and advanced development;

1 – 0.5–1%;

0 – more than 1%.

Education-Exporting Country:
Politics

p_{211} – *political (administrative) sustainability of the subject;*

2 – the political power has been unchanged for 10 years;

1 – has been unchanged for 5 years;

0 – a change in the political course.

p_{212} – *extent of interaction of the subjects;*

2 – the goods turn over dynamics (taking into account their balance) between the importing country and the exporting country has been positive over the past 3 years;

1 – has been constant over the past 3 years;

0 – the goods turnover decreases.

p_{213} – *legislation in the sphere of education;*

2 – agreements on the mutual recognition of education documents have been signed between the importing country and the exporting country;

1 – partial recognition of education documents;

0 – the absence of recognition of education documents.

p_{214} – *mutual attractiveness of the subjects;*

2 – the confessions of the importing country are widely represented in the exporting country;

1 – are represented to a limited extent;

0 – are not represented.

p_{215} – *level of administrative barriers;*

2 – visa-free entry to the exporting country;

1 – simplified procedure for obtaining a visa;

0 – visa is required.

Economics

p_{221} – *specific features of the demographic situation (over the past 5 years);*

2 – decrease in the population of the exporting country;

1 – the population of the country is constant;

0 – steady growth of the population of the country.

p_{222} – *economic situation (over the past 5 years);*

2 – steady growth of GDP;

1 – GDP remains constant;

0 – decrease in GDP.

p_{223} – *level of demand for the fields of study in the subject;*

2 – more than 75% of the fields of study taught in the exporting country are demanded by the economy of the importing country;

1 – 40–75% of the fields of study are in demand;

0 – less than 40%.

p_{224} – *logistical accessibility of the subject;*

2 – direct flight/train/bus to the importing country is available;

1 – one connecting flight/train/bus is necessary;

0 – two or more connecting flights/trains/buses are necessary.

Sociology

p_{231} – *number of graduates in the subject;*

2 – the share of graduates of the importing country with higher education degrees from the exporting country comprises more than 5% of the total population of the importing country with foreign higher education degrees received in the XXI century;

1 –1–5%;

0 – less than 1%.

p_{232} – *language attractiveness of the subject;*

2 – the common official language in the education-importing country and education-exporting country;

1 – large population groups in the importing country have a command of the language of the education-exporting country;

0 – other.

p_{233} – *the level of professional orientation activities carried out by the subject;*

2 – wide support of exhibitions, Olympiads, and competitive events aimed at attracting the people of the importing country to study (the share of the state scholarships for the importing country comprises more than 5% of the total number of state scholarships for foreign students);

1 – 1–5%;

0 – less than 1%.

p_{234} – *equality of the competence levels of applicants for admission in the subjects;*

2 – the ratio of the position of the exporting country in the world ranking of the level of secondary education to the position of the importing country is more than 1;

1 – within the range of 0.8–1;

0 – less than 0.8.

p_{235} – *competition of the subjects in the educational services market;*
2 – the share of the school eaves of the importing country admitted to study at the universities in the exporting country comprises more than 2% of the total number of foreign students in the year preceding to the year of the assessment;
1 – 0.5–2%;
0 – less than 0.5%.

Technology

p_{241} – *the level of use of distance education technologies (DET) by the subject;*
2 – 100% of the country is covered by the zone of stable internet connection;
1 – 90–100% coverage zone;
0 – less than 90%.

p_{242} – *level of technology development in the subject;*
2 – the country belongs to the type of «country with the developed economy»;
1 – a country with a developing economy;
0 – the least developed country.

p_{243} – *innovation dynamics in the subject;*
2 – the country spends more than 1% of its GDP on research and advanced development;
1 – 0.5–1%;
0 – less than 0.5%.

Education-Exporting University:

Politics

p_{311} – *political (administrative) sustainability of the subject (over the past 5 years);*
2 – positive dynamics of the total number of international students;
1 – the total number of international students remains at the same level;
0 – negative dynamics of the total number of international students.

p_{312} – *extent of interaction of the subjects;*
2 – the share of students from the importing country at the university is more than 5%;
1 –1–5%;
0 – less than 1%.

p_{313} – *legislation in the sphere of education;*
2 – the degrees awarded by the university are recognized around the world;
1 – the degrees awarded by the university are recognized in the importing country;
0 – the degrees awarded by the university are not recognized in the importing country.

p_{314} – *mutual attractiveness of the subjects;*
2 – the confessions of the importing country are the predominant population group in the region of the exporting university location;
1 – are represented to a limited extent in the region of the university location;
0 – other.

p_{315} – *level of administrative barriers;*
2 – visa-free entry;
1 – the university has a department providing visa support;
0 – the university does not provide visa support.

Economics

p_{321} – *specific features of the demographic situation (over the past 5 years);*
2 – the total number of students at the university decreases;
1 – remains constant;
0 – the total number of students increases.

p_{322} – *economic situation of the subject (over the past 5 years);*
2 – steady growth of the revenue received from foreign students training;
1 – the revenue remains at the same level;
0 – decrease in the revenue.

p_{323} – *level of demand for the fields of study in the subject;*
2 – more than 75% of the fields of study taught at the university are demanded by the economy of the importing country;
1 – 40–75% of the fields of study are in demand;
0 – less than 40%.

p_{324} – *logistical accessibility of the subject;*
2 – direct flight/train/bus to the city of the university location is available;
1 – one connecting flight/train/bus is necessary;
0 – two or more connecting flights/trains/buses are necessary.

Sociology

p_{331} – *number of graduates of the subject;*
2 – the share of graduates of the importing country with higher education degrees from the exporting university comprises more than 10% of the total number of foreign graduates of the university in the XXI century;
1 – 3–10%;
0 – less than3%.

p_{332} – *language attractiveness of the subject;*
2 – the common official language in the education-importing country and education-exporting country;
1 – the university offers language courses for applicants seeking admission.
0 – other.

p_{333} – *the level of professional orientation activities carried out by the subject;*
2 – exhibitions, Olympiads, and competitive events aimed at attracting people of the importing country to study at the university are conducted on a regular basis (no less than twice a year);
1 – less than twice a year;
0 – no events are conducted.

p_{334} – *equality of the competence levels of applicants for admission in the subjects;*
2 – the ratio of the position of the exporting country in the world ranking of the level of secondary education to the position of the importing country is more than 0.8;
1 – within the range of 0.5–0.8;
0 – less than 0.5.

p_{335} – *competition of the subjects in the educational services market;*
2 – the ratio of the number of the school eaves from the importing country admitted to study at the university to the total number of foreign students in the year preceding to the year of the assessment is more than 0.25;
1 – 0.05–0.25;

0 – less than 0.05.

Technology

p_{341} – *the level of use of distance education technologies (DET) by the subject;*

2 – 100% of the programs taught at the university for of all forms of study are available by means of the On-Line Education Environment;

1 – 90–100% of the programs;

0 – less than 90% of the programs.

p_{342} – *level of technology development of the subject;*

2 – the university ranks among the Top 500 in the world (QS, THE, or ARWU);

1 – ranks beyond 500;

0 – the university is not listed in the world rankings.

p_{343} – *innovation dynamics in the subject.*

2 – number of publications in the SCOPUS Database per 100 people is more than 5;

1 –3–5;

0 –less than 3.

3   Results

The suggested technique was tried for the following cases:

- the importing countries: Vietnam, Tajikistan, Turkmenistan, Uzbekistan;
- the exporting country: Russia;
- the exporting universities: Volgograd State Technical University (VSTU), Kazan National Research Technological University (KNRTU).

Based on the expert assessments of the elementary properties of politics, economics, sociology, and technology, the integral properties P_{ij} were determined by formula 5. The corresponding particular qualities of the subjects were found applying the known values of P_{ij} by the formula 4 ($A = 1,562; B = -2,125$). Formula 3 was used to determine the integral properties of Q_1, Q_2, Q_3, the weighting factors β_i were taken to be equal to unity. The assessment of the university attractiveness Q was calculated according to formula 2. The weighting factors α_i were taken to be equal to unity. The obtained values of Q_1, Q_2, Q_3, and the total quality Q of the system under assessment are presented in Tables 2 and 3.

Table 2. The results of the calculation of the assessment of the university capability in the educational services markets of student-importing countries (VSTU)

	Q_1	Q_2	Q_3	Q
Turkmenistan	−0,197	0,273	0,103	0,041
Vietnam	0,005	0,082	0,166	0,082
Tajikistan	0,503	0,671	0,301	0,480
Uzbekistan	0,766	0,555	0,607	0,639

Table 3. The results of the calculation of the assessment of the university capability in the educational services markets of student-importing countries (KNRTU)

	Q_1	Q_2	Q_3	Q
Vietnam	0,005	0,082	0,092	0,059
Turkmenistan	− 0,197	0,273	0,304	0,099
Tajikistan	0,503	0,671	0,428	0,529
Uzbekistan	0,766	0,555	0,589	0,632

The obtained integral index provides the assessment necessary for a university to make managerial decisions on where to apply the administrative and financial resources in an efficient way in order to improve the internalization index.

4 Conclusion

1. The analysis of the factors affecting the global student mobility has been conducted and the list of elementary properties has been determined, which allows constructing the hierarchical structure of the attractiveness of an education-exporting university taking into account the political, economic, social, and technological features of the countries of education import and export.
2. A technique for the quantitative assessment of the university attractiveness for international students has been developed, which allows the international departments of universities to make managerial decisions focused on the growth of the number of international students through the rational choice of education-importing countries.
3. The model can be easily changed and modified by including the parameters relevant for a particular university and time period, which significantly influence the international student mobility, or through excluding those of low impact.

References

1. Gurko, D.D., Trostyanskaya, I.B., Sema, E.Yu., Barsukov, A.A., Polikhina, N.A.: Obuchenie inostrannyh grazhdan v rossiiskih uchrezhdeniyah vysshego obrazovaniya. In: Teplova, Yu.N. (ed.) Education of Foreign Citizens in Russian Institutions of Higher Education. FGANU "Sociocenter", Moscow, 308 p. (2019). (in Russian)
2. Filimonova, N.Yu.: Internationalization of education: world and Russian experience. Aktualnye voprosy professionalnogo obrazovaniya [Actual Questions Professional Educ.] **3**(4), 54–57 (2016). (in Russian)
3. Arefiev A.L. (2019). Eksport rossiiskih obrazovatelnyh uslug: Statisticheskii sbornik. Vypusk 9. [Export of Russian educational services: Statistical collection. Issue 9.]. Center for Sociological Research, Moscow, 536 p. (in Russian)
4. Boyko, G.V., Poluektov, M.V., Zakharov, E.A., Fedin, A.P., Anufrieva, E.V.: Problems and prospects of training specialists for the road transport industry in modern conditions in the international aspect. Primo aspect **3**(43), 109–122 (2020). (in Russian, abstract in Eng.)

5. Vorob'eva, I.M.: [Academic Mobility of Students As an important tool for the formation of a global educational environment in the Russian university]. Molodoi uchenyi [Yang Sci.] **10**(90), 1113–1115 (2015). https://moluch.ru/archive/90/18763/. Accessed 24 May 2021
6. Naumov, R.A., Karaya, M.Z., Kovnir, V.N.: Mechanisms and the role of international academic mobility in Russian education. Kreativnaya ekonomika [J. Creative Econ.] **13**(10), 1893–1904 (2019). (in Russian, abstract in Eng.). https://doi.org/10.18334/ce.13.10.41244
7. Voloh, V.A., Grishaeva, S.A.: [International educational migration in modern Russia: features, problems and prospects]. Social'naya politika i sociologiya [Soc. Politic Sociol.] **16**(1) (120), 80–87 (2017). (in Russian)
8. Minin, M.G., Frantcuzskaia, E.O., Minich, A.S., Smyshlyaev, K.A., Smyshlyaev, A.V.: Export of higher education: innovations in physical education practice. Vysshee obrazovanie v Rossii = Higher Education in Russia **29**(6), 129–135 (2020). (in Russian, abstract in Eng.). https://doi.org/10.31992/0869-3617-2020-6-129-135
9. Pimonova, S.A., Fomina, E.M.: Short-term international academic mobility as a factor of higher education internationalization. Univ. Manag. Pract. Anal. **23**(4), 91–103 (2019). (In Russian, abstract in Eng.). https://doi.org/10.15826/umpa.2019.04.031
10. Saaty, T.L.: The Analytic Hierarchy Process. McGraw-Hill, New York. (Russian Translation: Vachnadze, R.G. (ed.) Radio i svyaz, Moscow 1993, 316 p.) (1980)
11. Saaty, T.L.: Relative measurement and its generalization in decision making why pairwise comparisons are central in mathematics for the measurement of intangible factors the analytic hierarchy/network process. Rev. R. Acad. Cien. Serie A. Mat. **102**, 251–318 (2008). https://doi.org/10.1007/BF03191825
12. Harrington, E.: The desirability function. Ind. Q. Control **21**(10), 494–498 (1965)
13. Taguchi, G., Chowdhury, S., Wu, Y.: Taguchi's Quality Engineering Handbook. John Wiley (2005). https://doi.org/10.1002/9780470258354
14. Lavnikova, I.V., Zheltobryukhov, V.F., Godenko A.E.: Optimization of polymer-analogous transformations in grafted chains of polycaproamide-polyglycidyl methacrylate copolymers. Russ. J. Appl. Chem. **77**, 1169–1171 (2004). (In Russian, abstract in Eng.). https://doi.org/10.1023/B:RJAC.0000044169.21417.ae
15. Godenko, A., Tarasova, I., Volchkov, V., Styazhin, V.: Systematic approach to quality assessment of hierarchy structure in education for management decision making. In: Kravets, A., Shcherbakov, M., Kultsova, M., Groumpos, P. (eds.) CIT&DS 2017. CCIS, vol. 754, pp. 375–385. Springer, Cham (2017). https://doi.org/10.1007/978-3-319-65551-2_27
16. Kalashnikov, S.Y., Godenko, A.E., Kalashnikova, Y.S., Tarasova, I.A.: System approach to the evaluation of a consumer appeal for the objects on the secondary housing market. In: IOP Conference Series: Materials Science and Engineering. The International Scientific Conference "Construction and Architecture: Theory and Practice for the innovation Development" (CATPID-2019), p. 066003 (2019)
17. Kolmogorov, A.N., Castelnuovo, G.: Sur la notion de la moyenne. G. Bardi, tip. della R. Accad. dei Lincei, 391 p. (1930)
18. Nagumo, M.: Uber eineklasse von mittelwerte. Japan. J. Math. **7**, 71–79 (1930). https://doi.org/10.4099/jjm1924.7.0_71
19. Homutova, E.G.: Sovremennye instrumenty menedzhmenta kachestva: uchebnoe posobie [Modern quality management tools: Tutorial]. Moscow: RTU MIREA, 181 p. (2020) (in Russian)
20. UNESCO Institute for Statistics (UIS). http://data.uis.unesco.org/. Accessed 29 Apr 2021

Cyber-Physical Systems and Big Data-Driven World. Design Creativity in CASE/CAI/CAD/PDM

Development of a Discrete Slicer for Additive Manufacturing

Andrey Andreev[✉], Marina Andreeva, Alexey Drobotov, Oleg Filimonov,
Anna Shmeleva, and Mikhail Denisov

Volgograd State Technical University, Volgograd, Russia
filimonovoleg@bk.ru
http://www.vstu.ru

Abstract. The paper proposes an improved discrete slicer algorithm for preparing
a 3D model for printing on multi-axis printers, as well as approaches to improving
slicing performance. The discrete-rotary slicer under consideration uses a selection
of cutting planes and provides better filling in the places where the models bend.
To test the algorithm and ways to improve performance in slicing, a prototype
of the slicer program was redesigned, and approximate methods for evaluating
the characteristics of model cross-sections were developed to assess the possible
reduction in slicing time when using multithreaded calculations.

Keywords: Additive printing technologies · 5-axis printer · Discrete slicer ·
Selection of cutting planes · Multithreaded calculations · Mesh representation of
surfaces

1 Introduction

Additive prototyping and manufacturing technologies are being used in an increasing
number of applications [1]. Along with the expansion of areas, additive technologies
themselves are developing. One of the areas of development is the creation of printing devices with additional degrees of freedom of movement of the print head, which
includes, for example, a 5-axis printer from Stereotech company [2, 3], as well as other
5-axis projects (for example, [4]).

For such devices, alternative software is required, including slicers-modules for
preparing the original 3D model for printing. These models perform slicing of the 3D
model into thin layers and calculating the trajectory of the working surface and the print
head to fill each layer. As traditional 3D printers use a traditional slicer with parallel
layers along the OZ axis, a 5-axis printer requires different types of slicers to prepare
different types of products. Some 5-axis slicers and algorithms are known [4–7], thought
they often either not well-described as commercial products ([4, 5]), or mostly suited
for production of metal details, not for 3D printers (as [6]). One of the slicers, suitable
for 5-axis 3D printing is the so-called discrete-rotary slicer [8–11]. Such a slicer cuts
the original 3D model in STL format into layers so that each subsequent layer can be
rotated at a certain angle (Fig. 1).

© Springer Nature Switzerland AG 2021
A. G. Kravets et al. (Eds.): CIT&DS 2021, CCIS 1448, pp. 267–281, 2021.
https://doi.org/10.1007/978-3-030-87034-8_20

This slicer allow to print products with overhanging structures without using supports, and also allows to obtain more durable prints.

In this paper, we consider modifications of the discrete-rotary slicer algorithm [12] with a choice of slicing planes [13], ways to improve the quality of slicing and increase the speed of its operation.

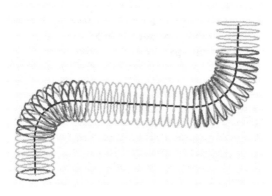

Fig. 1. Slicing of a model with a change in the slicing planes direction

2 The Algorithm of a Discrete-Rotary Slicer with the Selection of Slicing Planes

The algorithm described in [12], was used as a basis. Though it incorrectly processed a number of models, in particular, with sharp bends of the model (Figure 2 shows one of such cases).

Fig. 2. Problems with slicing of model with sharp bends («Pipe 2»)

In [13], an alternative algorithm is considered, in which, instead of calculating the angle of rotation of the current secant plane, the selection of secant planes from several options is proposed:

1) Search for the theoretical plane S_1.
2) Search for the real vector V_0, as the vector between the old (P_0) and new (Z_0) centroid, obtained by a single calculation of the centroid of the theoretical plane.
3) If the normals of the layers match, then the next layer is taken parallel to the previous one, and the iteration ends, otherwise it continues.
4) Search for a real plane (without rotation) - the first candidate.
5) Search for nine more candidates S_i for the role of the real plane (the number of candidates was chosen randomly).

    a. the rotation of the normal vector for the candidate plane was chosen like a fan along one plane inclined to the coordinate axes at an angle of 90 or 45 degrees (a total of 8 options for the orientation of this plane, depending on the inclination of the plane before rotation relative to the previous layer);

6) calculation of the cross-section sizes, that is, the lengths of the contour perimeters for all 10 candidates.
7) Selecting the section with the smallest perimeter as the new real plane.
8) Calculation of the centroid of the selected section (for the next iteration).

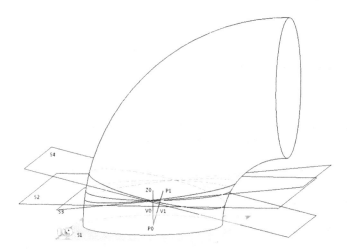

Fig. 3. Calculation scheme of the subsequent layer definition during slicing

Figure 3 schematically shows the selection of the cutting plane. In general, this algorithm improved the processing of a number of models, but it also had a number of disadvantages, which, in particular, include:

– the presence of gaps and gaps in a number of models in the places of kinks;
– incorrect operation on some models with complex geometry;
– the possible change in the thickness of the coils (layer thickness) is not taken into account);

– increased calculation time, especially for complex models.

Figure 4 shows an example of incorrect operation of the slicer using this algorithm. The essence of the error is that slicing the model at small angles does not change its direction, and after turning at an angle sufficient to start the rotation, the transition between these angles occurs too abruptly.

As you can see, an attempt to tilt the real plane was made, but the implementation of this tilt is not suitable.

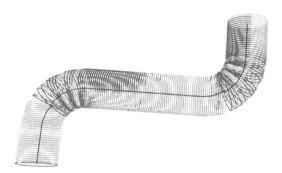

Fig. 4. Error when slicing the «Pipe 3» model

3   Modifications of the Slicing Algorithm

3.1   Test Models

To test the program, in addition to the models already presented, 36 more models were made. All of them have a three-letter code that means:

- 1 letter - pipe diameter S = 20 mm M = 50 mm L = 100 mm
- letter-length of straight sections S = 20 mm L = 300 mm
- letter - pipe bending radius S = 1/2 of pipe diameter M = pipe diameter L = 2 pipe diameter

3.2   Closing Large Gaps

The obvious solution was to modify the method of selecting the orientation of the new plane (see step 5a in Sect. 2). The solution is to take a few close vectors, rejected randomly, as the normals of the rejected planes.

Instead of a «vane» of vectors oriented in one not necessarily optimal plane, it would be logical to take a set of vectors evenly distributed in space around the central vector. In the case of a fixed angle of deflection, a "cone" without a bottom would be obtained. Hence, the first step parameter is the deflection angle. An angle of $2°$ was experimentally selected.

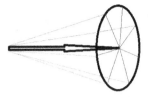

Fig. 5. The essence of the new approach to chose of the normal vector for the section plane

To distribute the vectors evenly over the surface of the cone means to take a certain step along the circumference of a certain "base of the cone", a multiple of 2π (or 360°) - see Fig. 5. Hence the second step parameter - the number of directions, i.e. 360° / step around the circle (Fig. 6).

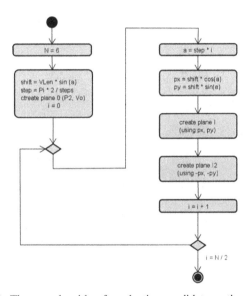

Fig. 6. The new algorithm for selecting candidate section planes

At first, 8 directions were considered (step 45°), then we stopped at 6 (step 60°) to reduce time. It makes no sense to reduce it to 4 (90° step).

As an intermediate step, an auxiliary plane normal to the main vector and passing through its end was used to construct the deflected vector. Passing with a step along the circle centered at the end of the main vector, we put a point on the auxiliary plane with the x and y coordinates proportional to the cosine and sine of the direction, respectively.

By inverting the point from 2D on the auxiliary plane to the main 3D coordinate system, we get the end of the rotated vector.

Based on the resulting rotated vectors (as normals) we build the rotated cross-section planes, with which we perform all the same operations as before - we count the lengths of the perimeters, choose the smallest section.

The proposed modification made it possible to improve the quality of slicing. Below are some examples of comparing the original version (on the left) with the received one – on the right) - Fig. 7.

Initially, up to a certain angle on the model in Fig. 7, the slicing angle did not change, after which there was a sharp change in the angle (with an obvious break), after which further slicing into layers occurred correctly.

Fig. 7. Slicing the "MSL" model

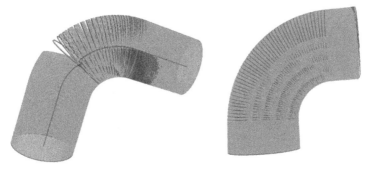

Fig. 8. Slicing the "SSM" model

The problem of the model in Fig. 8 was initially the same as the model in Fig. 8. For a long time there was no change in the angle, after which this change occurred abruptly.

The model in Fig. 9 had very large gaps due to sudden changes in the cutting angle. The problem was solved by reducing the pitch of the angles.

3.3   The Slicing Start Point

The next step was to work on the three proposed "real models", which were not sliced at all at the testing stage of the program. The slicer indicated that it did not detect any contours.

After the study, it was found out that the algorithm did not make a single complete iteration (it left the loop immediately), and the stop criterion was an empty section.

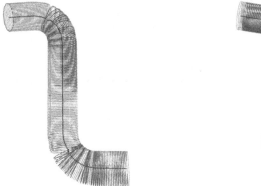

Fig. 9. Slicing the "Pipe 3" model

Hence, the conclusion was that from the very beginning, the algorithm did not "see" the model where the beginning was set.

After resaving the models so that their zero point coincides with the XY plane, they immediately became ready for slicing (Fig. 10).

This part initially did not have slicing due to the fact that this model did not have a contour in the XY plane, it was located at a distance of 150 mm from it. After setting the model to the zero point, the algorithm fully worked out the process.

The implementation of the search for the beginning of slicing is currently completely absent in the algorithm. The algorithm processes the model standing on the XY plane, starting to move up. Therefore, the task of choosing the correct direction of the "bypass" of the part falls on the person forming the STL model. This problem remains to be resolved in the future.

3.4   Removing Small Gaps

The next stage of the algorithm modernization was the control over the maximum size of the gap between the layers, which will eventually help to "close" the gaps by increasing the flow.

Here we need to make a small digression and say that a 3D printer can change the layer thickness during printing, although with some restrictions. If you need to print a wedge-shaped (trapezoidal) section, you can technically choose two approaches:

1. choose from several parallel layers of the same thickness, but different lengths, i.e. "ladder" - simple, but less " beautiful" and less durable;
2. slightly rotate the printing plane after each layer, making a thicker layer on the wide side, and a thin one on the narrow side, more difficult to implement and has restrictions on the permissible thickness-within up to 3.5 of the nominal thickness is considered acceptable, and generally stronger than the 1st option;
3. combine the second option with the first one when the steepness of the turn is too great.

Fig. 10. Slicing the real model "Part 7"

Fig. 11. Layer of variable thickness in one pass of the head

The thickened layer loses its shape, "stretching" or "contracting" vertically and can "stick" worse to the previous layer, so from practice it is considered acceptable to move the head no more than 3.5 times from the nominal thickness of the layer, as shown in Fig. 11. Thus, in the case of a minimum thickness of 0.2 mm, the maximum layer thickness does not exceed 0.7 mm.

Returning to the slicer, we noticed that the angle of rotation equal to 2°, on sufficiently wide sections, gives too much gap between the layers standing at an angle to each other. Figure 12 illustrates this. "Too big" means more than 3.5 of the layer thickness.

It became obvious that the angle of rotation of 2° (and any other fixed angle) is too large for some sections and too small for others. We need to calculate the allowable angle for each section individually. The analysis of the problem showed that to estimate the width of the gap, it is sufficient to estimate the distance of the points of the body on the cross-section (more precisely, on the perimeter of the cross-section) from the axis of rotation of the layer (see Fig. 13).

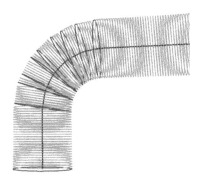

Fig. 12. Gaps between the rotated layers

If you know the dimensions of the cross section and the permissible gap (the gap between the outer edges of neighboring layers), then it is easy to calculate the upper bound for the angle of rotation, taking the value of the gap proportional to the sine of the angle (the base of the isosceles triangle is close to the opposite leg of the right triangle at a small angle).

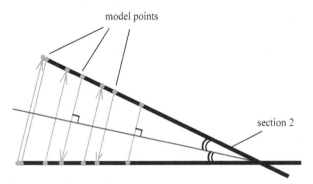

Fig. 13. The size of the gap depends on the distance of the point from the rotation axis of the layer and the angle of rotation

Hence, there are new parameters of the algorithm - the allowable gap between layers in mm (for example, 0.7), the maximum rotation of the planes of neighboring layers in degrees (for example, 10).

The angle of rotation of the cross section is now defined as the arcsin of the ratio of the outer gap to the max distance of the cross section point:

$$rotationAngle = arcsin(outer\_gap \, / \, max\_distance) \qquad (1)$$

The distance of the cross-section point is found when traversing the contour of the body that is obtained when performing the cross-section. To do this, another parameter is introduced - the number of points selected in the section, which by default is 8 and can be increased for bodies with a very large number of extraordinary parts in the section.

The points on the cross-section are taken with a certain step along the line forming the contour, and among the distances from them to the straight line (the axis of rotation), the maximum is selected as the size of the outer dimension of this section.

Testing of the algorithm showed that the angle of rotation is now selected adequately and adaptively, decreasing for large sections and increasing for small ones, which allows the algorithm to be used for a greater variety of models without manually selecting parameters. On small and degenerate sections, the angle is successfully limited to 10 degrees, which is enough, in our opinion, to print sufficiently curved narrow fragments of bodies.

As a result, after the final testing, the maximum gap was reduced to the layer thickness (0.2 mm), which made it possible to make the distances between the rotated layers the same as between the parallel ones (see Fig. 14, where the red layers are rotated by some angle relative to the previous layer located to the left of it).

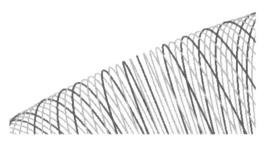

Fig. 14. Layers of the same thickness

4 Improving Performance of the Modified Discrete Slicer

One of the problems in implementing the algorithm with the choice of secant planes, both the original one and the one described in this paper, is the increase in slicing time due to additional calculations (estimation of sections by candidate planes) up to 2–4 times depending on model complexity. In [13], it was shown that, in principle, such an estimate can be made relatively quickly by approximate methods, and the time for this estimate could be reduced when using multithreaded calculations.

However, the results obtained in [13] were only marginally optimistic. Firstly, they did not take into account the modifications described above in this paper, that is, slicing was performed with errors, and secondly, the results of the evaluation of different planes speedup due to multithreading were quite modest. The second point is related to the features of the software prototype used. The prototype used was originally written in C# and used one of the existing geometry libraries for.NET. This, in turn, is due to the fact that both the original prototype used in [13] and the software for 5D printers of Stereotech, which is one of the interested parties in this study, at a certain stage was based on the same technologies and library. Also in the prototype, this library is used both for visualization and for performing actual geometric calculations using the same methods, which complicates both the calculation and its speedup. In [13] an attempt was made to move to a simplified estimation of sections, which gave a certain effect, but this work was not completed, since other calculations in the prototype still used the old scheme. In addition, some of the calculations in [13] were performed incorrectly for a number of models.

After the implementation of the algorithm modifications proposed above, we also considered the issue of separating the calculation and visualization and estimating both sections and centroids using ordinary simple geometric methods, since switching to another external library on the one hand takes time, on the other hand, we do not always know how a particular library is arranged, whether it is easily parallelized, what its limitations are, and so on.

These methods were embedded in the prototype code as a library that could be called along with the methods of the original geometric library. In fact, this interface of geometric methods may be implemented by different geometric libraries in the future, and the basic algorithm for slicing will remain unchanged.

Also, during the implementation of this mini-library, an estimate of the execution time of various steps for the models under consideration (profiling) was performed, which allowed us to find out that the calculation of centroids, as can be judged by its operational complexity as well, does not take much time and its parallel implementation does not make much sense.

4.1 Brief Description of the Implemented Methods for Section of the Mesh Model and Calculation of Centroids

The proposed algorithm for obtaining sections is based on the search for a polyline, which is formed from segments at the intersection of the triangles that make up the surface of the model in the mesh representation, and the section plane under consideration. These segments can be obtained as follows:

1. We define a set of triangles from the mesh representation of the model surface, the vertices of which are located on different sides of the plane we are considering (those triangles that are located entirely above or below the plane do not intersect with it and we are not interested in it).
2. We are looking for the intersection points of the edges of triangles whose vertices are points located on different sides of the plane with this plane.
3. Arrange the points by the angle relative to the center of mass of the section (the coordinates of the given normal vector of the plane).
4. Make a polyline passing through the found points and determine its length (or-the area of the polygon bounded by the polyline, the current version uses the length of the polyline).

To find the centroids, we simply find the average values of all the coordinates of the points that make up the polyline:

$$x = \sum_{i=0}^{n} x_i \quad y = \sum_{i=0}^{n} y_i \quad z = \sum_{i=0}^{n} z_i \tag{2}$$

4.2 Calculations Speedup Due to Simplified Implementation of Geometric Operations

A number of experiments were conducted with models of different sizes, and it showed that the proposed simplified calculation allows to speed up slicing by 9–50 times, depending on the size of the model. The results of some experiments are shown in Tables 1–2 (tests were conducted on CPU Core i5 7200U).

Table 1. Slicing time using external geometric library and approximate geometric operations

Model, layer thickness, mm	Sliced model using approximate operations	Calculation time using an external library, s	Calculation time using approximate operations, s	Speedup
Pipe3, 0.2		00.8890	00.0787	11,30
Pipe2 0.2		01.0840	00.0915	11,84
Pipe1 0.2		18.4467	00.5704	32,34
LSS 0,8		31.5477	00.6144	**51,34**
Overlap_long 0,8		18.4024	00.3625	50,76
Angled 0,7		13.0646	01.4146	9,24

4.3 Implementing Multithreading in Section Calculation

Multithreaded calculation of sections for different planes is described in [13] and uses built-in mechanisms of.NET – Parallel.For():

```
void SectionSize(int i)  {
    // Processing of the i-th secant plane …
}
// …
Parallel.For(0, N, SectionSize);
```

It is possible to fine-tune multithreading, taking into account the available physical cores along with the introduction of vector computing, and possibly even the use of the GPU, but in this paper these possibilities were not considered.

As a result of testing of multithreaded calculations in comparison with single - threaded ones for a number of models, the following results were obtained for different systems with a different number of cores (Tables 2–4).

Table 2. Slicing time with single-threaded and multithreaded estimation of sections on Core i5 7200U CPU with 2 cores and 4 threads

Model, layer thickness, mm	Time of single-threaded calculation, s	Time with multithreaded calculation, s	Speedup
Pipe3, 0.1	00.2155354	00.1783104	1,208765
Pipe2 0.1	00.1877088	00.1688788	1,1115
Pipe1 0.1	01.1734655	00.9968184	1,177211
LSS 0,1	05.4165081	05.0196731	1,079056
Overlap_long 0,1	03.9526902	02.6087500	**1,515166**
Angled 0,1	03.2761217	02.7220079	1,203568

Table 3. Slicing time with single-threaded and multithreaded estimation of sections on Core i7 920 CPU with 4 cores and 8 threads

Model, layer thickness, mm	Time of single-threaded calculation, s	Time with multithreaded calculation, s	Speedup
Pipe3, 0.2	00.0680042	00.0670030	1,014943
Pipe2 0.2	00.0950023	00.0910079	1,043891
Pipe1 0.2	00.6960375	00.4710216	1,477719
LSS 0,2	03.7491376	02.5971738	1,443545
Overlap_long 0,2	02.2311286	01.3170774	**1,694**
Angled 0,2	01.9375055	01.2200580	1,588044

As can be seen from Tables 2–4, the introduction of multithreading in the evaluation of secant candidate planes allows to noticeably reduce the calculation time for large models, and even for small models, there is a decrease in the evaluation time. This allows us to conclude that in general, the approach with the selection of planes in this case works fine and does not bring significant time overhead when using modern computing equipment, even at the level of a personal computer or an average workstation. But as well, results are quite similar for different system cores, 'cause we have only 6 tasks in parallel in all cases.

Table 4. Slicing time with single-threaded and multithreaded estimation of sections on Core i7 8750H CPU with 6 cores and 12 threads

Model, layer thickness, mm	Time of single-threaded calculation, s	Time with multithreaded calculation, s	Speedup
Pipe3, 0.5	00.0419969	00.0339924	1,235479
Pipe2 0.1	00.1380417	00.1200667	1,149708
Pipe1 0.1	00.1000078	00.0942608	1,060969
LSS 0,1	03.3955010	02.6922918	1,261194
Overlap_long 0,1	02.2983275	01.5723415	**1,461723**
Angled 0,7	00.3112504	00.2295177	1,356106

5   Conclusion and Directions for Further Development of the Slicer

The paper presents modifications of the previously proposed algorithm of the discrete-rotary slicer with the selection of cutting planes, which allow to improve the quality of slicing 3D models for subsequent printing on a 5-axis printer. The multithreaded calculation of sections for secant candidate planes is also considered, which reduces the sections estimation time. The implemented prototype of a simplified library for calculating sections and centroids demonstrates, on the one hand, that the selection of secant planes does not significantly increase the slicing execution time, and on the other hand, that its execution time can be noticeably reduced on multi-core and multi-processor computing systems.

The presented algorithm still needs to be refined and further research, and it is also necessary to develop a slicer library for implementation in the software of multi-axis printers. Future versions of the algorithm could be optimized in processing mashes [14], in using multithreading [15], take into account the model that is divided and branched into several components, printing hollow parts and rods with a complex shape, as well as dividing the model into parts for parallel slicing in different threads [16] and improvement of parallel slicing implementation in general, using various parallel technologies, as in [17].

References

1. Composites: Airbus continues to shape the future. Airbus SE: official website (2017). https://www.airbus.com/newsroom/news/en/2017/08/composites--airbuscontinues-to-shape-the-future.html. Accessed 20 Mar 2021
2. Stereotech - 5D Additive Manufacturing. https://stereotech.org/. Accessed 30 Apr 2021
3. Stereotech STE Slicer. https://github.com/stereotech/STE-Slicer. Accessed 14 Apr 2021
4. Five-Axis 3D printer Epit 5.1 https://www.epit3d.ru/. Accessed 05 May 2021
5. -Axis Slicer – Dotx Control Solutions. https://www.dotxcontrol.com/products/5-axis-slicer/. Accessed 05 May 2021
6. Sundaram, R., Choi, J.: A slicing procedure for 5-Axis LaserAided DMD Process ASME. J. Manuf. Sci. Eng. **126**(3), 632–636 (2004). https://doi.org/10.1115/1.1763180
7. Singh, P., Dutta, D.: Multi-direction slicing for layered manufacturing. In: Proceedings of DETC 2000, ASME, CIE-14626 (2000)
8. Cope, M. 5-Axis Programming: programming with tool vectors (2013). http://blog.hurco.com/blog/bid/309807/5-axis-programming-programming-with-tool-vectors? Accessed 30 Nov 2020
9. She, C.-H.: Design of a generic five-axis postprocessor based on generalized kinematics model of machine tool. Int. J. Mach. Tools Manuf. **47**(3–4), 537–545 (2007). She, C.-H., Chang, C.-C. (eds.). https://doi.org/10.1016/J.IJMACHTOOLS.2006.06.002
10. Liou, F., Ruan, J., Sparks, T.E.: Multi-axis planning system MAPS for hybrid laser metal deposition processes. https://www.researchgate.net/publication/267718640_Multi-Axis_Planning_System_MAPS_for_Hybrid_Laser_Metal_Deposition_Processes. Accessed 30 Apr 2021
11. Zhao, D., Li, T., Shen, B., Jiang, Y., Guo, W., Gao, F.: A multi-DOF rotary 3D printer: machine design, performance analysis and process planning of curved layer fused deposition modeling (CLFDM). Rapid Prototyping J. **6**, 1079–1093 (2020). https://www.researchgate.net/publication/340311998_A_multiDOF_rotary_3D_printer_machine_design_performance_analysis_and_process_planning_of_curved_layer_fused_deposition_modeling_CLFDM. Accessed 12 Apr 2021
12. Popov, A.Yu., Gushchin, I.A., Drobotov, A.V.: Model preparation algorithm for 3d printing with discrete rotation. In: 2019 International Conference on Industrial Engineering, Applications and Manufacturing (ICIEAM) (Sochi, Russia, 25–29 March, 2019), pp. 1–5 (2019)
13. Andreev, A.E., Drobotov, A.V., Makarov, A.M., Gushchin, I.A., Kizilov, V.G.: Speedup of the descrete slicer for additive manufacturing. In: Parallel Computational Technoligies (PCT2021), (Volgograd, Russia, 29 March – 01 April, 2021), pp. 143–150 (2021). http://omega.sp.susu.ru/pavt2021/proceedings.pdf. Accessed 05 May 2021
14. Minetto, R., Volpato, N., Stolfi, J., Gregori, R.M.M.H., da Silva, M.V.G.: An optimal algorithm for 3D triangle mesh slicing. Comput. Aided Des. **92**, 1–10 (2017). https://doi.org/10.1016/j.cad.2017.07.001
15. Kirschman, C.F., Jara-Almonte, C.C.: A parallel slicing algorithm for solid freeform fabrication processes. In: Proceedings of 1992 International Solid Freeform Fabrication Symposium, 3–5 August 1992, Austin, Tx, USA, pp. 26–33 (1992). https://doi.org/10.15781/T2NS0MF5K
16. Ma, X., Lin, F., Yao, B.: Fast parallel algorithm for slicing STL based on pipeline. Chin. J. Mech. Eng. **29,** 549–555 (2016). https://doi.org/10.3901/CJME.2016.0309.028
17. Getmanskiy, V., Andreev, A.E., Alekseev, S., Gorobtsov, A.S., Egunov, V., Kharkov, E.: Optimization and parallelization of CAE software stress-strain solver for heterogeneous computing hardware. Commun. Comput. Inf. Sci. **754,** 562–574 (2017)

Automatic Calculation of Material Laying Trajectories When Preparing 3D Models for Five-Axis FFF Printing with Continuous Fiber Reinforcement

Ilya Gushchin[1(✉)], Ivan Torubarov[1], Andrey Shvets[1], Alexey Yakovlev[1], Alexander Plotnikov[1], and Andrey Andreev[2]

[1] Automatization of Production Processes Department, Volgograd State Technical University, 28, Lenina Ave., Volgograd 400005, Russia
[2] Computers and Systems Department, Volgograd State Technical University, 28, Lenina Ave., Volgograd 400005, Russia

Abstract. The paper outlines the main directions for improving the strength of products in additive manufacturing using FFF technology, and studies methods for preparing control programs for 3D printing for additive manufacturing of products, including those using more than three degrees of freedom, as well as with reinforcement of products with continuous fiber. A method for automatically generating a control program for five-axis FFF printing of an arbitrary 3D model is described. A method of automatic generation for five-axis printing with continuous fiber laying has been developed, and software based on it has been created. Samples of products were made using the method of five-axis printing with continuous reinforcement.

Keywords: Additive manufacturing · FFF · 5D printing · Composite material · Continuous reinforcement · Continuous carbon fiber

1 Introduction

For medicine, the automotive industry, and the aerospace industry, the problem of mass production of lightweight and durable parts is always relevant. In the second half of the XX century to solve this problem, many polymer composite materials (PCM) based on fillers made of synthetic fibers (carbon, glass, aramid, boron, etc.) were developed. By 2015, according to some estimates, their share in aircraft designs reached 50% (and there is still a tendency to increase this indicator) [1]. So, in the same year, the Airbus A350 XWB aircraft began to be operated, in which the fuselage and wing (with a length of about 32 m and a width of about 6 m) are mostly made of carbon fiber [2].

Additive manufacturing (AM), based on the Fused Filament Fabrication (FFF) technology, allows us quickly and cost-effectively produce a small series of unique products, which favorably distinguishes additive technologies from traditional PCM production methods. Another distinctive feature is the production of not only complex shapes but

A. G. Kravets et al. (Eds.): CIT&DS 2021, CCIS 1448, pp. 282–295, 2021.
https://doi.org/10.1007/978-3-030-87034-8_21

also an arbitrary internal structure (for example, lattice), which is not available for traditional technologies at all. However, due to the layered structure, the AM part has an expressed anisotropy of mechanical properties. When a thermoplastic material melts, its macromolecules are pulled in the direction of flow, as a result of which the strength of the object along the layers is significantly higher than in the perpendicular direction [3]. The anisotropy of the properties, the low strength of the product, and the materials used limit the use of FFF for the production of final products.

Among the ways to increase their strength, the most effective at the moment is the reinforcement of the part with continuous fiber during the printing process [4]. In FFF technology, this approach has been implemented by companies such as Orbital Composites, Continuous Composites, Markforged, Anisoprint, and Arevo [5]. However, these solutions are still based on the classical principle of three-dimensional printing and do not eliminate a significant drawback: the continuous fiber is fused only inside the flat layers, and the interlayer strength remains at the level of the binding material. As a result, the strength increases along one plane, and vertically (relative to the plane of construction in 3D printing) is determined by the strength of the layer-by-layer extruded plastic.

One recent example of using 3D printers for mass production is antiviral filter adapters for anti-plague suits. Thanks to the accelerated preparation of production, the AM made it possible to launch the production of such adapters in a short time in order to provide the possibility of replacing the more expensive and missing original filters (Fig. 1 , a). However, the resulting adapters were characterized by product delamination in the thread area – a breakage that would not be prevented by laying a continuous fiber in the plane of the layer (Fig. 1 , b).

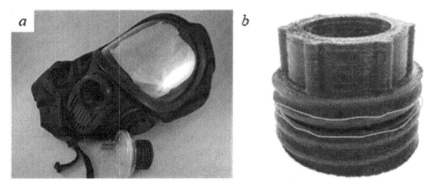

Fig. 1. a. Doctor's protection kit: anti-plague suit mask, anti-virus filter, and 3D printed adapter; b. Classic destruction of the printed adapter according to layers.

A rational solution to this problem can be the use of multi-axis printing for laying not flat, but "three-dimensional" layers in the form of cylindrical, conical, spherical, etc. surfaces. The use of continuous fibers in multi-axis printing will allow you to intertwine the reinforcing bundles inside the product and obtain isotropic strength properties, which will replace expensive and heavy aluminum parts. This approach will significantly expand the scope of the application of additive technologies.

When turning to multi-axis printing, the question of managing the equipment and automating the preparation of the parts, including "slicing" its 3D model in.stl format and obtaining the control program (g-code), arises separately. At the moment, all solutions for multi-axis printing are based on the Siemens NX [6] software, which provides the preparation of g-codes in a semi-manual mode, as will be shown later.

2   5D Tech

To realize the possibility of five-axis 3D printing, the authors created a new type of additive manufacturing device – a 5D printer that uses a new technology of multi-axis FFF printing (5D tech).

The classic FFF technology involves dividing a three-dimensional digital model into many thin, flat layers, which are transmitted to an additive manufacturing facility, where the object is created layer by layer according to this program. Each layer is applied on top of the previous layer until the object is completely built. At the same time, it is made of a thermoplastic polymer material, which is squeezed out in a softened form by the print head. In this case, auxiliary material can be used to support the overhanging elements (Fig. 2). This technology is characterized by the need to use supporting structures and low printing speed, while products with different mechanical properties in different directions (anisotropy) are obtained, low strength of the resulting products in the layer plane-not higher than the level of injection molding when using filaments filled with chopped fiber [7], across the layers-several times lower).

The essence of the developed technology of multi-axis FFF printing is to create a product not in flat layers, as in conventional 3D printers, but in three-dimensional curved

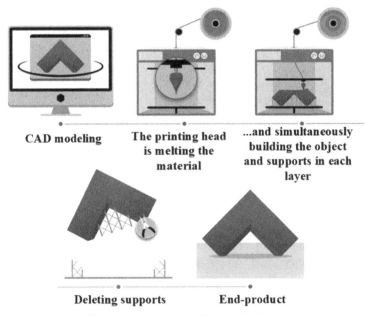

Fig. 2. The principle of FFF technology.

layers. The volumetric layer allows you to produce a solid three-dimensional structure of the product by orienting the polymer threads in different directions. The polymer thread in the orientation direction has greater strength than the cohesive connection between the individual threads. Therefore, the product obtained using the multi-axis FDM printing technology has isotropic high-strength properties, compared to the anisotropic properties of a 3D printed part. The production of parts of any shape with the application of polymer threads in different directions is possible only when using multi-axis processing (minimally, with five-axis processing). To distinguish products produced using 5 degrees of freedom from those printed on a 3D printer, the term 5D printing and 5D products are introduced.

The kinematics of the device were described in [8, 9], and the 5D printing process is depicted in detail in [8, 10]. In general, it consists of three stages (Fig. 3): the production of supporting equipment on a cylindrical receiving surface, the creation of the first part of the product, the core (usually cylindrical, but any other shape can be used), the imposition of material on the core along spatial trajectories. Thereat, the layer-by-layer building of objects with a curved axis occurs due to the control of the core tilt [11].

When preparing for printing, the 3D part model consisting of triangular faces is divided using the CSG (Constructive Solid Geometry) functions. Using the 3D triangular mesh boolean operations, such as subtraction and intersection, the original triangulated

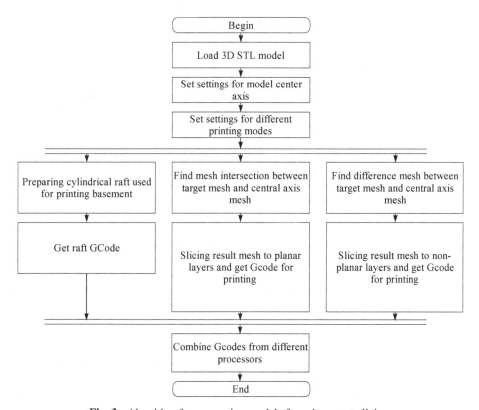

Fig. 3. Algorithm for processing models for subsequent slicing.

3D model is divided into 2 (or more). Further, each part of the model can be prepared in different ways by dividing the model into layers (slicing). Since multi-axis FFF 3D printers have the ability to change the position and orientation of the tool relative to the model, they can print parts using curved layers instead of flat ones. For example, in addition to slicing with planar layers, for multi-axis systems, you can use slicing with layers that have the shape of geometric primitives (cylinder, sphere, etc.) or with layers that have the shape of the 3D model itself. By combining different slicing methods, you can achieve certain characteristics of strength and surface quality of the printed part.

The result of each slicing method processor is a 3D printing program in the G-Code language. Individual parts of the G-Code from each of the processors are then combined into a common program for the multi-axis FFF 3D printer. The block diagram of the preparation is shown in Fig. 4.

As an example, we consider the printing method with the division of the original 3d model into a cylindrical base and a second part printed by curved layers having a cylindrical shape.

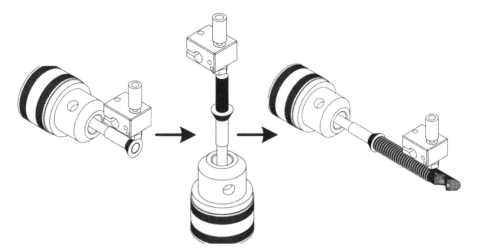

Fig. 4. Schematic diagram of the 3D printing process using 5 axis.

The three-point bending tests of the 5D printed ABS plastic samples showed a four-fold increase in strength compared to 3D-printed ones and a 32% increase compared to cast ones [8]. Additional reinforcement of 5D products with continuous fiber will make it possible to produce complex composite products of any shape that are stronger than similar aluminum parts while reducing weight.

3   Software for Multi-axis 3D Printing

For layer-by-layer division of a digital model and generation of trajectories of movement of the extruder there is a special software - slicers (for example, freely distributed Ultimaker Cura [12]). The functionality of all slicers is limited to the standard three-axis printing. On their basis, solutions for "multi-axis 3D printing" are proposed, which actually amount to reorienting the model on the platform by gradually tilting it as the object grows [13] or by printing supports from an auxiliary dissolvable material [14]. There are known attempts to achieve the curvature of the layers when reproducing various filling patterns on non-planar tooling [15], as well as printing on a flat platform with a pair of extruders with an adjustable slope [16]. However, in all the cases described above, the "slicing" of the model occurs in the usual way, and any "bending" additions are made to the g-code almost manually. In addition, the increase in strength due to curved layers can be only the most insignificant; the main advantage of an inclined platform is the ability to get rid of supports under overhanging elements and smooth the steps on inclined surfaces.

The only end-to-end software for preparing models for multi-axis processing remains the Siemens NX CAD, which also includes a module for additive manufacturing [6]. At the same time, all products must be created in the same design software, which imposes great restrictions on the distribution of these systems in production. In fact, if the end-user was not previously a user of the Siemens NX CAD, then in order to use the multi-axis AM systems of competitors, they must redesign all products in this design environment. Therefore, competitors can count on the introduction of their systems only among users of Siemens CAD Software. In addition, the preparation of the product in the Siemens NX system is manual, so it requires a highly qualified operator.

Siemens NX CAD applies manual and automatic decomposition (separation) of the product into elements, which the operator subsequently assigns a printing strategy (Fig. 5).

There is no information about analogs of the developed device and software that provide the functionality necessary for the automatic construction of product printing programs with the use of 5 degrees of freedom, either on the domestic or foreign market. Accordingly, there is no software for five-axis printing with reinforcement.

Fig. 5. Automatic and semi-automatic decomposition of parts into elements in Siemens NX.

4 Software for Preparing Models for 3D Printing with Reinforcement

Companies that have released solutions for 3D printing with continuous fiber reinforcement offer their own software for preparing models: for example, Eiger (Markforged

[16]) and Aura (Anisoprint [18]) slicers. Such solutions are generally identical: the AM device is a 3D printer operating on the standard three-axis FFF technology with a modified feed system that allows you to feed continuous fiber and fuse it into the layers of the product. In this case, the laying of both the main material (thermoplastic) and the fiber takes place in flat layers, into which the model is divided in the same way as in the Cura slicer.

To prepare models for FFF printing on 5 coordinates with the laying of reinforcing fiber, the authors created the software Stereotech STE Slicer [19] considering principles outlined in the work [20]. Its interface is based on Cura and is distributed under the LGPL-3.0 license. The software has a two-level architecture, the interface is separated from the printing program generators, which optimizes the speed of operation and allows us visually switch between three-and five-coordinate printing. A modification of the CuraEngine [21] generator is used as the generator of the three-coordinate printing program. A specially developed version of ATSS Glicer [22] is used as a five-coordinate printing generator.

The process of laying a continuous fiber has its own characteristics, which must be taken into account when calculating the trajectories (Fig. 6):

- The minimum length of the continuous fiber infill line cannot be less than the distance between the cutting mechanism and the nozzle end.
- At the beginning of the fiber laying, a straight section must be contained, which ensures the adhesion of the fiber to the polymer base.
- The distance between the parallel fiber lines must be 0.
- When the print head changes movement direction, rounding to the travel path must be added to prevent peeling and ensure that the print head moves smoothly.
- The layers below, above, and the areas inside the reinforced layer must be completely filled with polymer to ensure a strong solid composite matrix.
- The fiber must be placed in a fully formed polymer layer, i.e. all the main elements of the layer (walls, polymer infill, areas between the fiber filling, and other elements) must be printed.

Fig. 6. Layer with continuous fiber reinforcement.

Figure 7 shows the algorithm for calculating the fiber infill. For each segment of each polygon of the fiber infill area, the coordinates of all scanning lines with this segment are stored in a two-dimensional array with the scanning line - > intersections relation. To connect the lines to a single continuous path, a segment of the infill area polygon is added. Next, for each scanning line, the intersections are sorted and they are connected in pairs already in the filling line, which are then filtered by the minimum length of the straight section.

After generating the infill, the actual fiberfill area is calculated, and by subtracting the actual infill polygons from the original infill area, the areas that are filled with the polymer are determined. The code of the program that does this is shown below.

```
START
INPUT infill_line_width
...
INIT line_polygons (type: Polygons)
FOR S from 0 to lines_count by 1
    result_line := lines[S];
    INIT line_vector (type: Point);
    line_vector := result_line[1] - result_line[0];
    INIT line_vector_reversed (type: Point);
    line_vector_reversed := -line_vector;
    INIT line_poly (type: Polygon);
    INIT ratio (type: double);
    ratio := vSizeMM(line_vector) /
INT2MM(infill_line_width / 2);
    line_poly.add(result_line[0] + Point(line_vector.Y, -
line_vector.X) * (1 / ratio));
    line_poly.add(result_line[1] +
Point(line_vector_reversed.Y, -line_vector_reversed.X) *
(1 / ratio));
    line_poly.add(result_line[1] + Point(-
line_vector_reversed.Y, line_vector_reversed.X) * (1 /
ratio));
    line_poly.add(result_line[0] + Point(-line_vector.Y,
line_vector.X) * (1 / ratio));
    line_polygons.add(line_poly);
ENDFOR
line_polygons := line_polygons.offset(infill_line_width);
//expand result lines to make them intersect
line_polygons := line_polygons.unionPolygons(); //union
all polygons to get result polygon
line_polygons := line_polygons.offset(-
infill_line_width); //offset result polygon back to normal
width
result_gaps := in_outline.difference(line_polygons);
//find gaps between result polygon and basic infill area
...
END
```

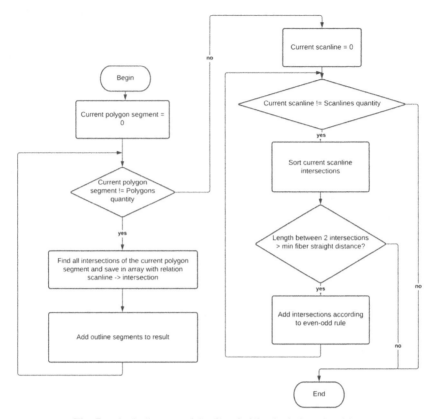

Fig. 7. Block diagram of the fiber infill calculation algorithm.

The layer view mode when preparing the model for five coordinates printing with a continuous fiber is shown in Fig. 8. This mode allows you to inspect the movement paths of the print head, as well as to determine the areas of the model in which the reinforcement will be performed.

The view mode for showing the order of laying the material within the selected layer is shown in Fig. 9. Infill lines made of continuous fiber are displayed in black.

The view mode of showing the reinforcement sections and the moment of material cutting is shown in Fig. 10. The fiber layout after the cut is displayed as a thin blue line.

The Reinforcement settings category has been added to configure the continuous fiber infill parameters (Fig. 11). It allows us to set the layer or height from which the reinforcement will start, as well as the height or number of reinforced layers.

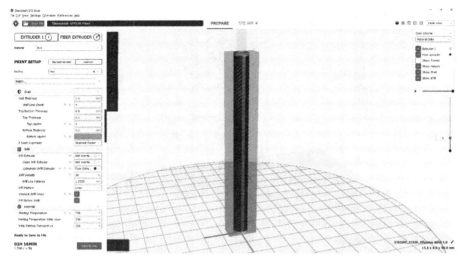

Fig. 8. Layer view mode.

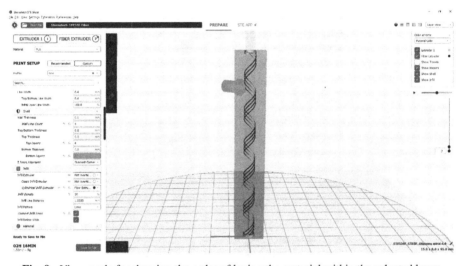

Fig. 9. View mode for showing the order of laying the material within the selected layer.

When set as an extruder for fiber infill lines, the software automatically connects the individual infill lines, ensuring the maximum possible continuous infill section. Next, the software recognizes the length of these infill sections and divides them into two groups. The infill lines that have a length less than the distance between the cutting mechanism and the end of the nozzle are printed with a polymer extruder, and the rest are printed with a fiber extruder. Next, a cut is added to the infill lines that are printed with fiber, after the cut, a non-extrusion movement is made (to layout the remaining fiber) and at the end, an extrusion is added to bring the fiber to the end of the nozzle.

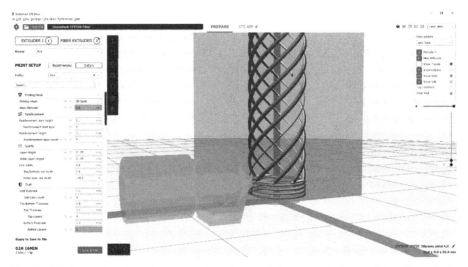

Fig. 10. Mode for showing reinforcement sections and the moment of material cutting. (Color figure online)

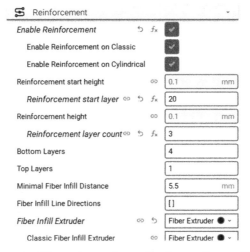

Fig. 11. Reinforcement settings category for configuring continuous fiber reinforcement.

The parameters sent to the generator: the distance between the cutting mechanism and the end of the nozzle, the height of the layers of the beginning and end of printing with fiber, the set of GCode commands for the operation of the fiber cutting mechanism, the fiber diameter, etc. are set by the profile of the printer and the profile of the extruder, which allows you to flexibly configure the generator, for example, for different fiber diameters or different locations of the cutting mechanism relative to the nozzle of the extruder.

5 Practical Work and Conclusions

Using the developed slicer, programs for the production of prismatic bars with a size of $100 \times 15 \times 8$ mm (Fig. 12a) with flat and cylindrical reinforcement, as well as antiviral filter adapters (Fig. 12b) with cylindrical reinforcement were generated. The pictures show samples of reinforced products made on a five-axis printer equipped with an additional extruder for laying out continuous fiber (Markforged prepreg with thermoplastic impregnation was used).

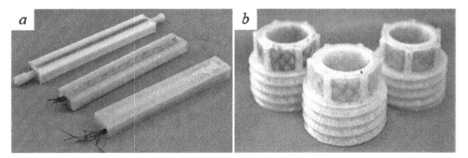

Fig. 12. Printed test products with continuous fiber reinforcement: a. Bending test samples; b. Antiviral filter adapter with sparse multi-layer reinforcement.

So, based on the results of the analysis, it is suggested that in order to obtain symmetric reinforcement for FFF printing of products with continuous fiber laying, it is rational to build a product not from flat layers, but from spatial intersecting trajectories, for which it is necessary to use additional degrees of freedom. To test the hypothesis, we developed our own software for the automatic generation of a part production program based on its 3D model, including the trajectories of the "tool" (the printer's print head) and the trajectories of the reinforcement fiber layout.

The next stage in the development of printing technology with volumetric reinforcement is the debugging of the software and manufacturing technology for fiber-reinforced products. After obtaining satisfactory results for printing more complex models with reinforcement, it is also necessary to conduct strength tests to assess the effect of continuous reinforcement at 5 coordinates in comparison with 3-coordinate fiber laying. First of all, static bending tests according to GOST 4648–2014 (ISO 178:2010) are of interest, for which the production of test samples in the form of prismatic bars has been started (Fig. 12a).

Acknowledgments. This work has been partially supported by a grant from the Skolkovo Foundation, project number MГ18/20. Also, the work has partially received funding from the Russian Foundation for Basic Research, project number 20–37-90133.

References

1. Gusev, Yu.A., Borshchev, A.V., Khrulkov, A.V.: Features of prepregs for automated calculation by ATL and AFP methods. Proc. VIAM **3**, 38–44 (2015). https://cyberleninka.ru/article/n/osobennosti-prepregov-dlya-avtomatizirovannoy-vykladki-metodami-atl-i-afp. Accessed 20 Mar 2021
2. Composites: Airbus continues to shape the future. Airbus SE: official website (2017). https://www.airbus.com/newsroom/news/en/2017/08/composites--airbus-continues-to-shape-the-future.html. Accessed 20 Mar 2021
3. Hambali, R.H., Smith, P., Rennie, A.: Determination of the effect of part orientation to the strength value on additive manufacturing FDM for end-use parts by physical testing and validation via three-dimensional finite element analysis. Int. J. Mater. Eng. Innov. **3**(3/4), 269–281 (2012)
4. Fidan, I., et al.: The trends and challenges of fiber reinforced additive manufacturing. Int. J. Adv. Manuf. Technol. **102**(5–8), 1801–1818 (2019). https://doi.org/10.1007/s00170-018-032 69-7
5. Mason, H., Gardiner, G.: 3D printing with continuous fiber: a landscape. CompositesWorld (2020). https://www.compositesworld.com/articles/3d-printing-with-continuous-fiber-a-landscape. Accessed 2 Apr 2021
6. Industrialize additive manufacturing. Siemens. https://www.plm.automation.siemens.com/media/global/de/Sessions%201-3_Additive%20Fertigung%20live_tcm53-55664.pdf. Accessed 2 Apr 2021
7. Yasa, E, Ersoy, K.: Additive manufacturing of polymer matrix composites. Aircr. Technol. **7**, 147–169 (2018). https://cdn.intechopen.com/pdfs/60211.pdf. Accessed 20 Mar 2021
8. Avdeev, A. V., et al.: Strength increasing additive manufacturing fused filament fabrication technology, based on spiral toolpath material deposition. Machines **7**(3), 18 (2019). https://www.mdpi.com/2075-1702/7/3/57. Accessed 2 Apr 2021
9. Pushkarev, V.V., Drobotov, A.V.: Layout of devices for volumetric printing with an extrudable melt of parts of complex shape. In: Izvestiya VSTU. The series "Progressive Technologies in Mechanical Engineering", Issue 10, 20 (123), pp. 121–123 (2019)
10. Popov, A.Yu., Gushchin, I.A., Drobotov, A.V.: Model preparation algorithm for 3D printing with discrete rotation. In: 2019 International Conference on Industrial Engineering, Applications and Manufacturing (ICIEAM) (Sochi, Russia, 25–29 March, 2019), pp. 1–5 (2019)
11. Andreev, A.E., Drobotov, A.V., Makarov, A.M., Gushchin, I.A., Kizilov, V.G.: Improving the performance of a discrete slicer for additive manufacturing. In: Parallel Computational Technologies (PCT'2021), pp. 143–150 (2021). http://omega.sp.susu.ru/pavt2021/proceedings.pdf. Accessed 2 Apr 2021
12. Ultimaker Cura. https://ultimaker.com/software/ultimaker-cura. Accessed 16 Nov 2020
13. Saunders, S.: TU Delft's multi-axis robotic 3D printing system makes it possible to print without supports. 3Dprint.com (2018). https://3dprint.com/215803/multi-axis-robotic-3d-printer/. Accessed 4 Apr 2021
14. O'Neal, B.: Multi-axis 3D printing technique improves FDM strength Over 2X. 3Dprint.com (2020). https://3dprint.com/272389/multi-axis-3d-printing-technique-improves-fdm-strength-over-2x/. Accessed 4 Apr 2021
15. McCaw, J.C.S., Cuan-Urquizo, E.: Curved-layered additive manufacturing of non-planar, parametric lattice structures. Mater. Des. **160**, 949–963 (2018). https://www.sciencedirect.com/science/article/pii/S0264127518307792. Accessed 24 Mar 2021

16. Zhao, D., Li, T., Shen, B., Jiang, Y., Guo, W., Gao, F.: A multi-DOF rotary 3D printer: machine design, performance analysis and process planning of curved layer fused deposition modeling (CLFDM). Rapid Prototyping J. **6**, 1079–1093 (2020). https://www.researchg ate.net/publication/340311998_A_multi-DOF_rotary_3D_printer_machine_design_perfor mance_analysis_and_process_planning_of_curved_layer_fused_deposition_modeling_C LFDM. Accessed 12 Apr 2021
17. Eiger 3D Printing Software. https://markforged.com/software. Accessed 14 Apr 2021
18. Aura. https://anisoprint.com/aura/. Accessed 14 Apr 2021
19. Stereotech STE Slicer. https://github.com/stereotech/STE-Slicer. Accessed 14 Apr 2021
20. Shapovalov, O.V., Andreev, A.E., Fomenkov, S.A.: Application of the parallel template library in the development of a geometric kernel. Bull. Comput. Inf. Technol. **11**(125), 8–12 (2014)
21. CuraEngine. https://github.com/stereotech/CuraEngine. Accessed 16 Nov 2020
22. Additive Technology Software Solution Glicer. https://www.atssgroup.com/. Accessed 16 Nov 2020

Constructing Equidistant Curve for Planar Composite Curve in CAD Systems

Oleg Y. Filimonov, Vitaly A. Egunov$^{(\boxtimes)}$, and Elena N. Nesterenko

Volgograd State Technical University, 28, Lenina ave., Volgograd 400005, Russia

Abstract. The paper describes an algorithm of the equidistant curve construction for planar and composite curves. Four base cases are defined and considered: connection, intersection, break, degeneration. For definition these cases use the rolling ball method which is also used for the processing of both cases, break and degeneration. The degeneration case is interesting because it allows to process the equidistant segments construction with the large offset value. The association of segments is considered which allows the equidistant segments to be processed without the intermediate processing of each segment. Results of constructing are shown in some figures. Results of the equidistant curves construction and the algorithm describing the main stages are shown.

Keywords: Equidistant curve · Parallel curve · Planar and composite curve · CAD systems · The rolling ball method

1 Introduction

Modern CAD systems have a wide range of different functions that allow to perform the construction of various geometric shapes. CAD systems functions could be used to solve other problems [11–14]. These systems also provide the performing of certain manipulations with beforehand created shapes. For example, calculating the volume of a 3D body or using the created bodies in boolean operations to generate a new one.

Some set of geometric operations in CAD systems are based on the equidistant concept. It is rather difficult to give a definition to this term, since its meaning can vary depending on both the dimension of the problem and the method of application. In this paper the construction of the equidistant curve to a planar composite curve is considered. The definition of the planar composite curve will be given later. However, an equidistant curve can also be constructed for a 3D curve. Moreover, this concept is generalized to various 3D surfaces. Another example of using the equidistant can be the solid body construction from a wire body or the thin-wall body construction [1, 7, 15, 18].

2 Existing Solutions

Almost all CAD systems implement their own methods for constructing equidistant curves, both 2D and 3D. The methods for constructing these curve is determined by the

© Springer Nature Switzerland AG 2021
A. G. Kravets et al. (Eds.): CIT&DS 2021, CCIS 1448, pp. 296–309, 2021.
https://doi.org/10.1007/978-3-030-87034-8_22

geometric kernel. Most of the geometric kernels are commercial, so their construction algorithms are often not public. The exception is OCCT (Open CASCADE Technology) and BRL-CAD. Of course, there are many other open source CAD systems, but almost all of them use OCCT.

The equidistant curve construction is usually performed for relatively simple curves or surfaces. For the most part, CAD systems handle such cases well and can even construct the equidistant to more complex geometric objects. Problems that results in incorrect construction are usually associated with a certain offset value. Incorrect construction is expressed in the incorrect equidistant curve displaying or, what is worse, in the incorrect operations performing over the equidistant curve because the geometry was damaged. This problem is typical for almost all geometric objects, since from a certain offset value when constructing an equidistant curve, self-intersection (equidistant curve of a parabola [5, 8] or an ellipse [8], a sine [17]), geometry degeneration (the equidistant of the circle when the offset value is equal to the circle radius) or the breaks can occur when we are talking about piecewise-smooth curves or surfaces. In addition, the offset value can be variable in some CAD systems, for example, in T-FLEX CAD [2, 15].

The algorithm proposed in this paper implements not only standard processing method (intersection, break), but also others. It allows to process some situations when the break between curves cannot be eliminated by tangent lines or by constructing an arc between them.

3   Equidistant Curve of a Composite Curve and Ways to Eliminate the Brake Between Curves

3.1   Mathematical Definition

To begin with, let us clarify the definition. In Russian literature and this paper "equidistant curve" has the same sense that "parallel curve" or "offset curve" in foreign literature [5, 7, 16, 18]. Thus, the terms "equidistant" and "parallel" are equivalent in this paper.

The equidistant curve of $C(t)$ is a curve $C_d(t)$ such that (see [1, 10] for details):

$$C_d(t) = C(t) + d \cdot n(t) \tag{1}$$

Where
$C_d(t)$ − equidistant curve of $C(t)$
$C(t)$ − base curve
d − offset value $(d > 0)$
$n(t)$ − unit vector

Unit vector n can be formed in various ways. For example, for a planar curve $n(t)$ is the cross product of two vectors tangent at point $C(t)$ and normal to the plane where the base curve is located.

Based on the definition of the equidistant curve, the equidistant curve of the composite curve can be defined. A composite curve and its equidistant are defined as a set of curves as follows:

$$C(t) = \{S_1(t), S_2(t), \ldots, S_n(t)\}, S_i(t_{end}) = S_{i+1}(t_{start}), i = \overline{1, n-1}$$
$$C_d(t) = \left\{S_1^e(t), \ S_2^e(t), \ldots, S_n^e(t)\right\} \tag{2}$$

where

$C_d(t)$ – equidistant curve of $C(t)$

$C(t)$ – basecurve

$S_i(t)$ – base curve segment

$S_i^e(t)$ – segment of equidistant curve

Curve $C(t)$ can be closed. In this situation we need to add the boundary condition, $S_n(t_{end}) = S_1(t_{start})$. It follows that an equidistant curve of a composite curve is a set of equidistant curves of all segments of the base curve. However, this method is not suitable for practical use. In fact, it is necessary to process the equidistant segments paired with each other to get the correct result. Because we can get a number of intersections or breaks when constructing the equidistant segments.

Notice that we suppose the equidistant curve construction for a single curve is correct and trouble-free. But the equidistant curve construction for a single curve is really complicated problem. For example, it is easy to construction an equidistant curve for a circle, but it is very hard to do this for a NURBS-curve because that requires knowledge of a curve structure, weights meaning, curvature and differential geometry [3, 6, 19, 20]. Moreover, the constructing task becomes more complicated if it is required to perform the equidistant curve construction for a curve is in a surface [4, 9].

3.2 Ways of Eliminating the Breaks Between Equidistant Segments

Processing pairs of adjacent equidistant segments is a way of connecting adjacent equidistant segments to each other. Most CAD systems have three methods to do this:

– Off. Do not connect the break;
– Linear. Connect the break with tangential lines;
– Circular. Connect the break with an arc.

The third method is most often used. The 3D analogue of this method is used for surface rounding and is called «the rolling-ball method». In this paper, a two-dimensional analogue of «the rolling-ball method» is used to connect the equidistant segments.

In two-dimensional space, its essence is as follows. The base curve equidistant is formed by moving a circle along it. The circle radius is equal to the offset value d. The trajectory of the circle center of the circle is an equidistant curve.

In this paper, we propose an algorithm that constructs the equidistant curve to a planar curve consisting of several segments. The algorithm is based on sequential processing of pairs of adjacent equidistant segments. The base curve has n-1 pairs of adjacent segments. If the base curve is closed, then the number of pairs is equal to the number of segments, i.e. n.

4   The Main Cases and Ways to Identify Them

When considering the interposition of adjacent equidistant segments, four basic cases can be defined.

- Connection (G0 continuity);
- Intersection;
- Break;
- Degeneration.

Notice that the above cases describe not any mutual arrangement of base curve segments, but only a limited set. Let's consider the cases in greater details. For convenience, denote the considered pair of the base curve segments (S_i, S_{i+1}) and the considered pair of the equidistant segments (S_i^e, S_{i+1}^e) in this way:

$$F = S_i, S = S_{i+1}, F^e = S_i^e, S^e = S_{i+1}^e \tag{3}$$

Connection. It is the simplest case of all. It is not required any processing of the equidistant segments pair in the connection case. The connection case is formed when $F^e(t_{end}) = S^e(t_{start})$. It means that the mutual arrangement of the equidistant segments remains the same as in the base curve.

Intersection. As the name implies the case occurs when equidistant segments are intersected. The intersection of equidistant segments is the most common case that can be occurred when constructing the equidistant curve of the base curve. Figure 1 shows the intersection case. Notice that in all figures the base curve segments are red and the equidistant curve segments are blue.

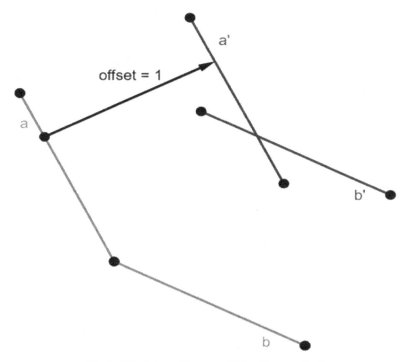

Fig. 1. The intersection case (Color figure online)

Break. A necessary condition for the break case formation is situation when there are no such parameters t_1 and t_2 belonging to the intervals of segments F^e and S^e respectively, that $F^e(t_1) = S^e(t_2)$. It means the pair of adjacent equidistant segments does not have common points, i.e. the equidistant segments are not intersected. Figure 2 shows the break case.

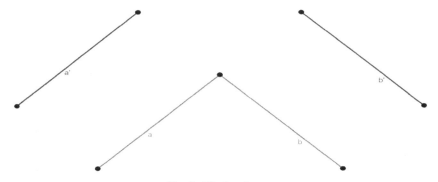

Fig. 2. The break case

A sufficient condition in order to identify a case as the break case is the non-existing of such the offset value $d > 0$ where the equidistant segments are intersected.

The degeneration case. The case describes a situation when one or two equidistant segments of pair cannot be constructed. It happens when the rolling ball moving on the first equidistant segment collides the second equidistant segment at point $S(t_{end})$ or does not collide it at all. In this case, the second equidistant segment can be replaced with the next one, if it exists. Visually, the degeneration case looks the same as the break case as shown in Fig. 3 (right). In fact, the degeneration case arises only from the certain offset value L. While $d < L$, the equidistant segments form the intersection case. Thus, a sufficient condition in order to identify a case as the degeneration case is the existence of such the offset value $d > 0$ that the equidistant segments are intersected. As you can see, the sufficient condition for the break case and the degeneration case are opposite. Figure 3 shows how the intersection case when increasing the offset value goes into the degeneration case.

The degeneration case is subdivided into 3 types:

– Degeneration of the first segment;
– Degeneration of the second segment;
– Degeneration of both segments.

If both segments are degenerated it geometrically means the rolling ball didn't collide any from a pair of base curve segments, or it collided the base curve segments at the ends of the intervals. In this case, the processing of the equidistant segments is not required, but the segments themselves can be used for processing in a different pair.

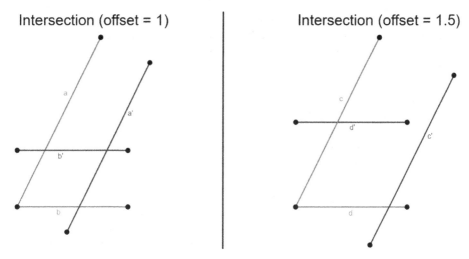

Fig. 3. The intersection case goes into the degeneration case

5   Equidistant Segment Processing Methods

The intersection case. The processing of the equidistant segments in the intersection case consists in changing the parametric interval of the equidistant segments. It is required to find the intersection point of the equidistant segments and parametrize it or perform the interval change. It means it need to obtain the values of parameters t_1, t_2 of the intersection point for F^e, S^e. It is required to change the parametric interval of the equidistant segments after obtaining the values of parameters. The parametric interval of the base curve segment is equal to the parametric interval of the equidistant segment. Thus, a change the parametric interval of the equidistant segments is an assigning a new boundary of the parametric interval. t_1 is the new end parameter F^e, and t_2 is the new start parameter S^e.

Notice that the processing of the intersection case in the algorithm assumes there is the only one intersection point.

The break case. Since there is no intersection between the equidistant segments in the break case, the processing comes down to connect the equidistant segments using an arc. The construction of an equidistant curve is based on the rolling ball model. It means that the curve connecting the equidistant segments to each other is an arc of a circle centered at the point $p = F(t_e) = S(t_s)$. Notice that the connecting circular arc must meet the following conditions:

$$
\begin{aligned}
F^e(t_{\text{end}}) &= \text{Circle}(t_{\text{start}}) \\
S^e(t_{\text{start}}) &= \text{Circle}(t_{\text{end}})
\end{aligned}
\tag{4}
$$

These conditions are necessary both for the correct displaying and for the correct performing others geometric operations. Otherwise, if we neglect these conditions the calculation of the points of the curve and tangent vectors will be incorrect, which may be undesirable or even critical for other algorithms.

The degeneration case. The processing of the degeneration case is divided into two steps. The first step is to determine which of two segments is degenerated, the second step is to redefine the parametric interval of one of the equidistant segments or do nothing if both segments are degenerated.

To begin with, if the rolling ball can move along the segment F or S, then this segment doesn't degenerate. It is because any movement of the rolling ball along the base curve segment constructs an equidistant segment or at least a part of it. Based on this fact, it is possible to make a test which will help to find the degenerate segment. Based on this fact, it is possible to create a test to find the degeneration segment. Let the rolling ball moves from a non-degenerate segment to a degenerate one. Let us make an assumption that F^e is non-degenerate, and S^e is degenerate. Let us place the center of the circle with the radius equal to the offset value d, at the start point of the F^e. If there is no intersection between the circle and the segment S, then the assumption is correct and F^e is really non-degenerate. However, if there is an intersection, then the assumption is wrong and a second check is required. If so, then let us make an opposite assumption that F^e is degenerate, and S^e is non-degenerate. It was said earlier that the rolling ball moves from a non-degenerate segment to a degenerate one. It means that in the second check the center of the circle is placed not at start point of S^e, but at end point of S^e, i.e. at point $S^e(t_{end})$. If there is no intersection between the circle and the segment F, then the second assumption is right and the S^e is non-degenerate. Otherwise, if in both tests there is intersection, then both segments are degenerate. Figure 4 shows the first (right) and the second (left) tests.

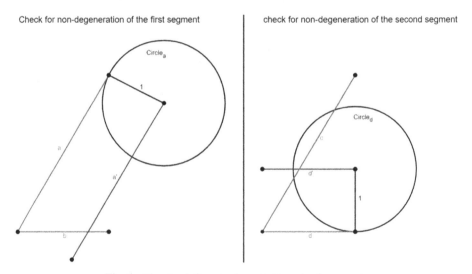

Fig. 4. The check for non-degenerate each of segments

As you can see, the circle in the first test (left) does not intersect the curve b, i.e. the circle can move along the curve a. In the second test there is an intersection and the circle cannot move along the curve d.

The second step of the degeneration case processing is to assign a new boundary of the parametric interval. Denote the non-degenerate segment and its equidistant curve as N and N^e, and the degenerate segments and its equidistant curve as D and D^e. It is required to know either a point of the curve N^e or a value of parameter at the same point to assign a new boundary of the parametric interval. If the circle moves from the curve N to the curve D, then the construction of the equidistant curve N^e ends at the instant of collision with the curve D. Figure 5 shows the collision the circle moving on the curve a' with the curve b, where the curve N is a', and the curve D is b.

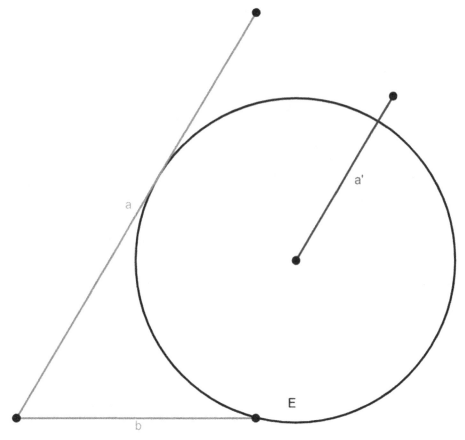

Fig. 5. Constructing a part of a non-degenerate curve

As you can see, the new boundary of the curve N^e is such parameter $t_{collision}$ that the minimum distance from the point $N^e(t_{collision})$ to the curve D is equal to the offset value d. It is also necessary that the following condition is met. For all values of parameter $t < t_{collision}$ of the curve N^e it is true that the minimum distance between the curve N^e with the parametric interval $[t_{start}, t_{collision})$ and the curve D is more than the offset value d. Obviously, it is possible to make such curves N1 and D that the curve N^e will has more than one collision point with its own parameter $t_{collision}$. However, the above condition will be met for one point of the curve N^e only. The parameter of this point is the new boundary of the curve N^e.

The use of numerical methods is required to calculate the point in which the circle collides with the curve D. Let us use the dichotomy method. Divide the parametric interval of the curve N^e into 2 parts (L and R) by the parameter t_{half}. Thus, $L - [t_{start}, t_{half}]$, $R - [t_{half}, t_{end}]$. Let us calculate the minimum distance between the N^e curve on the L interval and the curve D. We denote the obtained distance values as L_{min}, L_{max}. If the offset value d is in the range $[L_{min}, L_{max}]$, then the new interval on the next iteration will be the L interval, otherwise the R interval. Checking the R interval is not required because it is known that the circle collides with the curve D for sure. It means there is a point on the curve N^e in which the distance between the curve N^e and the curve D is equal to the offset value d. The above steps are repeated until the interval length is less than the required accuracy.

After reaching the required accuracy, the middle of the parametric interval is the new boundary of the curve N^e.

6 Association Between the Cases

Processing pairs of the base curve segments which follows one after the other is actually not as efficient as you think. In fact, there are situations in which it is required to process the curves created during the operation of the algorithm. For example, it could be a circular arc used to connect equidistant segments in the break case. Figure 6 shows a closed curve (a sequence of curves - a, b, c, d) and its equidistant segments, constructed accordingly with the processing of the four above cases.

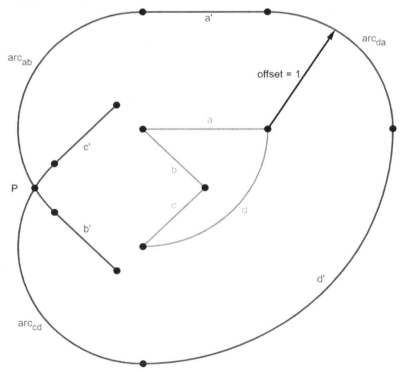

Fig. 6. Constructing an equidistant curve without processing a new pair (arc_{ab}, arc_{cd})

Let the offset value be 1. A pair of the segments (b, c) forms the degeneration case of third type where both segments are degenerate. The equidistant segments a' and d' have to be connected somehow because there is no processing of the double degeneration case. Figure 6 shows that the equidistant segments a' and d' (if we move from a' to d') are connected each other by two circular arcs formed by the processing of the pairs (a, b) and (c, d). Nevertheless, the circular arcs are intersected at the point P. This is because "the rolling circle" while constructing arc arc$_{ab}$ collides with the point where the segments c and d are connected. Because of that the remaining part of the circular arc have to be cut out. A similar situation occurs with the arc arc$_{cd}$. This example shows that the new curves which can be created in the processing have to be processed. This is the association between the cases when the processing of one case can generate new curves which have to be handled. The considered example is a special case of the association concept. The association concept means availability of a relation between two or more cases. An association between cases can be described as the intersection of arcs as shown in the above example. However, an association can be described in a different way. Notice that the association between cases is almost always reduced to the intersection case. Figure 7 shows constructing the equidistant curve using the modified algorithm where the circular arcs intersection are processed.

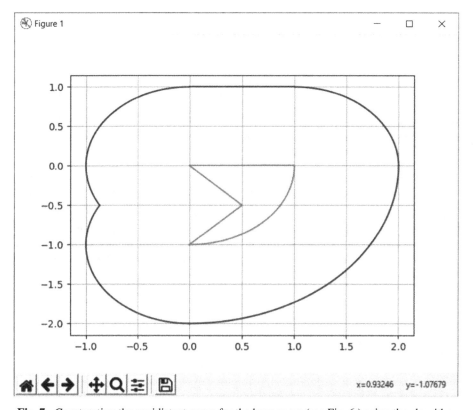

Fig. 7. Constructing the equidistant curve for the base curve (see Fig. 6.) using the algorithm

The detection such associations is important. First, it is required for correct processing. Second, the association processing improves the algorithm performance because the processing of some cases gets easier. Let us consider the following example shown in Fig. 8. Pairs (a, b) and (a_1, b_1) make the degeneration case in which the segment b is degenerate. Figure 8 shows the curve a' intersects the arc arc_{bc} at the point H. If we process a pair (a, b) then the parameter $t_{collision}$ for the curve a' will be such that $a'(t_{collision}) = H$. Thus, the degeneration case processing is optional and we can process the intersection case for the curve a' and the arc arc_{bc} instead.

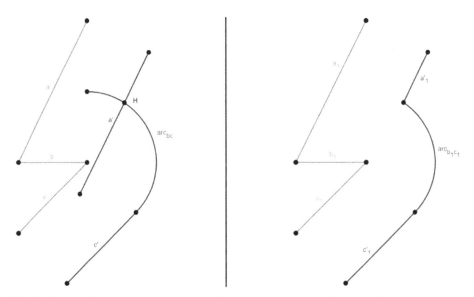

Fig. 8. The equidistant curve construction of the composite curve without associations processing (left) and with associations processing (right)

The associations searching between different pairs segments are not considered in this paper. However, it is important task because replacing the degeneration case with the intersection case will enable to reduce time taken by an algorithm on processing.

Notice that the associations searching are likely harder task than the equidistant curve construction. Such complexity is related to process pairs not only adjacent equidistant segments but also isolated from each other equidistant segments. It means that all pairs in the base curve must be processed. Figure 9 shows the algorithm flowchart.

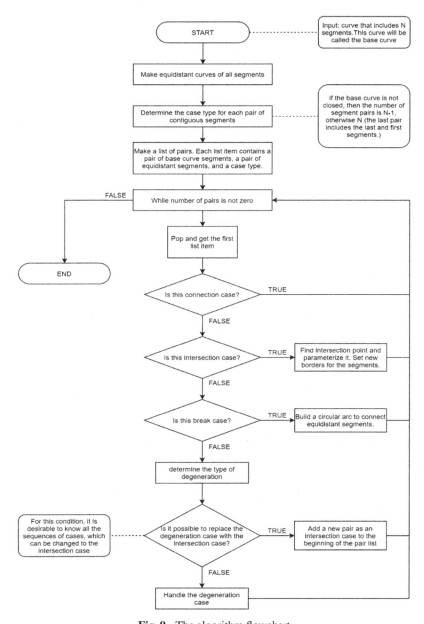

Fig. 9. The algorithm flowchart

7   Results

The proposed algorithm enables to perform the equidistant curve construction for a planar curve which is composite, i.e. piecewise-smooth. Figure 10 shows the equidistant curves construction.

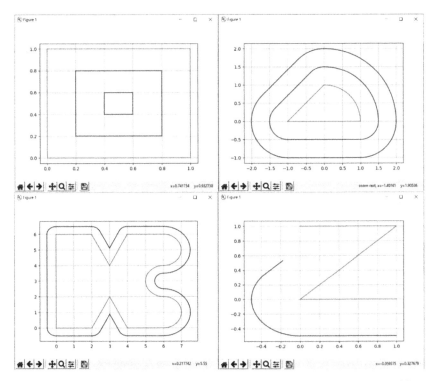

Fig. 10. Examples of the equidistant curves construction with the proposed algorithm

Nevertheless, some features of the base curve are neglected by the algorithm. For example, if the base curve has self-intersections then the algorithm will process the cases incorrectly. Moreover, self-intersection could be between as segments as within a single segment. There is a problem with the associations searching as far as it is required searching a sequence of the cases among which are one or more than one the degeneration case in order to replace it with the intersection case.

8 Conclusion

We proposed the algorithm of the equidistant curve construction for a planar composite curve. The algorithm can be used for various arrangement of curves. The equidistant curve construction is based on the rolling ball method. Use the rolling ball method allowed to define some cases and find the conditions for its identification. Analysis of some sequence of cases in the algorithm allows to change the processing of some pairs in order to replace the degeneration case with the intersection case that reduces time taken by an algorithm on processing.

References

1. Golovanov, N.: Geometric Modelling. Fizmatlit, Moscow (2002)

2. Kozlov S.: T-FLEX CAD 16. Part 1. Development of parameterization and drawing tools. CAD Graph. **5**(259), 38–44 (2018)
3. Piegl, L., Tiller, W.: The NURBS Book, 2nd edn. Springer, Heidelberg (1997)
4. Gálvez, A., Iglesias, A., Puig-Pey, J.: Computing parallel curves on parametric surfaces. Appl. Math. Model. **38**(9–10), 2398–2413 (2014)
5. Parallel curve of a curve. https://mathcurve.com/courbes2d.gb/parallele/parallele.shtml. Accessed 21 Apr 2020
6. Piegl, L., Tiller, W.: Computing offsets of NURBS curves and surfaces. Comput.-Aided Des. **31**(2), 147–156 (1999)
7. Parallel curve. https://en.wikipedia.org/wiki/Parallel_curve. Accessed 21 Apr 2020
8. Equidistant Curves. https://www.mathpages.com/home/kmath724/kmath724.htm. Accessed 21 Apr 2020
9. Brunnett, G.: Geometric modeling of parallel curves on surfaces. Comput. Suppl. **14**, 37–53 (1999)
10. Hartmann, E.: Geometry and Algorithms for Computer Aided Design. Department of Mathematics, Darmstadt University of Technology (2003)
11. Andreev, A., Egunov, V., Movchan, E., Cherednikov, N., Kharkov, E., Kohtashvili, N.: The introduction of multi-level parallelism solvers in multibody dynamics. In: Kravets, A.G., Groumpos, P.P., Shcherbakov, M., Kultsova, M. (eds.) CIT&DS 2019. CCIS, vol. 1084, pp. 166–180. Springer, Cham (2019). https://doi.org/10.1007/978-3-030-29750-3_13
12. Andreev, A., Chalyshev, M., Egunov, V., Doukhnitch, E., Kuznetsova, K.: Effective quaternion and octonion cryptosystems and their FPGA implementation. In: Kravets, A.G., Groumpos, P.P., Shcherbakov, M., Kultsova, M. (eds.) CIT&DS 2019. CCIS, vol. 1083, pp. 406–419. Springer, Cham (2019). https://doi.org/10.1007/978-3-030-29743-5_33
13. Getmanskiy, V., Andreev, A.E., Alekseev, S., Gorobtsov, A.S., Egunov, V., Kharkov, E.: Optimization and parallelization of CAE software stress-strain solver for heterogeneous computing hardware. In: Kravets, A., Shcherbakov, M., Kultsova, M., Groumpos, P. (eds.) CIT&DS 2017. CCIS, vol. 754, pp. 562–574. Springer, Cham (2017). https://doi.org/10.1007/978-3-319-65551-2_41
14. Nesmianov, I., et al.: Synthesis of control algorithm and computer simulation of robotic manipulator-tripod. In: Kravets, A., Shcherbakov, M., Kultsova, M., Shabalina, O. (eds.) CIT&DS 2015. CCIS, vol. 535, pp. 391–403. Springer, Cham (2015). https://doi.org/10.1007/978-3-319-23766-4_31
15. T-FELX CAD 17 - New possibilities for 3D modeling and for working 3D curves. Working with surfaces. https://www.tflex.ru/about/publications/detail/index.php?ID=4404. Accessed 21 June 2016
16. Hoschek, J.: Offset curves in the plane. Comput. Aided Des. **17**(2), 77–82 (1985)
17. Parallel curve. http://xahlee.info/SpecialPlaneCurves_dir/Parallel_dir/parallel.html. Accessed 21 June 2016
18. Max, K.: Agoston: Computer Graphics and Geometric Modelling, 1st edn. Springer, London (2005)
19. Joon Ahn, Y., Soo Kim, Y., Shin, Y.: Partial degree formulae for plane offset curves. J. Comput. Appl. Math. **167**(2), 405–416 (2004)
20. San Segundo, F., Sendra, J.R.: Approximation of circular arcs and offset curves by Bezier curves of high degree. J. Symbolic Comput. **44**(6), 635–654 (2009)

Data Processing Pipeline: From 3D Surface Scanning to Coke Drum Residual Life Assessment

Timur A. Janovsky[✉], Andrey V. Naidenko, Marina S. Kadykova, and Anton N. Kiselev

JSC "VNIKTIneftekhimoborudovanie", Volgograd, Russia
TAYanovsky@vnikti.rosneft.ru

Abstract. The working cycle of a coke drum is characterized by thermal discontinuity in time, in height and in diameter. Long-term operation leads to the appearance of cracks in the welded seams and deformation of the coke drum walls with the convex lateral deformation. Sophisticated problem is to search for convex lateral deformation on the data of 3D scanning of the inner surface of the coke drums after 10–20 years of their operation. The solution of this problem is necessary for a prompt assessment of the residual service life. The article presents a method for solving this problem in the form of a scanning data processing pipeline. Fragments of code and the results of experiments that characterize its sensitivity and accuracy are given.

Keywords: Coke drum · Body deformation · Convex lateral deformation · Residual life · 3D-scanning · Data analysis · Mathematical statistics · Machine learning

1 Introduction

The exhaustion surface loading capacity of the coke drum due to the loss of material plasticity may occur before the end of the service life of the coke chamber, which is determined by the permissible number of loading cycles. Therefore, monitoring of local deformations of the coke drum during its operation is a prerequisite for ensuring reliable and safe operation. The methodology for assessing the residual life [1–3] developed by JSC "VNIKTIneftekhimoborudovanie" provides for a visual inspection of the inner surface of cleaned of coke drum and an assessment of the local convex deformations revealed in this case by sagging deflection measuring - vertical deviation of the deformed section surface.

Sagging deflection was measured manually using a vertical laser beam or a vertical string or a rigid control rod installed across the deformed section (Fig. 1).

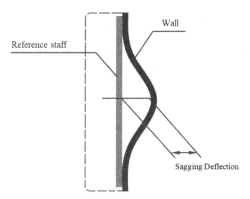

Fig. 1. Sagging deflection measuring on coke drum casing along the inner side (measuring-rod installed on unstrained sections of the body)

This method is unreliable and inaccurate, laborious and associated with the risk of injury to workers due to the height (over 20 m) and the large area of the inner surface of the coke drum.

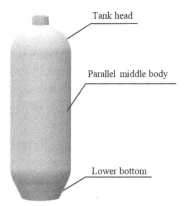

Fig. 2. Coke drum body

State-of-the-art 3D laser scanning technology allows to restore control of the deformation of the body. High accuracy and multiple measurements are sufficient for reliable machine assessment of deformations. If the cylindrical part of the body shown in Fig. 2 can be considered an ideal cylinder, neglecting local convex deformations and misalignment of the upper and lower bases up to 1 cm, then it is not difficult to find and determine the dimensions of the convex lateral deformation. It is enough to estimate the central axis of this cylinder and the radial distances to the points.

However, after 10–20 years of operation, the misalignment of the upper and lower bases can reach several cm as a result of the "tilt" of the cylindrical part of the body and banana effect syndrome extended along the height [4–6]. The search for convex lateral deformations in the cylindrical part of the body against the background of such "global" deformations and the effect of "retention hoops" in the zones of welded seams of shell sections becomes a sophisticated problem.

Let's consider the process of obtaining the initial data in the context of the problem statement. After cleaning the coke drum from the product, the Z + F IMAGER® 5016 3D laser scanner manufactured by Zoller + Frohlich GmbH is lowered inside it. It is sequentially fixed at 3 different heights and from these positions it performs multiple measurements of the coordinates of inner surface points of the coke drum. Measurements cover the entire 3-dimensional sphere except for the top cone, which contains base for attaching the scanner. Measurements are "stitched" together with specialized software Z + F LaserControl® and are written line-by-line to a text file. This input file is contains coordinates (x1, x2, x3) up to 2 million points of the inner surface of the coke drum.

The task is to find convex lateral deformations on the cylindrical part of the coke drum using a data processing pipeline of a given set of coordinates. It is necessary to evaluate the sagging deflection corresponding to the convex lateral deformations, as well as the horizontal and vertical length of the convex lateral deformations.

The control parameters of the data processing pipeline are:

- height and diameter of the cylindrical part of the coke drum;
- minimum sagging deflection (serves as a cutoff threshold);
- maximum convex lateral deformation height (serves as a cutoff threshold).

2   Background

A fairly large number of scientific and technical publications are devoted to the issues of modeling and operation of coke drums. They contain such aspects as the modeling of stresses and thermal regimes in coke drums [7, 8], the design of coke drums, service devices and automatic control systems [8–11], temperature monitoring and stress assessment in the metal of coke drums [12, 13], predictive analytics [14].

At the same time, there are few works directly devoted to the assessment of local convex deformations and the application of the results of 3D scanning. The analysis of open sources leads to the following results.

In the article by Mahmod Samman, Ediberto B. Tinoco, Fábio C. Marangone [15], a four-coke drum plant with a known fracture history is analyzed using stress and convex strain analysis techniques. Plastic deformations are calculated there directly from the differences between the original and deformed geometry, measured with a laser scanner.

M. Bazzi, G. Grimaldo and colleagues [16] write about a new laser technology that provides fast and accurate scanning of a delayed coking reactor. The result of the scan is "... data about the radius and position of the reactor, which are used to create convexity maps of the inner wall". In particular, the authors provide a polar plot of the coke drum surface data, which shows radius asymmetry at a particular height (Fig. 3).

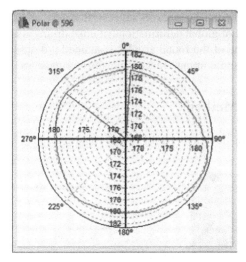

Fig. 3. Polar plot of the coke drum surface data. From [16]

This graph shows that the central axes of the actual reactor and the reference reactor are coincide. However, if the axis of the reactor is tilted due to severe temperature and power modes of operation, then the construction of the convexity map will be incorrect due to the radial shifted estimate.

M. Haragushi, M. Samman and collegues [17] proposed an alternative to the analysis of stress concentration factors (SCF) by finite-element methods. To avoid technical and practical limitations, the authors have developed a new method of deformation analysis - Plastic Strain Index (PSI). Evaluation procedure of reactor bulging ratio is carried out in several stages: laser scanning, visual inspection, data cleansing from statistical noise, processing and analysis of the obtained data. The result is a contour plot or radius map that represents the geometry of the inner surface.

However, the article does not specify the details of the scan data. On the other hand, there is a remark that the problem of displacement of the reactor vertical axis seriously complicates the process of constructing a radius map.

Finally, a similar topic presenting in the article by S. Ruparel and S. Bansode [18] - it describes closely results processing methods of laser scanning. The authors discuss the benefits of using 2D color contour plots, 3D surface maps, ranking of the most dangerous locations, multiple scans and statistical analysis, growth rate analysis and predictions of future fractures. At the same time, in contrast to [16], the stage of preprocessing the data obtained as a result of scanning is not mentioned. It is difficult to understand whether this is due to a simplified geometric interpretation of the cylindrical part of the coke drum or some other reason.

Thus, the analysis of published sources suggests that the search for local deformations against the background of global deformations of coke drums is a crucial scientific and technical task. But none of the found articles contained a description of how to solve this task suitable for programming. This article aims to make up for an annoying flaw.

3 Materials and Methods

The data processing pipeline includes 12 operations in 3 stages (Fig. 4).

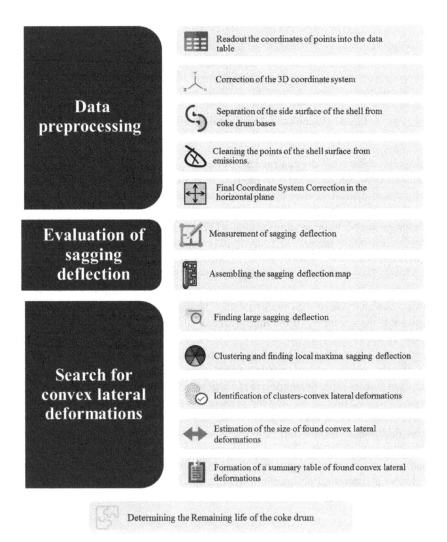

Fig. 4. 3D scanning data processing pipeline

Let us consider the content of each operation sequentially, accompanying it with fragments of program code in the R-language. For clarity, we will describe the parameters that the pipeline operates with and give an example of their values.

```
#The specified height and diameter of the cylindrical
part of the chamber, as well as the radius, m
L_Obechaika <-18
D_Obechaika <-5
R_Obechaika <-D_Obechaika/2
#Minimum depth and height of convex lateral deformation,
m
Depth_Gofra <-0.05
Hmax_Gofra <-1.0
#Height for reference point calculating, m
Hmax_Base <- 0.1*Hmax_Gofra
```

1. Reading Points into a Data Table.
   Coordinates (x_1, x_2, x_3) up to 2 million points of the inner surface of the coke drum from a text file
2. Coordinate system correction
   The zeros on the axes Ox_1 and Ox_2 are set by the medians of the values of the coordinates x_1 and x_2 of the entire set of points. The vertical axis Ox_3 direction is reversed. Now the axis is directed not downward (due to the fact that the scanner is lowered into the coke drum "upside down"), but upward. Zero of the Ox_3 axis is assigned to the lowest point of the entire set of measured ones, as shown in Fig. 5.

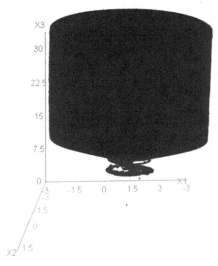

Fig. 5. Initial set of measurement points

3. Separating the side surface of the shell from the coke drum bases

Since the beginning of the vertical axis Ox_3 is set at the lowest measured point, and this point is random to a certain extent (for example, the scanner beam passed through the open lower hatch of the coke drum and reflected from some surface of the foundation), it is necessary to determine the value of the coordinate Ox_3, in which the lower base passes into the cylindrical part. Let us reduce this search to solving an optimization problem: to minimize the sum of squares of negative residuals between the set of points of the coke drum surface and the model cylinder with no bases with a given height and radius of the cylindrical part of the coke drum. The objective function does not respond to convex lateral deformations, but increases only when the radius of the surface points is less than the specified one - in order to avoid acquisition of points from the upper and lower conical bases. The problem is solved numerically - by searching on the grid for x_3 values. It means that we shift the model cylinder from bottom to top through the "cloud" of surface points. To achieve the required accuracy, the optimization problem is solved three times with a sequential decrease in the step along x_3 - from 0.1 to 0.001 m.

This makes it possible to correctly remove the points of the lower and upper bases of the coke drum.

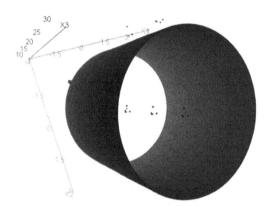

Fig. 6. Point cloud after clipping the top and bottom bases

4. Cleaning of points of a cylindrical surface from emissions

Part of the outliers, visible in Fig. 6, was formed around the central axis due to the capture of the attachment device corners by the scanner beam. All of these are points characterized by an abnormally small or abnormal radius distance. A simple statistical outlier test solves this problem. The result is shown in Fig. 7. A "convexity" is visible corresponding to the hole of the process fitting.

```
boxplot(Obechaika$R)
BPS<-boxplot.stats(Obechaika$R)
Out<-BPS$out
m <- max(Out[Out<R_Obechaika])
M <- min(Out[Out>R_Obechaika])
Obechaika <- Obechaika[Obechaika$R>m & Obechaika$R<M,]
```

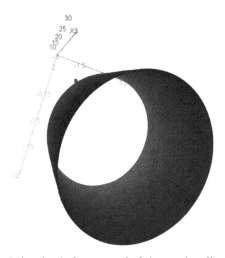

Fig. 7. Point cloud after removal of abnormal outlier points

5. Final correction of the coordinate system in the horizontal plane
   We shift the zero of the horizontal coordinate system to the center of the lower
   meter base of the cylindrical part. Additionally calculate the polar radius and angle
   to describe the points of the cylindrical surface.
6. Measurement of sagging deflection
   The procedure simulates the measurement of the sagging deflection using a control
   rod (Fig. 1). The height of the virtual "rod" is 20% greater than the maximum height
   of the desired convex lateral deformation: 10% of the height is added at the top and
   bottom to form "contact spots" of the virtual rod with the surface. Such a "rod" is
   used to perform machine measurement of the sagging deflection along the entire
   circumference of the cylindrical part. After passing the entire circle, the staff is
   displaced upwards by 0.1 meters and a new measurement along the circumference.
   These actions are performed until the rod reaches the top of the cylindrical part.
   Robust sample statistics are used to correctly process sample data and eliminate
   statistic noise during evaluating the sagging deflection.

```
#Cycle for shifting the analysis ring in 0.1 meter
increments
for(h in seq(from = h_Obechaika+Hmax_Base, to =
(h_Obechaika+L_Obechaika-(Hmax_Gofra+Hmax_Base)), by =
0.01))
{
#A ring is cut from the wall with a height Hmax_Base +
Hmax_Gofra + Hmax_Base
  Ring <-Obechaika[Obechaika$X3>=(h-Hmax_Base) &
Obechaika$X3<(h+Hmax_Gofra+Hmax_Base),]
#3 rings are cut out of it - the upper and lower support
rings and a ring of height Hmax_Gofra(=1.5м), which the
convex lateral deformation is sought
  Ring1 <-Ring[Ring$X3<h,]
  Ring2 <-Ring[Ring$X3>=h & Ring$X3<=(h+Hmax_Gofra),]
  Ring3 <-Ring[Ring$X3>(h+Hmax_Gofra),]
#Alternately, vertically elongated "spots" of points at
Arc_Degree degrees are cut from 3 rings to calculate
robust estimates of the sagging deflection in the "spot"
from the middle ring
  for (j in seq(from = -180, to = 180-Arc_Degree, by =
Arc_Degree))
    {
    sprintf("h = %f and j = %f", h,j)
    Spot1 <-Ring1[Ring1$alpha>=j & Ring1$alpha<(j+1),]
    Spot2 <-Ring2[Ring2$alpha>=j & Ring2$alpha<(j+1),]
    Spot3 <-Ring3[Ring3$alpha>=j & Ring3$alpha<(j+1),]
#The average of polar radius and of point heights from
the bottom support ring are determined. Lower anchor
point is obtained.
    R_Low  <- mean(Spot1$R)
    X3_Low <- mean(Spot1$X3)
#Upper anchor point
    R_High <- mean(Spot3$R)
    X3_High<- mean(Spot3$X3)
#The distance h from each point of the middle ring to the
line passing through the anchor points is calculated.
Moreover, this distance is with a sign: "+" means
convexity relative to the reference points, and "-" -
concavity
    X2X1 = X3_High-X3_Low
    Y2Y1 = R_High-R_Low
    SquareRoot =sqrt(X2X1*X2X1+Y2Y1*Y2Y1)
    Spot2$h <-(X2X1*(Spot2$R-R_Low)-Y2Y1*(Spot2$X3-
X3_Low))/SquareRoot
    minh <-0
```

```
    maxh <-0
#If in the middle of the "spot" the sagging deflection is
greater than the threshold value, then we determine the
boundaries of the convex lateral deformation vertically
    strela <- median(Spot2$h[Spot2$X3>(h+0.45*Hmax_Gofra)
& Spot2$X3<(h+0.55*Hmax_Gofra)])
    if(strela>=Depth_Gofra)
    {
        maxh <-max(Spot2$X3[ Spot2$h>NoSignDepth ])
        minh <-min(Spot2$X3[ Spot2$h>NoSignDepth ])
    }
#Determination of the maximum value from measurements -
this is the sagging deflection
    h_vct       <-c(h_vct,h+0.5*Hmax_Gofra)
    degree_vct <-c(degree_vct,j)
    strela_vct <-c(strela_vct,strela)
    minh_vct    <-c(minh_vct, minh)
    maxh_vct    <-c(maxh_vct, maxh)
  }
}
```

7. Assembling the sagging deflection map
   The table collects data of the sagging deflection value at points on a cylindrical surface, characterized by the height and rotate degree. Sagging deflection map is a graphical display of the table, which is shown in Fig. 8.

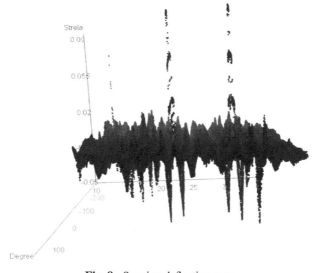

Fig. 8. Sagging deflection map

8. Search for large sagging defection

Points of the surface where sagging defection exceeds the threshold value are selected - the minimum sagging defection. The result is shown in Fig. 9.

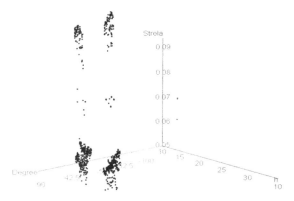

Fig. 9. Large sagging defection

9. Clustering and finding local maxima of the sagging defection
    Clusters of spatially close points should be distinguished among the multitude of surface points with high sagging deflection values. These are the required deformations - convex lateral deformations. The problem is solved by the well-known data clustering algorithm DBSCAN [19, 20] (Fig. 10).

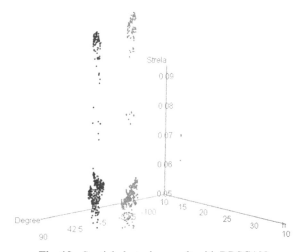

Fig. 10. Spatial clustering result with DBSCAN

10. Determination of the number of clusters-convex lateral deformations
11. Estimation of the dimensions of the found convex lateral deformations
     For each clusters-convex lateral deformation, sequentially calculate its length:

- horizontally - that is, the boundaries of the arc on which it is located;
- vertical - values of heights at which the convexity begins and ends,

as well as the maximum value of the sagging deflection and the coordinates of the corresponding point of the body in the polar coordinate system, which are considered the center of the convexity.
12. Formation of a summary table of found convex lateral deformations
   As a result, we obtain a table of the found local convex lateral deformations.

4   Results

To assess the efficiency of the data processing pipeline, the data of the experimental scan were loaded - the coordinates of 1,700,805 points of the inner surface of the coke drum which has been in operation for over 20 years at the petrochemical enterprise of PJSC NK Rosneft. Then the coordinates of a small subset of surface points were adjusted to form two seeded convex lateral deformations (Fig. 11):

- at a height of 20.35 m with a horizontal length of 70–100°, a vertical length of 0.5 m and a maximum sagging deflection of 0.09 m in the central part between 80 and 90°;
- at a height of 25.35 m with a horizontal length of 75–95°, a vertical length of 0.5 m and a maximum sagging deflection of 0.09 m in the central part between 80 and 90°.

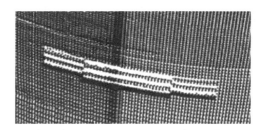

Fig. 11. Image of an artificially formed convex lateral deformation

The processing of the data by the data processing pipeline ended with the output of the results in the following form (Fig. 12).

No	h	degree	strela	min_h	max_h	min_degree	max_degree
1	13.347	-138	0.07022848	13.27660	13.33016	-139	-137
2	20.357	85	0.09129884	20.10288	20.75722	70	99
3	25.327	82	0.09278563	25.11002	25.72301	75	94

Fig. 12. Screenshot of the pivot table of the found convex lateral deformations

It indicates the height from the bottom of the cylindrical part of the body (in meters) and the polar angle, characterizing the position of the center of the convex lateral deformation, as well as the estimate of the sagging deflection. The final 4 columns of show the boundaries of the found convex lateral deformation vertically (in meters) and horizontally (range of arc degrees).

5   Discussion

According to Table 1 three deformations detected by the data processing pipeline was the test result. The first detected "deformation" with a depth of 7 cm is the hole of the process fitting located at a height of 13 m from the coke drum base plate. The small size of this "depression" (no more than 5 cm in diameter) did not prevent its detection. This positively characterizes the sensitivity of the data processing pipeline to local convex deformations. The higher the sensitivity of the method, the more accurately the sagging deflection of the convex lateral deformations is estimated. The resolution of the method is due to the density of the sagging deflection and the method of their calculation itself. A rigorous analytical assessment of this ability is impossible due to the use of methods of statistical data processing, but expertly it can be estimated at the level of 3 cm^2. If it necessary, this parameter can be improved by reconfiguring the method to smaller search resolution steps and a larger amount of calculations.

The other two are seeded defects for convex lateral deformations test. Their key characteristics were determined with a very high accuracy: the estimates of the sagging deflection were 0.0913 and 0.0928.

The absolute deviation of 0.0013 and 0.0028 m from 0.09 is understandable: these convex lateral deformations with a length of 0.5 m were measured vertically with control rods, the distance between the reference points of which is 1 m. "Deepening in the depression" effect arose and as a result - a somewhat large estimate of the sagging deflection, which cannot be considered erroneously overestimated - rather, the initial estimate of the sagging deflection of the convex lateral deformation during its artificial creation was imprecise. High accuracy of estimates of the sagging deflection boom is critically important in assessing the residual service life according to the methodology [1–3].

The absolute deviation of the estimates of the convex lateral deformation center along the vertical is up to 0.023 m. This accuracy is more than enough to determine the location of the convex lateral deformation.

Additional parameters of the convex lateral deformations were estimated with acceptable accuracy:

- absolute deviation of the assessment of the vertical length - up to 16 cm;
- absolute deviation of the assessment of the horizontal extent - up to 1 degree (about 4 cm).

At the same time, synthetic tests cannot replace the experience of using a new method of data processing pipeline in real examination of coke drum, especially those that have worked for more than 20 years and are subject to deformations. We also point out that a number of operations, in particular clustering, require further refinement of the parameters. In this sense, the data processing pipeline will have a rather long period of apprenticeship before it becomes a flawlessly working "at the touch of a button" tool for finding convex lateral deformations.

6   Conclusion

According to the authors, there is currently no opportunity in open sources to get acquainted in detail with the methods of 3D scanning data processing pipeline and analyzing deformations. We tried to satisfy this need by providing a complete description of the data processing process and code snippets. The systemic use of robust statistics in calculations makes the data processing pipeline insensitive to statistical noise of direct measurements and computational heuristics introduced in order to simplify and reduce the volume of computational operations with a large set of points. The presented synthetic tests indicate the acceptable sensitivity and accuracy of the presented method.

References

1. Martynov, N.V., Samokhin, Y.N., Serebryanny, V.B., Foliyants, A.E.: Extension of the service life of ultrasonic testing reactors with local deformations in the form of convex lateral deformations. In: Reliability of Equipment, Production and Automated Systems in the Chemical Industries. Abstracts of the 1st All-Union Scientific and Technical Conference, NHP-1-87, pp. 144–115 (1987)
2. Mukhin, V.N., Samokhin, Y.N., Stepanchikova, G.V., Kotov, N.V.: Estimation of the limiting size of the sagging deflection of the convex lateral deformation on the bimetallic coke drum of the delayed coking unit based on deformation criteria of destruction. NTIS "Oil refining and petrochemistry" **10**, 35–38 (1966)
3. Samokhin, Y.N., Mukhin, V.N., Serebryanny, V.B., Vatnik, L.E.: Increasing the residual service life of coke drum. Chem. Technol. Fuels Oils 5, 19–21 (1986)
4. The coke drum banana effect syndrome. https://coking.com/the-coke-drum-banana-effect-syndrome
5. Gonzalez, J., Gomez, S., Gomez, G.: Analysis of the mechanical behavior of a delayed coker drum with a circumferentially cracked skirt (2017). https://www.researchgate.net/publication/316945296_Analysis_of_the_mechanical_behavior_of_a_delayed_coker_drum_with_a_circumferentially_cracked_skirt
6. Li, Z.L., Wang, H.H., Liu, W., Jin-Shui, Z., Zhang, G.Q.: Finite element simulation, safety assessment and countermeasure of the coke drum leaning process during the quenching stage. Atlantis Press (2017). https://www.atlantis-press.com/article/25872326.pdf
7. Valenca, P.H.A., Waturuocha, A., Wisecarver, K.: 2D axisymmetric temperature profile modeling of a delayed coking drum during pre-run warm up. Russell School of Chemical Engineering, University of Tulsa, Tulsa, OK, USA. https://www.comsol.it/paper/download/258311/amorim_paper.pdf
8. Optimal Design of Coke Drum Skirt Slots and Analysis of Alternative Skirt Support Structures for Thermal-Mechanical Cyclic Loading. University of Alberta, Edward Lee Wang, 2017. https://era.library.ualberta.ca/items/eaf1387f-68b8-453e-9711-52e300a0e300/view/2eaf74c1-7f96-4e93-9f8a-585ca38abb0d/Wang_Edward_L_201705_MSc.pdf

9. S. Parkhe, A.K.: Design and analysis of pressure vessel subjected to pressure-temperature variation. IJE Trans. A Basics **31**(1), 58–64 (2018). http://www.ije.ir/article_73092_975cca1 3c1fd19ec15da05aca974bc0a.pdf

10. Automated batch control of delayed Coker/Richard Lucas, Whiting, IN (US), Patent No.: US 10,696,902 B2, Date of Patent, 30 June 2020. https://patentimages.storage.googleapis.com/ f6/8f/21/1c2e08d5be3ad9/US10696902.pdf

11. Abishek Mukund, H.: Systems and methods for optimizing refinery Coker process. TX (US); Matthew Stephens, Houston, TX (US); Nadav Cohen, Yavne (IL), Pub. No.: US 2020/0311547 A1, 1 October 2020. https://patentimages.storage.googleapis.com/39/dd/d9/ 212d4f42290877/US20200311547A1.pdf

12. Clark, R.D. Rutt, D.K.: Coke drum life improvement – a combined approach. Prepared for presentation at the AIChE 2002 Spring National Meeting, 10–14 March 2002, New Orleans, Louisiana, Advances in Coking Session (2002). http://www.cia-inspection.com/resources/ wp-content/uploads/2010/09/aiche2002.pdf

13. Soare, M., Minea, I-S., Predoi, M.V., Bunescu, C., Diba, C.: Fatigue damage assessment of coke drums based on temperature monitoring., Nuclear NDT Res. Serv. SRL, Bucharest, Romania, August 2019. https://nuclearndt.ro/wp-content/uploads/2019/10/HP-August-2019- Nuclear-NDT-Article.pdf

14. ZhiYuan, M.C., Selere, N., Seng, L.C.: Equipment failure analysis for oil and gas industry with an ensemble predictive. https://arxiv.org/ftp/arxiv/papers/2012/2012.15030.pdf

15. Samman, M., Tinoco, E.B., Marangone, F.C.: Comparison of stress and strain analysis techniques for assessment of bulges in coke drums. In: Proceedings of the ASME 2014 Pressure Vessels & Piping Conference PVP2014-28139, 20–24 July 2014, Anaheim, California,USA. https://citeseerx.ist.psu.edu/viewdoc/download?doi=10.1.1.654.4083&rep=rep1&type=pdf.

16. Bazzi, M., Grimaldo, G., Peacock, M., Sjerve, E.: Coke drum laser profiling (2013). https://www.semanticscholar.org/paper/Coke-Drum-Laser-Profiling-Bazzi-Gri maldo/a81466a3ca8136897d667a7d56845463f98b62b7#related-papers

17. Haraguchi, M.I., Samman, M, Tinoco, EB, Marangone, F.D.: Coke drums inspection and evaluation using stress and strain analysis techniques. In: Conference: Rio Oil & Gas Expo and Conference 2012, Rio de Janeiro, Brazil (2021). https://www.researchgate.net/pub lication/281843212_COKE_DRUMS_INSPECTION_AND_EVALUATION_USING_S TRESS_AND_STRAIN_ANALYSIS_TECHNIQUES

18. Ruparel S., Bansode S.: Fitness for service evaluation of bulging in delayed coke drums. https://ru.scribd.com/document/169481729/ME-47

19. Ester, M., Kriegel, H.-P., Sander, J., Xu, X.: A density-based algorithm for discovering clusters in large spatial databases with noise. In: Simoudis, E., Han, J., Fayyad, U.M.: Proceedings of the Second International Conference on Knowledge Discovery and Data Mining (KDD-96), pp. 226–231. AAAI Press (1996). ISBN 1-57735-004-9

20. Ricardo, J.G.B., Campello, D., Moulavi, A., Zimek, J.S.: Hierarchical density estimates for data clustering, visualization, and outlier detection. ACM Trans. Knowl. Discovery Data (2015). T. 10, rel. 1. ISSN 1556-4681. https://doi.org/10.1145/2733381

Using Virtual Reality Systems for Crime Scene Reconstruction

Igor Trushchenkov[1], Vladimir Bulgakov[1(✉)], Kirill Yarmak[1], Elena Bulgakova[2], and Irina Trushchenkova[1]

[1] Moscow University of the Ministry of Internal Affairs of the Russian Federation named after V.Y. Kikot, 12 Academician Volgin Street, Moscow 117437, Russia
[2] Kutafin Moscow State Law University (MSAL), 9 Sadovaya-Kudrinskaya Street, Moscow 125993, Russia

Abstract. Scientific and technological progress has a great impact on modern society, including one of the social institutions - law enforcement agencies. The most important task is the introduction of new computer technologies into the training system of law enforcement officers. This process is associated with effective work in conditions as close as possible to professional activity. Mastering such important complex competencies as the ability to conduct an investigation of the scene of an incident is a rather difficult task, the solution of which is possible only by modeling typical situations of investigating various crimes in a complex multi-object environment. In order to simulate the situation of real places of incidents on the basis of available virtual reality devices, the authors have developed a system of virtual training grounds intended for training law enforcement officers.

Keywords: Virtual reality systems · Forensic simulator · Crime detection and investigation · Virtual training ground

1 Introduction

Forensic experts are trained in how to properly use forensic tools, for example, to identify and fix fingerprints. However, it is difficult to teach on-site tactics - how to inspect crime scenes and see the full picture. This is because to the fact, that almost all places of the incidents are different. Why was this man killed? What tool was used to do this? Who is the killer? Police officers must answer these and other questions and the answers will always vary.

Understanding what happened, based on the analysis of different scenarios, objects and traces - is the main task of the police officer's training system [7, 9, 10]. Historically, forensic training grounds are used in police educational organizations – simulated places of various incidents such as murders, thefts, robberies and others. However, it is technically impossible to create training grounds for huge places - for example, a large house, or, moreover, a residential area, a highway or a railroad.

A. G. Kravets et al. (Eds.): CIT&DS 2021, CCIS 1448, pp. 325–335, 2021.
https://doi.org/10.1007/978-3-030-87034-8_24

Thus, it is impossible to teach forensic tactics at training grounds about all the different situations that occur in real life. But in solving this problem, simulated training grounds in virtual reality can help [1]. In addition, such technologies create the possibilities of restoring the places of resonant crimes - unsolved murders, terrorist acts or disasters. From photographs or video recordings, it is possible to recreate such places in VR, so that investigators can analyze them again and again at any time, until the crime will be solved.

2   Background

Virtual reality, in our opinion, is a virtual world created by hardware and software components, which can be felt by the organs of human perception, using such senses as touch, sight and hearing. The perception of objects in the virtual world is sensually close to the perception of similar objects in the material reality.

The user's movement in the virtual world and his interaction with three-dimensional objects performed according to the physical laws, implemented by using software algorithms. Of course, it is important, that user should be in convenient conditions to reach the effect of complete immersion.

In addition, the use of VR technologies provides opportunities that were initially unavailable in the real world [14]. For example, virtual reality allows you to analyze the scene from any side and height, instantly move long distances, etc. [2]. This creates the possibilities of obtaining more information about the event under investigation [11].

In educational organizations and police departments in different countries, various simulators in virtual reality have previously been developed [19–23]. Similar developments are also underway in Russia [24]. However, until recently, there was no simulator in our country with the opportunities of modeling of crime scenes for police work with photorealistic quality of visualization and inspecting in VR.

3   Possibilities of the Virtual Reality Forensic Simulator CSI VR

Since 2017, we have been testing mobile virtual reality headsets available on the market in order to create a training system for the law enforcement agencies of the Russian Federation. The solution of the set tasks for three-dimensional modeling of the real scene of the incident is associated with the need to use a complex of technical and software tools, which should include a virtual reality headset, a personal computer, and software.

A virtual reality headset must have the following characteristics:

- the displayed image must have quality of the visualization close to the real world;
- when turning and tilting the head, delays are unacceptable;
- the device must provide the possibility of comfortable use for a long time;
- the system must be equipped with position sensors for tracking user's movements, as well as controllers for interacting with virtual objects.

We studied such characteristics of the devices under consideration as the quality of the displayed image, the duration of the time of comfortable use, the possibility of interacting with objects in the virtual world, and others. The best results were shown by the devices "Oculus Rift S" [6].

At the same time, the possibilities of creating a software environment for modeling virtual spaces of photographic quality were studied. The best results were achieved using the high-performance 3D rendering software Unreal Engine [3]. Using this system and its programming environment – Blueprints - the CSI VR virtual reality forensic simulator was created (Fig. 1).

Fig. 1. The interface of the forensic simulator in virtual reality "CSI VR".

The developed software environment includes two main components: the Constructor and the Virtual Learning System. The Constructor allows to create three-dimensional areas (Fig. 2–3). The size of the simulated territories is limited only by the power of the computer used.

Fig. 2. 3D area constructor interface.

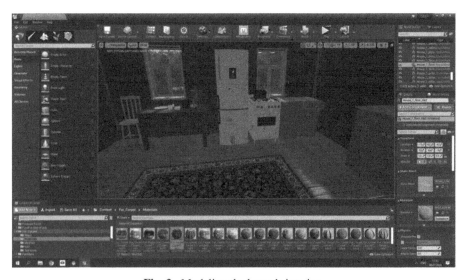

Fig. 3. Modeling the house's interior.

Currently, the system has ready to use six test virtual areas:

– virtual forensic laboratory (Fig. 4),
– the road traffic accident scene,
– the accident on the railway scene (Fig. 4),
– the plane crash scene (Fig. 7),
– death as a result of a fall from a height scene (Fig. 6),
– the murder scene (Fig. 5).

Fig. 4. "Virtual Forensic Lab". In this area, the trainee can explore different types of forensic objects and traces, as well as special tools used by forensic experts.

Fig. 5. The murder scene. This zone contains the setting of the scene of the murder by an unknown person in a private house on the outskirts of the city. Based on the objects and traces left here, the trainees need to recreate an approximate portrait of the criminal and a picture of what happened.

All resources of the virtual areas can be changed by the user, and there is no restriction on the creation new ones. For this purpose, the Constructor includes a large library of three-dimensional models and textures - vehicles, elements of houses, household and computer equipment, kitchen utensils, office supplies, lighting devices, clothes, etc. The

Fig. 6. The accident on the railway scene. This zone is an area of 1.5 km², where was found a man who was hit by a train. According to the plot of the case, the driver of another train saw a body on the rails, stopped in front of him and called the police. Students need to inspect the site of the incident and offer their version of what happened.

library also contains a section of forensic objects - models of police tools and equipment, corpses with various injuries, damaged vehicles, various types of weapons, fingerprints and shoe soles, drops, stains and smears of blood, bullet holes, scratches, dents, etc.

Fig. 7. The plane crash scene. This huge area represents the crash site of the plane in the forest. The investigation of such a scene with a large number of corpses and objects is a complicated task. Students have the opportunity to virtually visit the site of such a disaster.

The Virtual Learning System, which contains a lot of scripts, preprogrammed using the Blue prints environment [4], allows to explore in VR the territory created in the Constructor. It has such capabilities, as:

- moving in virtual space as in the real world;
- interaction with objects (take, inspect, move, etc.) (Fig. 8);
- using of inspection tools (flashlight, laser measure device, digital camera, forensic ruler, etc.) (Fig. 9).

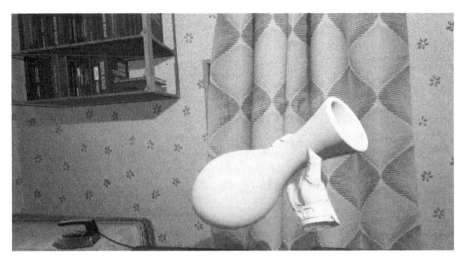

Fig. 8. Interaction with objects.

The capabilities of the Virtual Learning System are not limited only to moving and viewing of the crime scene, but also to analyze objects. A feature is the ability to use a special forensic suitcase, which contains in a set of technical and forensic tools. It allows to document and investigate the situation of the scene with future demonstration of virtual photos or print them. Competencies in the detection (identification) of objects and traces at the crime scene are important during the process of training future criminologists and forensic experts [8].

Finished projects have photorealistic rendering quality and allow to convey even the smallest details of real furnishings, objects and traces.

At the same time, the image observed by the user is shown on an interactive white-board to other students, which allows for group lessons [5]. The sound is also transmitted to external speakers and is available for an audience.

This virtual learning system can be integrated into the electronic information and educational environment of an educational organization and fully complies with the requirements for the formation of professional competencies of the modern educational standard of the Ministry of Science and Higher Education of the Russian Federation. The modern Standard states that during the training process, it is allowed to replace equipment with its virtual counterparts [18].

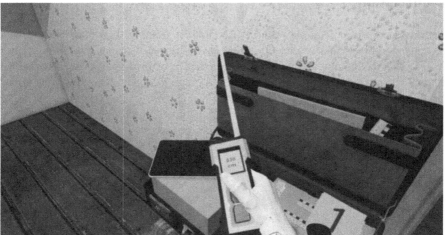

Fig. 9. Virtual set of technical and forensic tools – "Forensic Suitcase".

4 Implementation and Results

Over the three years since the beginning of the development of the Simulator, we have tested more than 300 cadets - future forensic experts of the police of the Russian Federation.

The developed system has shown significant results of use in the learning process:

– Due to the fact that the virtual world is perceived by the senses close to reality, the cadets memorized the material taught much better. Studying a large accident site with a huge number of objects teaches you to better understand, think, analyze the fullpicture of traces in its relationship and draw the right conclusions.

– Thanks to the possibilities provided by the simulator, the trainees were able to virtually "visit" the accident sites, which cannot be created at a training grounds, but they are encountered in real life (for example, at the scene of a train accident). The experience gained will be important for their future police work.
– The system is perceived not as a duty to learn something, but as a game. It should be noted that the cadets themselves speak only positively about the proposed organization of training. In their words, "it is interesting to study in such a way."

As an experiment, we recreated the place of a real murder from photographs that took place thirty years ago. Having studied this place in virtual reality, the students were able to correctly indicate the places where the criminals left traces, reached conclusions about what happened and compose verbal portraits of the suspects that are very close to real ones. This indicates the possibilities of using the simulator in old and resonant crimes investigation.

5 Conclusion

The considered virtual complex can be used both in training future law enforcement officers and in practical activities during the investigation of crimes by existing police officers. This technology can be used in the practice of investigative and operational departments, inquiry departments, forensic and training centers, other divisions of law enforcement agencies.

Using of the CSI VR simulator in the training process will improve the quality of training police officers for practical activities, crime detection and investigation. Also, training in virtual reality could be effectively in distant learning during the Covid-19 pandemic.

References

1. Truschenkov, I.V.: Three-dimensional modeling of the scene of the incident using virtual reality systems. Actual problems of legal theory and practice, collection of scientific articles, p. 135. Border, M. (2020)
2. Truschenkov, I.V.: Possibilities of using modern high-resolution technical devices for fixing and demonstrating the situation of a crime scene. Theory and practice of forensic examination: international experience, problems, prospects. Collection of scientific papers of the II International Forum, p. 347. M. (2019)
3. The official website of the Unreal Engine. http://unrealengine.com/
4. Documentation of the Unreal Engine. https://docs.unrealengine.com/en-US/index.html
5. Bulgakov, V., Trushchenkov, I., Bulgakova, E.: Spherical panoramic photo shooting and virtual reality demonstration of a crime scene. In: Kravets, A.G., Groumpos, P.P., Shcherbakov, M., Kultsova, M. (eds.) CIT&DS 2019. CCIS, vol. 1084, pp. 217–225. Springer, Cham (2019). https://doi.org/10.1007/978-3-030-29750-3_17
6. The official website of Oculus VR. LLC. http://oculus.com
7. Grant, H.: Social Crime Prevention in the Developing World. Exploring the Role of Police in Crime Prevention, vol. VI, 51 p. Springer, Heidelberg (2015). https://doi.org/10.1007/978-3-319-13027-9

8. Jahankhani, H. (ed.): Cyber Criminology. ASTSA, Springer, Cham (2018). https://doi.org/10.1007/978-3-319-97181-0
9. Savona, E.U.: Crime and Technology. New Frontiers for Regulation, Law Enforcement and Research. Springer, Netherlands, vol. XIV, 142 p. (2004). https://doi.org/10.1007/978-1-4020-2924-0
10. Leclerc, B., Savona, E.U. (eds.): Crime Prevention in the 21st Century. Springer, Cham (2017). https://doi.org/10.1007/978-3-319-27793-6
11. Jacobs, C.: Interactive Panoramas. Techniques for Digital Panoramic Photography, vol. XIII, 248 p. Springer, Heidelberg (2004). https://doi.org/10.1007/978-3-642-18665-3
12. The Criminal Code of the Russian Federation of June 7, 1996, No. 63-FZ. https://fzrf.su/kod eks/uk/. Accessed 7 July 2018. Accessed 27 June 2018
13. Federal Law "On Police" of 07.02.2011 N 3-FZ (Ed. 12/19/2016). Article 11
14. Jung, T., tom Dieck, M.C. (eds.): Augmented Reality and Virtual Reality. PI, Springer, Cham (2018). https://doi.org/10.1007/978-3-319-64027-3
15. Mihelj, M., Novak, D., Beguš, S.: Virtual Reality Technology and Applications, vol. X, 231 p. Springer, Netherlands (2014). https://doi.org/10.1007/978-94-007-6910-6
16. Bishop, C.: Pattern Recognition and Machine Learning. Springer, New York, vol. XX, 738 p. (2006)
17. Deng, Z., Neumann, U.: Data-Driven 3D Facial Animation, vol. VIII, 296 p. Springer, London (2008). https://doi.org/10.1007/978-1-84628-907-1
18. Federal State Standard of Higher Education in the direction of training 40.03.01 Jurisprudence. Registered in the Ministry of Justice of Russia on September 7, 2020 No. 59673, paragraph 4.3.1
19. Cho, J., Jung, T., Macleod, K., Swenson, A.: Using virtual reality as a form of simulation in the context of legal education. In: tom Dieck, M.C., Jung, T.H., Loureiro, S.M.C. (eds.) Augmented Reality and Virtual Reality. PI, pp. 141–154. Springer, Cham (2021). https://doi.org/10.1007/978-3-030-68086-2_11
20. Edifor, E., Swenson, A., Aiyenitaju, O.: A virtual reality framework for upskilling in computer programming in the business context. In: tom Dieck, M.C., Jung, T.H., Loureiro, S.M.C. (eds.) Augmented Reality and Virtual Reality. PI, pp. 181–192. Springer, Cham (2021). https://doi.org/10.1007/978-3-030-68086-2_14
21. Lee, C., Fang, Y., Huang, Y., Lee, S., Chen-Chung Yeh, W.: Application of wearable devices in crime scene investigation and virtual reality. In: 2019 IEEE Symposium Series on Computational Intelligence (SSCI), pp. 206–210 (2019). https://doi.org/10.1109/SSCI44817.2019.9002700
22. Kim, H.-S., Kim, H.-J., Lee, Y.-S., Lee, J.: Criminal profiling simulation training and assessment system based on virtual reality. J. Korea Comput. Graph. Soc. 24(3), 83–92 (2018). 1975–7883(pISSN)/2383–529X(eISSN)
23. Mayne, R., Green, H.: Virtual reality for teaching and learning in crime scene investigation. Sci. Justice 60(5), 466–472 (2020). https://doi.org/10.1016/j.scijus.2020.07.006. Epub 2020 Jul 29 PMID: 32873386
24. The Academy hosted testing of the "Chameleon" virtual reality system. The official website of the Nizhny Novgorod academy of the Ministry of internal affairs of Russia. https://xn--80az.xn--b1aew.xn--p1ai/Press-sluzhba/Novosti/item/14343047/

Cyber-Physical Systems and Big Data-Driven World. Intelligent Technologies in Urban Design and Computing

Collection and Consolidation of Big Data for Proactive Monitoring of Critical Events at Infrastructure Facilities in an Urban Environment

Anton Finogeev[1]([✉]) [iD], Danila Parygin[2] [iD], Sergey Schevchenko[3] [iD],
Alexey Finogeev[1] [iD], and Danish Ather[4]

[1] Penza State University, Krasnaya Str. 40, 440026 Penza, Russia
[2] Volgograd State Technical University, Lenina Ave. 28, 400005 Volgograd, Russia
[3] National Technical University «Kharkiv Polytechnic Institute», 2,
Kyrpychova str., Kharkiv, Ukraine
[4] Sharda University, Plot No. 32-34, APJ Abdul Kalam Road, Knowledge Park III, Greater
Noida, Uttar Pradesh 201310, India

Abstract. The article proposes and investigates the concept of proactive monitoring of critical events at the distributed objects of engineering communications of the city and in the urban road environment. The purpose of monitoring is to determine, assess and predict the dynamics of the risks of critical events, depending on changes in indicators and factors correlating with them. The main characteristics of distributed monitoring objects, the classification and analysis of critical events, the reasons for their occurrence and possible influencing factors are given. For predictive analysis and assessment of risks of critical events, collection, consolidation and analysis of big sensor and social data is carried out, reflecting the dynamics of changes in the indicators of monitored objects and external factors of influence. Big data includes indicators of monitored objects, information about events and possible causes of their occurrence, factors influencing the risks of their development. Cyber-physical (sensor) data is unloaded from spatially distributed photo and video recording complexes, video surveillance cameras, weather stations, measuring instruments and sensors of objects and pipelines of engineering networks. Cyber-social (social) data is collected from open sources of information on the Internet and mobile communications of the civilian population. The monitoring system is using a multi-agent approach, which involves the use of software agents directly on distributed data collection sources and robots for collecting data from open sources on the Internet, brokers for consolidation and protection of transmitted data, a component of a distributed information warehouse.

Keywords: Proactive monitoring · Critical events · Big sensor data · Multi-agent approach · Data mining · Predictive analysis · Risks · Monitoring system

1 Introduction

Monitoring and control of the state of geographically distributed objects in the modern urban environment refers to the tasks of managing complex systems. An increase in

© Springer Nature Switzerland AG 2021
A. G. Kravets et al. (Eds.): CIT&DS 2021, CCIS 1448, pp. 339–353, 2021.
https://doi.org/10.1007/978-3-030-87034-8_25

the complexity of any systems is accompanied by the growth and complication of their structure, an increase in the number of controlled parameters, an increase in control and monitoring procedures, which leads to an increase in the number of reporting levels and a complication of the hierarchy of controlling bodies. The process of transition to information and analytical decision support systems for ensuring the quality and safety of life of the population is being implemented within the framework of digital transformation and the transition to an intelligent urban environment in the concept of Smart & Save City [1, 2]. The concept of Smart & Save City is based on the integrated use of digital and telecommunication technologies for the management of infrastructural objects and processes in the life support course and safe life of the urban population [3].

As a basic management technology in the infrastructure of a "smart" city, it is advisable to use the model of decentralized proactive management [4]. The model is implemented using intelligent analytical components for assessing and analyzing the risks of disruption to life safety, depending on the spatial location of infrastructural objects, anthropogenic specifics of management processes, technical difficulties in collecting heterogeneous data, numerous participants and eyewitnesses of events [5]. Intelligent components are being implemented in all areas of city management, including the municipal management system, the system for ensuring the safety and warning of the population, the health care system and medical services, the road safety system, the system for generating and distributing energy resources, and in the housing sector and public utilities, etc. [6].

2 Background

Within the framework of the proactive management model, the functions of monitoring critical events, coordination, planning and regulation of the processes of safe human life are implemented. The essence of proactive management is reduced to the use of predictive analytics tools for the selection or synthesis of preventive measures to prevent or minimize risks and/or trends in the dynamics of their development [7]. The goal is to predict the risks of negative events by means of intelligent and predictive analysis of situations, as well as to identify the causes of their occurrence and influencing factors in order to promptly respond to emergency and emergency situations, restore the health and functionality of life support systems of the population. In proactive systems, a person is assigned the function of a dispatcher, since the functions of collecting, analyzing data and controlling are implemented by software and hardware systems [8]. The basic principle is to implement event-driven processes to handle critical events according to a "detect-forecast-decide-act" scheme.

The transition to proactive technologies means the introduction of digital control systems using cyber-physical and cyber-social systems for distributed data collection and analysis. Sensory and measuring devices connected by sensor networks to the Internet of Things act as cyber-physical components [9]. Cyber-social components are software tools for collecting data in open sources of the Internet, monitoring social networks, chats, blogs, forums and messengers in order to track the facts of critical events and social reactions of the population to them and the actions of the relevant structures and authorities.

With the growth of the population and urban infrastructure facilities, the number of critical events, accidents and emergency situations grows. The realization of the risks of such events often leads to serious consequences associated with material damage, damage to health and death of people. For example, with an increase in the length of roads, the complication of road infrastructure, an increase in the number of vehicles, the likelihood of road accidents increases [10]. The implementation of proactive traffic light control technologies based on retro-perspective traffic data in order to reduce the number of road accidents is given in [11]. A proactive traffic control system is used to solve traffic congestion problems based on predicting traffic incidents [5].

Critical events can be prevented using predictive risk analysis of their occurrence and development. To do this, it is necessary to have prompt and most complete information about the current state of the facilities of engineering networks and the processes occurring in them and the environment, as well as about the possible causes of critical events. However, most of the events refer to uncertain and difficult to predict incidents, and their analysis also requires an investigation of the factors influencing them. A predictive analysis toolkit is necessary for early detection of such combinations of values of parameters of observed objects and processes in combination with combinations of values of influencing factors that lead to critical events (incidents, incidents, failures, failures, accidents, emergency situations, etc.) [12]. Factors are determined by a set of variables, which are mostly discrete. The main problem in the analysis of data on events and factors is their heterogeneous nature [13]. Researchers can use data segmentation to reduce heterogeneity using expert technologies without guaranteeing optimal division into homogeneous groups of events [14]. For such segmentation, it is better to use cluster analysis methods.

It is advisable to use cluster analysis as one of the preliminary tasks along with classification. For example, the authors of [15] used clustering to categorize road crashes, and then analyzed the results using a negative binom to assess an influencing factor such as the age of the driver. In [16], clustering was chosen as the first stage of grouping data into segments in order to find the relationship between the characteristics of an accident using the Probit model. Poisson models [17] and negative binomial negative binomial (NB) models [18] are used to find the relationship between incidents and causal factors.

Traditional methods of regression analysis (linear regression, binomial regression and Poisson regression) are mainly used when the relationship between accidents and influencing factors is fairly obvious. The limitations of these methods are large errors in the presence of hidden patterns and relationships between events and factors, especially when working with big heterogeneous data [19]. Problems arise when the number of parameters of the observed objects and possible influencing factors grows exponentially; therefore, the dimension of the phase space should be reduced by selecting only sensitive variables. Erroneous results also appear when there are assumptions and predefined relationships between the dependent and independent variables in the regression model [20]. Poisson models can give better results than linear regression models when handling non-negative, random, and discrete characteristics.

For the intellectual analysis of large heterogeneous data on critical events that have both physical (sensor data from devices and sensors) and social nature (eyewitness data), it is necessary to use simultaneously several methods of data mining [21, 22], such as classification, clustering, regression, benchmarking, decision trees, etc.

In [23], the analysis of data on two-lane rural highways in Granada, Spain was carried out using the decision rule from the decision tree method. The paper [24] presents the results of the analysis of incident data in Slovenia using the classification algorithm and regression tree (CART). Similar trees are considered in article [25] for the analysis of incident records received from the Iranian traffic police, which also uses the cluster analysis technique based on the K-means algorithm and the Apriori association rules algorithm. Clustering is used at the first stage to group data into homogeneous segments, and an algorithm for generating association rules is implemented for clusters.

In scientific research, many clustering algorithms are used [26, 27]. When analyzing critical events, the method of hierarchical clustering, the method of K-means, and the method of hidden classes (LCC) [28] can be used, which provides several criteria for choosing a cluster, but can have high computational complexity. For the purposes of this study, a combination of this method and a modified version of the K means method, which is called the K mode method [29], is best suited. This is due to the fact that the K-mode method is better suited for clustering large heterogeneous data with many attributes, but because of this, there is a problem of determining the number of clusters, which is solved using the cluster selection criteria in the LCC method.

3   Causes of Critical Events at Distributed Urban Infrastructure Objects

Distributed infrastructure objects of the urban environment include elements of an interconnected space that solve common problems of ensuring the life of the population, and additional components to support their functioning. A distributed system is one for which the relation of the location of its elements is essential from the point of view of its functionality.

In distributed systems of different types, both similar and unique critical events can occur. With different types of events and belonging to different classes, the reasons for the development and occurrence of emergency situations and the factors influencing them can be common. For example, power line breaks and traffic accidents were caused by weather conditions, namely icing due to freezing rain or sleet. In addition, events in one system can cause the occurrence or a factor influencing the performance of another, since most of them are interrelated and interdependent to varying degrees.

For all classes of distributed infrastructure objects, events can be classified into three large groups:

1. Events caused by anthropogenic causes and factors of influence. Most often, they arise in the process of erroneous human actions during the operation of the system and are the most difficult to predict, because of their uncertainty, randomness and chaos. An exception is deliberate action to cause damage to objects.
2. Events caused by natural causes and factors of influence. These events are mainly caused by geological, meteorological phenomena, the actions of animals or birds,

etc. The reasons and factors here are better predictable, since it is possible to continuously monitor most of the possible influencing factors (temperature, pressure, humidity, wind speed, precipitation level, etc.), with the exception of difficult-to-predict phenomena (earthquakes, tornadoes, landslides, etc.), etc.

3. Events caused by man-made causes and factors of influence. These include equipment failures and malfunctions, breakdowns, accidents, wear and tear, etc. This class of factors is the most easily predictable, especially with constant monitoring of equipment operation and periodic preventive examination of its condition.

Based on this classification, it is possible to conditionally divide the factors of the occurrence of critical events into poorly, medium- and well-predicted for a more accurate analysis at the stage of predictive assessment of their impact on the occurrence and development of critical events at distributed objects.

It is possible to divide the influencing factors according to the class of the main sources of data collection for their analysis and forecasting in three directions: a) data sources for the analysis of anthropogenic causes and factors are mainly Internet Web sites, social networks, instant messengers, b) data sources for analysis natural factors are mainly equipment and applications that are not direct components of infrastructure facilities, c) data sources for the analysis of anthropogenic factors are mainly components and devices as part of the infrastructure facilities themselves.

Let's consider the main distributed infrastructure objects and highlight the main critical events, the reasons for their occurrence and the factors influencing their occurrence and development.

1. The road transport infrastructure of the city includes a set of mobile objects (vehicles), static objects of the road environment (a set of communication routes, transport structures and devices that ensure the movement of vehicles).

   Massive critical events in the road infrastructure include road traffic accidents (RTA). They, in turn, are the cause of a large number of other events related to the death of people, injury, material damage, blocking of road traffic, etc. Naturally, these events can occur independently of road accidents, depending on other factors. The main reasons and factors of critical events here include: weather conditions, road and road traffic, vehicle malfunctions, human factor, the quality of the road surface, markings and road signs, their location, traffic light modes, road sections lighting, time of day, repair work and much more [30]. All factors are divided into objective and subjective. Factors of the first type are design parameters and road condition, traffic intensity, road arrangement, correct location of road signs, warning boards, traffic control devices, time of day and year, weather conditions. Subjective factors include the condition of drivers and pedestrians, their violation of traffic rules.

2. Engineering heat supply networks are designed to create comfortable temperature conditions in various kinds of buildings. They include boiler and thermal power plants, pipelines for transportation and distribution of coolant, pipeline fittings, heating devices, instrumentation complexes, control systems, communications and auxiliary facilities.

   Critical events here include accidents in heating networks, especially in the winter season, which lead to the impossibility of living in unheated premises and evacuating the population. Accidents are the consequences of damage to heating mains, boiler and heating equipment [31].

The first reason for damage is the temperature difference, when, when heated, the metal of the pipelines expands and any corrosion defect or microcrack can provoke a breakthrough [32]. As preventive measures, hydraulic tests are used during the inter-heating season, acoustic tomography of networks, control openings of sections with measurement of metal thickness, the use of two-layer pipes with an insulating gasket between them and a wire monitoring system for leaks in places of rupture of the inner pipe.

The second reason is the destruction of highways due to uneven load in different areas during soil mixing, especially during thaws and frosts with sudden temperature changes when groundwater freezes and thaws. As a preventive measure, pipes are laid in covered concrete trays with the installation of a waterproofing coating.

The third reason is the "fatigue" of the metal from which the pipes are made. A preventive measure is compliance with the standard pipeline service life, compliance with the laying technology, overhaul, and industrial safety expertise.

The fourth reason is damage to pipelines during the repair of other underground objects, such as water supply networks, sewerage networks, electrical networks and communication cables, especially when using horizontal drilling rigs and attempting unauthorized tapping.

The fifth reason is destruction from vibration, which is typical when pipelines are located under roads or railways, next to subway tunnels. Vibration causes cracks in concrete trays, waterproofing crumbles, groundwater rises to pipelines, which causes a corrosion process.

The sixth reason is electrochemical corrosion, especially when pipelines are adjacent to power electrical cables. The cable becomes a source of stray currents, which, in combination with ground water, create breakdowns and corrosion centers.

Note that some of the causes of critical events in water supply networks are similar to those considered earlier for heat supply networks [33]. These are hydraulic shocks due to pressure surges in the pipe, deformation of pipelines as a result of temperature fluctuations and mechanical damage, violation of the tightness of joints as a result of poor-quality connections, defects and "fatigue" of pipes, pipeline fittings and accessories.

3. Networks of city lighting are necessary for the safe and comfortable operation of buildings and adjacent territories, lighting of pedestrian zones and highways at night. The main reason for the problems is the insufficient elaboration of the unified concept of the urban lighting system, with the exception of the lighting of motor roads [34]. Independent lighting of architectural objects of the urban environment and the massive introduction of advertising light sources leads to a distortion of the city's appearance. To solve the problem, a developed lighting plan is required for each of the conceptual parts of the urban environment (historical buildings, public and recreational areas, industrial buildings, apartment buildings with storey buildings) with control of such a phenomenon as "light pollution". The essence of the phenomenon lies in the irrational use of artificial light sources, especially advertising sources, which at night completely change the habitat of humans and animals.

4. Gas supply networks include a complex of structures, technical devices and pipelines providing gas supply and distribution between industrial, municipal and household consumers. The system includes: gas distribution stations and gas control points of various types (street, intra-apartment, courtyard, inter-workshop, inter-village), gas networks of the city, consisting of rings of low, medium and high pressure gas pipelines and connecting gas pipelines with automatic gas control installations, subsystems of control, management and operation.

   The causes of critical events on gas pipelines and gas equipment are: internal physical phenomena (non-stationary gas-dynamic processes that determine the dynamics of gas emission into the atmosphere) and external influences that lead to the destruction of a section of a pipeline or a high-pressure vessel [35]. As a result of these events, compression waves are formed due to the expansion in the atmosphere of the gas ejected under pressure, the ignition of gas, equipment and gas pipelines occurs, the formation and scattering of fragments of destroyed areas, equipment, buildings and structures, the thermal effect of fire on the surrounding Wednesday. The main danger is represented by damaging factors for the population, personnel, the environment and the object itself (air blast wave of the explosion, thermal radiation, fire, fragments and fragments).

   The reasons can also be: mechanical damage to external and underground gas pipelines; loss of strength of welded joints and breaks; corrosion damage to gas pipelines; damage to gas pipelines by vehicles and as a result of natural phenomena. The reasons for the failure of gas equipment include: cessation of the supply of energy resources; physical wear, corrosion and erosion, mechanical damage, thermal deformation of equipment and pipelines; staff errors; external influences of a natural and man-made character.

5. Power supply systems are designed to transfer electrical energy from sources to consumers. The system includes power transmission lines, substations, switches and switchgears, control and measuring equipment, dispatch control systems. The power supply system is closely related to the city lighting system.

   Disruption of power supply to residential and industrial objects of the urban environment is also accompanied by consequences that are dangerous to human life and health. Power supply problems arise as a result of: overloaded power lines, short circuit, lightning strike, switching on electrical appliances with high impulse power consumption (argon welding equipment, heaters, electric motors, etc.), the presence of poor-quality electrical wiring, failures and malfunctions of electrical equipment. -substations, power line break [36].

4   Material and Methods of Proactive Monitoring

Formulation of the problem. In the process of research, it is necessary to develop methods and software and tools for collecting, consolidating and intelligent analysis of large sensory and social data based on a multi-agent approach. The main goal is to ensure the safety of the life and activities of the urban population through proactive monitoring and prevention of the risks of the occurrence and development of critical events at the distributed facilities of the city's utilities and in the road transport infrastructure. The system for monitoring critical events at distributed infrastructure facilities should provide [37]:

- Two-way communication with the external environment.
- Functionality for collecting and consolidating data, operating in real time.
- Functionality of predictive analytics operating in near real-time mode.
- Network interfaces for organizing the interaction of various devices for collecting and processing data.
- Intelligent processing of big data in the data center.
- Functionality of secure storage and personalized access to data and monitoring results.

The methodology for proactive monitoring of critical events at distributed infrastructure facilities of the urban environment includes three main stages (Fig. 1).

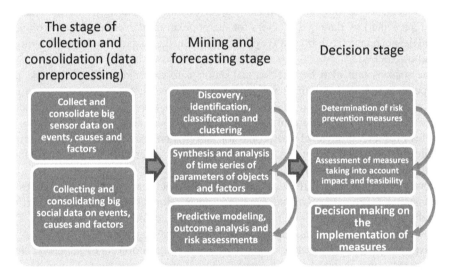

Fig. 1. Methodology for monitoring critical events.

1. The stage of collection, processing and consolidation of heterogeneous large sensory and social data on critical events, causes and factors of influence:

   - Detection, identification, classification and clustering of critical events based on the collection and processing of sensory and social data.
   - Determination, analysis and classification of possible causes of their occurrence, as well as external and internal factors of influence on events.

2. Stage of data mining and forecasting the risks of occurrence and development of critical events:

- Assessment of the sensitivity of the risks of critical events to influencing factors and possible causes by the method of multivariate analysis of variance in order to reduce the dimension by selecting the most significant causes and factors.
- Presentation of the dynamics of changes in the parameters of the observed objects and influencing factors at specified time intervals before and after the event in the form of time series spectra for predictive modeling of the risks of the occurrence and development of critical events.
- Synthesis of predictive models for studying the spectrum of time series and predictive risk assessment.
- Comparative analysis of forecasting results with similar results obtained earlier for similar and similar events within the framework of a previously created classification and taking into account temporal and spatial characteristics.

3. The stage of choosing preventive measures and making decisions on their implementation:

- Selection and/or synthesis of preventive measures to prevent the risks of events of this type, assessment of ways to solve the problem, taking into account the consequences and economic feasibility.
- Making a decision on the implementation of the selected measures.

At the first stage, technologies for data collection and preliminary processing are implemented. Data preprocessing is associated with removing noise, data duplicates, processing missing values, removing irrelevant attributes, consolidating data from different sources, bringing heterogeneous data to a homogeneous structure and a single format for loading into the storage and subsequent analysis.

At the next stage, it is necessary to perform identification, classification and clustering of critical events and factors influencing them, taking into account the current state of the environment.

After clustering, the problem of reducing the dimension of the phase space of the parameters of the objects of monitoring and the factors influencing the dynamics of their change is solved. For this, from the set of parameters of objects and events, those that fall into the area of unacceptable values at the moments of time of the critical event are selected and correlations between them and possible influencing factors are established by the method of analysis of variance. To rank the factors, the sensitivity of the parameters of objects to their influence is assessed taking into account the temporal and spatial characteristics of the event. A cluster of essential factors is formed, associated with a specific object and a critical event, and a hypothesis is accepted about the connection of this factorial cluster with clusters of similar objects and similar events. For the formed cluster, a set of interval values of factors is fixed, the combination of which can cause the risk of occurrence and development of critical events of this type.

The next step is predictive modeling of the dynamics of change in factors in the formed clusters. The aim is to determine the future moments of time of a critical event at similar objects and to assess the risks of the appearance of a combination of values of factors that leads to its occurrence. For this, in our case, it is proposed to use the representation of the dynamics of changes in the parameters of the monitoring objects and the values of the influence factors in the form of a spectrum of time series. Time series describe dynamic processes that can be predicted by a sequence of values of some quantities for which the moment in time at which they were obtained is known [38, 39]. To predict events based on the analysis of a time series, it is first necessary to construct an adequate function of its description.

In the process of analyzing the time series in the spectrum, the deviations of the values of the studied variables from the range of permissible values, moments and time intervals for deviations are determined. Changes in influencing factors at similar points in time. Comparative analysis of time series of object parameters and influencing factors in the selected spectrum makes it possible to establish correlations between them, to clarify the results of the sensitivity assessment obtained at the stage of analysis of variance. The absence of a strong correlation means the wrong choice of influencing factors or the falsehood of the hypothesis about the connection of the cluster of factors with the object and the event. For a refined set of correlating factors and parameters of the object, at the next step of the analysis, such characteristics are determined as: a) the presence of a trend, b) the presence of seasonal short-term and cyclical long-term fluctuations, c) the presence of noise (random fluctuations in values). According to these characteristics, the time series of object parameters and factors are compared in order to identify the so-called trend, seasonal, cyclical and noise factors.

To predict the dynamics of changes in the values of factors and parameters of the monitoring object, a model is used that connects the probability of equality of the value of the indicator Z_k in the next time interval with it in the previous interval:

$$P\left[I_{i,t+1} = Z_\kappa\right] = f(x_{it}), \tag{1}$$

where $I_{i,t+1}$ – factor value for the i-th object in the next time interval $t + 1$, x_{it} – set of early factor values.

To predict events, it was decided to use the composition of the decision tree C5.0 and CHAID models is selected to improve the forecast accuracy:

$$f(x) = F(f_1(x), f_2(x)), \tag{2}$$

where f_1 is the C5.0 model, f_2 is the CHAID model, F is the aggregation function. For a more accurate assessment of the algorithm, an analysis of the dynamics of accuracy was carried out on the time series of changes in the influence factor. The solution of the problem was carried out in 2 stages. At the first stage, the stability of the accuracy dynamics was assessed based on the training sample of factor values for a randomly selected type of events occurring on the object during a given time interval. A sample of data on the values of the factor for the previous time interval was used as a test to assess the accuracy and stability of the algorithms on new observations.

5 Results of Collection and Consolidation of Sensory Data

As shown above, the first stage of monitoring is the collection and processing of data received from sensor devices and from open sources on the Internet. For example, the following operations are implemented in the road traffic monitoring system [40]:

1. Collecting data from photo radar systems and road video surveillance cameras for statistical research of indicators of critical events.
2. Collecting data from external systems and navigation services (weather stations, geoinformation services for satellite navigation, intelligent transport systems, etc.) to identify factors that influenced the occurrence and development of road incidents.
3. Collection of data from mobile communications of road users and outside observers. The peculiarity lies in the fact that such data are heterogeneous, poorly structured, have a subjective interpretation of events and a lot of duplicate information from different sources.
4. Collection of data in open sources of the Internet (social networks, chats, blogs, forums, instant messengers, web resources). The problems of using data are similar, but the problem of delay is also added, since the information is laid out with a delay from the moment of the real event.

Most of the event data are discrete and have geospatial and time stamps. Consolidation of data about the same events is the process of integrating information from multiple sources. It includes a number of procedures, including finding associations and correlations, cleaning and normalizing, eliminating duplicates, combining different types of information, assessing the relevance and reliability of data, etc. To analyze a multitude of critical events at distributed objects, for example, on many sections of pipelines or sections of roads, the problem of sensor consolidation of the same type of data from a variety of sensors or photoradar complexes and other sensor devices is solved. Sensory console-dation can be performed at different levels: at the level of signals (telemetric and diagnostic data on the operation of monitoring tools), at the level of features of the monitoring object, at the level of critical events and at the level of decision making. The most difficult task here is the consolidation of images or video sequences obtained from a variety of devices of different quality and resolution. In the road monitoring system, data on critical events refers to [41]:

- Number of targets (vehicles), date, time, coordinates and registration numbers.
- Date, time and coordinates of the place of fixation of road incidents and targets.
- Data on the recorded offenses (type, characteristics of the event and the object at the time of the incident (speeding, crossing a solid line, crossing a stop line, passing a prohibitory signal, not allowing a pedestrian to pass, etc.).
- Identifier and coordinates of the fixing device.
- Identifier of the offense and vehicle data file.

To solve the problems of proactive monitoring of events on a set of sections of any distributed infrastructure object, in our case, a multi-agent approach is used [42, 43], according to which software agents are loaded into the sensor nodes. Also, agents search, collect and process data about events in open sources of the Internet [44]. Within the framework of the multi-agent approach, agent behavior models are defined in the form of functions that control the procedures for processing, protecting and storing data on distributed nodes. Several agents can work on one node, performing different functions. The task of sharing the hardware resources of a node between agents is implemented by means of the operating platform [45].

6 Conclusion and Future Work

The modern trend in the management of complex systems is the use of elements of artificial intelligence, including methods of data mining, machine learning and predictive modeling. The proactive monitoring concept allows to prevent the risks of emergence and development of accidents and catastrophes on the basis of predictive analysis of events. The essence of proactive monitoring is the registration and identification of events, the intellectual analysis of big data and time series of events, prognostic modeling and risk assessment of emergencies and emergencies. The result of the introduction of proactive technologies is the transfer of decision-makers from the management subsystem to the configuration and control subsystem with the transfer to them of the settings, control and diagnostics functions of the monitoring tools. In fact, the control subject moves to the level of coordination and supervisory control of the operational monitoring process in complex geographically distributed systems.

Currently, there are no comprehensive solutions for proactive monitoring of events in complex geographically distributed systems of a region or city. The complexity of proactive monitoring tasks here is related to the length and spread of controlled objects over a large territory. The main problem is the collection and consolidation of large data from open distributed sources for analysis and forecasting the time series of events and factors of influence in order to support decision-making to minimize the risks of emergency and non-regular situations.

Intellectualization of sensor nodes with the help of software agents makes it possible to implement proactive monitoring technologies to improve the safety of human life through:

- Assessing and forecasting the risks of critical events.
- Control of monitoring objects in real time.
- Tracking changes in factors of influence on negative events.
- Predictive modeling of time series of events.
- Localization of places of accidents and taking preventive measures.

The proactive event monitoring system and software agents are implemented using open source technologies: Apache HBase, Apache Hadoop, Apache Storm, Apache Spark, libraries of mining algorithms and machine learning MLlib (Apache Spark) and Ma-hout (Apache Hadoop), libraries for working with graphs GraphX (Apache Spark). The MLlib library includes the implementation of a number of intelligent analysis algorithms for execution in a distributed mode (classification, regression, clustering, collaborative filtering, etc.). The Mahout library implements algorithms such as Fuzzy k-Means, Canopy, Dirichlet and Mean-Shift with Map-Reduce support.

At present, the methodology and algorithms are being implemented in the subsystems of pro-active monitoring of the road transport infrastructure and in the intelligent SCADA system for detecting critical events in the engineering network of the city's heat supply. In the future, it is planned to spread the proposed approach for proactive monitoring of other distributed infrastructure facilities, such as power supply networks, water supply and sewerage networks, gas supply and urban lighting. Also, mobile applications are being developed to warn and notify citizens of probable critical events at distributed monitoring facilities, taking into account from the location, by analogy with the emergency warning system of the Ministry of Emergencies. The mobile application, via push notifications, warns citizens about the need to observe increased caution when entering the zone of possible critical events and about the probable time of the onset of a critical event.

Acknowledgments. The research was supported by the grants the Russian Science Foundation, RSF 20-71-10087. The results of part 4 were obtained within the Russian Foundation for Basic Research grants (project № 19-013-00409).

References

1. Bibri, S.E., Krogstie, J.: Smart sustainable cities of the future: an extensive interdisciplinary literature review. Sustain. Urban Areas **31**, 183–212 (2017)
2. Myeong, S.: A study on determinant factors in smart city development: an analytic hierarchy process analysis. Sustainability **10**, 2606 (2018)
3. Iker, Z., Alessandro, S., Saioa, A.: Smart city concept: what it is and what it should be. J. Urban Plan. Dev. **142**, 4015005 (2016)
4. Bakhmut, A.D., Krylov, A.V., Krylova, M.A., Okhtilev, M.Y., Okhtilev, P.A., Sokolov, B.V.: Proactive management of complex objects using precedent methodology. In: Silhavy, R. (ed.) CSOC2018 2018. AISC, vol. 764, pp. 298–307. Springer, Cham (2019). https://doi.org/10.1007/978-3-319-91189-2_29
5. Li, Y., et al.: Proactive behavior-based system for controlling safety risks in urban highway construction megaprojects. Autom. Constr. **95**, 118–128 (2018)
6. Parygin, D.: Implementation of exoactive management model for urbanized area: real-time monitoring and proactive planning. In: Proceedings of the 2019 8th International Conference on System Modeling and Advancement in Research Trends, pp. 310–316. IEEE (2019). https://doi.org/10.1109/SMART46866.2019.9117298
7. Gitelman, L.D., et al.: Proactive management in the power industry: tool support. Int. J. Sus. Dev. Plan. **12**(8), 1359–1369 (2017)
8. Lawrence, M.: "What Is Proactive Monitoring?" Small Business - Chron.com. http://smallbusiness.chron.com/proactive-monitoring-73438.html
9. Civerchia, F., Bocchino, S., Salvadori, C., Rossi, E., Maggiani, L., Petracca, M.: Industrial Internet of Things monitoring solution for advanced predictive maintenance applications. J. Ind. Inf. Integr. **7**, 4–12 (2017). https://doi.org/10.1016/j.jii.2017.02.003
10. Russian Federal State Statistics Service. https://rosstat.gov.ru. Accessed 17 Apr 2021
11. Manikonda, P., Yerrapragada, A., Annasamudram, S.: Intelligent traffic management system, pp. 119–122. https://doi.org/10.1109/STUDENT.2011.6089337. Accessed 21 Jan 2020
12. Carrez, F., Moessner, K., Zoha, A.: Predicting complex events for pro-active IoT applications. In: Proceedings of the 2015 IEEE 2nd World Forum on Internet of Things (WF-IoT), Milan, Italy, 14–16 December 2015, pp. 327–332 (2015)
13. Savolainen, P., Mannering, F., Lord, D., Quddus, M.: The statistical analysis of highway crash-injury severities: a review and assessment of methodological alternatives. Accid. Anal. Prev. **43**, 1666–1676 (2011)
14. Depaire, B., Wets, G., Vanhoof, K.: Traffic Accident Segmentation by Means of Latent Class Clustering, Accident Analysis and Prevention, vol. 40. Elsevier, Amsterdam (2008)
15. Karlaftis, M., Tarko, A.: Heterogeneity considerations in accident modeling. Accid. Anal. Prev. **30**(4), 425–433 (1998)

16. Ma, J., Kockelman, K.: Crash frequency and severity modeling using clustered data from Washington State. In: IEEE Intelligent Transportation Systems Conference, Toronto, Canadá (2006)
17. Miaou, S.P., Lum, H.: Modeling Vehicle Accidents and Highway Geometric Design Relationships, Accident Analysis and Prevention, vol. 25. Elsevier, Amsterdam (1993)
18. Miaou, S.P.: The Relationship Between Truck Accidents and Geometric Design of Road Sections–Poisson Versus Negative Binomial Regressions, Accident Analysis and Prevention, vol. 26. Elsevier, Amsterdam (1994)
19. Chen, W., Jovanis, P.: Method of identifying factors contributing to driver-injury severity in traffic crashes. Transp. Res. Rec. **1717**, 1–9 (2002)
20. Chang, L.Y., Chen, W.C.: Data mining of tree based models to analyze freeway accident frequency. J. Saf. Res. **36**, 365–375 (2005)
21. Tan, P.N., Steinbach, M.: Introduction to Data Mining. Pearson Addison-Wesley, Boston (2006)
22. Sivarajah, U., Kamal, M., Irani, Z., Weerakkody, V.: Critical analysis of big data challenges and analytical methods. J. Bus. Res. **70**, 263–286 (2017)
23. Abellan, J., Lopez, G., Ona, J.: Analyis of traffic accident severity using decision rules via decision trees. Expert Syst. Appl. **40**, 6047–6054 (2013)
24. Rovsek V.: Identifying the Key Risk Factors of Traffic Accident Injury Severity on Slovenian Roads using a Non-Parametric Classification Tree, Transport. Taylor and Francis, UK (2014)
25. Kashani, T., Mohaymany, A.S., Rajbari, A.: A data mining approach to identify key factors of traffic injury severity. PROMET-Traffic Transp. **23**, 11–17 (2011)
26. Basu, S., Davidson, I., Wagstaff, K. (eds.): Constrained clustering: advances in algorithms, theory, and applications. CRC Press, Boca Raton, 441 p. (2009)
27. Han, J., Kamber, M.: Data Mining: Concepts. Morgan Kaufmann Publishers, USA (2001)
28. Oña, J.D., López, G., Mujalli, R.: Analysis of traffic accidents on rural highways using latent class clustering and Bayesian networks. Accid. Anal. Prev. **51**, 1–10 (2013)
29. Chaturvedi, A., Green, P., Carroll, J.: K-modes clustering. J Classif. **18**, 35–55 (2001)
30. Factors affecting the likelihood of an accident. http://road-traffic-safety.blogspot.com/2011/01/dtp-factory.html. Accessed 22 Apr 2021
31. 6 reasons why: what provokes bursts of heating networks and can they be avoided. https://tvk6.ru/publications/news/40336. Accessed 23 Apr 2021
32. Stankov, S., Jovanović, Z., Icić, Z.: Temperature measurements using PLC and SCADA systems. Energy Technol. [Energetske tehnologije] **7**(4), 13–22 (2010)
33. Causes of accidents on water pipelines. https://mygazeta.com/life-image/reasons-failures-on-waterpipelines.html. Accessed 24 Apr 2021
34. City lighting - norms, principles of construction. https://yandex.ru/turbo/elektrik-a.su/s/osveshhenie/naruzhnoe/osveshhenie-goroda-400. Accessed 21 Apr 2021
35. Assessment of emergency situations on the gas pipeline. http://www.tehgazpribor.ru/data_sheet/proekt/226-emergency-situations-onthegaspipeline. Accessed 05 Apr 2021
36. Problems of power supply in large cities and megalopolises. http://www.ruscable.ru/article/Problemy_elektrosnabzheniya_krupnyx_gorodov_i. Accessed 05 Apr 2021
37. Want, R.: Comparing autonomic and proactive computing. IBM Syst. J. **42**(1), 129–135 (2003)
38. Mylnikov, L.A., Seledkova, A.V., Krause, B.: Forecasting characteristics of time series to support managerial decision making process in production-And-economic systems. In: Proceedings of 2017 20th IEEE International Conference on Soft Computing and Measurements, SCM 2017, pp. 853–855 (2017)
39. Kane, M.J., Price, N., Scotch, M., Rabinowitz, P.: Comparison of ARIMA and random forest time series models for prediction of avian influenza H5N1 outbreaks. BMC Bioinform. **15**, 1–9 (2014). https://doi.org/10.1186/1471-2105-15-276

40. Finogeev, A., Finogeev, A., Fionova, L., Lyapin, A., Lychagin, K.: Intelligent monitoring system for smart road environment. J. Ind. Inf. Integr. **15**, 15–20 (2019). https://doi.org/10.1016/j.jii.2019.05.003.Accessed21Jan2020

41. Finogeev, A., Finogeev, A., Shevchenko, S.: Monitoring of road transport infrastructure for the intelligent environment «Smart Road». In: Kravets, A., Shcherbakov, M., Kultsova, M., Groumpos, P. (eds.) CIT&DS 2017. CCIS, vol. 754, pp. 655–668. Springer, Cham (2017). https://doi.org/10.1007/978-3-319-65551-2_47

42. Parygin, D., Usov, A., Burov, S., Sadovnikova, N., Ostroukhov, P., Pyannikova, A.: Multi-agent approach to modeling the dynamics of urban processes (on the example of urban movements). Commun. Comput. Inf. Sci. **1135**, 243–257 (2020)

43. Parygin, D., Nikitsky, N., Kamaev, V., Matokhina, A., Finogeev, A., Finogeev, A.: Multi-agent approach to distributed processing big sensor data based on fog computing model for the monitoring of the urban infrastructure systems. In: Proceedings of the 5th International Conference on System Modeling & Advancement in Research Trends, pp. 305–310. IEEE (2017)

44. Ustugova, S., Parygin, D., Finogeev, A., et al.: Monitoring of social reactions to support decision making on issues of urban territory management. In: Proceedings of the 5th International Young Scientist Conference on Computational Science (YSC 2016), pp. 243–252. Elsevier, Poland (2016)

45. Finogeev, A., Bershadsky, A., Finogeev, A., Fionova, L., Deev, M.: Multiagent intelligent system of convergent sensor data processing for the smart & safe road. In: Chatchawal, W. (ed.) Intelligent System, Ch. 5, pp. 102–121. IntechOpen (2018)

Digital Technologies for Surveying Buildings and Structures

Irina Petrova(⌐) ⓘ, Oleg Mostovoy, and Viktoriia Zaripova ⓘ

Astrakhan State University of Architecture and Civil Engineering, 18 Tatishchev Street, Astrakhan 414056, Russia

Abstract. The paper dwells on the issues of applying digital technologies in surveying and technical diagnostics of buildings and structures. It analyzes in detail the business process of surveying buildings and structures, marks out the main stages of the process and interaction between the participants, considers a set of problematic aspects and issues of concern that degrade the quality of preparing a technical statement on the structure condition. The need for creating an ontology knowledge base on building structure defects has been justified. Collecting information for a knowledge base is a strategically important and the most challenging task in the automation of the in-office work stage. Automation of the in-office work stage will allow for avoiding mistakes, repetitions and typing errors, reducing the reporting time, increasing control over the documentation workload quality, reducing the time of the survey works, performed by the contractor, freeing up the employees' time for fulfilling other tasks, boosting productivity and providing the organization with competitive advantages.

Keywords: Surveying of buildings and structures · Business process · Categories of technical condition

1 Introduction

Rapid development of the new digital technologies and cyber-physical systems, taking place in the 21st century, has resulted in significant changes in the construction industry, related to the working methods and organization of business processes. Indeed, a new term 'Construction 4.0' has appeared (it was introduced in 2016 in Germany [1]), describing new opportunities for the companies that want to increase their competitiveness, decision-making quality and timely completion of projects. Digitalization of the construction industry has strong potential and sustainable development prospects.

Review [2] presents a bibliometric analysis of 260 research papers, specifying the modern technologies and changing approaches to construction works:

- Internet of Things.
- CAD technologies (BIM).
- 3D printing.
- Big Data.

A. G. Kravets et al. (Eds.): CIT&DS 2021, CCIS 1448, pp. 354–366, 2021.
https://doi.org/10.1007/978-3-030-87034-8_26

- Artificial intelligence and robotics.
- Virtual and Augmented reality.
- New materials related to industrialization.

Summing up the results of analysis of the number of publications, given in [2], allowed to construct a chart, showing significant growth of publications on digitalization of the construction industry (Fig. 1), and a diagram of the distribution of the publications by topic (Fig. 2).

The charts show that the above-listed topics largely contribute to the development of the construction industry all across the globe.

Surveying of buildings and structures holds a special place in the construction sector of the economy, since various natural and technological factors, influencing building structures in operation, and assessment of the new construction impact on the exiting real estate are important factors that determine the integrity and security of buildings and structures.

So, introducing automation in building surveying is seen especially important in the light of a large number of real estate items with significant obsolescence and physical deterioration and the modern fast pace of construction.

Rapid development of digital technologies in the construction industry allowed to improve lots of building surveying aspects significantly and change business processes [3].

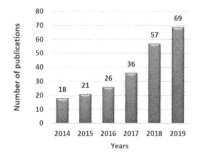 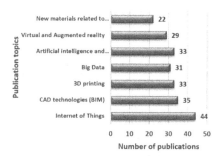

Fig. 1. Growth chart of publications related to digitalization of the construction industry. **Fig. 2.** Diagram of distribution of the publications by topic.

2 Digital Technology Application in Surveying of Buildings and Structures

Below are digital technologies that are especially actively applied in surveying buildings and structures.

2.1 Internet of Things

The concept 'Internet of Things' (IoT) [4] was formed in 1999 at Massachusetts Institute of Technology (MIT). It is one of the key technologies of the future.

The Internet of Things is a global infrastructure of the information society that ensures the provision of advanced services through connecting objects (physical and virtual) on the basis of the existing and developing joint information and communication technologies [5].

Five IoT technologies are used in surveying buildings and structures [6, 7]: radio frequency identification (RFID), wireless sensor networks (WSN), middleware, cloud computing, and IoT application software.

Using cloud technologies together with IoT allows for real-time data transmission for systems that monitor the condition of a building or structure both at the design and construction stage and in service [8].

2.2 CAD Technologies (BIM)

Databases are widely used to create, process and store comprehensive information at each stage of the life cycle of a building. Progress in the sphere of building information modelling (BIM) gives a real boost to this work. The information accumulated in the bases will be necessary for efficient surveying of buildings and structures at all stages of the life cycle.

Despite the advances in the sphere of digital technologies, the current practice of expert assessment of construction projects is still two-dimensional and paper-based. Employees have to compare and interpret a large volume of two-dimensional plans and drawings in order to check whether the given structures meet the building regulation. This results in slower work, mistakes and inaccuracies [9]. Unfortunately, BIM is not of frequent use in the expert assessment of the existing buildings and structures. Study [9] has shown that BIM can be applied to inspect the building standards compliance, with the surveying time being reduced significantly.

The main problem, encountered when introducing BIM, is connected with the comprehensive introduction of this technology at all stages of the life cycle: design – construction – operation of a building [10].

As a result of the continuing introduction of BIM, the construction industry will stop being document-oriented and become data-oriented. It will become critically important to compare and contrast the data in order to extract timely and valuable business ideas from them.

2.3 Big Data

The term 'big data' appeared in 2008 in a special issue of Nature [11]. The article mentioned an explosive growth of the global information volume and stated that new instruments and more developed technologies would help master it.

Building surveyors have always worked with their own data, collected either from various resources or through their own internal resources within the scope of the project, and used these data as a basis for their estimates. That is why if a person left the organization, these data were lost.

Using big data leads to a decreasing volume of manual work, done by a surveyor, for example, in measurement or reporting.

As a result of the continuing introduction of BIM, the construction industry stopped being document-oriented and become data-oriented. It became critically important to compare and contrast the data in order to extract timely and valuable business ideas from them. The data are used in the construction industry throughout the whole life cycle of design – construction – operation. It allows for preventing risks in construction, making more accurate forecasts on the facility condition and assessing the collapse probability.

2.4 Artificial Intelligence and Robotics

The most striking example of using robots in building surveying is the active use of unmanned aerial vehicles (drones) to collect information during the real-time monitoring and inspection of construction sites [12]. Unmanned aerial vehicles can conduct visual and thermographic surveys of high-rise buildings and large areas. It helps specialists draw up reports quicker and more accurately. For example, a drone with a thermal imaging camera can analyze and detect potential problems of a building heat leakage, water ingress under the roof, etc., with the greatest degree of accuracy.

A comprehensive and systematic review of the use of drones in construction is given in [13, 14].

Using building structures with incorporated sensors, connected in an artificial neural network, is a promising trend – it will allow for precise identification of the type and place of a failure based on pattern recognition technology. For example, article [15] presents information on the assessment of using convolutional neural networks (CNN) for automatic detection and localization of building key defects (fungus, damage, spots) by images.

2.5 Virtual and Augmented Reality

Over the last decade, the tools for surveying buildings and structures have changed a lot. For example, there have appeared 3D laser scanners which allow to perform accurate measurements quickly and save a big amount of data. The laser scanning method allows for performing accurate measurement within a short time and getting full information on the facility in a single array of the point cloud or a 3D project. It makes the process of using and managing information when developing a BIM model and drawing up a damage report considerably easier and allows for getting any data from one single source [16, 17]. Once a BIM facility database is created, augmented reality (AR) can make the facility servicing easier, especially the tasks in the areas with multiple components, located close to each other. AR can combine real and virtual information about the facility, which allows for detecting areas and elements in the buildings that need to be maintained [18].

Rapid development of these technologies allows specialists to collect and process high-accuracy data promptly, which improves the general economic efficiency of building surveying.

3 Applying Digital Technologies in Construction in Russia

In 2017, the national program "Digital Economy of the Russian Federation" was developed in Russia [19]. Paper [20] discusses the role of digitalization in the sphere of construction in Russia and shows that BIM is the most popular technology in this industry. Paper [21] presents a review of the BIM regulatory documents in Russia.

The Ministry of Construction, Housing and Utilities of Russia has approved a program of introducing information modeling technologies that oblige to use BIM technologies at the stages of design, construction and operation of the state-sponsored capital construction projects. Information modeling will be obligatory for all the government-contract projects, financed through the budget of the Russian Federation [22]. According to this program, BIM shall cover all the life cycle of a facility. In modern Russia, however, BIM technologies are most commonly used in design, less frequently – in construction and are almost never used at further stages of the life cycle.

Automation of different processes in construction is an important factor that will allow to improve the production efficiency, reduce the operating costs, improve the quality of design, construction, surveying and engineering investigations. Stages and methods of engineering surveying buildings and structures are described in detail in [23, 24].

The present article considers automation of surveying of buildings and structures, the algorithm of which is presented in Fig. 3. The objective of this business process is to develop a directive decision on further operation of the facility, based on the results of a survey of buildings and structures (preconstruction, fieldwork stage, in-office work stage).

The main tasks for surveying building parts and structures are:

- To identify the most critical defects and damages, detected during the engineering investigation.
- To conduct necessary laboratory investigations and calculations for identifying the causes of their occurrence.
- To examine for compliance with the design parameters.
- To classify the condition of specific structural components and the facility in general.

Determining the remaining lifetime of the buildings with a significant working life forms the basis for making a decision on repairing, reconstruction or demolition of the facility if critical defects were identified and is a consequence of the downgrading of.

A building surveyor is to determine the number of the most significant qualities from the set of parameters that describe the building condition. This requires specific qualification and experience, favouring the development of a specialist's personal and heuristic knowledge. Using this knowledge, an expert can make efficient decisions even in case of fuzzy or incomplete data. Consequently, it is advisable to enhance and expand professional capabilities for the specialists that survey buildings using digital technologies. A computer-assisted search for an expert decision can help in the work of both newcomers and experienced experts.

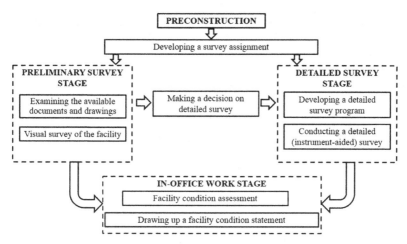

Fig. 3. Process of surveying buildings and structures.

At the in-office work stage, documents, measurement results and analysis of all the information available are collected, and a technical statement on the building structure condition is drawn up. This stage is quite time-consuming and lasts from a few days to a few weeks, depending on the culture of archiving the reporting documentation and the number of works. The average cost of this stage of the works is about 1/3 of the cost of a detailed survey. That is why automation of works at this stage is an important and relevant task.

4 In-Office Work Stage in Surveying Buildings and Structures as a Business Process

The functional model of the business process of the in-office work stage in surveying buildings and structures is described by the IDEF0 method (Integration Definition for Function Modeling) [25, 26].

Systems analysis of the in-office work in building surveying suggests that there's a large number of information flows, both from the external environment (construction rules and regulations (SNiP), All-Union State Standards (GOST), design documents) and the information about the facility under survey itself (survey assignment, survey program, design and service documents for the facility under survey, engineering investigations, contract between the customer and survey provider). It significantly complicates the process of getting and processing information, used to draw up an assessment report (statement) on the condition of the facility under survey and to make a directive decision on further operation of the building. The business process resources are the staff of the surveying organization, computers and software (Fig. 4).

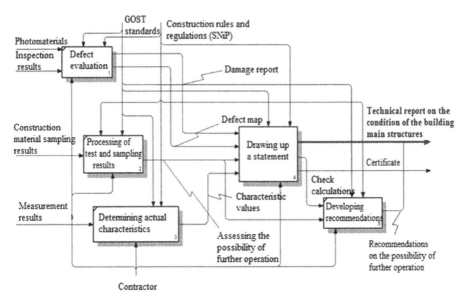

Fig. 4. In-office work stage (AS IS).

At the in-office work stage, the contractor analyses, processes and systematizes the data, received through preliminary and detailed surveys.

In the course of work, the contractor uses various regulations and reference materials:

- On climate references (depending on the location of the facility under survey), necessary for thermotechnical calculations of the enclosing structures.
- On various structural schemes and elements, necessary to describe and make checking calculations.
- On the data, necessary to describe defects and recommendations for their elimination.

Once all the data are analyzed and processed, the facility condition is then classified and a technical statement on the current condition of the facility is drawn up; a facility certificate is filled in and a survey report is drawn up.

Most of the mistakes occur at the stage of compiling a technical statement on the facility condition. It is connected with the fact that in the existing market conditions, surveyors seek to reduce the period of work execution as much as possible. As a result, there is no time left for control and verification of completed reports.

5   In-Office Work Stage Automation

It is necessary to automate the in-office stage in order to reduce the labor and working costs and to exclude mistakes in compiling a technical statement on the facility condition. The authors have developed a BPMN (Business Process Management Notation) chart to show the process of compiling a technical statement on the facility condition (Fig. 5).

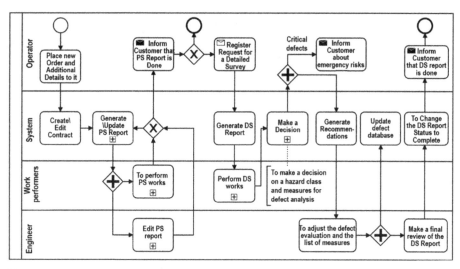

Fig. 5. BPMN chart of the process of compiling a technical statement on the facility condition.

After the customer's request, an operator enters data on the new order and additional details to it into the automated system. The system generates a new contract, creates a report form and generates a preliminary survey (PS) task.

The contractors carry out preliminary survey (PS) works (Fig. 6):

- Work performers carry out works on visual inspection of the objecton, recording the facility characteristics and defects and enters data into the system.
- Engineer examines the data obtained, edits the PS report and formulates a statement upon the PS results.

The operator requests the customer for additional information. If there is such and the customer provides it, the operator adds the documents to the contractual documentation and in the automated system. Once the changes are introduced, the system updates the PS report.

After the statement is edited and compiled, the system changes the report status to Complete. The operator informs the customer that the PS report has been drawn up.

If no additional work is needed upon the PS results, the customer takes over the works and receives the PS report.

If a detailed examination is necessary upon the PS results and the customer signs all necessary legal documents, the operator updates the contract terms, and the system creates a report and generates a detailed survey (DS) task.

The contractors carry out detailed survey (DS) works (Fig. 7):

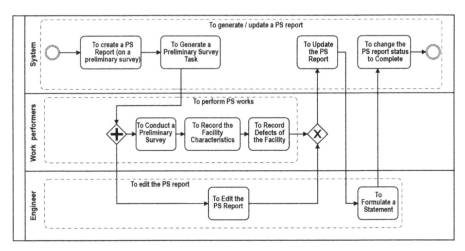

Fig. 6. BPMN chart of the sub-processes on PS works and generation/updating of PS reports.

- Work performers carry out works on surveying structures in the dug pits and defects, measuring the dimensions, determines strength properties of the materials with instrumental non-destructive methods, performs the testing opening and sounding of the structures, samples the materials for further laboratory studies and enters data into the system.
- Land surveyor performs a geodesic survey to assess the position of the building and its structures and enters data into the system;
- Geologist conducts a subsoil survey and soil sampling and sends data to the laboratory;
- Laboratory workers examine the given samples of the materials, soil, etc., and enter the examination results into the system.

Analysis and assessment of the detected defects is a crucial stage of the works, carried out by the system (Fig. 8). The system uses the obtained data to classify the facility under study and choose the defects, corresponding to the detected ones, from the defect database. Based on the data analysis, the system assigns a class of hazard to the defects obtained and generates recommendations for their elimination. If high-hazard defects (emergency state) were detected, the system issues warning on the necessity to inform the customer and on the emergency state in accordance with the legal requirements.

An engineer examines the data received, edits the detailed survey (DS) report, adjusts the defect evaluation and recommendations, introduces changes in the defect database and compiles a statement upon the DS results.

After the statement is edited and compiled, the system changes the report status to Complete. The operator informs the customer that the DS report has been drawn up. The customer accepts the contract works and receives the DS report.

Working with the ontology defect knowledge base is a key point of the system work (Fig. 9). Filling and updating the defect knowledge base is carried out by experts with high experience in this sphere. Their job includes analysis of practical and theoretical

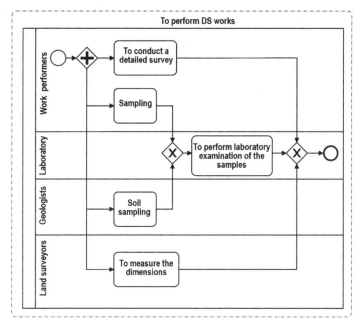

Fig. 7. BPMN chart of the DS sub-process.

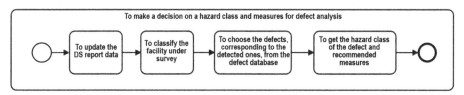

Fig. 8. BPMN chart of the sub-process of making a decision on a hazard class and measures for defect analysis.

studies in technical diagnostics of building parts and structures, examination of regulatory and technical documents and scientific literature, collection and generalization of heuristic knowledge and specialists' considerations. Based on the obtained and examined data, experts evaluate/reevaluate hazard classes of defects and make changes in the classification of facilities and defects. Collecting information in the knowledge base is a strategically important and the most challenging task in the automation of the in-office work stage.

Parallel accounting of the estimates and measures for hazard elimination, used in the report, is also carried out to minimize the experts' time expenditure and constantly update the defect knowledge base. In this case, assessments and measures are added to the knowledge base as a draft and an expert can take them into consideration in further updating of the base.

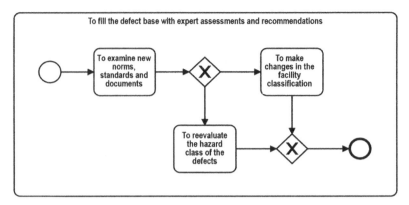

Fig. 9. BPMN chart of the sub-process of filling the defect base with expert assessments.

Introduction of an automated system excludes the human factor in most of the works on drawing up a technical report. It will allow for:

- Avoiding mistakes, repetitions and typing errors, reducing the reporting time, increasing control over the documentation workload quality.
- Reducing the time of a survey, carried out by the contractor, boosting productivity and providing the organization with competitive advantages.
- Improving the precision of control over some parameters (geometric, geodesic, structural), calculation and assessment of the strength properties of the building structures under survey.

6   Conclusion

- Introduction of digital technologies speeds up decision-making and improves the quality of managing the main business processes.
- The business process of surveying buildings and structures has been considered; BPMN charts on surveying buildings and structures, carried out with an automated system, have been shown.
- Introduction of an ontology defect knowledge base, constantly updated as a result of both making real estate reports and examining regulatory and technical documents and scientific literature, with classification by hazard classes will allow to get a true picture of the surveyed facility condition (the judgmental human factor is excluded).
- The need for automation of the in-office work stage has been justified.

References

1. Berger, R.: Roland Berger Digitization in the Construction Industry: Building Europe's Road to "Construction 4.0." Roland Berger GMBH, Munich (2016)

2. Forcael, E., Ferrari, I., Opazo-Vega, A., Pulido-Arcas, J.A.: Construction 4.0: a literature review. Sustainability **12**, 9755 (2020)
3. Gissane, R.: Modern technology and changing approaches to building surveying (2021). https://www.pbctoday.co.uk/news/construction-technology-news/building-surveying-technology/89564/. Accessed 2 May 2021
4. Adat, V., Gupta, B.B.: Security in Internet of Things: issues, challenges, taxonomy, and architecture. Telecommun. Syst. **67**, 423–441 (2018)
5. Recommendation ITU-T Y.4000/Y.2060 (06/2012) Overview of the Internet of things (2012). https://www.itu.int/ITU-T/recommendations/rec.aspx?rec=11559&lang=en. Accessed 13 Apr 2021
6. Botta, A., De Donato, W., Persico, V., Pescape, A.: Integration of cloud computing and Internet of Things: a survey. Future Gener. Comput. Syst. **56**, 684–700 (2016)
7. Daissaoui, A., Boulmakoul, A., Karim, L., Lbath, A.: IoT and big data analytics for smart buildings: a survey. Procedia Comput. Sci. **170**, 161–168 (2020). https://doi.org/10.1016/j.procs.2020.03.021
8. Kai, K., Jiarui, L., Jianping, Z.: BIM- and IoT-based monitoring framework for building performance management. J. Struct. Integr. Maint. **3**(4) (2018). Computing in Structural and Construction Engineering
9. Kim, K.P., Freda, R., Nguyen, T.H.D.: Building information modelling feasibility study for building surveying. Sustainability **12**(11), 4791 (2020). https://doi.org/10.3390/su12114791
10. Sun, C., Jiang, S., Skibniewski, M.J., Man, Q., Shen, L.: A literature review of the factors limiting the application of BIM in the construction industry. Technol. Econ. Dev. Econ. **23**, 764–779 (2017)
11. Big data: the next Google. Nature **455**, 8–9 (2008). https://doi.org/10.1038/455008a
12. Lattanzi, D., Miller, G.: Review of robotic infrastructure inspection systems. J. Infrastruct. Syst. **23**, 1–16 (2017)
13. Zhou, S., Gheisari, M.: Unmanned aerial system applications in construction: a systematic review. Constr. Innov. **18**, 453–468 (2018)
14. Grosso, R., Mecca, U., Moglia, G., Prizzon, F., Rebaudengo, M.: Collecting built environment information using UAVs: time and applicability in building inspection activities. Sustainability **12**, 4731 (2020). https://doi.org/10.3390/su12114731
15. Perez, H., Tah, J.H.M., Mosavi, A.: Deep learning for detecting building defects using convolutional neural networks. Sensors **19**(16), 35–56 (2019)
16. Koch, C., Neges, M., König, M., Abramovici, M.: Natural markers for augmented reality-based indoor navigation and facility maintenance. Autom. Constr. **48**, 18–30 (2014)
17. Tobias, M.: Applications of laser scanning, augmented reality and BIM in existing facilities (2019). https://www.gim-international.com/content/article/applications-of-laser-scanning-augmented-reality-and-bim-in-existing-facilities. Accessed 2 May 2021
18. Liu, F., Seipel, S.: Precision study on augmented reality-based visual guidance for facility management tasks. Autom. Constr. **90**, 79–90 (2018)
19. The program "Digital Economy of the Russian Federation" (2017). http://government.ru/rugovclassifier/614/events/. Accessed 2 May 2021
20. Aleksandrova, E., Vinogradova, V., Tokunova, G.: Integration of digital technologies in the field of construction in the Russian Federation. Eng. Manage. Prod. Serv. Sciendo **11**(3), 38–47 (2019)
21. Kuzhakova, Z.U., Baiburin, A.Kh.: Review of the BIM regulatory documentation in the Russian Federation. In: Bulletin of the South Ural State University. Ser. Construction Engineering and Architecture, vol. 20, no. 3, pp. 70–79 (2020)

22. RF Government Decree of 05.03.2021 N 331: The establishment case in which developers, technical customer facing, provide or carry out preparation of justification of investments, and (or) the person responsible for the operation of capital construction projects, secure the development and maintenance of information model of the object capital construction. https://docs.cntd.ru/document/573842519. Accessed 2 May 2021
23. GOST 31937-2011 Buildings and constructions. Rules of inspection and monitoring of the technical condition, Standartinform, p. 89 (2014). https://files.stroyinf.ru/Index2/1/4293781/4293781963.html. Accessed 2 May
24. Ushakov, A., Zinkevich, E.S.: Methods of diagnostics of technical condition of structures of buildings and structures. J. Constr. Prod. **2**, 35–40 (2020)
25. Ross, D.T.: Application and extensions of SADT. Comput. IEEE **18**, 25–34 (1985)
26. Feldmann, C.G.: The Practical Guide to Business Process Reengineering Using IDEF0. Dorset House Publishing, New York (1998)

Database of Architectural Patterns, Heritage Objects and Plots for Conceptual Design of Urban Objects

Irina Petrova$^{(\boxtimes)}$ iD, Viktoriia Zaripova iD, and Kseniia Proshunina iD

Astrakhan State University of Architecture and Civil Engineering, 18, Tatishcheva Str., Astrakhan 414056, Russia

Abstract. The article discusses an information system for supporting the conceptual design of urban objects on the basis of architectural patterns, which meet requirements for construction in the historical and cultural environment. The system allows you to select architectural samples with an emphasis on restrictions on the regulation of urban areas near cultural heritage sites, competently and harmoniously implement the consistency of the architecture of the historical environment with the new building object included in it, and maintain a balance of the architectural and stylistic characteristics of this environment. The system provides three linked databases: plots, heritages, and architectural patterns, to process orders for construction near the cultural heritage sites. The selection of samples is carried out by the operator according to the identification number of the site in the cadastral quarter and the planned building area. As a result, the user will receive a list of the most suitable patterns, selected according to the client order's parameters and the requirements related to the heritage sites nearby.

Keywords: Heritage · Pattern · Information system · Historical and cultural environment · Design · Sustainable development

1 Introduction

1.1 Challenge of Cultural Heritage Preservation in Dynamic Urban Development

A harmonious relationship between the preservation of cultural heritage and the socio-economic development of the urban environment is an urgent problem. The historical and cultural landscape is considered not only a heritage that must be preserved for future generations but also a resource for the sustainable development of society [1]. Due to a long period of lack of attention to historical sites, the material wear and tear of architectural monuments reached its climax. Buildings are destroyed from dilapidation and desolation. Cities are losing units of history and, along with them, their historical origins. A significant problem arises in the preservation of the identity of the historical town formation with its cultural heritage and valuable environmental objects in the context of the development of modern architecture. The historical heritage is invaluable and must be preserved as a sustainable historical formation [2, 3].

© Springer Nature Switzerland AG 2021
A. G. Kravets et al. (Eds.): CIT&DS 2021, CCIS 1448, pp. 367–384, 2021.
https://doi.org/10.1007/978-3-030-87034-8_27

Today, in order to preserve the historical and cultural heritage, projects of protection zones are adopted, that regulate the development regulation zone and the requirements for economic activities near cultural heritage sites. It makes it possible to control the chaotic architecture in historical settlements. Many cities in the territory of Russia need competent restoration of historical environmental spaces by means of compensatory facilities being introduced, that are being erected on empty territories.

Work on a projected object near the territory of a cultural heritage object is a capacious research process, that requires significant analysis of the architectural and spatial environment and the interaction of a specific environment with an observer. Information technology is a source of innovation for the development of research methods, accelerating the issuance of competent design documentation for a capital construction object being built and, due to this, preserving the historical and cultural heritage [4]. In the conceptual design of a capital construction facility, the work of designers must be automated. Automation will reduce design time and labor costs on the one hand and eliminate possible errors in the choice of configuration and geometric dimensions of the planned object.

1.2 Digital Technologies for Heritage Conservation and Urban Cultural and Historical Landscape Management

Many works are devoted to research on the creation of information systems for immovable monuments of history and culture. The need arises to expand the systematic and flexible organization of expertise in this area due to the complex nature of preserving cultural heritage. A new approach was proposed in [5] based on the ontology of the subject area of cultural heritage preservation. The approach allows efficient processing of heterogeneous data (object description, location characteristics, components, material properties, survey and measurement results, damage typologies, events causing damage, etc.).

A digital information system to support the conservation and management of the cultural landscape is studied in [6, 7]. The system provides a more holistic, dynamic, and specific cultural perspective on heritage for landscape conservation professionals.

The information system [8]contains a set of information about immovable monuments of history and culture. The system is intended for effective multipurpose use, both in an autonomous mode and in conjunction with computer-aided design systems application-oriented.

The information system for the preservation of the archaeological heritage in the Kaliningrad region is considered in [9]using the methods of GIS analysis.

Agata software in [10] allows real-time interaction with high-resolution polygonal models and annotating various raster and vector information directly on them.

A process-oriented approach to the management of World Heritage cities is proposed in [11], a management method has been created that makes it possible to introduce UNESCO directives into the actual management system of World Heritage sites.

Relational database MQNUfakt provides users with a wide range of information in the field of preservation of cultural heritage, a description of the observed damage, reports, and information on the materials used [12].

A new form of metadata and a risk management structure for architectural heritage based is proposed in a virtual environment on information modeling of buildings [13].

Decision-making for the protection of cultural heritage is a multi-criteria process involving many parameters and stakeholders. A methodological approach was proposed in [14] for scientific decision-making support based on integrated documentation protocols as a source of necessary data for a cultural heritage object. Evaluation of a number of criteria is carried out in an expert way, which will allow entering weight coefficients into the system using mathematical models.

French researchers pay particular attention to tools that combine at least two of the following three aspects: digital representation of the city (for example maps, 3D modeling, etc.), multimedia data (text data, audio stories, images, video, etc.), and digital and text data [15].

The analysis showed that most of the works are devoted to the issues of digitalization and 3-D presentation of cultural heritage objects in a certain area. A significantly smaller part of the works is associated with the consideration of the urban cultural landscape as a whole in the context of sustainable transformation and integration of modern architecture in the historical environment.

The developed information system for supporting project activities in the historical and cultural environment has great potential, which contributes to the preservation of heritage and the competent development of the historical center of the urban fabric. The formation of space in the historical and cultural environment will result from the application of an information system for supporting project activities that meet the characteristics of a historical city, taking into account legal and economic realities. The system will preserve the uniqueness of the historical urban environment and ensure the sustainable development of the urban agglomeration.

The purpose of the article is to develop computer-aid support (information system) to the design of new buildings in the historical and cultural environment. The system will help to select the optimal construction solution with regard to the bounding factors of neighboring historical heritage objects.

The information system will find practical application in the historical cities of Russia. The system will make it possible to monitor compliance with the established regulations in the protected zones, which is a mandatory basis for con-ducting construction and economic activities near the territories of cultural heritage sites, and competently introduce the design model of the capital construction object into the free areas of the city's historical center.

2 Methodological Basis for the Development of Information Technology to Support the Design of New Buildings in the Historical and Cultural Environment

2.1 Visual Interaction of the Object-Monument and the Background Environment

Research work is a must in the vicinity of the cultural heritage site. Protection zones with established regulations ensure the preservation of the cultural heritage object in its historical environment and in the adjacent territory, in accordance with the requirements of Federal Law N 73 "Cultural heritage objects (historical and cultural monuments) of the peoples of the Russian Federation".

Determination of the parameters of a new capital construction object in the historical environment is associated with the analytical process of the formation of the landscape space of the city and the visual perception of this space by a person. The methodology landscape-visual analysis on the compositional perception of the environmental space is given in, taking into account the anthropometric indicators of a person [16]. The picture of the visual interaction of the cultural heritage object with the projected background environmental object is shown in Fig. 1 in the area of regulation of development and economic activity.

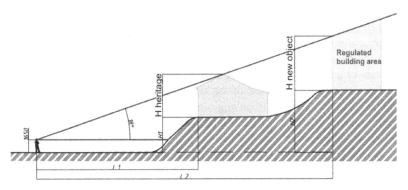

Fig. 1. Visual interaction of the object-monument and the background environment.

$$H_{object} = \sqrt{\left(\frac{L_2}{\cos(18°)}\right)^2 - L_2^2} - H_2 + 1{,}65, \qquad (1)$$

L_1 – the distance from the observer to the cultural heritage site; L_2 – the distance from the observer to the object under construction in the area of regulation of the building; H_1 – the difference between the ground level at the observer's point and the level of the foundation of the cultural heritage object; H_2 – the difference between the ground level marks at the observer's point and the level of the base of the object being erected; H_{object} – the height of the object being erected in the area of regulation of the building.

The results of the landscape-visual analysis form the basis for entering data into the developed information system for supporting project activities in the historical and cultural environment.

2.2 Formation of Architectural Patterns in the Historical and Cultural Environment

The study of the urban fabric space was considered within the boundaries of the historical settlement of the city of Astrakhan in the Russian Federation. During the study of historical objects of the environment, the authors identified the planning features of the urban planning solution: rectangular or close to the rectangular cutting of quarters, land allotment for plots has similar areas, the surviving buildings can be typed and defined into a system of modules.

The authors propose to use the theory of spatial patterns, which is widely used in economic geography, as well as in the development of settlement systems and in urban planning [17, 18].

Preliminary studies were carried out to form the types of objects (patterns) of capital construction classified in relation to the configuration of territorial areas. Plots are classified according to size types. The basic size of ordinary households in the plots of historical formation "Armenian Sloboda, XVIII - early XX centuries" ranges from 20 m–25 m in depth, which corresponds to half the depth of historical quarters, in the width of households - from 7 m to 35 m. The most common standard sizes of ordinary households are dimensions from 15 m to 20 m.

To preserve the unique identity of the historical and cultural environment of the territory under consideration, a method of introducing standard architectural solutions (patterns) is proposed. In the methodology, indicators of landscape-visual analysis are taken into account. Indicators allow us to perceive the scale of the environment. This technique provides for the consolidation of the development of the city block with standard modules - patterns, for maximum expediency and efficient exploitation of the land of the city center.

Pattern (English Pattern - sample, pattern, system), in the work of the authors, is defined as a reference standard project, adapted to the historical and cultural environment and applicable as compensatory construction on plots free from building.

The methodology for the formation of typical architectural solutions is based on the principles of land use and development of adjacent areas, modern regulatory and legislative documentation, sanitary requirements, fire safety, and improvement [20]. The set of types of households (patterns) is formed on the basis of the standard sizes of the sites of the historical settlement. Six principal names of patterns were proposed in the development of an experimental prototype of the developed information system. The scheme of the basic planning organization of homeownership is developed for each individual pattern. Data on patterns are summarized in Table 1.

Table 1. Types of architectural patterns.

Pattern name	Description
A.1.2.1.1	Type of building an object with a firewall and a driveway arch (right/left), the position of the street building along the building line, two-story, the position of the courtyard building indented from the borders of adjacent territories, one-story
A.2.2.0.0	Building type object with a firewall and a driveway arch (central), the position of the street building indented from the building line, two-story
B.1.2.1.1	Building type object with a firewall, the position of the street building along the building line, two-story, the position of the yard building indented from the borders of adjacent territories, one-story
B.2.1.0.0	Building type object with a firewall, the position of the street building indented from the building line, one-story

Regulations are set in the area of regulation of development near cultural heritage sites, imposing restrictions on new construction in terms of height parameters, style architectural solutions, and special requirements. The base of patterns of the design organization can be replenished in accordance with these regulations.

The following rules were formed for designing patterns:

- The building with its street facade is oriented along the red line while maintaining the line of the historical buildings of the quarter.
- The building can be presented with a basement and an attic floor.
- The architectural solution of the street building should not be knocked out of the context of the historical buildings, the use of bright colors in large masses is prohibited.
- The number of the story's in the street and courtyard buildings is limited by the heights obtained as a result of landscape-visual analysis and compliance with the requirements for insolation.
- The provision of access to the inner courtyard space is observed for the possibility of operating the territory, due to emergencies.
- Fire-fighting materials are proposed to be used for the construction of walls, while the boundaries of adjacent households should have a firewall, passages less than the width of the passage should be excluded between buildings.
- Car parks for residents should be organized in the depths of the household through the use of basements.

A graphical diagram showing the principal criteria for a typical homeownership pattern is shown in Fig. 2, Fig. 3 shows examples of patterns. The patterns are classified according to the position of the street and courtyard buildings and their absence. Currently, 50 patterns have been developed for construction projects in the city of Astrakhan.

General information about the nature of the existing development should form an idea of the ecological space for the placement of potential development in it and lay the fundamental criteria for establishing a stylistic solution for potential development within the boundaries of these territories.

The existing buildings within the boundaries of the study area are represented by buildings objects at different time intervals. New architectural solutions should be chronologically linked to heritage sites.

Projected capital construction objects near the location of cultural heritage objects should have an architectural and compositional solution visually linked to the architecture of cultural heritage objects, with a color scheme that does not contrast with the cultural heritage object and does not create dissonant perception.

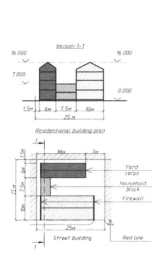

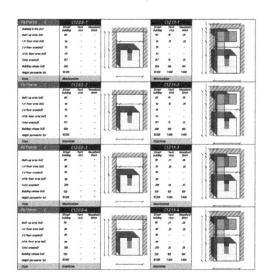

Fig. 2. Homeownership scheme.   **Fig. 3.** Fragment of the pattern database archive.

2.3 Information System for Supporting Project Activities Based on Patterns in the Historical and Cultural Urban Environment

The information system for supporting project activities is represented by a system that allows you to develop solutions for the issuance of finished project documentation based on certain stages and rules for the development of individual components. Variants of the draft design for the customer are formed from the pattern base. The information system design methodology is based on an ontological model that analyzes the subject area and is necessary for structuring the relationship of entities and instances and the development of information system databases.

The study reflects the hypothesis about the possibility of automating project activities to streamline the architecture of compensatory construction and the formation of an integrated urban environment.

The diagrams in Fig. 4 and Fig. 5 explain the existing process of work in design organizations using standard methods for designing buildings in a historical and cultural environment and at the same time using an information system.

The impact of the developed information system on work performance was assessed in the study. On average, 6 months with the participation of team members of 6 people are spent on the development of a draft design of a capital construction object using the traditional design method. The use of an information system with a ready-made database of patterns reduces the time for processing information and issuing a design solution to the customer up to 3 days from the date of the conclusion of the contract and the provision of the necessary information.

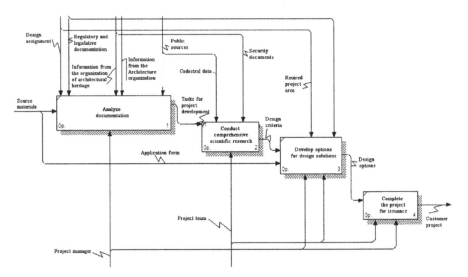

Fig. 4. Diagram of a business process in a design organization "as is".

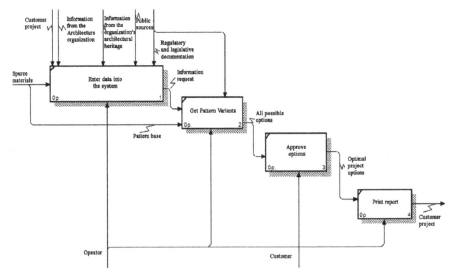

Fig. 5. Diagram of the business process of the project organization "to be".

Databases are formed for structuring information and optimal operation of the information system:

- Database of parcels and permissible heights for new construction.
- Database of cultural heritage objects.
- The base of patterns.

The relationship between these databases is shown in Fig. 6.

Database development is based on a preliminary analysis of the subject area, main and auxiliary functions, a description of the environment for each function. The use of this information provides a rationale for using the necessary entities, attributes in modeling.

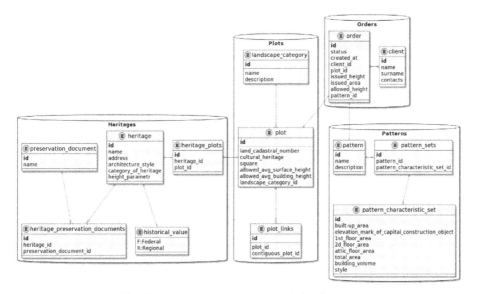

Fig. 6. ER system database connectivity diagram.

3   Experimental Prototype of the Information System

The authors have created an experimental prototype of an information system for supporting project activities in a historical and cultural environment using the software https://coda.io/ to confirm the hypothesis. The experimental prototype represents a working model of project support, formed in a real situation in the cadastral quarter of the historical center of the city of Astrakhan (Russia) (see Fig. 7, 8, and 9).

An experimental prototype of the information system is made on the basis of a cadastral quarter in a historical environment. There are cultural heritage objects in the quarter. The presence of such objects burdens new construction on vacant plots of the quarter.

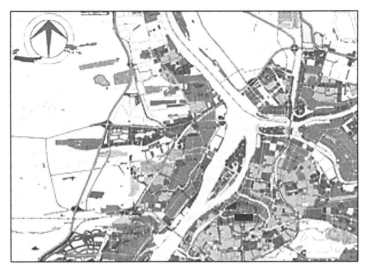

Fig. 7. Location of the historical settlement "Armenian Sloboda" in the city of Astrakhan.

30:12:0101359

Fig. 8. Location of the investigated cadastral quarter 30: 12: 0101359 in the historical settlement "Armenian Sloboda" in the city of Astrakhan.

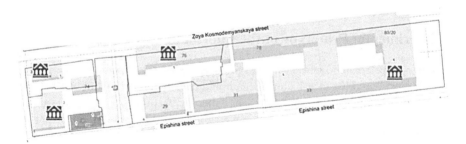

Fig. 9. Cadastral quarter 30: 12: 0101359. G. Astrakhan, Russia.

The concept of the information system assumes the organization of project activities of conflict-free compensatory construction in the historical and cultural environment and increasing the efficiency of making design decisions.

The procedure for working in the information system for a specialist in a design organization is as follows. The specialist forms an application and receives possible options for architectural solutions and their design characteristics based on the information in the order letter. In the order letter, the cadastral number of the territorial plot for the construction of a capital construction object and the building area planned by the customer are indicated.

A specialist of a design organization begins work in the information system by entering data on the building site, information on sites with cultural heritage objects. Cultural heritage sites have already been described in the database. If necessary, the operator can add a new cultural heritage site and link it to the site, as well as supplement the list of protection documents of cultural heritage sites (see Fig. 10).

The plot of the cultural heritage site cannot be used for construction. The proximity to it imposes a number of restrictions on the areas adjacent to it. This data is recorded in the system. For example, the site 30: 12: 0101359: 1 selected by the operator is not a cultural heritage site, but is linked to two adjacent sites, one of which is a cultural heritage site (see Fig. 11).

Fig. 10. Form of viewing and entering information about the object of cultural heritage.

PLOTS

30:12:0101359:1

Search
30:12:0101359:1
30:12:0101359:2
30:12:0101359:3
30:12:0101359:4
30:12:0101359:5
30:12:0101359:6
+

AREA *
m2
226.00

HERITAGE *

AVERAGE MARKING OF PLOT
M
-19.375

PERMISSIBLE HEIGHT MARKING
M
-9.175

PERMISSIBLE HEIGHT PARAMETER
M
10.200

LAND CATEGORY
Lands of settlements (land of settlements)
for the operation of cafes

CONTIGUOUS PLOTS

Cadastral number	Heritage	Area	Average marking of plot	Permissible height marking	Permissible height parameter	
30:12:0101359:2	☑	1013.63	--	--	--	The estate of the court councilor Sergeev, 1830-1840, 1887

Fig. 11. Form for viewing and entering information about plots.

The design organization operating the information system, before starting operation, must fill in the database of patterns that it intends to use for construction. If necessary, the operator can supplement this base with new architectural patterns. The main criteria for this are the height of the building, the area it occupies, and the intended architectural

PATTERN

Fig. 12. Form for viewing and entering information about patterns.

style of the building. The operator can attach a gallery of images to the passport of each pattern (see Fig. 12).

An application is made for each client's request. The application contains information about the construction site and the desired parameters: height and building area (see Fig. 13). After that, the application in the "Received" status is displayed in the application journal (Fig. 14).

Fig. 13. Application entry form.

Fig. 14. Application journal.

In the application form, the system automatically displays information on adjacent areas. The system calculates the maximum allowable height for the designed object according to the parameter of the allowable height of the cultural heritage object, calculated by the formula (1) if the adjacent site belongs to the cultural heritage object. The height is chosen according to the minimum of the permissible heights from all included cultural heritage objects in the case of placing several cultural heritage objects in adjacent areas. The building height desired by the customer, permitted by the approved documentation, is selected in the absence of a cultural heritage object in adjacent areas. The system allows the operator to select patterns suitable for height and area. In this case, the operator has the opportunity to view the mini-card of each pattern. After the operator has selected a pattern, the system automatically fills in the application form with the data of the selected pattern (see Fig. 15).

Request

Fig. 15. Autocomplete the application form.

Sets of draft design documentation are selected and supported by the operator on the basis of the pattern identification number from the electronic archive of the design organization (see Fig. 16).

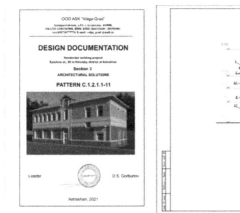
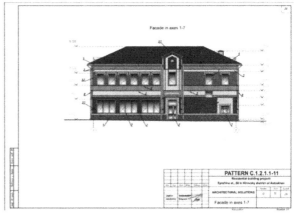

Fig. 16. Project documentation.

The operator can send a short report on the work for verification to the customer.

4   Discussion of Results

Project activities take a significant amount of time. The customer's wait after writing an application for project development can reach several months. The design process in the historic urban environment is delayed due to preliminary studies and the creation of a project with optimal data to meet the requirements of protected areas of the cultural heritage site. The proposed information system significantly reduces the design time. Formation and constant updating of the system databases is the most time-consuming stage. The design organization can independently replenish the base of standard projects, thereby increasing the quality of design solutions. The selection of typical projects from the pattern base takes a split second and makes it possible to select multiple ready-made architectural solutions from the archive of the design organization.

The interaction of the project organization with the administrative structures of the city is necessary to improve the efficiency of the system for supporting project activities in the historical and cultural environment. This will make it possible to update information about the belonging of the building understudy to a cultural heritage object, registration data of a cultural heritage object, documentation on the definition of protected zones with the regulation of easements in the zones of regulation of development and economic activity; readable topographic surveys. Currently, contracts are being concluded with responsible institutions to support the developed information system.

The results issued by the information system confirm the principle of "conformity of conflict-free compensatory construction in the historical and cultural environment", which is important for the implementation of objects in the environment of historical settlements.

Possible directions for improving the experimental prototype of the system:

- Use of geoinformation technologies and virtual reality technologies.
- Development of a network version of the information system for the possibility of mutual use by design and management organizations.
- Development of an Internet resource that allows the urban community to participate in the formation and sustainable development of the cultural landscape of the city.

The information system has received experimental approbation in the historical and cultural environment near the cultural heritage site "The estate of the court councilor Sergeev, 1830-1840, 1887". The capital construction object was implemented according to the preliminary design "Pattern C.2.1.0.0-14", represented by a one-story volume in the eclectic style, with the position of the street building along the red line, without the presence of yard and utility blocks (see Fig. 17).

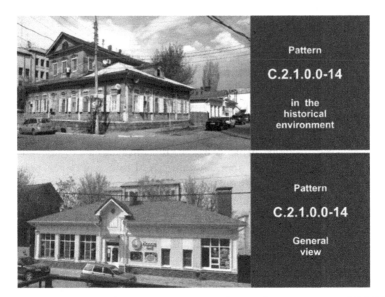

Fig. 17. Implementation of the project in the historical environment pattern C.2.1.0.0-14

5   Conclusion

The erection of new buildings in the historical and cultural environment must be designed with the preservation of the identity of the historical environment: with its cultural heritage objects, valuable environmental objects, and regulations of protection zones.

To preserve the unique identity of the historical and cultural environment of the territory under consideration, the authors proposed a method for introducing standard architectural solutions (patterns), taking into account the indicators of landscape-visual analysis, which makes it possible to perceive the scale of the environment and formulated rules for the design of architectural modules - patterns, for maximum feasibility and effective exploitation of the land of the urban center.

The proposed information system for supporting the conceptual design of objects under construction is intended to increase the efficiency of making design decisions during the construction of a new building near a cultural heritage site. The information system supports project activities based on architectural samples, that are adapted to the historical and cultural environment. The composition of the databases is determined by this system.

The interconnections between the designed object, the nearest cultural heritage objects, and adjacent territories are formed in the information system. The relationship of building sites with architectural monuments is determined. A number of alternative conceptual projects (patterns) are provided to the user depending on the requested building area and the cadastral number of the site.

References

1. Ashrafi, B., Kloos, M., Neugebauer, C.: Heritage impact assessment, beyond an assessment tool: a comparative analysis of urban development impact on visual integrity in four UNESCO World Heritage Properties. J. Cult. Herit. **47**, 199–207 (2021). https://doi.org/10.1016/j.cul her.2020.08.002
2. Jurkovic, M., Čaldarović, O., Behaim, J., Kranjec I.: The perception and social role of Heritage Buildings in modern society (2019). https://doi.org/10.1484/m.dem-eb.5.118099
3. Figueiredo, V.: Cultural heritage, city, sustainability: what is the role of urban legislation in preservation and development? Ambiente & Sociedade **17**, 91–110 (2014). https://doi.org/10.1590/S1414-753X2014000200007
4. Gombault, A., Allal-Chérif, O., Décamps, A.: ICT adoption in heritage organizations: crossing the chasm. J. Bus. Res. **69**(11), 5135–5140 (2016)
5. Cacciotti, R., Valach, J., Kuneš, P., Čerňanský, M., Blasko, M., Kremen, P.: Monument damage information system (MONDIS): an ontological approach to cultural heritage documentation. ISPRS Ann. Photogramm. Remote Sens. Spat. Inf. Sci. II-5/W1, 55–60 (2013). https://doi.org/10.5194/isprsannals-II-5-W1-55-2013
6. Yang, C., Han, F.: A digital information system for cultural landscapes: the case of Slender West Lake scenic area in Yangzhou, China. Built Heritage **4**(1), 1–14 (2020). https://doi.org/10.1186/s43238-020-00004-8
7. López, M., Antonio, S., Cabreraab, T., Linares, M., Pulgarb, G.: Guidelines from the heritage field for the integration of landscape and heritage planning: a systematic literature review. Landsc. Urban Plan. **204**, 103931 (2020)
8. Tkachenko, I.G.: Research and development of the information system of immovable monuments of history and culture. Thesis. Rostov-on-Don. p. 161 (2001)
9. Puzakova G.S.: Information systems in the preservation of the archaeological heritage in the Kaliningrad region (2021). https://www.archaeolog.ru/media/periodicals/agis/AGIS-5/Puzakova/page1.html. Accessed April 3
10. Francisco, S., Francisco, J., Melero, M., Victoria, L.: A complete 3D information system for cultural heritage documentation. J. Cult. Herit. **23**, 49–57 (2017)
11. Lidija, P., Marko, H., Janvan, D.B.: Process orientation of the world heritage city management system. J. Cult. Herit. **46**, 259–267 (2020)
12. Fitz, S.: MQNUfakt the federal environmental agency's database for the protection of historic monuments and cultural heritage. In: Science, Technology and European Cultural Heritage. Proceedings of the European Symposium, Bologna, Italy, 13–16 June 1989–1991, pp. 830–833 (1991)
13. Jongwook, L., Junki, K., Jaehong, A., Woontack, W.: Context-aware risk management for architectural heritage using historic building information modeling and virtual reality. J. Cult. Herit. **38**, 242–252 (2019)
14. Kioussia, A., et al.: A computationally assisted cultural heritage conservation method. J. Cult. Herit. **48**(March–April), 119–128 (2021)
15. Jaillota, V., Istasseb, M., Servignec, S., Gesquièrea, G., Rautenbergd, M., Leforte, I.: Describing, comparing and analysing digital urban heritage tools: a methodology designed with a multidisciplinary approach. Digit. Appl. Archaeol. Cult. Herit. **17**(1), e00135 (2020)
16. Proshunina, K.A., Petrova, I.: Information system of project activities in the historical and cultural environment. Eng. Constr. Bull. Caspian Reg. **1**(31), 78–83 (2020)
17. Christopher, A., Hirschen, S., Ishikawa, S., Coffin, C.: Shlomo angel houses generated by patterns, vol. 219. Center for Environmental Structure (1969)
18. Leitner, H.: Pattern Theory: Introduction and Perspectives on the Tracks of Christopher Alexander, Graz (2015)

19. A Pattern Language: Towns, Buildings, Construction, p. 1216. Oxford University Press, Oxford
20. Skokan, A., Gnezdilov, A., Stadnikov, V., Skorokhod, M.: A method of conflict-free renovation of a regular quarter of a historic Russian city (2021). http://www.robotarchitects.ru/projects/stadnikov/1012/. Accessed April 13

Computer-Aided Evaluation of Individual Traffic Road Safety Along a Given Route Within the Framework of the "Driver-Car-Road-Environment" System

Dmitry Skorobogatchenko[1]([⊠]), Vitaly Borovik[2], Roman Chugumbaev[3], and Anastasia Borovik[1]

[1] Volgograd Technical State University, Volgograd, Russia
[2] State Public Enterprise of Volgograd Region «Directorate of Highways», Volgograd, Russia
[3] Russian Transport University, Moscow, Russia
romanry@ya.ru

Abstract. The paper substantiates the need to develop a system for the assessment of individual road traffic safety in urban conditions when analyzing the factors constituting the "driver-car-road-environment" (DCRE) system. The authors suggest an assessment technique of road traffic accidents, which makes it possible to analyzw a number of factors influencing road accidents. In particular, the simulation includes the characteristics of the driver, technical condition of the vehicle, road conditions, weather, and climatic factors. Fuzzy neural networks such as ANFIS are used as a tool for the implementation of a computer-aided assessment system of road traffic safety. The authors provide the results of statistical analysis of a number of variables of the DCRE system, and it helps us create membership functions within the fuzzy inference system. In the final part of the paper, the results of road traffic safety assessment for various driver types in various road conditions are presented on the example of the road network of the city of Volgograd.

Keywords: Road safety assessment · Fuzzy neural networks · Road conditions

1 Introduction

The increase in demand for transport services contributes to the continuous growth of the level of motorization (see Fig. 1). Over the past 20 years, the motorization rate in Russia alone has almost tripled and grew to more than 330 cars per 1000 people by the beginning of 2020 [1]. The growth in the number of individual vehicles is especially strong in large urban agglomerations, which is associated with both an increased population density and a relatively high level of average wages.

The logic of the motorization growth requires the corresponding development of infrastructure in the form of required density of the road network, expansion of parking space, and improvement of traffic control. However, as practice shows, the rate of development of transport infrastructure lags behind the rate of motorization, which is

A. G. Kravets et al. (Eds.): CIT&DS 2021, CCIS 1448, pp. 385–404, 2021.
https://doi.org/10.1007/978-3-030-87034-8_28

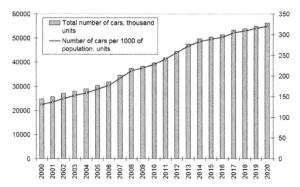

Fig. 1. Analysis of changes in the number of passenger cars and the total number of vehicles in Russia presented dynamically, for 2000–2020

especially important for the urban road network, the extensive development of which is significantly limited [2]. The structure of the road network of Russian cities was created and then developed with the priority of servicing public transport and for the estimated level of motorization of 60 vehicles/1000 people. The consequence of this is the fact that modern urban agglomerations are on the verge of depletion of road capacity (see Fig. 2).

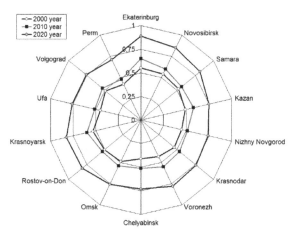

Fig. 2. Analysis of the traffic ratio in 14 cities of Russia with the population of over one million people presented dynamically for 2000–2020

Thus, today we can speak about the existence of a problematic situation, which consists in the inconsistency of the capacity of the city road network with the annually increasing traffic needs caused by the growth in the total number of vehicles. This circumstance, in turn, leads to a number of serious socio-technical, economic, and environmental consequences. Let's consider them in more detail. An increase in traffic density leads to a drop in the average speed of traffic (see Fig. 3), which is typical not only for Russian cities but also for European urban agglomerations, comparable in scale [3].

This circumstance, in turn, leads to economic losses of road users, the additional load on road infrastructure, noise, and air pollution [4].

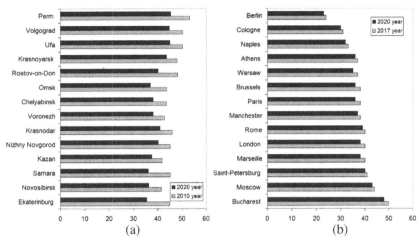

Fig. 3. Analysis of the fall in the average speed of vehicles in megacities: a) according to data from 14 cities of Russiawith the population of over one million people presented dynamically for 2010–2020; b) according to data from 14 large cities in Europepresented dynamically for 2017–2020

Despite significant spatial differences in large Russian cities, their main environmental problems are associated with a high concentration of population and transport in relatively small areas [5]. At the same time, there is no doubt that it is motor transport that is one of the main sources of air pollution in urban agglomerations (see Fig. 4).

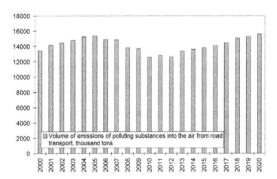

Fig. 4. Analysis of emissions of pollutants emitted into the atmosphere by road transport in Russia presented dynamically for 2000–2020

However, perhaps the most serious problem associated with the increase in traffic density is the growth of road accidents in the urban environment. The current accident rate (see Fig. 5) is several times higher than the damage from other anthropogenic accidents and entails negative social and economic consequences, which are determined by the damage resulting from the death and injury of people, damaged vehicles, damage to goods and damage to transport infrastructure [6].

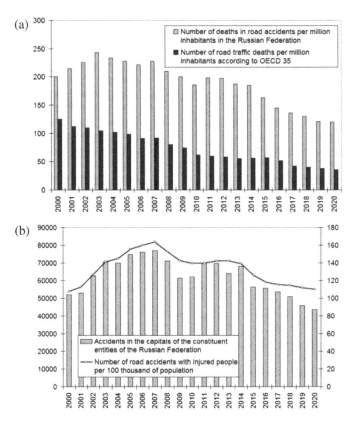

Fig. 5. Analysis of road traffic safety: a) number of fatal crashes per 1 million inhabitants in Russia in comparison with the average indicator of 35 developed countries of the Organization for Economic Cooperation and Development b) Analysis of road accidents by cities - capitals of the constituent entities of the Russian Federation

As the analysis of accident statistics shows [7], road safety depends to the greatest extent on road conditions, speed limits observed by drivers, and their psychophysiological characteristics (see Fig. 6).

Thus, today, when designing a smart and comfortable urban environment, issues connected with the development and design of systems for assessment and improvement of road traffic safety, taking into account traffic conditions in urban agglomerations, which make it possible to suggest recommendations on safe speed mode of the vehicle based on the accident rate forecast for a specific route.

The aim of the study is to develop an integrated computer-aided system for the assessment of individual traffic safety along a given route of the road network within the combination of DCRE factors.

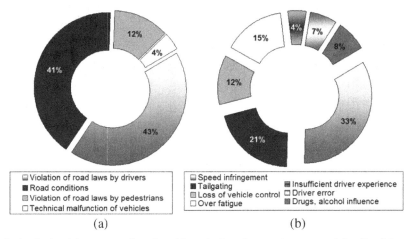

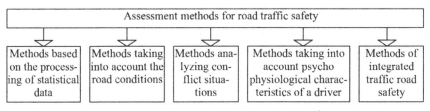

Fig. 6. Analysis of the causes of road accidents in the urban environment: a) details of the causes of an accident according to road police data b) including an expanded structure of traffic violations by drivers

2 Review of Methods of Problem Solution

By the current moment, a number of methods for the assessment of road traffic safety have been developed (see Fig. 7). The most widely used assessment methods are based on the analysis of road conditions.

Fig. 7. Classification of the main assessment methods for traffic road safety

However, integrated methods, as well as techniques using individual factors in the assessment, such as the physiological characteristics of the driver or the design specificity of vehicles, also deserve close attention.

Since the design of an assessment system of road traffic safety is carried out within the framework of the DCRE system, so when analyzing the existing approaches to automation, the greatest attention should be paid to integrated approaches [8]. The classification of the main tools used to automate the assessment of road accidents is shown in Fig. 8.

Automation of the assessment of the factors of the DCRE system is founded on the use of statistical analysis methods predicting the occurrence of road accidents, localizing hazardous areas, and identifying factors which have the most significant influence on the accident.

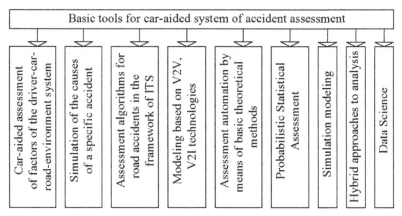

Fig. 8. Analysis of the main instruments used to automate the assessment of road accidents and road traffic safety

The data for the analysis is supplied either by computer-aided road data banks or directly by users who are participants in road accidents, while entry is available by means of mobile applications [9]. The approaches within this area are aimed at the prediction of the potential number of accidents in each region and identification of potentially dangerous factors, their analysis is necessary for the design of road infrastructure and traffic improvement. It should be noted also that road data banks allow us systematizing independently the nuclei of accidents and on the basis of client and server applications, carry out road accident analysis.

The mechanism assessment of car accidents within the design of intelligent transport systems is used to ensure road safety, reduce environmental problems and optimize urban traffic. This approach presents a global trend for the assessment of road accidents in modern urban agglomerations and allows us to improve radically the quality of road traffic [10]. The practice of the use of tools in this direction for final users is designed, as a rule, in the form of client/server applications.

Within the direction of computer assistance of the main theoretical methods, a set of mathematical models was developed, which makes it possible to analyze and predict the dynamics of the main indicators of road safety. The most popular is the approach to computerizing the assessment method of road accident rate and is based on the record of the influence of road conditions [11].

The direction of simulation of a specific incident is based on the assessment of various factors that led to an accident, such as braking distance, speed, state of the braking system, etc. As an example, we can mention such software systems as CARAT, AUTO-GRAF, PC-Crash, ANALYSER PRO [12]. Methods for the analysis and reconstruction of the circumstances of an accident are based on mathematical models that describe two main processes that occur in an accident with cars, i.e. the process of d and the process of the crash. Both processes are described by models built on a scientific basis, which use the well-known laws of mechanics and are based on one or another experimental data [13].

The simulation of accidents by means of V2V, V2I technologies is based on the fact that the state of the parameters under the control of a car (speed, steering system, braking system, etc.) is communicated wirelessly to neighboring cars or road infrastructure [14]. The automation of accident assessment is based on the processing of data from vehicles equipped with some communication device with infrastructure or unmanned vehicles and allows reducing the impact of human factor, as the main source of accidents, and to make the characteristics of traffic homogenous.

Probabilistic-statistical tools for the assessment of road accidents are presented by regression models for the evaluation of the number of road accidents, as well as the number of deaths and injuries in them, based on a set of socio-economic indicators. At present, the statistics on road accidents with injured people and deaths are mainly used to forecast road accidents. The most common methods are extrapolation, forecasting taking into account seasonality, modeling the recurrence of accidents.

The methods of big data analysis can be seen as a modern continuation of the approach to statistical data processing [15]. The data on road traffic accidents come from photo radars, complexes of photo and video recording of offenses and vehicles, as well as from open sources on the Internet and mobile devices of participants in the events. As platforms for the collection and analysis of such applications as Apache HBase, Apache Hadoop, Apache Storm, Apache Spark, libraries of data mining algorithms and machine learning MLlib and Mahout are used. This area should also include machine learning tools and soft computing. A review of approaches using machine learning methods in the analysis of road accidents is presented in the paper [16]. The use of a multilayer perception is considered one of the most suitable structures for the solution of the problems of road accident forecasting and transport control strategies [17]. An overview of models for soft computing is presented here [18].

Such software products as VISSIM, SUMO, and MATSim are successfully used for simulation. A feature of the direction is the visualization of the data of the traffic flow model in the emergency-hazardous section and the desire to create a three-dimensional model of the recognizable environment of dangerous zones. As an example of the use of computer-aided assessment systems of road traffic safety based on a comprehensive evaluation of DCRE factors, we can cite a study [19], being technically a set of digital simulation models. The largest part of them were introduced into practice as basic normative documents. Specificity of this line of research is the possibility to assess quantitavely the set of factors which have the greatest significancy in the road transport situation on a specific road segment.

Hybrid approaches include a set of methods combining several of the listed tools. So the use of the synthesis of expert and simulation modeling, mechanisms of interaction between expert systems and decision support systems, systems for automating the assessment of road accidents, combining GIS technologies, analytical models, and databases are known [20]. There are a number of articles that, despite the fact that they consider road traffic safety within an integrated DCRE system, emphasize the reliability of specific system parameters. As an example, we can cite studies devoted to the assessment of the reliability of vehicles and the response of drivers at the assessment of road accidents, as well as a set of simulation models for road accident assessment including the description of road parameters, road conditions, and the qualities of drivers [21].

The weakest link in the DCRE system is human being. In this respect, a significant part of techniques to the automation of safety assessment considers the DCRE as a biotechnical system allowing the identification of physiological and psychological characteristics of drivers [22].

Summing up the analysis of tools and means for assessment of road safety, it should be noted that the predominance of an integrated approach and the desire of researchers to take into account the maximum number of factors that can be done only within the framework of the DCRE system should be noted. The most promising tools are the use of Big Data mining tools.

3   Assessment Model of Road Traffic Safety

At the first stage of work, we determined the structure of variable factors that characterize road safety within the DCRE system and conducted statistical studies for each variable. The main components of the DCRE were studied in sufficient detail and were described in a variety of scientific studies [23]. The structure of the variables that form the factors of the DCRE system from the point of view of traffic safety assessment is shown in Fig. 9.

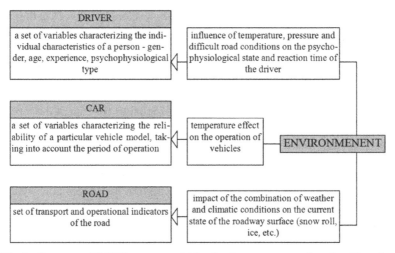

Fig. 9. Structure of DCRE system variables for the assessment of road traffic safety

On the basis of the collected statistical information, we shall analyze the main variables that form the basis of the components of the DCREsystem.

As it was stated earlier, the least reliable factor in the DCRE system is the driver. The analysis of the "driver" subsystem in the formation of an emergency situation shows that the risk of an accident is maximal when the driver is young or old. Meanwhile, if we analyze young drivers and middle-aged drivers, the risk of road accidents for men is significantly higher than for women, while among older drivers the opposite tendency prevails, i.e. the risk of road accidents for older women is higher than for men of the same age. It is agreed by the researchers that changes in driver characteristics are largely influenced by age [24]. Mental and emotional stress, which changes with age, has a significant impact on the driver's behavior. The results of the study of individual characteristics of the driver's behavior are shown in Fig. 10.

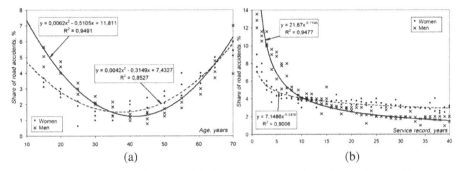

(a)   (b)

Fig. 10. Analysis of the accident rate of the factor "driver": a) dependence of the accident on age and gender of the driver; b) dependence of the accident on experience and driver's gender

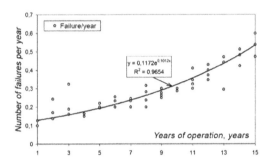

Fig. 11. Reliability analysis for the "car" factor

The safety of the "car" factor in the DCRE system is affected by such factors as the increase in pedestrians, the traffic of cyclists, the organization of traffic, the state and dimensions of engineering structures, intersections at the same level, vehicles standing on the side of the road, geometric parameters and the state of vehicle elements. Generally, at the description of the reliability of the "car" factor in the DCRE system, the effectiveness of its safety system takes into account the age [25]. The analysis results of vehicle failures are presented in Fig. 11.

When assessing such factor as "road", it is recommended to use a system of variables which is usually defined as "road conditions". In this situation, the most significant variables which influence traffic safety in the DCRE system are the intensity of the traffic flow and the speed of the vehicle (see Fig. 8) (Fig. 12).

The main external factors affecting all other elements of the DCRE system are the environment or meteorological conditions [26]. Weather and climate influence significantly the general psycho-physiological state of both the driver and the pedestrian. The paper [27] presents the change in the psycho-physiological parameters of the driver, leading to an accident, depending on the temperature. Qualities of roads and road structures under the influence of weather and climate are studied by many scientists. And if

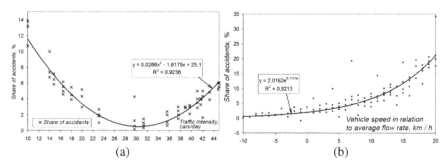

Fig. 12. Analysis of accidents depending on the conditions for the factor "road": a) dependence of road accidents on traffic intensity on multi-lane roads; b) dependence of the accident on the increase in speed in relation to the flow

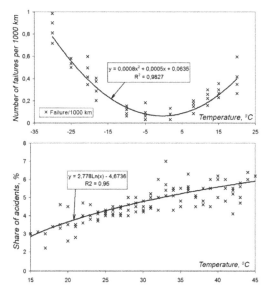

Fig. 13. Influence of the factor "environment" on the behavior of the driver and the work of transport

the influence of the state of the pavement on road safety or the temperature gradient on the transport and operational state of the road has been studied well [28], then the temperature's effect or influence of atmospheric pressure on the driver's behavior has to be taken into account, making the variables of DCRE system. As an exemplification of the author's thesis, Fig. 13 and 14 show the author's studies of the influence of temperature on the operation of vehicles and the behavior of the driver.

At the second stage, on the basis of the collected statistical data for the variables that form the structure assessment system of road traffic safety within the framework DCRE the membership functions of the Gaussian type were constructed.

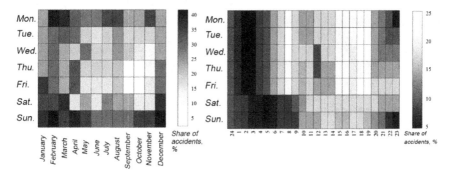

Fig. 14. Influence of time, day of the week, and period of the year on road accidents

The leading parameters for their construction are center and width. It is the expertly specified form of the membership functions of the Gaussian type that will be corrected in the learning process, which will be discussed below. As an exemplification of the operation of the model, Fig. 15 shows the membership functions of two leaf variables included in the complex variable "Driver's predisposition to road accidents". In a similar way, membership functions are constructed for all the leaf variables of the DCRE elements that determine the accident rate.

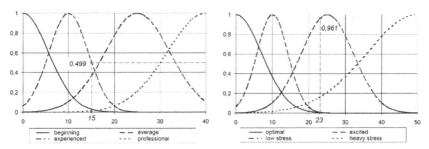

Fig. 15. Generation of membership functions as exemplified by the variables "driver's experience" and "psycho-emotional state of the driver"

Further, for all the membership functions of the system variables, the normalization procedure takes place, that is, the transfer from the natural dimension of the axis to the normalized one from 0 to 1. For functions of the Gaussian type, we will illustrate the normalization by the example of the variable "driving experience" and "psycho-emotional state of the driver "(See Fig. 16).

It should be taken into account that a number of variables have the reverse order of the axis. Consequently, it is not possible to combine the axis with variables that have a straight directivity of the axis. In this regard, all variables with the reverse order of the axis, after the normalization, are reduced to the direct order of the axis. An example is shown in Fig. 17.

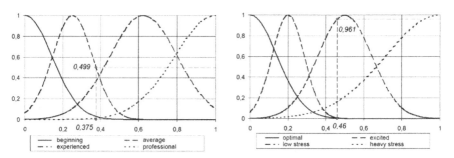

Fig. 16. Normalization of membership functions as exemplified by the variables "driver's experience" and "psycho-emotional state of the driver"

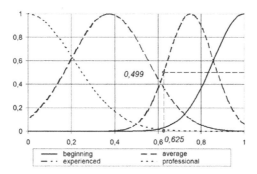

Fig. 17. Membership functions to the direct order of the axis exemplified by the variable "driver experience"

The parameters of membership functions of complex integrated variables such as "Predisposition of the driver to road accidents", "Vehicle performance", "Route safety" and "Environmental impact" are calculated according to the general formula:

$$b = \sum_{i=1}^{n} a_i w_i, \tag{1}$$

where b—parameter (center or width) of the membership function of integral variable; a_i—parameter (center or width, respectively) of the membership function of the i-th leaf variable included in the integral one; w_i—the weight of the i-th leaf variable included in the integral one; i—number of leaf variables.

As an exemplification, let us present the development of a complex variable "Driver's predisposition to road accidents" on the basis of two leaf variables "driver's experience" and "psycho-emotional state of the driver" normalized and given above (see Fig. 18).

At the third stage, the development of the system for the prediction of individual road traffic safety takes place, which is based on fuzzy inference. Its implementation is based on the following stages: development of the rules of fuzzy inference systems, fuzzification of input variables, aggregation of sub-conditions in fuzzy rules, activation of conclusions in their fuzzy rules, subsequent accumulation, and defuzzification of output variables.

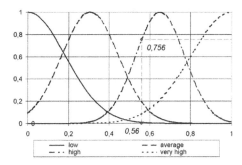

Fig. 18. Generation of the integrated variable "driver's predisposition to road accidents"

Let us exemplify the functioning of the method based on fuzzy inference, using the example of predicting the accident rate in the DCRE system. To facilitate perception, we will restrict ourselves to just two rules and ten values of the membership functions (Fig. 19):

Rule 1:

Predisposition of the driver to an accident = "high" ∧ Performance of the vehicle = "moderately dangerous" ∧ Safety of the traffic route = "unsatisfactory" ∧ Level of environmental impact = "increased" → Accident rate = "high"

Rule 2:

The driver's predisposition to road accidents = "average" ∧ Vehicle characteristics = "moderately safe" ∧ Safety of the traffic route = "satisfactory" ∧ Environmental impact level = "average" → Accident rate = "average"

The definitive advantage of the applied method is the ability to use a significant number of variables, combining them in feature trees, as well as taking into account qualitative information, which is very significant when describing processes in the industry. However, the technique also has its weak points. In particular, as the main drawback of forecasting systems based on fuzzy logic, it is worth mentioning the subjectivity of construction of the form of membership functions and the grid of rules, as well as the low variability of the system, which must be eliminated by adjusting the features of membership functions and rules.

To eliminate these disadvantages the authors developed a fuzzy adaptive system in which statistical material through synthesis with the fuzzy inference features will eliminate subjectivity and determinism inherent in the method. As a tool for the increase of the adaptability of the method, it is advisable to use fuzzy neural networks, which allow solving numerous problems of the road industry.

The general view of the model for forecasting the road accident rate in the DCRE system is presented in Fig. 20.

Fuzzification takes place on the first layer of the FNN (Fig. 20):

$$\mu^{(k)}(x_i) = \frac{1}{1 + \left(\dfrac{x_i - c_j^{(k)}}{\sigma_j^{(k)}}\right)^{2b_j^{(k)}}} \tag{2}$$

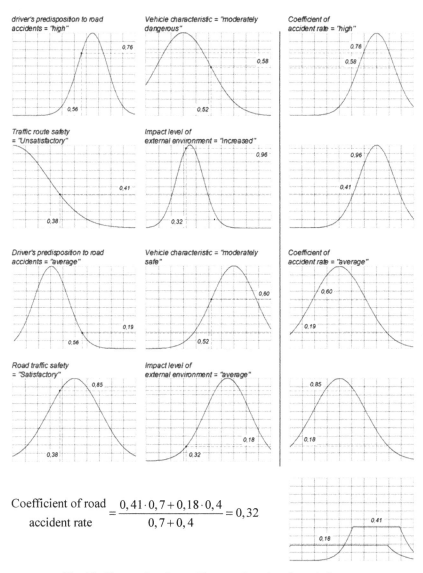

$$\text{Coefficient of road}\atop\text{accident rate} = \frac{0,41 \cdot 0,7 + 0,18 \cdot 0,4}{0,7 + 0,4} = 0,32$$

Fig. 19. Forecasting the accident rate based on fuzzy inference.

where k—number of membership functions (k = 1…M); j—number of variables (j = 1…N); $c_j^{(k)}$, $\sigma_j^{(k)}$, $b_j^{(k)}$—parameters that determine, respectively, the center, width, and shape of the k-th membership function of the j-th variable.

In Layer 2, the values of the variables xi are aggregated according to the formula:

$$w_k = \prod_{j=1}^{N} \frac{1}{1 + \left(\dfrac{x_i - c_j^{(k)}}{\sigma_j^{(k)}}\right)^{2b_j^{(k)}}} \tag{3}$$

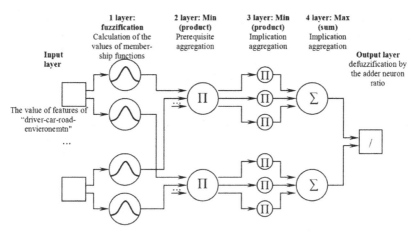

Fig. 20. General scheme of the structure of the FNN (fuzzy neuron net) for forecasting of road traffic safety in the DCRE system in the road industry

The parameters wk (k = 1...M) calculated similarly are simultaneously supplied further into Layer 3 (for the multiplication by weights) and into Layer 4 for the computation of their sums in the neuron f2.

Layer 3 calculates the centers for k-rules by means of the formula:

$$y_k = p_{k0} \tag{4}$$

where pk0 can be considered as the center of the membership function ck.

Then, the aggregation of implication takes place via the algebraic product: $w_k \times y_k(\mathbf{x})$.

The fourth layer is presented by two neurons f1 and f2 that aggregate the results:

$$f_1 = \sum_{k=1}^{M} w_k \times y_k(\mathbf{x}) = \sum_{k=1}^{M} \left[\left(\prod_{j=1}^{N} \mu^{(k)}(x_i) \right) \times c_k \right] \tag{5}$$

$$f_2 = \sum_{k=1}^{M} w_k = \sum_{k=1}^{M} \left[\prod_{j=1}^{N} \mu^{(k)}(x_i) \right] \tag{6}$$

Layer 5 is presented by a single neuron which is in the process of defuzzification:

$$y(x) = \frac{f_1}{f_2} = \frac{\sum\limits_{k=1}^{M} w_k \times y_k(\mathbf{x})}{\sum\limits_{k=1}^{M} w_k} = \frac{\sum\limits_{k=1}^{M} \left[\left(\prod\limits_{j=1}^{N} \mu^{(k)}(x_i) \right) \times c_k \right]}{\sum\limits_{k=1}^{M} \left[\prod\limits_{j=1}^{N} \mu^{(k)}(x_i) \right]} \tag{7}$$

The FNN learning algorithm can be consiquently divided into two phases.

At the first stage, the parameters of the center of the output membership functions in Layer 3 are subject to training. In order to do this, when fixing the parameters of the membership functions of Layer 1, the parameters of the weights are determined on the basis of the following formula:

$$y(x) = \sum_{k=1}^{M} w'_k p_{k0} \tag{8}$$

It should be noted that the output signals y are replaced by reference signals d from p training samples (training examples x(l), d(l)) where l = 1... p. Then:

$$wp = d, \tag{9}$$

where w—the matrix A simplified by means of polynomial replacement.

Further, the solution of the system of equations is carried out on the basis of pseudo-inversion of matrices. At the second stage, after fixing the values of the linear parameters yk = pk0 the actual y outputs and the error vector are calculated ε = y − d.

For practical implementation, a Web application was developed using the Node.js framework in JavaScript, also using CSS and HTML. Node.js is a server-based JavaScript platform. JavaScript acts on the client-side, and Node on the server-side.

The scheme of the developed application is shown in Fig. 21.

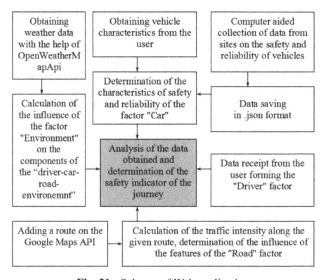

Fig. 21. Scheme of Web application

Using the Google Maps API, a map has been added to the application, on which the route is laid. As was mentioned above, there is a need to obtain information about the safety characteristics of the vehicle. This data will be taken from the autoreview.ru website. For this, an automated data collection tool was developed using the Scrapy Python framework and saving of the received data into a JSON file, which will be used further in order to take information from it. Scrapy is the most complete set of tools for loading web pages, processing them, and saving them to files and databases. Free OpenWeatherMapApi will be used to obtain data on the current weather, which is necessary to determine the factors of the "Environment" component. Weather data is also provided in JSON format.

4   Conclusion and Discussion

After training the FNT according to the algorithm described in the paper [29], based on statistical data for a number of cities in the Southern Federal District, the accident rate forecast for the city of Volgograd was carried out, the data for which did not participate in the FNS learning process (Fig. 22).

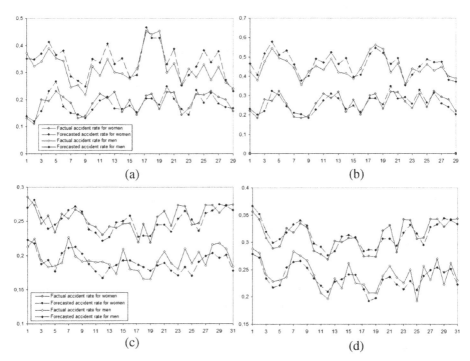

Fig. 22. Forecast of the accident rate on the roads of Volgograd: a) for drivers under 25 inthe daytime, June; b) for drivers under 25 inthe nighttime, June; c) for drivers 35–50 years old, in the daytime, February d) for drivers 35–50 years old, in the nighttime, February.

At the analysis of the dependences under analysis, it is apparent that the accident rate alters during the week with peaks in the morning and on Saturday. Also, the graphs show distinctly the difference in accident rates for men and women of different ages. You should also pay attention to the increase in the accident rate for the same age and gender groups, caused by traffic conditions at night.

The tendency of an increase in the accident rate of drivers with a high driving proficiency, due to severe environmental conditions, in particular, driving at night in winter is particularly noteworthy.

Thus, the authors have developed a system for a comprehensive computer-aided assessment of accidents, which makes it appropriate to take into account driver's individual characteristics, driving conditions, and specificity of the impact of weather and climatic factors, the results of which lead to the following conclusions:

1) Unlike existing methods for the assessment of road traffic safety, the functioning of which is based on road conditions and/or weather and climate [30], the automated system developed by the authors allows taking into account both the complex influence of environmental factors and the state of the road and attention to the individual psychophysiological characteristics of the personality of the driver and the characteristics of the vehicle. The accident rate, calculated within the methodology suggested by the authors, is the result of the influence of the entire set of factors of the DCRE system.

2) The functioning of the model for the forecast of the accident rate is implemented in such a way that it takes into account the mutual influence of the factors of the DCREsystem. So, in particular, when determining the individual accident rate, the influence of weather and climate is taken into account both on the individual characteristics of the driver's behavior and on the work of the mechanical part of vehicles, as well as the joint influence of the entire set of factors on individual road traffic safety.

3) The function of forecasting individual traffic safety, implemented in the system, has a dynamic character. The assessment of road traffic safety is carried out taking into account the characteristics of climate, traffic, season, and route for a specific time of a certain day of the week and automatically changes when the specified parameters are changed, allowing to obtain fairly accurate results due to training the FNN underlying it.

The dependencies which are studied by the authors can be used for the development of measures allowing to reduce the accident rate on the roads of urban agglomerations and consequently to increase road transfport efficiency what contribute directly to the social and economic development of the regions.

References

1. Federal State Statistics Service. https://rosstat.gov.ru/. Accessed 20 Dec 2020. (in Russian)
2. Salini, S., Ashalatha, R.: Analysis of traffic characteristics of urban roads under the influence of roadside frictions. Case Stud. Transp. Policy **8**(1), 94–100 (2020). https://doi.org/10.1016/j.cstp.2018.06.008
3. Dhamaniya, A., Chandra, S.: Influence of operating speed on capacity of urban arterial mid-block sections. Int. J. Civ. Eng. **15**(7), 1053–1062 (2017). https://doi.org/10.1007/s40999-017-0206-7
4. Lu, J., Li, B., Li, H., Al-Barakani, A.: Expansion of city scale, traffic modes, traffic congestion, and air pollution. Cities **108**, 102974 (2021). https://doi.org/10.1016/j.cities.2020.102974
5. The volume of emissions of harmful (polluting) substances into the atmospheric air from road transport. State statistics of EMISS. https://fedstat.ru/indicator/42723. Accessed 20 Dec 2020. (in Russian)

6. Petrov, A., Petrova, D.: Equivalence of distribution of social and economic damage caused by road accidents in the territories of the largest countries of the world: a new pattern? Transp. Res. Procedia **36**, 577–585 (2018). https://doi.org/10.1016/j.trpro.2018.12.150. (in Russian)
7. Indicators of road safety. http://stat.gibdd.ru/. Accessed 20 Dec 2020. (in Russian)
8. Korchagin, V., Lyapin, S., Klyavin, V., Sitnikov, V.: Increase of road traffic safety of cars based on the analysis of accidents and accident simulation. Fundam. Res. **6**(2), 251–256 (2015)
9. Tyulkin, E.: Automation of the process of statistical research of road accident factors. Bull. Civ. Eng. **5**, 248–253 (2015)
10. Torrisi, V., Ignaccolo, M., Inturri, G.: Innovative transport systems to promote sustainable mobility: developing the model architecture of a traffic control and supervisor system. In: Gervasi, O., et al. (eds.) ICCSA 2018. LNCS, vol. 10962, pp. 622–638. Springer, Cham (2018). https://doi.org/10.1007/978-3-319-95168-3_42
11. Banushkina, N., Pechatnova, E.: Improvement of the efficiency of road accident predicting on motor roads outside settlements based on the development of an expert system. Bull. Altay State Univ. **1**, 86–90 (2015)
12. Azemsha, S., Galushko, V., Skirkovsky, S.: Improvement of expert analysis of road traffic accidents using computer simulation programs. Sci. Technol. **4**, 18–24 (2015)
13. Evtyukov, S., Vasiliev, Y.: Examination of road accidents: methods and technologies. S. Petersburg: SPbGA-SU, 310 (2012)
14. Barik, S., Mohanty, S., Agarwal, R., Pramanik, J., Samal, A.K.: A proposed wireless technique in vehicle-to-vehicle communication to reduce a chain of accidents over road. In: Swain, D., Pattnaik, P.K., Gupta, P.K. (eds.) Machine Learning and Information Processing. AISC, vol. 1101, pp. 105–112. Springer, Singapore (2020). https://doi.org/10.1007/978-981-15-1884-3_10
15. Hu, L., Zhao, Y.: Research on the architecture of road traffic accident analysis platform based on big data. In: Abawajy, J., Choo, K.-K., Islam, R. (eds.) ATCI 2017. AISC, vol. 580, pp. 28–34. Springer, Cham (2018). https://doi.org/10.1007/978-3-319-67071-3_6
16. Singh, J., Singh, G., Singh, P., Kaur, M.: Evaluation and classification of road accidents using machine learning techniques. In: Shetty, N.R., Patnaik, L.M., Nagaraj, H.C., Hamsavath, P.N., Nalini, N. (eds.) Emerging Research in Computing, Information, Communication and Applications. AISC, vol. 882, pp. 193–204. Springer, Singapore (2019). https://doi.org/10.1007/978-981-13-5953-8_17
17. Kouziokas, G.N.: Neural network-based road accident forecasting in transportation and public management. In: Nathanail, E.G., Karakikes, I.D. (eds.) CSUM 2018. AISC, vol. 879, pp. 98–103. Springer, Cham (2019). https://doi.org/10.1007/978-3-030-02305-8_12
18. Kannojiya, A.K., Maurya, R., Rajitha, B.: Survey on soft computing methods for accident condition and severity predictions. In: Pandian, A.P., Ntalianis, K., Palanisamy, R. (eds.) ICICCS 2019. AISC, vol. 1039, pp. 584–591. Springer, Cham (2020). https://doi.org/10.1007/978-3-030-30465-2_65
19. Eremin, V.: Conceptual model of the functioning of the VADS system as the basis of computer simulation. CAD GIS Autom. Roads **1**(2), 90–93 (2014)
20. Eliseev, M., Mazunova, L., Eliseeva, I.: Statistical and correlation analysis of weather factors in an interactive information system for road safety improvement. Proc. NSTU im. R.E. Alekseeva **2**(129), 28–41 (2020)
21. Lazarev, S., Oreshin, N., Mamleev, D.: Assessment of the quality of safe functioning of a car in the road-transport system "driver-car-road-environment" according to static properties. Manag. Activ. Ensure Road Saf. State Prob. Ways Improv. **1**(2), 278–284 (2019)
22. Bennajeh, A., Bechikh, S., Said, L.B., Aknine, S.: A fuzzy logic-based anticipation car-following model. In: Thanh Nguyen, N., Kowalczyk, R. (eds.) Transactions on Computational Collective Intelligence XXX. LNCS, vol. 11120, pp. 200–222. Springer, Cham (2018). https://doi.org/10.1007/978-3-319-99810-7_10

23. Babkov, V.: Road conditions and traffic safety. Transport 183 (1991)
24. Lyon, C., Mayhew, D., Marie-Axelle, G., Robertson, R., Vanlaar, W., Woods-Fry, H., Thevenet, C., Furian, G., Soteropoulos, A.: Age and road safety performance: Focusing on elderly and young drivers. IATSS Res. **44**(3), 212–219 (2020). https://doi.org/10.1016/j.iat ssr.2020.08.005
25. Oreshin, N., Cherepkov, S., Menyuk, D.: Assessment of the quality of the safe functioning of a car in the road-transport system "driver-car-road-environment" by operational properties. Manag. Activ. Ensure Road Saf. State Prob. Ways Improv. **1**(2), 342–348 (2019)
26. Saidullozoda, S., Mambetalin, K., Umirzokov, A., Mallaboev, U.: Assessment of the reliability of the system "Driver-car-road-environment" in mountainous conditions. Bull. South Ural State Univ. Ser. Mech. Eng. **1**(20), 38–46 (2020). https://doi.org/10.14529/engin200105
27. Kozlov, V., Skrypnikov, A., Abasov, M., Nikitin, V., Samtsov, V.: Influence of weather and climatic factors on the systems of the complex "Driver-car-road-environment." Transp. Transp. Facilit. Ecol. **1**, 30–36 (2019)
28. Frauke W.: Conceptual model of the industry sector in an energy system model: a case study for Denmark. Frauke Wiese, Mattia Baldini. J. Clean. Prod. **203**, 427–443 (2018). https://doi.org/10.1016/j.jclepro.2018.08.229
29. Kravets, A., Skorobogatchenko, D., Salnikova, N., Orudjev, N., Poplavskaya, O.: The traffic safety management system in urban conditions based on the C4.5 algorithm. In: Moscow Workshop on Electronic and Networking Technologies, MWENT 2018 – Proceedings, vol. 1, pp. 1–7 (2018)
30. Borovik, V., Borovik, V., Skorobogatchenko, D.: Model of the strategy for reducing the road accident rate in the city. Transp. Res. Procedia **36**, 68–76 (2018)

Development of a Methodology for Complex Monitoring of the Development of Urban and Suburban Areas Based on the Intellectual Analysis of Earth Remote Sensing Data and Geospatial Technologies

Vitaliy Malikov, Natalia Sadovnikova⬤, Danila Parygin$^{(\boxtimes)}$ ⬤,
Alexander Aleshkevich, and Oksana Savina

Volgograd State Technical University, Lenina Ave. 28, 400005 Volgograd, Russia
npsn1@ya.ru

Abstract. Over the past half century, mankind is increasingly faced with the problems of rational use of the Earth's territories and its resources without negative impact on the environment and the person himself. The organization of human life activity requires solving the issues of urban planning and the correct distribution of zones for the construction of industrial facilities, recreation, waste disposal zones, communications, routes, etc. Balanced planning is based on monitoring the current state of infrastructure and territory. This article proposes a methodology for integrated monitoring of the development of urban and suburban areas. It is proposed to use Earth remote sensing data as a basis for the study. The issues of collection, integration and intelligent processing of satellite images are considered. The definition and segmentation of objects in images to create digital maps is performed based on machine learning algorithms.

Keywords: Area monitoring · Machine learning · Remote sensing data · Urban area · Intelligent analysis

1 Introduction

Over the past few decades, the world has seen an upsurge in the use of digital maps. This is due to the rapid development of geographic information technologies and geographic information systems (GIS). This direction offers a fundamentally new approach to working with spatial data, which have recently been used in most areas of human life. Problems of studying geoinformation technologies, methods of processing and storing geospatial data, their interpretation in various studies takes an important place in geoinformatics.

These data, when properly processed, carry a huge store of information for any scientific and practical direction. Special tools inside software solutions are created so that not only specialists can work with them, but also ordinary users: builders, marketers, officials, environmentalists, businessmen, etc.

A. G. Kravets et al. (Eds.): CIT&DS 2021, CCIS 1448, pp. 405–417, 2021.
https://doi.org/10.1007/978-3-030-87034-8_29

Spatial data, by which Russian legislation understands various data about spatial objects (their shape, location, properties, etc.), including those presented using coordinates (Article 3 of the Federal Law of December 30, 2015 No. 431-FZ) are necessary in a variety of areas, primarily for making management decisions. The availability of spatial data and the possibility of using modern services for their processing are of fundamental importance.

Spatial data are more intensively and widely used to implement the powers of executive authorities at the regional level than at the federal level. At the same time, a group of powers is highlighted, for the implementation of which they are most often used. These are monitoring, planning and management decision-making, and the provision of public services. According to forecasts, the greatest demand for spatial data will be presented by the electric power industry, housing and communal services, the financial sector, the construction industry, and the transport complex. In this regard, the problem of this study is associated with the development of methodological and software tools for obtaining relevant spatial data on area infrastructure facilities and natural environment objects.

2   Remote Sensing as the Main Source of Spatial Data

Remote sensing of the Earth (ERS) is the process of conducting observations of the Earth's surface, carried out by ground, space and aviation facilities, which are equipped with special imaging equipment. Remote sensing of the Earth is a scientific area, a subsection of geography. It includes knowledge and methods of obtaining information at a distance about objects on the earth's surface. They are also called non-contact information retrieval methods [1].

The results of the application of such methods are primary data or ERS data, representing raster images of the earth's surface with accompanying measurements of the energy and polarized characteristics of the radiation of the objects under study. These measurements are required to determine the location, type, and some properties of the objects of analysis. In addition, remote sensing data have a characteristic of time, in connection with which it is possible to analyze their variability under certain conditions [2].

As mentioned earlier, remote sensing data is considered to be images of the earth's surface taken by artificial earth satellites. These images must be pre-processed before being used in research. The general algorithm for processing remote sensing data is a two-stage work with the received satellite images:

1. Preliminary processing of remote sensing data, which consists in geometric, atmospheric and radiometric correction of the image, as well as in its geographic referencing.
2. Thematic processing, which determines what tasks will be solved based on the received satellite information. This processing includes various methods of image enhancement (contrast adjustment, noise suppression, border extraction, etc.).

ERS data is usually called "ERS materials" after preparatory work. ERS materials have the characteristics of space and time, which makes it possible to carry out all kinds of research on their basis. For example, information about the natural resources of the area of interest, about the objects of transport and industrial infrastructures, etc. can be obtained as a result of thematic processing of remote sensing data [3–5]. In addition, the presence of the characteristics of the time of the data obtained will allow tracking the existing trends in the development of the objects and phenomena under study [6]. In this regard, ERS is used in many areas of human activity:

- In geology (obtaining topography of territories, data on temperature, soil moisture, vegetation, etc.).
- In meteorology (obtaining data on precipitation, air temperature, cyclones and anticyclones, etc.).
- In oceanology (obtaining the topography of the oceans, data on the temperature of water, its color, etc.).
- In the cryosphere (obtaining data on icebergs, glaciers, etc.).
- In the military industry (intelligence), etc.

The effectiveness of the use of remote sensing methods in the study of large territories in comparison with the use of ground-based studies is explained by the solution of such a global problem as the impossibility of simultaneous observation of several objects located at a great distance from each other. Especially when it comes to hard-to-reach places.

In addition, this method of studying the earth's surface allows accumulating a huge amount of data on vast territories in the shortest possible time. A striking example of this fact is the speed of the Meteosat satellite, which forms a raster image of a quarter of the Earth's surface within half an hour.

The advantages of ERS methods over other ground-based methods of studying the Earth's surface are becoming obvious [7]:

- The scale of the images obtained - the ability to shoot large areas with a high degree of detail.
- Relevance of data - fast acquisition of images by space satellites allows to form an information base with a time characteristic. This will make it possible to obtain data on objects of the earth's surface for any available period.
- Data availability - the ability to obtain images with a resolution of 2 m, in which it is quite easy to recognize architectural objects, green areas, roads, etc. (freestanding people can be recognized at a resolution of 0.3 m to 1 m).
- Objectivity of data - it is possible to fake satellite images, but it does not make sense, since there are a small number of companies that provide satellite tracking. For any attempts to change the data, one of the companies will be able to track this fact.
- Ability to survey any part of the Earth's surface without special instructions and orders from any state to which this area belongs.

This activity is controlled by the provisions of the Moscow Convention of December 3, 1986 on the transmission and use of remote sensing data from space, as well as the UN and its affiliated agencies that promote international cooperation in the field of remote sensing, provide technical support and coordination, as well as manage requests for remote sensing access.

3   The Use of Remote Sensing and GIS in the Management of Urban Areas

Effective management of the urban environment is directly dependent on the availability of up-to-date spatial data. The field of satellite observation of the Earth is rapidly developing, and the achievements of this scientific direction are increasingly finding their application in a variety of practical problems. The use of these technologies will improve the performance indicators of the analysis of urban infrastructure, which includes monitoring of the urban environment land use, mothe urban development process, the trends of area use, the urban environmental infrastructure, and much more [8].

In addition, problems arise against the background of rapid growth and development of cities associated with the efficiency of the use of territories. This is due to the ambiguity of the choice of construction options, the organization of public and cultural spaces, green and industrial zones, as well as the justification of the investment attractiveness of certain projects [9].

Also, there are problems in the field of thematic mapping associated with the identification of some objects of territories, including those of a dynamic nature. This leads to an incorrect analysis of the studied area [10].

It is necessary to have an information base with accurate and up-to-date spatial data for comprehensive monitoring of the area development. As a rule, geoinformation technologies, Earth remote sensing data (satellite images), as well as special methods of processing this kind of information are used when conducting this kind of research [11].

4   Practices for Using Spatial Data

The study of the practice of using spatial data on the territory of the Russian Federation testifies to the versatile use of information in this format. Thus, 15 best practices for using spatial data were selected according to a report prepared by the National Research University Higher School of Economics [12], which are focused on storing and updating spatial data on real estate objects, urban planning zones, cultural heritage and protected areas, agricultural land, the state of the environment, etc. The presented spatial data are available for use by a wide range of individuals and institutions (government agencies, local authorities) and provide an opportunity to make decisions on planning urban planning, investment and other economic activities [13]. The developed tools (geographic information systems) are created to solve information and computational problems related to the processing of spatial data. They are applicable in the field of management and planning, inventory of resources, monitoring, analysis, forecasting and other tasks in the field of territorial planning.

Studies by foreign authors in the field of spatial data application are of great practical importance. Thus, P.M. Mwati determines the impact of land use and land cover change in the city of Nairobi on the environmental quality of the city using spatial data [14].

The team of scientists (H. Taubenbökom, N.J. Kraff, M. Wurm) [15] based on satellite images created three-dimensional models of buildings in areas that are considered cities of arrival (areas of the urban poor). The researchers were able to create a morphological index of the settlement type based on the density, orientation, size, height and heterogeneity of the building pattern using a methodology for classifying the shape and distribution of buildings.

Research by H. Taubenböck, A. N. Tiwari also touch on the growth of urbanized areas using GIS technologies [16, 17]. Spatial data are becoming the most important source of information for mapping, monitoring, and analysis of further urban development.

The exponential growth of impenetrable surfaces arising from the growth of cities and transport infrastructure is monitored using spatial data in the article by T. Leichtl [18]. Adjusting the volume of impermeable surfaces will avoid negative effects such as increased runoff and flood risk, reduced groundwater recharge or increased urban heat island effect.

D. Abuya, M. Oyugi, E. Oyaro define the impact of land use change on urban infrastructure (roads, water supply and sanitation) in Ruaka, Kenya using spatial data in their study [19].

A description of a number of projects aimed at introducing spatial data for the rational development of city territories is given in the article by S. Boag [20]. Thus, the Keyne Eye application is an intelligent urban planning tool that enables an automated planning management system. Very high resolution satellite imagery allows the analysis of changes in land plots in accordance with the permitted planning.

The use of spatial data for the organization of competent planning of the water supply network in urbanized areas is shown on the example of a project carried out in Malawi, Lilove region [21].

The use of spatial data is implemented in various areas of urban planning. The Madrid City Council uses spatial data to monitor green areas (vegetation cover) in urban areas, thereby controlling the level of urban heat, improving the quality of life, and reducing potential hazards associated with climate change and human activities in the city.

5   Methodology for Complex Monitoring of the Development of Urban and Suburban Areas

The task of using remote sensing data for solving the problems of developing territories is reduced to the problem of thematic processing of remote sensing data. It should be carried out in such a way as to expand the area of analysis of urban infrastructure, to introduce into its analysis territories and objects (construction sites, arrays of green spaces, etc.) that change over time. For example, the density of buildings, the aggressiveness of the urban environment and its ecological state can be investigated in addition to analyzing the level of buildings in various areas of the city. All these indicators make it possible to compile a general characteristic of the development of the city, to assess the effectiveness of its management, to increase the efficiency of accounting for the state and composition of the territory's objects using automatic mapping by remote sensing. They can also be used as the main decision-making tools for the development of urban infrastructure [22].

Satellite remote sensing plays a fundamental role in supporting urban spatial planning, existing policies, and in mapping and monitoring human settlements and urban growth. Examples of developments can be:

- A map of the spatial location of various land cover types and the state of the natural environment - for site selection, zoning regulation, resource allocation, environmental monitoring and urban growth management.
- Classification map of the spatial distribution of settlement types - to improve road infrastructure and other services such as schools and clinics in these areas.
- Urban transformation map - for planning the provision of services to the population and assessing the impact of the development of settlements on the environment.
- Map showing low-cost housing units - for planning community service delivery and assessing the environmental impact of human settlements development.
- Settlement transformation map - to support financial audits by municipalities.
- Urban communications map - to optimize water, sewage, telecommunications and electricity transmission routes, etc.

Evaluation of the effectiveness of the use of the territory and planning its development is one of the most important tasks solved with the use of spatial data and GIS [23]. It is possible to analyze the needs for new infrastructural facilities, identify the shortcomings of existing layouts, and obtain information to analyze the efficiency of the use of the territory using these technologies. The efficiency of using the territory is rather low in most Russian cities. Valuable urban areas tend to be occupied by low-income and unaesthetic industrial facilities that pollute the air and displace residential development to the outskirts of cities. The use of GIS technologies and systems for supporting the tasks of planning the territory [24] will provide the necessary information for the optimal location of various objects.

A model of a system for forming a database of segmented objects based on satellite imagery data is proposed as part of the implementation of the methodology for integrated monitoring of the growth and development of urban and suburban areas (Fig. 1). The system of integrated monitoring of the development of urban and suburban areas offers the following tools:

1. Segmentation of green areas in urban and suburban areas. The problems of the lack of parks, squares, forest belts and other types of urban and suburban green areas appear in the context of rapid growth and urban development. In this connection, this tool will allow experts to control the processes of land use in urban and suburban areas in order to preserve and improve the ecological situation of the studied area.
2. Segmentation of possible landfills. The problem of the proliferation of landfills, as well as spontaneously forming landfills, is global throughout the world. The presence of a tool that allows to determine the location of such objects will help to form a historical component for each of the objects, as well as to identify unauthorized dumps for taking operational measures to destroy them.
3. Segmentation of non-stationary trade objects. The proliferation of non-stationary shopping facilities is a contemporary problem for many Russian cities. The main violations of the law are associated with such objects: illegal installation of these

objects (thereby seizure of administrative land), illegal insertion into power grid facilities (i.e. theft of electricity), installation of an object in the wrong from the point of view of traffic laws (for example, in front of pedestrian crossings). In addition, the pollution of nearby territories can be associated with such retail outlets, since such facilities do not have appropriate communications. This tool can be useful for detecting illegal actions on the part of property owners.

4. Segmentation of highways. Traffic jams are a common occurrence in any large city. They often arise due to improper organization of urban transport policy. The road segmentation tool will allow to determine the places for the creation or reclassification of objects for the organization of unimpeded traffic.

5. Segmentation of buildings and structures. This tool provides a huge range of urban management tasks. Experts can get the following digital views based on the data provided by the building and structure segmentation function:

   - Definition of dormitory and central areas, private sectors, garage cooperatives, etc.
   - Determination of price categories for buildings located in different areas of the analyzed area.
   - Development of infrastructure in different areas of the analyzed area, etc.

6. Segmentation of parking spaces. The lack of parking spaces is also a significant problem for large cities. This problem arose at a time when a car for a city dweller was no longer a luxury. In modern realities, every sleeping area, city center and other public places must be equipped with parking spaces. The parking lot segmentation tool can be used to organize parking spaces correctly.

The system includes separate modules that use trained neural networks to identify objects on digital maps using the "Satellite map" layer, as can be seen from Fig. 1. These models were implemented based on the standard machine learning algorithm in the Python 3.8 programming language, as well as using the Tensorflow and Keras machine learning libraries, the OpenCV library for image processing and numerical algorithms, and the numpy library for high-level mathematical calculations [25].

The construction and training of such models consists in the formation of a dataset consisting of a large number (~1000–10000) images of the selected analyzed objects. Educational and training image uploads are selected based on the generated dataset. Next, an algorithm based on the OpenCV and numpy libraries is performed to select the mask of the desired objects, which will later be used to build and train a neural network.

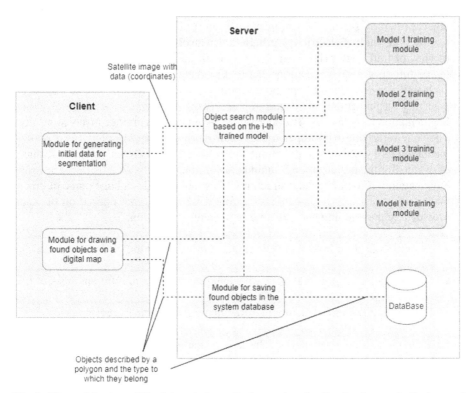

Fig. 1. The architecture of the integrated monitoring system for the development of urban and suburban areas.

The construction of models is based on the use of layers of convolutional neural networks, "folding" images in order to find the main features for the analyzed class of objects, as well as layers that perform operations inverse to the first layers, i.e. "Unfolding" the found features and forming the final matrix of weights. The probabilities of belonging of each pixel of the image to one of all classes are defined in this matrix.

Thus, the system for integrated monitoring of the development of urban and suburban areas includes subsystems that identify objects on satellite images based on implemented and trained models of neural networks, specializing in a certain type of objects. Examples of object recognition on a selected area of a digital Google Map when the map is zoomed are shown in Fig. 2.

All 6 models were built on the basis of about 100 images, divided into training, test and verification datasets. Eight new images were obtained from each input image: the image was rotated 90° at each step (4 images) and mirrored (4 images). The accuracy of the defined objects of each model varies from 77 to 84%.

Fig. 2. Examples of object recognition on a selected area of a digital Google Map: trees (green areas), non-stationary objects (red areas), roads (purple areas). (Color figure online)

6 Analysis of Urban Development Based on Remote Sensing Data

The proposed method is based on the analysis of consumer properties of the territory and takes into account the real possibilities of existing urban infrastructure facilities to provide the required level of quality of life for residents [26]. A sufficient number and availability of infrastructure facilities of various types ultimately determine the quality of the living environment for people and safety, especially in emergency situations when life support issues are especially important.

Building analysis can be performed using several methods:

- By dividing the territory into cells measuring 250 by 250 m (standard distance to the stop).
- Through quarterly assessment.

The analysis of development by cells is excellent for analyzing the amount of a city's territory occupied by buildings. The use of cells 1000 by 1000 m is suitable for determining the average density of streets, since this indicator is measured in km/km2, or the direct division of the total length of all streets by the total area of the territory. The grid-based approach is effective for large-scale calculations performed simultaneously for several cities or when universal comparison of parameters is required.

An approach to the automated determination of quarters is required to form in order to obtain a detailed picture of specific coefficients associated with the justification of some planning decisions for quarters and blocks when assessing the territory according to remote sensing data. The quarter represents several land plots on which buildings are located, and which are fully or partially surrounded by streets and/or territories occupied by natural objects (water bodies, abrupt changes in the relief, etc.). If the quarters are not analyzed, then it will not be possible to objectively draw up recommendations that can be used, for example, for the preparation of territorial planning documents. On the other hand, different quarters were built at different times, their size depends on the needs and judgments of the time when they were built, and the typology of buildings. Finding patterns and determining those that are required in different conditions will be required on the basis of the available quarters. The following algorithm was developed to determine the quarters from remote sensing data:

1. Obtaining data on road segmentation.
2. Obtaining data on the segmentation of buildings and structures.
3. Obtaining data on the segmentation of green areas and water bodies.
4. Overlay of the received data.
5. Groups of buildings and structures within the contour of roads / green zones and water bodies should be allocated in separate quarters.

The calculation of the building factor is to find the ratio of the sum of the foundations of all buildings that intersect with the block to the area of the block.

The application of the obtained algorithm allows for the available data to determine the coefficient of the territory development. At the moment, the algorithm has been implemented for five cities: St. Petersburg, Berlin, Singapore, Kolkata and Montreal (Fig. 3) [27].

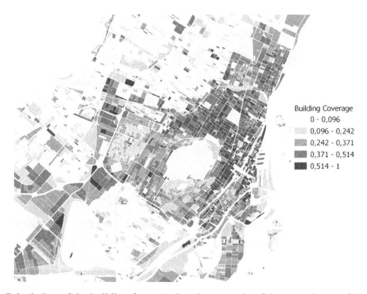

Fig. 3. Calculation of the building factor (using the example of the central part of Montreal).

7 Conclusion

The proposed system can be used as a data source for other systems, methods and algorithms for assessing various indicators of the urban area. The authors of the article [28] are faced with the complexity of calculating structural indicators based on the GIS data of the OpenStreetMaps system due to the complexity of their processing for calculating indicators. The use of remote sensing data will make it much easier to calculate target indicators, thanks to the ability to superimpose the results of image processing on each other and select the necessary objects for analysis.

The proposed system of integrated monitoring of the development of urban and suburban areas allows collecting data that determine the presence of a sufficient number of life support facilities, their correct location and accessibility ultimately determine the quality of the living environment of people [29]. Segmentation tools allow assessing the morphology of urban development, which is determined by the planning and zoning of the area.

Acknowledgments. This work has been supported by the Russian Science Foundation (RSF) grant (project No. 20–71-10087). The authors express gratitude to colleagues from UCLab involved in the development of UrbanBasis.com project.

References

1. Taubenböck, H., Esch, T.: Remote sensing – An effective data source for urban monitoring. http://earthzine.org/2011/07/20/remote-sensing-an-effective-data-source-for-urban-monitoring/. Accessed 16 Mar 2021
2. Khabarov, D.A., Adiev, T.S., Popova, O.O., Chugunov, V.A., Kozhevnikov, V.A.: Analysis of modern technologies for remote sensing of the Earth. Moscow Econ. J. **1**, 33–40 (2019)
3. Lezhnin, S.A.: Remote method for assessing the formation of young stands on the deposits of the Mari forest Trans-Volga region using satellite images, Yoshkar-Ola (2013)
4. Miroshnichenko, S., Titov, V.S., Yashchenko, A.A.: Method for automatic localization of extended geospatial objects in space images. Proc. High. Educ. Inst. Instrum. **56**(6), 17–23 (2013)
5. Zhilyakov, E.G., Likhosherstny, A.: Method of neural network recognition of objects on aerospace images of the earth's surface. Radio Electron. Issues **4**(1), 86–93 (2012)
6. Youssef, A.M., Pradhan, B., Tarabees, E.: Integrated evaluation of urban development suitability based on remote sensing and GIS techniques: contribution from the analytic hierarchy process. Arab. J. Geosci. **4**(4), 463–473 (2011)
7. Popkin, G.: Technology and satellite companies open up a world of data. Nature **557**(7706), 745–748 (2018)
8. Taubenböck, H., Dech, S.: Remote Sensing and Urban Planning: A Common Future. http://www.vector1media.com/article/features/13931-remote-sensing-and-urban-planning-a-common-future. Accessed 19 Mar 2021/03/19
9. Akanbi, A.K., Kumar, S., Fidelis, U.: Application of Remote Sensing, GIS and GPS for efficient Urban Management Plan, A case study of part of Hyderabad city. https://www.researchgate.net/publication/259335189_Application_of_Remote_Sensing_GIS_and_GPS_for_efficient_Urban_Management_Plan_A_case_study_of_part_of_Hyderabad_city. Accessed 20 Mar 2021

10. Sivakumar, V.: Urban mapping and growth prediction using remote sensing and GIS techniques, Pune, India. Int. Arch. Photogram. Remote Sens. Spat. Inf. Sci. **8**, 140–167 (2014)
11. Kresnikova, N.I., Vasilievykh, N.A.: Application of remote sensing data and geoinformation technologies to ensure territorial planning. Proc. Univ. "Geodesy Aer. Photogr." **62**(2), 212–217 (2018)
12. Belogurova, E.B., Vorobiev, V.E., Gvozdev, O.G.: Spatial Data: The Needs of the Economy in the Context of Digitalization. Higher School of Economics, Moscow (2020)
13. Savina, O.V., Sadovnikova, N.P., Parygin, D.S.: Analysis of options for using objects of a municipality property complex in urban area development management. IOP Conf. Ser. Mater. Sci. Eng. **962**, 032061 (2020)
14. Mwathi, P.M.: Effects of land use and land cover dynamics on environmental quality of Narobi city and its environs//University of Nairobi. http://erepository.uonbi.ac.ke/handle/11295/97377. Accessed 29 Mar 2021
15. Taubenböck, H., Kraff, N.J., Wurm, M.: The morphology of the arrival city - a global categorization based on literature surveys and remotely sensed data. Appl. Geogr. **92**, 150–167 (2018)
16. Taubenböck, H.: Remote Sensing for the Analysis of Global Urbanization. https://www.researchgate.net/publication/334318755. Accessed 01 Apr 2021
17. Tiwary, A.N.: GIS and remote sensing in urban development planning: issues and challenges of developing world. Int. J. Sci. Res. **5**(4), 45–62 (2016)
18. Leichtle, T.: Remote Sensing for Impervious Surface Estimation. http://conference.euspaceimaging.com/vhr-remote-sensing-for-impervious-surface-estimation/. Accessed 11 Apr 2021
19. Abuya, D., Oyugi, M., Oyaro, E.: Management of the effects of land use changes on urban infrastructure capacity: a case study of Ruaka Town, Kiambu County, Kenya. Am. J. Geogr. Inf. Syst. **8**(4), 158–190 (2019)
20. Boag, S.: From Urban to Rural Enabling Sustainable Urban Planning and Development Using Satellite Imagery. https://www.gim-international.com/articles/case-study/from-urban-to-rural-enabling-sustainable-urban-planning-and-development-using-satellite-imagery. Accessed 10 Apr 2021
21. Engineer, I.T.: Remote sensing and urban spatial planning. https://www.ee.co.za/article/remote-sensing-urban-spatial-planning.html. Accessed 01 May 2021
22. Taleai, M., Mesgari, S.M., Sharifi, M.A., Sliuzas, R.V., Barati, N.: A spatial decision support system for evaluation various land uses in built up urban area. https://www.researchgate.net/publication/228948588_A_Spatial_Decision_Support_System_for_evaluation_various_land_uses_in_built_up_urban_area. Accessed 21 Apr 2021
23. Noor, N.M., Abdullah, A., Rosni, N.A.: Leveraging of remote sensing and GIS on mapping in urban and regional planning applications. IOP Conf. Ser. Earth Environ. Sci. **20**(1), 012004 (2014)
24. Medvedeva, O.E.: The economic mechanism for optimizing land use in cities, Moscow (2005)
25. Sharma, D.K., Malikov, V., Parygin, D., Golubev, A., Lozhenitsina, A., Sadovnikova, N.: GPU-card performance research in satellite imagery classification problems using machine learning. Procedia Comput. Sci. **178**, 55–64 (2020)
26. Zelenskiy, I.S., Parygin, D.S., Ather, D., Soplyakov, I.N., Antyufeev, A.Yu., Prigarin, E.A.: Software and algorithmic decision support tools for real estate selection and quality assessment. J. Phys. Conf. Ser. **1661**(1), 012201 (2020)
27. Zuev, A.Yu., Parygin, D.S., Sadovnikova, N.P.: Study of the dependence of city development indicators from urban form. IOP Conf. Ser. Mater. Sci. Eng. **962**, 032089 (2020)

28. Zuev, A., Parygin, D., Sadovnikova, N., Aleshkevich, A., Boiko, D.: Analysis methods of spatial structure metrics for assessment of area development effectiveness. In: Alexandrov, D.A., Boukhanovsky, A.V., Chugunov, A.V., Kabanov, Y., Koltsova, O., Musabirov, I. (eds.) DTGS 2020. CCIS, vol. 1242, pp. 273–288. Springer, Cham (2020). https://doi.org/10.1007/978-3-030-65218-0_21

29. Parygin, D.: Rebalancing cycle of ensuring needs for an exoactive management system. In: Proceedings of the 2020 International Multi-Conference on Industrial Engineering and Modern Technologies, art. no. 9271512. IEEE (2020)

Intelligent Technologies in Social Engineering. Data Science in Social Networks Analysis and Cyber Security

A Secure and Stable Routing Protocol for VANET Under Malicious Attacks

Amani A. Sabbagh$^{(\boxtimes)}$ and Maxim V. Shcherbakov

Volgograd State Technical University, 400005 Volgograd, Russian Federation

Abstract. Changing over digital age is becoming the driving force for modern approaches to provide a safe road system. Vehicular ad hoc networks (VANETs) are new networks that are used in intelligent transportation systems (ITS). The interest in this type of networks lies in the promising challenge to enhance safety in vehicular transportation systems trying to reduce driving problems. Routing is one of the most important operations in VANET as it deals with data exchange between nodes through wireless channels, which increases in requirements of security due to wireless systems have far more susceptibility to adversary's malicious attacks than the classic wired systems. Hence, we propose a stable and secure routing protocol that combines the features of clustering algorithm and cuckoo search algorithm to establish an efficient, secure and stable routing. In our proposed protocol, k-means clustering is used for cluster formation and a cuckoo search algorithm is used for selecting the cluster head. The selection of cluster head depends on five weight parameters, the most important of which are speed of node and trust factor with neighborhood nodes. The weight parameters are used as a fitness function along with the cuckoo search algorithm to ensure a stable and secure route. The simulation is carried out in simulator NS-3 and it demonstrates that the proposed routing protocol significantly improves the packet delivery ratio, average delay, packet loss ratio, overhead and throughput while compared to popular routing protocol AODV under malicious attacks.

Keywords: Clustering · Cuckoo search · Weight parameters · Security and black hole

1 Introduction

Currently, Vehicular Ad-hoc Networks (VANETs) technology has grabbed considerable attention and is emerging as a notable research field for various research engineers. VANETs are constructed by pertaining to the rules of Mobile Ad-hoc Networks (MANETs) [1]. VANET is a special type of MANET but VANETs are superior to MANETs in overcoming the energy constrained limitations. MANETs are limited to utilize lesser energy but VANETs utilize extended life batteries which are kept in vehicles, parking places or road crossings. VANETs are capable of self-organizing the vehicles to mobile nodes. The communication

© Springer Nature Switzerland AG 2021
A. G. Kravets et al. (Eds.): CIT&DS 2021, CCIS 1448, pp. 421–435, 2021.
https://doi.org/10.1007/978-3-030-87034-8_30

in VANETs could be Vehicle to Vehicle (V2V) or Vehicle to Roadside (V2R) [2]. there are several techniques available for V2V connectivity optimization, clustering is an important and effective optimization technique. Clustering is the process of grouping nodes with common attributes with each other into subgroups. The attributes are determined in advance based on the system requirements and the goal to be achieved. In general, the Clustering process in VANETs can be classified into two types: static and dynamic [3]. The static clustering of VANETs depends on vehicle-to-infrastructure (V2I) communications. Road Side Units (RSU) are the communication units with vehicles in VANET which are fixed along the road side. They play the role of the head of the groups to manage the clustering process of vehicles. But it is difficult to depend on static clustering in VANETs because of the high cost of establishing several infrastructures and the large distance between RSUs, so that high mobility vehicles couldn't always connect to RSUs [3]. Whereas, VANET's dynamic clustering is based on vehicle-to-vehicle (V2V) communications. Each cluster is responsible for selecting the cluster head from among the cluster nodes according to some important attributes that the head should have [4]. The most of recent research prefer the dynamic clustering method over the static for several reasons, including: V2V communications are more flexible and independent from roadside conditions. In addition, most developing countries or rural areas suffer from a lack of roadside infrastructure and the inability to establish it due to the high cost [5]. VANET has some special characteristics such as frequently network topology changes, lack of infrastructure for the analysis of nodes behaviors and constrained resources which makes it suffer from many security and connectivity issues [6,7]. VANETs are also susceptible to many attacks namely Sybil attack [8,9], bogus information, Denial of Service (DoS), Man in the middle (MIM) attacks, replay attacks, malicious coding and location tracking [10,11]. All these attacks gain unauthorized access and provide unauthorized results. cryptographic method and trust-based method are some of the exiting methods to improve the security concept in VANET. Cryptographic methods provide the integrity and confidentiality requirements of routing. In addition, they have role in establishing route, protecting exchanged data packets and route maintenance during communication. The development of routing protocols to ensure security in VANET networks has taken a great deal of researches and several methods have been suggested, but the search is still going on to reach the best solution that adapts to the conditions of the Vanet environment with the lowest cost and ensures the establishment of secure route within acceptable time in the network. Some of the solutions was proposed by Cerri and Ghioni as A-SOADV [12] they presented A-SAODV, a prototype implementation of the SAODV routing protocol to optimizes it by reducing the communication load. Zapta introduced secured AODV (SAODV) [13], which is used in MANET based on authentication and integrity of signaling packets. In [14] Eichel and Roman proposed a novel approach to secure AODV protocol which is named as AODV Security Extension (AODVSEC). It is an improved version of the SAODV based on the certificate and public key infrastructure. This means using the central administration. While others introduced a new approach in [15] for establishing trustworthy routes in AODV. Pirzada proposed a novel and pragmatic method for establishing trustworthy routes in an AODV based ad-hoc network without necessitating the use of cryptography. It based on an agent to populate the trust reputation in each node to every other node making the scenario a semi-centralized environment also. Thus, we need to develop new mechanisms against malicious nodes away from central or semi-central environments so that the cost of establishing VANET and the load on the network are reduced.

2   Security Issues in VANETs

The characteristics of ad hoc networks such as flexibility, decentralization, topology changes, and the wireless medium to establish communications between nodes [7]. These characteristics make it suitable for linking between vehicles, and themself exploited by attackers to gain control of the network. The malicious acts carried out by the attacker cause weak links between the nodes on the network by isolating the nodes from each other and then transmitting misleading messages on the network, which makes the network lose the effectiveness of the network due to the lack of information needed by the cars in a desired time [16].

2.1   VANET Security Requirements

Some of VANET's special features make it vulnerable to many malicious attacks, which imposes strict restrictions to properly handle security issues, otherwise failure to meet security requirements will lead to inevitable attacks in VANETs. Taking into account that securing and processing security requirements increases the overhead on the network due to the increased processing of exchanged data on the network [7]. The basic security requirements are divided into five main categories: availability, authentication, confidentiality, data integrity, and non-repudiation [17,18].

2.2   Types Attack in VANET

The large spread of the VANET networks to cover the largest possible geographical area and the participation of huge number of vehicular in one network, led to the emergence of new security risks against these networks. To overcome these security risks and provide a secure connection for the exchange of data between nodes, a comprehensive knowledge of the characteristics and methods of attacks on the network is necessary. Attacks on VANET are classified according to their objectives and methods into four types: [19]

1. on availability: such as Denial of Service (DOS) Attacks, Malware Attack, Black hole Attack and others.
2. on confidentiality: such as Eavesdropping Attack and Traffic Analysis Attack.
3. on authentication: such as Sybil Attack and GPS spoofing.
4. on integrity: such as Masquerading Attack and Message Tampering Attack.
5. on Non-repudiation: such as Repudiation Attack.

2.3   Trust Management in VANET

Routing plays an important role in VANET networks as it is responsible for establishing the connection and choosing the path for exchanging data between nodes. Due to the lack of infrastructure in the Vanet network, nodes cooperate with each other to manage the routing of data among themselves. In other words, the nodes take on the role of a router to provide the routing services. So, attacks against routing can damage it easily and decrease network performance significantly. The most traditional security mechanisms such as cryptography and authentication can provide protection at some level, but they alone cannot overcome malicious node attacks. Recently, the trust method has received great attention by researchers in order to solve security problems and overcome security challenges and find trust-based security solutions without the need to request and verify certificates or add any signature or encryption methods, in message packets, which leads to Low load in VANET networks [20]. Trust models depend mainly on the reputation of the node between the nodes, i.e., how node operates in the network, and provide information on a suitable confidence value for all vehicles. Establishing trust is a challenge as malicious nodes try to disrupt correct path discovery, transfer data to the wrong destination, or spoof data in the network. There is a several types of trust models, which can be classified depending on the source of information used for trust establishment or also depending on the entity that performs the trust establishment. Each of them calculates the value of trust differently from the other [21,22]. We can classification trust models depending on the source of information into: direct models, indirect models and hybrid models. While trust models depending on who makes the trust establishment can be divided into Infrastructure based models and Self-organized models. We can divide any trust process into following components: Trust factors, Trust calculation, Trust Threshold, and Routing [20].

1. Trust factors. Are the factors that determine whether a node is legitimate or not. It depends on how the malicious node works in attacking and damaging the network. For example, Black hole attack which drops all the packets it should forward [23].
2. Trust calculation. The trust value of a node is calculated using a given trust formula based on the number of normal and abnormal actions of a node. This value is compared with the trust threshold to determine whether the node is malicious or not.
3. Trust Threshold. It is an important factor of trust process in detection the abnormal node. Trust threshold is used to differentiate between abnormal and normal node. The trust threshold is defined as half the maximum value of the trust authors in [20], defined value is between 0.4 and 0.8. While in [24], authors suggested that trust threshold is 0.5.
4. Routing in this process, the routing algorithm joins or removes a node from the routing route, based on the node's trust value if it is above or below predefined trust threshold.

3   Proposed Routing Algorithm

3.1   K-means Clustering Algorithm

K-means clustering is one of the simplest and popular unsupervised machine learning algorithms in Data Science to classify unlabeled datasets. A cluster refers to a collection of data points aggregated together because of certain similarities. It is widely used in ad-hoc networks because it effectively manages routing problems due to its fast convergence and easy implementation. It is a static and location-based approach. The algorithm relies on the initial centers of clusters and then on the squared Euclidean distance to determine the centers of clusters. Let us assume c clusters are available in a data group [25]. Then the k-means algorithm includes the following steps:

1. Select C nodes to the space illustrated by the objects which are going to get clustered. Such nodes are picked as the primary centroid group.
2. Assign every object to the set which contains the nearest centroid.
3. Once every object is assigned, compute the C centroid location.
4. Repeat the steps 2 and 3 till the centroids stop their movement. This technique is called object segregation to clusters from which the standard to be reduced has to be done again.

3.2   Cuckoo Search Algorithm

Cuckoo search algorithm (CSA) is one of the latest nature-inspired metaheuristic algorithms. It is developed in 2009 by Xin-She Yang [26]. CSA is a behavior algorithm which is effective to solve optimization problem based on breed behavior of some cuckoo types. So, in the first need to review cuckoo behavior. The main step of CSA can be described as follows:

1. Starting with a random population of "n". So, some host nests are generated.
2. In randomly chosen nest each and parasitic cuckoo lays one egg, which represents a solution.
3. The best nest with high quality egg (the solution with the best fitness) will be hatched in the nest and will be used as nest in next generation.
4. The host bird maybe discovers the cuckoo's egg and throws away the alien egg with a probability p [0, 1] and creates a new nest so that the nest number is not reduced.
5. This process is repeated from step 2 a finite number of iterations.

3.3   Stable Routing Protocol

VANETs are characterized by high speed and frequent network topology change, which in turn makes routing extremely difficult in front of the challenges of ensuring a good proportion of timely delivery of safety application packages that need a high stability topology. Our proposed routing protocol depends on clustering with k-means and cuckoo search algorithm to make fewer topology changes by formatting clusters and select a cluster head. The elected CH is responsible for coordinating communication between the members of the cluster inside and coordinating communication with CHs outside. The stability of the cluster head is very important to ensure the stability of the cluster, which represents a serious challenge due to the high movement of vehicles that leads to the reconfiguration of the cluster again due to the exit of the cluster head from the cluster, and consequently the loss of communication and the loss of messages or delay of delivery, which means an increase in overheads on the network and failure to achieve the goal the desired VANET networks. Speed is one of the important mobility characteristics in VANET networks and an important factor in the stability of the cluster, as the speed of the vehicle affects the stability of the node, and therefore the relatively small speed means that the network topology changes slowly compared to the fast speed, which leads to a relatively small connection life or immediate deterioration of the connection and deterioration network performance. Therefore, we suggested adding the degree of speed factor to the head selection method. If the cluster head with high speed is chosen, it will lead to instability of the connection. Therefore, it is better to choose a node with relatively small differences speed to the rest of the neighboring vehicles. we calculated the degree of speed factor as follows:

$$SF'_v(t+1) = \gamma SF_v(t) + (1 - \gamma)SF_v(t+1) \tag{1}$$

Where

$$SF_v(t) = \frac{S_v(t) - S(t)}{S(t)} \tag{2}$$

$S_v(t)$: the instantaneous speed of vehicle V at time t. $S(t)$: is the harmonic mean speed of all the vehicle 's neighbors at time t.

$$SF_v(t+1) = \frac{S_v(t+1) - S(t)}{S(t)} \tag{3}$$

$S_v(t+1)$: the instantaneous speed of vehicle V at time t+1.

$$S_v(t+1) = S_v(t) + (t+1)A_{(v)} \tag{4}$$

$A(v)$ is acceleration of vehicle V.

3.4   Secure Routing Protocol

A routing is considered secure if it can overcome packet drops and intentional modifications by attackers. Each node calculates trust value of neighbor list to determine the abnormal node. Hence, trust value is combined in the routing process in various ways to find a trustworthy routing path and avoid malicious node. So, trust value plays basic role in route selection process [27]. Attacks against routing protocols have been extensively studied by researchers, for example grey hole, Black hole attack and Sink hole attack [20] These attacks can cause one or multiple of the following actions: packet drop, packet modification, and routing disruption. For example, black hole and grey hole try to drop packets and do not forward it to the destination node. Hence, the process of trust will be divided into:

1. Trust Factors. To calculate the trust value, we need to know the behavior and the outcomes of attacks. Then we can determine the factors which is taken into calculate the trust value. in our routing protocol, we study a black hole attack. So, the trust factors below were taken into account:
   (a) number of all packets received.
   (b) number of all packets sent.
2. Calculation of Degree Trust. In our proposed algorithm we used hybrid model to calculate the trust value for several reasons, among which are often the value of trust cannot be calculated directly from the node, so the node may need to help from other nodes in the network to perform the evaluation of trust due either to a lack of knowledge about the required node, or because of the mobile environment and the changing topology, Or because of the less interactions between the nodes, so we combined indirect trust with direct trust to obtain a comprehensive trust value. We depended on moving average model to calculate trust value at each iteration:

$$Trust'_{a,b}(t+1) = \gamma Trust_{a,b}(t) + (1 - \gamma)Trust_{a,b}(t+1) \tag{5}$$

Where

$$Trust_{a,b}(t) = \alpha DTrust_{a,b}(t) + \beta IDTrust_{a,b}(t) \tag{6}$$

Where $Trust_{a,b}(t)$ is trust value of node b for node a at time t. α and β are weighted factors, where values of α and β are 0.7 and 0.3, respectively. Where $\alpha + \beta = 1$ And γ is the weighted factor used to balance the measurement in the current and the previous iterations and is specified in a range $0 < \gamma < 1$.

$$DTrust_{a,b}(t) = \frac{\sum packets received by node a}{\sum packets sent by node b} \tag{7}$$

$DTrust_{a,b}(t)$ is the direct trust value of node b for node a at time t.

$$IDTrust_{a,b}(t) = \frac{1}{n} \sum_{i=1}^{i=n} DTrust_{i,b}(t) \tag{8}$$

$IDTrust_{a,b}(t)$ is the indirect trust value of node b for node a at time t. n represents the number of neighbors' nodes of a which are also the neighbors of b.

3. Trust Threshold. We used trust threshold is equal to 0.5.

4. Routing. The main process of our routing protocol is the route selection by elect cluster head with highest value of trust to avoid black hole attack when sending data. When the node wants to establish the communication with another node, it will send RREQ to neighborhood nodes. Each node received RREQ message, it will calculate the total number of received and forwarded packets, in addition to RERR, control and CBR packets. The trust values of each node are stored in a record table, which has the information regarding the trust value for all neighbors that are involved in data forwarding. Our proposed secure and stable routing against black hole depends on k means clustering to format the initial clusters quickly, cuckoo search algorithm to elect the cluster head based on fitness function which consists of five parameters. Our proposed routing algorithm avoids black hole nodes in route selection and keep the network performance in good level.

Begin: rout discovery process

step 1. For each source vehicle S – destination vehicle D , do

step 2. Initiate the process of local broadcast route discovery

step 3. Execute Algorithm 1: K-Means Cluster Formation

step 4. Choose the list of the succeeding hop node from S

step 5. For every neighbouring vehicle N of the current vehicle C do

step 6. If (N! = D) then validate

step 7. If $(RREQ < range$ of $Tx)$

step 8. Receive RREQ then

step 9. Update RREQ in the routing table

step 10. Calculate distance from intermediate node to source node Else

step 11. Ignore RREQ

step 12. Repeat the steps 6 and 7 till the source S reaches destination D

step 13. Initialize the size of the population to P. Get available population of P paths, x = 1, 2......, P

step 14. For x=1:P for (RREP from destination to source node) Execute Algorithm 2: Cuckoo Search algorithm

step 15. Calculate the fitness $W(a, b, c) = h1 * DF(a, b, c) + h2 * AF(b, c) + h3 * RF(b, c) + h4 * SF(b, c) + h5 * Trust(b, c)$

step 16. Increment x.

step 17. Choose Optimized node as CH with best fitness value in that K-means cluster formation group

step 18. CH node sends advertisement message to group nodes

step 19. Nodes which receive the advertisement message will become the cluster member for that CH

step 20. This process continues throughout in the network

step 21. Final data transmission will be done through selected CHs to reach the destination vehicle.

step 22. End procedure

From the previous section, i.e., cluster formation using k-means algorithm and CH selection using modified CSA, we consider the smallest weight parameter as the CH. The five parameters responsible for the selection of CH are derived through the fitness function W(a, b, c):

$W(a, b, c) = h1 * DF(a, b, c) + h2 * AF(b, c) + h3 * RF(b, c) + h4 * SF(b, c) + h5 * Trust(b, c)$ where

(a) DF(a, b, c) : it is the distance factor between source node a, neighbour node b and destination node c, which is calculated as the mean value of three nodes.

(b) AF(b, c): it is the angle factor between two nodes which decides if a node b is moving near or moving from the targeted destination c where the angle between two nodes.

(c) RF(b, c) it is road factor which decides if two nodes on the same road.

(d) SF(b, c) it is speed factor which determines the node with relatively small differences speed to the rest of the neighbouring vehicles.

(e) Trust(b, c) it is trust factor which decides the trust value of trust.

4 Performance Evaluation

4.1 Scenario Description

The simulation for the proposed model is carried out using Network Simulator (NS-3) and analysis is presented below. We evaluate the performance and validate the effectiveness of proposed protocol through this simulation. A comparative study on the metrics, with existing protocol namely AODV are also presented in the graphs below. The simulation parameters we considered are stated in Table 1.

Table 1. Simulation parameters

Parameter	Value
Simulator	NS-3.23
Topology	Manhattan grid road network 5×5 with 2000 m edge
Number of nodes	50 to 250
Number of blackhole	10
Packet size	512 bytes
Traffic type	CBR, UDP
Topology generation tool	Bonn Motion
Routing algorithm	AODV, proposed protocol
Mac protocol	802.11b standard
Simulation time	200 s

We used the following parameters to analyse the performance of network under black hole attacks [28]:

1. Packet Delivery Ratio (PDR). is defined as the ratio of the overall successful number of data packets delivered at the targeted destination to the overall number of data packets generated.

2. Average Delay. decides the average time that is needed for the packets from source to the application layer present at the destination node. They are expressed in seconds.
3. Packet Loss Ratio (PLR). can be defined as the ratio of the number of lost packets to number of sent packets.
4. Throughput. It is defined as the packets received at the destination out of total number transmitted packets. The unit used is kbps. The routing protocols with high throughput are more efficient.
5. Overhead. can be defined as the number of routing bytes required by the routing protocols to construct and maintain its routes.

4.2   Results and Discussions

We implemented the proposed routing protocol and compared it with the popular AODV algorithm in NS-3 using the simulation parameters discussed in the scenario description section previously. In this section, we estimate parameters such as packet delivery rate (PDR), average latency, packet loss rate, overhead and throughput depending on the number of vehicles in question under 10 attackers of black hole. The following Figs. 1, 2, 3, 4 and 5 show that the proposed algorithm is highly scalable and robust as the expected results were obtained with an evolving number of vehicles despite of the network is exposed to black hole attacks.

As shown in Fig. 1 and Fig. 2, the proposed protocol is superior to the popular protocol AODV in terms of PDR and PLR. This improvement is made possible because of the CS algorithm and the weighted parameters (fitness functions) namely distance, angle, road, speed and trust that positively influenced to increase the packet delivery rate of the data packets by selecting highly secure and stable routes with lesser number of link failures that in influences packet loss. The cause of data packets loss was partially because of inadequate bandwidth, failure in the links, overheads, collision of data packets and black hole attacks that drop packets.

From the Fig. 3, the proposed protocol had produced better results compared to the AODV protocol in terms of routing overhead. The optimal route and CH selection didn't take higher overhead on spending control packets to form a cluster and selection of cluster in the other words, the proposed protocol selects the best route and cluster head in shorter period of time with minimum control packets in the presences of black hole attack.

The Fig. 4 depicts the average delay on the basis of the number of vehicles considered in this study. As per Fig. 2, it is evident that when the number of vehicles increases, the average delay increases as well. The application of CSA with weighted parameters supported in selecting the optimal route in lesser time period while compared to AODV protocol.

From the Fig. 5, the proposed routing protocol had produced better results compared to the AODV protocol. The optimal route selection takes longer time in AODV protocol whereas the proposed protocol selects the best route in shorter

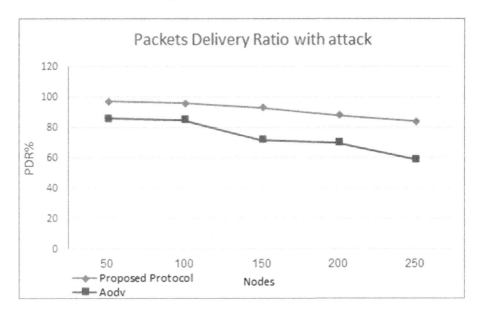

Fig. 1. Packet Delivery Ratio under 10 black hole attacks

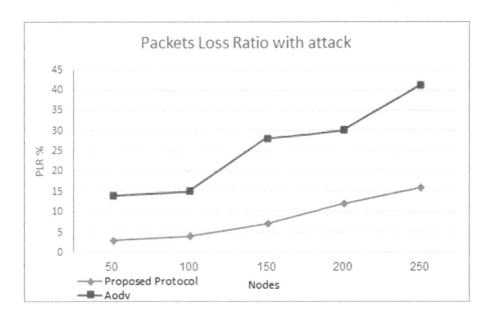

Fig. 2. Packet Loss Ratio under 10 black hole attacks

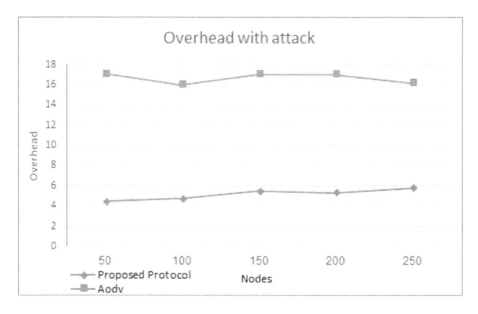

Fig. 3. Overhead under 10 black hole attacks

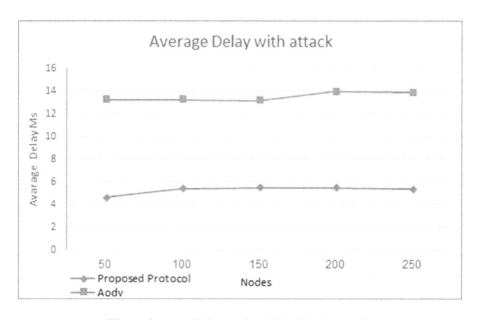

Fig. 4. Average Delay under 10 black hole attacks

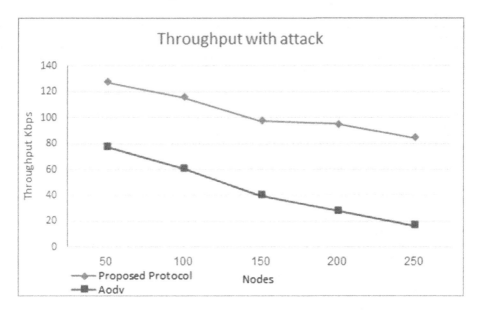

Fig. 5. Throughput under 10 black hole attacks

period of time. The advantage of swift convergence rate increased the throughput of the proposed protocol while compared to the existing AODV.

5 Conclusions

Vehicular ad hoc networks are powerless against different attacks because of the wireless nature and other characteristics of VANET. Moreover, these networks face some challenges in central administration making it further more challenging in ensuring efficient and secure routing. Hence, in this paper, we introduce a routing protocol for VANETs that smartly utilizes k-means clustering and a cuckoo search algorithm. In our proposed protocol, k-means clustering algorithm is responsible for cluster formation whereas cuckoo search algorithm is responsible for cluster head selection based on fitness function by computing the weights using five weight factors such as distance, angle, road, speed and trust. Simulation results depict that the proposed protocol had produced superior performance compared to the AODV protocol in terms of packet delivery ratio, average delay, packet loss ratio, overhead and throughput under blackhole attacks. The fitness functions used in the CSA helps to identify the optimal as well as stable and secure route in a shorter period of time. The proposed protocol outperformed the AODV protocol because of its distinct characteristics, specifically, the utilizing of speed factor and trust value in fitness function calculation which helps to identify the optimal as well as stable and secure route in a shorter period of time.

References

1. Singh, S., Agrawal, S.: VaNet routing protocols: issues and challenges. In: Recent Advances in Engineering and Computational Sciences (RAECS), pp. 1–5. IEEE (2014)
2. Isaac, J.T., Camara, J.S., Zeadally, S., Marquez, J.T.: A secure vehicle-to-roadside communication payment protocol in vehicular ad hoc networks. Comput. Commun. 31(10), 2478–2484 (2008)
3. Mukhtaruzzaman, M., Atiquzzaman, M.: Clustering in VANET: algorithms and challenges. arXiv preprint arXiv:2009.01964
4. Bali, R.S., Kumar, N., Rodrigues, J.J.: Clustering in vehicular ad hoc networks: taxonomy, challenges and solutions. Veh. Commun. 1(3), 134–152 (2014)
5. Bouchachia, A.: Intelligence for nonlinear dynamics and synchronisation, vol. 3. Springer, Cham (2010). https://doi.org/10.2991/978-94-91216-30-5
6. Bylykbashi, K., Elmazi, D., Matsuo, K., Ikeda, M., Barolli, L.: Effect of security and trustworthiness for a fuzzy cluster management system in VANETS. Cogn. Syst. Res. 55, 153–163 (2019)
7. Kaur, R., Kaur, H.: Performance evaluation of routing protocols in VANET. Int. J. Future Gener. Commun. Netw. 8(6), 239–246 (2015)
8. Xiao, B., Yu, B., Gao, C.: Detection and localization of sybil nodes in VANETs. In: Proceedings of the 2006 Workshop on Dependability Issues in Wireless Ad Hoc Networks and Sensor Networks, pp. 1–8 (2006)
9. Guette, G., Ducourthial, B.: On the sybil attack detection in VANET. In: IEEE International Conference on Mobile Adhoc and Sensor Systems, pp. 1–6. IEEE (2007)
10. Parno, B., Perrig, A.: Challenges in securing vehicular networks. In: Workshop on Hot Topics in Networks (HotNets-IV), Maryland, USA, pp. 1–6 (2005)
11. Nekovee, M.: Modeling the spread of worm epidemics in vehicular ad hoc networks. In: IEEE 63rd Vehicular Technology Conference, vol. 2, pp. 841–845. IEEE (2006)
12. Cerri, D., Ghioni, A.: Securing AODV: the A-SAODV secure routing prototype. IEEE Commun. Mag. 46(2), 120–125 (2008)
13. Guerrero Zapata, M.: Secure ad hoc on-demand distance vector (SAODV) routing, Internet Draft: draft-guerrero-manet-saodv-05. txt
14. Eichler, S., Roman, C.: Challenges of secure routing in MANETs: a simulative approach using AODV-SEC. In: 2006 IEEE International Conference on Mobile Ad Hoc and Sensor Systems, pp. 481–484. IEEE (2006)
15. Pirzada, A.A., Datta, A., McDonald, C.: Trustworthy routing with the AODV protocol. In: International Networking and Communication Conference, pp. 19–24. IEEE (2004)
16. Tyagi, P., Dembla, D.: A taxonomy of security attacks and issues in vehicular ad-hoc networks (VANETs). Int. J. Comput. Appl. 91(7), 22–29 (2014)
17. Raya, M., Hubaux, J.-P.: Securing vehicular ad hoc networks. J. Comput. Secur. 15(1), 39–68 (2007)
18. Yadav, V., Misra, S., Afaque, M.: Security of wireless and self-organizing networks: security in vehicular ad hoc networks, Security of Self-Organizing Networks: MANET, pp. 227–250. WMN, VANET, CRC Press, USA, WSN (2010)
19. Kaur, R., Singh, T.P., Khajuria, V.: Security issues in vehicular ad-hoc network (VANET). In: 2nd International Conference on Trends in Electronics and Informatics (ICOEI), pp. 884–889. IEEE (2018)

20. Ishmanov, F., Bin Zikria, Y.: Trust mechanisms to secure routing in wireless sensor networks: current state of the research and open research issues. J. Sens. (2017)
21. Montenegro, J., Iza, C., Aguilar Igartua, M.: Detection of position falsification attacks in vanets applying trust model and machine learning. In: Proceedings of the 17th ACM Symposium on Performance Evaluation of Wireless Ad Hoc, Sensor, & Ubiquitous Networks, pp. 9–16 (2020)
22. Patel, N.J., Jhaveri, R.H.: Trust based approaches for secure routing in VANET: a survey. Procedia Comput. Sci. **45**, 592–601 (2015)
23. Duan, J., Yang, D., Zhu, H., Zhang, S., Zhao, J.: TSRF: A trust-aware secure routing framework in wireless sensor networks. Int. J. Distrib. Sens. Netw. **2014**, 1–14 (2014). https://doi.org/10.1155/2014/209436
24. Jøsang, A., Ismail, R., Boyd, C.: A survey of trust and reputation systems for online service provision. Decis. Support Syst. **43**(2), 618–644 (2007)
25. Zhang, Q., Almulla, M., Ren, Y., Boukerche, A., An efficient certificate revocation validation scheme with k-means clustering for vehicular ad hoc networks. In: IEEE Symposium on Computers and Communications (ISCC), pp. 000862–000867. IEEE (2012)
26. Yang, X.-S., Deb, S.: Cuckoo search via lévy flights. In: World Congress on Nature & Biologically Inspired Computing (NaBIC), pp. 210–214. IEEE (2009)
27. Garg, K., Misra, M.: Trust based security in manet routing protocols: a survey. In: Proceedings of the 1st Amrita ACM-W Celebration on Women in Computing in India, pp. 1–7 (2010)
28. Khairnar, M., Vaishali, D., Kotecha, D., et al.: Simulation-based performance evaluation of routing protocols in vehicular ad-hoc network. arXiv preprint arXiv:1311.1378

Proactive Modeling in the Assessment of the Structural Functionality of the Subject of Critical Information Infrastructure

Elena Maksimova[1](✉) ⓘ and Natalia Sadovnikova[2](✉) ⓘ

[1] Russian Technological University MIREA (RTU MIREA), Central Federal Distrikt, Vernadsky Avenue, 78, Moscow 119454, Russia
maksimova@mirea.ru
[2] Volgograd State Technical University, Lenin Avenue, 28, Volgograd 400005, Russia
sadonnikova.natalia@vstu.ru

Abstract. With the introduction of Federal Law No. 187 [1], methodological issues of ensuring information security of processes, systems, and technologies were updated. The introduced regulatory documents regulate these issues without taking into account a systematic approach. In addition, the assessment of information security (IS) of the subject of critical information infrastructure (SCII) does not take into account infrastructure destructive, the appearance of which is possible due to inter-object systems of relationships and interactions at the level of the subject of CII. SCII is a complex multi-component dynamic system. In a number of works, cognitive modeling and a scenario approach were used to justify and implement a comprehensive assessment of information security. To ensure its safety, it is necessary to make management decisions. For the development of the information security management system, it is proposed to use proactive modeling. As one of the indicators of the effectiveness of proactive management at the level of ensuring the safety of SCII, we can consider the coefficient of structural functionality of the SCII. To evaluate this indicator, we propose a developed model and a methodology for working with it. Expected indicators of the competitive advantages of the using of proactive security management of the SCII: stabilization of the processes of ensuring the security of the SCII at all stages of the life cycle, reduction of the costs of ensuring the security of the components of the SCII, including in the dynamic model.

Keywords: Information security · Subject · Critical information infrastructure · Destructive impacts · Proactive modeling · Structural functionality

1 Problem Statement

With the introduction of Federal Law No. 187 [1], methodological issues of ensuring information security of processes, systems, and technologies were updated. The introduced regulatory documents regulate these issues without taking into account a systematic approach. In addition, the assessment of information security (IS) of the subject of critical information infrastructure (SCII) does not take into account possible destructive,

© Springer Nature Switzerland AG 2021
A. G. Kravets et al. (Eds.): CIT&DS 2021, CCIS 1448, pp. 436–448, 2021.
https://doi.org/10.1007/978-3-030-87034-8_31

the appearance of which is possible due to inter-object systems of relationships and inter-actions at the level of the subject of CII. In a number of works [2–7], cognitive modeling and a scenario approach [8–12] were used to justify and implement the solution of this issue at the level of a comprehensive assessment of information security. At the level of solving information security management issues, it is proposed to use the methodology of proactive modeling.

2   Research Methodology

The methodology of proactive modeling is currently a professional approach to opti-mization of the management of any organizational structure. It is based on the basic knowledge of scientific enterprise management and is focused on achieving the final result. In such a systemically formed approach, the goal set and the result obtained are inseparable [13].

Managing critical processes, ensuring the achievement of the goal of ensuring the safety of the SCII, it is necessary to consistently take into account the achieved results [8, 13, 14]. In practical implementation, it turns out that it is easier to set goals and objec-tives than to manage based on them. This situation is associated with the «impatient» approach of many managers to the management of information security, to solve «acute» issues aimed at quickly eliminating vulnerabilities.

In general, the information security management model can be formalized as the implementation of individual goals that allow achieving a common goal and displaying it in the form of logical and linguistic connections:

$$M = \left\{ N_c, \ F_N, \ M_k, \ \left(C^B, \ Z^B \right), \ \left(C^H, \ Z^H \right) \right\}$$

where N_c is the finite set of selected goals from the set of goals; F_N is the formalized representation of the goal by the decision-maker; M_k is the set of criteria, functions, and functional that reflect the achievement of the goal; C^B, C^H – goals of the higher and lower levels of the goal hierarchy; Z^B, Z^H – significance, goal preference on a set of goals, subordination ratio.

The manager, who gives priority to solving current issues, promptly implements reactive management – a management method in which planning of necessary actions is carried out before the beginning or in the process of their implementation. Thus, the planned actions change quite often, largely due to the lack of sufficiently clear goals. Management is reduced to the correct response to current events, but to the wrong response to events related to the goal [14].

The method of proactive management of information security can be aimed at pre-venting incidents, negative trends and force majeure. At the CII level, proactivity is based on the constant study of critical processes for the effective solution of security problems, in particular, problems related to reducing the level of the destructive impact of an infrastructure nature. Proactive management during implementation models (observing, measuring, and analyzing) the progress of critical processes, warns about possible.

3 Discussion

CII is a complex system, the cognition (study) of which requires the joint involvement of different types of models, many theories, many scientific disciplines (the organization of interdisciplinary research). SCII – structurally limited system interaction between CII objects. To display system complexity, it is advisable to use various methods: formalized description (topological, graph analytic, logical, set-theoretic, linguistic), verbal (goal setting, expert assessments, intuitive experience), special modeling (cognitive, structural-linguistic, situational).

SCII is a system of hierarchically related objects organized in a certain way, which can be described, among other things, using the apparatus of reliability theory [13–15]. SCII as a system has an individual character depending on the infrastructure of a particular subject and the selected subsystems of interacting objects.

Formalization and adjustment of the algorithms for managing information security systems operating in dynamic environments associated with the possibility of implementing information security threats, including destructive effects, should be carried out for a period of time when the state of the infrastructure is not significantly transformed. At the same time, the self-organizing SCII systemically has the properties of sensory-informative perception (measurement) of individual structural and component complexity, independently and purposefully adjusted according to the results of systemometry data. The process of establishing the most important and significant relationships between the components of the SCII analytically reflects the functionality of the components of the management goal aimed at the ideal:

$$S \equiv F(A, R, Z, C, T) \to \text{ideal} \ll \text{synergy of EM and IM} \gg$$

where S – the components of the management goal; A – the set of components in the SCII; R-multiple mutual connections between the components of the SCII; Z – the structural and compositional indicator of the connectivity of the SCII; C – the environment; T – the total duration of the SCII; EM – the natural model of the life cycle of the SCII; IM – an artificially organized model of the life cycle of the SCII.

A large number of indicators are considered in the model "Assessment of information security" to assess the safety of SCII [6, 7, 16–18].

The draft model for assessing the information security of a subject of critical information infrastructure under destructive influences is made in accordance with the IDEF0 functional modeling methodology, designed to formalize and describe the process of improving the level of information security. The contextual IDEF0 diagram of the process of increasing the level of information security is shown in Fig. 1.

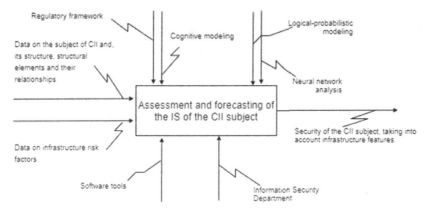

Fig. 1. Contextual IDEF0 diagram of the process of assessing and predicting information security.

It is important to note that the functionality of the SCII is taken into account only at the infrastructure-context level and does not take into account the infrastructure composition of the SCII. That is, the assessment of the infrastructure sustainability of the SCII at the level of the infrastructure of the subject is not considered. In this regard, in the framework of proactive modeling of the assessment of the functionality of the subject of CII, we will consider the cognitive model at the level of subsystems. The result of this model should be:

1. Assessment of the infrastructure integrity coefficient of the SCII (as the initial data for assessing the strength of the concept V1 "Assessment of the functionality of the SCII»)– *K(inf_int)*.
2. Evaluation of the structural functionality coefficient of the SCII (as the initial data for evaluating the strength of the concept V1 "Evaluation of the SCII functionality»)- *K(str_func)*.
3. A set of scenarios for achieving the required level of functionality of the CII subject, depending on the type of infrastructure.

The evaluation of the infrastructure integrity coefficient of the CII (as the initial data for evaluating the strength of the concept V1 "Evaluation of the functionality of the CII") *K(inf_int)* is proposed to be performed taking into account the topology of the subsystem of interacting CII objects.

Under the topology of the subsystem of interacting CII objects, we will understand the physical location of CII objects relative to each other and the way they are connected by communication lines. It is important to note that the concept of topology refers primarily to local networks, in which the structure of connections can be easily traced. In global networks, the communication structure is usually hidden from users and is not too important, since each communication session can be made in its own way [15].

As ways of organizing the information infrastructure, we will define the types of topologies considered for information systems [15, 19]:

Network topology-a scheme for connecting CII objects.

According to [19], the network topology can be:

1. Physical-describes the actual location and connections between network nodes.
2. Logical-describes the walking of the signal within the physical topology.
3. Information-describes the direction of information flows transmitted over the network.
4. Exchange management is the principle of transferring the right to use the network.

There are many ways to connect network devices, including the following types of topologies: fully connected, cellular, shared bus, star, ring, snowflake.

One of the indicators that influence the assessment of information security of the SCII is the integrity of the SCII. This indicator is directly determined by the integrity of the subsystems of the interacting SCII objects. The integrity of the subsystems of the interacting SCII objects is the property of the SCII subsystem to remain unchanged in time at the qualitative level when making authorized changes at the infrastructure level (adding or removing an element from the information infrastructure).

Assessment of the integrity of subsystems of interacting objects of the SCII is a set of calculated, experimental and organizational measures aimed at assessing the compliance of the actual or projected state of the information infrastructure with the relevant requirements.

The structural characteristics of the system make it possible to assess the quality of its structure and elements from the point of view of the general system approach at an early stage of the system creation. To assess the integrity of the information infrastructure, we will use the following topological characteristics [20]:

1. Structure connectivity - A^s.

This characteristic allows you to identify the presence of breaks in the structure, hanging vertices, etc. The connectivity of the graph elements is determined by the connectivity matrix $C = \|c_{ij}\|$, the elements of which are determined based on the total adjacency matrix:

$$A^s = \sum_{k=1}^{n} A^k$$

where n is the number of vertices of the graph, $A^k = A^{k-1}A$ (in particular $A^2 = A \cdot A$), where A is the adjacency matrix of the graph.

The matrix element $A^k = \|a^k{}_{ij}\|$ defines the number of paths of length k from vertex i to vertex j.

Element of the connectivity matrix:

$$c_{ij} = \begin{cases} 1, \textit{если } a^s_{ij} \geq 1; \\ 0, \text{если } a^s_{ij} = 0. \end{cases}$$

2. Structural redundancy - *R*.

The structural redundancy of R is a parameter that reflects the excess of the total number of links over the minimum necessary one. R is defined as follows:

$$R = 0.5 \div (n-1) \sum_{i=1}^{n} \sum_{j=1}^{n} a_{ij} - 1$$

For systems with redundancy that have a ring structure or a structure of the "complete graph" type, $R > 0$, for systems without redundancy, $R = 0$, for systems that are disconnected, $R < 0$.

Typically, systems with a larger R are potentially more reliable.

To characterize systems with high redundancy, the parameter ε^2 is also introduced, which takes into account the uneven distribution of connections. In this case, the arcs of a directed graph are considered without taking into account the directionality.

$$\varepsilon^2 = \sum_{i=1}^{n} g_i^2 - \frac{4m^2}{n},$$

where n is the number of vertices, g_i is the degree of the i-th vertex, and m is the number of edges of the graph.

This indicator characterizes the underutilization of the structure's capabilities in achieving maximum connectivity.

3. Structural compactness:

$$f(Q, Q_{oth}, d).$$

The proximity of elements i, j to each other is determined by the minimum length of the chain (path) d_{ij}. Structural compactness is determined by several parameters.

Absolute compactness:

$$Q = \sum_{i=1}^{n} \sum_{j=1}^{n} d_{ij}, i \neq j.$$

Relative compactness:

$$Q_{omH} = \frac{Q}{Q_{min}} - 1,$$

where $Q_{min} = n(n - 1)$ is the minimum compactness value for a "complete graph" system structure.

Structure diameter:

$$d = \max_{ij} d_{ij}.$$

An increase in the values of these parameters indicates that:

– increasing the inertia of the processes carried out in the system;
– increasing the number of links separating the elements;
– reducing the reliability of the system.

4. The degree of centralization in the structure - σ.

To assess centralization, use the centrality index:

$$\sigma = \frac{(n - 1)(2Z_{max} - n)}{Z_{max}(n - 2)},$$

where Z_{max} is the maximum value of the value:

$$Z_i = \frac{Q}{2 \sum_{j=1}^{n} d_{ij}}, i = 1, 2, \ldots, n; i \neq j.$$

Thus:

$$\sigma = \begin{cases} 1, & \text{for structures of systems that have the maximum degree} \\ & \text{of centralization, i.e. the structure is radial;} \\ 0, & \text{for structures with a uniform distribution of connections} \\ & \text{(complete graph, ring).} \end{cases}$$

The assessment of the integrity function of the information infrastructure can be considered as one of the indicators for assessing its security.

The proposed assessment, for example, will allow the timely application of a sufficient set of measures to neutralize the following threats to information security [21]:

- the threat of abuse of the opportunities provided to consumers of cloud services;
- threat of code or data injection;
- the threat of exploiting the weaknesses of cryptographic algorithms and vulnerabilities in the software of their implementation;
- threat of access to protected files using a workaround;
- the threat of changing the operating modes of the hardware elements of the computer;
- the threat of distortion of the information entered and output to the peripheral devices;
- the threat of disruption of the availability of the cloud server, etc.
- The coefficient of structural functionality of the SCII - $K(str\_func)$.

This indicator is not a standard topological characteristic from the point of view of the system approach and the theory of system reliability.

To evaluate $K (str\_func)$, it is necessary to construct a graph model "Evaluation of the structural functionality of the subject of the CII" in the form of a digraph.

For this model:

- The weights of the Oij relationships are determined by the expert method based on the type of relationship.
- The weight of the vertexes F(Oi) is set based on the significance category of the corresponding object in the scale [0,1] according to the following rule:

$$\left(SIGN_{CAT[O_I]} \equiv 0 \Rightarrow f[O_I] \equiv 0\right) \wedge \left(SIGN_{CAT[O_I]} \equiv 3 \Rightarrow f[O_I] = 0.3\right)$$
$$\wedge \left(SIGN_{CAT[O_I]} \equiv 2 \Rightarrow f[O_I] = 0.6\right) \wedge \left(SIGN_{CAT[O_I]} \equiv 1 \Rightarrow f[O_I] = 1\right).$$

The values of the weights of the links «Oi-F(Sj) » are equal to +1 for all i, j:

$$V(Oi\_F(Sj)) \equiv +1.$$

The values of the weights of the links «F(Sj) - V1» are +1 for all j:

$$V(F(Sj)\_V1) \equiv +1.$$

The developed graph model can be linearized into a perceptron with a given target vertex Fm (S) - the structural functionality of the SCII. Then, based on the values: m - the number of layers, n_i-the number of connections on the i-th layer, w_{ij}^k-the weight of the connection between the objects O_i and O_j on the k-th layer, we can estimate the maximum (max(Fm(S)), minimum (min(Fm(S)) and corresponding (Fm(S)) values of the structural functionality of the SCII:

$$max(Fm(S)) = n1 + n1 \cdot (n1 - 1) + \sum_{i=1}^{m} n_i \cdot n_{i-1} = n_1^2 + \sum_{i=3}^{m} n_i \cdot n_{i-1}, \quad (1)$$

$$min(F_m(S)) = n1 - n1 \cdot (n1 - 1) - \sum_{i=1}^{m} n_i \cdot n_{i-1} = 2 \cdot n_1 - n_1^2 - \sum_{i=3}^{m} n_i \cdot n_{i-1},$$
(2)

$$|Fm(S)| = n_1 + \sum_{i=1}^{n1} \sum_{j=1}^{n1} w_{ij}^2 \cdot F\left(O_i^2\right) + \sum_{k=2}^{m} \sum_{i=1}^{n} \sum_{l=1}^{n} w_{ij}^k \cdot F\left(O_i^k\right) j \neq j.$$
(3)

4 Experimental Research

Let us consider the study of the proposed model for a particular case. Let there be 10 CII objects in the SCII structure. Suppose that as a result of the decomposition of the infrastructure, 4 subsystems of interacting objects are allocated (see Fig. 2).

Based on the results of the analysis of the presented infrastructure, a graph model «Assessment of the structural functionality of the subject of the CII» is constructed (see Fig. 3).

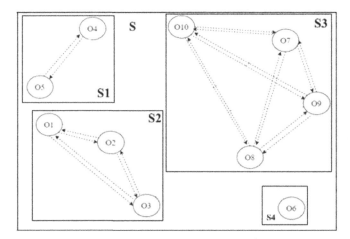

Fig. 2. Decomposition of the infrastructure of the CII subject.

The graph model (see Fig. 2) is represented as a multilayer perceptron (see Fig. 4). Let's assume that there are CII objects with the following categories of significance:

$$Cat(O1) \equiv Cat(O2) \equiv Cat(O3) \equiv 3 \Rightarrow F\_zn(O1)$$
$$\equiv F\_zn(O2) \equiv F\_zn(O3) \equiv 0,35,$$

$$Cat(O4) \equiv Cat(O5) \equiv 2 \Rightarrow F\_zn(O4) \equiv F\_zn(O5) \equiv 0,7,$$

$$Cat(O6) \equiv H/3 \Rightarrow F\_zn(O6) \equiv 0,1,$$

$$Cat(O7) \equiv Cat(O8) \equiv Cat(O9) \equiv Cat(10) \equiv 3 \Rightarrow F\_zn(O7)$$
$$\equiv F\_zn(O8) \equiv F\_zn(O9) \equiv F\_zn(10) \equiv 0,35.$$

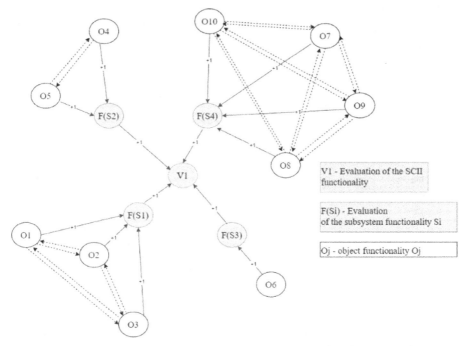

Fig. 3. Graph model «Assessment of the structural functionality of the CII subject».

Let's also assume that the weight of the connections between all interacting objects is «weakly positive», i.e. F(Oij)= 0,2.

Calculated by formula 3, the value of K(str_func) = 1.56. The maximum value of this coefficient is in the limit [5.49, 7.8]. In the triangular fuzzy representation, the estimate of the value of the structural functionality coefficient can be represented as:

$$K(str\_func) = [5.49, 1.56, 7.8],$$

where the first number is the minimum of the maximum possible values of the structural functionality coefficient of the SCII, the second number is the expected value of the structural functionality coefficient of the SCII, and the third number is the maximum possible value of the structural functionality coefficient of the SCII.

Since according to the general approach to the concept of «the coefficient of structural functionality of the subject of critical information infrastructure», the maximum level of information security can be maintained with a minimum value of this coefficient, we can say that with the calculated value of K(str_func), the infrastructure state of the research SCII will not affect the overall assessment of information security.

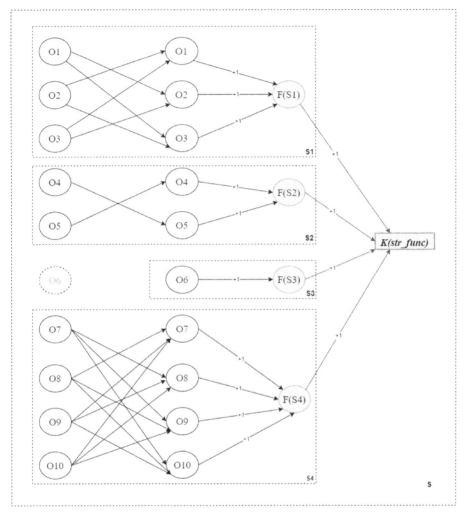

Fig. 4. Representation of the graph model «Assessment of the structural functionality of the CII subject» in the form of a multi-layer perceptron.

5   Conclusion

1. The subject of critical information infrastructure is a complex multi-component dynamic system. To ensure its safety, it is necessary to make management decisions. It is proposed to use proactive modeling as a methodological basis for the development of an information security management system.
2. As one of the indicators of the effectiveness of proactive management at the level of ensuring the safety of SCII, the coefficient of structural functionality of the SCII can be considered. To evaluate this indicator, a model and a methodology for working with it have been developed.

3. Expected indicators of the competitive advantages of the using of proactive security management of the SCII: stabilization of the processes of ensuring the security of the SCII at all stages of the life cycle, reduction of the costs of ensuring the security of the components of the SCII, including in the dynamic model.

Acknowledgments. The reported study was funded by the Russian Ministry of science (information security) (grant IS, project No. 3/2020).

References

1. On the Security of the Critical Information Infrastructure of the Russian Federation: Federal Law No. 187-FZ of July 26, 2017 (With Amendments and Additions), http://www.consultant.ru/document/cons_doc_LAW_220885/. Accessed 24 Mar 2021
2. Azhmukhamedov, I.M.: Information Security System Analysis and Fuzzy Cognitive Modeling. LAP, Moscow (2012)
3. Azhmukhamedov, I.M.: Analysis and management of complex security based on cognitive modeling. Manag. Large Syst. **29**, 5–15 (2010)
4. Azhmukhamedov, I.M.: Dynamic fuzzy cognitive model of the impact of threats on the information security of the system. Inf. Technol. Secur. **2**, 68–72 (2010)
5. Maximova, E.A.: Cognitive modeling of destructive malicious actions on objects of critical information infrastructure. Proc. Educ. Inst. Commun. **6**(4), 91–103 (2020)
6. Maksimova, E.A.: Assessment of Information Security of the Subject of Critical Information Infrastructure Under Destructive Influences. VolSU, Volgograd (2020)
7. Maksimova, E.A.: "Smart decisions" in development of a model for protecting information of a subject of critical information infrastructure. In: Popkova, E.G., Sergi, B.S. (eds.) ISC 2020. LNNS, vol. 155, pp. 1213–1221. Springer, Cham (2021). https://doi.org/10.1007/978-3-030-59126-7_132
8. Roberts, F.S.: Discrete Mathematical Models with Applications to Social, Biological, and Environmental Problems. «The science», Moscow (1986)
9. Kosko, V.: Fuzzy cognitive maps. Int. J. Man-Mach. Stud. **24**, 65–75 (1986)
10. Sadovnikova, N.P., Kikteev, A.S.: Application of agent-based modeling for constructing strategic development scenarios, Izvestiya VolgSTU. Actual Probl. Control Comput. Eng. Comput. Sci. Tech. Syst. **4**(91), 144–147 (2012)
11. Bashilov, A.M., Korolev, V.A., Arzhenovsky, A.G., Globin, A.N., Glechikova, N.A.: Proactive modeling of the dynamic complexity of agrotechnocenoses. Bull. Agrar. Sci. Don **3**(51), 45–54 (2020)
12. Kaivosoja, J., Jackenkroll, M., Linkolehto, R., Weis, M., Gerhards, R.: Automatic control of farming operations based on spatial web services. Comput. Electr. Agricult. **100**, 110–115 (2014). https://doi.org/10.1016/j.compag.2013.11.003
13. Balashova, T.I.: Ensuring network fault tolerance by increasing the reliability of its topology. Modern Probl. Sci. Educ. **6** (2014). http://science-education.ru/ru/article/view?id=16846. Accessed 2 May 2021
14. Viktorova, V.S., Stepanyants, A.S.: Multilevel modeling of system reliability. Sens. Syst. **6**(181), 33–37 (2014)
15. Gromov, Y.Y.: Reliability of Information Systems. Publishing House of GOU VPO TSTU, Tambov (2010)

16. Klimov, S.M., Polikarpov, S.V., Ryzhov, B.S., Tikhonov, R.I., Shpyrnya, I.V.: Methodology for ensuring the stability of the functioning of critical information infrastructure in the conditions of information impacts. Cybersecur. Issue. **6**(34), 37–48 (2019)
17. Kosolapov, O.V.: Stability as one of the main characteristics of the system. Izvestiya Ural State Mining University **4**, 77–81 (2013). https://e.lanbook.com/journal/issue/290438
18. Gadzhiev, B.R., Gibina, E., Proyudova, T.B., Shchetinina, D.P.: Topology and stability of local-world networks. Software Products and Systems **4**, 51–54 (2009)
19. Computer Technologies. https://www.sites.google.com/site/informtexxim/home/5. Accessed 25 Apr 2021
20. Structural and Topological Characteristics of Systems-Programming in C, C# and Java (vscode.ru). https://vscode.ru/articles/struct-topolog-charact-system.html. Accessed 25 Apr 2021
21. Data Bank of Information Security Threats. https://bdu.fstec.ru/threat/. Accessed 25 Apr 2021

Data Processing Based on the Structure Oriented Evaluation Online Tool from SERVQUAL Model

Uranchimeg Tudevdagva[1,2(✉)], Bolorsaikhan Omboosuren[3], and Wolfram Hardt[1]

[1] Chemnitz University of Technology, 09111 Chemnitz, Germany
uranchimeg.tudevdagva@informatik.tu-chemnitz.de
[2] Mongolian University of Science and Technology, 14191 Ulaanbaatar, Mongolia
[3] Mongolian National University of Medical Sciences, 14210 Ulaanbaatar, Mongolia

Abstract. SERVQUAL and SURE are multidimensional, non-parametric evaluation models for evaluating of complex processes and systems. While SERVQUAL uses standard statistical procedures for the evaluation of observational data, such as those implemented in SPSS, for example, the SURE model has its own data processing tool, which was developed with the help of general measure theory for the evaluation of logically structured processes. This paper shows how data records obtained in sense of SERVQUAL model can be analyzed with the SURE data processing tool. As example, an evaluation of SERVQUAL data from the health care sector is considered. Data collected from 5138 students based on SERVQUAL model and processed by the SURE model online tool.

Keywords: Evaluation model · Higher education · Service quality · Structure oriented evaluation · SURE model

1 Introduction

The Mongolian National University of Medical Sciences (MNUMS) is a gem of an institution that has been a pioneer in medical education in Mongolia since its founding in 1942- and 79-years history. Mission: To become one of the top 100 medical universities in the Asia-Pacific Region. Over 13,200 degree seeking students are enrolled in the MNUMS across our eight schools: Medicine, Biomedicine, Dentistry, Traditional Medicine, Nursing, Pharmacy, Graduate Studies, and Public Health and 3 regional Medical colleges. With approximately 13,000 alumni who occupy over 90% of the medical professionals in the health care service across the country, the MNUMS continues to be a leader in providing an environment that empowers physicians and medical professionals to contribute to the development of the society. The MNUMS has been recognized by the state in so many areas that reflect our commitment to excellence in education and health care. In 2017, Medical bachelor degree program accredited by ASIIN, International Accreditation agency based in Dusseldorf, Germany. Currently we implement block-integrated curriculum with capacity-based program [1].

© Springer Nature Switzerland AG 2021
A. G. Kravets et al. (Eds.): CIT&DS 2021, CCIS 1448, pp. 449–462, 2021.
https://doi.org/10.1007/978-3-030-87034-8_32

The Mongolian National University of Medical Sciences aims to complete three core missions including research, education, and social contribution, to respond to the demands of reforms designed to raise their competitiveness internationally by cultivating research-oriented universities. Out of them, research is apt to change in response to global trends.

The Mongolian National University of Medical Sciences must introduce the internationally accepted new systems that promote and maintain academic freedom, cutting-edge knowledge of the world, and the best practical use of modern technologies. With approximately 13,000 alumni who occupy over 90% of the medical professionals in the health care service across the country, the Mongolian National University of Medical Sciences continues to be a leader in providing an environment that empowers physicians and medical professionals to contribute to the development of the society. We welcome students from a variety of backgrounds, as we recognize that international students provide diverse perspectives and contribute to a dynamic learning atmosphere. Undergraduate course /Medical doctors' curriculum/are offered to International Admissions by us.

School of Medicine has over 3200 undergraduate students, 140 graduate students and 380 postgraduate students, 142 faculties, 23 clinical departments including 3 traditional departments with 15 professor's teams. Since 1999, our school had implemented an integrated PBL based curriculum with 21 blocks. This curriculum has been accredited by the National Council for Higher Education Accreditation and evaluated successfully by the Association for Medical Education in the Western Pacific Region in 2011.

From this academic year, we are implementing 2 years premedical, plus 4 years of medical curriculum for all medical and dental students. All students will study anatomy, physiology, biochemistry, microbiology, immunology, genetics and plus various other studies including biostatistics, epidemiology, pharmacology, and laboratory classes in their initial 2 years pre-medical training. From the third year until the fifth year, students study clinical studies, based on the "block-integrated curriculum." Clinical studies are based within the hospital complex with attachments to Medicine, Surgery, Pediatrics, and other direct patient care specialties. From last year, students have done their clerkship at the rural hospitals throughout Mongolia.

Managing the quality of service in higher educational institution is an important issue. To meet the students' requirements and achieve institutional goals is a complex task. As a result of employers' opinion about alumni's knowledge and skills is poor, we may conclude quality of higher education has problems [2].

Evaluating E-learning. A case study MNUMS, Audit results for ophthalmology department course execution, Internal and external auditing study on the University's main activities, The evaluation of service quality of the health education organizations, Results of the Service Quality Survey of the Nursing Schools, Nowadays condition to determine of training technology Health sciences university of Mongolia is clinical chair's activity, realization of result evaluation, Comparative study of some special professional training gaps between medical universities, Survey on satisfaction of graduating medical students with special curriculum in public schools, Survey on satisfaction of Students, The matter of using key performance indicator for evaluating and monitoring of university activity, The comparative study of student's social status, personally valuable things and satisfaction, Result of self-report of faculty members on the teaching perspectives inventory et all [3].

Although the access to higher education (HE) and tertiary level enrolment rate is relatively high on the global stage in Mongolia, the Mongolian HE has been working on addressing the issue of low-cost, low-quality academic programmes that are often not relevant to the labour market. Graduate unemployment is a major issue given that an estimated 40% of HE graduates were unemployed in Mongolia [4].

It is essential that students learn to harness the power of the internet while internalizing the course content and applying it throughout their lives far beyond classroom doors. The aim of the research is to evaluate teaching methods, development of MOOCs, and student attendance rates. A total of students participated in the current study. Student attendance of MNUMS's e-learning was 91.9% as compared to 90–100% for other 24 (30.4%) colleges and universities. As we studied about 5 elements of e-learning, we found out that the legal environment is favorable; the university has administrative information system, e-learning system and public network. Online learning library is used by 3 (27.3%) out of 11 branch schools, therefore, it is not being used by its full potential. As a result, lecture content and structures are assured as indicated, hand out materials and advices are given. 64.6% of the students used mobile phone and tablet, around 35% used computer for online study. Teachers spend around 4–6 h giving advice to students, checking homework and evaluating their performance. Overall performance of online learning was good. E-learning is done by an ineffective learning form. Passive learning has been used in online teaching.

Methodology SERVQUAL

Data collection designed based on SERVQUAL model. The SERVQUAL model in our study which looks at the gap between the expectations of the trainees or clients and the perception of actual services they received in order to define and evaluate quality [5]. As the higher education system is rapidly developing in the increasingly globalized world, the universities of highly developed countries such as countries from the European Union, the US, Japan and even China, South Africa, Malaysia, Greece and Iran, are using SERVQUAL model to evaluate their training service quality [6, 7]. Therefore, the purpose of our research was to evaluate the quality of training services provided by public nursing schools using SERVQUAL (Model of Service Quality), which is widely used throughout the world [8]. The online survey was conducted using random sampling among 2568 students studying in 8 urban and rural medical schools between 8 December 2020 and 23 December 2020.

In 1985 A. Parasuraman, professor of Miami University, US, first developed this model (Model of Service Quality) to study the quality of services which were slightly modified to produce a questionnaire with 27 questions on perceptions and expectations organized into two chapters and five basic indicators, which are used for determining the quality of training services [9]. By doing so, the researchers were able to replace their traditional one-dimensional method of evaluating quality with a multidimensional one, which allows viewing the quality from multiple angles. This helps in locating areas which need improvement or areas where resources could be better utilized [10].

Mongolian case emphasizes the governance of the quality assurance system as the major issue, whereas the Omani case focuses on decontextualisation of imported programmes and standards, and academics' resistance to accept them, and costly and lengthy processes of international accreditation [11].

Methodology SURE
In this paper the SURE model data processing was applied to process data which collected via SERVQUAL model.

Structure Oriented Evaluation Model: The structure-oriented evaluation (SURE) model originally developed for measure quality of e-learning [12]. Later the SURE model extended to implement into various type evaluations of complex systems and data processing of different evaluation models [13]. Main concept of the SURE model is to start evaluation process with definition of evaluation key and sub goals. Defined key and sub goals are visualized via logical series and parallel structures. And following steps of the SURE model is developed based defined logical structure. Therefore model called: structure oriented model. The checklist for data collecting creating based on logical structures. The collected data by adapted checklist processing by SURE calculations rules. The SURE calculation rules developed based on defined logical structure in frame of measure theory [12].

It became possible due to the structural organization of main questions of SERVQUAL model.

The SURE data processing computes four different evaluation scores.

- $Q^*_e(A_{ij})$ – evaluation score for each sub goal
- $Q^*_e(B_i)$ – evaluation score for each key goal
- $Q^*_e(C)$ – evaluation score for each response
- $Q^*_{e,k}(C)$ - evaluation score for logical structure

Below show all calculation rules which applied to compute above listed evaluation scores.

Due to the mixed nature of service quality for data processing the structure oriented evaluation (SURE) model for evaluation data processing was applied. The structure oriented evaluation model consists of eight steps for implementation [12–15]. In first, step key goals of evaluation should be defined. Based on SERVQUAL model [16, 17] here the defined five key goals:

According to this model, there are 5 dimensions, namely Assurance (B_1), Responsiveness (B_2), Empathy (B_3), Reliability (B_4), and Tangibles (B_5). These five dimensions are defined as key goals of SURE evaluation (Fig. 1).

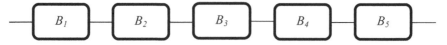

Fig. 1. Logical structure of key goals.

Main condition for key goal structure is the successful achievement of all defined key goals. Each key goal should receive evaluation score bigger than zero (>0). If just one of the defined key goals evaluates as unsuccessful (=0) then the total evaluation of defined structure will receive an evaluation score of zero.

Series logical structure is strongest structure of the SURE model. Therefore, the evaluator should take care of key goals in this logical structure.

By the SURE model, after definition of key goals structure the sub goals structure should be defined. Following checklist of the SERVQUAL model sub goals are defined (Figs. 2, 3 and 4).

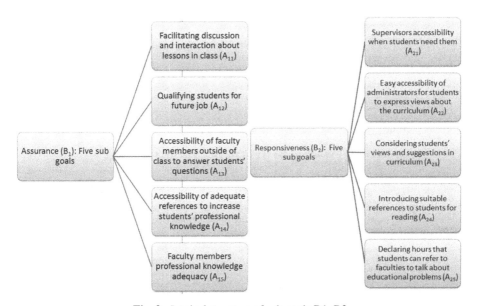

Fig. 2. Logical structure of sub goals B1, B2

Figure 5 shows logical structure of sub goals. If any of the goals from defined sub goals achieves its target, the corresponding key target evaluates as successful.

Number of sub goals are flexible. But by previous cases of evaluation and experiences in different application confirm that better to keep sub goals in limited numbers. Seven is almost a lot for sub goals. In our case we are processed data which collected by SERVQUAL method early, that means cannot change and reduce sub goals here.

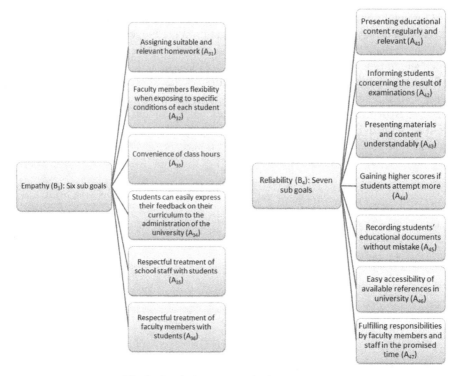

Fig. 3. Logical structure of sub goals B3, B4

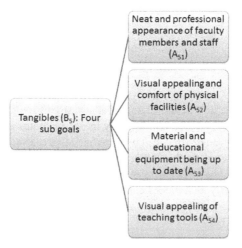

Fig. 4. Logical structure of sub goals B5

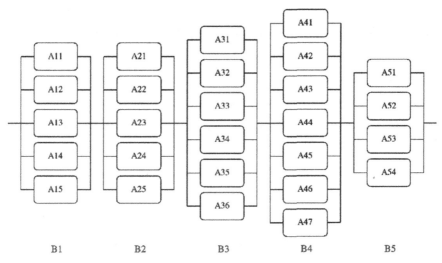

Fig. 5. Logical structure of sub goals.

2 Data Processing

Based on SERVQUAL model, the key goal structure consists of five key goals: Assurance (B_1), Responsiveness (B_2), Empathy (B_3), Reliability (B_4), and Tangibles (B_5). Data was collected by the online survey from 5138 students studying in 8 urban and rural medical schools from 8 December to 23 December, 2020.

Data was processed objectively by online calculator of the SURE model [18]. Due to the big size, the collected data set was not included into paper. Data was processed by calculation rules of the SURE model. The calculation rules of the SURE model developed based on evaluation goal structures and frame of measure theory [19].

Figure 6 shows main screenshot of online calculator with corresponding data for data processing. In edit field with note "Enter checklist data" entered comma separated vector (CSV) data. This data starts with numbers 5 by means evaluation data has five key goals. Next row: 5, 5, 6, 7, 4, show that numbers of sub goals of five key goals. Following row: 1, 5 numbers are for scale interval of evaluation measurement. Remaining numbers are collected data by SERVQUAL model from students.

Next to edit field for data entered, there are three different small rectangles with corresponding options for selection of color scale type, checklist data display format and evaluation table type. Before pressing SEND button evaluator should configure these options by their request.

Color scale type has four different options:

- Red-yellow-green
- Red-white-blue
- Gray scale
- No color scale

Evaluator can select one of the given options and evaluation scores will be shown by selected option.

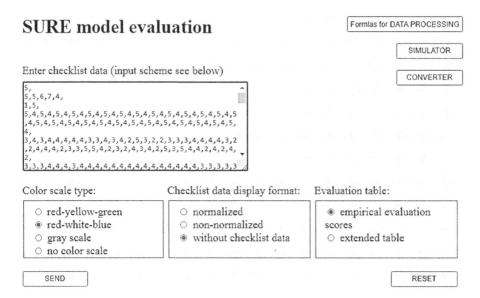

Fig. 6. Start window of the online calculation tool

Checklist data display format has three options for selection:

- Normalized
- Non-normalized
- Without checklist data

Normalized will show the collected data in an interval between 0 to 1 after normalization. Non-normalized version is for table with data in original scale, from 1 to 4 for instance. Without checklist data option will not include any data into to result table. Sometime this option is useful, due to the too big data set.

Following figures show evaluation scores of key goals and as well as sub goals (Figs. 7, 8 and 9) after computation of given data by online tool [18].

B_1. *First key goal:* Assurance
B_2. *Second key goal:* Responsiveness
B_3. *Third key goal:* Empathy
B_4. *Fourth key goal:* Reliability
B_5. *Fifth key goal:* Tangibles

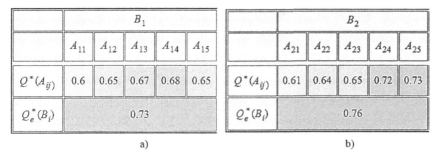

Fig. 7. Evaluation scores: a) Assurance; b) Responsiveness

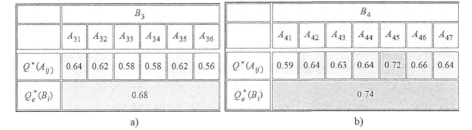

Fig. 8. Evaluation scores: a) Empathy and b) Reliability

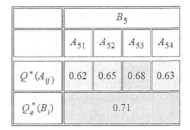

Fig. 9. Evaluation score of Tangibles

Based on all collected data the SURE model calculates general evaluation score for whole logical structure (Fig. 10).

Empirical evaluation score $Q_e^*(C)$

$$Q_e^*(C) = 0.705047$$

Asymptotic confidence intervals $[q_{e,0}^*, q_{e,1}^*]$ for $Q_e(C)$ at confidence level
$1 - \alpha = 0.90, 0.95, 0.99$

and sample standard deviation σ_e^* with $\sigma_e^* = \sqrt{\frac{1}{n-1} \sum_{k=1}^n (Q_{e,k}^*(C) - Q_e^*(C))^2}$.

$1 - \alpha$	$q_{e,0}^*$	$Q_e^*(C)$	$q_{e,1}^*$	σ_e^*
0.90	0.7003		0.7098	
0.95	0.6994	0.705	0.7107	0.2065
0.99	0.6976		0.7125	

Sample size $n = 5138$

Fig. 10. General evaluation score

3 Analyze on Evaluation Results

The SURE model calculates evaluation scores for all sub goals, key goals and general evaluation score. Here we analyze evaluation results.

- General evaluation score is 0.70. This number tells that in general the evaluated process achieved its target in 70%. The success of the process measured as 70 from 100.
- Next focus moves to key goals. How good reached key goals their target? Evaluation score of first key goal is 0.73, second goal is 0.76, third is 0.68, fourth is 0.74 and fifth is 0.71. All key goals have reached their targets. Second key goal received the highest values. Third key goal, to the contrary, got the lowest score. Third key goal was measured Empathy with sub goals: Assigning suitable and relevant homework (A_{31}); Faculty members flexibility when exposing to specific conditions of each student (A_{32}); Convenience of class hours (A_{33}); Students can easily express their feedback on their curriculum to the administration of the university (A_{34}); Respectful treatment of school staff with students (A_{35}), and Respectful treatment of faculty members with students (A_{36}). To analyze achievement of third key goal, have to check evaluation scores of corresponding sub goals. Sub goals: Convenience of class hours (A_{33}) and Students can easily express their feedback on their curriculum to the administration of the university (A_{34}) are evaluated with score 0.58. That means students cannot satisfy with class hours and communication between students and administration of university is running not smoothly. Second key goal: Responsiveness was evaluated with best score 0.76. The second key goal consists of sub goals: Supervisors accessibility when students need them (A_{21}); Easy accessibility of administrators for students to express views about the curriculum (A_{22}); Considering students' views and suggestions in curriculum (A_{23}); Introducing suitable references to students for reading (A_{24}), and Declaring hours that students can refer to faculties to talk about educational problems

(A_{25}). Sub goals: Introducing suitable references to students for reading (A_{24}), and Declaring hours that students can refer to faculties to talk about educational problems (A_{25}) are evaluated with score 0.72 and 0.73 which are most high score in amount of sub goals. Based on this score can conclude that students are satisfying with faculties support in education issues and reading references.

- One more analysis can be done on the evaluation scores of sub goals. The best evaluation score received sub goal $A_{25,}$ value is 0.73 for Declaring hours that students can refer to faculties to talk about educational problems. Worst evaluation score received sib goal $A_{36,}$ value is 0.56 for Respectful treatment of faculty members with students. Until this we described evaluation results based on the SURE data processing. Below explains data processing based on SPSS software.

Table 1. Five SERVQUAL dimensions correlation

	1	2	3	4	5
Reliability	0.643**				
Assurance	0.515**	0.590**			
Empathy	0.514**	0.461**	0.684**		
Responsiveness	0.529**	0.473**	0.577**	0.684**	
Tangibles	0.455**	0.389**	0.490**	0.506**	0.723**
SERVQUAL	0.328**	0.417**	0.322**	0.343**	0.266**

$p < 0,001$. weak* (0.–0.3); moderate ** (0.3–0.7); strong *** (0.7–1.0).

- Table 1 shows some data processing by SPSS software. There is a strong direct positive ($r = 0.723$) correlation between tangibles, responsiveness and empathy have moderate direct positive ($r = 0,684$) correlation which has statistical significance ($p < 0.001$). Other factors are directly related ($r = 0.389–0.643$) to moderate, and less likely to be statistically significant.

- The service quality value that indicates the outcome (-0.29) or process (-0.30) is negative (Table 2). In particular, improving the coherence of multi-stakeholder interactions in the delivery of educational services, and paying more attention to communication approaches, will reduce the gap between expectations and perceptions received after receiving intangible services through the process ($P < 0.001$).

Table 2. Outcome and process indicators of educational service of MNUMS

Indicator		Perception	Expectation	Service quality	P
Outcome	Responsiveness	3.76	3.47	−0.29	P < 0.001
Process	Reliability	3.71	3.40	−0.30	P < 0.001
	Assurance				
	Empathy				
	Tangibles				

4   Conclusion

The aim of this paper was to apply the structure oriented evaluation model for data processing of the SERVQUAL model. The logical structure of the SURE model designed based on the SERVQUAL model.

By data processing, general evaluation measured as 0.70 from 1.00, that means there are some space to improve quality of the service in the future. If measure in procent it can reflect us 70% achievement, which is not really high. Main focus of improvement should go to sub goals: A_{36}, A_{33}, A_{34}, and A_{41}. First three sub goals are from third key goal Empathy defined as Respectful treatment of faculty members with students, Convenience of class hours, Declaring hours that students can refer to faculties to talk about educational problems. In conclusion most students were not really satisfied with communication and with faculty members. Moreover, students want more convenient environment for studying. Last sub goal is from fourth key goal Reliability defined as Presenting educational content regularly and relevant. It shows that students could not fully enjoy the teaching methods or content delivery types.

The fact that the quality of educational services does not reach the level expected by the client has direct strong positive ($r = 0,723$) correlation to intangibles (innovation of the school's educational technology) and direct moderate positive ($r = 0,684$) correlation to empathy. Improving the coherence and consistency of teacher-student interactions in the delivery of training services by branch campuses and faculty departments will help in reducing the gap between perceptions and expectations. The global pandemic situation COVID-19 has brought unprecedented changes in the qquality assurance of higher education in Mongolia. The planned onsite visits of accreditation have been postponed during the quarantine and the social distance periods since February 2020. However, a partial online accreditation process has begun with interviews and meetings involving evaluators and professional committees. It has been indeed a challenge for evaluators and higher education institutions to check and provide evidence online, even though evaluators manage to conduct online interviews with employers, graduates, academics, and managers. Mongolian National council for education accreditation has undertaken the following actions towards the digital transition: (1) Issued a temporary regulation on online accreditation; (2) organised professional committees' meetings online; (3) developing online accreditation procedures, learning from the international best practices; (4) improved their social media outreach provide updated information by improving their online presence and visibility; (5) developing new criteria and procedures to accredit online degree programmes and e-courses to address the critical issue of quality of e-learning; and (6) holding a series of capacity building activities online.

This work was focused to analyze collected data by SERVQUAL models by two different data processing methods: the SURE data processing rules and SPSS software. Evaluation results by these two different methods are quite close in meaning and it confirms that if data collected by questions which have structures can be processed by the SURE data processing rules or by online tool of the SURE model. Evaluation scores of the SURE model are shows in interval between 0 and 1 and it easy to explain and understand to all interested groups for evaluation results.

References

1. ASIIN: General criteria for the accreditation of degree programs, engineering, informatics, architecture, natural sciences, mathematics, individually and in combination with other subject areas (2015). http://www.asiinev.de/media/kriterien/0.3_Criteria_for_the_Accrediation_of_Degree_Programmemes_2015-12-10.pdf
2. MECSS: Statistical yearbook education, 2016–2017. Ulaanbaatar: Ministry of Education, Culture, Science, and Sports (2017). http://www.mecss.gov.mn/data/1702/HigherSta1617ab
3. ASIIN: Self evaluation report Accreditation of Medical Doctors Bachelors Program, Ulaanbaatar, Mongolia (2016)
4. MECSS: Statistical report of higher education sector, 2018–2019. Ulaanbaatar: Ministry of Education, Culture, Science, and Sports (2019). https://mecss.gov.mn/news/1388/
5. Bolorsaikhan, O., Otgontsetseg, O., Purevdorj, Ts., Dalkh, Ts.: Results of the service quality survey of the nursing schools. New medicine Mar, pp. 25–30 (2012)
6. Kebriaei, A., Roudbari, M.: Quality gap in educational services at Zahedan university of medical sciences: students viewpoints about current and optimal condition. Iranian J. Med. Educ. **5**, 53–60 (2005)
7. Bradley, R.B.: Analyzing service quality: The case of post-graduate Chinese students (2007). http://lub-swww.leeds.ac.uk/researchProgs/fileadmin/user_upload/ documents/Barnes.pdf
8. Bolorsaikhan, O., Tseveenmyadag, M., Tserendagva, D., Purevdorj, T.: Quality gaps in educational services in state health colleges: viewpoints of students. Med. Educ. **46**(Suppl. 2), 10–11 (2012)
9. Parasurman, A., Zeithmal, V.A., Berry, L.L.: SERVQUAL: A multiple-Item scale for measuring consumer perceptions of services quality. J. Retailing **64**, 12–20 (1988)
10. Berry, L.L.: Relationship marketing of services-growing interest, emerging perspectives. J. Acad. Mark. Sci. **26**, 767–786 (1995). Results of the service quality survey of the nursing schools. https://www.researchgate.net/publication/287078369_Results_of_the_service_quality_survey_of_the_nursing_schools. Accessed 04 May 2021
11. Bolorsaikhan, O., Orkhon, G.: Higher Education in the Gulf: Quality Drivers, Chapter 10. How internationalization facilitates the development of national quality assurance of higher education in Mongolia and Oman (2021)
12. Tudevdagva, U., Hardt, W.: A measure theoretical evaluation model for e-learning programs. In: Proceedings of the IADIS on e-Society 2012, 10–13 March 2012, Berlin, Germany, pp. 44–52 (2012)
13. Tudevdagva, U.: Structure Oriented Evaluation Model for E-Learning. Wissenschaftliche Schriftenreihe Eingebettete Selbstorganisierende Systeme, Universitätsverlag Chemnitz, July 2014, p. 123. ISBN 978-3-944640-20-4. ISSN 2196-3932

14. Tudevdagva, U., Bayar-Erdene, L., Hardt, W.: A self-assessment system for faculty based on the evaluation SURE model. In: Proceedings of the 5th International Conference on Industrial Convergence technology, ICICT2014, 10–11 May, 2014, Asan, Korea, pp. 266–269. IEEE Computer Society (2014). ISBN 978-99973-46-29-2
15. Tudevdagva, U.: Structure-Oriented Evaluation an Evaluation Approach for Complex Processes and Systems. Springer, Cham (2020). ISBN 978-3-030-44805-9. ISBN 978-3-030-44806-6 (eBook). https://doi.org/10.1007/978-3-030-44806-6
16. Bennett, A., Jooste, C., Strydom, L.: Managing Tourism Service: A South African Perspective. Van Schaik, Pretoria (2005)
17. Bosch, J.K., Tait, M., Venter, E.: Business Management: An Entrepreneurial Perspective. Lectern, South Africa (2006)
18. Online calculator of the SURE model (2021). http://uranchimeg.com/sure/eva.php
19. Tudevdagva, U., Hardt, W.: A new evaluation model for eLearning programs, Technical report CSR-11-03. Chemnitz (2011)

Expert and Technical Support for Investigation of Thefts Involving Malware Usage

Evgeny Kravets[1]([✉]), Alexey Alexeev[1], Sergey Nikonovich[2], Taulan Boziev[3], and Nikolai Bukharov[4]

[1] Volgograd Academy of the Russian Ministry of Internal Affairs, Volgograd, 130 Istoricheskaya Street, Volgograd 400089, Russia
[2] Military University of the Ministry of Defense of the Russian Federation, St. B. Sadovaya, 14, Moscow 123001, Russia
[3] State Institute of Economics, Finance, Law and Technologies, 5 Roschinskaya Street, Gatchina, Leningrad Region 188350, Russia
[4] Saint-Petersburg University of the Ministry of the Interior of the Russian Federation, Letchika Pilyutova Street, Saint-Petersburg 198206, Russia

Abstract. The specific features of investigative activities related to IT crimes are the requirements for special knowledge in different areas (electronics, programming, telecommunications and others) and meticulous preparation for their application. In recent years, telecommunication networks are more commonly used for attempting to steal financial property. Thus, it has become necessary to examine technical and software opportunities and their usage for countering such legal offences. This article aims to provide forensics reasoning for measures detecting the main attributes of high-technology crimes of this category. It studies questions of applying special knowledge for CDR analysis, examination of computer devices and computer forensics.

Keywords: Criminal proceedings · Special knowledge · Malware · Theft investigation · Forensics · Expert · Investigator

1 Introduction

The constant development and improvement of computer technology leads to its widespread distribution, an increase in the level of its availability for various segments of the population, and the development of communication technologies makes it possible to connect to the Internet almost anywhere. But, like most achievements of scientific and technological progress, computer technology has a downside - it is actively used by cybercriminals to commit crimes [1].

One of the most common types of criminal use of computer technology is the creation and distribution of malware. Since the first virus was written in November 1983 [2], many threats have emerged.

In recent years, there has been a steady increase in the number of crimes associated with theft of funds from the accounts of payment cards of bank customers. One of the

© Springer Nature Switzerland AG 2021
A. G. Kravets et al. (Eds.): CIT&DS 2021, CCIS 1448, pp. 463–473, 2021.
https://doi.org/10.1007/978-3-030-87034-8_33

methods of theft that is gaining popularity among cybercriminals is the use of special malicious programs created for various operating platforms, in particular the Android OS [3].

The aim of this paper is a research of experts' knowledge application for investigation of thefts involving malware usage.

2 Types of Computer Malware

There are different types of computer malware that can be used for a wide variety of purposes. When money is stolen from bank and other payment accounts, Trojan-type malware is used. These programs are spread by humans, unlike viruses and worms, which spread spontaneously. The tasks of the Trojans are to collect information and transfer (copy) it to an attacker, destroy information or maliciously modify it, disrupt the performance of a computer device, and use the resources of a computer device for illegal purposes.

To steal money from bank and other accounts of citizens, cybercriminals use various types of "Trojan" malware created for different operating systems. At the same time, according to information from Kaspersky Lab, 98% of such malicious programs were created specifically for the Android operating platform. Among them are programs of the families "Android.bankbot", "Trojan-SMS.AndroidOS.Svpeng", "Trojan-SMS.AndroidOS.FakeInst" [4].

Despite a number of operating features, the tasks of these programs are similar - to gain access and the ability to remotely control another user's mobile device. As an illustrative example, let us consider the algorithm of operation of a Trojan-type malicious program "Android.BankBot.34.origin".

After installation on a mobile device, "Android.BankBot.34.origin" places a shortcut on the main screen of the operating system with an icon of one of the popular applications. This shortcut is later removed if the malicious program is launched directly by the owner of the infected mobile device. If the user does not launch the malicious program on his own, this shortcut is saved. The malicious program is able to automatically start its work by loading with the operating system. After launching, the program asks the user for access to the functions of the administrator of the mobile device, and starts tracking user activity and waits for the latter to launch a number of popular applications (WhatsApp, Viber, Instagram, Facebook, Twitter and others).

As soon as one of the specified programs is launched, "Android.BankBot.34.origin" will display its own window over its interface, simulating a request for entering confidential information (login and password, phone number or credit card information). The data obtained in this way is transmitted to the management server.

To transmit stolen information to cybercriminals, as well as to receive commands from them, "Android.BankBot.34.origin" connects to the control server located in the anonymous "Tor" network. During the first communication session with a remote center, the malicious program registers an infected mobile device, transmitting basic information about it (IMEI identifier, model name).

Having received the necessary command from the server, "Android.BankBot .34.origin" can perform the following actions:

- start or stop interception of incoming and outgoing SMS;
- execute a USSD (Unstructured Supplementary Service Data) request;
- add a certain number to the blacklist, messages from which will be hidden from the user (by default, the list contains service numbers of a number of telephone operators, a mobile banking system of a well-known Russian bank, as well as a popular payment platform);
- clear the list of blocked numbers;
- send information about the applications installed on the device to the server;
- send an SMS message;
- send the malware identifier to the server;
- display a dialog box or message on the screen in accordance with the parameters received from the command and control server (for example, a command can contain a text to be displayed on the screen, the number of fields for data entry, etc.).

Thus, the malicious Trojan Android.BankBot.34.origin (Fig. 1), "registered" on the user's mobile device, allows attackers to read complete information about this device and the software installed on it, and most importantly, to intercept and block the access of a legitimate user. and send SMS messages on his behalf without his knowledge. The given program capabilities for unauthorized blocking, copying and modification of information clearly characterize its harmfulness.

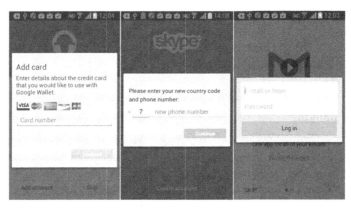

Fig. 1. Android.BankBot.34.origin displays its own window on top of its interface, simulating a request for entering confidential information [5]

The further mechanism of theft is manifested in the interaction of such a malicious computer program with the remote banking program installed on the victim's computer device.

3   Examination of Call Detail Records of the Victim

One of the ways to apply special knowledge for investigating money thefts from a bank client's card committed using malware is to study technical documents on phone communications of the victim during the period of theft (call detail records, billing) [6].

3.1 Call Detail Records

The victim's Call Detail Records (CDR) (Fig. 2) can be a valuable source of information on the method of money theft, if this crime has been committed using cellphone technologies. Thus, a proper analysis that helps to obtain valuable data requires expert's knowledge on functioning of cellphone networks, mobile devices and applications.

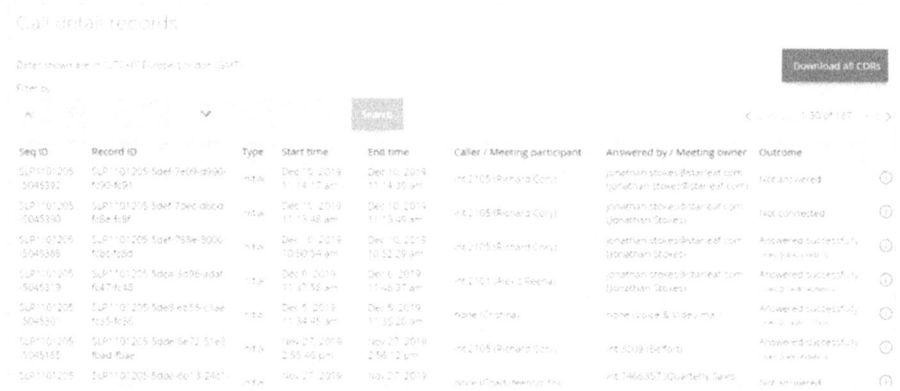

Fig. 2. An example of call detail records [7]

In this case, special knowledge can be applied for both procedural (participation of the specialist in document examination, interview of the specialist) and non-procedural activities, e.g., the investigator's consultations with the specialist during investigative preparations [8].

3.2 Mobile Banking

A mobile bank is software functioning on cell network terminals (mobile phones, tablets) that enables bank account management via text messages and USSD (Unstructured Supplementary Service Data) commands sent to a number belonging to the bank: getting information on bank card status, making various payments, transferring money from one client's card to others. The providing organization is responsible for cellphone services (voice data, short message service (SMS), multimedia message service (MMS) and others). Thus, mobile bank services can be used if the mobile device has connection with the cellphone operator. Internet access is not required for applications of this type.

Bank card operations involving mobile banks apps are performed the following way: a person (who is both a bank client and a cellphone operator subscriber) sends a USSD command or a certain text message to a special number (that shows all money transactions related to the client's bank card), transferred to the provider's server. Then, the provider sends the text message or the USSD commands to the bank's processing center that in most cases in Russia is located in Moscow. The center processes the command (message) and performs a required operation with the card account.

Thus, a money theft from the victim's bank card can be performed through unsanctioned transactions caused by malware that can access all incoming text messages on the victim's cellphone, send text messages and USSD commands as well as through exploiting services of mobile bank applications.

3.3 Banking Remote Services

Most banks also have a computer system providing remote services that can be accessed by inputting a username and a password. These credentials can be obtained from a bank office operator by submitting a special request or from bank terminals and ATMs (Automated teller machine) by showing a bank card – in the case, the ATM (terminal) will print out a check showing the username and the password. Having access to the Internet and connecting to the remote service system, bank clients can manage all their accounts (persona, transactional, deposit), pay housing and phone bills or transfer money.

Unlike mobile bank apps, this service requires Internet access. Besides, clients who use remote banking services can also get information on all their accounts and transactions. In other words, this application offers more functions compared to a mobile bank.

Thus, for stealing money via remote bank service systems, the perpetrators require access to the credentials – the username and the password. This information can also be obtained using malware.

3.4 Trojan Malware for Stealing Money from Bank

It should be noted that "harmfulness" criteria of computer programs are stipulated by the disposition of Article 273, Russian Criminal Code: "Creation, dissemination or use of computer programs or other computer information deliberately intended for unsanctioned destruction, blocking, modification or copying of computer information or for neutralizing means of computer information security" [9].

Several types of malware can be distinguished, which are used for various purposes. For stealing money from bank and other accounts, Trojan malware is applied. These programs are spread by people, compared to self-replicating worms and viruses. Trojan malware collects information, sends (copies) it to the perpetrators, destroys or modifies data, causes malfunctioning of computer devices or uses their resources for illegal purposes.

Different types of Trojan malware targeting various operating systems can be used for stealing money from bank or other accounts, with the majority of such programs specially designed for Android OS.

3.5 Expert and Technical Support of Examination Procedure

During the initial stage of investigation, victims often claim they have not received any text messages with a transaction request or sent any messages confirming the payment. No data can be found on the cellphone as well - victims claim that the cellphone did everything required for money transfer via mobile banking "on its own" [10]. The main task of the specialist examining phone communication is to establish the fact of money withdrawal and distinguish what technologies were applied for this. Most malware programs, used on mobile operating systems for stealing money from payment cards, remotely intercept and send text messages from the victim's phone. However, if such messages were received or sent though the victim's phone number, information on them can be found in call data records [11].

Article 186.1 of the Criminal Procedural Code clearly defines the order of requesting CDR for criminal investigation [12]. Yet obtaining and examining these records is one of the primary investigative activities, so it seems reasonable to get these data during the procedural verification (e.g., as part of operational search activities). For CDR examination, it also seems reasonable to request assistance of a specialist from the phone operator's IT department or other organization involved in preparing and managing billing data for cellphone networks.

In this situation, an expert has the following tasks:

1. To study all phone communications of the victim during the period of illegal money withdrawal from the payment card and explain these data to the investigator;
2. To document all incoming and outgoing text messages between the victim's phone number and service number(s) of the bank, specifying their exact sequence and receiving/sending time;
3. To document information on IMEI (International Mobile Equipment Identity) of phone devices related to the victim's phone number during the period of theft, as well as directly before and after this period (nearest communications) and prepare concluding remarks on similarities or differences of IMEI numbers;
4. To obtain and analyze data on addresses of base stations that have protocoled the victim's phone communications during the period of theft, as well as directly before and after this period.

Thus, examination of phone communications and the specialist's explanations must establish the following facts:

- whether commands to make and confirm the payment were sent from the victim's number;
- whether these messages were sent from the victim's phone number or some other device;
- the place from which these text messages were sent.

If technical information contained in the phone records requires additional explanation, the investigator can initiate another method of using special knowledge – interviewing the specialist [13].

4   Examination of the Victim's Computer Device

An important method of applying special knowledge for investigating malware-related thefts involves the expert's examination of personal computer, laptop, tablet, smartphone, other devices. belonging to the victim. Initial examination of such devices can be performed during examination of evidence items. However, it seems more reasonable to do this during the pre-investigation verification, i.e., during the crime scene examination.

The analysis of investigational practice shows that this type of crime poses several organizational and technical issues that the investigator needs to address during the examination. The main reason for inefficient crime scene examination is lacking competence of people performing this procedure [14].

4.1 Stages of Examination Procedure

At the initial stage of the investigation, the primary objective is to establish the way and mechanism of theft, in particular, to document the fact of malware usage. This requires a legally and technically correct examination of the computer device used by the victim. Its results determine subsequent qualification of the criminal offence and planning of further investigative activities [15]. However, an investigator or other person performing the procedural verification often lack necessary knowledge and skills.

Second stage is documenting. Correct and complete documenting of relevant data contained in the mobile device requires assistance of a specialist aware of technical specifics of mobile terminals. Understanding the functioning algorithm of malware used for stealing money from bank clients' cards is a prerequisite for assigning the specialist to examine the mobile device.

Finally, the main information that needs to be detected on the victim's computer device and documented during the examination is the presence of a malware program (programs) and traces of its usage. The functioning principle of malware used for stealing money from bank accounts is similar for all operating platforms: the malware collects data and gains remote control over the victim's bank account that leads to money withdrawal. By installing a Trojan program on the mobile terminal, perpetrators get extensive information on the device and its software and, most importantly, get the opportunity to intercept and send text messages without the victim's knowledge.

In investigative practice, a distinguishing example of malware's "harmfulness" was the wide-scale money theft from accounts of bank clients who used mobile bank apps on their phone devices. A Trojan program, installed on a mobile phone under the guise of an updated version of a popular app, collected data on mobile bank service package, sent them to the server, analyzed the user's activity; by doing this, the perpetrators received information on the user's bank card. Then, through remote administering of the victim's phone and mobile bank opportunities, the perpetrators sent text messages requesting money transfer from the victim's payment card. Unknown to the user, the incoming text message from the bank server requiring payment confirmation was intercepted by the malware. In response to this message, the Trojan program sent a message confirming the transfer that contained (if necessary) a single-use confirmation code [16].

4.2 Examination Procedure Activities

While examining computer equipment, priority should be given to personnel of the local forensic center who specialize in computer expertise. Yet this opportunity is limited due to extensive amount of work and small number of such employees. If there is no opportunity to get the assistance of forensic center experts, it is possible to use the help of other state agencies (for instance, the Federal Service for Supervision of Communications, Information Technology and Mass Media), and non-government organizations (e.g., technical specialists of Internet providers, cellphone operators, IT companies) [17].

Thus, the specialist's objectives during the examination include detection and identification of a malware, its functioning and evidence of its usage.

The expert examining the computer device should perform the following activities:

- determine external attributes model and size of the device, IMEI data of cellphone terminals (tablets, smartphones), phone number and sim card used during the examination;
- define system parameters of the device: installed operating system, program apps, performance settings (Central Processing Unit (CPU), Random Access Memory (RAM) etc.). Special attention should be given to presence (absence) of remote bank applications and antiviruses. It is necessary to specify properties of these apps, time and date of their installation and last usage;
- directly detect a malware on the device or traces of its usage, document the fact of unsanctioned payments. To do this, the specialist examines logs of remote bank service programs and antivirus software. In the first case, it is necessary to document data on all payments made during the period of interest. In the second case, information on all detected threats and warnings needs to be protocoled. During the examination, it also seems reasonable to additionally scan the system for malware, making sure scanning parameters are properly set (without deleting threats or taking other measures against them) so that malware programs and traces of their usage do not get deleted by accident;
- to study and protocol during examination of cellphone terminals (tablets, smartphones) text message and call logs during the period of money theft (unsanctioned transfers from the victim's account). Every incoming and outgoing text message is protocoled and described in detail (time, date, recipient, full text of the message as well as time, date and recipients of incoming (outgoing) phone calls);

Photographic recording of examination results must be taken while performing all the activities listed above. While detecting malware programs using antivirus software, video recording must be provided.

It is worth noting that in practice, specialists assigned to perform the examination do not always have the necessary competence. In order to properly fulfill this tasks, examination of mobile devices can involve representatives of expert agencies and other organizations specializing in malware expertise. They have all skills and knowledge required to get the full picture of the committed crime [18].

5 Computer Forensics

Despite the importance of experts' involvement in examination of computers, the main way of applying special knowledge for investigating criminal case on money theft via computer malware is forensic expertise.

Given the specifics of the studied object, it is necessary to clearly and correctly define the purpose of the expertise and its expected results. It is important to ask the expert clear and unequivocal questions.

Questions for the expert must meet the following criteria:

– legally and technically correct formulations;
– compliance with factual capacities, competence and available equipment of the expert (expert agency);
– clear and unambiguous representation of the expertise purpose and expected results.

The following list of questions (Fig. 3) seems to be the optimal (we provide a screenshot of the target computer program for consultation with specialized experts).

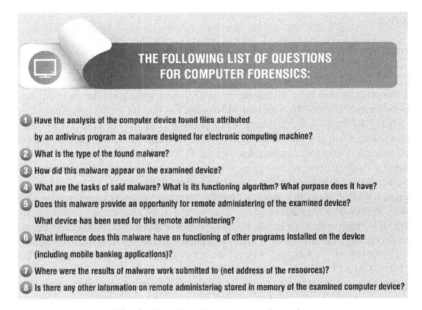

Fig. 3. Questions for computer forensics.

Other questions can be added to this list depending on the investigative situation. But if the expert answers these questions, the investigator will get an understanding of the malware spread, its administrator, theft method, recipient and specific of illegal money transfer.

On-scene detection of offence consequences and operational search activities involves mobile forensic complexes that can collect data and provide express on-site examination while maintaining device integrity (data storage units can be further used as evidence). It is important for the specialist to establish chronological sequence of relevant data formation, access and malicious use. There are ways to restore the chain of criminal events second by second and find malware that cannot be detected by antivirus programs [19].

6 Conclusion

The expert's participation in computer device examination is essential for the initial stage of investigating thefts committed using malware. An obligatory criterion for assigning the specialist is competence in mobile terminal technologies and malware functioning. In total, these conditions ensure proper qualification of the criminal offence, planning and performing investigative activities at further stages.

It should be noted that meticulous examination of the crime mechanism, identification of all accomplices involved in the theft (including not only the final link in the criminal chain - people who withdrew stolen cash - but also those who spread the malware and operated it) can be achieved only due to computer forensic reports of high quality.

References

1. Kravets, A.G., Al-Ashval, M.: Mobile corporate networks security control. In: 2016 International Siberian Conference on Control and Communications, SIBCON 2016 - Proceedings, Article № 7491811 (2016)
2. The computer virus is born, 10 November 1983. https://www.edn.com/the-computer-virus-is-born-november-10-1983/. Accessed 14 May 2021
3. Bui, N.D., Kravets, A.G., Nguyen, T.A., Nguyen, L.T.T.: Tracking events in mobile device management system. In: IISA 2015 - 6th International Conference on Information, Intelligence, Systems and Applications, Article № 7388127 (2016)
4. Protecting Android from mobile threats. https://www.kaspersky.ru/resource-center/preemptive-safety/android-device-security. Accessed 14 May 2021
5. Android.BankBot.34.origin Access mode. https://vms.drweb.com/virus/?i=4249551&lng=en. Accessed 14 May 2021
6. Saltykov, S., Rusyaeva, E., Kravets, A.G.: Typology of scientific constructions as an instrument of conceptual creativity. In: Kravets, A., Shcherbakov, M., Kultsova, M., Shabalina, O. (eds.) CIT&DS 2015. CCIS, vol. 535, pp. 41–57. Springer, Cham (2015). https://doi.org/10.1007/978-3-319-23766-4_4
7. Call Detail Record (CDR) analysis Access mode. https://support.starleaf.com/managing/monitoring-starleaf/call-detail-record-cdr-analysis/. Accessed 14 May 2021
8. Vanathi, B., Shanmugam, K., Uthairaj, V.R.: A secure m-commerce architecture for service provider to improvize quantity and quality of the products using fingerprint authentication and gender classification. Asian J. Inf. Technol. **15**(2), 232–242 (2016)
9. Russian Criminal Code. http://base.garant.ru/10108000/. Accessed 14 May 2021
10. Wass, S., Pournouri, S., Ibbotson, G.: Prediction of cyber attacks during coronavirus pandemic by classification techniques and open source intelligence. In: Jahankhani, H., Jamal, A., Lawson, S. (eds.) Cybersecurity, Privacy and Freedom Protection in the Connected World. Advanced Sciences and Technologies for Security Applications, pp. 67–100 (2021)
11. Korobkin, D.M., Fomenkov, S.A., Kravets, A.G.: Methods for extracting the descriptions of sci-tech effects and morphological features of technical systems from patents. In: 2018 9th International Conference on Information, Intelligence, Systems and Applications, IISA 2018, Article № 8633624 (2019)
12. Russian Federation Criminal Procedural Code Access mode. https://www.zakonrf.info/upk/. Accessed 14 May 2021

13. Sarmento, A.G., Yeo, K.C., Azam, S., Karim, A., Al Mamun, A., Shanmugam, B.: Applying big data analytics in DDos forensics: challenges and opportunities. In: Jahankhani, H., Jamal, A., Lawson, S. (eds.) Cybersecurity, Privacy and Freedom Protection in the Connected World. Advanced Sciences and Technologies for Security Applications, pp. 235–252 (2021)

14. Kosiński, J., Krasnodębski, G.: Cybercrime predicting in the light of police statistics. In: Jahankhani, H., Jamal, A., Lawson, S. (eds.) Cybersecurity, Privacy and Freedom Protection in the Connected World. Advanced Sciences and Technologies for Security Applications, pp. 55–65 (2021)

15. Hyland, J.M., Hyland, P.K., Corcoran, L.: Cyber aggression and cyberbullying: widening the net. In: Jahankhani, H. (ed.) Cyber Criminology. ASTSA, pp. 47–68. Springer, Cham (2018). https://doi.org/10.1007/978-3-319-97181-0_3

16. Jakobs, L.E., Sprangers, W.J.: A European view on forensic expertise and counter-expertise. Crim. Law Forum **11**, 375–392 (2000)

17. Bulgakova, E., Bulgakov, V., Trushchenkov, I., Vasilev, D., Kravets, E.: Big data in investigating and preventing crimes. In: Kravets, A.G. (ed.) Big Data-driven World: Legislation Issues and Control Technologies. SSDC, vol. 181, pp. 61–69. Springer, Cham (2019). https://doi.org/10.1007/978-3-030-01358-5_6

18. Kravets, E., Birukov, S., Pavlik, M.: Remote investigative actions as the evidentiary information management system. In: Kravets, A.G. (ed.) Big Data-driven World: Legislation Issues and Control Technologies. SSDC, vol. 181, pp. 95–103. Springer, Cham (2019). https://doi.org/10.1007/978-3-030-01358-5_9

19. Kravets, E., Gladkova, S., Shinkaruk, V., Ovchinnikov, V., Bukharov, N.: Method of acquiring the video conference using the skill in investigative actions. In: Kravets, A.G., Groumpos, P.P., Shcherbakov, M., Kultsova, M. (eds.) CIT&DS 2019. CCIS, vol. 1083, pp. 359–368. Springer, Cham (2019). https://doi.org/10.1007/978-3-030-29743-5_29

Biometrics Databases as Forensic Registers

Yuriy Bokov[1], Daniyar Kairgaliev[2(✉)], Sergei Kolotushkin[3], Polina Shmarion[4],
and Irina Titovets[4]

[1] Volgograd State University, 100 Universitetskiy av., Volgograd 400062, Russia
`bokov@volsu.ru`
[2] Volgograd Academy of the Russian Ministry of Internal Affairs, Volgograd, 130
Istoricheskaya str., Volgograd 400089, Russia
[3] Research Institute of the Federal Penitentiary Service of Russia, 15 «a» Narvskaya str.,
Building 1, Moscow 125130, Russia
[4] MIREA — Russian Technological University, Vernadskogo av., 78, Moscow 119270, Russia

Abstract. This article studies issues of preparing biometrics-based forensic registers, relevant for law enforcement theory and practice. It examines the structure of biometric parameters that must be subject to forensic registering.

Keywords: Forensics · Biometrics · Biometric data · Law enforcement · Forensically relevant data

1 Biometric Parameters in Forensic Registering Systems

An analysis of historical development of forensic registering systems demonstrates that register systems containing personal data were used even during the empiric stage of forensic science. The very first registering methods were based on individual human traits. Eventually, all means of registering – fingerprinting, verbal description and signaletic photography – rely on the empiric notion that every person has some kind of physical individuality distinguishing them from other people, even if they are similar-looking at first sight. In our opinion, there is no coincidence in this tendency, as individual characteristics help to directly identify a person and, consequently, are the most valuable data for crime clearance and investigation tasks. Earlier, many biometric parameters could not have been used due to objective reasons. On the one hand, it was unknown that certain parameters can be applied for human identification; on the other hand, some methods and means for documenting and examining biometric data were not developed. Nowadays, theoretical basics for identifying many biometric parameters have been established, as well as previously unavailable methods for data documenting and examination. Forensic scientists are actively working on improving theoretical aspects of studying personal traits and applying this knowledge to solving and investigating crimes [1].

It is uncommon that criminals leave traditional forensic traces (fingerprints, shoe prints, micro-objects, etc.) on the scene. It is also worth noting that such trace evidence can be of use only if there is a list of people suspected of the crime. Thus, it has become

A. G. Kravets et al. (Eds.): CIT&DS 2021, CCIS 1448, pp. 474–482, 2021.
https://doi.org/10.1007/978-3-030-87034-8_34

essential to design new technologies, means and methods that would provide more information on various personal traits required for identification, as part of crime clearance and investigation. One potential solution involves better representation of multiple personal traits and their interrelations in forensic registering systems. To do this, it is necessary to increase the number of documented personal traits, as well as to introduce registers of social, psychological and biological human traits. Researchers point out that identification of objects through databases is one of the most important objectives of forensic registering. Multiple biological traits are defined by their personal biological specifics that constitute biological individuality. Obtaining complex data on human biological characteristics makes it possible to solve the key task of forensics – personal identification. In order to properly arrange forensic registering of biometric data, it is essential to address several organizational and methodological issues, define common terminology, structure, system and registering forms. Even now, scientific debates continue in forensic literature over the subject of forensic registering.

1.1 Biological Substructure of Human Personality

It is considered indisputable in modern forensic science that human personality must be analyzed in the context of all physical, biological, psychological and social traits as well as intrinsic systemic relations between them. Meanwhile, it is biological trats that have the greatest influence of personality development. Many personal traits and characteristics are determined by biological aspects. Biological substructure of human personality is comprised of the following elements: anthropological traits (race, sex, age, etc.); physical attributes (body size, structure and mechanical properties); external anatomy (facial features, specifics of other external body parts, skin line morphology, etc.); functional and anatomical specifics (voice acoustics, movements of body and body parts); biochemical characteristics (contents of blood, saliva, sweat, semen, body tissues, scent-forming sweat and grease traces, etc.); pathological anomalies of said elements [2].

We have to admit that as of now, not all of these biometric characteristics are effectively used for solving and investigating crimes; besides, some of them are still not represented in forensic registering systems. Yet, forensic identification is one of the most challenging tasks of crime investigation. Law enforcement practice shows that the amount of information on any person, available to investigation (inquiry) agencies, is comprised of various objects that require different registering.

As for biometric parameters in forensic registering systems, it remains unclear what should be considered as the registering object: persons themselves, their biometric parameters and distinctive features, materially documented biometric parameters, mathematical models of biometric parameters or traces containing biometric data. Some researchers believe the registering object is the forensically relevant data as a specific sum of objects' identifying traits required for correct crime prevention, clearance and investigation, not some material or immaterial carrier of such data. However, this definition ignores the specifics of forensic registering objects and their individuality. According to another point of view, forensic registering objects should include people, dead bodies and human traces, weapons and their traces, items, etc. Others divide registers by objects, in particular distinguishing the following groups: registers of people and bodies; registers of felony crimes; registers of stolen items and vehicles; registers of crime traces and other material evidence. In this case, the main criterion for distinction is the connection between the object and the crime.

This position seems imperfect to us, as such an approach would exclude data obtained beyond criminal proceedings, e.g., during voluntary fingerprinting or, in the nearest future, genotype registering. In terms of biometric data, it is necessary to distinguish two categories of objects: carriers of registering data and sources of such data.

Thus, in registering systems containing biometric parameters, a person should be considered either the registration object or the information source object. The list of information carrier objects that initiate a separate type of forensic registering should be comprised of various biometric parameters. This list can be expanded as new opportunities for registering various human traces (evidence) arise, focusing on certain biometric parameters. Such material carriers of information can include, for example, biological materials containing DNA data, prints in a fingerprint chart, trace evidence or video recordings providing information on the person's gait and gestures [3].

Some biometric parameters examined in this article have already been registered in forensic systems but are scattered over different register types (informational, operational search, forensic), disrupted (i.e., have no systemic links) and maintained on different levels. Current informational registers providing biometric data include, for instance, fingerprint registers.

2   Structure of Biometric Registering Systems

In our opinion, biometric databases can be established and developed within forensic registering systems. Firstly, they already have various charts and trace collections containing biometric data. Secondly, forensic units of law enforcement agencies are better technologically and methodologically prepared for working with such data. Within the forensic registering system, it is possible to distinguish a relative subsystem of biometric registering, understood as biometrics-based registering of people for identification purposes. We believe that further integration of biometric data in the forensic registering system requires a complex systemic approach. Data determining biological individuality, i.e., forming the basis of identifying information, need a complex examination, taking into account their correlation with social, psychological and other personal characteristics.

The forensic registering systems is being managed by data centers of Russian Ministry of Internal Affairs, where fingerprint cards and other data on convicted criminals are collected. These forensic registers contain fingerprint and hand traces that are of operative interest, for purposes of crime clearance and investigation.

The fingerprint register is closely related to the operational register of names, as registering in both of these lists is performed simultaneously. The operational register of names provides identifying data and other information about registered persons.

Biometric data is most fully represented in registers managed by forensic units of Russian law enforcement agencies. The fingerprint register implemented in the forensic unit system includes two types of data arrays: trace collections containing evidence from unsolved crime scenes and quantitively limited fingerprint cards of people capable of committing crimes on a certain territory. The former registers are created on municipal and regional levels, while the latter are typical for lower (district and municipal) levels [4].

Recently, new registers containing biometric data have been established: DNA register of biological objects, craniological register, etc. Mandatory forensic registering is applied to hand prints of unidentified persons, collected from crime scenes; DNA data of biological objects, collected from crime scenes; DNA of unidentified bodies.

2.1 Biometric Data Hierarchy

Biometric data representing physical, physiological and other human characteristics should form the informational core of forensic registers containing personal data. Meanwhile, the biometric data hierarchy should be established basing on the following criteria: uniqueness of a biometric parameter and its ability to distinguish individuality of one person only; permanence of biometric information for a long-term period or the whole lifespan; extent of information and relation between the data carrier size and its informational capacity; ability to register (document), save, collect and structure such data depending on distinguished identifying traits; informational relevance for diagnostical and identification objectives.

In our opinion, the concept of biometrical forensic registering should be structurally implemented as a system consisting of three data blocks, including information on physical, physiological and other properties. The architecture of system components (blocks) should be designed depending on the extent of data relevance and ability to accurately address firstly identification objectives and secondly - various diagnostical tasks.

The first block is the upper level that provides information on physical and physiological parameters. Static biometric parameters, most relevant for identification, include DNA, papillary patterns on hands and feet, irises. These biometric parameters are unique, highly stable, do not change with time and are inseparable from the person. Moreover, they are present almost from the moment of birth and can be applied for identifying both living persons and dead bodies. This group can also include such biometric parameters as facial appearance and palm geometry. Their relevance for forensic registering is slightly smaller due to ability to change (transform) facial appearance using make-up or plastic surgery and low uniqueness rate of palm geometry information.

The second block is made of dynamic physiological parameters. Dynamic parameters include human specifics typical for subconscious movements detectable when a certain action is being performed (gait, gestures, facial expression, intonation, handwriting, signature, speech, typing, etc.). It is well known that physiological characteristics can be influenced by different factors, become intentionally distorted or simply change with time; however, forensic practice confirms their applicability to completing not only diagnostical but also, in some cases, identification tasks [5].

Constituents of the third block are human traits and skills that generally are demonstrated during criminal activity. Individuality and sustainability of habits and skills shown while committing a crime makes it possible to use these data in forensic registering systems. Scientists propose to study human traits and skills through their materially documented representation, as objects and material traces of a crime (Fig. 1).

As for particular biometric parameters, it should be noted that parameters like DNA, irises and fingerprints provide not only data sufficient for identification but also much information on hereditary traits, predisposition to certain diseases, substance abuse, etc. DNA is present in almost all cells of a human body and can be extracted from a

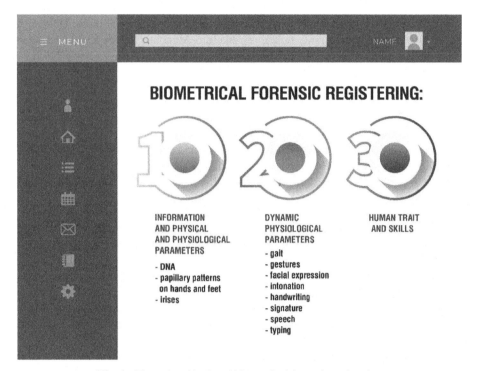

Fig. 1. Three data blocks of biometrical forensic registering

microscopic amount of biomaterial (in theory even from one cell). In terms of human data volume-carrier size ratio, DNA can be ranked the first, followed by irises and finger papillary patterns [6].

3   Approaches to Implementing Biometric Registering Systems

In order to address systematicity issues in forensic registering, it is necessary to unite available biometric data around the key element, i.e., the human. We believe that all registers containing biometric data should be integrated in one system and connected via informational links, with a code or an individual number acting as the "identifier" for various data arrays. For such an identifier, it is possible to use the DNA code - a sequence of letters and digits that resulted from decrypting hypervariable DNA parts. As for biometric information confidentiality, we support the proposal on organizing and forming biometric registers, according to which biometric and personal information (identifying data) should be stored separately. In this case, biometric data arrays will include only "nameless" material with a certain registration number. Access to this information and, consequently, to personal data must be provided only upon a special request from the initiator, thus maintaining sufficient level of data secrecy.

Forensic register databases cannot work effectively without a telecommunication system that makes information available to users (law enforcement personnel) directly at their workplaces and enables, for instance, to quickly check crime scene traces through a database, identify a person or confirm authenticity of a document.

3.1 Modus Operandi Registering

Traces and objects serve as material representations of criminal skills and are directly related to specific ways of committing crime. Modus operandi (M.O.), a criminal pattern, demonstrates regular characteristics of criminal activities and people who commit them. Total repeatability of all crime-related characteristics is impossible. Ways of committing crimes repeat themselves if certain determining factors (crime purpose and motive, objective circumstances, criminal's personal characteristics, criminal offence object, etc.) remain unchanged; however, as determining factors change both quantitively and qualitatively, M.O. inevitably changes as well, maintaining, however, certain repeating traits [7].

The sum of repeating elements of crime is represented by traces that can be found during the crime scene examination or other investigative activities, enabling to get forensically relevant information for crime clearance and investigation. According to forensic literature, low efficiency of M.O. registering is caused by the fact that registering process has not adopted latest ICT opportunities for detecting, collecting and using evidence of criminal activities. These opportunities include video surveillance at ATMs, casinos, cash registers in supermarkets, etc. More and more often, facial appearance of people involved in committing a crime gets recorded by video and security surveillance. Video materials obtained from surveillance cams can provide information on such biometric parameters as facial appearance, gait, gestures, facial expressions, articulation, etc.

3.2 Biometric Data Documenting Types

Documenting these biometric parameters of criminals in the forensic registering system should be based on the possibility of using these data for solving forensic tasks. For instance, documenting visual appearance characteristics for video data banks should follow common rules ensuring documentation of both static and dynamic human traits. All registering methods traditionally used in forensics are applicable to biometric parameters analyzed in this article. Depending on the biometric data documenting type, descriptive, graphic (photographs, audio and video recordings), collective and combined methods can be used for registering. Combined method is most commonly used, as modern computer equipment enables to create structured databases for various textual and graphic information. For example, visual appearance registering combines verbal description (information cards) with photo or video recording; registering of speech (voice) phonograms of unidentified persons uses authentic object collections; registering of DNA data and craniological information requires collections of respective authentic objects as well.

Getting back to managing forensic registers containing biometric data, we should emphasize that nowadays all forensic registers, regardless of their management specifics and information they contain, are gradually switching to automated data processing and output. Biometric technologies, in its modern understanding, can be implemented only using computer hardware and software. New data processing technologies have eventually changed registering processes. This is why nowadays automation is the most common type of register management. New biometric parameter registers, containing digital biometric data, should be based on automated informational search systems that are widely applied for law enforcement activities [8].

4 Integrated Biometric Data Banks

Integrated data banks are the next step of database improvement. They enable to process various data arrays, regardless of their specifics, while request answers provide relevant information covering all data types. Apparently, all currently disparate databases continuing biometric information need to be united as integrated databases.

Informational links can be established between the following registers: informational registers of fingerprints and names; operational search registers of felony criminals, register of criminals by their appearance (photo- and video registers), register of crimes by their M.O.; fingerprint registers managed by forensic units; as well as forensic registers of hand traces, biological objects' DNA, speech (voice) phonograms, subjective portraits and craniological registering.

Informational compatibility of databases containing biometric parameters can be maintained through software-level standardization by using a standard shell and a set of programs providing access to other arrays that use common data format.

Presenting and manipulating knowledge in any specific area requires obtaining necessary information in full volume, considering all interrelations. Extraction of knowledge is understood as interaction between a knowledge engineer and an information source (experts, special literature, etc.) that does not require computer equipment. To perform this procedure, a knowledge engineer who knows methods of cognitive psychology, system analysis, mathematical logic and others needs to recreate a system domain model, used by specialists. The most rational and promising way of integrating forensically relevant information, currently applied in various registers, involves developing a common system of forensic registering.

Introducing biometric parameters to the forensic registering system is a part of a more complex task currently addressed by law enforcement reforms. They include gradual implementation of the informational analytical system that consists of several subprograms: "Reconstructing and reequipping information centers", "Developing the federal-level system of interregional automated data banks for fingerprint information and regional-level network of hardware and software complexes", "Establishing the automated information search system of biometric identification by image" [9].

Uniting different registering types in the common integrated systems does not mean simple adding up of pieces of data they provide – this process enables a shift to a qualitatively new level of forensically relevant information. It requires considering a person as a holistic system, in which all traits and characteristics are interrelated and mutually dependent, and establishing correlation ties between different registers and different data types. In the nearest future, it will become possible that if trace evidence is collected from a crime scene, analyzed and input in the common system of forensic registers, missing data pieces will be restored thanks to mutual transition between trace systems. This approach grants a real opportunity to eventually solve the hardest task of forensics – identifying an unknown criminal using limited amount of trace evidence

[10]. A developed system of biometric registers can enable to prepare an adequate informational model of suspected criminal's identity. Creating integrated databases that provide systematized and structured biometric information is a challenging task, as it requires getting a detailed description of an object, defining a system of its stable traits sufficient for identification, formalizing and encoding data. This can be achieved only by joint work of programmers, knowledge engineers, specialists in general forensics and forensics of certain biometric parameters [11].

The developers expect that implementation of common ICT law enforcement system will facilitate informational support of crime solving and investigation and prevention activities enabling real-time delivery of accurate and detailed operative, search and forensic data, integrated in MoIA system [12]. As of now, functioning of this system has already proved its efficiency in several Russian regions. The system is still in development, yet it already has a positive impact on countering criminal offences. In areas where several system segments were put into operation, many indicators have significantly improved. In regions where the system is being implemented, crime clearance shortly after the incident grew 20% in average, investigative work became more effective, preliminary investigation period decreased [13].

5 Conclusion

The common integrated system is supposed to be available to all Russian law enforcement agencies (Federal Security Service, Prosecutor's Office, Federal Customs Service, etc.). Later, this network will be able to use data arrays of other state agencies and institutions. Russia has a complex system of agency-managed data banks containing trace evidence of criminal activities. These data banks can be forensically structured, thus establishing the common integrated network used by law enforcement, controlling and supervisory agencies for getting complex information on objects of interests [13].

A promising way of applying biometric data in law enforcement activities involves exchange of forensically relevant information by forming and managing an inter-governmental forensic data banks, as well as providing international level of data exchange and joint usage of integrated biometrics databases with international agencies, such as Europol and Interpol. Implementing the concept of law enforcement systems will undoubtedly develop informational, hardware, software and communicational groundwork for further introduction of new biometric technologies to law enforcement activities.

References

1. Kravets, E., Birukov, S., Pavlik, M.: Remote investigative actions as the evidentiary information management system. In: Kravets, A.G. (ed.) Big Data-driven World: Legislation Issues and Control Technologies. SSDC, vol. 181, pp. 95–103. Springer, Cham (2019). https://doi.org/10.1007/978-3-030-01358-5_9
2. Kanade, S., Petrovska-Delacrétaz, D., Dorizzi, B.: Obtaining cryptographic keys using multi-biometrics. In: Campisi, P. (ed.) Security and Privacy in Biometrics, pp. 123–148. Springer, London (2013). https://doi.org/10.1007/978-1-4471-5230-9_6

3. Kravets, A.G., Bui, N.D., Al-Ashval, M.: Mobile security solution for enterprise network. In: Kravets, A., Shcherbakov, M., Kultsova, M., Iijima, T. (eds.) Knowledge-Based Software Engineering, pp. 371–382. Springer, Cham (2014). https://doi.org/10.1007/978-3-319-11854-3_31

4. Jain, A.K., Nandakumar, K., Nagar, A.: Fingerprint template protection: from theory to practice. In: Campisi, P. (ed.) Security and Privacy in Biometrics, pp. 187–214. Springer, London (2013). https://doi.org/10.1007/978-1-4471-5230-9_8

5. Vielhauer, C., Dittmann, J., Katzenbeisser, S.: Design aspects of secure biometric systems and biometrics in the encrypted domain. In: Campisi, P. (ed.) Security and Privacy in Biometrics, pp. 25–43. Springer, London (2013). https://doi.org/10.1007/978-1-4471-5230-9_2

6. Scheirer, W.J., Bishop, W., Boult, T.E.: Beyond PKI: the biocryptographic key infrastructure. In: Campisi, P. (ed.) Security and Privacy in Biometrics, pp. 45–68. Springer, London (2013). https://doi.org/10.1007/978-1-4471-5230-9_3

7. Quyên, L.X., Kravets, A.G.: Development of a protocol to ensure the safety of user data in social networks, based on the backes method. In: Kravets, A., Shcherbakov, M., Kultsova, M., Iijima, T. (eds.) Knowledge-Based Software Engineering, pp. 393–399. Springer, Cham (2014). https://doi.org/10.1007/978-3-319-11854-3_33

8. Zhang, D., Yong, X., Zuo, W.: Sparse representation-based classification for biometric recognition. In: Zhang, D., Yong, Xu., Zuo, W. (eds.) Discriminative Learning in Biometrics, pp. 61–77. Springer, Singapore (2016). https://doi.org/10.1007/978-981-10-2056-8_3

9. Vasilev, D., Kravets, E., Naumov, Y., Bulgakova, E., Bulgakov, V.: Analysis of the data used at oppugnancy of crimes in the oil and gas industry. In: Kravets, A.G. (ed.) Big Data-driven World: Legislation Issues and Control Technologies. SSDC, vol. 181, pp. 249–258. Springer, Cham (2019). https://doi.org/10.1007/978-3-030-01358-5_22

10. Yemelyanova, E., Khozikova, E., Kononov, A., Opaleva, A.: Counteracting the spread of socially dangerous information on the internet: a comparative legal study. In: Kravets, A.G. (ed.) Big Data-driven World: Legislation Issues and Control Technologies. SSDC, vol. 181, pp. 135–143. Springer, Cham (2019). https://doi.org/10.1007/978-3-030-01358-5_13

11. Tamburrini, C.: What's wrong with forensic uses of biobanks? In: Lenk, C., Sándor, J., Gordijn, B. (eds.) Biobanks and Tissue Research: The Public, the Patient and the Regulation, pp. 127–140. Springer, Dordrecht (2011). https://doi.org/10.1007/978-94-007-1673-5_9

12. Kravets, A.G., Orudjev, N.Y., Salnikova, N.A.: Software for predictive maintenance and repair of the enterprise office equipment. In: 2019 International Multi-Conference on Industrial Engineering and Modern Technologies, FarEastCon 2019, Article № 8934186 (2019)

13. Kravets, A.G., Bui, N.D., Nguyen, L.T.T.: Resource-oriented architecture of mobile devices QoS-based management system. In: 2017 8th International Conference on Information, Intelligence, Systems and Applications, IISA 2017, 2018-January, pp. 1–5 (2018)

14. Korobkin, D.M., Fomenkov, S.A., Kravets, A.G.: Extraction of physical effects practical applications from patent database. In: 2017 8th International Conference on Information, Intelligence, Systems and Applications, IISA 2017, 2018-January, pp. 1–5 (2018)

Intelligent Technologies in Social Engineering. Educational Creativity and Game-Based Learning

Tools for Convergence, Actualization and Personalizing Educational Programs and Content

Mikhail Deev[1] ⓘ, Anton Finogeev[1] ⓘ, Leyla Gamidullaeva[1] ⓘ,
Sergey Schevchenko[2] ⓘ, and Alexey Finogeev[1](✉) ⓘ

[1] Penza State University, Krasnaya Street 40, 440026 Penza, Russia
fanton3@ya.ru
[2] National Technical University «Kharkiv Polytechnic Institute», 2,
Kyrpychova street, Kharkiv, Ukraine

Abstract. The article deals with the synthesis of tools for optimizing the process of training specialists in an intellectual educational environment. The complex of tools is being developed in a hyper-converged computing ecosystem to support open personalized learning technologies. The complex is necessary to update the training programs for specialists and content in accordance with the changing requirements of federal educational standards and the requirements of employers in labor markets. The developed tools search, collect, consolidate and intelligent analyze the requirements for specialists, which can be found in Internet sources, for example, on the websites of enterprises or recruiting agencies, as well as in the corresponding sections of social networks and messengers. At the next stage, the process of setting up and synchronizing educational programs is implemented, taking into account the consolidated information and predicted data on the required competencies in the short and medium term in the region. Setting up the educational process in the information environment takes place in a convergent learning model by updating educational programs and personalizing the trajectories of training specialists. The convergent model determines the convergence of educational programs and content for different specialties in accordance with the processes of digitalization of all spheres of human life, which is reflected in the requirements for competencies in professional and educational standards on the part of employers. The processes of actualization and personalization make it possible to increase the efficiency and quality of training specialists by reducing the risks of obtaining a low-quality and morally outdated education. The architecture of the adaptive management system of the educational environment includes components: a) Learning Management System (LMS), b) Education Content Management System (ECMS), c) Learning Activity Management System (LAMS), d) tools for searching, collecting and analyzing employers' requirements, e) cloud storage of educational content.

Keywords: Intelligent learning environment · Convergent model · Actualization · Personalization · Learning management system · Educational content management system

© Springer Nature Switzerland AG 2021
A. G. Kravets et al. (Eds.): CIT&DS 2021, CCIS 1448, pp. 485–495, 2021.
https://doi.org/10.1007/978-3-030-87034-8_35

1 Introduction

The modern open and distance education technologies define the need to digitize the process of training specialists using intelligent information technologies. The innovative process of transition to the model of open education is based on the principles of interaction between participants (administrators, students and teachers) in a single information and educational environment. To organize such an environment, a powerful platform is required with support for big data technologies and mechanisms for adaptive adjustment of training and retraining programs for specialists, taking into account new technological, digital and economic realities. These realities cover all institutional processes in regional labor markets and dictate to all participants the need to search for new models of the educational process. This situation is especially relevant for the federal education system, where, due to the specifics, there is a significant inertial lag when educational standards change. On the other hand, it is educational institutions that must quickly respond to changing trends in the state's economy. High-quality training of in-demand specialists ensures sustainable development of enterprises and preserves their competitive advantages. The features of the learning process in an open educational environment are:

- Independent work with electronic educational resources (e-learning) in the mode of ubiquitous access.
- Distance learning with support for online interaction with teachers for all types of classes, consultations, testing through instant messengers and video conferencing (Zoom, Skype, Google Meet, etc.).
- Use of mobile systems (m-learning) for training.
- Support of interaction in network communities with students, teachers and employers to adjust the educational process.
- Use of Internet resources and cloud technologies (cloud learning) to search for educational and methodological materials.
- Use of gaming and augmented reality technologies for obtaining practical skills.

The educational information environment provides support for horizontal links between all participants in the educational process and stakeholders. Horizontal ties determine the sustainability of the educational system, which is achieved through the continuous updating of educational programs and methodological resources, leading to changes in the competence requirements of professionals on the part of employers. The current situation is characterized by a trend towards convergence of the required competencies for specialists in various industries, which is associated with information and telecommunication technologies and transition to digitalization of all spheres of human life. The convergence management can be implemented within the framework of the convergent model [1] using a feedback mechanism, which is a set of tools for adaptive adjustment of the educational environment based on the regional labor markets analysis [2]. At the same time, the educational environment should be built on the basis of open and accessible learning technologies [3]. This means the use of mobile technologies to support all forms of the educational process. New technologies and tools are needed to update electronic educational resources, synthesize personalized trajectories for training specialists in the process of changing educational standards and the emergence of new requirements of employers.

2 Background

An innovative approach to education involves solving four basic problems: a) providing personalized access to the information environment with identification and tracking of the student's personality, b) managing educational data and electronic resources, c) visualizing interactive teaching materials and resources in a collective mode, d) immersing in learning environment with virtual and augmented reality tools for mastering practical skills. An example of the synthesis of a personal information environment is the Smart Classroom model [4]. Here, users' smartphones, smartwatches and wearable RFID tags are used to personalize, locate, and gauge student responses during learning. The approach allows synthesizing predictive behavioral models of students to assess their emotional response to the impact of teachers and testing systems in order to select the necessary actions to improve academic performance and learning efficiency [5]. The process of managing educational data and resources is closely related to the use of technologies for collecting and analyzing big data [6]. The big data toolkit is becoming popular in the educational field [7, 8]. It combines many technologies, tools and methods for big data processing [9].

Educational big data forms a field in which attention is paid to the analysis of the educational process [10]. For example, big data analysis is used to monitor and predict student performance [11]. Support for transparency, confidentiality, personalized access, minimization of adverse impacts, etc. is of particular importance. [12]. The educational process analysis includes the operations of measuring, collecting, analyzing and presenting data to the students, optimizing and personalizing the learning process [13]. An open information environment is becoming a virtual space where you can learn and teach anywhere and anytime [14]. Online training is implemented through videoconferencing systems (Zoom, Google Meet, Skype, etc.), as well as using instant messengers and social media tools.

Many educational institutions create their own developments for remote work, presentation of multimedia resources for the preparation and assessment of knowledge and competencies [15]. For open access to training courses, regardless of place of residence and student status, the concept of MOOC (Massive Open Online Course) is being implemented. Thanks to cloud and web technologies, the cost of content for MOOC courses is reduced, which allows providers to provide it for free [16]. Research in the field of creating an environment for training specialists is being carried out in the direction of the transition from traditional forms of the educational process to mixed forms of electronic, mobile and cloud learning. An important task here is the introduction of virtual and augmented reality technologies to gain practical skills [17]. The work [18] defines the basis for the use of augmented reality tools. The positions and interaction of the trainees and the objects under study in such an environment is realized using RFID and GPS sensors [19].

The introduction and use of artificial intelligence technologies is also an educational trend. In [20], the problems of implementation and exchange of knowledge on the organization and application of intelligent educational systems are considered. The article [21] presents an intellectual learning characteristics and the problems that need to be overcome in the development of educational environments. The article [22] discusses in detail the adaptive training systems of the new generation. The article [23] provides a definition of intellectual education and presents its conceptual basis. The authors consider the features of intelligent educational environments and present their own architecture of such an environment. In [24], the definition and criteria of the intellectual educational environment are presented in the framework of the development of technologies for ubiquitous education. It offers a platform for developing components of intelligent learning environments and supporting online education. The article [25] discusses in detail examples of the use of information and communication technologies for intelligent educational environments. A typical framework for developing a smart educational platform is proposed in [26]. An intelligent system includes intellectual and interactive content, means of personalizing the educational process [27]. Features are the ability to adapt to the level of training of the student and the implementation of the functional analysis of the learning process. Smart boards [28], smart classrooms [29], RFID and NFC nodes, touch sensors and other devices of the Internet of Things [30] can be used as smart components of the educational environment. To organize the operation of such an environment with multiple devices, a scalable telecommunications and computing infrastructure is required, which is a hyper-converged ecosystem [31]. Other problems in the development and use of educational platforms are described in article [32]. The work [33] examines technological and social constraints, which are a factor in the introduction of such mechanisms of intellectual education.

3   Materials and Methods: Convergence, Actualization and Personalization of Education

Open and distance education technologies are driving the learning environment beyond educational institutions. Training of specialists in such an environment requires a change in the educational process in order to implement a new convergent model of the educational process with the continuous updating of educational programs and content and the synthesis of individual learning trajectories for specialists.

The convergence of educational trajectories of different specialties occurs when the requirements of professional standards and employers change in the same way, which determines a new convergent educational model. The convergence process is realized as a result of the interpenetration and functioning of complex systems under certain conditions [34]. For example, the digitalization process currently determines the need for compulsory mastering of competencies related to information and telecommunication technologies by specialists in almost all areas of knowledge. The result is the convergence of educational programs, the creation of a single content, the use of similar methods and teaching technologies for specialists. The converged educational model means the consolidation of many similar educational resources and technologies in a single information environment.

Let us define the problem of assessing the convergence of educational content. Educational content is a hierarchical structure that consists of related sections, topics and concepts. Therefore, it is easy to represent it in the form of a variety of graph models. Teachers from different educational institutions actually work according to uniform educational standards and often create or use similar electronic educational resources in the educational process. Thus, in the information space of the Internet there are many similar resources that can be used to train specialists. One of the tasks of the transition to a converged model is the search, analysis and integration of many similar resources into the educational environment. It can also be thought of as a content graph model that has similar (isomorphic) subgraphs of related topics and sections. Thus, the task of assessing the degree of similarity of educational resources is reduced to the task of finding and determining isomorphic subgraphs. At the same time, by the isomorphism of educational content we mean the identity and identity of its parts studied in different disciplines for different specialties. To solve this problem, we use the algorithmic typing method, which is often used in computer-aided design problems. It consists in splitting the general content graph model into parts with minimization of identical (isomorphic) subgraphs, which will later serve as components in the process of synthesizing a new educational resource.

In such an environment, there is a constant updating of existing educational programs and content in order to meet changes in society and the economy, the emergence of new requirements for the competencies of specialists. The validity of updating is determined by changes in the competence requirements of professional and educational standards and employers. The results are the modernization of educational programs and content to reduce the risks of receiving low-quality and obsolete education. The task of updating is solved after the appearance of new standards, their changes, after changes in the requirements for competencies on the part of employers. In the course of updating, the tasks of synchronizing the models of the life cycles of educational programs and content for the development of new competencies are solved.

The main problems of updating include:

- Vagueness or impossibility of formulating the required competencies on the part of employers.
- Differentiation in the formulations of knowledge, abilities and skills as components of competencies.
- Lack of qualified specialists in regions.
- Lack of necessary competencies in the educational programs of regional educational institutions.
- The changes in the employer's requirements to the knowledge of specialists.
- The time gap between changes in employers' requirements and actualization of federal educational and professional standards.
- The need for bureaucratic coordination of the changes introduced with the relevant ministries and departments, with the requirements of standards.

Information on competencies for updating can be found in Internet sources, such as enterprises, recruitment agencies sites, on forums and chats of social networks and messengers, etc. Due to the huge number of possible information sources on the Internet for monitoring and analyzing data, it is here that big data and mining technologies are in demand [35].

Open and distance education technologies are driving the learning environment beyond educational institutions. Personalized training of specialists is a way of designing and implementing the educational process, in which the student is the subject of educational activity [36]. The model of personalization of training is based on the hypothesis that the educational process will be more effective when focusing on the individual characteristics of the student. The trainee has the ability to plan educational trajectories, select educational goals, manage time and the rate of assimilation of knowledge, select tasks and ways to solve them, choose individual or group training, etc. The process of personalization of learning is implemented in the educational environment through the synthesis of individual trajectories and the selection of educational resources, taking into account the level of qualifications and characteristics of the students. As an example of a digital platform for the implementation of personalized learning, we note the Russian development "SberClass", developed by the specialists of the joint-stock company "Sberbank" within the framework of the program "Digital platform for personalized education for schools". The platform implements personalized learning technology that allows you to create individual trajectories for students, as well as automatically track students' progress and problems using elements of artificial intelligence.

4   Results: Components of an Intelligent Educational Environment

An intelligent educational environment includes many tools for collecting, consolidating and analyzing big educational data. To organize the environment, a platform is being developed in the form of a hyper-converged computing ecosystem, within which tools are functioning for updating educational content, synchronizing the life cycles of educational programs, personalization of educational trajectories. The intelligent environment includes:

1. Computing facilities of the data processing center.
2. Tools for collecting, consolidating and loading educational resources.
3. Tools for searching, collecting and analyzing educational data and employers' requirements.
4. Tools for the synthesis and customization of individual trajectories for training specialists.
5. Tools for updating educational programs and content.
6. Applications for access and work with educational resources and technologies.
7. Instrumentation for monitoring and managing the educational process.
8. Instruments of administration and information security.

The tools are intended for collecting, processing and analyzing big data, managing learning processes, modernizing electronic educational resources, synthesizing personalized learning paths, adapting educational programs. The architecture is based on modular solutions that are connected as needed. The power of the ecosystem varies through horizontal scalability and integration of standalone modules, and functionality is provided by software agents. The main components of the ecosystem are:

– Learning Management System (LMS), which is used for management the elements of the educational space, customize the trajectories of training specialists, etc.

- Educational Content Management System (ECMS), which is used for management of electronic educational content. This system is based on CMS Alfresco.
- Learning Activity Management System (LAMS), which is used for administrative management.
- A system for searching, collecting and analysis of employers' requirements, which implements analytical technologies for working with big data and is necessary for the prompt correction of training trajectories.
- System for storing educational content in the cloud storage and providing access to electronic educational resources.

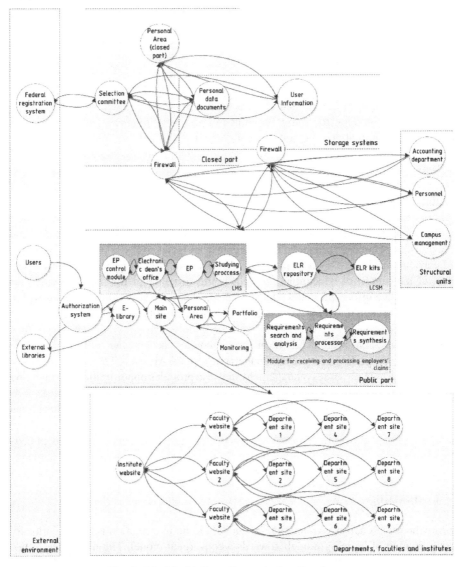

Fig. 1. Model of information and educational space.

The components automate the learning process in accordance with the convergent model of the educational environment (Fig. 1).

In an intelligent environment for managing the life cycles of educational programs and content, as well as for the synthesis and customization of individual educational trajectories, tools are used that are part of the learning management system [37]. This toolkit is also necessary to automate administrative tasks, including the functions of user registration, control of access to content, synthesis of reports, and work with educational content. Access to educational content for students and teachers is realized through the web portal. Here you can also select and enroll in training courses, work with educational and methodological materials, technologies for intermediate and final testing, knowledge assessment, maintaining electronic journals and diaries, synthesis of statements and reports for administration. Various multimedia resources are integrated into educational content, such as text of lectures and presentations, lecture audio and video courses, materials for practical and pre-laboratory classes, electronic tests, collaboration tools, links to external materials, etc. To manage the training of specialists, the LMS system Moodle (Modular Object-Oriented Dynamic Learning Environment) was chosen as a system. After analyzing the basic functionality, the functionality of the system was expanded, educational and methodological content was filled, group policies were set up and users were registered. LMS Moodle storage structure includes categories and courses.

Learning content is placed directly in courses. Categories group courses according to subject matter. The course uses a set of tools to support the educational process: questionnaires, lectures, polls, forums, tests, hyperlinks, books, SCORM packages, files, etc. To import e-courses, scripts have been developed that implement representational state transfer technology requests. Scripts represent classes in PHP. The folder structure and curriculum files are used as input. Folders are imported as nested categories. The result of the import of educational content is the structure of training categories for navigation in the information and educational space and the structure of courses within the category, broken down by years and semesters of training.

For Web publishing of educational and methodological materials, an educational content management system has been implemented based on the replicated content management system CMS (content management system) Alfresco. The system serves as a tool for electronic resources management, and also provides opportunities for finalizing and optimizing the information and educational environment. Additional software tools (web scripts and dashlets) have been developed to manage the life cycles of educational content.

The system of collection, consolidation and analysis of employers' requirements acts as a feedback mechanism for setting up the information and educational environment.

5 Conclusion

During the research, it was noted that the modern trend in education is the evolutionary transformation of learning models towards a convergent model. The main idea of this model lies in the convergence of the trajectories of training specialists in different sectors of the economy, which is associated with the processes of digitalization and informatization of all spheres of human life. The platform and ecosystem for the implementation and development of the converged model is the information and educational environment with intelligent means and technologies for synchronizing the life cycle models of educational programs and content with the changing requirements of educational and professional standards and employers' requirements. The goals of synchronization processes are the actualization of educational content and learning technologies, as well as personalization of the educational environment through the synthesis and adaptive adjustment of the trajectories of training specialists. The result of project research of the study is the development of new technologies for managing big educational data for the modernization of educational programs and content based on the collection and analysis of changing requirements for competencies on the part of employers. The processes of actualization and personalization in a converged educational model help to reduce the risks of receiving low-quality and outdated education, the risks of releasing unclaimed specialists in the labor market.

The analysis of research in this area showed that there is a problem of obtaining unnecessary competencies by specialists, since educational institutions cannot quickly change educational programs and content. Also relevant is the need to manage the processes of personalization of educational trajectories for specialists in different fields of activity, taking into account the requirements of educational standards and employers. The methods and tools of the information and educational ecosystem are considered as a platform for the implementation of this process. As an example of the implementation of methods and tools, we note the experience of the Penza State University. The development of an information and educational environment has been implemented since 2015. Educational content is hosted by LMS Moodle. The main component for managing the learning process in a higher educational institution with the possibility of online control and monitoring of the work of students and teachers in the educational environment is the electronic dean's office system.

Acknowledgments. The results of the work were obtained with the financial support of the Russian Foundation for Basic Research within the framework of the grant No. 19-013-00409-a. The research results presented in Sect. 3 were obtained at the expense of the Russian Science Foundation (project No. 20-71-10087).

References

1. Finogeev, A., Gamidullaeva, L., Bershadsky, A., Fionova, L., Deev, M., Finogeev, A.: Convergent approach to synthesis of the information learning environment for higher education. Educ. Inf. Technol. **25**(1), 11–30 (2019). https://doi.org/10.1007/s10639-019-09903-5
2. Hussin, A.: Education 4.0 made simple: ideas for teaching. Int. J. Educ. Literacy Stud. **6**(3), 92–98 (2018)
3. Elhoseny, H., Elhoseny, M., Abdelrazek, S., Riad, A.M., Hassanien, A.E.: Ubiquitous smart learning system for smart cities. In: Proceedings of the IEEE 8th International Conference on Intelligent Computing and Information Systems, ICICIS 2017, Cairo, Egypt, 5–7 December 2017, pp. 329–334 (2017). https://doi.org/10.1109/INTELCIS.2017.8260058

4. Liu, S., Chen, Y., Huang, H., Xiao, L., Hei, X.: Towards smart educational recommendations with reinforcement learning in classroom. In: Proceedings of the IEEE International Conference on Teaching, Assessment, and Learning for Engineering, TALE 2018, Wollongong, Australia, 4–7 December 2018, pp. 1079–1084, (2018). https://doi.org/10.1109/TALE.2018.8615217

5. Soltanpoor, R., Yavari, A.: CoALA: Contextualization framework for smart learning analytics. In: Proceedings of the IEEE 37th International Conference on Distributed Computing Systems Workshops, ICDCSW 2017, Atlanta, United States, 5–8 June 2017, pp. 226–231 (2017). https://doi.org/10.1109/ICDCSW.2017.58

6. Kellen, V., Recktenwald, A., Burr, S.: Applying Big Data in higher education: a case study. Data Insight Soc. BI Exec. Rep. 13(8), 3 (2013)

7. Murumba, J., Micheni, E.: Big Data analytics in higher education: a review. Int. J. Eng. Sci. 6(6), 14–21 (2017)

8. Huda, M., Maseleno, A., Atmotiyoso, P.: Big Data emerging technology: insights into innovative environment for online learning resources. Int. J. Emerg. Technol. Learn. 13(1), 23–36 (2018)

9. Eynon, R.: The rise of Big Data: what does it mean for education, technology, and media research? Learn. Media Technol. 38(3), 237–240 (2013)

10. Dumbill, E.: Defining Big Data. Forbes Site (2014). http://www.forbes.com/sites/edddumbill/2014/05/07/definingbig-data/

11. Khan, S.U., Bangash, S.A.K., Khan, K.U.: Learning analytics in the era of big data: a systematic literature review protocol. In: Proceedings of the International Symposium on Wireless Systems and Networks, ISWSN 2017, Lahore, Pakistan, 19–22 November 2018, pp. 1–7 (2017). https://doi.org/10.1109/ISWSN.2017.8250033

12. Long, P., Siemens, G.: Penetrating the fog: analytics in learning and education. Educause Rev. Online 46(5), 31–40 (2011)

13. Muthukrishnan, S.M., Yasin, N.B.M., Govindasamy, M.: Big data framework for students' academic performance prediction: a systematic literature review. In: Proceedings of the IEEE Symposium on Computer Applications and Industrial Electronics (ISCAIE 2018), Penang Island, Malaysia, 28–29 April 2018, pp. 376–382 (2018). https://doi.org/10.1109/ISCAIE.2018.8405502

14. Maseleno, A., Sabani, N., Huda, M., Ahmad, R., Jasmi, K.A., Basiron, B.: Demystifying learning analytics in personalised learning. Int. J. Eng. Technol. 7(3), 1124–1129 (2018)

15. Martin, A., Thawabieh, M.: The role of Big Data management and analytics in higher education. Bus. Manag. Econ. Res. 3(7), 85–91 (2017). Academic Research Publishing Group

16. Hussein, H.S., Elsayed, M., Mohamed, U.S., Esmaiel, H., Mohamed, E.M.: Spectral efficient spatial modulation techniques. IEEE Access 7, 1454–1469 (2019). https://doi.org/10.1109/access.2018.2885826

17. Khalid, F., Ali, A.I., Ali, R.R., Bhatti, M.S.: AREd: anatomy learning using augmented reality application. In: Proceedings of the 2019 International Conference on Engineering and Emerging Technologies (ICEET), Lahore, Pakistan, 21–22 February 2019, pp. 1–6 (2019). https://doi.org/10.1109/CEET1.2019.8711843

18. Aguilar, J., Sánchez, M., Cordero, J., Valdiviezo-Díaz, P., Barba-Guamán, L., Chamba-Eras, L.: Learning analytics tasks as services in smart classrooms. Univ. Access Inf. Soc. 17(4), 693–709 (2017). https://doi.org/10.1007/s10209-017-0525-0

19. Verma, P., Sood, S.K., Kalra, S.: Smart computing based student performance evaluation framework for engineering education. Comput. Appl. Eng. Educ. 25, 977–991 (2017). https://doi.org/10.1002/cae.21849

20. Lister, P.J.: A smarter knowledge commons for smart learning. Smart Learn. Environ. 5(1), 1–15 (2018). https://doi.org/10.1186/s40561-018-0056-z

21. Gros, B.: The design of smart educational environments. Smart Learn. Environ. **3**(1), 1–11 (2016). https://doi.org/10.1186/s40561-016-0039-x
22. Essa, A.: A possible future for next generation adaptive learning systems. Smart Learn. Environ. **3**(1), 1–24 (2016). https://doi.org/10.1186/s40561-016-0038-y
23. Zhu, Z.-T., Yu, M.-H., Riezebos, P.: A research framework of smart education. Smart Learn. Environ. **3**(1), 1–17 (2016). https://doi.org/10.1186/s40561-016-0026-2
24. Hwang, G.-J.: Definition, framework and research issues of smart learning environments - a context-aware ubiquitous learning perspective. Smart Learn. Environ. **1**(1), 1–14 (2014). https://doi.org/10.1186/s40561-014-0004-5
25. Price, J.K.: Transforming learning for the smart learning environment: lessons learned from the Intel education initiatives. Smart Learn. Environ. **2**(1), 1–16 (2015). https://doi.org/10.1186/s40561-015-0022-y
26. Al-Majeed, S., Mirtskhulava, L., Al-Zubaidy, S.: Smart education environment system. Comput. Sci. Telecommun. **4**(44), 21–26 (2014)
27. Vesin, B., Mangaroska, K., Giannakos, M.: Learning in smart environments: user-centered design and analytics of an adaptive learning system. Smart Learn. Environ. **5**(1), 1–21 (2018). https://doi.org/10.1186/s40561-018-0071-0
28. Yushendri, J., Rindani, F., Cristhian, A.A., Rustamin, Dewi Agushinta, R.: Design the Smart Board system in ubiquitous computing for teaching and learning process. In: Proceedings of the International Conference on Science in Information Technology: Big Data Spectrum for Future Information Economy, ICSITech 2015, Yogyakarta, Indonesia, 27–28 October 2015, pp. 89–94 (2015). https://doi.org/10.1109/ICSITech.2015.7407783
29. Huang, L.S., Su, J.Y., Pao, T.L.: A context aware Smart classroom architecture for smart campuses. Appl. Sci. **2019**, 9 (1837). https://doi.org/10.3390/app9091837
30. Shapsough, S., Hassan, M., Shapsough, S.E., Zualkernan, I.A.: IoT technologies to enhance precision and response time of mobile-based educational assessments. In: Proceedings of the International Conference on Computational Science and Computational Intelligence, CSCI 2016, Las Vegas, United States, 15–17 December 2016, pp. 202–205 (2016). https://doi.org/10.1109/CSCI.2016.0045
31. Kassab, M., Defranco, J.F., Voas, J.: Smarter education. IT Prof. **20**, 20–24 (2018). https://doi.org/10.1109/MITP.2018.053891333
32. Bagheri, M., Movahed, S.H.: The effect of the Internet of Things (IoT) on education business model. In: Proceedings of the 12th International Conference on Signal Image Technology and Internet-Based Systems, SITIS 2016, Naples, Italy, 28–30 November 2016, pp. 435–441 (2016). https://doi.org/10.1109/SITIS.2016.74
33. Moreira, F., Ferreira, M.J., Cardoso, A.: Higher education disruption through IoT and Big Data: a conceptual approach. In: Zaphiris, P., Ioannou, A. (eds.) LCT 2017. LNCS, vol. 10295, pp. 389–405. Springer, Cham (2017). https://doi.org/10.1007/978-3-319-58509-3_31
34. Bainbridge, M.S., Roco, M.C.: Managing Nano-Bio-Info-Cogno Innovations. Converging Technologies in Society, vol. 390. Springer, Cham (2005)
35. Daniel, B.: Big Data and analytics in higher education: opportunities and challenges. Br. J. Edu. Technol. **46**(5), 904–920 (2014). https://doi.org/10.1111/bjet.12230
36. Personalized Learning: A Working Definition - Education Week. Education Week, 22 October 2014
37. Deev, M.V., Finogeev, A.G., Gamidullaeva, L.A., Bershadsky, A.M., Kravets, A.G.: Life-cycle management of educational programs and resources in a smart learning environment. Smart Learn. Environ. **5**, 1–14 (2018)

Model for Creating an Adaptive Individual Learning Path for Training Digital Transformation Professionals and Big Data Engineers Using Virtual Computer Lab

Stanislav Grishko$^{(\boxtimes)}$ (iD), Mikhail Belov (iD), Evgeniya Cheremisina (iD), and Petr Sychev

Dubna State University, Universitetskaya st.19, 141980 Dubna, Russian Federation
`{grishko,belov,chere}@uni-dubna.ru`

Abstract. The paper formulates key aspects of a strategy for training highly qualified and in-demand IT professionals in the fields of advanced analytics and Big Data processing for solving the most urgent problems of digital transformation and data-driven business. It analyzes the problems of modern distance education (e-learning) and ways to overcome them with the use of an innovative training data center based on the principles of self-organization and cybernetics 2.0. The model presented is designed to help in the creation of individual educational trajectories and knowledge management. It is based on fuzzy logic and makes it possible to automate control of the educational process, with consideration for different mentalities and capabilities, while reducing the work of the teacher.

Keywords: IT education · Learning path · Knowledge management · Educational process improvement · Educational data center · Virtual computer laboratory · e-learning problems · Distance learning · Training of IT professionals · Data scientist · Machine learning · Fuzzy logic · Artificial intelligence · Big data analytics

1 Introduction

The main competencies of a digital transformation professional and Big Data engineer are a set of professional skills and personal qualities, such as the ability to research business processes; develop digital strategy and evolve appropriate distributed data processing solutions using load balancing, high availability or cloud computing technologies; design data models or create particular machine learning algorithms; self-organization, self-development and self-learning; working effectively in groups to solve cases and actual tasks; and develop new methods, technologies and software applications for working with Big Data and mastering Business Intelligence solutions. To teach these competencies, institutions need to make changes in educational processes. In traditional computer classes, there is no opportunity to teach complex skills based on practical learning, because the processing and analysis of data, as well as the development of corresponding multiplatform program solutions to support digital transformation, require a

© Springer Nature Switzerland AG 2021
A. G. Kravets et al. (Eds.): CIT&DS 2021, CCIS 1448, pp. 496–507, 2021.
https://doi.org/10.1007/978-3-030-87034-8_36

symbiosis of multicomponent software and hardware, which is impossible to implement on a standard computer in class.

During the traditional intramural learning process, direct interaction between the teacher and the student is required, as well as forming teams and organizing joint work.

In distance learning, it is especially important to implement an automated learning process management system that allows for controlling the quality of material assimilation and the formation of new skills, based on the personal characteristics of the student, including their basic knowledge.

This article presents a variant on the implementation of the management of the educational process, which is part of the automated software package for training IT professionals for digital transformation in the environment of the Virtual Computer Lab of Dubna State University. This allows us to launch the process of competence formation using artificial intelligence technologies, virtualization, containerization, DevOps, and cloud solutions [1–4].

2 Brief Description of the Learning Process and Solution Architecture as an Example of the Training Course "Distributed Big Data Analytics"

It is obvious that the classical e-learning system is not able to form knowledge, skills, and abilities at such a level of complexity. The process of mastery consists of professional functions, from system deployment to solving subject-oriented and algorithmic problems, that a student must perform independently or in a workgroup.

The training system in the Virtual Computer Lab is designed in such a way that each course allows students to learn one or more professional functions, including:

- Exploring, cleaning, and preprocessing data for digital transformation solutions
- Development and approval of technical specifications for the creation of methodological and technological Big Data infrastructure
- Coordination and controlling of the digital transformation project based on Big Data analytics
- Big Data management and distributed processing
- Data quality management
- Data protection and privacy management
- Development of multiplatform software solutions with AI based on direct access to Data Lakes

Each professional function is divided into granular competencies represented as a unitary task. All tasks are evaluated by the expert group with relative units of complexity, called a Complexity Task (CT), when created. A CT is an entity that is used to manage the complexity of tasks included in the course; it allows one to manage the volume of the total load on students, avoid overwork, and predict the feasibility of the planned work. The evaluation process can be either centralized or decentralized. If the assessment process is centralized, the complexity of the tasks is determined by an expert group that includes teachers, graduate students, and undergraduates. In a decentralized approach, each task is evaluated by a group accompanied by a teacher in the first lesson. The teacher manages the learning process using the Kanban workflow improvement method (see Fig. 1).

Fig. 1. Kanban board for "Distributed Big Data Analytics Course"

The first lesson is considered introductory. The teacher explains the main organizational points and students configure their access to all the necessary systems. At the beginning of the course, all tasks are placed in a column called *To Do*. Students move the task from the *To Do* column to the column called *In Progress* while completing the task. After that, students move completed tasks from the *In Progress* column to the *Review* column. The teacher evaluates the results of the work and, if there are no comments on the results, transfers the task to the *Done* column or leaves a comment with notes on the task and returns it to the *In Progress* column. This process is shown as a graph (see Fig. 2).

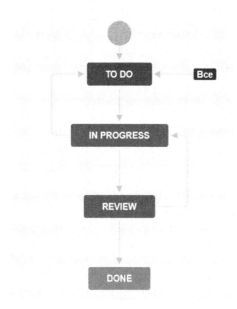

Fig. 2. General complexity task lifecycle

As part of the demonstration of the process, it is proposed to consider the course "Distributed Big Data Analytics". This course allows one to teach the professional function "Big Data management and distributed processing"; namely, exploring, cleaning and preprocessing data for digital transformation solutions. The professional function is divided into granular competencies, which in turn are divided into subtasks. Consider an example of the task of implementing an integration service:

Granular competencies:

- Infrastructure preparation

  - Hardware preparation
  - Generating data from heterogeneous sources
  - Configuring the software and environment

- Implementation of a data processing and storage system

  - Implementation of the integration service

    - Development of a prototype of the integration service in the DEV circuit – 5 CTs (see Fig. 3)
    - Development of an integration service in the DEV circuit – 8 CTs
    - Transfer of the integration service to the PROD contour – 5 CTs
    - Monitoring setup – 2 CTs

- Implementation of the data quality assessment mechanism
- Implementation of data visualization using BI tool

Fig. 3. Example of complexity task in the virtual computer lab

In this way, at the first stage of the work, a completely transparent system is implemented, the main task of which is to build and manage the learning process. The operation of this system is as follows:

1. Select the desired course
2. Divide into tasks
3. Evaluate each task in terms of CTs
4. Plan tasks for the duration of the course

Students can track the status of their assignments at any time and participate in the process of moving through the stages of the CT lifecycle. One of the important components of the Virtual Computer Lab is the system of reporting and stabilization of the training process, based on fuzzy logic methods.

2.1 The Task Completion Report System

In addition to tracking the progress of assignments, the teacher and students can plan their work together in real time so that they have time to complete all assignments by the beginning of the credit week. The task completion report system (see Fig. 4) allows one to reproduce the workflow within the training course, increase the transparency of the educational process, reduce the burden on the teacher, and develop independence in students. The ideal plan τ is calculated by the formula:

$$y = -\frac{S}{(t_1 \div t_2)}x + S,$$

where S is the sum of CTs of all tasks $(t_1 \div t_2)$, which is the number of days for which tasks must be completed. The trajectory helps one evaluate the current process and identify critical deviations from the ideal plan at any given time. Deviation from the plan can be reduced by stabilizing the process (i.e., by conducting a comparative analysis of possible solutions and forming a new training trajectory).

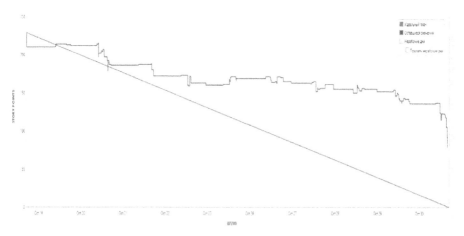

Fig. 4. An example of a task completion report

3   The Task of Stabilizing the Process

As a quadratic function of control quality on a finite time interval $(t_1 \div t_2)$, it is proposed to use the function $F(t_2)$:

$$F(t_2) = \int_{t_1}^{t_2} C_0[\Delta H(\tau)]^2 d\tau,$$

where τ is the ideal plan for closing tasks, $\Delta H(\tau)$ is the deviation from the ideal plan, and $C_0 > 0$ is a scale factor.

Given that the control action is limited in modulus, and its implementation is performed in a hardware-software environment as $R = (R_H, R_S)$, the optimal control problem is formulated as:

$$F(t_2) = \int_{t_1}^{t_2} C_0[\Delta H(\tau)]^2 d\tau => min,$$

when $U \in U_{accept}, R \in R_{accept}$, where U_{accept} и R_{accept} are acceptable sets of control actions and technical solutions, the space of R_H is hardware, and R_S is software.

4   Solving the Stabilization Problem Using Fuzzy Logic Methods

The characteristic of a fuzzy set is the membership function. This is denoted by $MF_c(x)$, which indicates the degree of membership in a fuzzy set C, which is a generalization of the concept of the characteristic function of an ordinary set. Then a fuzzy set C is a set of ordered pairs of the form $C = \left\{\frac{MF_c(x)}{x}\right\}$, $MF_c(x)[0, 100]$. A value of $MF_c(x) = 0$ means that it does not belong to the set, while 100 indicates full ownership.

To solve the stabilization problem, it is necessary to formalize the fuzzy variables *low, medium,* and *high* for the following fuzzy concepts with triangular membership functions (see Fig. 5):

– Total number of CTs of the remaining tasks
– Amount of time left until the end of the course
– Complexity of the course

Fig. 5. Formalized fuzzy concepts

For example, the imprecise definition "There are many days left until the end of the course" has the following form of a set:

$$C = \left\{ \frac{0}{0.50}; \frac{10}{0}; \frac{20}{0.60}; \frac{40}{0.70}; \frac{60}{0.80}; \frac{80}{0.90}; \frac{100}{1} \right\},$$

where if the course lasts 80 days, and 16 days have passed, then 64 days belong to the set "There are many days left until the end of the course" with a degree of 60.

Also, a rule base was compiled, which is the basis for the operation of fuzzy inference (see Fig. 6).

		Complexity_Task_Left		
		low	medium	high
Time_Left	low	not_change	reduce	reduce
	medium	increase	not_change	reduce
	high	increase	not_change	not_change

Fig. 6. Rule base for fuzzy inference

The result is a fuzzy model that allows one to manage the complexity of the training course (see Figs. 7, 8).

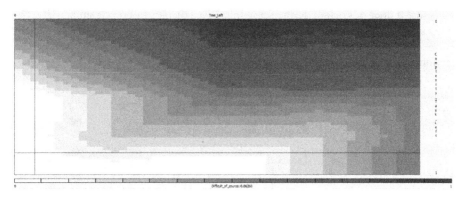

Fig. 7. Two-dimensional model for curriculum complexity management

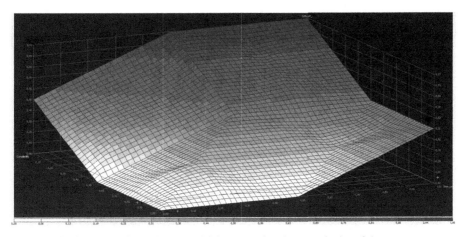

Fig. 8. Three-dimensional model for managing the complexity of the course

5   Approbation of Results

As an example of this method, we planned several tasks with a total complexity of 220 CT. The course lasted 4 months, or 80 working days. Entering all the information in the model shows that there is a lot of time and a lot of CT (see Fig. 9).

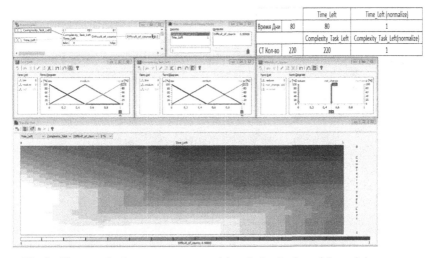

Fig. 9. The complexity management model at the beginning of the training course

After a month (20 working days), the group completed several tasks with a total complexity of 74 CT. Having entered all the information in the model, we do not need to make changes to the course complexity (see Fig. 10).

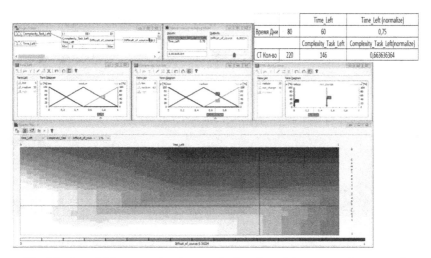

Fig. 10. A model for managing the complexity of a training course after a month

Two months later, the group completed 79 CT and 41 CT remained to be completed. The graph shows that one needs to increase the complexity of the course by adding tasks with a total complexity of 33 CT (see Fig. 11).

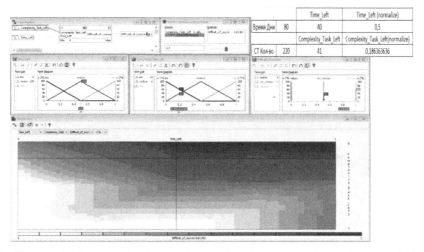

Fig. 11. A model for managing the complexity of a training course that needs to be stabilized

After adding tasks with a total complexity of 33 CTs to the course, the learning process has stabilized, and changes no longer need to be made (Fig. 12).

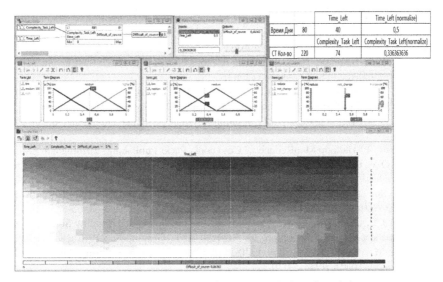

Fig. 12. A stable model for managing the complexity of a training course

6 Conclusion

The approach developed here to manage the educational process is an important part of the innovative solution for training Digital Transformation Professionals and Big Data Engineers in the cloud environment of the Virtual Computer Lab of Dubna State University. This approach allows one to train students effectively based on a professional functions' paradigm, evaluate the current process, and determine critical deviations from the ideal plan at any time and stabilize deviations from the educational process in time. It provides for unmatched flexibility, mobility, and innovation in IT education. Globally, the Institute of System Analysis and Control has improved the educational process and laid the foundation for overcoming one of the most acute problems in modern education: slow and weak responses to changes in the external environment.

References

1. Grade, A., Mehrotra, S.: Apache Spark Quick Start Guide. Packt Publishing, Birmingham (2019)
2. Belov, M.A., Cheremisina, E.N., Potemkina, S.V.: Distance learning through distributed information systems using a virtual computer lab and knowledge management system. J. Emerg. Res. Solutions ICT **1**(2), 39–46 (2016). Bitola
3. Belov, M.A., Kryukov, Y.A., Miheev, M.A., Lupanov, P.E., Tokareva, N.A., Cheremisina, E.N.: Improving the efficiency of mastering distributed information systems in a virtual computer lab based on the use of containerization and container orchestration technologies, Sovremennye informatsionnye tekhnologii i IT-obrazovanie. T.14, vol. 4, pp. 823–832, Moscow (2018)
4. Belov, M.A., Krukov, Y.A., Mikheev, M.A., Tokareva, N.A., Cheremisina, E.N.: Essential aspects of it training technology for processing, storage, and data mining using the virtual computer lab. In: CEUR Workshop Proceedings, vol. 2267, pp. 207–212 (2018)

5. Cheremisina, E.N., Belov, M.A., Tokareva, N.A., Grishko, S.I., Sorokin, A.V.: Embedding of containerization technology in the core of the Virtual Computing Lab. In: CEUR Workshop Proceedings, vol. 2023, pp. 299–302 (2018)
6. Foster, I., Kesselman, C.: The Grid2: Blueprint for a New Computing Infrastructure. Morgan Kaufmann Publishers, San Francisco (2003)
7. Singh, G.: Hadoop 2.x Administration Cookbook. Packt Publishing, Birmingham (2017)
8. Alapati, S.R.: Expert Hadoop Administration. Addison-Wesley, New York (2016)
9. Deshpande, T.: Hadoop Real-World Solutions Cookbook. Packt Publishing, Birmingham (2016)
10. Gunarathne, T.: Hadoop MapReduce v2 Cookbook. Packt Publishing, Birmingham (2015)
11. Yarullin, D.V., Faizrakhmanov, R.A., Fominykh, P.Y.: Automation of demand planning for IT specialists based on ontological modelling. In: Kravets, A.G., Bolshakov, A.A., Shcherbakov, M. (eds.) Society 5.0: Cyberspace for Advanced Human-Centered Society. SSDC, vol. 333, pp. 35–45. Springer, Cham (2021). https://doi.org/10.1007/978-3-030-63563-3_4
12. Bulgakova, E., Bulgakov, V., Trushchenkov, I.: Use of Playing and Training Software Complexes in the Lawyers Preparation. In: Kravets, A.G., Groumpos, P.P., Shcherbakov, M., Kultsova, M. (eds.) CIT&DS 2019. CCIS, vol. 1084, pp. 366–377. Springer, Cham (2019). https://doi.org/10.1007/978-3-030-29750-3_29
13. Smirnova, E., Lazarou, E., Vatolkina, N., Dascalu, M.-I.: Preparation of PhD students for engineering disciplines' teaching. In: Kravets, A.G., Groumpos, P.P., Shcherbakov, M., Kultsova, M. (eds.) CIT&DS 2019. CCIS, vol. 1084, pp. 351–365. Springer, Cham (2019). https://doi.org/10.1007/978-3-030-29750-3_28
14. Ignatyev, V., Soloviev, V., Beloglazov, D., Kureychik, V., Andrey, K., Ignatyeva, A.: The fuzzy rule base automatic optimization method of intelligent controllers for technical objects using fuzzy clustering. In: Kravets, A.G., Groumpos, P.P., Shcherbakov, M., Kultsova, M. (eds.) CIT&DS 2019. CCIS, vol. 1084, pp. 135–152. Springer, Cham (2019). https://doi.org/10.1007/978-3-030-29750-3_11
15. Moshkin, V., Yarushkina, N.: Modified knowledge inference method based on fuzzy ontology and base of cases. In: Kravets, A.G., Groumpos, P.P., Shcherbakov, M., Kultsova, M. (eds.) CIT&DS 2019. CCIS, vol. 1084, pp. 96–108. Springer, Cham (2019). https://doi.org/10.1007/978-3-030-29750-3_8
16. Nguyen, V.T., Kravets, A.G., Duong, T.Q.H.: Predicting research trend based on bibliometric analysis and paper ranking algorithm. In: Kravets, A.G., Bolshakov, A.A., Shcherbakov, M.V. (eds.) Cyber-Physical Systems. SSDC, vol. 350, pp. 109–123. Springer, Cham (2021). https://doi.org/10.1007/978-3-030-67892-0_10
17. Viet, N.T., Kravets, A.G.: Analyzing recent research trends of computer science from academic open-access digital library. In: Proceedings of the 2019 8th International Conference on System Modeling and Advancement in Research Trends, SMART, pp. 31–36 (2019)
18. Gamidullaeva, L., Finogeev, A., Vasin, S., Deev, M., Finogeev, A.: The information and analytical platform for the big data mining about innovation in the region. In: Kravets, A.G., Groumpos, P.P., Shcherbakov, M., Kultsova, M. (eds.) CIT&DS 2019. CCIS, vol. 1083, pp. 230–242. Springer, Cham (2019). https://doi.org/10.1007/978-3-030-29743-5_18
19. Krushel, E., Stepanchenko, I., Panfilov, A., Berisheva, E.: Big data in the stochastic model of the passengers flow at the megalopolis transport system stops. In: Kravets, A.G., Groumpos, P.P., Shcherbakov, M., Kultsova, M. (eds.) CIT&DS 2019. CCIS, vol. 1083, pp. 118–132. Springer, Cham (2019). https://doi.org/10.1007/978-3-030-29743-5_9

20. Surnin, O., Sigova, M., Sitnikov, P., Ivaschenko, A., Stolbova, A.: Adaptive analysis of merchant Big Data. In: Kravets, A. G., Groumpos, P. P., Shcherbakov, M., Kultsova, M. (eds.) CIT&DS 2019. CCIS, vol. 1083, pp. 105–117. Springer, Cham (2019). https://doi.org/10.1007/978-3-030-29743-5_8
21. Sokolov, A., Shcherbakov, M.V., Tyukov, A., Janovsky, T.: A new approach to reduce time consumption of data quality assessment in the field of energy consumption. In: Kravets, A.G., Groumpos, P.P., Shcherbakov, M., Kultsova, M. (eds.) CIT&DS 2019. CCIS, vol. 1083, pp. 49–62. Springer, Cham (2019). https://doi.org/10.1007/978-3-030-29743-5_4

E-learning Evaluation Based on SURE Model: Case of Mongolian University of Pharmaceutical Sciences

Uranchimeg Tudevdagva[1,2], Selenge Erdenechimeg[3(✉)], and Bazarragchaa Sodnom[3]

[1] Chemnitz University of Technology, 09111 Chemnitz, Germany
[2] Mongolian University of Science and Technology, 14191 Ulaanbaatar, Mongolia
[3] Mongolian University of Pharmaceutical Sciences, 18133 Ulaanbaatar, Mongolia
`selenge.e@monos.mn`

Abstract. The evaluation of e-learning is an important issue of online teaching. Teaching medical sciences and pharmacy courses is challenging for teachers and students to complete, and excellent internships are restricted. Faculty members of the Mongolian University of Pharmaceutical Sciences were not prepared for digital change in a short time. But due to the Covid-19, the pandemic government announced a lockdown for an extended period, and to keep the education process, and the university needs to change teaching mode. In the second semester of the 2019–2020 academic year, all subjects in 4 majors of the Mongolian University of Pharmaceutical Sciences were taught online, and training conducted asynchronously using xcloud software. Whereas, from the 2020–2021 academic year, teachers started uploading their lecture and seminar files in xcloud in advance and teaching their courses in synchronous form using programs such as Google meet and zoom. In this study, we aim to assess the advantages and disadvantages of e-learning, the learning environment, and teacher performance, as well as the factors that influence e-learning.

Keywords: Evaluation goal structure · Adapted checklist · SURE score · Online courses · Online teaching

1 Introduction

1.1 Educational Evaluation

Ralph W. Tyler is an American educator whose work was focused on educational evaluation. He worked on curriculum and instruction design and published a very famous book about the basic principles of curriculum and instruction. Tyler's assessment method is accepted not only by American educational institutions, but his work also wide distributed as an object-oriented evaluation model [1]. Assessment has become, over the years, an essential key to the improvement of the quality of education. It is one of the most reliable ways of identifying problems, whether at the system level, the school level, or the individual student [2, 3].

A. G. Kravets et al. (Eds.): CIT&DS 2021, CCIS 1448, pp. 508–519, 2021.
https://doi.org/10.1007/978-3-030-87034-8_37

As for Mongolia, the quality of education at all levels has become one of the most pressing social issues. The outcome of the quality of education is assessed and evaluated by educational institutions at all levels. Still, it does not reflect the individual's knowledge, skills, and practices [4].

Assessment is the process of gathering the information needed to decide on an educational policy, a school, a curriculum, or a student. In other words, the data collected through evaluation plays an essential role in decision-making at all levels of educational institutions [5]. Assessment is categorized into formative assessment and summative assessment, and the assessment provides the learner and teacher with information that can be used as feedback to improve learning. Formative assessments are made during the learning process, while summative assessments are made at the end of a particular learning process [6].

Formative evaluations are essential in improving the quality of higher education and take the form of student self-assessment, peer assessment, teacher and student assessment. These assessments aim to identify successes and shortcomings in the learning process and support students' learning [7].

The researchers described the formative evaluation of the training as follows. Including Wolf (1987), it is a general assessment of the competencies acquired during the training process. Coldeway (1988), evaluation is the act of assessing the quality, importance, and advantages of something. Scriven (1993. p.1), An assessment is an action taken to determine the importance and benefits of a learning activity. Scriven was the first person who had distinguished differences between "formative evaluation" and "summative evaluation." Davidson (2005), Every time we try to do something new, we must consider its value and benefits. Stufflebeam & Shinkfield (2007), Evaluating is the actions that guarantee relevance in terms of importance, benefits, advantages, productivity, cost savings, reliability, ease of use, and fairness. Stufflebeam described the differences between Scriven's two types of assessments as follows. "Formative evaluation" is a decision-making evaluation, and "Summative evaluation" is a more accountable and results-based evaluation [8].

1.2 E-learning Evaluation

One of the visible results of internet development and intelligent mobile devices is a new type of teaching and learning: e-learning. E-learning becomes possible and could distribute well only due to the development of electrical appliances and the internet. An evaluation of e-learning is developing as a new branch of educational assessment.

In the last years' e-learning has rapidly been implemented into all levels of education, from preschools to high schools. Relating to this action number of e-learning courses and online courses is jump up dramatically. This change in the education sector requires speed-up research on e-learning evaluation. Table 1 shows a small statistic about visible online content linked to e-learning. The number of online courses, compared to November of 2012, increased by around 34%.

E-learning is quite simple to understand and implement. The use of a desktop, laptop, smartphone, and the internet form a significant component of this learning methodology. Many universities have strived to increase distance learning capabilities, highlighting the potential benefits of e-learning [9]. More than 1.5 billion students and youth across the planet are or have been affected by school and university closures due to the COVID-19 pandemic. This pandemic has forced the global physical closure of businesses, sports activities, and schools by pushing all institutions to migrate to online platforms. E-learning provided rapid growth and proved to be the best in all sectors, especially in education, during this lockdown. Online learning uses the internet and some other essential technologies to develop materials for educational purposes, instructional delivery, and management of programs [10].

Table 1. Short statistic of online search result

E-course	Online course	Date
507 000 000	293 000 000	November 2012
1 360 000 000	1 190 000 000	August 2013
1 400 000 000	1 250 000 000	October 2013
1 510 000 000	1 290 000 000	November 2013
1 520 000 000	1 310 000 000	December 2013
1 670 000 000	1 520 000 000	January 2014
2 270 000 000	9 950 000 000	April 2021

Hrastinski stated that the two types of online learning, namely asynchronous and synchronous online learning, are majorly compared. For online learning to be effective and efficient, instructors, organizations, and institutions must comprehensively understand the benefits and limitations [11]. A systematic review by the World Health Organization (WHO) [12] examined global e-learning. It blended learning methods and their effect on knowledge, skills, attitudes, and satisfaction compared to other methods (traditional, alternative e-learning/blended learning, no intervention). The effectiveness of e-learning was mainly evaluated by comparing e-learning to different learning approaches, such as traditional teaching methods, or assessing students' and teachers' attitudes [13].

1.3 Structure Oriented Evaluation Model

One of the visible results of internet usage is a new type of teaching and learning: e-learning. By own characteristics, e-learning is different than traditional classroom teaching. Therefore, researchers developed various types of evaluation models and methods for e-learning. Several evaluation methods and models became an essential background for an idea for a new model for e-learning. For example, ECBCheck is one of the quality improvement schemes for E-Learning programs, and it is widely applying to a different kind of accreditation for e-learning programs [14]. ECBCheck stands for Open Certification Standard for E-Learning in Capacity Building. It was developed by Ulf-Daniel Ehlers [15].

The structure-oriented evaluation model (SURE) was developed to measure the quality of e-learning in multi-dimensional space [16–19]. The SURE model consists of eight steps. Evaluators should follow defined steps to apply the SURE model in the evaluation process. The central core of the SURE model is evaluation goals structures. At the beginning of the evaluation, process evaluators should focus on the definition of critical goals. The essential goal means a goal that must be reached during the evaluation process. The structure-oriented evaluation model aims to figure out the achievement of defined vital goals. The SURE evaluation score will be successful or more significant than 0, only if all defined key goals reached their target successfully. We applied product space and product rules to calculate the evaluation score of key goals [16]. Therefore, all defined key goals should reach an evaluation score bigger than zero. After the definition of critical goals evaluator should focus on the meaning of sub-goals. Goals that work to support the achievement of the corresponding key goal are calls as sub-goal. Based on defined goals, a structured evaluator should develop an adapted checklist for data collection. This part is like other educational evaluation models and methods. Data collection is run via an adapted list. Collected data processes applying the SURE calculation rules.

2   Evaluation of Online Courses

2.1   The SURE Model

The structure-oriented evaluation model is applied for the evaluation of online courses. To implement the SURE model, one must follow pre fined eight steps [16].
   Step 1. Definition of critical goals. Here we defined four key goals:

- Quality of lecture.
- Quality of practical lessons: Seminars/Practices/Laboratories.
- Quality of teaching.
- Quality of teacher skills for online education.

   Key goals are visualizing as a series logical structure by the SURE model (Fig. 1).

Fig. 1. Logical structure of key goals.

   Step 2. Definition of sub-goals. To reach defined key goals here need to define sub-goals. Sub goals are goals that work in a sense to match the corresponding key goal.
   The first key goal consists of 5, the second key goal consists of 6, the third key goal consists of 4, and the fifth key goal consists of 5 sub-goals (Fig. 2) (Table 2).
   Step 3. Confirmation of goal structures. Defined goal structures are checked by evaluators and confirmed.

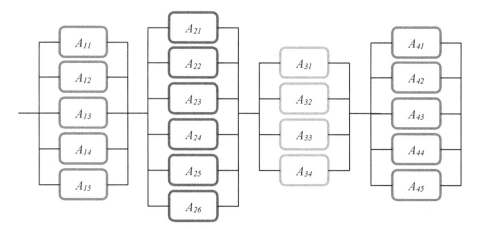

Fig. 2. Logical structure of sub goals.

Table 2. Sub goals definition

Key goals	Sub goals	Definition
B1	A11	Content of lecture
	A_{12}	Lecture lesson
	A_{13}	Time management of teacher during lecture
	A_{14}	Online synchronic lecture
	A_{15}	Offline video lecture
B_2	A21	Theoretical knowledge
	A_{22}	Practical skills
	A_{23}	Learner centered learning
	A_{24}	Professional concept
	A_{25}	Online synchronic practice
	A_{26}	Offline video practice
B_3	A31	Preparation for lesson
	A_{32}	Teaching methods
	A_{33}	Oral skills
	A_{34}	Technical skills
B_4	A41	Quality of preparation
	A_{42}	Quality of files for lessons
	A_{43}	Motivation for students
	A_{44}	Communication with students
	A_{45}	Feedback speed and style

Step 4. Creation of adapted checklist. Based on sub goals definition here formulating questions for checklist. The definition sub goals should transfer to questions. Measurement scale for data collection defined as below:

- Dis-agree at all $= 1$
- Agree up to 30% $= 2$
- Agree 31–50% $= 3$
- Agree 51–75% $= 4$
- Agree 76–100% $= 5$

All questions for data collection were created based on sub-goals definitions. For example, below are questions for the third key goal with four sub-goals:

- A11, The preparation of teacher for online teaching was perfect
- A12, The format and methodology of delivering the course content was excellent
- A13, Presentation proficiency was outstanding
- A14, Technical skills, and ability were good

Step 5. Confirmation of checklist. The adapted list should test by evaluators. Only after complete verification of all evaluators can we move to the next step.

Step 6. Data collection. The adapted checklist was transferred to an online questionnaire via Google form. Created form sent to students with an invitation to take part in the evaluation process.

Step 7. Data processing. For data processing, used online calculator of the SURE model [20]. Data processing rules of the SURE model are one of the highlights of the model. The SURE model processes data with mathematical rules developed based on goal structures defined in the first two steps. That means data will process precisely in a logical structure, which was essential for formulating questions.

$$C = \bigcap_{i=1}^{r} B_i = \bigcap_{i=1}^{r} \bigcup_{j=1}^{S_i} A_{ij} \tag{1}$$

$$(C) = \prod_{i=1}^{r} Q(B_i) = \prod_{i=1}^{r} (1 - \prod_{j=1}^{S_i} (1 - Q(A_{ij}))) \tag{2}$$

$$Q_e(C) = \sqrt[r]{\prod_{i=1}^{r} Q_e(B_i)} = \sqrt[r]{\prod_{i=1}^{r} \left(1 - \sqrt[S_i]{\prod_{j=1}^{S_i} (1 - Q(A_{ij}))}\right)} \tag{3}$$

Formula (1–3) are the main formulas defined for data processing of the SURE model [16].

2.2 Evaluation Results

In Mongolia University of Pharmaceutical Sciences studies 1062 students for professional Pharmacy, 97 students for professional Traditional medicine, 41 students for professional Pharmaceutical Engineering and Technology, and 77 students for professional Nursing.

The checklist was the same for all students. In total, we collected data from 693 students. From them, 60 students from Traditional medicine, 25 students from professional Pharmaceutical Engineering and Technology (PET), 552 students from Pharmacy, and 56 students from Nursing. Evaluation scores of the SURE data processing are shown in Table 3 as a collection of four different professionals.

Table 3. The SURE evaluation scores for four professionals

		A11	A12	A13	A14	A15	A21	A22	A23	A24	A25	A26	A31	A32	A33	A34	A51	A52	A53	A54	A55
Pharmacy	Q(A)	0.69	0.66	0.68	0.63	0.65	0.64	0.61	0.62	0.62	0.61	0.59	0.65	0.68	0.72	0.71	0.73	0.73	0.66	0.67	0.69
	B	B₁ = 0.75					B₂ = 0.68						B₃ = 0.73				B₄ = 0.75				
		Q(C) = **0.70**																			
Traditional	Q(A)	0.69	0.68	0.68	0.58	0.61	0.62	0.58	0.62	0.62	0.56	0.55	0.63	0.68	0.73	0.71	0.73	0.71	0.66	0.68	0.7
	B	B₁ = 0.73					B₂ = 0.65						B₃ = 0.74				B₄ = 0.72				
		Q(C) = **0.68**																			
PET	Q(A)	0.74	0.7	0.75	0.74	0.71	0.55	0.59	0.63	0.62	0.61	0.56	0.64	0.65	0.72	0.64	0.78	0.79	0.67	0.62	0.71
	B	B₁ = 0.8					B₂ = 0.64						B₃ = 0.71				B₄ = 0.79				
		Q(C) = **0.71**																			
Nursing	Q(A)	0.65	0.63	0.67	0.58	0.6	0.56	0.49	0.56	0.53	0.53	0.53	0.57	0.6	0.67	0.61	0.69	0.66	0.59	0.59	0.64
	B	B₁ = 0.68					B₂ = 0.6						B₃ = 0.64				B₄ = 0.68				
		Q(C) = **0.62**																			

A. *Pharmacy.*

The general evaluation score is 0.70, which is not so high expected of professors who teach selected courses. Key goals are like general score: B1 = 0.75, B2 = 0.68, B3 = 0.73 and B4 = 0.75. There is no key goal that could reach over 80%. That means professors need to do detailed analyses on each key goal and focus on weak online teaching points.

The worst score of 0.59 received is "Offline video practice (A26)". That means students cannot accept or adapt to studying from video by themselves.

We need a more detailed study to determine why this score is the worst and how it can be improved in the following courses. The best evaluation score of 0.73 received is "Preparation level (A41)" and "Files for lessons (A42)" from the fourth key goal, "Teacher skills for e-learning (B4)". Students are satisfied with teaching skills for online teaching. Students respect the efforts of teachers in the preparation of online courses. However, 0.73 is not one, and there is a lot of space for improving teacher skills for e-learning. Further reasons can be not well-developed self-study ability of students or quality of video lessons could not meet expectations of students.

One of the most exciting evaluation results is 157 students evaluated online courses with a maximum score of 1, against this 17 assessed students online courses with the worst score of 0. Here, a big variance can be observed. This result shows more analyses on other questions relating to the learning environment, quality of internet connection speed, and other issues is needed to be done, which can influence the evaluation to such an extent.

B. *Traditional medicine.*

The overall evaluation was 0.68, which is insufficient. Key goals are similar to general score: B1 = 0.73, B2 = 0.65, B3 = 0.74 and B4 = 0.72. There is no key goal that could reach over 80%. That means professors need to do a detailed analysis on each key goal and focus on weak points of online teaching. The worst score of 0.55 received is "Offline video practice (A26)". That means students cannot accept or adapt to studying from video by themselves.

Further reasons can be not well-developed self-study ability of students or quality of video lessons could not meet expectations of students. We need a more detailed study to determine why this score is the worst and how it can be improved in the following courses. The best evaluation score of 0.73 received is "Presentation skill of instructor (A33)" from the third key goal "Teacher's instruction performance (B3)" and "Preparation level (A41)" from the fourth key goal, "Teacher skills for e-learning (B4)". Students are satisfied with teaching skills for online teaching. Students respect the efforts of teachers in the preparation of online courses. However, 0.68 is a tiny percentage, and we need to learn new ways to conduct seminars and workshops online.

C. *Pharmaceutical Engineering and Technology.*

The overall evaluation was 0.71, which means that students evaluated 71% on e-learning. Key goals are: B1 = 0.8, B2 = 0.64, B3 = 0.71 and B4 = 0.79. The highest evaluation was 0.8 for lectures, 0.64 for seminars, internships, laboratory classes, 0.71 for teacher performance, and 0.79 for teaching skills. The worst evaluation score was 0.55 given for "Consolidation of theoretical knowledge (A21)" online access to seminars, internships, and laboratory classes (B2). This concludes that seminars, internships, and laboratory courses cannot consolidate the theoretical knowledge gained through online lectures. The best evaluation score was 0.79 for "Files for lessons (A42)" from the fourth key goal, "Teacher skills for e-learning (B4)". Students are satisfied with teaching skills for online teaching. Students respect the efforts of teachers in the preparation of online courses.

D. *Nursing.*

The overall evaluation score was 0.63, which meant that students rated e-learning as insufficient. Key goals are like general score: B1 = 0.68, B2 = 0.6, B3 = 0.64 and B4 = 0.68. The worst score of 0.49 was for "Skills Development (A22)" online seminars, workshops, and laboratory courses (B2). This shows that online seminars, internships, and laboratory courses are insufficient to consolidate the theoretical knowledge and skills acquired through only lectures. As a nursing profession, it is a profession where you work with patients, learns everything by hand, and gain skills, so e-learning shows that it is not effective. The best evaluation score was 0.69 for "Preparation level (A41)" from the fourth key goal, "Teacher skills for e-learning (B4)" (Fig. 3).

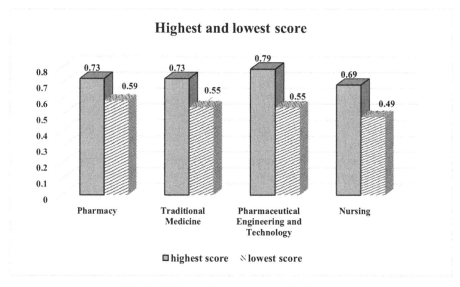

Fig. 3. Highest and lowest score of evaluation

The graph proves that the most outstanding scores for these professions are "Teacher's instruction performance (B3)" and "Teacher skills for e-learning (B4)".

The worst scores were for 'Online seminars, workshops and laboratory courses (B2)', with 'Skills Development (A22)', 'Offline video practice (A26) and Consolidation of theoretical knowledge (A21)'. Consequently, it is necessary to pay more attention to improving the preparation and efficiency of online seminars, internships, and laboratory courses in the above four professions (Fig. 4).

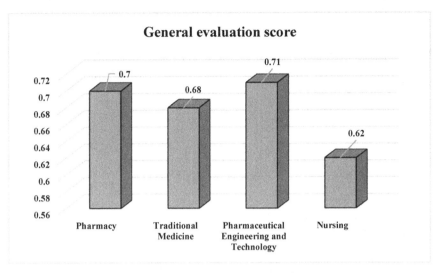

Fig. 4. Comparison of general evaluation score

Comparing to the general evaluation scores, the Pharmaceutical Engineering and Technology and Pharmacy grades were relatively high at 0.71 and 0.7, while the Nursing grade was the lowest. The evaluation of e-learning by students who major in nursing shows that the lectures, seminars, internships, laboratory courses, the performance of the teachers, and the teacher's skills are not enough. This, in turn, may be related to the feature of the nursing profession.

Conclusions

For the first time, a survey was conducted among students majoring in Pharmacy, Traditional medicine, Engineering and Technology of Pharmaceutical Sciences, and Nursing to evaluate the process of transferring to e-learning without adequate preparation due to the requirements of the situation. One thousand sixty-two students studied professional "Pharmacy," but only 552 students sent responses, and it was 51.98% of total enrolled students. Of them, 500 were female, and 52 were male students. Out of 97 students studying in a physician of traditional medicine, 60 students or 61.85% (50 female, ten male), 25 students or 60.97% (17 female, eight male) out of 41 students studying in Pharmaceutical Engineering and Technology, 56 students or 72.72% out of 77 students studying in Nursing % (54 female, two male) students took part in the evaluation process. Thus, 693 students were involved in the survey or 54.27% of the total number of students at the Mongolian University of Pharmaceutical Sciences. Some students not participating in the process were the hard accessibility to the Internet in rural areas.

This paper describes the evaluation process and the four different professions of the Mongolian University of Pharmaceutical Sciences. For evaluation of these professions, applied same evaluation model: SURE. This is the first test of e-learning evaluation for selected courses. Professors who included to evaluation process the first time did self-evaluation for their online teaching. The whole process supported and guided the SURE expert; therefore, this is a good lesson and experience for professors.

General evaluation results were from 62% to 72%, by means faculty members have enough space to improve and develop their online courses. This first self-evaluation show faculty members a way to evaluate e-learning and learned lessons that will be applied for other processions and online courses in the future. Moreover, this case motivated professors to self-evaluate their classes based on scientific evaluation models and methods.

References

1. Tyler, R.W.: Basic Principles of Curriculum and Instruction. The University of Chicago Press, Chicago (1949)
2. Kellaghan, T., Greaney, V.: Using assessment to improve the quality of education, UNESCO: International Institute for Educational Planning, UNESCO (2001)
3. Smith, E.R., Tyler, R.W.: Appraising and recording student progress (1942)
4. Alumni Tracking Survey and Employer Satisfaction Survey Handbook. Higher Education Reform Project: Ulaanbaatar (2015)
5. Ganbold, D.: Evaluation reform or evaluation of student learning, Ulaanbaatar (2017)
6. Purevdorj, C.: Teaching Management, "Munkhiin useg", Ulaanbaatar, pp 10–11 (2010)
7. Ichinkhorloo, S.: Theory and methodology of Universities, Mongol Soyombo Printing, Ulaanbaatar, p 117 (2009)
8. Ariunbolor, D., Myadagmaa, R., Tuul, P., Bulga, P., Batbayar, D.: Handbook-Methodological recommendations for updating and evaluating the training process. Ulaanbaatar, pp 1–97 (2017)
9. Qandil, A., Abdel-Halim, H.: Distance e-learning is closer than everybody thought: a pharmacy education perspective. Health Prof. Educ. **6**(3), 301–303 (2020)
10. Radha, R., Mahalakshmi, K., Sathish, K., Saravanakumar, A.R.: E-learning during lockdown of covid-19 pandemic: a global perspective. Int. J. Control Autom. **13**, 1088–1099 (2020)
11. Olasile, B., Emrah, S.A.: Covid-19 pandemic and online learning: the challenges and opportunities. Interact. Learn. Environ. (2020). https://doi.org/10.1080/10494820.2020.1813180
12. Al-Shorbaji, N., Atun, R., Car, J., Majeed, A., Wheeler, E.: eLearning for undergraduate health professional education. A systematic review informing a radical transformation of health workforce development. World Health Organization (2015)
13. Frehywot, S., Vovides, Y., Talib, Z., Mikhail, N., Ross, H., Wohltjen, H.: E-learning in medical education in resource constrained low- and middle-income countries. BMC Hum. Resour. Health **11**(4) (2013). https://doi.org/10.1186/1478-4491-11-4
14. Official web site of ECB check orgnazition. e-learning programme certification (2021). http://www.ecb-check.org/
15. Open ECBCheck Low cost, community based certification for E-learning in Capacity Building A Reader by Ulf Ehlers. http://www.ecb-check.net/files/2013/01/Open-ECBCheck_handbook.pdf. ISBN 978-3-939394-64-8
16. Tudevdagva, U., Hardt, W.: A measure theoretical evaluation model for e-learning programs. In: Proceedings of the IADIS on e-Society 2012, Berlin, Germany, 10–13 March 2012, pp.44–52 (2012)
17. Tudevdagva, U.: Structure Oriented Evaluation Model for E-Learning, Wissenschaftliche Schriftenreihe Eingebettete Selbstorganisierende Systeme, Universitätsverlag Chemnitz, July 2014, p. 123 (2014). ISBN 978-3-944640-20-4, ISSN 2196-3932

18. Tudevdagva, U., Bayar-Erdene, L., Hardt, W.: A self-assessment system for faculty based on the evaluation SURE model. In: Proceedings of the 5th International Conference on Industrial Convergence technology, ICICT 2014, 10–11 May 2014, Asan, Korea, pp. 266–269. IEEE Computer Society (2014). ISBN 978-99973-46-29-2

19. Tudevdagva, U.: Structure-oriented evaluation an evaluation approach for complex processes and systems, Gewerbestrasse 11, 6330, p.92. Springer, Cham (2020). ISBN 978-3-030-44805-9, ISBN 978-3-030-44806-6 (eBook). https://doi.org/10.1007/978-3-030-44806-6

20. Online calculator of the SURE model (2021). http://uranchimeg.com/sure/eva.php

E-Learning Evaluation Based on SURE Model: Case of Mongolian University of Science and Technology

Uranchimeg Tudevdagva[1,2(✉)] and Narantsatsral Delgerkhuu[2]

[1] Chemnitz University of Technology, 09111 Chemnitz, Germany
uranchimeg.tudevdagva@informatik.tu-chemnitz.de
[2] Mongolian University of Science and Technology, 14191 Ulaanbaatar, Mongolia

Abstract. This paper describes self-evaluation of online course of "Introduction to cultural studies" during quarantine period in public university of Mongolia. Due to the Covid-19, pandemic situation, and the teaching style had to switch from traditional classroom teaching to online teaching without any preparation. This action happened in many countries and the teaching faculties met with challenges which had to be solved. The Mongolian University of Science and Technology has its own learning management system Unimis for e-learning, but due to the massive access of all students and professors to system some weaknesses of the system were found. The Unimis was not able to handle all requests from teaching faculties therefore professors heeded to use other software for teaching, such as Zoom, Microsoft Team, Moodle and others for instance. Issues of online teaching are divided into three main parts. First is the teaching environment like learning management system, different software for preparation of digital content; second is readiness of professors and last not least is readiness of students for e-learning. The self-evaluation of "Introduction to cultural studies" online course is aimed to figure out second and third issues of e-learning during pandemic. Findings from evaluation will apply for improvement of online course for further teaching.

Keywords: Evaluation goal structure · Adapted checklist · SURE score · Online courses · Online teaching

1 Introduction

1.1 E-learning

There are models and methodologies for education developed by many researchers since 1950s [1–5]. E-learning, in the last decade, just like its precursor the Internet, has greatly transformed the way we live, work and learn. Unlike the pre-Internet period, people can now decide where, when, what and how they learn as a result of newly developed e-learning technologies and applications, which continue to improve each year. This chapter aims to identify and evaluate current, as well as future, technologies, applications and platforms being deployed by individuals, higher education institutions and

© Springer Nature Switzerland AG 2021
A. G. Kravets et al. (Eds.): CIT&DS 2021, CCIS 1448, pp. 520–532, 2021.
https://doi.org/10.1007/978-3-030-87034-8_38

organizations around the world to enhance and facilitate the learning process. We then proceed to look at the current state of the art of E-learning in the 21st century [6].

Any time you learn something from an electronic source, which is e-learning—electronic learning. In a more formal sense (and for the purposes of this book), e-learning is any course or structured learning event that uses an electronic medium to meet its objectives. It can have many of the same elements of more traditional learning (text, audio, tests, homework), but a computer is used to meet or enhance the learning objectives [7].

Technology has greatly revolutionized the way we live, work, and think. And with the advent of the internet age, it has further changed the way we learn, making what was only in the realm of scientific imagination twenty years ago possible. [8] E-learning can both be highly interactive and simultaneously isolating because of the inherent difficulties of developing cohesiveness and true connectedness among students. Nonetheless the experiences in this field are varied and ever increasing. The last decade has witnessed a significant growth in the number of international e-learning conferences, workshops and symposia involving practitioners, experts, researchers, newcomers and providers from around the world where best practices are shared as well as knowledge, expertise and abilities [9].

Many researchers have shown that online delivery can produce creativity, high order thinking, reflection in action, and skill proficiency. It can even boost these educational values through active and engaging learning experiences. Furthermore, it has been argued that ICT assist problem and task-based learning so that they get more communicative and interactive; this way the restrictions of face-to-face learning can be overcome. This produces various learning styles such as blended, interactive and innovative learning models. In addition to this, it has been argued that this form of learning gives students the opportunity to learn according to their preferred learning techniques. This way they can become more self-directed and more responsible for their learning [10].

In spite of the fact that ICT has progressed sufficiently to allow educators to exemplify many features of face-to-face learning in an online learning environment, researchers insist that it still has restrictions when it comes to being functionally capable of replacing face-to-face learning. ICT based learning environments need to be customized to suit the various learning styles and modes, particularly focusing on the communication efficiency as well as learners' participation and commitment. [11] In addition to this, it needs to improve technical limitations in order to reproduce characteristics of a discipline and achieve pertinent educational values.

The disadvantages of e-learning are that technology - mediated learning has no direct social interaction, no interpersonal relationships and the ability to isolate learners from society or at least negatively impact the social aspects of the learning process. [12] The transition to online training is less difficult, but there are downsides, technical difficulties, as well as lack of communication and cooperation, difficulty concentrating, too much screen time, lack of logistics infrastructure and unrealism. [13] Students stressed the importance of more workload, loss of laboratory classes and general social constraints during the crisis. Positive attributes include ease of attendance, time savings, home comport, learning opportunities, new skills and flexibility to learn and participate.

1.2   The SURE Model

The SURE abbreviation came out by principle to select letters from definition StrUture oRiented Evaluation model. The structure-oriented evaluation model targeted to apply for e-learning and online courses [14–18]. Comparison with existing evaluation models the SURE model describes evaluation process in logical orders and included all necessary steps for any evaluation for e-learning.

Main aim of the structure-oriented evaluation model is to give opportunity to all level of evaluators, lecturers and teachers who teach their courses online to do self-evaluation for own e-learning process. Moreover, the SURE model can be applied to more complex evaluation like service and system of e-learning with multi-dimensional metrics.

The SURE model is described in eight steps. Output of previous step becomes input for the following step. First step begins with definition of key goals of evaluation. The logical structure of key goals become basis for definition of sub goals. The definition of sub goals is the second step of the SURE model. Key and sub goals structures have to be confirmed by the evaluation team and this calls third step of the model. The confirmed logical structures become fundament for creation of questionnaire for data collection. Output of the fourth step is questionnaire for data collection and this created questionnaire should be confirmed by evaluators during fifth step of the model. Only checked and confirmed questionnaire should be used for data collection. Sixth step is the data collection part, for data collection it is better to use objective online forms. In this step different online software for data collections can be used. After data collection, the data processing should start. The data processing in frame of the SURE model runs based on the defined calculation rules which are developed based on key and sub goal structures [14]. Data processing part is the seventh step of the SURE model. Eighth step of the model is reporting part. After computation of collected data the SURE model returned four different evaluation scores:

- The SURE evaluation score, general score for evaluation;
- Evaluation scores for each key goal;
- Evaluation scores for each sub goals;
- Evaluation scores of each responses.

2   Evaluation Based on the SURE Model

The evaluation process based on the SURE model start with definition of evaluation goals.

2.1   Definition of Key Goals

As key goals of evaluation three goals are defined:

- Quality of lecture (B_1);
- Quality of seminars (B_2);
- Quality of teaching (B_3).

Figure 1 shows key goal structures as in series logical structure.

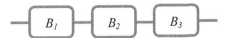

Fig. 1. Key goals of evaluation.

2.2 Definition of Sub Goals

Key goals can include sub goals:

- Quality of lecture (B₁)

  - o Content of lecture (A₁₁)
  - p Online live lecture (A₁₂)
  - q Offline recorded lecture (A₁₃)

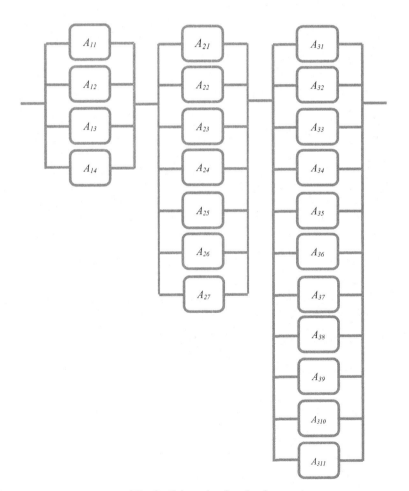

Fig. 2. Sub goals of evaluation

r   Lecture materials for self-study (A_{14})

- Quality of Seminars (B_2)

    o   Transformation of theory into practice (A_{21})
    p   Practical skills (A_{22})
    q   Student centered teaching (A_{23})
    r   Online live lesson (A_{24})
    s   Offline recorded lesson (A_{25})
    t   Seminar materials for self-study (A_{26})
    u   Team work (A_{27})

- Quality of teaching (B_3)

    o   Preparation for lesson (A_{31})
    p   Teaching skills (A_{32})
    q   Presenting skills (A_{33})
    r   Technical skills (A_{34})
    s   Quality of preparation (A_{35})
    t   Quality of files for lessons (A_{36})
    u   Motivation for students (A_{37})
    v   Communication with students (A_{38})
    w   Feedback speed and style (A_{39})
    x   Assessment (A_{310})
    y   Bonus for activation (A_{311})

Figure 2 shows sub goal structures as in parallel logical structures.

2.3   Confirmation of Goal Structures

This step is omitted here because logical structures were developed in cooperation with SURE expert and professor who teach evaluating course. By other words logical structures of evaluation goals defined in cooperation together with SURE expert and teaching professor. Therefore, special confirmation is not needed.

2.4   Creation of Questionnaire

Based on sub goals definition in this step evaluators developed questions for data collection. Table 1 shows questions for second key goal as example.

Table 1. Question for sub goals

Goal		Disagree at all	Agree up to 50%	Agree 51–70%	Agree 71–90%	Agree 91–100%
A21	During the seminar, I was able to consolidate the theoretical knowledge I gained from the lectures					
A_{22}	Seminary classes have improved my skills					
A_{23}	The seminar was student-centered					
A_{24}	It was convenient to go directly to the seminar online according to the schedule					
A_{25}	It was a good idea to watch the workshop on video and study it					
A_{26}	I was not able to attend the seminar online, but it was clear from the seminar materials in the LMS (e-learning course)					
A_{27}	It was effective for the students to speak as a team during the seminar					

2.5 Confirmation of Questionnaire

The created questionnaire was checked by SURE expert and teaching professor. As the evaluation team the SURE expert and teaching professor confirmed the created questionnaire for data collection.

2.6 Data Collection

For data collection we are applied the Google form due to the open and free software for online survey. Questions of questionnaire was designed as Google form and the link sent to students.

2.7 Data Processing

Data processing starts with cleaning of original collected data. Response with missing answer and empty lines will be deleted. Original data includes text answer; therefore, text data have to convert to numeric data: from 0 to 4. After cleaning of original data converted numeric data should be transferred to comma separated vector (CSV) format. The online converter of the SURE model is applied for transformation of original data to CSV format [19].

Соёл судлал_OriginalData - Excel

FILE HOME INSERT PAGE LAYOUT FORMULAS DATA REVIEW VIEW

B3 | эрэгтэй

	A	B	C	D	E
1	Timestamp	Таны хүйс	Курс	Лекц [Лекцийн агуулга т	Лекц [Лекц хуваарийн д
2	3/15/2021 11:15:21	эмэгтэй	5 ба 5-аас дээш курс	91-100 хувь санал нийлж	91-100 хувь санал нийлж
3	3/15/2021 11:46:41	эрэгтэй	3-р курс	71-90 хувь санал нийлж	71-90 хувь санал нийлж
4	3/15/2021 11:48:42	эрэгтэй	4-р курс	91-100 хувь санал нийлж	91-100 хувь санал нийлж
5	3/15/2021 11:51:11	эрэгтэй	4-р курс	71-90 хувь санал нийлж	71-90 хувь санал нийлж
6	3/15/2021 11:52:48	эмэгтэй	1-р курс	71-90 хувь санал нийлж	91-100 хувь санал нийлж
7	3/15/2021 11:53:03	эрэгтэй	1-р курс	91-100 хувь санал нийлж	91-100 хувь санал нийлж
8	3/15/2021 11:54:51	эмэгтэй	5 ба 5-аас дээш курс	91-100 хувь санал нийлж	91-100 хувь санал нийлж
9	3/15/2021 11:56:59	эмэгтэй	3-р курс	71-90 хувь санал нийлж	91-100 хувь санал нийлж
10	3/15/2021 11:58:53	эмэгтэй	1-р курс	91-100 хувь санал нийлж	91-100 хувь санал нийлж

Fig. 3. Original data from Google form

Figure 3 shows the original data which was collected via Google form online from students. To collect response from students we used qualitative measurement. To process data by online calculator of the SURE model needs to be transferred from qualitative measurement to quantitative measurement.

Figure 4 shows data after transformation from qualitative measurement to quantitative measurement. The quantitative data from figure show that some evaluation values

Соёл судлал_OriginalData - Excel

FILE HOME INSERT PAGE LAYOUT FORMULAS DATA REVIEW VIEW

F69 | 0

	A	B	C	D	E
1	Лекц [Лекцийн агуулга т	Лекц [Лекц хуваарийн д	Лекц [Лекцийг бичлэгээс	Лекц [Лекцийн хичээлд	Семинар [Семинарын хи
2	4	4	4	4	4
3	3	3	3	3	1
4	4	4			3
5	3	3	3	3	3
6	3	4	4	4	3
7	4	4	3	4	4
8	4	4	4	4	3
9	3	4	4	3	3
10	4	4	4	3	2
11	2	4	3	4	3
12	4	2	3	4	3
13	4	4	4	4	4
14	4	4	4	4	4
15	3	3	3	3	3

Fig. 4. Data is quantitative measurement

are missing. There are two ways to solve this issue. All not complete responses and empty rows can be deleted. Or, missed steps in data processing can be filled by calculating the average from existing responses of corresponding students. For example, Fig. 4 shows missing data on cell by C4 and D4. Those missing data are filled by average value of other responses from that student.

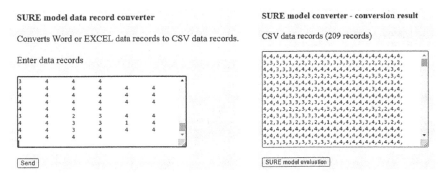

Fig. 5. Converting data to CSV format

Cleaned data should be converted to CSV format. For data converting can be applied to online converter. Figure 5 shows how the online converter is applied. When online converter is called, it will open an empty editor window. Cleaned data should be put into the empty editor window and **Send** button should be pressed. After pressing the **Send** button, the converter returns the data already in CSV format which shows in right window (Fig. 5).

Data in CSV should be sent to online SURE calculator [20] to computer evaluation scores. For that **SURE model evaluation** button can be pressed, which is below the converted data (Fig. 5). After pressing the **SURE model evaluation** button, a new window for data processing comes out (Fig. 6). On top of CSV data show texts:

Enter evaluation structure parameter:

r,

s1,s2,...,sr,

x0,x1,

Evaluation data:

These are the lines which should be replaced with real data.

- r, is number of key goals
- s1, s2,..., sr are numbers of sub goals
- x0, x1, are measurement intervals

In our case these are:

- 3,
- 4, 7,11,
- 0, 4,

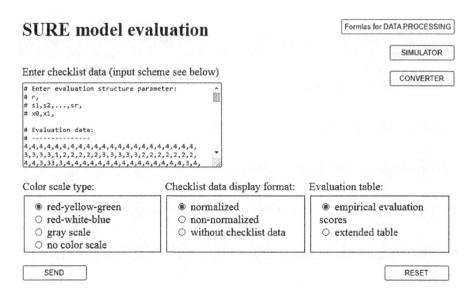

Fig. 6. Online calculator

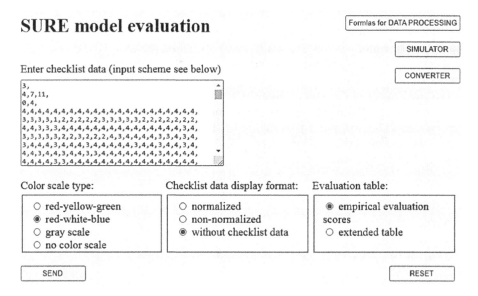

Fig. 7. Data processing is ready to start (Color figure online)

Figure 7 shows the replaced data in editor window. To start computing of the data, color of scale type, display format and view of evaluation table need to be selected. In Fig. 7 it can be seen that red-blue-white, without checklist and empirical evaluation scores are selected each for color of scale type, for display format and view of evaluation table.

	B_1				B_2							B_3										
	A_{11}	A_{12}	A_{13}	A_{14}	A_{21}	A_{22}	A_{23}	A_{24}	A_{25}	A_{26}	A_{27}	A_{31}	A_{32}	A_{33}	A_{34}	A_{35}	A_{36}	A_{37}	A_{38}	A_{39}	A_{310}	A_{311}
$Q^*(A_{ij})$	0.83	0.82	0.72	0.78	0.74	0.75	0.77	0.79	0.7	0.75	0.75	0.86	0.85	0.88	0.82	0.86	0.85	0.78	0.81	0.81	0.8	0.86
$Q_t^*(B_i)$	0.87				0.86							0.9										

$Q_t^*(C) = 0.8687$

Fig. 8. The SURE evaluation scores

Figure 8 shows the computed evaluation scores based on the SURE model using calculation rules of structure-oriented evaluation model. The online SURE calculator returns four evaluation scores: SURE score as general evaluation result, evaluation scores of each key goals, evaluation scores of each sub goals and evaluation scores of each students.

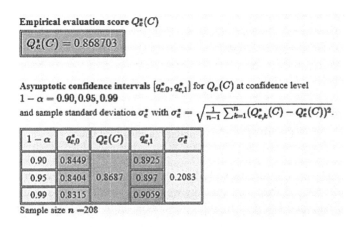

Empirical evaluation score $Q_e^*(C)$

$Q_e^*(C) = 0.868703$

Asymptotic confidence intervals $[q_{e,0}^*, q_{e,1}^*]$ for $Q_e(C)$ at confidence level $1 - \alpha = 0.90, 0.95, 0.99$
and sample standard deviation σ_e^* with $\sigma_e^* = \sqrt{\frac{1}{n-1} \sum_{k=1}^n (Q_{e,k}^*(C) - Q_e^*(C))^2}$.

$1-\alpha$	$q_{e,0}^*$	$Q_e^*(C)$	$q_{e,1}^*$	σ_e^*
0.90	0.8449		0.8925	
0.95	0.8404	0.8687	0.897	0.2083
0.99	0.8315		0.9059	

Sample size $n = 208$

Fig. 9. Confirmation of confidence intervals for empirical evaluation score

Moreover, online calculator computes confidence intervals for the general evaluation score (Fig. 9). Following this table, evaluator can examine whether the computed score is significant or not. Figure 9 shows that 208 responses were processed, due to the big number all responses not be included into the result table.

2.8 Reporting

In this step evaluator can produce different report or can start discussions on received evaluation results. The SURE score of evaluation is computed as 0.86. That means the general evaluation of 208 students for this course is 86% successful. The SURE model doing normalization with all collected original data before data processing. Therefore, all evaluation scores after data processing belongs to interval between 0 and 1. It makes easy to understand evaluation scores for all interested groups in evaluation results. That means if general evaluation is computed as 0.86 one, we can explain it success of online lessons is 86%. Third key goal "Quality of teaching" is $B_3 = 0.9$, which means very high. This shows that the students were satisfied with quality of teaching.

3 Summary of Evaluation Process

Online course "Introduction to cultural studies" was taught to bachelor students. Invitations to participate in the evaluation process was sent to all students. 212 students responded to the invitations, 4 from them were deleted after data cleaning process. In total 208 answers were computed by the online calculator of the SURE model (Fig. 10).

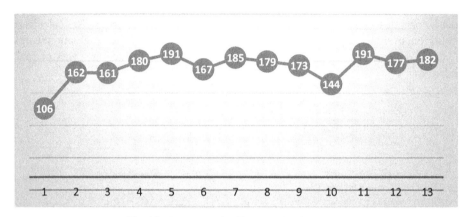

Fig. 10. Progress of online teaching by Teams

The first week of online course had a low attendance, fifth and eleventh weeks had a high attendance. 52% of freshmen students were surveyed. The students evaluated sub goals A_{13} and A_{14}, and key goal B_1 with evaluation score 0.87. This evaluation score shows that students confirm that content of online lecture was easy to understand and more preferred compared to recorded lecture. There are relatively few opportunities to study independently by watching lecture recordings. In terms of seminar classes, they were rated as student-centered.

The sub evaluation goals $A_{21}-A_{23}$ are evaluated by scores from 0.74 up to 0.77. These are comparatively low scores and we had idea that this can be linked to internet access of students. Therefore, here we included some results about internet access of students. The 90.1% of students had access to mobile phones. 65.3% had access to home internet, 59.9% to mobile data, from which 50.5% were from rural areas and 49.5% from urban areas. These numbers can be proof our idea that from mobile data access students cannot stay longer with online platform due to the cost problems. The Mongolian University of Science and Technology (MUST) has contracted with mobile phone companies to provide students with mobile phone numbers with data. However, the study questioned whether students were able to use it. According to the survey, it was almost never used and every day students bought data.

The sub goals $A_{31}-A_{39}$ and key goal B_3 evaluated by score 0.9. The students evaluated the lecturer's presentation and interpretational skills as good, the lesson as well prepared. It was concluded that the workload for students to complete an e-assignments is easy. The final result was 0.86. It was a good result for our online class.

4 Conclusion

Due to the COVID-19 pandemic, the Mongolian University of Science and Technology (MUST) is in its third semester of e-learning. We used SURE model with its online calculation program in our research and evaluated an online class. From the results of the research, it is very clear and easy for lecturers to determine how effective their lessons are and to see on what to focus in the future by using this evaluation model. I am very satisfied with the assessment of my online class "Introduction to cultural studies" using the SURE model. We will plan correspondingly on what to do and on what to pay attention to in the future. The use of lecturers' online platforms, the quality of online teaching and the use of them have improved from the previous year. There is a need to organize regular lecturer training and digital skills trainings to conduct e-learning. The reason for students not being able to attend e-learning is the lack of internet data of students without computers. Provide digital skills training to students as well.

Research shows that in addition to e-learning, other internet resources need to be used in the classroom. Because students spend a lot of time in the internet and become followers of many blogs. In addition, lecturers using LMS and Teams software, it will be more effective to use blogs and podcasts that students are interested in following. Facebook and Twitter influencers started podcasting on their own. It is increasing day by day and disappearing. Professional podcasters have emerged. Newspaper, TV and radio institute-wide content is distributed to the public. We need in the development of education.

1. University professors and researchers need to work with student. Become a MENTOR
2. There is an urgent need for youth education cooperation.
3. There is a need for a common understanding, consensus and cooperation of lecturers and Update, Upgrade for Introduction to Cultural Studies class.

References

1. Alkin, M.C.: Evaluation theory development. Evaluation Comment **2**, 2–7 (1969). Alkin, M.C.: Wider context goals and goal-based evaluators. Evaluation (1972)
2. Kirkpatrick, D.L.: Techniques for evaluation training programs. J. Am. Soc. Training Directors **13**, 21–26 (1959)
3. Scriven, M.: Conceptual revolutions in evaluation. Evaluation Roots, pp. 167–179 (2012)
4. Tyler, R.W.: Basic Principles of Curriculum and Instruction. The University of Chicago Press, Chicago (1949)
5. Warr, P., Bird, M., Rackham, N.: Evaluation of management training: a practical framework, with cases, for evaluating training needs and results. Gower Press (1970)
6. Hamada, M.: E-learning: new technology, applications and future trends. Nova Science Publishers, Incorporated (2013)
7. Elkins, D., Pinder, D.: E-learning fundamentals: A practical guide. American Society for Training and Development (2015)

8. Liang, K., Zhang, Y., He, Y., Zhou, Y., Tan, W., Li, X.: Online behavior analysis-based student profile for intelligent E-learning. J. Electr. Comput. Eng., 1–7 (2017). https://doi.org/10.1155/2017/9720396

9. Tabot, A., Oyibo, K., Hamada, M.: E-Learning new technology, applications and future trends, pp. 2–14. Department of Computer Science, African University of Science and Technology, Abuja, Nigeria Software Engineering Lab. The University of Aizu, Aizuwakamatsu, Fukushima, Japan (2013)

10. Tinetti, F.G., et al.: IEEE 2014: Proceedings of the 2014 International Conference on E-Learning, E-Business, Enterprise Information Systems, & E-Government. Mercury Learning and Information, pp. 52–53 (2014)

11. Hussain, M., Zhu, W., Zhang, W., Abidi, S.M.R.: Student engagement predictions in an e-learning system and their impact on student course assessment scores. Hindawi Computational Intelligence and Neuroscience Volume 2018, p. 21, Article ID 6347186 (2018). https://doi.org/10.1155/2018/6347186

12. Bell, J.: E-learning: your flexible development friend? Dev. Learn. Organ. Int. J. **21**(6), 7–9 (2007). https://doi.org/10.1108/14777280710828558

13. Ariunaa, Kh.: Evaluating the quality of distance training services in covid-19: tam model analysis, p. 4. Mongolian University of Science and Technology. School of Business administration and Humanity. Professor Seminar (2021)

14. Tudevdagva, U., Hardt, W.: A measure theoretical evaluation model for e-learning programs. In: Proceedings of the IADIS on e-Society 2012, 10–13 March 2012, Berlin, Germany, pp. 44–52 (2012)

15. Tudevdagva, U.: Structure Oriented Evaluation Model for E-Learning. Wissenschaftliche Schriftenreihe Eingebettete Selbstorganisierende Systeme, Universitätsverlag Chemnitz, July 2014, p. 123 (2014). ISBN 978-3-944640-20-4. ISSN 2196-3932

16. Tudevdagva, U., Bayar-Erdene, L., Hardt, W.: A self-assessment system for faculty based on the evaluation SURE model. In: Proceedings of The 5th International Conference on Industrial Convergence technology, ICICT 2014, 10–11 May 2014, Asan, Korea, pp. 266–269. IEEE Computer Society (2014). ISBN 978-99973-46-29-2

17. Tudevdagva, U.: Structure-Oriented Evaluation an Evaluation Approach for Complex Processes and Systems. Springer, Cham (2020). ISBN 978-3-030-44805-9. ISBN 978-3-030-44806-6 (eBook). https://doi.org/10.1007/978-3-030-44806-6

18. Tudevdagva, U., Shambaljamts, T., Mongolia, U., Senden, D.: The evaluation of distance teaching during COVID quarantine at MUST. In: Proceedings of International Symposium on Computer Science, Computer Engineering and Educational Technologies, ISCSET 2020, Laubusch, Germany, pp. 90–93 (2020). ISBN 978-3-95908-223-5

19. Online converter of the SURE model (2021). http://www.uranchimeg.com/sure/eva_convert.html?

20. Online calculator of the SURE model (2021). http://uranchimeg.com/sure/eva.php

Lee's Wave Algorithm Developed in Tower Defense (TD) Game

Alexandr Bershadskii and Vitalina Epp[⊠]

Penza State University, 40, Krasnaya Street, Penza 440026, Russian Federation
bam@pnzgu.ru

Abstract. The article describes the use of the classic Lee algorithm (finding the shortest path) in the development of a gaming application in the Tower Defense game. Finding the shortest path is a task that arises in various spheres of human activity, and is very important. The shortest path will save time or other valuable resources, so algorithms are needed to find it. One of the algorithms designed to find the shortest path is the wave algorithm. The waveform algorithm gives a global solution, which means that this solution will be the best possible one.

Due to the interactivity of computer games, they are increasingly used for learning, of course, not every game can be suitable for teaching any kind of skills and knowledge; in order for the game to become educational, it is necessary to think about how the game process could contribute to the study.

Learning the wave algorithm through a game application makes the learning process more interesting and allows you to consider a lot of different examples. In addition, the application builds traces without errors, which will allow the user to check himself when constructing a route manually.

Testing game situations showed all the boundary conditions of the algorithm. Examples of different game situations show many options for constructing the shortest path.

Keywords: Lee's algorithm · Finding the shortest path · Tower defense · Educational programs · Game application

1 Introduction

Finding the shortest path is a task that arises in various spheres of human activity and is very important. The shortest path will save time or other valuable resources, so algorithms are needed to find it. One of the algorithms for finding the shortest path is the wave algorithm. Works on the study of the wave algorithm date back to 1977 [5]. A huge contribution to the study and application of the wave algorithm in the design of printed circuit boards was made by Russian scientists Dendobrenko B.N. [1], Bershadsky A.M [3, 4] The waveform algorithm gives a global solution, which means that this solution will be the best possible.

Learning the wave algorithm through a game application makes the learning process more interesting and allows you to consider many different examples. Attempts to apply

A. G. Kravets et al. (Eds.): CIT&DS 2021, CCIS 1448, pp. 533–544, 2021.
https://doi.org/10.1007/978-3-030-87034-8_39

classical design algorithms have already been effectively tested in the games "Sea Battle" [10], RPG games [10], in the formation of a decision tree for the behavior of opponents [8].

2 Lee's Wave Algorithm

Wave tracing algorithm (wave algorithm, Lie algorithm) - an algorithm for finding the shortest path on a planar graph [1]. The algorithm works on a discrete working field (DCF), which is a bounded closed figure, most often rectangular or square, but not necessarily. The set of all cells of the DRP are divided into subsets: "passable" - when searching for a path, they can be passed, "impassable" - the path through this cell is prohibited, the starting cell is the "source" and the finish cell is the "receiver". The source is the cell in which the wave originates, the receiver is the cell into which the wave should come. This designation is conditional since you only need to know the cells between which you need to make a path.

The algorithm includes three stages:

- Initialization.
- Stage of wave propagation.
- The stage of laying the track.

During initialization, an image of a plurality of cells of the processed field is built, attributes of passability and impassability are assigned to each cell, the start and finish cells are remembered.

At the stage of wave propagation on a set of free cells, a wave of influence is simulated from one cell to another, which is subsequently connected by a common path. The wave originates from the source and follows to the receiver. In order to be able to follow the passage of the influence wavefront, its fragments at each stage are assigned some weights calculated by formula 1.

$$Pk = Pk - 1 + \varphi(f1, f2, \ldots, fg) \tag{1}$$

Pk и Pk − 1 – weights of cells of the kth and (k − 1) th fronts;

φ(f1,f2,...,fg) – weight function, which is an indicator of the quality of the path, each parameter of which fi ($i = 1,2,\ldots, g$) characterizes the path in terms of one of the quality criteria (path length, number of intersections, etc.) [1].

The weights of the cells of the previous fronts should not be greater than the weights of the subsequent ones. The front extends only to neighboring cells that have either a common side (von Neumann's neighborhood) or a common point (Moore's neighborhood) with the cells of the previous front. The process of wave propagation continues until the wave reaches the receiver or at the n-th step, there is no cell for wave propagation, in this case, it is impossible to build a path.

If the wave reaches the receiver, the stage of laying the path begins. The path is laid from the receiver to the source so that the weight of the next cell is as small as possible. In the case when several cells have the same minimum weight, the concept of "track coordinates" is introduced [1]. Each direction is assigned a priority. The direction with the lowest priority value is preferred. Moving from the receiver to the source, so that the values of the weights of the cells decrease monotonically and, taking into account the path coordinates, we obtain a trace of the minimum length, and regardless of how the path coordinates are selected, the trace will always be of the minimum length. Figure 1 shows the propagation of the wave and the resulting path, where A is the start point and B is the endpoint.

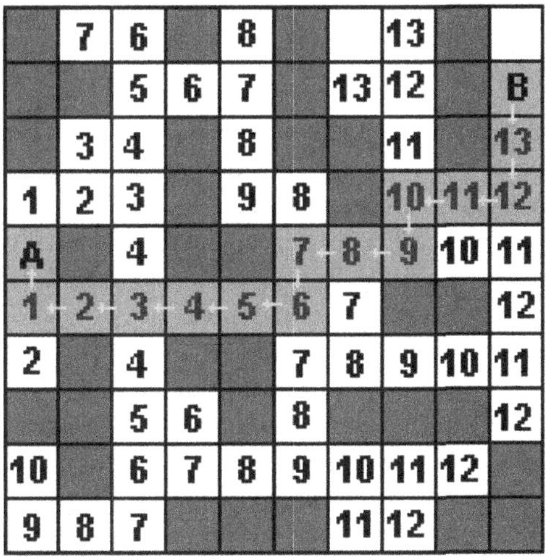

Fig. 1. Lee's wave algorithm illustration.

The scope of the wave algorithm is quite wide, since finding the shortest path is a problem that arises in various fields of human activity.

The main application of the wave algorithm is automated tracing of printed circuit boards, connecting conductors on the surface of microcircuits. Another application of the wave algorithm is finding the shortest distance on the map in computer strategy games [1]. Depending on the area of application, its features must be taken into account.

So, when routing printed circuit boards, several criteria arise by which it will be possible to evaluate the effectiveness of routing. Firstly, the traces should be of minimum length, so there is less chance of a short circuit, and secondly, close laying of conductors should be avoided, since this creates a parasitic capacitance, which can lead to a short circuit, thirdly, the intersections of the traces should be minimal, or there should be no intersections at all if the printed circuit board is single-layer; fourthly, the routes should be with a minimum number of bends, since routes with a large number of bends are more difficult to manufacture. Compliance with all criteria is ensured with the introduction of additional weight on the cells in which the laying of the route is not desirable.

When using the algorithm in computer games, there are other criteria that must be considered for finding a route, and these criteria can be completely different, depending on the game.

The designed application is a TD (Tower Defense) game. The game in the TD genre sets the task of dealing with the advancing enemies. The selection of the type of towers and their location is an integral strategy of the game.

The training application should allow the user to look at various examples of how the wave algorithm works, namely, how the arrangement of towers changes routes, for it is necessary to understand how the wave algorithm works in order to further implement its work in the program code. Figure 2 shows a block diagram of the wave algorithm.

3   TD (Tower Defense) Game

Finding the shortest path is a challenge that occurs in different genres of games: strategy games, tower defense, and many others. But for the process of learning the wave algorithm, tower defense games are more visual.

The designed application is a TD (Tower Defense) game. The game in the TD genre sets the task of dealing with the advancing enemies. The selection of the type of towers and their location is an integral strategy of the game.

The training application should allow the user to look at various examples of how the wave algorithm works, namely, how the arrangement of towers changes routes, for it is necessary to understand how the wave algorithm works in order to further implement its work in the program code. Figure 2 shows a block diagram of the wave algorithm.

In the game application, you need to display the DRP in the form of a game map, as well as in a numerical representation, the constructed path and path coordinates (coordinates for binding the game map to the DRP). Towers will serve as obstacles in the path of enemies, but towers cannot block the entire path. Towers, depending on their level and type, will have an additional weight of the cell and the cells adjacent to them.

The users of this game application are students studying the wave algorithm.

The main functions that are incorporated in the game application are characteristic both for the training application and for the game application, namely:

Setting up a tower (To set up a tower, you need to choose the type of tower and the cell in which the player wants to place it).

Upgrading a tower (When upgrading a tower, improve its parameters, such as radius, damage, strength, and unique ones, depending on the type of the tower itself).

Selling a tower (To sell a tower, select a tower on the playing field and press the right mouse button).

Changing the way coordinates (To change the way coordinates, you need to use the buttons responsible for each direction (left, right, up, down) to set a number indicating the priority of this side).

Viewing the constructed path (The constructed path is shown on the playing field and on the matrix with the weights of the cells).

Viewing statistics of built paths (Statistics are saved in a file).

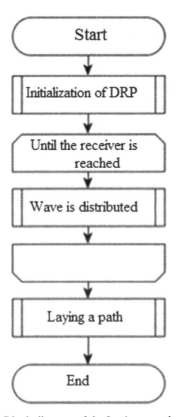

Fig. 2. Block diagram of the Lee's wave algorithm.

Characteristics collected for statistics of built paths:

1. Wavenumber.
2. Number of the enemy in the wave for which this path was built.
3. Path length.
4. Time to build a path.
5. The danger of the way (Danger of the way increases if the enemy passes through the tower, by 5 units and additionally to the level of the tower, if next to the tower, then only by the value of the level of the tower).

The number of towers located on the playing field at the time of building the path.

One of the first tasks that had to be solved was the display of the game map. The game card is represented in the form of a two-dimensional matrix that contains values, these values determine what type the cell belongs to 0 - passable cell; 1 - impassable cell; 2 - starting square; 3 - finish square.

When the map is stored as a matrix, it can be used as a discrete working field for the waveform algorithm.

The wave propagation starts from the finishing cell, the value 0 is entered into it. After all cells of the wavefront are checked, the front is increased by 1 and the algorithm is repeated. When the wave arrives at the starting cell, the wave propagation stops.

To build a path, cells are viewed that have a common side with the starting one, and the cell that has the minimum weight of them is selected, if there are several such cells, then the one with the higher priority direction is selected.

When installing towers, it is necessary to add additional weight to the cell in which the tower is installed, as well as additional weight to neighboring cells, this will make laying a path through these cells less preferable, making it difficult for enemies to pass the path. The path between two towers should be less preferred than the path next to one tower, so the weights of adjacent towers must add up to each other.

The game application window displays the following elements:

1. Green squares - the playing field, which represent free cells in which towers can be installed.
2. Gray squares represent impassable cells.
3. The square with the letter S denotes the starting position, from this cell the enemies come out.
4. The square with the letter F indicates the finish position, when the enemy reaches this cell, the player takes 1 life.
5. The number of lives is shown on the top right of the playing field, it also shows the time until the wave comes out, the number of points that the user scored, as well as how much money he has to build and improve towers.
6. Buttons with towers - contain a number reflecting the cost of the tower, if the player has enough money to build, then the price will be shown in yellow, otherwise in red.
7. To the right of the towers there is a matrix that represents the weights of the cells of the playing field, and also shows the starting, finishing cells, and impassable cells by the X symbol. The selected cell is displayed in the matrix in red, on the playing field the selected cell has an orange frame.
8. Above the matrix there are buttons for setting the track coordinates, the coordinate value is increased by one when the button is pressed, and the button that had this increased value gets the previous value of the button whose priority was changed.

To set up a tower, you must select the type of tower, and then select the cell in which the towers will be located. During the placement, students see changes in waveforms and changes in path length. When the wave timer is reset, the enemies will begin to appear and move from start to finish.

When enemies appear, the path of the last one who came out is shown. The path is shown in yellow squares on the playing field, and a matrix appears to the right of the matrix containing the cell weights, showing the numerical wave propagating from the finishing cell, and the constructed path in red.

All possible situations were considered when on the playing field:

- 0 tower.
- There are towers of the same type.
- There are towers of different types.
- There are towers of different types and levels.

Let's first check the correctness of building the path on an empty playing field (without installed towers).

Figure 3 shows that the numerical wave propagates from the finish cell. Since there are no towers on the playing field, the weights of the cells are added evenly. The numerical wave is built correctly. Upon reaching the starting cell, the wave propagation ended, therefore, the cells with the values -1 remain in the matrix, which shows the wave propagation. As mentioned earlier, the cells with such a value are passable cells, but in these cells, there will be a weight already greater than the maximum on the map.

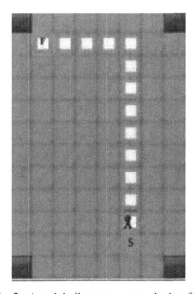

Fig. 3. A path built on an empty playing field

Now we will show the correctness of building the path when installing towers on the playing field. Let's set up some towers and see how the numerical wave will propagate Fig. 4.

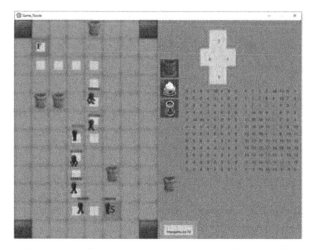

Fig. 4. Building a path with towers on the playing field.

When towers were added, the numerical wave began to spread unevenly, since the cells with towers and the cells adjacent to them had additional weight. Figure 5 shows a numerical wave matrix and a matrix with initial cell weights.

X	0	0	4	40	4	0	X	X	1	2	7	48	13	8	X
0	F	0	4	4	4	0	0	1	0	1	6	9	10	7	8
0	0	0	0	0	0	0	0	2	1	2	3	4	5	6	7
4	8	8	4	0	0	0	0	7	10	11	8	5	6	7	8
4	44	44	4	0	0	0	0	12	55	56	11	6	7	8	9
4	8	8	4	0	0	0	0	17	20	19	12	7	8	9	10
0	0	0	0	0	0	0	0	12	11	10	9	8	9	10	11
0	0	0	0	4	4	4	0	13	12	11	10	13	14	15	12
0	0	0	0	4	40	4	0	14	13	12	11	16	55	18	13
0	0	0	0	4	4	4	0	15	14	13	12	17	-1	19	14
0	0	0	0	0	8	0	0	-1	15	14	13	14	15	-1	15
X	0	0	0	0	0	0	X	X	-1	15	14	15	-1	-1	X

Fig. 5. Matrix of initial weights (left) and matrix with a numerical wave (right).

With an increase in the level of the tower, the weight of the cell in which it is located, as well as the weight of the neighboring cells, increases. Figure 6 shows a path paved on the playing field, which contains towers of various levels and types.

The game application collects statistics of the constructed paths, which is later used by students to analyze the algorithm. The construction time of the path is slightly different

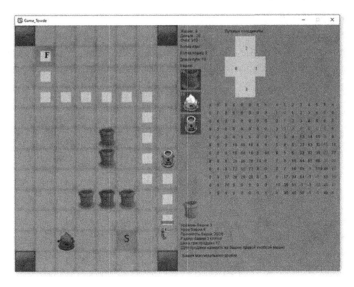

Fig. 6. The path built at different levels and types of towers.

even for the same paths due to the measurement error, but the error does not exceed ten-thousandths of a millisecond. With higher hazard indicators of the path, the time for building the route also increases, for example, the statistical indicators for the playing field, which is covered by towers, are shown in Fig. 7.

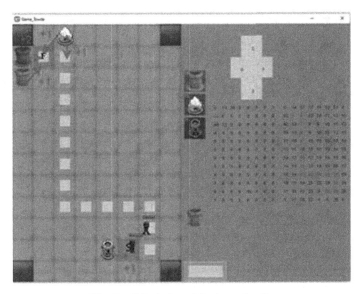

Fig. 7. Calculation of the hazard path.

4   Conclusion

Measurements were made of the construction time of the track, at various values of the danger of the track. Figure 8 shows a graph of the dependence of the construction time of a path on its hazard.

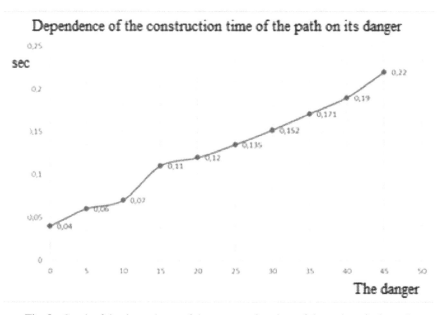

Fig. 8. Graph of the dependence of the construction time of the path on its hazard.

As can be seen in Fig. 8, with an increase in the hazard indicator of a path, the time of its construction also increases. This is due to the fact that a more dangerous path runs next to the towers or directly through the cells in which the tower is located, which leads to the fact that the numerical wave in these cells increases by more than 1, as happens on empty cells, the number of iterations is increased.

Figure 9 shows a graph of the dependence of the time to build a path on the length of the path.

With the help of the development of educational game applications, the following tasks were solved:

1. In-depth study of classical algorithms.
2. Increasing interest in the basic disciplines of the specialty.
3. Improving the quality of software development.
4. Design and development of non-trivial functions for gaming applications.
5. Collected statistical indicators of the constructed path.

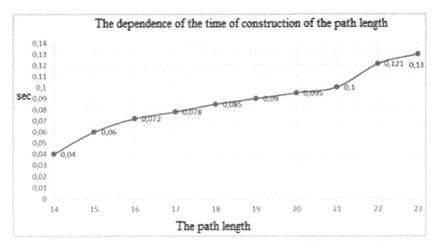

Fig. 9. Graph of the dependence of the construction time of the path on its length.

References

1. Dendobrenko, B.N., Malika, A.S.: Automation of Designing REA: Textbook for Universities, p. 384. Higher School (1980)
2. Bershadsky, A.M., et al.: Algorithms for solving design problems on a computer. In: Sapozhkova, K.A. (ed.) Study Guide. Penz. Polytechnic Institute, Penza (1984)
3. Epishin, I.V., Pikulin, V.V., Shcherban, A.B.: Methodological Instructions for Conducting EIRS in the Field of Automated Design of EVA, p. 53. Penz. Polytechnic Institute, Penza (1983)
4. Jesse, S.: The Art of Game Design: A Book of Lenses, Second Edition - Alpina Digital (2019)
5. Parshin, I.S., Epp, V.V.: Implementation of behavioral design templates on the example of a game application. Cult. Technol. **5**(1), 20–36 (2020)
6. Gregory, J.: Game Engine Architecture (3nd edn.), p. 1018. A K Peters/CRC Press, Boca Raton (2018)
7. Spallazzo, D., Mariani, I.: Location-Based Mobile Games. Design Perspectives. Springer, New York (2018)
8. Yannakakis, G.N., Togelius, J.: Artificial Intelligence and Games. Springer, New York (2018)
9. Quick, J.M.: Learn to Implement Games with Code. CRC Press, Boca Raton (2016)
10. Macklin, C., Sharp, J.: Games, Design, and Play. Addison-Wesley Professional, New York (2016)
11. Shestopalov, K.K.: Basics of Computer-Aided Design: Textbook. Allowance. MADI, Moscow (2017)
12. Kudryavtsev, E.M.: Fundamentals of Computer-Aided Design: A Textbook for Students Higher Study Institutions. Publishing Center "Academy", Moscow (2011)
13. Norenkov, I.P.: Computer-aided design systems: a tutorial for technical colleges. construction principles and structure. Higher shk, Moscow (1986)
14. Encarnacho, J.: Computer-aided design. Basic concepts and architecture of systems: per. from English. Radio and communication, Moscow (1986)
15. Zykov, A.G., Polyakov, V.I.: Computer Design Algorithms. ITMO University SPb, Moscow (2014)
16. Harari, F.: Graph Theory (3rd edn.). KomKniga, URSS, Moscow (2006)

17. Norenkov, I.P.: Fundamentals of Computer Aided Design: A Tutorial for Universities. Publishing house of MSTU im.N.E. Bauman, Moscow (2006)
18. Zykov, A.A.: Fundamentals of Graph Theory. Vuzovskaya kniga, Moscow (2004)
19. Cormen, T.H., Leiserson, C.I., Rivest, R.L., Stein, C.: Algorithms: Plotting and Analysis. Williams, Moscow (2013)

User Engagement Assessment for Adaptive Learning Systems

Angelina Voronina$^{(\boxtimes)}$, Olga Shabalina, Alexander Kataev, and Natalia Sadovnikova

Volgograd State Technical University, Volgagrad, Russia
angelina.vaa@gmail.com, o.a.shabalina@gmail.com,
alexander.kataev@gmail.com, npsn1@ya.ru

Abstract. Modern trends in educational software development are associated with adaptive learning systems, i.e. systems that can personalize the user's interaction with the system. One of the key quality indicators for educational software, which is characterized by intensive user interaction with the system, is engagement. The paper discusses applicability of the known methods of assessing engagement to adapt learning process in learning systems, as well as the metrics used by these methods and ways of interpreting them in terms of engagement. A method of combined engagement assessment is presented, which makes it possible to take into account various aspects of possible manifestation of user engagement while interacting with the learning system. Metrics, indicators and rules for their convolution are proposed that are applicable to the online assessment of engagement in adaptive learning systems. Ways of using the developed method to adaptation of the learning process in learning systems are consider.

Keywords: Adaptive learning system · Quality of the learning system · Engagement · Engagement assessment · Engagement assessment method · Online engagement assessment

1 Introduction

Modern trends in educational software development are associated with adaptive learning systems, i.e. systems able to personalize the user interaction with the system [1]. The key problem in adaptive systems development is development of models and methods of adaptation that can actually improve the system quality, and accordingly, the effectiveness of the learning process in the system. One of the key quality indicators for educational software, which is characterized by intensive user interaction with the system, is engagement. Research shows that user engagement in the interaction with the learning system is positively correlated with the learning outcomes, and thus directly affects the quality of the system [2]. Thus, the results of the user engagement analysis can be used to adapt the learning process in learning systems, aimed at retaining and increasing the user engagement, and, accordingly, to improve the system quality in terms of the effectiveness of the learning process.

© Springer Nature Switzerland AG 2021
A. G. Kravets et al. (Eds.): CIT&DS 2021, CCIS 1448, pp. 545–558, 2021.
https://doi.org/10.1007/978-3-030-87034-8_40

2   User Engagement as Quality Indicator for Learning System

User engagement is understood as emotional, cognitive and/or behavioral connection between the user and software system during their interaction [3]. User engagement is one of the key quality indicators of interactive software, which is characterized by intense user interaction with the system. Known methods for assessing engagement differ in the data sets that are used to analyze engagement, the methods of collecting this data and their interpretations in terms of engagement [4]. To assess engagement, information is used about how the user was engaged while interacting with the system, which can be obtained directly from the user (self-reporting), from the results of online observations of user actions (web-analytics), from observations of external manifestations of user behavior (physiological approach, physiological approach), from the data of neurophysiological signals received from the corresponding sensors installed on the user's body (neurophysiological approach, neuro-physiological approach) [4].

Self-reporting involves obtaining information directly from the user, allowing to draw a conclusion and how much he was involved in the process of interacting with the application. Such self-reporting methods as discrete method, the spatial method or free response method can be used to assess engagement. The discrete method is based on the user's choice of some terms (words and / or phrases) from the set provided to him, reflecting his engagement.The spatial approach is based on a two-dimensional or three-dimensional representation of experiences, emotions, events that the user experienced while interacting with the application. Examples of this approach are semantic differential scales and the Affect Grid [5]. A free response rating is a direct engagement assessment by the user.

The physiological approach means assessing user engagement by the results of observing his actions and external manifestations of his behavior while interacting with the application. Facial expression analysis (emotion analysis), speech analysis and eye tracking analysis are used to assess engagement in such cases. The neurophysiological approach uses data from respiratory and cardiovascular accelerations and decelerations, muscle spasms, and other signals received from appropriate sensors installed on the user's body to assess engagement [6].

The classification of characteristics and methods for assessing engagement, was proposed in [7], as shown in Fig. 1.

Educational software is a category of software, which, by definition, is based on user interaction, therefore, the user's engagement in the interaction process with the learning system directly affects the quality of the system. To manage the quality of learning systems, the developer needs to assess the user engagement at all stages of the system Life Cycle (LC). Assessment of engagement at the Software Development Stage (a priori assessment of engagement) can be useful to the developer, since at this stage he can improve certain aspects of the system in order to increase the engagement of potential users. User engagement can also be assessed for already developed learning systems (a posteriori assessment), as the results of such assessment can be taken into account when developing new versions of the syhstem.

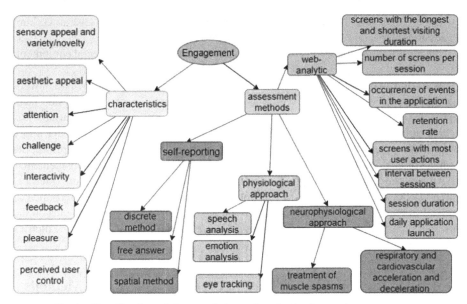

Fig. 1. Classification of characteristics and methods of assessing engagement

3   Analysis of the Applicability of Methods for Assessing Engagement in Adaptive Learning Systems

Recently, studies have appeared on using the results of engagement assessing for adapting the learning process in learning systems, aimed at retaining and increasing engagement, and, finally, at improving the system quality in terms of the effectiveness of the learning process [8]. In an adaptive learning system, the adaptation of the learning process runs online, and, accordingly, the adaptation mechanisms cannot be connected with any change in the system itself. The volumes of content of many learning systems are quite large and the learning process in such systems can take a lot of time (more than one working session).

To adapt the learning process between the sessions in such systems, the posteriori engagement assessment methods can be used, which do not require changes in the system itself. However, to adapt the learning process within a single session, only those engagement assessment methods are applicable, the results of which can be used online.

Engagement assessment methods based on measurements of the user's neurophysiological parameters require specialized equipment. Such equipment may be expensive, difficult to obtain, and special knowledge may be required to operate such equipment. Implementation of such methods for assessing engagement in adaptive learning systems significantly limits the number of potential users of such systems. Thus, to assess the applicability of methods for assessing engagement for adapting the learning process in learning systems, the following criteria have been defined:

1.   The ability to use the results of the assessment without changing the system itself;

2. The ability to use the results of the assessment during one and / or several working sessions;
3. The ability to use the results of the assessment without the use of special equipment.

According to the selected criteria, the physiological approach and the method of web-analytics appear applicable for online assessment of engagement. The physiological approach is based on emotion analysis, speech analysis, and eye movement analysis (oculography). As a rule, the user interaction with the learning system does not imply sound accompaniment and / or comments from the user on his actions. Therefore, the methods of oculography and analysis of emotions were chosen to assess engagement.

All assessment methods operate with quantitative or qualitative indicators (metrics) that are collected in the process of user interaction with the system and interpreted in terms of of engagement. Thus, the result of the engagement assessment depends on the choice of metrics that are matched to the corresponding method, and on how the metrics and/or their convolutions are interpreted.

4   Ways to Interpret Metrics of Engagement Assessment Methods

4.1   Analysis of Ways to Interpret Oculography Metrics

Oculography is widely used to study user behavior in the process of interacting with a software system and to analyze his activities such as reading, scanning, and processing of visual stimuli [9]. User interaction with such systems is based on visual perception and information processing. As the user performs visual tasks such as searching or perceiving a scene, the eyes alternate between fixations and saccades. Fixations are used to maintain visual focus on one stimulus, while saccades reorient the eye to focus on the next desired position. Saccades are rapid eye movements and are considered the fastest rotational movement of any external part of our body, reaching angular velocities of up to 900 degrees per second and usually lasting from 20ms to 100ms. Saccades and fixations are the main metrics of eye movement [10]. Oculographic metrics and their possible fixation-based interpretations proposed in [11, 12] are presented in Table 1.

Oculographic metrics and their saccades-based interpretations [11, 12] are presented in Table 2.

Pupil dilation [12] is interpreted as a change in the user's mood or attitude, or the solution of complex cognitive tasks. In [13] the metric of eye movement "blinking frequency" is given. Lower blink rates of a user indicate higher exertion or attention, while higher rates are associated with fatigue.

All oculographic metrics are measurable and can be obtained during video surveillance of the user while he interacts with the system.

4.2   Analysis of Ways to Interpret Emotion Analysis Data

The user's emotional state usually has external observable manifestations, such as facial expressions, gestures, posture, etc., which can be monitored during video surveillance of the user in the process of his interaction with the system. The observed manifestations

Table 1. Interpretations of fixation oculography metrics in the context of engagement

Metric	Metric interpretation
Overall number of fixations	A high commit value indicates a less efficient search for interface elements on the web page (possibly due to suboptimal interface layout) [11]
	A higher number indicates more visual effort to complete the task [12]
Fixation rate	Higher values indicate higher efficiency associated with less effort to find the corresponding item [12]
Fixations per area of interest	More fixation on a particular area indicates that that area is more visible or more important to the user than other areas [11]
Fixation duration	Longer fixation indicates difficulty in retrieving information, or it means that the subject is more attractive [11]
	A higher value indicates areas that the user considers important [11]
Fixation spatial density	Commitments concentrated in a small area indicate a focused and effective search. Uniformly distributed commits reflect widespread and ineffective search [12]
	Lower spatial density indicates more targeted searches [11]
Repeat fixations – «posttarget fixations»	More fixations outside of the target after the target has been locked indicate that it lacks meaning or visibility [12]
Time to first fixation on-target	A faster time to first fixate on an object or area means that it has better attention-grabbing properties [12]

of the emotional state are non-measurable, and, accordingly, the problem of recognizing the user's emotional state is reduced to the problem of interpreting these observed manifestations in terms of certain emotions associated with these observations. In [14], a method is described for interpreting emotions obtained by analyzing the user's facial expressions to determine the engagement of students. Seven basic emotions are selected as metrics: anger, disgust, fear, happiness, sadness, surprise, and neutrality. A convolutional neural network is used to predict the likelihood of emotions occurring, with the emotion most likely to be dominant. To assess the level of engagement, the user concentration index is introduced, calculated as multiplication of the dominant emotion probability by a coefficient reflecting the user's concentration at the current time (emotion weight). Depending on the value, the concentration index is interpreted as the level of engagement and is assessed on the scale {"Very engaged", "Nominally engaged", "Not engaged"}.

Table 2. Interpretations of saccade-based oculography metrics in the context of engagement

Metric	Metric interpretation
Number of saccades	More saccades means more searching [11]
	It is associated with mental stress and helps to understand how the complexity of the material affects eye movements [12]
Saccade amplitude	Larger values indicate more significant signs [11]
Regressive saccades	Regressions indicate the presence of less significant features [11]
	Regression rate describes non-linear reading [12]
Saccades revealing marked directional shifts	Any saccade greater than 90 degrees from the saccade that preceded it shows a rapid change in direction. This may mean that the user's goals have changed or the interface layout does not meet the user's expectations [11]

In [15], engagement is considered directly as one of the emotional states of the user, determined on the basis of emotions. For emotion recognition, multimodal algorithms are proposed. The interpretation of emotions is based on the PAD-model (Pleasure, Arousal and Dominance) of the user's emotional states. Interpretations of the emotion analysis metrics are shown in Table 3.

Table 3. Interpretations of emotion analysis metrics in the context of engagement

Metric	Metric interpretation
Concentration index	User engagement
Dominant emotion	
The weight of emotion	
Emotions	Engagement as one of the emotional states

Emotion analysis metrics can be obtained during video surveillance of the user in the process of his interaction with the system and are themselves interpretations of the user's external observable manifestations.

4.3 Analyzing of Ways to Interpret Web-analytics Metrics

Web-analytics is based on the analysis of user behavioral indicators. Metrics used for web-analytics include such ones as daily application launch, session duration, interval between sessions, retention rate, number of screens per session, screens with the longest and shortest visit duration, screens with most user actions (gestures), occurrence of events in the application (within a certain time frame). Interpretations of the web-analytics metrics most often used to assess the quality of applications in the context of engagement are proposed in [16–18] (Table 4).

Table 4. Interpretations of web-analytics metrics in the context of engagement

Metric	Metric interpretation
Session intervals	Shows how often users use the application [16]
	Shows how "sticky" (sticky, that is, the user wants to use it more) the application is [17]
Daily application launch	Shows the key users of the application [16]
Session duration	Shows the level of user engagement during the session. Shorter session duration does not necessarily mean low engagement. The user can quickly find what he was looking for and end the session [16]
	More active participation means longer session duration [18]
Number of screens per session	Knowing what users are doing in an application, what screens they open, and how they use them can be essential in spotting UI issues. The metric shows whether some parts of the application perform better than others, which allows to properly focus development efforts [16]

Web-analytics metrics are measurable, so engagement assessment depends on how these metrics are interpreted.

The classification of metrics is shown in Table 5.

Table 5. Classification of metrics

Metric	Metric characteristic	Characteristic of the engagement assessment method based on the metric
Oculographic metric	Measurable	Interpretable
Emotional metric	Interpretable	Interpretable
Web-analytics metric	Measurable	Interpretable

5 Development of a Method for Combined Online Engagement Assessment

The results of assessing engagement based on oculography, emotion analysis and web-analytics metrics depend on the chosen methods of interpreting the metrics themselves.

The subjectivity of assessments based on interpretations is always high, and the degree of confidence in the results of such assessment ("reliability") may not be sufficient to make decisions based on these results. In case of assessing engagement based on the analysis of the user's emotional state, the determination of the emotional state by external manifestations is itself interpretable, therefore the reliability of such an assessment may be deliberately unacceptable.

In case of assessing engagement for making decisions in adaptive learning systems, confidence in the results of the assessment is very important. The decisions on adapting learning process to a specific user, made on the results of the assessment that does not reflect the real level of engagement of this user, may not only not increase the effectiveness of the learning process, but even lead to the user's unwillingness to continue learning.

Joint analysis of physiological state and behavior of the user of the adaptive learning system allows to take into account various aspects of possible manifestation of the user engagement, and, in case of consistency of the analysis results, to increase confidence in the results of the engagement assessment. A method for assessing engagement has been developed, which is applicable for adapting the learning process in adaptive learning systems, based on a combination of oculography, emotion analysis and web-analytics methods. Metrics are proposed that are applicable to the online engagement assessment, engagement indicators, methods of their interpretation, and rules for the convolution of indicators.

The user interaction with the learning system engages fixing his eyes on certain areas of the screen that display the most significant information in terms of learning process (so called area of interest). From the point of view of assessing engagement, the number of fixations per area of interest determines the user's interest. Therefore, to assess engagement by the oculography method, the metrics based on commits were selected: the total number of commits and the number of commits per area of interest collected while the user interacts with some screen of the learning system. As an oculographic indicator of engagement on one screen of the system, the following relation is proposed:

$$p_j = \frac{f_j}{\varphi_j}, \tag{1}$$

where p_j - the oculographic indicator of engagement on the j-th screen;

f_j - the number of commits per area of interest on the j-th screen;

φ_j - the total number of commits on the j-th screen.

Research shows [19] that emotional reactions a person experiences during the learning process can influence this process. A negative or positive emotional state of the user in the process of interacting with the learning system may reflect his engagement. Decisions on adapting the learning process in adaptive learning systems are usually made at times predetermined by the system developer, and the time intervals after which the adaptation is carried out are not necessarily equal. The number of values of the engagement indicator calculated over a certain time interval is determined by the number of screens with which the user interacted and the given frequency of emotion recognition. Accordingly, the oculographic indicator of engagement for the selected time interval is determined as following:

$$P_i^O = \frac{\sum_{j=1}^{n_i} p_{ij}}{n_i},$$ (2)

where P_i^O - oculographic indicator of engagement in the i-th time interval;
p_{ij} - oculographic indicator of engagement on the j-th screen of the i-th time interval;
n_i - the number of screens passed by the user in the i-th time interval.

There are various classifications to describe the user's emotions. The main emotions of a person, distinguished by most software libraries, include such emotions as happiness, sadness, neutral expression, anger, surprise, contempt. When choosing individual emotions as metrics, the interpretation of each emotion in terms of engagement is obviously ambiguous. Therefore, the user's emotional state, determined by the results of dividing a set of basic emotions according to Russell's model, was chosen as a metric for assessing engagement by emotions [20]. The following emotions are attributed to the positive state: happiness; neutral expression; surprise; to the negative - sadness; anger; contempt. A positive emotional state can be interpreted as the user's engagement, while a negative one can be interpreted as a lack of engagement. Thus, as an indicator of emotional engagement in the selected time interval, the following relation is proposed:

$$P_i^E = \frac{E_i^p}{E_i},$$ (3)

where P_i^E - an indicator of emotional engagement in the i-th time interval;
E_i^p - the number of emotions related to a positive state in the i-th time interval;
E_i - the total amount of emotions in the i-th time interval.

In the case when the learning process in the learning system is not completed during one session, to adapt the learning process between sessions, some indicators calculated by the metrics of web-analytics, can be additionally interpreted in terms of engagement. As an indicator of web-analytics, it is proposed to use the ratio of the duration of the current session to the average duration of all previous sessions:

$$P_k^w = \frac{t_k(k-1)}{\sum_{j=1}^{k-1} t_j},$$ (4)

where P_k^w – web-analytics metric after the k-th session is completed;
k - session number;
t_j - the duration of the j-th session.

Due to the ambiguity of possible interpretations of quantitative indicators of engagement, a combined engagement assessment is determined using fuzzy inference mechanism. To assess engagement, the linguistic variable *Engagement* is defined, described by the following set of terms:

$$Engagement \in \{low, \ below \ average, \ average, \ above \ average, \ high\},$$ (5)

on a given domain of definitions:

$$X = [0; 1]. \tag{6}$$

Thus, the generalized assessment of user engagement in the process of interacting with the learning system, depending on the number of sessions, is determined by the values of two (one session) or three (more than one session) linguistic variables:

$$Engagement_I = < Engagement_O, Engagement_E, Engagement_W >, \tag{7}$$

where $Engagement_I$ - generalized assessment of engagement;
$Engagement_O$ - assessment of engagement based on oculographic indicator;
$Engagement_E$ - assessment of engagement based on emotional state;
$Engagement_W$ - engagement score based on web-analytics metric.
The $Engagement_I$ value is determined based on a set of fuzzy inference rules:

If (Engagement$_O$ = "Engagement$_O$") and (Engagement$_E$ = "Engagement$_E$") and gagement$_W$ = "Engagement$_W$"), then (Engagement$_I$ = "Engagement$_I$").

$$\tag{8}$$

Examples of fuzzy inference rules for determining Engagement$_I$:

R1: If Engagement$_O$ = low and Engagement$_E$ = low and Engagement$_W$ = average, then Engagement$_I$ = below average.
R2: If Engagement$_O$ = below average and Engagement$_E$ = low and Engagement$_W$ = below average, then Engagement$_I$ = below average.
R3: If Engagement$_O$ = above average and Engagement$_E$ = average and Engagement$_W$ = high, then Engagement$_I$ = above average.

The process of assessing the engagement during one T_k session of the user's work with the adaptive learning system is shown in Fig. 2.

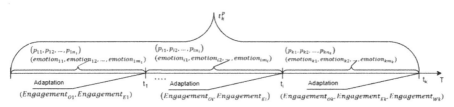

Fig. 2. The process of assessing engagement during one session of a user with an adaptive learning system

The process of assessing engagement using the combined online assessment method over several sessions of work with the adaptive learning system is shown in Fig. 3.

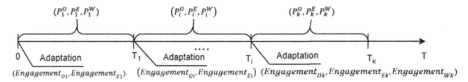

Fig. 3. The process of assessing engagement using a combined online assessment method over several sessions

6   Implementation of the Combined Online Engagement Assessment Method

The proposed method is implemented in a web application designed to assess engagement in adaptive learning systems. The initial data for the application are oculographic data, emotion recognition data and web analytics data, the result of the work is engagement assessment at predrfined points in time.

The results of assessing engagement using the proposed method depend on how the linguistic variables will be set. The values given in Table 6 were selected as the initial values of the parameters of the membership functions.

Table 6. Membership function parameters

Fuzzy variable	Membership function parameter			
	c (oculographic, emotional, generalized)	c (web-analytic)	σ (oculographic, emotional, generalized)	σ (web-analytic)
Low	0	0	0.05	1
Below average	0.25	2.5	0.05	1
Average	0.5	5	0.05	1
Above average	0.75	7	0.05	1
High	1	10	0.05	1

The membership function graph corresponding to the selected values of the function parameters for the linguistic variable $Engagement_W$ is shown in Fig. 4.

The membership function graph corresponding to the selected values of the function parameters for the linguistic variable $Engagement_O$, $Engagement_E$, $Engagement_I$ is shown in Fig. 5.

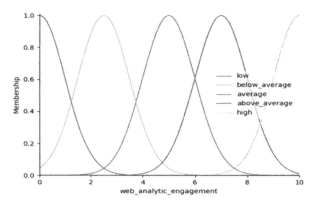

Fig. 4. Membership function graph for a linguistic variable EngagementW

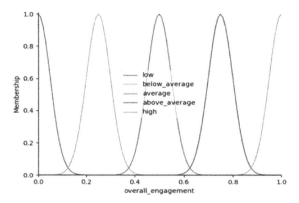

Fig. 5. Membership function graph for a linguistic variable EngagementO, EngagementE, EngagementI

To clarify fuzzy variables, it is necessary to conduct a series of experiments on organizing the learning process of a group of users using some selected learning system, accompanied by the collection of oculographic data, emotion recognition data and web analytics data from the computer's webcam in the process of user interaction with the system. The data collected should be fed into a developed engagement scoring module that will measure user engagement at predetermined points in time. At the same points in time, the engagement of each user will be assessed by experts (external observers) by external observable signs and by the users themselves. Based on the results of the analysis of the obtained sets of alternative estimates of engagement (a set of estimates by the method, a set of expert estimates, a set of self-assessment results), the fuzzy variables will be set in such a way that the result of the engagement assessment obtained using the method does not contradict the results of expert assessments and user self-esteem.

The experiment process is shown in the Fig. 6.

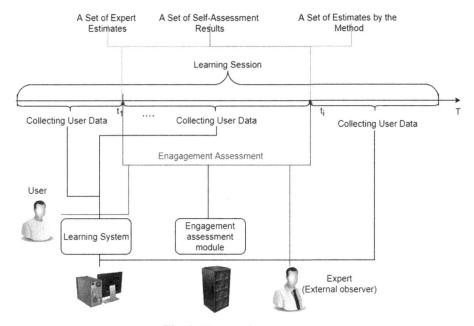

Fig. 6. The experiment process

7 Conclusion

The proposed method for the combined online engagement assessment is based on the analysis of both the user's actions in the leanring system and his current physiological state, and the joint interpretation of the results in terms of engagement. The method is intended for use in adaptive learning systems, in which engagement is considered as an indirect assessment of the success of the learning process when the user interacts with the system, and the results of the engagement assesment are used to adapt the learning process. for this user. As part of further research, a series of experiments will be carried out to organize the learning process in a learning system specially designed for this purpose, with an assessment of user engagement. Based on the experimental results analysis, the values of linguistic variables will be clarified and the module for assessing engagement will be finalized.

References

1. Shabalina, O.A., Davtyan, A.G., Kataev, A.V., Alimov, A.A.: Adaptive educational games as a trend in the development of educational software. ITNOU: Inf. Technol. Sci. Educ. Manag. **4**(8), 11–16 (2018). (in Russian)
2. Rebelo, F., Noriega, P., Duarte, E., Soares, M.: Using virtual reality to assess user experience. Hum. Fact. J. Hum. Fact. Ergon. Soc. **54**(6), 964-982 (2012)
3. User engagement. https://whatis.techtarget.com/definition/user-engagement. Accessed 16 Nov 2019

4. Lalmas, M., O'Brien, H., Yom-Tov, E.: Measuring User Engagement: Synthesis Lectures on Information Concepts, Retrieval, and Services, pp. 11–58 (2015)
5. Russell, J.A., Weiss, A., Mendelsohn, G.A.: Mendelsohn affect grid: A single-item scale of pleasure and arousal. J. Pers. Soc. Psychol., 493–502 (1988)
6. Murphy, D., Higgins, C.: Secondary Inputs for Measuring User Engagement in Immersive VR Education Environments, pp. 1–6 (2019)
7. Voronina, A.A., Shabalina, O.A., Kataev, A.V.: Methods for assessing the engagement of users of interactive applications. ITNOU: Inf. Technol. Sci. Educ. Manag. **4**(14), 70–74 (2019). (in Russian)
8. Shabalina, O.A., Kataev, A.V., Voronina, A.A.: Adaptation to user engagement in an adaptive learning game. Modeling Optimization Inf. Technol. Electron. Sci. J. **8**(2) (29), 9 (2020). (in Russian)
9. Lorigo, L., et al.: Eye tracking and online search: lessons learned and challenges ahead. J. Assoc. Inf. Sci. Technol., 1041–1052 (2008)
10. Sluganovic, I., Roeschlin, M., Rasmussen, K.B., Martinovic, I.: Using reflexive eye movements for fast challenge-response authentication. In: Proceedings of the 2016 ACM SIGSAC Conference on Computer and Communications Security (2016)
11. Poole, A., Ball, L. J.: Eye tracking in human-computer interaction and usability research: current status and future prospects (2006)
12. Sharafi, Z., Sharif, B., Guéhéneuc, Y.: Eye-tracking metrics in software engineering. In: Conference Paper (2015)
13. Fritz, T., et al.: Using psycho-physiological measures to assess task difficulty in software development. In: Proceedings of the 36th International Conference on Software Engineering, pp. 402–413. ACM (2014)
14. Sharma, P. et al.: Student Engagement Detection Using Emotion Analysis, Eye Tracking and Head Movement with Machine Learning (2019)
15. Kołakowska, A., et al.: Emotion recognition and its application in software engineering. In: 6th International Conference on Human System Interactions (HSI), pp. 532–539 (2013)
16. The Best Metrics and Tools for Measuring User Engagement. https://hackernoon.com/the-best-metrics-and-tools-for-measuring-user-engagement-fb083d9a9be7. Accessed 19 Mar 2021
17. Metrics to Measure User Engagement in Mobile Apps. https://appfollow.io/blog/metrics-to-measure-user-engagement-in-mobile-apps. Accessed 19 Mar 2021
18. Key Metrics to Measure User Engagement in Mobile Apps. https://www.newgenapps.com/blog/mobile-app-analytics-10-key-metrics-to-measure-user-engagement/. Accessed 19 Mar 2021
19. Distance learning. Informational portal. http://www.distance-learning.ru/db/el/0ACA1C9C4A5FA253C32576E7001E115C/doc.html. Accessed 19 Mar 2021. (in Russian)
20. A Guide to Human-Computer Interaction: Emotional Technologies. https://lpgenerator.ru/blog/2017/10/22/putevoditel-po-cheloveko-kompyuternomu-vzaimodejstviyu-emocionalnye-tehnologii/. Accessed 19 Mar 2021. (in Russian)

Cybersecurity Specialists' E-learning Problems

Svyatoslav Birukov[1], Dmitry Vasilev[2]([✉]), Lubov Kokoreva[3], Polina Shmarion[4],
and Sergey Nikonovich[5]

[1] Volgograd State University, 100 Universitetskiy Avenue, Volgograd 400062, Russia
[2] Volgograd Academy of the Russian Ministry of Internal Affairs, 130 Istoricheskaya Street,
Volgograd 400089, Russia
[3] Moscow Regional Branch, Moscow University of the Ministry of Internal Affairs of Russia
named after V.Ya. Kikotya, Moscow region, Ruzsky urban district, pos. Staroteryaevo Index,
Volgograd 143100, Russia
[4] MIREA—Russian Technological University, Vernadskogo Avenue, 78,
Moscow 119270, Russia
[5] Military University of the Ministry of Defense of the Russian Federation, St. B. Sadovaya, 14,
Moscow 123001, Russia

Abstract. This article studies problems of data security e-learning systems. It covers the definition of e-learning and its attributes, as well as analyzes classifications of e-learning systems described in scientific literature, their advantages and downsides. It offers the main notions that need to be studied by cadets and attendees of non-technical programs within the Ministry of Internal Affairs educational system. It provides brief definitions and key methods of data protection that do not require special training.

Keywords: Data · Threat · Authorization · Cryptography · Electronic digital signature · Firewall

1 Introduction

In recent decades, information technologies have rapidly developed in all social spheres. Information is gradually becoming a more important strategic resource for the state and a demanded good. Like any other goods, data also need safety and reliable protection.

Data vulnerability in computer systems is caused by huge concentration of calculating resources, their spatial dispersion, long-term storage of large data volumes, simultaneous access of multiple users to computer system resources. Every day new threats are arising, so information security problems become more and more relevant [1].

Establishment of common information space, almost universal application of personal computers and introduction of computer systems determine the necessity to address the complex problem of data protection.

Various institutions of higher and professional education provide courses covering data security issues. Their content and educational approaches vary depending on specialty and preparedness of students.

© Springer Nature Switzerland AG 2021
A. G. Kravets et al. (Eds.): CIT&DS 2021, CCIS 1448, pp. 559–571, 2021.
https://doi.org/10.1007/978-3-030-87034-8_41

As higher educational institutions of Ministry of Internal Affairs are humanities-focused, it is necessary to determine how detailed this topic should be approached. This task requires taking into consideration not only the present situation concerning data security but also certain practical aspects. For instance, investigators regularly work with confidential data, however getting into technical specifics on data protection seems unreasonable, as these activities are beyond their responsibilities.

2   Data Security

Data protection in computer systems involves regular usage of systems, and methods as well as taking measures and actions to systemically uphold required safety of data stored and processed through computer equipment. The protected objects include data, storage devices and informational processes that need protection according to certain safety purposes.

Data security is understood as protection of information from unlawful familiarization, transformation and destruction, as well as protection of information resources from actions damaging their functionality. Data safety can be achieved by maintaining main properties of information: confidentiality, integrity, reliability and availability.

Confidentiality is the property indicating necessity for limiting data access to a certain group of people. In other words, it guarantees that transferred data would be known to lawful users only.

Integrity is the property of data to maintain content and/or structure during storage and transfer, so that they remain unchanged compared to some fixed state. Information can be created, transformed and destroyed only by an authorized person (a lawful user with access rights).

Reliability is the property understood as strict belonging of data to the subject that is either the source or submitter of these data.

Availability is the ability to provide users the well-timed and unobstructed access to required data [2].

Countering multiple threats to data security requires complex application of various organizational, legal, engineering and technical, hardware and software, cryptographical and other means and activities.

2.1   Information Security Complex

Organizational activities on data security include recruiting and training personnel to prepare and operate data and software, as well as regulating development and functioning of computer systems.

Legal measures and methods include effective laws and regulations imposing data handling rules and responsibility for their violation.

Engineering and technical means are diverse and consist of physical, technological, hardware, software, cryptographical and others. They establish the following lines of protection: controlled territory, building, area, specific devices and data storages.

Hardware and software security means are used directly in computers and computer networks and include various network-integrated electronic and electromechanical devices. Specialized programs and packages implement such protection functions as limiting and controlling access to resources, registering and analyzing ongoing processes, events and users, preventing potential damage to resources, etc.

Cryptographic protection involves changing (transforming) information, making it implicit through special algorithms or hardware and encryption keys.

Software security is aimed at protecting data from the most common threats: unauthorized access, copying and malware (viruses). Computer systems are protected against unsanctioned intervention by so-called "three A's" (Authentication, Authorization and Accounting).

Authorization (sanctioning, permission) is the procedure, during which a user entering the system is recognized and gets rights specified by the system administrator to access certain resources (computers, discs, folders, peripheral equipment). Authorization is performed by software and consists of identification and authentication.

Identification means providing an identifier: a non-secret name, word or number for user registering. The subject inputs the username that is compared with the list of identifiers. The user who has an identifier registered in the system is considered as rightful (lawful). Identifiers are synonymous to logins: a combination of letters and digits, unique for a given system.

Authentication is the procedure confirming that the input identifier actually belongs to the subject, performed by comparing the username and the password. After the authentication, subjects are granted access to system resources according to permissions given to them [3].

The most common authorization methods are based on passwords (secret combinations of symbols). Launching a program or performing certain activities on a computer or in a network can be password-protected. Apart from passwords, plastic cards and smart cards can also be used for authentication.

Accounting involves registering user's network activities, including attempts to access certain resources. In order to prevent unsanctioned actions, the controlled compliance with access rights requires regular collection, documenting and providing upon request information on any access to protected computer resources. The main registering form is software-managed special logs - files on external storage devices.

There are different methods to prevent unsanctioned copying of data:

1. Countering reading of copied data. These methods are based on making certain features while recording data on storage devices (non-standard marking, storage device formatting, hardware key installation), so that copied data cannot be read on devices not belonging to the protected system. In other words, these methods maintain compatibility of storage devices only within a specified computer system.
2. Countering and hindering usage of copied software and data. The most effective protection method of this type involves storing data in a cryptographically transformed form. Another way to counter unsanctioned running of copied programs is to use software environment control unit. This unit is created during program installation and includes characteristics of environment, in which the program is located (computer device or data storage device characteristics), and means to compare these characteristics.

2.2 Varieties of Antivirus Programs

Special antivirus software has been developed to protect computer systems from mal-ware. Antiviruses detect malware, offer to disinfect files and delete uncurable ones. There are several types of antivirus programs [4]:

1. scanners, or phages, are programs that search files, memory and boot sectors for virus signatures (unique program code of a particular virus), check and treat files;
2. monitors (type of scanners) check Random Access Memory (RAM) during operating system boot, automatically inspecting all files when they are getting opened or closed in order to prevent opening and recording infected files, as well as to block viruses;
3. immunizers prevent file infection by detecting suspicious activities during computer work, typical for early stages of infection (i.e., before the virus replicates) and inform the user on it;
4. inspectors memorize initial state of programs and catalogues before they were infected and compare it with their current condition on schedule (or upon user's request);
5. doctors not only detect infected files but also cure them by removing virus software from files, restoring their initial condition;
6. blockers track events and intercept suspicious activities (performed by a malware), prohibit such activities or request user's permission.

An effective way to counter various threats to data security is to apply cryptographic transformation. As a result, protected data become unavailable for familiarization and direct usage by unsanctioned persons.

For blocking threats coming from public systems, special hardware or software appliances are used, known as firewalls. A firewall enables to divide common network in two or more parts and implement a set of rules for transferring data package between parts of public network. Network protection fully blocks incoming traffic but allows internal users to freely communicate with the outside world. Firewalls are generally used to protect local networks from interventions from the Internet and perform four main functions:

1. filtering data on several levels;
2. using proxy servers that act as intermediaries and establish connection between access object and subject for further data transfer, while maintaining control and registering;
3. transmitting addresses in order to conceal actual internal addresses from outside parties;
4. registering events in special logs. The log analysis helps to document attempted violations of network data exchange and find the perpetrator.
5. SIEM systems (Event Collection and Correlation System) track suspicious activity both inside the circuit and outside.

To accomplish their task, modern SIEM systems use the following sources of information (Fig. 1) [5].

Intrusion Detection System (IDS), unlike firewalls, which operate on the basis of predefined policies, are used to monitor and detect suspicious activity. Thus, IDS can be called an important addition to the network security infrastructure. It is with the help of an intrusion detection system that an administrator will be able to detect unauthorized access (intrusion or network attack) to a computer system or network and take steps to prevent an attack [6].

IPS (Intrusion Prevention System) is based on IDS, that is, each IPS includes an IDS module.

Fig. 1. Sources used in SIEM systems.

In terms of their functions, the systems are similar, but there are also differences:

- IDS is a "passive" solution that monitors network packets, ports, compares traffic with a certain set of rules and alerts when malicious actions are detected;
- IPS blocks malicious attacks from attempts to penetrate the network. If there is a risk of intrusion, the network connection is disconnected, or the user's session is blocked and access to IP addresses is stopped, account, service or application.

3   Problems of E-learning Systems

E-learning has been deeply integrated in modern educational process. It brings quali-tative changes to traditional views on educational purposes, replacing acquisition and reproduction of teacher-provided information with students' independent search and assessment; changes to educational content by providing new knowledge and skills not through one-dimensional gradual retelling of textbook materials but through hypertex-tual implementation of individual learning trajectories; changes to educational methods by establishing an educational network as an intermediary between students and faculty stuff (Fig. 2). There is no doubt that defining the notion of e-learning and its differences from other education types, revealing its psychological and pedagogical tendencies and developing classifications of e-learning systems are of great interest to pedagogical theory and practice.

Fig. 2. Sample of the virtual classroom in BigBlueButton's platform [7].

Some researchers believe a full-fledged e-learning system consists of three standard modules: the learning management system (LMS), educational content (e-courses) and authoring tools. LMS is generally understood as an online platform enabling to upload various formats of electronic educational materials, differentiate access to files, control learning progress and task performance, facilitate interaction between participant via network communication, create electronic educational materials [8]. Educational content is commonly understood as a set of functional data blocks, interconnected according to specified rules. Authoring tools are means to developing educational content (e-textbooks, presentations, simulations, video trainings, test) that is uploaded to the LMS. There are several types of authoring tools: course editors, presentation programs, tools for creating tests, surveys and questionnaires, screen capture software, online seminar tools. As we can see, this model represents e-learning as a hierarchy comprised of learning tools only. On the contrary, other theorists focus on qualitative attributes of e-learning: interactivity, hypermedia, mobility, variability, multifunctionality, availability. It is worth noting that these characteristics describe not only procedural but also content-related aspects of e-learning.

In Russia, the definition of e-learning is stipulated by law – organization of educational activities involving information, contained in databases and applicable to educational programs, and implementation of information-processing technologies, equipment and ICT networks maintaining transfer of said data through communication lines in order to establish interaction between students and faculty stuff. Given this definition, we can conclude that e-learning process adopts educational databases technologies; educational information processing equipment and technologies; network technologies transferring educational information via their channels; network technologies for inter-action between students and faculty stuff. This allows to classify e-learning resources, learning systems using computer equipment, distant learning systems and systems of indirect student-teacher interaction as e-learning systems. This definition focuses on diversity of e-learning systems and considers distant learning to be a type of electronic education [9].

Classification of electronic courses by their purpose distinguishes managing, demonstrational, generating, operating, controlling and modeling types (Fig. 3).

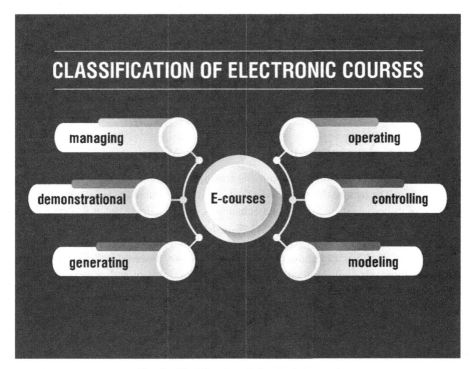

Fig. 3. Classification of electronic courses

Managing and demonstrational programs are aimed at managing learning process during classes, additional individual and group work. Demonstrational programs also give an opportunity to provide on-screen dynamic illustrations. Generating ones prepare a set of topic-related tasks, allowing to perform in-person tests or individual work, while providing each student with specific tasks according to their personal abilities. Operating programs give students an opportunity to set and perform tasks themselves via a computer, graphically illustrate studied notions, etc. Controlling ones are aimed at managing current or final examinations of students, helping to score assessment points, get feedback during the education, dynamically check performance of each students, compare study results with task difficulty, individual aspects of students, education rate, volume and type of study materials. Modeling programs imitate complex experiments and introduce students to research labs used by scientists, designers, architects, etc.

4 Improvement Data Protection Skills via Built-In Operating System Features

One of the basic ways to protect data is to use built-in OS functions. Modern operating systems have powerful built-in tools for security, authentication, authorization, audit of user activity, malfunction protection, cryptographic security of OS objects, network attack prevention. These functions are easy to apply and do not require profound technical skills from their users. This factor is important for teaching non-technical students, as federal standards for their education do not provision in-depth study of specialized disciplines that develop data protection knowledge skills.

Choosing the method of delivering topic materials requires determining objectives, number and format of classes. For instance, the main objective of the topic titled "Data protection via built-in operating system means" is to provide general knowledge on forms and methods of data protection via built-in OS tools, establish practical skills on cryptographic and password data protection, access rights differentiation and standard system recovery.

4.1 Data Protection via Built-In Operating System Means

Given these objectives, it seems reasonable to study this topic during a lecture and a practical class. The lecture should provide the basic description of OS functioning and an overview of its built-in data protection mechanisms. The practical class is recommended to be fully devoted to learning the simplest and most effective data protection tools, provided as part of OS delivery package.

In terms of methods for conducting the topical lecture, it seems sufficient to choose a classical approach, with gradual, structured material delivery and demonstration of specific examples. This is why we should give more attention to methods and order of practical study.

The key attribute of these practical learning methods is that during the class students must have full, unlimited access to all operating system resources, i.e., they should be given administrator rights. Thus, it seems necessary to isolate the system used for study from the main workstation system that is planned to be applied for performing educational tasks. The easiest way to establish a fully isolated system is to apply virtual machines.

Virtual machine technology helps to get rid of all restrictions and make experiments imitating system functioning as realistic as possible. Meanwhile, any mistakes that can be possibly made by students will not cause a malfunction of the workstation's main system. Thus, the abovementioned practical class should begin with launching the virtual machine and pre-installed operating system.

Before students start performing practical tasks, they need to be persuaded that the skills they are about to learn will help them in their professional daily activities.

The main structure of the practical class can be divided in four stages [10] (Fig. 4).

Fig. 4. Structure of the practical class.

At the first stage, students need to learn the basics of password protection via built-in OS mechanisms. To do this, they are supposed to perform the following tasks:

1. Create two additional user accounts in the system, giving them individual names and passwords.
2. Use one of the new accounts to enter the system and save several files in user's personal folders (e.g., My Documents folder) and in random location on the hard drive.
3. Enter the system from another account and try to access previously saved files.

Upon completing these tasks, students should individually make conclusion on efficiency of this protection method [11].

Modern operating systems give administrators vast opportunities for flexible setting of users' access to different computer resources. Detailed study of all administering options is time-consuming and requires specific skills. However, students do not need special knowledge for learning basic access differentiation.

4.2   Access Restriction Method

During the second stage, students are learning the access differentiation method that restricts access to certain files and folders in addition to default rules formed automatically when a new account is made [12].

When performing this task under the supervision of a faculty member, students make a list of users and their access rights (to read, save, change files etc.) to files or folder chosen in advance. The first thing that must be taken into consideration is that all activities at this stage are performed by the administrator, not a common user.

For consolidating obtained knowledge, students should enter the system in turns, trying to access said folders and files. The main conclusion students are supposed to make after this task is that access differentiation enables effective protection of data from common users working on a same computer, yet this mechanism cannot be used against users with administrator rights.

It is necessary to focus students' attention on the fact that an account password must be chosen responsibly. A password must contain at least 8 symbols, including uppercase and lowercase letters and special symbols, and should not be a derivative of existing words. Besides, students need to realize that even if only one user works on the computer, automatic login option should not be activated, because in this case any person, who turns on the computer, gets access to all files and parameters of this account [13].

4.3   Standard Encryption Function

For better protection of data against unsanctioned access, students are expected to learn built-in encryption functions. Before getting to practical tasks, students need to be briefly reminded about main principles of cryptographical transformation and special importance of encryption keys. For learning the built-in OS mechanism for folder and file encryption, students asked to enter the system from one of the accounts and then create a random file at any location, setting its encryption parameters in file properties.

For checking efficiency of this protection method, students can try to access encrypted files and folders as another user or as the administrator. While performing this task, it is necessary for them to understand that if files are copied or a user password is changed, access to encrypted files will become impossible without the key. This is why it is obligatory to save the key formed by the system after the encryption, which can also be password-protected.

Sometimes, operating system integrity is damaged due to malfunctions, malware or perpetrators' activities. The fourth stage of the class helps to develop skills on operating system recovery via built-in tools. At first, students need to realize that no operating system, no matter how sophisticated, is flawless and can guarantee perfectly stable computer functioning. There is always a possibility that an improper combination of hardware and user-installed software will lead to operating system failure [14].

Besides, operating system boot can become impossible because of users and third parties. IT specialists can help with its recovery, but this will require additional time and resources – which is unacceptable if the information required for user's work is stored on this computer only.

As Microsoft Windows is the most commonly used operating system in Russia, it seems reasonable to study recovery tools provided by this system during the class. At first, students should learn system recovery options that involve restore points. To do this, they create a restore point and then recover computer status on that moment via Windows GUI. Students need to pay attention that if properly set, operating system will create restore points automatically; however, in some cases it is reasonable for users to make their own points, e.g., while installing or updating drivers, setting up unknown software, etc. Besides, this method is applicable only in case of a successful OS boot.

Often, operating system cannot boot at all due to a failure, making it impossible to restore the system through Windows environment. This is why students need to learn additional ways to start this operating system. To do this, they reboot the system, activate the menu of additional options for OS boot and then, supervised by a faculty member, choose one of the following options.

Last Known Good Configuration option is the first mechanism that can be recommended in case of an OS failure. If selected, it loads the last configuration of device drivers and register, during which Windows demonstrated stable work. This configuration does not have a component that could have caused the malfunction: it will be deleted when the last known good configuration is being loaded, without a possibility for its recovery. If this option was unable to solve the malfunction, it seems worthy to run the OS in safe mode.

Safe mode launches the minimal number of services and drivers required for Windows to function. It helps to recover the system from a restore point, delete software that could have caused the malfunction, delete drivers, etc. Running Windows in safe mode also helps to find out, on which level the problem has appeared. Students also must take into consideration that if the system is working properly in safe mode, the malfunction was caused by bootable files.

Safe Mode with Command Prompt option enables to launch the command prompt instead of standard Windows graphical shell. This mode can be helpful in case of problems with the file manager and of utmost importance if the GUI is blocked by malware. When studying this mode, students should pay attention to two useful utilities than can be run from the command prompt: CHKDSK and SFC. The former checks hard drives for file system errors, including physical damages, and corrects them, while the latter checks system files and enables users to look for damages and restore damaged system files. It has to be noted that these utilities can be run only from the administrator's account.

After learning to run several types of safe modes, students need to familiarize with Windows Recovery Environment opportunities. To do this, they should choose Troubleshoot option in the boot menu. This environment contains many tools designed for restoring computer functionality, including means to automatic boot recovery, restore point recovery, system image recovery, RAM diagnostics and the command prompt option. It seems unreasonable to study all recovery tools during the class, yet some of them should be highlighted, so that students can understand which purpose each of these tools serves.

At the end of the class, a faculty member must summarize its results by making a group discussion of studied methods of data protection via built-in operating system mechanisms. This method of conducting practical classes allows students, who have no special knowledge on data security and recovery, to learn skills of password protection, access differentiation and basic built-in methods of data encryption and recovery, available at any computer device. These skills will be useful not only to specialists dealing with confidential information but also to everyone who use computer equipment in their professional activities.

It is also worth mentioning that while selecting tools for this practical class, preference was given to built-in software, pre-installed on every computer and provided by almost all operating systems. This will help future specialists to apply obtained skills in their professional activities, regardless of software they are going to use.

5   Conclusion

Data security issues are becoming more relevant every year. Many believe these problems can be solved through technical means only – by installing firewalls and antivirus software. However, the main prerequisite for reliable protection is awareness of existing threats and ways to counter them. This applies not only to IT specialists but to everyone dealing with various information systems in their professional activities. Famous "forewarned is forearmed" principle works in computer security as well: if a threat is promptly detected, many unpleasant consequences can be avoided. This is why security measures must be upheld at all network points, when any subjects are working with data.

References

1. He, J.: The Rules of Judicial Proof. In: Methodology of Judicial Proof and Presumption. Masterpieces of Contemporary Jurisprudents in China (2018). 280 p.
2. Bulgakova, E., Bulgakov, V., Trushchenkov, I., Vasilev, D., Kravets, E.: Big data in investigating and preventing crimes. In: Kravets, A. (eds.) Big Data-driven World: Legislation Issues and Control Technologies. Studies in Systems, Decision and Control, vol. 181, pp. 61–69 (2019)
3. Luo, Y., Cheung, S.S., Lazzeretti, R., Pignata, T., Barni, M.: Int. J. Inf. Secur. **17**, 261–278 (2018)
4. Kravets, A.G., Kravets, A.D., Korotkov, A.A.: Intelligent multi-agent systems generation. World Appl. Sci. J. **24**(24), 98–104 (2013)
5. Vasilev, D., Kravets, E., Naumov, Y., Bulgakova, E., Bulgakov, V.: Big data-driven world: legislation issues and control technologies. Stud. Syst. Decis. Control **181**, 249–258 (2019)
6. Dronova, O., Smagorinskiy, B.P., Yastrebov, V.: Counteraction to e-commerce crimes committed with the use of online stores. In: Kravets, A. (eds.) Big Data-driven World: Legislation Issues and Control Technologies. Studies in Systems, Decision and Control, vol. 181, pp. 121–131 (2019)
7. Sample of the virtual classroom in BigBlueButton's platform. https://support.bigbluebutton.org/hc/en-us/articles/1500005315982-Show-recordings-from-deleted-activities. Accessed 14 May 2021
8. Kravets, E., Birukov, S., Pavlik, M.: Remote investigative actions as the evidentiary information management system. In: Kravets, A.G. (ed.) Big Data-driven World: Legislation Issues and Control Technologies. SSDC, vol. 181, pp. 95–103. Springer, Cham (2019). https://doi.org/10.1007/978-3-030-01358-5_9

9. Bui, N.D., Kravets, A.G., Nguyen, T.A., Nguyen, L.T.T.: Tracking events in mobile device management system. In: IISA 2015 - 6th International Conference on Information, Intelligence, Systems and Applications, article № 7388127 (2016)

10. Saltykov, S., Rusyaeva, E., Kravets, A.G.: Typology of scientific constructions as an instrument of conceptual creativity. In: Kravets, A., Shcherbakov, M., Kultsova, M., Shabalina, O. (eds.) CIT&DS 2015. CCIS, vol. 535, pp. 41–57. Springer, Cham (2015). https://doi.org/10. 1007/978-3-319-23766-4_4

11. Klimmt, C.: Virtual worlds as a regulatory challenge: a user perspective. In: Cornelius, K., Hermann, D. (eds.) Virtual Worlds and Criminality, pp. 1–18 (2011)

12. Kravets, A.G., Al-Ashval, M.: Mobile corporate networks security control. In: 2016 International Siberian Conference on Control and Communications, SIBCON 2016 - Proceedings, article № 7491811 (2016)

13. Kopyltsov, A.V., Kravets, A.G., Abrahamyan, G.V., Katasonova, G.R., Sotnikov, A.D., Atayan, A.M.: Algorithm of estimation and correction of wireless telecommunications quality. In: 2018 9th International Conference on Information, Intelligence, Systems and Applications, IISA 2018, article № 8633620 (2018)

14. Kravets, A.G., Skorobogatchenko, D.A., Salnikova, N.A., Orudjev, N.Y., Poplavskaya, O.V.: The traffic safety management system in urban conditions based on the C4.5 algorithm. In: Moscow Workshop on Electronic and Networking Technologies, MWENT 2018 - Proceedings, 2018-March, article № 8337254, pp. 1–7 (2018)

Intelligent Technologies in Social Engineering. Intelligent Assistive Technologies: Software Design and Application

User Experience Analysis Based on a Virtual Mark-up Approach

Anton Ivaschenko$^{(\boxtimes)}$ and Arkadiy Krivosheev

Samara State Technical University, Molodogvardeyskaya, 244, Samara, Russia

Abstract. The paper presents some results of interactive user interfaces implementation in practice. Virtual mark-up approach is used to classify the professional status of the users and respectively adapt the user interface. New software components are introduced as a part of Augmented Reality system that capture the user's behavior, compare it to the typical patterns and generate virtual elements when necessary. The resulting solution is capable of providing alerts and notifications for novice users and hiding the redundant information for experts and thus personalizing the user interface. Artificial neural network provides classification based on the results of user performance in script execution according to pre-defined scenarios. The proposed approach is illustrated by an example of electrical meters surveying mobile application. Research results illustrate the possibility to improve and personalize the augmented reality user interfaces based on the analysis of user activity.

Keywords: Personalization · User interface · Augmented reality · Artificial neural networks · Cyber-physical systems

1 Introduction

Modern user interfaces design and implementation remains one of the challenging problems nowadays. Application of Augmented Reality allows improving the functionality and attractiveness of software applications but at the same time causes new challenges for usability and use experience consideration.

This paper continues the research in the area of interactive user interfaces development. On the basis of accented visualization concept there is proposed a virtual mark-up approach that utilizes artificial neural networks for user's experience classification and adaptation of the user interfaces to provide better usability. The details can be found below in this paper.

2 State of the Art

Modern theory of computer user interfaces (UI) design and development cover a number of problem domains including software development, visual representation, social computing and philosophy of computer-human interaction [1, 2].

© Springer Nature Switzerland AG 2021
A. G. Kravets et al. (Eds.): CIT&DS 2021, CCIS 1448, pp. 575–586, 2021.
https://doi.org/10.1007/978-3-030-87034-8_42

Considering the powerful tools of web and mobile UI implementation, IT companies try to organize the information space around the user in the most comfortable, easy to use, and entertaining manner. UI design is used as an engine for market competition and targeted advertising of many other innovations and services, making it a mandatory component of any new solution and system.

These trends are developing under the concept of the user experience (UX) design, which studies the process of supporting user behavior through usability, usefulness, and desirability provided in the interaction with a product [3, 4]. It extends the theory of computer-human interaction in a certain way and provides useful methods and technologies for software developers to deliver convenient solutions.

A new technology of Augmented Reality (AR) brings new possibilities and new challenges in this sphere [5–8]. AR solutions are not limited with the "rectangular frames", consider the user's mobility (e.g. it should not make the user walk backward) and physical constrains, and require user immersion in experience. These and other features are not fully studied at the moment, therefore many users experience difficulties and discomfort when using AR based devices. Based on a number of efficient applications of AR solutions in practice [9–12] there can be specified a set of recommendations on how to achieve the benefits and provide long and efficient maintenance of AR interfaces and based on them IT solutions.

According to the definitions and role of Augmented Reality its efficient use in practice is closely related to the users' creativity analysis and support [13, 14]. Modern software requires creativity to be developed, but at the same time is perceived as a source of inspiration. The capability of modern software solutions to excite the creativity of the users becomes in demand. The main task of user creativity stimulation is performed by the user interface. The role of user interfaces in creativity support is discussed in [15, 16].

Special aspects of computer-human interaction in cyber-physical systems used for decision-making support are studied in [17, 18]. It is proposed to place the user inside the "loop of computer-human interaction" and adapt the user interface considering the features of user perception. To provide this possibility the system should consolidate related data in solid virtual scenes [19].

In such a way the user becomes involved into an interactive process of data processing and visualization not only in the role of visual services consumer, but also as a designer of surrounding mixed reality. Thereby modern user interface based on Augmented Reality include multiple active virtual and real objects [20] that interact and influence each other by generating impact and receiving feedback. As a result both humans and software systems develop the skills of learning and adaptation that can be implemented on a technical level using the modern technologies of Artificial Intelligence [21, 22].

It is important to note that improving and personalization of Augmented Reality User Interfaces is an effective facility to provide and stimulate creativity [23], which is highly demanded in most software systems for cooperative interaction and decision-making support.

This paper presents the results of implementation and analysis of machine learning implementation as a part of virtual mark-up method for user experience analysis and support. The approach is based on a concept of accented visualization [24, 25] and continues the research initially presented in [26]. Starring with the synopsis of the proposed method the paper presents an intelligent solution for the virtual mark-up in augmented reality.

3 Virtual Mark-up Approach

The proposed approach is based on a concept of accented or focused visualization. The idea is to formalize the entities of <focus, context, and overlay context> for each user. Focus points on the object that is processed by the user or attracts his attention. The context describes the current situation and considers the history of previous actions and events that have led to it. Overlay context includes virtual entities (textual items, marks, or highlights) that attract user attention to the required scene objects when needed.

The method allows changing the user focus to target values using the overlay context as a management tool. Therefore it refers to the soft manipulation techniques and provides higher user involvement and independence. These features increase the usability of AR based systems and contribute to their implementation in practice.

The method can be used to identify the deviations of the user's focus for his/her experience analysis.

Generalized AR scene contains virtual and real objects and control elements $w_{i,k}$, where $i = 1..N_k^w$ is the number of an element and $k = 1..N^s$ is the scene number.

We describe such a scene as:

$$s_k = \{w_{i,k}\}. \tag{1}$$

Attention of the viewer at a certain point in time is given to one or several objects. It can be captured by tracking the actions in the user interface or determined using specific censors, e.g. eye-tracker. Each fixed change of the user's attention can be described by an event represented by a Boolean variable:

$$v_{i,j,k} = v_{i,j,k}\left(w_{i,k}, t'_{i,j,k}\right) = \{0, 1\}. \tag{2}$$

The sequence of these events represents the user's focus.

The required operating work process is formulated in a standard scenario:

$$c_{k,n} = \{e_{i,k,n,m}\}, \tag{3}$$

where $e_{i,k,n,m} = e_{i,k,n,m}(w_{i,k}, t_{i,k,n,m}, \Delta t_{i,k,n,m})$ is an expected event of the user's required focus, $t_{i,k,n,m}$ - the moment of focus attraction to the object or control $w_{i,k}$ according to the scenario $c_{k,n}$, $\Delta t_{i,k,n,m}$ - the corresponding possible deviation.

Effective process requires correspondence of $e_{i,k,n,m}$ and $v_{i,j,k}$, which means minimum of the issues of unprocessed scenario stages:

$$K(c_{k,n}) = \sum_{i,m} e_{i,k,n,m} \cdot \left(1 - \delta\left(\sum_{j} v_{i,j,k} \cdot \delta\left(t'_{i,j,k} \in (t_{i,k,n,m}, t_{i,k,n,m} + \Delta t_{i,k,n,m})\right) \geq 1\right)\right) \to 0, \tag{4}$$

where $\delta(x) = \begin{cases} 1, x = true; \\ 0, x = false. \end{cases}$

This statement means that each $e_{i,k,n,m}$ should receive at least one $v_{i,j,k}$. It can be used to differentiate experienced users from the novice and adapt user interface for newcomers.

Virtual mark-up approach is illustrated by Fig. 1. Initial data described the current context that contains a combination of real objects and virtual entities and the user's focus, which can be determined on the basis of analysis of his/her activity and attention. On the basis of this information the Matcher module considers several options and generates an overlay layer with necessary hints and active elements. Identification of the user professionalism at early stages helps improving the user interface by generation of hints and alerts when required.

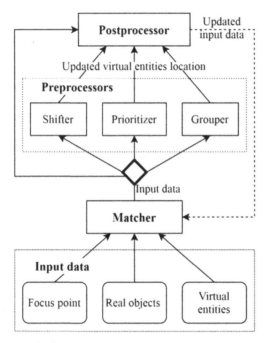

Fig. 1. Virtual mark-up solution architecture

Application of the proposed approach in practice was performed in a distributed system for electric meters surveying using handheld mobile devices for photographing and image recognition of the readings. This is an example of cyber-physical system: photos are taken by human operators using a mobile device with Augmented Reality application and later processed by an artificial neural network. Both are characterized by high uncertainty and require implementation of cooperation of human and software components in united information space.

Solution User Interface is presented in Fig. 2.

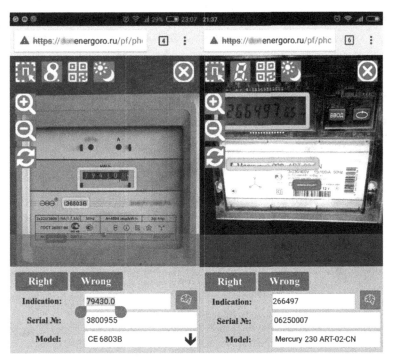

Fig. 2. Examples of meters reading recognition

In this case we have a web interface of the system for collecting and transmitting meter readings. The use of the system is logged, the time is not particularly taken into account, since in places with poor Internet coverage, and there can be long time delays. For several training approaches in different cities, we have records of the actions of professional (experienced) users. And there are a lot of records of actions of non-professional (ordinary) users.

According to the customer's feedback, we understand that it is difficult for users to use the system due to the interface. The following approach illustrate how we can identify inexperienced users in order to show them further tips on the interface or on re-referral to training.

4 Implementation

The proposed approach was implemented as a part of mobile application for electrical meters surveying. The controls of AR based used interface were marked according to Fig. 3.

To solve the problem, a dataset of 400 records of the actions of experienced users and 1000 records of actions of inexperienced users was collected. To stratify the resulting set, it was decided to generate 600 records of experienced users by statistically processing real records, then constructing a Markov chain and creating a chain of user actions based on the resulting chain. The resulting Markov chain is shown in Fig. 4, additional

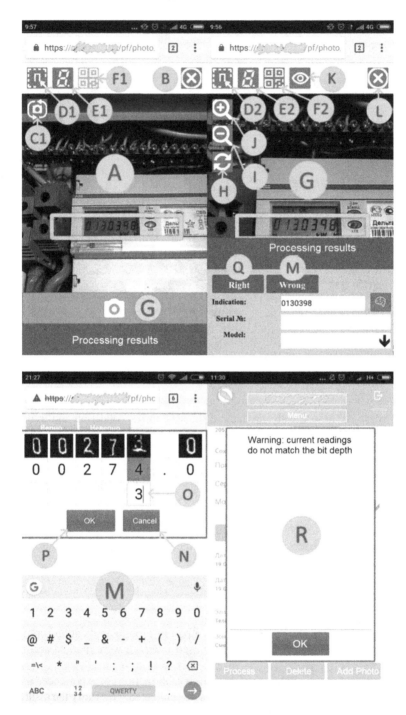

Fig. 3. User interface objects

information on actions is given in Table 1. As a result, 2000 records were obtained, which were divided into a training set (1600 records) and a test set (400 records).

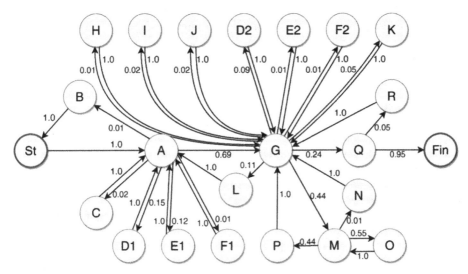

Fig. 4. Experienced user actions

Table 1. Types of the transfer.

Source node	Description	Target node	Description
St	Start screen	J	Scaling "+"
A	Photo creation screen	K	Tariff selection (day/night/general)
B	Return to start screen	L	Return to the photo creation ("A")
C	Main/front camera selector	M	Screen for adjusting photo processing
D1, D2	Manual selection on the photo/video stream of the zone with readings	N	Cancel correction of results
E1, E2	Type of counter selection	O	Adjustment of results
F1, F2	QR code search	P	Confirmation of the adjustment
G	Processing results	Q	Confirmation of photo processing
H	Cyclic rotation of a photo	R	Error screen
I	Scaling "−"	Fin	Finish

To solve the classification problem, a neural network was created, consisting of two recurrent layers with long short-term memory (LSTM) and two fully connected layers. After each recurrent layer for regularization, there is an exclusion layer with cutting off 20% of the data during training. The network architecture is shown in Fig. 4.

The training took place in a Python virtual environment using Keras version 2.3.1 and Tensorflow version 1.15.2 packages. "Adam" was chosen as the optimization algorithm for training, the binary cross entropy "binary_crossentropy" was chosen as the loss function, the values of the other parameters were left by default. The results of training the neural network over 20 epochs are shown in Fig. 5.

One can notice that the results stabilize after 5 epochs, the precision of determining inexperienced users reaches 69.1%, and the recall is 84%. The reason of insufficient results is that the actions of experienced and novice users may be similar, which makes it impossible to classify the user with a high probability by one record of actions. The solution to the problem is to classify several records of user actions at once, and calculate the final result based on the largest number of results on these records. The results of such an experiment are shown in Figs. 6 and 7.

Classification based on 7 records leads to an increase in accuracy and completeness up to 85% and 99.5%, respectively, i.e. after a couple of hours of user work, it is possible to determine the level of his knowledge of the system with 85% accuracy and, if necessary, issue a hint to the interface or send a message to the system administrator about the need to additionally train this user.

Layer (type)	Output Shape	Param #
lstm_1 (LSTM)	(None, 128, 50)	14800
dropout_1 (Dropout)	(None, 128, 50)	0
lstm_2 (LSTM)	(None, 50)	20200
dropout_2 (Dropout)	(None, 50)	0
dense_1 (Dense)	(None, 50)	2550
dense_2 (Dense)	(None, 1)	51

Total params: 37,601
Trainable params: 37,601
Non-trainable params: 0

Fig. 5. Neural network architecture

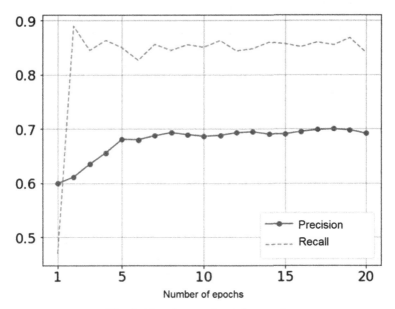

Fig. 6. Neural network training results

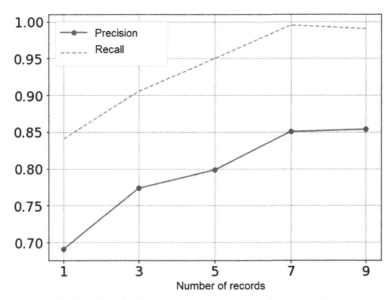

Fig. 7. Classification improvement based on history analysis

By analogy with experienced users, a Markov chain was built for inexperienced users in order to study their behavior and find key differences, see Fig. 8.

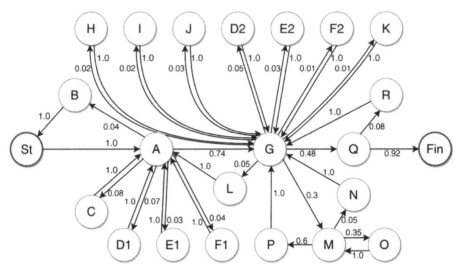

Fig. 8. Novice user actions

Let us consider the screen A. Comparing to experienced users in equal conditions, inexperienced ones use the C camera rotation button 4 times more often; use the D1 highlighting button 2 times less often; use the E1 counter type selection button 4 times less often; and use the F1 QR code search button 4 times less often. Also, the chance of an inexperienced user to proceed from this screen to the next G screen or return to the St screen is slightly higher than that of an experienced user. This suggests that inexperienced users tend to learn the secondary features of the system.

For the G screen the situation is broadly the same. Inexperienced users are 1.5–2 times more likely to flip the H images and use the J zoom; specify the D2 display area twice less often; specify the K tariff type 5 times less often; and specify the E2 type of meter 3 times more often. It is worth noting that the choice of the type of meter, the tariff and the selection of the indication area has the greatest impact on the recognition result among the other options available to the user. This means that the rare use of these actions by inexperienced users leads to worse results. Even so, inexperienced users are less likely to introduce corrections using the M screen even when needed, and the likelihood of moving from the G screen to the Fin screen is 2 times higher than that of experienced users.

Summing up the subtotal, we can see that inexperienced users tend to finish working with the program as soon as possible, even at the cost of an incorrect result. The main problem is that they do not know the key functional on which the obtaining of a high-quality recognition result depends.

The proposed solution gives the possibility to identify these users and help them understand the interface. These results illustrate the possibility to improve and personalize the augmented reality user interfaces based on the analysis of user activity.

5 Conclusion

Modern intelligent technologies can significantly improve the usability of user interfaces. Classification of the users based on the analysis of their behavior can be an advantageous instrument for user interfaces adaptation and personalization especially in such areas like Augmented Reality, where the knowledge on usability patterns and requirements is still limited due to a number of reasons.

Application of accented visualization concept and virtual mark-up approach is one of the promising solutions for user interfaces personalization. It allows classification of the professional status of the users and adapting the user interface. Next steps are concerned with an extension of a methodology practical use in real projects, probation and testing of the developments in practice.

Acknowledgment. The paper was supported by RFBR, according to the research project № 20-08-00797.

References

1. Norman, D.A.: Emotion & Design: Attractive things work better. Interact. Mag. **ix**(4), 36–42 (2002)
2. Soegaard, M., Dam, R.F.: The encyclopedia of human-computer interaction, 2nd Ed. Interaction Design Foundation (2014)
3. Schmidt, A., Etches, A.: Useful, usable, desirable: applying user experience design to your library. ALA Techsource, Chicago (2014). 168 p.
4. Marcus, A. (ed.): DUXU 2015. LNCS, vol. 9186. Springer, Cham (2015). https://doi.org/10.1007/978-3-319-20886-2
5. Babich, N.: UX design principles for augmented reality (2020). https://xd.adobe.com/ideas/principles/emerging-technology/ux-design-principles-for-augmented-reality/. Accessed 24 Apr 2021
6. Stumpp, S., Knopf, T., Michelis, D.: User experience design with augmented reality (AR), pp. 1032–1040 (2019). https://doi.org/10.34190/ECIE.19.019
7. Javornik, A.: Augmented reality: research agenda for studying the impact of its media characteristics on consumer behaviour. J. Retail. Consum. Serv. **30**, 252–261 (2016)
8. Ejaz, A., Ali, S.A., Ejaz, M.Y., Siddiqui, F.A.: Graphic user interface design principles for designing Augmented Reality applications. Int. J. Adv. Comput. Sci. Appl. **10**(2), 209–216 (2019)
9. Schmalstieg, D., Reitmayr, G.: The world as a user interface: augmented reality for ubiquitous computing. In: Gartner, G., Cartwright, W., Peterson, M.P. (eds.) Location Based Services and TeleCartography. Lecture Notes in Geoinformation and Cartography. Springer, Heidelberg (2007). https://doi.org/10.1007/978-3-540-36728-4_28
10. Ke, C., Kang, B., Chen, D., Li, X.: An Augmented Reality based application for equipment maintenance. Lect. Notes Comput. Sci. **3784**, 836–841 (2005)
11. Navab, N.: Developing killer apps for industrial Augmented Reality. Technical University of Munich, IEEE Computer Graphics and Applications IEEE Computer Society (2004)
12. Singh, M., Singh, M.P.: Augmented reality interfaces. Natural web interfaces. IEEE Internet Comput. **17**, 66–70 (2013)

13. Kravets, A., Groumpos, P., Shcherbakov, M., Kultsova, M.: Creativity in intelligent technologies and data science third conference. In: Proceedings, Part I: Third Conference, CIT&DS (2019). https://doi.org/10.1007/978-3-030-29743-5.(2019)

14. Volkmar, G., Muender, T., Wenig, D., Malaka, R.: Evaluation of natural user interfaces in the creative industries. In: CHI 2020 Extended Abstracts, Honolulu, HI, USA, pp. 1–8 (2020). https://doi.org/10.1145/3334480.3375201

15. Zabramski, S., Ivanova, V., Yang, G., Gadima, N., Leepraphantkul, R.: The effects of GUI on users' creative performance in computerized drawing. In: ACM International Conference Proceeding Series. pp. 142–151 (2013)

16. Kim, J., Bouchard, C., Omhover, J.-F., Aoussat, A.: Designing a graphical interface for creativity support tools for designers: a case study. Int. J. Web Eng. Technol. **7**, 173–199 (2012)

17. Holzinger, A.: Extravaganza tutorial on hot ideas for interactive knowledge discovery and data mining in biomedical informatics. In: Ślęzak, D., Tan, A.-H., Peters, J.F., Schwabe, L. (eds.) BIH 2014. LNCS (LNAI), vol. 8609, pp. 502–515. Springer, Cham (2014). https://doi.org/10.1007/978-3-319-09891-3_46

18. Holzinger, A.: Interactive machine learning for health informatics: when do we need the human-in-the-loop? Brain Informatics **3**(2), 119–131 (2016). https://doi.org/10.1007/s40708-016-0042-6

19. Julier, S., Livingston, M.A., Swan J.E., Bailot, Y., Brown D.G.: Adaptive user interfaces in augmented reality. In: Proceedings of the Software Technology for Augmented Reality Systems, pp. 1–8 (2003)

20. Pechenkin, V., Korolev, M., Kuznetsova, K., Piminov, D.: Analysis of three-dimensional scene visual characteristics based on virtual modeling and parameters of surveillance sensors. In: Dolinina, O., Brovko, A., Pechenkin, V., Lvov, A., Zhmud, V., Kreinovich, V. (eds.) ICIT 2019. SSDC, vol. 199, pp. 552–562. Springer, Cham (2019). https://doi.org/10.1007/978-3-030-12072-6_45

21. Egmont-Petersen, M., de Ridder, D., Handels, H.: Image processing with neural networks – a review. Pattern Recogn. **35**(10), 2279–2301 (2002)

22. Goodfellow, I., Bengio, Y., Courville, A., Bengio, Y.: Deep learning, vol. 1, p. 925. MIT Press, Cambridge (2016)

23. Dhengre, S., Mathur, J., Oghazian, F., Tan, X., Mccomb, C.: Towards enhanced creativity in interface design through automated usability evaluation. In: Eleventh International Conference on Computational Creativity ICCC20, pp. 366–369 (2020)

24. Ivaschenko, A., Sitnikov, P., Katirkin, G.: Accented visualization in digital industry applications. In: Dolinina, O., Brovko, A., Pechenkin, V., Lvov, A., Zhmud, V., Kreinovich, V. (eds.) ICIT 2019. SSDC, vol. 199, pp. 366–378. Springer, Cham (2019). https://doi.org/10.1007/978-3-030-12072-6_30

25. Ivaschenko, A., Kolsanov, A., Nazaryan, A.: Focused visualization in surgery training and navigation. In: Arai, K., Kapoor, S., Bhatia, R. (eds.) SAI 2018. AISC, vol. 858, pp. 537–547. Springer, Cham (2019). https://doi.org/10.1007/978-3-030-01174-1_40

26. Ivaschenko, A., Orlov, S., Krivosheev, A.: Accented visualization user interfaces in augmented reality. In: Kravets, A.G., Bolshakov, A.A., Shcherbakov, M.V. (eds.) Cyber-Physical Systems. SSDC, vol. 350, pp. 213–223. Springer, Cham (2021). https://doi.org/10.1007/978-3-030-67892-0_18

Mobile Interface Personalization During the Application Usage Based on Patterns Ontology Model for People with Special Needs

Anastasiia Potseluiko[1]([✉]) and Ekaterina Azarova[2]

[1] Volgograd State Technical University, Volgograd, Russia
[2] Volgograd State University, Volgograd, Russia

Abstract. The paper is devoted to the problem of interface adaptation for people with special needs during interface usage. After creating the interface according to the user's health problems and device characteristics the interface can be improved by applying interface patterns. This work evolves our previous researches on the development of adaptive user interfaces and presents the second part of the interface adaptation algorithm. Much attention in this work was given to the analysis of existing pattern-based adaptation methods, patterns classification and recommendations to their application. The second part of the algorithm was developed and described based on the ontological representation of the interface patterns and the information about user's device and user's behaviour and preferences. The set of adaptation rules was presented, an example of the adaptation mechanism reaction on user's behaviour was described. In the paper, we implemented the set of patterns to be applicable and the corresponding ontology set of rules.

Keywords: Assistive technologies · Adaptive user interface · Mobile applications · Ontological user modeling · Interface patterns · User behaviour

1 Introduction

According to the worldwide statistics [2] nearly 20% people in the world have some kind of disability. Despite the fact that the WHO prognoses the increasing of people with disabilities amount, the quality of their life can be improved with the help of the IT-sphere. Unfortunately, the mobile applications, web sites and desktop applications mostly are not user-friendly to people with disabilities. Developers often are not aware of the problems which can be caused by inappropriate usage of interface creation techniques. Also, the problem of post-interface adaptation is ignored.

The problem of collecting the best recommendations for interface creation was tried to being solved by W3C organization [1]. The W3C guide contains the set of best practices for creating adaptive interfaces and advises how to improve

© Springer Nature Switzerland AG 2021
A. G. Kravets et al. (Eds.): CIT&DS 2021, CCIS 1448, pp. 587–597, 2021.
https://doi.org/10.1007/978-3-030-87034-8_43

the accessibility of the existing interfaces for people with disabilities of different types.

Large software companies such as Google [3] encourage to make applications more accessible and provide special features for people with disabilities in Google Chrome, Android and YouTube. Microsoft [7], Apple [4] and Android [6] have their own guides on how to develop accessible software with their tools and libraries.

Despite the fact that accessibility plays an important role in the software development process not all of the developers apply the recommendations of the leading companies to their own application creation. The main goal of our research is to facilitate the process of adaptive interfaces development and further interface usage by implementing the interface adaptation method based on the ontology model, set of adaptation rules and the method of user's behaviour tracking.

2   State of the Art

In recent years accessibility became an essential part of software development. The leading companies such as Google, Apple, Facebook and Microsoft promote the accessibility to be a must-have part of any application. Since interface adaptation is not a trivial issue different approaches were created to increase accessibility. In our research we divided the approaches into four groups:

- Methods based on the ontology model.
- Methods based on the interface patterns.
- Methods based on the context information collection.
- Side software solutions.

The first group of methods is described in papers [13, 19]. A distinctive feature of this interface adaptation method is the usage of an ontological model which is used to store personalized information. The authors used an ontological model to support decision making in the context of the user interface. A user profile is an ontology or a set of ontologies of areas associated with a user: user diseases, preferences, device characteristics, characteristics of an adaptive interface, etc. Authors also used a set of semantic rules, which allowed them to solve the interface adaptation problem by reasoning on the semantic network.

Next group of methods works with a set of patterns. A pattern, according to the W3C recommendations [1], is a set of best practices that have been proven to be effective in solving a problem. Practice in the context of an interface can mean the appearance of an interface element, its characteristics, how an application or its components react to user actions. Each pattern can be represented as a combination of three components: the name of the pattern, the problem that the pattern solves, and the solution to the problem.

In the developed software MyUI [12], the authors propose to use 4 types of patterns: main patterns, interaction patterns, general patterns and switching patterns.

In contrast to this approach, software [19] implements interface patterns in the form of an ontological model. Patterns in this case are divided into two types: general patterns and interaction patterns.

The last group of the methods uses the special kind of the information about a user and an environment. The example of usage the context information is presented in the work [20]. In order to make the interface more user-friendly, the application can use more than the information entered by the user. The second way to obtain information is from the environment or by reading device parameters.

The researchers suggest taking into account the parameters of users' devices, their experience with the application, as well as external factors. Each of the pieces of contextual information is presented in the form of a model: a user model, an environment model, and a device model. This approach is useful when additional information can be extracted from the user's environment or about his device. Using this approach alone for adapting interfaces for people with disabilities is not enough and can be used as an addition to the main method.

3   Strategies of an Interface Adaptation

An important part of customizing a user interface is a strategy for responding to changes in the user context. It should be noted that the user is always placed in a certain context while using mobile applications. According to [21], each context has its own specific aspects, which can be divided into four categories:

- Aspects related to the user (preferences, goals and objectives on the interface, physical condition, emotional state, etc.).
- Technical aspects (screen resolution, network connection, browser type, battery power, etc.).
- Environmental aspects (location, lighting, noise, etc.).
- Social aspects (privacy rules, collaboration, etc.).

When any of the aspects is changed, the context of using the interface also changes. Interface adaptation can also be carried out using various methods:

- Change at the presentation level of the interface by changing the parameters of the interface elements (color, size, position of objects, font size, etc.).
- Change at the level of behavior by changing the type or structure of navigation, activating or deactivating interface elements.
- Change at the content level of the interface by adjusting the text, its semantic content, changing images or explanatory inscriptions on the interface.

Various adaptation strategies are possible and can be classified according to the impact they have on the user interface:

- Saving: for example, simple scaling of user interface elements.
- Rearrangement: for example, changing of interface layout.

– Simplification of understanding: for example, the same interface element, but with a changed presentation.
– Enlargement (also called progressive enhancement): for example, adding new interface elements for the convenience of the user.
– Shrinking (also known as gradual degradation): for example, removing unnecessary or unused interface components.

In our research we did the patterns classification according to above-mentioned grouping. This classification helped to specify the problem of patterns applicability and led to the patterns conflicts resolving algorithm.

4   Patterns Ontology Model

During our long-time research the set of ontologies were created and described in papers [8,9,11,18].

The meta-ontology presented on picture Fig. 1 was extended and now contains the Pattern ontology. Pattern is selected by user directly of with the help of tracking the user context information. Selected pattern impacts on the user interface.

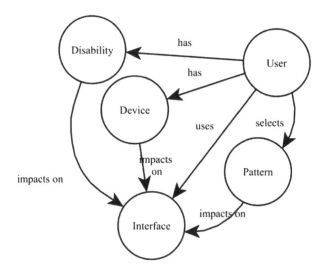

Fig. 1. The meta-ontology model.

The newly created ontology which contains the information about interface patterns is presented on the picture Fig. 2 below.

The patterns ontology can be defined as follows:

$$O_P = <C_P, InstP, R_P, I_P>, \tag{1}$$

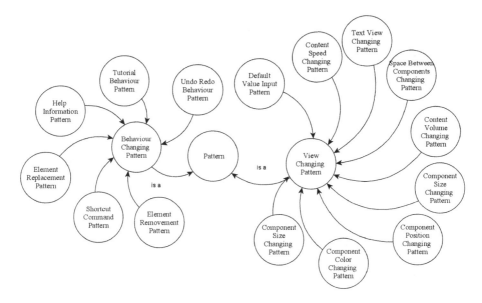

Fig. 2. The patterns ontology model.

where C_P – finite set of concepts of the patterns ontology; $Inst_P$ – a finite set of patterns ontology instances, $Inst = \varnothing$; R_P – a finite set of relations between the patterns ontology components; I_P – a finite set of interpretation rules.

Patterns in the ontology model are separated into two huge groups. The first group contains patterns that are only changing the view of the interface elements. This group of patterns implements the first three adaptation strategies and does not have any impact on an interface element functionality and behaviour. The second group contains patterns that are changing the behaviour of the interface elements. This group of patterns corresponds with the two last adaptation strategies: enlargement and shrinking. Each pattern has its own index of impact. The higher indexed pattern brings more significant changes to a user interface. It means that the highest indexes will have patterns that implement the last two strategies.

5   Example of Patterns Representation

Each group of patterns contains pattern instances. Each instance is connected with corresponding interface elements. The examples of actual patterns instances representations from both pattern groups are presented below.

The first example of pattern is the font resizing pattern. The description of the pattern is represented in the Table 1.

The ontological representation of the pattern is shown on picture below (Fig. 3). The interface contains two textual interface elements. Each text element has the current font size. Each instance of a text element is tracked using

Table 1. The example of the font resizing pattern

Pattern	Font resizing pattern
Problem	The user may have difficulty reading or entering text at the set size entering text at the set size
Pattern group	Text view changing pattern
Context (condition)	$2 <= visualimpairment < 3$ or user selects the appropriate setting
Solution	Allow to increase font size up to 200'%'
Realization	Get every text component of connected UI element and increase the font size

a text resizing pattern that contains the current font size, as well as two restrictions on the font size - the font size cannot be less than 8 and greater than 32 according to the W3C recommendation [1].

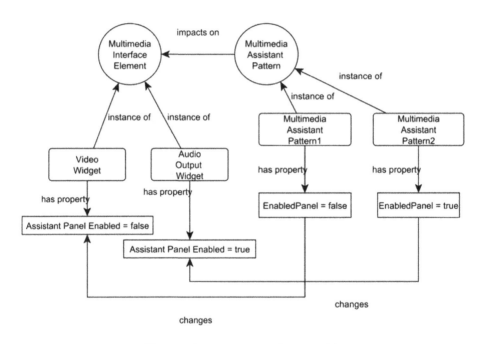

Fig. 3. The patterns ontology model.

The corresponding Jena rule is presented below (2):

$$[increaseTextFontSizePattern : (?usermain : hasNecessityToIncreaseText$$
$$dis : VisionDisability), (?usermain : hasInterface?interface),$$
$$(?interfaceinterface : hasElement?element),$$
$$(?elementrdf : type$$
$$interface : ActualTextContentElement) \rightarrow$$
$$\rightarrow (?elementinterface : hasTextSize?newTextSizeValue)] \quad (2)$$

where $?user, ?interface, ?element, ?newTextSizeValue$ – Jena variables; $main : hasDiseaseProblem, main : hasInterface, dis : VisionDisability; interface : hasElement, interface : hasTextSize, rdf : type$– ontology relations with ontology prefixes; $ActualTextContentElement$ – ontology instance of $Interface$ domain.

The second example of pattern is the multimedia assistance pattern. The description of the pattern is represented in the Table 2.

Table 2. The example of pattern description

Pattern	Multimedia assistance pattern
Problem	The user wants to play, pause or stop the playback of multimedia content
Pattern group	Help information pattern
Context (condition)	For all users or user selects the appropriate setting
Solution	Add 'Stop', 'Restart' and 'Play' buttons to all multimedia interface elements
Realization	Get all the multimedia elements of the interface and activate the panel with buttons to control the content of the elements

The ontological representation of the pattern is shown on picture below (Fig. 4). The interface contains two elements of the multimedia type: video and audio. Each widget has a property for activating a panel with buttons "Stop", "Restart" and "Play". Each instance of a media widget is tracked and can be modified using a pattern. According to the [1] each multimedia element can be paused, stopped or replayed again.

The corresponding Jena rule is shown below (3):

$$[multimediaAssistantPattern : (?usermain : hasInterface?interface),$$
$$(?interfaceinterface : hasElement?element),$$
$$(?elementrdf : type$$
$$interface : ActualMultimediaContentElement) \rightarrow$$
$$\rightarrow (?interfaceinterface : hasMultimediaControlButtons?element)] \quad (3)$$

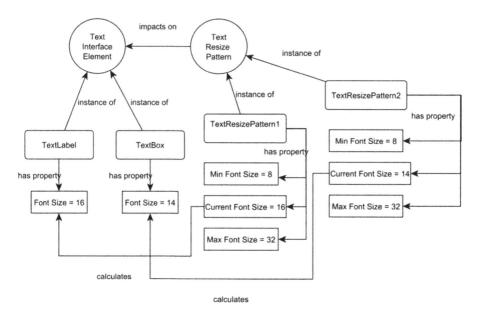

Fig. 4. The patterns ontology model.

where *?user*, *?interface*, *?element* – Jena variables; *main* : *hasInterface*, *dis* : *Deafness*; *interface* : *hasElement*, *interface* : *hasMultimediaControl Buttons*, *rdf* : *type*– ontology relations with ontology prefixes; *ActualMulti mediaContentElement* – ontology instance of *Interface* domain.

6   Algorithm for Pattern Applying

A simplified process for responding to changes in the user context is shown in the figure below Fig. 5. The goal of the main algorithm is to determine the type of context changes, resolve conflicts, choose an adaptation strategy, and control possible interface degradation.

At the first stage, the adaptation system receives an event that was generated and sent from the application. This event can be, for example, an event about changing user preferences about the font size, an event about connecting a trackball, an event about changing the battery level, etc. First, the system determines to which category a given event should be categorized. The next step is to check the possibility of inconsistencies, for example, the user wants to use a green font, but the interface has many elements with a green background.

If conflicts were found, then it is necessary to discard potential changes in the event that a conflict arose with higher priority aspects. If a conflict has arisen with less priority aspects, then the changes adopted when taking them into account should be revised or discarded if revision is impossible. In case of a

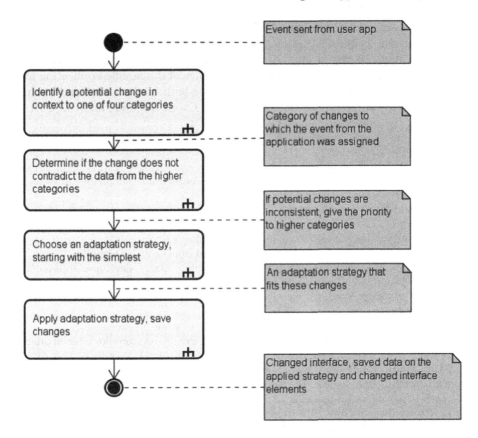

Fig. 5. The general method of patterns appliance.

conflict of changes in equal aspects, a user should select the preferred adaptation option by his own.

After determining the aspect of new changes and resolving conflicts, an adaptation strategy that has the lowest level of interference on the interface must be chosen. For example, if the user reads the text on the screen for too long, the application can try increasing the font size instead of immediately changing the textual representation on the screen to the voice of the text.

After applying the adaptation strategy, the application saves the current state of the interface, the interface elements affected by the adaptation, as well as the strategy and the aspect that led to the changes in the interface. On the next circle the ontology database is working with updated data.

7   Conclusion and Future Work

The ontology model of interface patterns introduced. The set of rules for pattern applicability was described. The main principle of patterns prioritization was developed based on the classification of the adaptation strategies.

Next, we are planning to test the patterns ontology model on consistency and resolving the conflict situations. The algorithm for saving the user context information must be tested also. In the near future, it is planned to apply the developed approach for adaptation of user interface of the mobile application for support of mobility and communication of people with intellectual and development disabilities in rehabilitation centres in the Czech Republic and the USA.

References

1. W3C official website, World Wide Web Consortium. http://www.w3.org/standards/webdesign/accessibility/
2. The World Bank official website, The World Bank. http://www.worldbank.org/en/topic#1
3. Google. http://www.google.com/intl/en/accessibility/
4. Apple official website, Apple Inc. http://support.apple.com/accessibility/
5. Apple official developer website, Apple Inc. http://developer.apple.com/documentation/uikit/accessibility/
6. Android Developers official website. http://developer.android.com/guide/topics/ui/accessibility
7. Microsoft official website. http://www.microsoft.com/en-us/accessibility
8. Kultsova, M., Romanenko, R., Anikin, A., Poceluico, A.: An ontology-based adaptation of user interface for people with special needs. In: Proceedings The AINL FRUCT 2016 Conference, November 2016
9. Kultsova, M., Romanenko, R., Anikin, A., Poceluico, A.: An ontology-based approach to automated generation of adaptive user interface based on user modeling. In: Proceedings of IISA 2016 Conference, July 2016
10. Kultsova, M., Romanenko, R., Zhukova, I., Usov, A., Penskoy, N., Potapova, T.: Assistive mobile application for support of mobility and communication of people with IDD. In: Proceedings of MobileHCI 2016 Conference, September 2016
11. Kultsova, M., Zhukova, I., Potseluico, A., Skorikov, A., Romanenko, R.: A two-phase method of user interface adaptation for people with special needs. In: Proceedings of CITDS2017 Conference, September 2017
12. Peissner, M., Shuller, A., Spath, D.: A design patterns approach to adaptive user interfaces for users with special needs. In: Proceedings of HCII Conference, pp. 268–277, July 2011
13. Skillen, K.-L., Chen, L., Nugent, C.D., Donnelly, M.P., Burns, W., Solheim, I.: Ontological user profile modeling for context-aware application personalization. In: Bravo, J., López-de-Ipiña, D., Moya, F. (eds.) UCAmI 2012. LNCS, vol. 7656, pp. 261–268. Springer, Heidelberg (2012). https://doi.org/10.1007/978-3-642-35377-2_36 As references [13] and [14] are the same, we have deleted the duplicate reference and renumbered accordingly. Please check and confirm.
14. Gamecho, B., et al.: Automatic generation of tailored accessible user interfaces for ubiquitous services. IEEE Trans. Hum. Mach. Syst. **45**(5), 612–623 (2015). Oct
15. AEGIS Ontology. http://www.aegis-project.eu
16. Elias, M., Lohmann, S., Auer, S.: Towards an ontology-based representation of accessibility profiles for learners. In: Proceedings of Second International Workshop on Educational Knowledge Management, vol. 1780, November 2016

17. Lempert, L.B., Kravets, A.G., Lempert, B.A., Poplavskaya, O.V., Salnikova, N.A.: Development of the intellectual decision-making support method for medical diagnostics in psychiatric practice. In: 9th International Conference on Information, Intelligence, Systems and Applications, IISA (2018)

18. Kultsova, M., Potseluico, A., Dvoryankin, A.: Ontology based personalization of mobile interfaces for people with special needs. In: Proceedings CITDS 2019 Conference, September 2019

19. Shahzad, S.K.: Ontology-based user interface development: user experience elements pattern. J. Univ. Comput. Sci. **17**(7), 1078–1088 (2011)

20. Hussain, J., et al.: Model-based adaptive user interface based on context and user experience evaluation. J. Multimod. User Inter. **12**(1), 1–16 (2018). https://doi.org/10.1007/s12193-018-0258-2

21. Paterno, F.: The Encyclopedia of Human-Computer Interaction, 2nd Edn. http://www.interaction-design.org/literature/book/the-encyclopedia-of-human-computer-interaction-2nd-ed/

Development of Specialized Methods and Algorithms for Preventive Monitoring of Reliability

Maxim Dyatlov[1]([⊠]), Olga Shabalina[1], Alexey Todorev[1], Rodion Kudrin[2], Yuriy Komarov[1], and Konstantin Katerinin[1]

[1] Volgograd State Technical University, Volgograd, Russian Federation
[2] Volgograd State Medical University, Volgograd, Russian Federation

Abstract. The project is aimed at solving an urgent scientific problem of fundamental and applied importance – support of the professional activities of vehicle drivers in conditions close to the real labor process. As part of this work, it is planned to conduct a professional study and develop a methodology for diagnosing and developing the psychophysiological qualities of drivers using a specialized hardware and software complex. An analysis of the current state of the road transport industry shows that the existing methods of escorting professional drivers do not fully take into account the psychological, psychophysiological and socio-personal characteristics of this profession. This significantly reduces the quality of professional selection of vehicle drivers and leads to the appearance of potentially dangerous and emergency situations on the roads. Ultimately, the shortcomings of professional selection and escort of drivers lead to human and material losses in road transport.

Keywords: Driver of urban passenger transport · Psychophysiological health · Professional reliability · Software platform · Hardware and software complex · Professional selection methodology · Levels of professional suitability

1 Introduction

An analysis of the current state of the road transport industry shows that the existing methods for the selection of professional drivers do not fully take into account the psychophysiological characteristics of this profession.

This leads to the appearance of potentially dangerous and emergency situations on the roads and to human and material losses during road transport [1–4].

The professional activity of a driver of urban passenger transport, which has been studied for a long time, however, does not have a full-fledged scientifically grounded method of professional selection.

The importance and necessity of its development is determined by the modern features of this work – a rather rare combination of monotony with periodically arising extreme levels of tension, the need to maintain a high level of attention for a long time and the ability to quickly process information.

A. G. Kravets et al. (Eds.): CIT&DS 2021, CCIS 1448, pp. 598–611, 2021.
https://doi.org/10.1007/978-3-030-87034-8_44

At the same time, the driver has a fairly high level of current psycho-emotional stress, due to numerous risks of a different nature. Features of this kind are currently not typical for most types of labor activity, which emphasizes the level of requirements for the selection, training and constant ongoing monitoring of the functional readiness of professional drivers. All of the above problems of traffic safety can be successfully resolved through joint comprehensive research by specialists of different scientific profiles and the analysis of the results of the data they receive.

Systemic research allows obtaining the most complete scientific data on the psychophysiological capabilities and functional states of the driver, which is especially important for specialists in dangerous and responsible professions. The development trend of this fundamental research ensures effective interaction of psychophysiological and technical disciplines and is fruitful both for solving current problems of psychophysiology of driver's labor and for accumulating research potential in the study of complex ergatic systems in the future.

In January 2018, the Government of the Russian Federation (RF) approved the Road Safety Strategy in the RF for 2018–2024. The strategy is the basis for planning in the implementation of road safety policy and should provide a holistic (systematic) approach to solving the problem of road traffic injuries. The objectives of the Strategy are to improve road safety, as well as to strive for zero fatalities in road traffic accidents by 2030. The creation of specialized automated imitation hardware and software systems will allow diagnosing, analyzing and developing the professional qualities of specialists in operator professions, thereby purposefully reducing the influence of the "human factor" in the "man-technician" system.

2 The List of the Most Significant Psychophysiological Qualities of Urban Passenger Transport Drivers

The management of passenger vehicles (buses, trolleybuses) is associated with certain features, which are determined by high requirements for safety, efficiency and quality of passenger transportation. Occasionally, the profession of a passenger vehicle driver under the influence of external factors is extreme [5–8]. Despite the complexity and responsibility of the work of a passenger transport driver, his suitability for this profession is currently determined only by medical and educational selection [9–17].

The choice of the methodology for determining the most significant psychophysiological qualities (MSPQ) was determined by the nature of the labor process. The developed questionnaire includes 2 questions and a list of 53 psychophysiological qualities (Table 1) [18, 19].

Each psychophysiological quality was included in the proposed list on the basis of observation, conversations with experts in the field of passenger road transport, analysis of available literary sources and regulatory documentation, considering the features of the professional activities of operator work specialists.

The essence of the expert assessments was to assign, on a scale from 0 to 10 points, each of the psychophysiological qualities necessary for the efficient and safe work of a driver of urban passenger transport. The psychophysiological qualities indicated in the questionnaire, in the opinion of the respondents, to one degree or another determine the success of the drivers' labor activity. At the same time, 10 points were assigned to the most significant factor. The study involved 43 experts in the field of psychophysiology and 34 in the field of road transport.

Table 1. Questionnaire for expert assessments of the MSPQ of the driver of urban passenger transport.

N	Psychophysiological qualities	Scoring the degree of importance	Quality content
1	Adapting vision to light and dark		A complex of physiological processes that ensure the effective operation of vision in bright light (day vision), at dusk (twilight vision), and in very low light (night vision)
2	Visual acuity		An indicator of vision, which characterizes the ability to distinguish between small details or the minimum distance between two points
	...		...
53	Simple sensorimotor reaction		Reciprocal elementary movement to a suddenly appearing, but known in advance

When answering the second question of the questionnaire, the expert was asked to add psychophysiological qualities, which, in his opinion, are necessary for drivers of urban passenger transport (bus, trolleybus), but were not indicated in the general list of qualities.

According to the results of the assessment by the experts in the amount of 77 people of the list of 53 psychophysiological qualities presented in the questionnaire, the consistency of the testimony of the group of the surveyed was checked using the Kendall coefficient of concordance. The analysis of the consistency of expert testimony showed a significant correlation both in each of the two groups of specialists separately, and in the entire expert group as a whole.

To process the results of expert assessments, a macro developed in MS Excel was used.

The results of the answers of the expert groups on the determination of the MSPQ necessary for the efficient and safe operation of the driver of urban passenger transport are shown in Table 2.

Thus, for drivers of urban passenger transport, whose work is associated with high vehicle speeds and significant neuro-emotional stress, the speed of sensorimotor reactions, the properties of higher nervous activity, emotional intelligence, and visual and vestibular analyzers come to the fore.

Table 2. MSPQ of the driver of urban passenger transport based on the results of expert assessments.

MSPQ (significance for profession, points)	MSPQ (significance for profession, points)
1. Reaction to a moving object (9.72)	13. Perception of movement (9.01)
2. Accuracy of movements (9.62)	14. Distribution of attention (9.00)
3. Strength of the nervous system (9.60)	15. Visual acuity (8.97)
4. Coordination of movements (9.50)	16. Physical static endurance (8.92)
5. Concentration of attention (9.44)	17. Field of view (8.91)
6. Balance of nervous processes (9.37)	18. Flexibility of thinking (8.82)
7. Complex sensorimotor reactions (9.26)	19. Technical thinking (8.77)
8. Simple sensorimotor reaction (9.19)	20. Perception of space (8.71)
9. Mobility of nervous system (9.16)	21. Volume of attention (8.69)
10. Emotional intelligence (9.15)	22. Adaptation of vision to light and dark (8.69)
11. Vestibular stability (9.10)	23. Operational field of view (8.69)
12. Operational thinking (9.04)	24. Physical dynamic endurance (8.58)

3 The Method of Testing the Most Significant Psychophysiological Qualities of Drivers in the Conditions of Computer Simulation of Road Traffic

The highest efficiency and predictive value at the stage of professional selection, as a rule, is provided by diagnostic methods that are close to the conditions of professional activity.

At present, experimental psychophysiological devices and individual test methods are used to study the degree of development of the professionally important qualities (PIQ) of specialists in operator professions, which include the profession of a driver of urban passenger transport. However, the existing methods for the most part are universal, they do not take into account the specifics of a particular profession, which significantly reduces the reliability of the selection results.

To increase the efficiency of the selection of professional drivers, it is necessary to develop methods for assessing professional qualities in conditions close to real ones. Such conditions can be implemented in hardware and software complexes (HSC) that allow simulating driving and assessing the user's ability to professionally drive a vehicle [20, 21].

For successful driving in hazardous and difficult road conditions, the driver must have certain psychophysiological qualities in order to quickly and accurately respond to a large number of visual, sound and other stimuli.

As a result of the analysis of the professional activities of drivers of passenger transport, a model of imitation test tasks (ITT) was developed for computer diagnostics of the degree of development of MSPQ.

The concept of testing the driver's MSPQ in the conditions of computer simulation of road traffic was formed on the basis of the following conditions:

1. Simulation of road traffic and the implementation of test tasks in conditions close to the professional activity of the driver.
2. Use in test equipment of specialized peripheral devices, similar to vehicle controls.
3. Availability of ITT with different levels of complexity of implementation.
4. Diagnostics and development of separate groups of driver's MSPQ.

The layout of the ITT facilities is shown in Fig. 1.
Configurable test parameters:

– high-speed intervals of movement;
– time of passing the test;
– the level of complexity of the "track" (along the curvature of the trajectory);
– the value of the dangerous distance from the "road hole";
– the value of the dangerous distance from the "parked car";
– frequency of "parked cars" appearance;
– frequency of occurrence of "road pits".

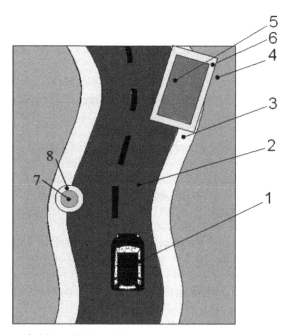

Fig. 1. Arrangement of objects ST (simulation test): 1 – "car" of the subject; 2 – contour "road" (safe zone); 3 – contour of the "roadside" (danger zone); 4 – contour of "near-road space" (critical zone); 5 – contour of a fixed or movable obstacle (critical zone); 6 – contour of a dangerous distance along the perimeter of a fixed or movable obstacle (danger zone); 7 – contour of the "road pit" (critical zone); 8 – contour of the dangerous distance along the perimeter of the "road pit" (danger zone).

Implementations of the model have been developed: "Driving on an empty road" (ITT ER), "Driving along a road with fixed obstacles" (ITT FO) and "Driving along a road with movable obstacles" (ITT MO). The subject controls the "Car" object using the "Computer steering wheel" manipulator.

The architecture of the HSC for traffic simulation (HSC TS), which implements the required functionality, has been developed (Fig. 2).

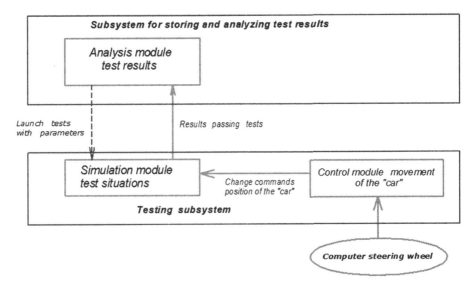

Fig. 2. Architecture HSC TS (hardware-software complex traffic simulation).

The hardware part of the HSC TS is a prefix for motion simulation, including the "Computer steering wheel".

The software includes modules for controlling the movement of the car, simulating test situations and evaluating the results of monitoring user actions while driving.

Test Situations Simulation Module – HSC module that simulates the testing process and simulates the traffic process.

Vehicle motion control module – a module that processes vehicle control signals from the "Computer steering wheel" manipulator and controls the movement of a vehicle in virtual space.

Test results analysis module – a module designed to analyze the test results of drivers.

The developed HSC TS has the following capabilities:

– user testing in a virtual three-dimensional space using a "computer steering wheel";
– registration of errors made by the user during the execution of the ITT;
– calculation of criteria for maneuvering in relation to hazardous and critical zones of the ITT facilities, as well as the resulting criterion for the reliability of maneuvering.

The recorded indicators can be used to assess the level of formation of some MSPQ in conditions close to the professional activity of a driver of urban passenger transport at the stages of professional selection, pre-trip express diagnostics and professional differentiation.

4 Methods for the Professional Selection of Drivers of Urban Passenger Transport by Psychophysiological Indicators

On the basis of the identified MSPQ, a methodology for the professional selection of drivers of urban passenger transport was developed. For the first fifteen MSPQ from the rating of significance, psychophysiological diagnostic methods have been developed and selected, which make it possible to assess the degree of development of each of the studied characteristics. The methodology for the professional selection of drivers includes instrumental and measuring diagnostic methods and psychophysiological test questionnaires, presented in Table 6. From the existing test methods, those were selected that met the requirements of validity, reliability, predictive value and availability of use.

After all the registered parameters have been determined according to the test results, partial indicators of the degree of development of individual psychophysiological properties are calculated:

- the highest estimated score of one diagnosed MSPQ, points:

$$n = N/p_{max};$$
(1)

- reduced maneuvering factor ($0 \leq K_{CS} \leq K_{CS\ MAX}$):

$$K_{CS} = npR;$$
(2)

- coefficient of assessment of individual psychological personality traits

$$0 \leq K_{EPI} \leq K_{EPI\ MAX} : K_{EPI} = K_{IE} + K_{NEU};$$
(3)

- driver applicability factor based on instrumentation testing

$$0 \leq K_{MEA} \leq K_{MEA\ MAX} : K_{MEA} = \sqrt[3]{\frac{K_{CS} \cdot K_{VR} \cdot K_{VA}}{K_{CSmax} \cdot K_{VRmax} \cdot K_{VAmax}}} \cdot K_{MEAmax}, \quad (4)$$

N – the highest estimated score of the total number of diagnosed MSPQ; p_{max} – total number of diagnosed MSPQ; p – number of diagnosed MSPQ.

The resulting coefficient of professional suitability of urban passenger transport drivers by psychophysiological indicators ($0 \leq K_S \leq 100$) is determined by the formula:

$$K_s = 100 \cdot K_{MEA} \cdot \frac{\left(K|_{EQ} + K_{EPI}\right)}{K_{MEAmax} \cdot \left(K|_{EQmax} + K_{EPImax}\right)},$$
(5)

Figure 3 shows a method for distributing MSPQ according to the coefficients of professional suitability and determining the maximum values of the coefficients depending on the number of MSPQ determining them (Table 3).

Table 3. Methods for diagnosing the degree of development of MSPQ drivers urban passenger transport and registered parameters.

MSPQ number in the overall rating	Methods for diagnosing the degree of development of MSPQ	Designation and name Registered parameter (value ranges)
1	HSC TS (ST RFO)	R – maneuvering reliability criterion $(0 \leq R \leq R_{MAX})$
2		
4		
5		
7		
8		
12		
13		
14		
11	Vestibulometry methods (medical checkup)	K_{VR} – coefficient of the level of development of vestibular stability $(0 \leq K_{VR} \leq K_{VR\,MAX})$
15	Tables D. A. Sivtseva and S. S. Golovina (medical checkup)	K_{VA} – visual acuity development coefficient $(0 \leq K_{VA} \leq K_{VA\,MAX})$
3	Eysenck test EPI (A)	K_{IE} – coefficient of assessment of levels of introversion-extraversion $(0 \leq K_{IE} \leq K_{IE\,MAX})$; K_{NEU} – coefficient for assessing the levels of neuroticism (emotional stability-instability) $(0 \leq K_{NEU} \leq K_{NEU\,MAX})$
6		
9		
10	Goleman emotional intelligence test (EQ)	K_{EQ} – emotional intelligence development coefficient $(0 \leq K_{EQ} \leq K_{EQ\,MAX})$

The method of professional selection of drivers of urban passenger transport by psychophysiological indicators consists of several main stages.

1st stage. Determination of the list of MSPQ.
2nd stage. Psychophysiological testing using apparatus-measuring methods and psychophysiological test questionnaires.

3rd stage. Determination of particular indicators of the degree of development of individual psychophysiological properties.

4th stage. Determination of the coefficient of professional suitability of urban passenger transport drivers by psychophysiological indicators.

The development of a methodology for the professional selection of drivers of urban passenger transport was carried out in accordance with the basic principles, on the implementation of which the effectiveness of the implemented measures depends: complexity, dynamism, activity and practicality.

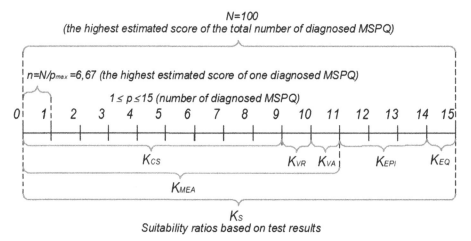

Fig. 3. Method of distributing MSPQ according to the coefficients of professional suitability and determining the maximum values of the coefficients depending on the number of MSPQ determining them.

5 Procedure for Approbation and Substantiation of the Effectiveness of the Developed Methodology

For a quantitative assessment of the degree of compliance of the PIQ and individual psychological characteristics of drivers with the level of professionalism in labor activity, the method of questioning and expert assessment was used. A group of experts was formed from specialists from the municipal unitary enterprise (MUE) "Metroelektrotrans" of the city of Volgograd, who have a high level of professional training and experience of practical work at this enterprise for more than 10 years. At the time of the survey, each of the experts was a mentor or supervisor of at least one of the assessed drivers.

In the developed questionnaire, the level of professionalism of the trolleybus driver was determined by 9 characteristics.

A group of subjects was formed, consisting of 32 trolleybus drivers with at least a year of work experience in their specialty. The age of the participants at the time of enrollment in the study ranged from 26 to 59 years. Among the surveyed 11 people (34.4%) are women and 21 people (65.6%) are men.

The assessment of the degree of compliance of these characteristics with the levels of professionalism of the tested trolleybus driver, according to the mentor or leader, was carried out on a five-point scale (5 points – the highest degree of compliance of these characteristics).

The resulting estimated score for each driver was formed as the arithmetic mean of the scores based on the results of the assessments of two experts.

The resulting interval of expert estimates was divided into two levels of driver professionalism.

The normal distribution of the analyzed samples was checked using the Shapiro-Francia test (since $n < 50$). It was concluded that the empirical distribution approximates the normal distribution for samples with $p > 0.05$. For samples that were classified as abnormally distributed, the median Me was calculated.

The normative values of the diagnosed psychophysiological indicators were determined according to the Order of the Ministry of Health and Social Development of the Russian Federation, the analysis of literature sources on the psychophysiology of driving activity and the obtained values of the diagnosed psychophysiological characteristics.

The standard values of the coefficient of professional suitability were determined according to the results of instrumental-measuring testing and psychophysiological test questionnaires, as well as the standard values of the resulting coefficient of professional suitability according to psychophysiological indicators (Tables 4, 5, 6, and 7).

Table 4. Standard values of the coefficient of professional suitability based on the results of instrumental and measuring testing.

The coefficient of professional suitability according to the results of instrumental and measuring testing K_{MEA}, scores	Professional suitability level
0–19	Unsuitability
20–39	Limited validity
40–59	Suitability
60–69	Conformity
70–73,33	Vocation

The values of particular indicators of the degree of development of individual psychophysiological properties and the resulting coefficient of professional suitability of the tested drivers were calculated (Table 7 and Fig. 4).

As a result of the analysis of the results obtained, it was revealed that among the surveyed trolleybus drivers, 13 people (40.6%) have an average EQ (81–120 points), 19 people (59.4%) have a high EQ (121–168 points). In the group of "professional" drivers, 8 people (66.7%) have a high EQ, and in the group of "pre-professional" drivers, 11 people (55.0%). No drivers with low EQ scores (42–80 points) were found among the study participants.

Table 5. Standard values of the coefficients of professional suitability according to the results of psychophysiological test questionnaires.

Level factor development of emotional intelligence K_{EQ}, scores	Rating coefficient individual psychological traits personality K_{EPI}, scores	Professional suitability level
0–1,32	0–3	Unsuitability
1,33–2,66	4–8	Limited validity
2,67–4,01	9–12	Suitability
4,02–5,33	13–16	Conformity
5,34–6,67	17–20	Vocation

Table 6. Standard values of the resulting coefficient professional suitability for psychophysiological indicators.

Resulting factor professional suitability K_S, scores	Professional suitability level
0–8	Unsuitability
9–22	Limited validity
23–41	Suitability
42–74	Conformity
75–100	Vocation

Table 7. Values of coefficients of professional suitability depending on the level of professionalism and gender of the driver.

Professional suitability factor	Values of the coefficient of professional suitability, scores (M ± σ or Me)		
	«Pre-professionalism» (n = 20)	«Professionalism» (n = 12)	General group (n = 32)
K_{MEA}, scores	57,08	56,97	57,07
K_{EPI}, scores	14,22 ± 2,77	16,88	14,96 ± 2,83
K_{EQ}, scores	4,12 ± 0,57	4,36 ± 0,42	4,21 ± 0,52
K_S, scores	53,62	63,76	56,74

According to the results of processing the data of the Eysenck questionnaire EPI (A), individual psychological personality traits of the tested drivers were revealed. The most common types of temperament are phlegmatic people – 15 people (46.9%) and sanguine people – 12 people (37.5%). The melancholic type corresponded to 5 study participants (15.6%). High marks on the extraversion-introversion scale (13–24 points) were scored by 12 people (37.5%), which corresponded to the extroverted personality type. Low

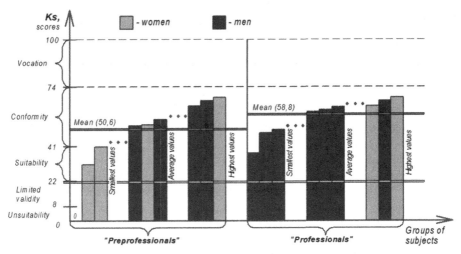

Fig. 4. Point assessment of the resulting coefficient of professional suitability of the groups of tested trolleybus drivers.

scores on the extraversion-introversion scale (0–10 points) were scored by 13 people (40.6%), which corresponded to the introverted personality type. Average points on the extraversion-introversion scale (11–12 points) were scored by 7 people (21.9%). In the group of "professional" drivers, 3 people (25.0%) were extroverts, 4 people (33.3%) were introverts, and 5 people (41.7%) scored average points on the extraversion-introversion scale. In the group of "preprofessional" drivers, 9 people (45.0%) corresponded to the extraverted and introverted personality types, and 2 people (10.0%) scored average points on the extraversion-introversion scale. High scores on the neuroticism scale, which corresponds to emotional instability (14–24 points), were scored by 5 study participants (15.6%). Low scores on the neuroticism scale, which corresponds to emotional stability (0–11 points), were scored by 25 study participants (78.1%). Average scores on the neuroticism scale (12–13 points) were scored by 2 study participants (6.3%). In the group of "professional" drivers, 1 person (8.3%) scored high points on the neuroticism scale, and 11 people (91.7%) scored low. In the group of "preprofessional" drivers, 4 people (20.0%) scored high scores on the neuroticism scale, 14 people (70.0%) had low scores, and 2 people (10%) had average scores.

One driver from the group of "pre-professional" had visual acuity below the values required for professional drivers of urban passenger transport (better seeing eye – 0.5 units, worse seeing – 0.5 units). Currently, a prerequisite is the values for a better seeing eye – 0.8 units, worse than a seeing one – not less than 0.4 units according to the tables of Sivtsev or Golovin.

The analysis of the results of the performance of the ITT FO by the subjects showed the presence of psychophysiological features that determine the success of the driver's actions in dangerous traffic situations. All test drivers performed the ITT on the HSC TS with the values of the reliability criterion for maneuvering R > 0.86.

6 Study Results

A methodology for the professional selection of drivers of urban passenger transport based on the assessment of the most significant psychophysiological qualities has been developed and tested.

Coefficients have been developed that determine the degree of development of the most significant psychophysiological qualities and the resulting coefficient that allow differentiating urban passenger transport drivers into groups of suitability for professional activity.

The reliability and validity of the choice of quantitative criteria for assessing professional suitability and methods for their calculation is confirmed by the empirical results of the study. The values of the resulting suitability factor of 96.9% of the tested trolleybus drivers are in the upper range of the "suitability" level values and a wide range of the "compliance" level values (with the values of the intensity of vestibulo-vegetative reactions at the "suitability" level for all tested drivers).

References

1. Kur'yanova, O.: Primeneniye professional'nogo otbora dlya realizatsii individual'nogo podkhoda pri podgotovke voditeley transportnykh sredstv. Avtotransportnoye predpriyatiye **6**, 14–22 (2016)
2. Bubnova, A., Sheveleva, A., Klauchek, S.: Individual-typological peculiarities of the functional organization of the cerebral cortex and the dynamics of the efficiency of operator activity. Int. Res. J. Clin. Med. **2**, 69–73 (2016)
3. Kuz'menko, M.D.: Kriterii i professional'noy prigodnosti spetsialistov operatorskogo profilya v osobykh usloviyakh deyatel'nosti, Vektor nauki Tol'yattinskogo gosudarstvennogo universiteta. Seriya: Pedagogika, psikhologiya **1**(12), 125–128 (2013)
4. Nersesyan, L.S.: Rol'intellektual'no-myslitel'nogo komponenta v razlichnykh operatorskoy deyatel'nosti, Pedagogicheskoye obrazovaniye i nauka. - M.: Nekommercheskoye partnerstvo «Mezhdunarodnaya akademiya nauk pedagogicheskogo obrazovaniya » **8**, 28–32 (2012)
5. Petukhov, I.V.: Model' i sistema otsenki uspeshnosti operatorskoy deyatel'nosti v cheloveko-mashinnykh sistemakh upravleniya. Nauchno-tekhnicheskiy vestnik Povolzh'ya **3**, 156–162 (2011)
6. Surnina, O.Ye.: Tip rabotosposobnosti i psikhofiziologicheskiye osobennosti cheloveka, Psikhologicheskiy vestnik Ural'skogo gosudarstvennogo universiteta. Vyp. 7. Izd-vo Ural'skogo. Universiteta, Yekaterinburg, pp. 209–222 (2009)
7. Sukhodol'skiy, G.V.: Inzhenerno-psikhologicheskaya ekspertiza dorozhno-transportnoye proisshestviy. Institut prikladnoy psikhologii «Gumanitarnyy tsentr». Khar'kov 156p (2006)
8. Blows, S., Ameralunga, S., Norton, R.: Risky driving habits and motor vehicle driver injury. Acc. Anal. Prevent. **37**(4), 619–624 (2005)
9. Lee, H.C., Lee, A.H.: Identifying older drivers at risk of traffic violations by using a driving simulator: a 3-year longitudinal study. Am. J. Occup. Therapy **59**(1), 97–100 (2005)
10. Mukhin, Ye.M., Litvinova, N.A., Prokhorova, A.M., Berezina, M.G.: Osobennosti reagirovaniya kardiorespiratornoy sistemy voditeley v usloviyakh sensomotornoy deyatel'nosti, Valeologiya, Rostov-na-Donu **1**, 23–29 (2016)
11. Mitin, I.N., Shcheblanov, V.Yu.: Otsenka psikhofiziologicheskikh kharakteristik bezavariynoy deyatel'nosti voditeley., Meditsina katastrof **1**(77), 45–48 (2012)

12. Kurganov, V.M.: Psikhologicheskiye kachestva i nadezhnost' voditelya. Voprosy psikhologii **6**, 118–127 (2004)
13. Zhukov, I.Yu., Mitin, I.N.: Psikhologicheskiye indikatory neblagopriyatnogo prognoza bezavariynoy deyatel'nosti voditeley, Meditsina katastrof **3**(75), 36–39 (2011)
14. Aydarkin, Ye.K., Ovchinnikov, K.V.: Psikhofiziologicheskaya kharakteristika lits s razlichnym vegetativnym statusom, Valeologiya **2**, 23–32 (2006)
15. Kabalevskaya, A.I. Sovremennyye metody issledovaniya voditel'skoy deyatel'nosti v transportnoy psikhologii. Rossiyskiy nauchnyy zhurnal **3**(28), 205–210 (2019)
16. Yulkin, Ye.S.: Psikhologiya avariynosti na avtomobil'nom transporte i puti yeyo resheniya. [Tekst], Vestnik Tverskogo gosudarstvennogo universiteta. Seriya «Pedagogika i psikhologiya» **1**, 184–191 (2011)
17. Ushakov, I.B.: Adaptatsionnyy potentsial cheloveka, Vestnik Rossiyskoy akademii meditsinskikh nauk **3**, 8–13 (2004)
18. Dyatlov, M.N., Shabalina, O.A., Komarov, Yu.Ya., Kudrin, R.A.: Razrabotka testovyh zadanij dlya komp'yuternoj diagnostiki stepeni razvitiya sensomotornyh reakcij s uchyotom osobennostej professional'noj deyatel'nosti voditelej, Izvestiya VolgGTU. Ser. Aktual'nye problemy upravleniya, vychislitel'noj tekhniki i informatiki v tekhnicheskih sistemah. Volgograd **6**(185), 33–39 (2016)
19. Shabalina, O.A., Kudrin, R.A., Agazadyan, A.R., Todorev, A.N., Dyatlov, M.N.: Ocenka professional'noj prigodnosti voditelej passazhirskogo avtotransporta v usloviyah imitacii dorozhnogo dvizheniya. Vestnik Volgogradskogo gos. med. un-ta (Vestnik VolgGMU) **2**(62), 126–129 (2017)
20. Todorev, A.N., Shabalina, O.A., Dyatlov, M.N., Kudrin, R.A., Komarov, Yu.Ya.: Comparison of testing results of drivers on the road traffic simulator and on the set of psychological tests [electronic resource]. In: Proceedings of the IV International research conference «Information technologies in Science, Management, Social sphere and Medicine» (ITSMSSM 2017), Berestneva, O.G., et al. (eds.). [Published by Atlantis Press] (Ser. Advances in Computer Science Research (ACSR); vol. 72), pp. 430–433 (2017). https://www.atlantis-press.com/proceedings/itsmssm-17
21. Dyatlov, M., Shabalina, O., Todorev, A., Kudrin, R., Sentyabryov, N.: Method of preliminary computer evaluation of professional readiness of the vehicle driver. In: Kravets, A.G., Groumpos, P.P., Shcherbakov, M., Kultsova, M. (eds.) CIT&DS 2019. CCIS, vol. 1084, pp. 378–392. Springer, Cham (2019). https://doi.org/10.1007/978-3-030-29750-3_30

Methodology for Preclinical Laboratory Research Using Machine Learning

Vadim Loshmanov[1]([✉]), Viktor Petraevskiy[1], and Pavel Fantrov[2]

[1] Volgograd State Technical University, 28 Lenin avenue, Volgograd 400005, Russia
loshmanov.vadim17@gmail.com, petvikt@mail.ru
[2] Volgograd State University, 100 Universitetskiy avenue, Volgograd 400062, Russia
pavelfantrov@volsu.ru

Abstract. Currently, a considerable amount of research is being carried out on the development of new drugs. Therefore, it is necessary to improve existing approaches to search for new chemical compounds with pharmacological activity. Such studies have been carried out for several years. During this period, a considerable amount of information is accumulated, which is quite difficult for one or even a group of experienced specialists to process and analyze. With such a volume of data, obtaining a sufficient degree of accuracy of the neural network data model is possible. The article discusses the methodology for conducting preclinical laboratory research. The Preclinical Validation Study method was conducted using the Ocular Disease Intelligent Recognition (ODIR) database of approximately 4,000 color fundus images and specialist diagnostic results. As a result, the accuracy of the constructed model was obtained together with the optimal hyperparameters. The article also considers the analysis of the data source ChEMBL (chemical database of bioactive molecules with drug-like properties), based on which it is planned to develop a method for predicting the presence of the pharmacological activity of a chemical substance. As a result of the study, a frequency prediction of the chemical compounds' activity concerning five types of targets was developed.

Keywords: Neural networks · Deep learning · Hyperparameters tuning · Laboratory research · Trend prediction · LSTM · Pharmacological activity · ChEMBL

1 Introduction

Currently, the pharmacological industry is actively developing in Russia, an integral part of preclinical laboratory studies' conduct. Due to the specifics of this area, there are a limited number of solutions to automate the process of analyzing the results of preclinical laboratory studies. In this regard, it becomes necessary to develop methods for processing data obtained during the tests.

As part of the state implementation of the Neuronet program of the National Technological Initiative, the development of the Neurofarm segment is envisaged. In this segment, in December 2018, events began to be held, one of which is "Permitting the Federal Import of Unregistered Medical Devices into the Russian Federation for

© Springer Nature Switzerland AG 2021
A. G. Kravets et al. (Eds.): CIT&DS 2021, CCIS 1448, pp. 612–625, 2021.
https://doi.org/10.1007/978-3-030-87034-8_45

Research, Including Scientific Purposes" at the legislative level [1]. Currently, a considerable amount of research is being carried out using unregistered medical devices and analysis on the development of new drugs. Therefore, it is necessary to improve approaches in the search for new chemical compounds with pharmacological activity. One way to introduce innovative methods into the drug research process is using an actively developing area in information technology, such as data mining using deep machine learning methods. Analyzing and analyzing the data obtained from this experience is challenging to study. With such a volume of information, it is possible to get the degree of accuracy of the neural network model (NNM).

The application of machine learning (ML) in the field of drug development is currently one of the priority areas for the development of bioinformatics [2].

The determination of the interaction of the test chemical compound with the target is of great importance for detecting the pharmacological activity of the substance, predicting side effects and drug resistance of the target [3]. However, the study of the drug-target interaction through biochemical experiments is very expensive and requires a sufficiently long amount of time. And recently, in the context of filling various genomic, chemical, and pharmacological databases, there is an opportunity to develop innovative solutions for predicting drug-target interactions [4]. At the same time, you should not rule out risks that can have a significant impact on the results of artificial intelligence (AI) using in such researches [5]. The current COVID-19 crisis can be quite severe influence decisions using AI [6], which are used in cases of pneumonia, therefore, you should not lose sight of the impact of third-party factors [7].

2 Preclinical Validation Study ML-Based Method

2.1 Analysis of Basic Ophthalmic Preclinical Laboratory Tests

Ophthalmology was chosen as the main one for the development of the concept of a system for the identification of the pharmacological properties of a new drug. In this direction, there are many open sources, based on which it is possible to develop and evaluate models for the classification and identification of changes in the patient's condition during the use of the investigational medicinal product [8].

Ophthalmoscopy (visual assessment of the state of blood vessels and the retina of the eye) is an examination of the fundus (the inner surface of the eye lined with the retina), which makes it possible to identify many ophthalmic pathologies and, in some cases, diseases of other body systems (for example, nervous, cardiovascular, endocrine) since their first symptoms can manifest themselves in this area of the visual system. With ophthalmoscopy, the retina is examined and its structures: the optic nerve, blood vessels, the macular area, and peripheral areas. In addition, the opacity of the vitreous body or lens is assessed [9]. The result of ophthalmoscopy is an image of the patient's fundus (Fig. 1), based on which the changes, their qualitative and quantitative characteristics are assessed [10].

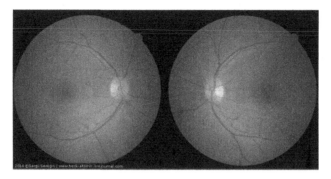

Fig. 1. Ophthalmoscopy result [10].

2.2 Formation of a Training Sample

Data from the Ocular Disease Intelligent Recognition (ODIR) source containing about 4000 color fundus images and the results of specialist diagnostics [11] are presented in the form of a general catalog of images. Their names include identifiers and a link to a CSV file, which correlates the names of image files, patient data, and diagnoses for the left and right eyes (Table 1). Python script was written to form a sample of images in which the fundus is normal and if the patient has a cataract.

Table 1. Description of a sample of fundus images (fragment).

Id	Age	Sex	Image of the left eye	Image of the right eye	Left eye diagnosis	Right eye diagnosis
32	59	Male	119_left.jpg	119_right.jpg	Cataract	Drusen
131	60	Female	254_left.jpg	254_right.jpg	Cataract	Macular epiretinal membrane
56	69	Female	294_left.jpg	294_right.jpg	Cataract	Normal fundus
345	65	Female	330_left.jpg	330_right.jpg	Cataract	Normal fundus
742	68	Male	448_left.jpg	448_right.jpg	Cataract	Moderate non proliferative retinopathy

2.3 Software Implementation of the Ophthalmic Pathology Classification Module

A convolutional neural network for classifying fundus images for pathologies was developed during the study using the Python programming language and the TensorFlow and Keras libraries. The developed module receives a training and test set of photographs of the fundus at the input, divided into classes based on the presence or absence of pathology. The output is a trained neural network model with a description of its parameters, loss function, and accuracy. The convolutional neural network architecture (Fig. 2) consists of 4 repeating convolutional and downsampling layers, a fully connected layer of 512 neurons, and two neurons of the output layer.

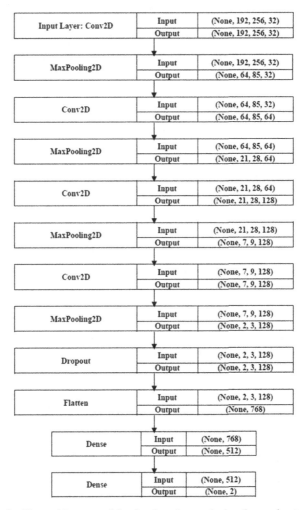

Fig. 2. The architecture of the developed convolutional neural network.

The ReLU (Rectified Linear Unit) activation function was used because it is less demanding on computational resources, in contrast to, for example, hyperbolic tangent or sigmoid, and is better suited for the development of deep neural networks [12].

2.4 Tuning Model Hyperparameters

The main task of machine learning is to build a model, initialize its parameters and then optimize them until the accuracy approaches its maximum possible value. At the same time, hyperparameter optimization methods aim to select the correct parameters of the model architecture, at which its efficiency will be close to maximum [13]. The following function can describe the goal of the optimization problem for model hyperparameters:

$$X^* = \arg\min_{x \in X} f(x), \tag{1}$$

where $f(x)$ is the objective function to be minimized (for example, MSE root mean square error); x is the optimal hyperparameter at which the objective function reaches its optimal value [14].

2.5 Grid Search

Grid search is the most used method for optimizing a set of hyperparameters. GS can be considered an enumeration method that evaluates the Cartesian product of all user-specified hyperparameter combinations. GS is easy to implement and parallelize, but it is ineffective for high-dimensional hyperparameter sets [15].

In the current study, the implementation of the GS algorithm - "GridSearchCV", from the Scikit-learn library [16] was used. This implementation estimates the model mean square error (MSE) based on parameters from a given list. At the output, we get the most practical combination of hyperparameters, with an assessment of the corresponding model using the cross-validation method.

2.6 Experiment

To improve the efficiency of the model, the following set of hyperparameters was chosen, based on which the optimization will be carried out: the number of epochs, batch size, kernel size, learning rate, and momentum (Table 2).

Table 2. List of values of checked hyperparameters.

Hyperparameter	Value
Epochs	[16, 32, 64, 128, 256]
Batch size	[4, 8, 16, 32, 64, 128, 256]
Kernel size	[1, 3, 5]
Learning rate	[0.01, 0.1, 0.2, 0.3, 0.4, 0.5]
Momentum	[0, 0.1, 0.2, 0.3, 0.4, 0.5, 0.6, 0.8, 0.9]

The loss function has been changed to Stochastic Gradient Descent (SGD). This change was made because the SGD optimizer, instead of performing computations on the entire dataset, which is already redundant, only computes a random dataset.

At the same time, the Scikit-learn library allows you to fine-tune the learning rate and impulse optimizer when using the SGD function [17]. The data was split into three parts for cross-validation. Due to the large volume of estimated hyperparameters, the experiment was carried out in three stages.

Stage 1 - Finding the Optimal Values of the Intersection of the Parameters of the Number of Epochs/Batches Size. As part of this stage, a set containing the number of epochs and the batch size indicated in Table 3 was submitted to the input of the GS algorithm. As a result, the optimal values of the sought hyperparameters were found: the number of epochs is equal to 256, the batch size is 8 (Fig. 3).

Table 3. List of values of checked hyperparameters.

Hyperparameters	Image size	Sample size	Accuracy of the training sample	Test sample accuracy
Hand selected	192 × 256	4000	90%	81%
Optimized by GS algorithm	192 × 256	4000	95%	88%

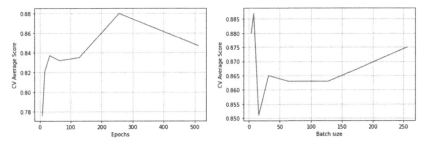

Fig. 3. Plots of model cross-validation estimates versus the number of epochs/batches size.

Stage 2 - Choosing the Optimal Value for the Kernel Size. As part of the second stage, the number of validated values of the number of epochs and the batch size was previously reduced for the model following the first stage results. The checked values of the kernel size are shown in Table 3. As a result, the optimal kernel size was obtained equal to 3. The average score of the model cross-validation was 0.894 (Fig. 4).

Stage 3 - Finding the Optimal Values of the Intersection of the Learning Rate Coefficient/Pulse Optimizer Parameters. In the third stage, the optimal value of the kernel size, the number of epochs, and the batch size were predefined for the model according to the results of the second and third stages. The tested values of the learning rate coefficient and the impulse optimizer are shown in Table 3. As a result, the optimal values of the sought hyperparameters were found: the learning rate coefficient - 0.1, the impulse optimizer - 0.1 (Fig. 5).

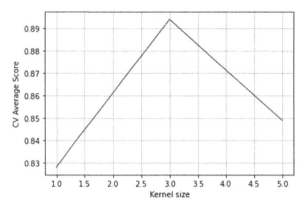

Fig. 4. The plot of the dependence of the results of the assessment of cross-validation of the model and the size of the kernel.

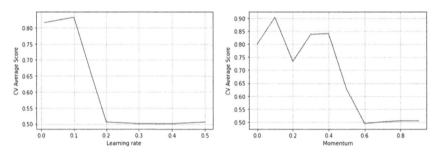

Fig. 5. Plots of model cross-validation estimates versus learning rate/momentum optimizer.

2.7 Estimating the Model with Optimal Hyperparameter Values

A classification model for ophthalmic pathology was constructed using the optimal hyperparameter values obtained in the current study (Fig. 6). According to the experiment results, the accuracy of the model during training was 95%, and the accuracy of the test sample was 88%. From the results obtained, we can conclude that the experiment on selecting the optimal values of the model hyperparameters was successful. In comparison with the previously obtained results, the classification accuracy increased by 8.64%.

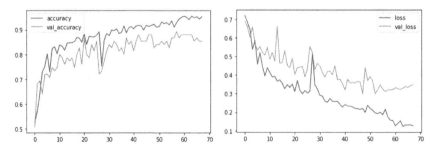

Fig. 6. Plots of accuracy and loss functions of the model with optimal values of hyperparameters.

The training was carried out using the cloud resource Data Sphere (Yandex Cloud) on the computing power of Intel Broadwell 8 vCPU, Nvidia Tesla V100. There was no retraining of the neural network during the study.

3   Pharmacological Target Prediction NNM-Based Method

The purpose of this section of the article is to prepare a training sample and train a model of the developed method for predicting the presence of the pharmacological activity of a chemical concerning a specific target.

To achieve this goal, to need to structure the publicly available data on the analysis of the pharmacological activity of chemical compounds. First, the data were filtered by the type of target concerning which the research is being carried out. This choice will allow the future to reduce the error in the obtained results of the developed method. This section analyzes drug development research to select the main types of targets used. Further, a forecast of the frequency of checking the activity of developed drugs concerning the five most frequently studied targets using neural network models is constructed.

3.1   Dataset Description

Synthesis of novel chemical compounds possessing pharmacological activity is a priority direction of modern development medicine and pharmacology. In 2009, based on The European Bioinformatics Institute (EBI) chemical database was developed from pharmacologically active molecules with drug similar properties [18]. The database contains data manifestations of pharmacological activity of compounds appropriately to targets. Selection for current research is formed from the above-described source.

The sample used in research consists of 274400 pharmacologically active compounds taken from publications from 1976 to 2020. Structure sampling (Fig. 7) includes identification chem. compounds number, molecule name, chem. characteristics of the compound, its formula in the format SMILES (Simplified Molecular Input Line Entry

	Molecule ChEMBL ID	Molecule Name	Molecule Max Phase	Molecular Weight	#RO5 Violations	AlogP	Compound Key
2	CHEMBL3735304	NaN	0	335.79	0	4.90	15b
3	CHEMBL3734995	NaN	0	287.75	0	3.26	17
4	CHEMBL4542238	NaN	0	480.57	0	3.61	23d
5	CHEMBL589601	NaN	0	740.98	1	3.03	33
6	CHEMBL3326598	NaN	0	579.02	1	3.83	Mo10

Fig. 7. The researching sample of these pharmacologically active chemical compounds.

System), target identification number, with according to which manifests the researching pharmacological activity, quantitative and qualitative indicators of this activity, article identification number, in which had a mention of the current chemical connection, journal name, year and month of work publication.

The target in the current context is macromolecular biological structure, presumably related to a particular function, the violation of which leads to disease and for which it is necessary to commit a certain impact. The most common targets are receptors and enzymes [19].

3.2 Dataset Preliminary Processing

Preliminary processing of the sample includes removal of non-disabled data, the grouping of published works by target type, and publication date (Fig. 8).

	Date	Target Type	count
0	1976-01-01	ORGANISM	21
1	1976-02-01	ORGANISM	27
2	1976-03-01	ORGANISM	23
3	1976-04-01	ORGANISM	25
4	1976-05-01	ORGANISM	27
...	...	...	...
1162	2020-08-01	ORGANISM	1620
1164	2020-09-01	ORGANISM	1697
1166	2020-10-01	ORGANISM	1732
1168	2020-11-01	ORGANISM	1677
1170	2020-12-01	ORGANISM	1725

Fig. 8. Statistics of studies of the chemical compounds' activity in relation to the type of target.

The result is statistics of studies of pharmacologically active chem. compounds with relating to several of the most common target types (Fig. 9).

3.3 Analysis of Frequency Statistics of Target Studies

In this study, it is necessary to analyze the search statistics for chemical compounds that potentially have pharmacological activity in relation to five types of targets: single-cell proteins, organisms, complex proteins, protein-protein interaction, and nucleic acids [20]. To solve this problem, a recurrent neural network with LSTM using Python, TensorFlow, and Keras libraries [21] was built.

NN Architecture. During the experiment, a neural network was trained, which has a visible layer with one input, a hidden layer with four LSTM blocks, and an output layer that predicts one value. For LSTM blocks, the activation function was applied sigmoid (Fig. 10).

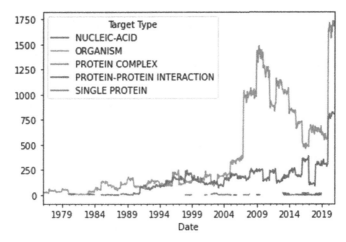

Fig. 9. Drug development research trends.

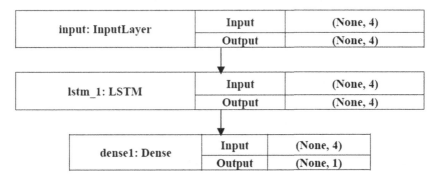

Fig. 10. The neural network architecture.

3.4 Model Assessment and Prediction Results

As a visual evaluation of the results of the prediction, we plot the time series for the frequency of using single-cell protein as a target in the analysis of the pharmacological activity of the synthesized chemical compound and denote it in blue. Further, we add to the graph the results obtained using the neural network model. The predictions for the training dataset are orange and for the test dataset are green. We can see at the resulting graph (Fig. 11), the data obtained using the constructed prediction model almost completely overlaps the graph of the original data, which indicates a high accuracy of the model. Table 4 also shows the RMSE values for each target type, indicating the amount of input data.

Further, trend prediction were built for each type of target over the next year (2021). Their graphs are shown in Fig. 11.

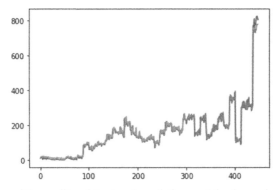

Fig. 11. Evaluation of the quality of the trend prediction model using a single cell protein as a target.

Table 4. Assessment of the built models.

Target type	Dataset volume	RMSE (train)	RMSE (test)
Organism	202519	22.93	121.89
Nucleic acid	26	0.43	1.30
Single protein	70747	19.19	56.42
Protein complex	947	4.02	5.70
Protein-protein interaction	161	1.65	1.49

From the graph (Fig. 12), it can be concluded that this year studies aimed at detecting pharmacological activity when interacting with target organisms (viruses, bacteria) will prevail. At the same time, the number of studies on other types of targets will remain at the same level.

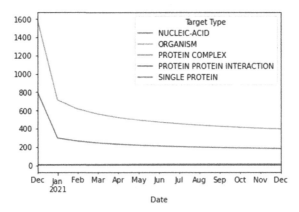

Fig. 12. Prediction of target trends of pharmacological activity over the next year.

4   Software for the Preclinical Laboratory Studies

Software for collecting data on the results of preclinical laboratory studies has been developed, presented in the format of a web application written using ASP.NET Core technologies and PostgreSQL. In this software, the user will be provided with the functionality for loading an image (for the current experiment, a photograph of the patient's fundus), highlighting its area, and adding a class of the selected object (Fig. 13).

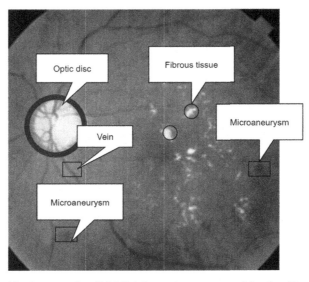

Fig. 13. An example of highlighting an image area and its classification.

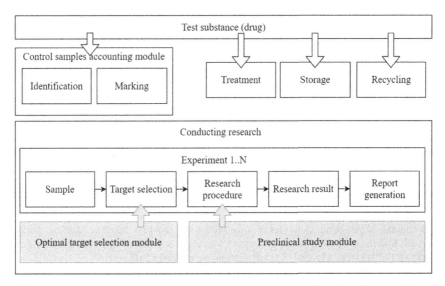

Fig. 14. Implementation of the developed methods in the preclinical studies workflow.

After the user has uploaded the data and formed a training sample, it will train a convolutional neural network model, which is part of the preclinical research module based on the developed method. The implementation of the developed modules in conducting preclinical laboratory studies is shown in Fig. 14.

5 Conclusion

In this paper, a methodology for automated preclinical laboratory research is considered. As part of the development of this methodology, the analysis of statistics and prediction of the frequency of the analysis of the pharmacological activity of chemical compounds concerning five types of targets was carried out using neural network models. Based on the study, it can be assumed that the correct approach would be to develop the predicting method described in the second section of the article, using data in which the type of targets used is an organism. Since there is already a relatively large sample of data and according to the constructed prediction, the number of scientific publications on this topic will remain at the same high level in the coming year.

In the future, it is planned to structure data from the source understudy, to develop and test a methodology for predicting the presence of pharmacological activity of a chemical concerning a specific pathology, using the results of the current study. The development of this task can be in adding new types of pathologies and expanding the classification, and in the future adaptation of the resulting model to images of a higher expansion, which will allow the developed software to be universal concerning the devices with which photographs of the patient's fundus are obtained. At the same time, the study results make it possible to develop an integrated approach to determining the pharmacological activity of new drugs acting in the treatment of various eye pathologies.

In the future, it is planned to expand the training sample and conduct a repeated experiment. At the same time, the developed methods can already be introduced into the concept of a software system for identifying the pharmacological properties of a chemical compound. Within the framework of this concept, it becomes possible to form data sets necessary for the automation of preclinical laboratory studies. And further, based on the processed results of ophthalmoscopic tests (electroretinography, tonometry, and Doppler sonography), using the developed method for classifying ophthalmic pathologies, a more accurate model can be built that will be used to support decision-making in determining the pharmacological activity of a drug.

Acknowledgment. This research was supported by the Russian Fund of Basic Research (grant No. 20–37–90105, grant No. 19–07–01200).

References

1. Al-Gunaid, M.A., et al.: Analysis of drug sales data based on machine learning methods. In: 7th International Conference on System Modeling & Advancement in Research Trends (SMART–2018), pp. 32–38. IEEE UP Section, New Delhi (2018)
2. Qehaja, B., Abazi, B., Hajrizi, E.: Enterprise technology architecture solution for eHealth system and implementation strategy. IFAC PapersOnLine **52**(25), 370–375 (2019)

3. Peng, J., Li, J., Shang, X.: A learning-based method for drug-target interaction prediction based on feature representation learning and deep neural network. BMC Bioinform. **21**(13), 394 (2020)
4. Kobrinskii, B.A., Grigoriev, O.G., Molodchenkov, A.I., Smirnov, I.V., Blagosklonov, M.A.: Artificial intelligence technologies application for personal health management. IFAC PapersOnLine **52**(25), 70–74 (2019)
5. Organ, J., Stapleton, L.: Information systems risk paradigms: towards a new theory on systems risk. IFAC SWIIS **46**(8), 116–121 (2013)
6. Naude, W.: Artifcial intelligence vs COVID-19: limitations, constraints, and pitfalls. AI Soc. **35**, 761–765 (2020)
7. Kiener, M.: Artificial intelligence in medicine and the disclosure of risks. AI Soc., 1–9 (2020). https://doi.org/10.1007/s00146-020-01085-w
8. Kravets, A.G., Al-Gunaid, M.A., Loshmanov, V.I., Rasulov, S.S., Lempert, L.B.: Model of medicines sales forecasting taking into account factors of influence. J. Phys. Conf. Ser. **1015**, 8 (2018)
9. Kravets, A.G., Kolesnikov, S., Salnikova, N., Lempert, M., Poplavskaya, O.: The study of neural networks effective architectures for patents images processing. In: Kravets, A.G., Groumpos, P.P., Shcherbakov, M., Kultsova, M. (eds.) CIT&DS 2019. CCIS, vol. 1084, pp. 27–41. Springer, Cham (2019). https://doi.org/10.1007/978-3-030-29750-3_3
10. Nagasato, D., et al.: Deep neural network-based method for detecting central retinal vein occlusion using ultrawide-field fundus ophthalmoscopy. Hindawi J. Ophthal. **2018**, 1–6 (2018)
11. Ocular Disease Recognition. https://www.kaggle.com/andrewmvd/ocular-disease-recognition-odir5k
12. Understanding Activation Functions in Neural Networks. https://medium.com/the-theory-of-everything/understanding-activation-functions-in-neural-networks-9491262884e0
13. Yang, L., Shami, A.: On hyperparameter optimization of machine learning algorithms: theory and practice. Neurocomputing **415**, 295–316 (2020)
14. Hutter, F., Kotthoff, L., Vanschoren, J.: Automatic Machine Learning: Methods, Systems, Challenges. Springer, New York (2019)
15. Injadat, M., Moubayed, A., Nassif, A.B., Shami, A.: Systematic ensemble model selection approach for educational data mining. Knowl.-Based Syst. **200**, 105992 (2020)
16. Pedregosa, F.: Scikit-learn: machine learning in Python. J. Mach. Learn. Res. **12**, 2825–2830 (2011)
17. Lei, Y., Hu, T., Li, G., Tang, K.: Stochastic gradient descent for nonconvex learning without bounded gradient assumptions. IEEE Trans. Neural Netw. Learn. Syst. **31**(10), 4394–4400 (2020)
18. ChEMBL. www.ebi.ac.uk/chembl
19. Sun, L., Xi, J., Xia, Q., Li, Z., Kumail, A.: Optimal control strategy of multi-stage pharmaceutical. IFAC PapersOnLine **52**(10), 370–375 (2019)
20. Zhang, R., Zou, Q.: Time series prediction and anomaly detection of light curve using LSTM neural network. J. Phys. Conf. Ser. **1061**, 012012 (2018)
21. Greff, K., Srivastava, R.K., Koutník, J., Steunebrink, B.R., Schmidhuber, J.: LSTM: a search space odyssey. IEEE Trans. Neural Netw. Learn. Syst. **28**(10), 2222–2232 (2016)

Author Index

Printed in the United States
by Baker & Taylor Publisher Services